THEGREENGUIDE
New York City

Fifth Avenue Photo: © Oliver Malms/iStockphoto.com

MICHELIN

THEGREENGUIDE **NEW YORK CITY**

Editorial Director	Cynthia Clayton Ochterbeck
Editor	Jonathan P. Gilbert
Contributing Writer	Anne-Marie Scott
Production Manager	Natasha G. George
Cartographer	Peter Wrenn
Photo Editor	Yoshimi Kanazawa
Proofreader	Karolin Thomas
Interior Design	Chris Bell
Layout	Michelin Travel Partner, Nicole D. Jordan
Cover Design	Chris Bell, Christelle Le Déan
Cover Layout	Natasha G. George

Contact Us	Michelin Travel and Lifestyle North America
	One Parkway South
	Greenville, SC 29615
	USA
	travel.lifestyle@us.michelin.com
	www.michelintravel.com
	Michelin Travel Partner
	Hannay House
	39 Clarendon Road
	Watford, Herts WD17 1JA
	UK
	✆01923 205240
	travelpubsales@uk.michelin.com
	www.ViaMichelin.com

Special Sales	For information regarding bulk sales, customized editions and premium sales, please contact us at:
	travel.lifestyle@us.michelin.com
	www.michelintravel.com

Note to the reader Addresses, phone numbers, opening hours and prices published in this guide are accurate at the time of press. We welcome corrections and suggestions that may assist us in preparing the next edition. While every effort is made to ensure that all information printed in this guide is correct and up-to-date, Michelin Travel Partner accepts no liability for any direct, indirect or consequential losses howsoever caused so far as such can be excluded by law.

CONTENTS

Peter Wrenn/Michelin

DISCOVERING NEW YORK CITY

YOUR STAY IN THE CITY

Welcome to New York City

Financial powerhouse, international diplomatic center, cultural mecca, fashion capital, gateway to the United States… There are hardly enough superlatives or definitions to describe New York City, the 305 square-mile metropolis occupying a scattering of islands at the southern tip of New York State. Its world-famous buildings, museums, landmarks and neighborhoods draw some 45 million visitors each year.

MANHATTAN: DOWNTOWN *(pp70–145)*

On Manhattan Island south of 34th Street, Downtown jumbles together a welter of diverse neighborhoods. Economic and administrative engines of the city, the Financial District and Civic Center occupy the island's southernmost tip, where ferries depart for the Statue of Liberty.

Just north, Chinatown and Little Italy rub shoulders with trendy TriBeCa, SoHo, Greenwich Village and the gritty Lower East Side. Gentrified neighborhoods around Union and Madison Squares give way to tranquil Chelsea, on the cusp of Midtown.

MANHATTAN: MIDTOWN *(pp146–191)*

The Empire State Building looms above Fifth Avenue at the southern edge of Midtown, defined here as the area between 34th Street and 59th Street/Central Park South. You'll find some of New York's finest and most famous buildings here, including the New York Public Library, the Chrysler Building in East Midtown, and the elegant UN Headquarters along the East River. Bustling Times Square, Broadway and the Theater District are all located here. Elegant Park Avenue leads north from Grand Central Terminal through East Midtown.

MANHATTAN: UPTOWN *(pp192–229)*

Central Park, with its vast green spaces, occupies the heart of Uptown Manhattan, which includes all of the island north of 59th Street. The posh Upper East Side encompasses fine old buildings, cultural institutions and the Madison Avenue shopping mecca. The Upper West Side boasts the world-famous Lincoln Center, plus Columbia University and lovely Riverside Park. Farther north lies historic Harlem.

New York Harbor, the Statue of Liberty and Manhattan's skyline

MAJOR MANHATTAN MUSEUMS *(pp230–271)*

Manhattan's preeminent museums merit a chapter all to themselves. Here you'll find extensive practical information and descriptions for the Metropolitan Museum of Art (and the Cloisters), the American Museum of Natural History, the Museum of Modern Art, The Frick Collection, the Guggenheim Museum, the Morgan Library, the Whitney Museum of American Art and several others.

THE BRONX *(pp272–279)*

Spread across a finger of mainland across the Harlem River north of Manhattan, The Bronx is home to several noteworthy sights including waterside Pelham Bay Park. The world-famous Bronx Zoo and the New York Botanical Garden are located here, as is Yankee Stadium, home of the New York Yankees.

BROOKLYN *(pp280–293)*

Perched on the western tip of Long Island, Brooklyn retains a close-knit feel in its eclectic mix of neighborhoods, and outstanding cultural institutions like the Brooklyn Museum in Prospect Park and the cutting-edge Brooklyn Academy of Music. The up-and-coming DUMBO area at the foot of the venerable Brooklyn Bridge embraces the new, while shabby-yet-loveable Coney Island preserves the old.

QUEENS *(pp294–302)*

New York's largest borough occupies much of the western part of Long Island. Its tightly packed neighborhoods hold a bustle of immigrant communities and ethnic enclaves. Queens is a great place to sample international cuisines ranging from Greek (in Astoria) to South American, Indian (Jackson Heights) or Asian (Flushing). Cultural offerings

The Cloisters

The Metropolitan Museum of Art, The Cloisters Collection, 1925

here include The Noguchi Museum, the P.S.1 Contemporary Art Center and the outstanding Museum of the Moving Image.

STATEN ISLAND *(pp303–307)*

Still relatively undeveloped (though its population is fast growing), quiet Staten Island is a pleasant bedroom community linked to Manhattan by the fun (and free) Staten Island Ferry; the Verrazano-Narrows Bridge connects the island to Brooklyn. Sights in Staten Island include Historic Richmond Town, a living history experience of life from the 17C onward; and the surprising Jacques Marchais Museum of Tibetan Art.

EXCURSIONS *(pp308–331)*

Excursions from New York City usually foray north to the scenic Hudson River Valley and its stately mansions, estates and arts centers; to the US Military Academy at West Point and to the historic home of Franklin D. Roosevelt. Long Island is also worth exploring for the ritzy Hamptons beach communities and charming seaside villages and gardens.

Grand Central Terminal
©Jeremy Edwards/iStockphoto.com

PLANNING YOUR TRIP

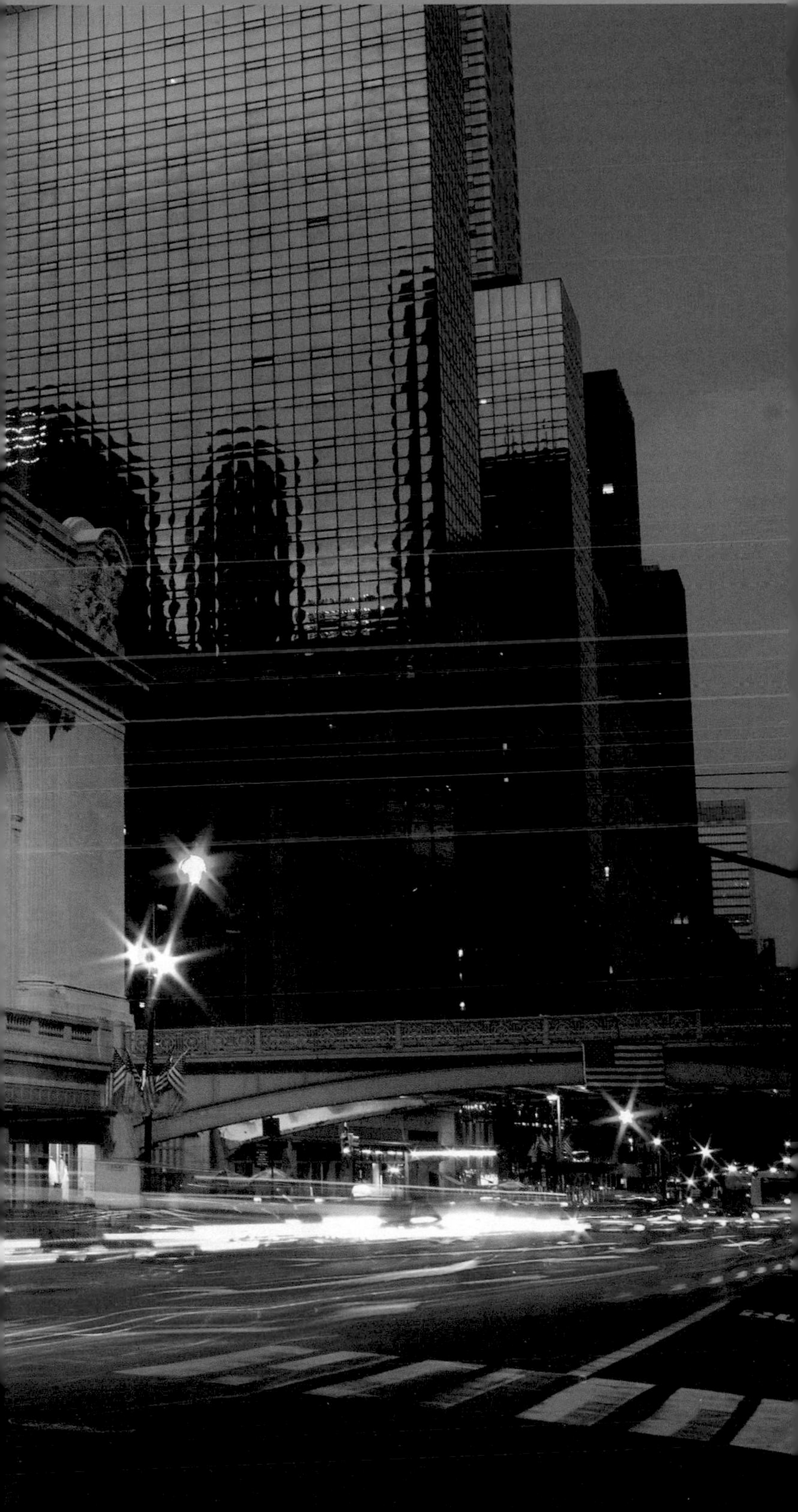

When and Where to Go

WHEN TO GO

New York's four distinct seasons each lend a particular character to the city. The mild months of April, May, September and October are especially pleasant. Hotels are heavily booked during these times and advance reservations are recommended.

Spring – A brief and generally unpredictable season, spring brings New Yorkers out of doors to enjoy the mild temperatures (42° to 62°F). From late March through May, sunny days may give way to rain or to snow showers (not uncommon in April).

Summer – The weather can be unpleasantly muggy in the summer and many New Yorkers head out of town, leaving the city calmer and less crowded. Daytime temperatures can reach into the 90s, especially in July and August. The many shady green parks throughout the city, alive with free summer events, provide a welcome respite from the heat.

Fall – Warm temperatures (47° to 68°F), crisp, clear days and the brilliant colors of the trees (especially the reds and oranges of the maples) make this a favored time to visit New York. Fall also heralds the opening of the city's renowned cultural season.

Winter – Although winds blowing in off the Hudson and East Rivers can cause bitterly cold days, New York's winters are usually not too severe. Temperatures hover around 32°F, and the days are short but often clear and bright. The holiday season in New York is festive, indoors and out, with seasonal performances and decorations. January and February bring fewer crowds, with low-season discounts; it's a great time to land tickets to Broadway shows.

WHERE TO GO
TWO-DAY ITINERARY

For those with time for just a tiny bite at the Big Apple, this itinerary includes quintessential landmarks plus tantalizing ideas for your next visit.

FIRST DAY

Get a good overview by way of the bus or boat tours, then explore the highlights of Midtown: world-class visual and performing arts, architecture and shopping.

Morning	Double decker bus or Circle Line boat tour
Lunch	Grand Central Terminal★★★
Afternoon	Fifth Avenue★★★, Rockefeller Center*aaa*, Metropolitan Museum of Art★★★
Evening	Broadway★★, Times Square★★, Lincoln Center★★

SECOND DAY

After a bracing trip to the nation's beloved Lady Liberty, spend the rest of the day wandering the diverse neighborhoods of Lower Manhattan.

Morning	Ferry to Statue of Liberty★★★, Financial District★★
Lunch	In Chinatown★★
Afternoon	SoHo★ shopping or Chelsea★★ galleries
Evening	Dine in TriBeCa★, jazz in Greenwich Village★★

NEW YORK CITY TEMPERATURE CHART *(recorded at Central Park)*			
	Average high	**Average low**	**Precipitation**
January	38°F (3°C)	26°F (-3°C)	3.9in (9.9cm)
April	61°F (16°C)	44°F (7°C)	3.9in (9.9cm)
July	85°F (29°C)	70°F (21°C)	4.5in (11.4cm)
October	66°F (19°C)	50°F (10°C)	4.5in (11.4cm)

Central Park in summer

© Yadid Levy/age fotostock

FOUR-DAY ITINERARY

For visitors with a bit more time, this itinerary covers the best of New York's museums, neighborhoods and landmarks, plus dining, shopping and nightlife.

FIRST DAY

After a morning of art in Midtown, rest your feet on a boat tour, followed by a night at the theater.

Morning Rockefeller Center★★★, Museum of Modern Art★★★
Lunch In Midtown
Afternoon Circle Line boat tour
Evening Dine in Theater District★, see a Broadway show

SECOND DAY

Enjoy a day of iconic landmarks, museums and shopping, punctuated by a picnic break in Central Park.

Morning Empire State Building★★★ Stroll along Fifth Avenue★★★, Central Park★★★
Lunch Picnic in Central Park (look for food markets on the Upper West Side)
Afternoon American Museum of Natural History★★★
Evening Dine on the Upper West Side, Lincoln Center★★ performance

THIRD DAY

Explore the unique and historic neighborhoods of Lower Manhattan following a morning boat ride to Liberty Island and Ellis Island.

Morning Statue of Liberty★★★ and Ellis Island★★
Lunch Stone Street Historic District in the Financial District★★
Afternoon Civic Center★, Brooklyn Bridge★★★, Chinatown★★, Little Italy★
Evening Dine in TriBeCa★, jazz in Greenwich Village★★

FOURTH DAY

Uptown landmarks and art museums are on tap today. Later, unwind with dinner and a live cabaret show.

Morning UN Headquarters★★★, Grand Central Terminal★★★, East Midtown★★
Lunch In Midtown or the Upper East Side
Afternoon Metropolitan Museum of Art★★★ or Guggenheim★★
Evening Dine on the Upper East Side, cabaret at The Carlyle

What to See and Do

SIGHTSEEING
TOURS

If you have little time at your disposal, we recommend the two- or four-day itineraries described at the front of Planning Your Trip. You can also choose from a wide variety of guided tours offered in the city. Here's a selection:

City Tours

Double Decker and Trolley Tours – These tours of New York aboard double-decker buses and trolleys allow visitors to board at any of over 50 stops located at major attractions in Manhattan and Brooklyn, each lasting about 2–3hrs. Tours run every 30min year-round daily (except Jan 1 & Dec 25) 8.30am–5pm in Lower Manhattan, 9am–4pm in Uptown, and 10.30am–3pm in Brooklyn; $54 all loops ($49 online). The same ticket allows free reboarding for 2 consecutive days. An upgrade *($88)* includes the Statue of Liberty cruise, the Empire State Building and admission to the South Street Seaport Museum. *Tickets sold online or at Gray Line Visitors Center, 777 Eighth Ave. between W. 47th & W. 48th Sts.*

Gray Line *212-445-0848 or 800-669-0051. www.newyorksightseeing.com.*

Helicopter Tours – Offering a panoramic view of Manhattan and the five boroughs, these unforgettable flights last a brief 15–20min. Tours depart year-round starting at 9am, weather permitting, from the heliport at Pier 6 along the East River in Lower Manhattan *(last flight 6.45pm Mon–Sat, 4.45pm Sun; reservations required; $150–$215 per person plus $30 security fee).* Contact Liberty Helicopters (*212-967-6464 or 800-542-9933; www.libertyhelicopter.com*).

Neighborhood Tours

The following organizations offer a number of different walking tours through New York's distinct neighborhoods, exploring the city's diverse history and architecture:

Adventure on a Shoestring – *212-265-2663.* About 25 tours year-round weekends. Any tour $5.

Big Onion Walking Tours – *888-606-9255. www.bigonion.com.* Year-round daily 2hr tours of historic districts and ethnic neighborhoods. $15. *See schedule online.*

Context – *800-691-6036. www.contexttravel.com.* Small-group walking tours led by scholars covering history, art, architecture and cuisine. $55–$65.

Double-decker tour bus

© Christian De Grandmaison/Dreamstime.com

World Yacht Dinner Cruises

Spectacular views of the Manhattan skyline from aboard *World Yacht*. Three-hour cruises take place each evening May–Dec *(Apr, Wed–Sun)*. Depart from Pier 81, W. 41st St. at the Hudson River. Dinner packages start from $101.98 Mon–Thu & $106.52 Fri–Sun; lunch and Sun brunch packages also available. *800-498-4270. www. worldyacht.com. Jackets required for evening cruises; no jeans, shorts or sneakers.*

Foods of New York Tours, Inc – *917-408-9539. www.foodsofny.com.* Year-round 3hr tours of Greenwich Village (*daily*), Chelsea/Meatpacking District (*Thur–Sun*), SoHo (*Thur–Sat*) and Chinatown (*Mon & Sat*). Call or check online for schedule. *$47 and $65.*

Grand Tour of Midtown – *212-883-2420. www.grandcentralpartnership.org.* Year-round Fri 12.30pm. The 90 min tour departs from the Sculpture Court at 120 Park Avenue at E. 42nd Street.

Harlem Spirituals, Inc. (*see Harlem*) – *212-391-0900 or 800-660-2166. www.harlemspirituals.com.*

Municipal Art Society – *212-439-1049. www.mas.org.* Two-hour themed or architectural walking tours. Also private tours (*by appointment: 212-935-3960*). For details, call or go online. *$15.*

New York Like a Native – *718-393-7537. www.nylikeanative.com.* Offers a variety of Brooklyn tours of varying duration year-round. Call or check website for schedule and rates.

NYC Discovery Tours – *212-465-3331.* Themed tours of the city year-round, such as historic taverns at Christmas. Call for details. *$18–$22.*

Rent a New Yorker Tours – *212-982-9445. www.rentanewyorker.com.* Private tours (*$60 per hour, minimum 3hrs*). Call for schedule and reservations.

SCENIC CRUISES AND FERRIES

Tours of New York Harbor with panoramic views of the Statue of Liberty and the city's skyline are offered by the following boat lines:

Bateaux New York – European-style glass-enclosed boats depart year-round daily from Pier 61, W. 23rd St. Lunch cruises (*2hr; from $51.90*) and dinner cruises with entertainment (*3hr; from $117.90*). No jeans or sneakers. Call or go online for schedules. *866-817-3463. www.bateauxnewyork.com.*

Circle Line – Full Island Cruise (*3hrs; $35*); **Harbor Lights Cruise** (*2hrs; $31*); **Seaport Liberty Cruise** (*1hr 15min; $27; spring, summer & fall*); **Beast Speedboat Rides** (*30 min; $24; summer only*). All cruises depart from Pier 83, W. 42nd St. Call or go online for schedule. *212-563-3200. www.circleline42.com.*

NY Waterway Cruises depart year-round from Pier 78, W. 39th St.; 1hr 30min. *$26.* Call or go online for schedule. *800-533-3779. www.nywaterway.com.*

Spirit Cruises – Depart year-round daily from Pier 61, W. 23rd St. Lunch cruises (*2hrs*) from *$41.90.* Dinner cruises (*2hrs 30min*) from *$76.90.* Gospel lunch, jazz and dance cruises offered. *(fee) 866-483-3866. www.spiritofnewyork.com.*

Staten Island Ferry – *See Staten Island.*

World Yacht Cruises – *See sidebar above.*

ENTERTAINMENT TOURS

On Location Tours (*212-683-2027; www.screentours.com*) offers tours of familiar sites from TV shows and movies set in NYC.

The following tours give visitors a behind-the-scenes look at some of the city's renowned entertainment venues: **Radio City Grand Tour** and **NBC Studio Tour** (*see Central Midtown*); **Lincoln Center Tour** (*see Upper West Side*); **Carnegie Hall Tour** (*see East Midtown*); **Madison Square Garden Tour** (*tours every half* hour daily 11am–3pm & depart from the box office: Seventh Ave. at W.33rd St.; ☞$18.50; ✆212-465-5800; www.thegarden.com).

TELEVISION SHOWS

Tickets for shows in New York City are free, but are often hard to come by since some shows have waiting lists over a year long. Check the specific shows below for the procedure for getting tickets.

Late Show with David Letterman – *Ed Sullivan Theater, 1697 Broadway. ✆212-247-6497. www.cbs.com.* Visit website for details. For stand-by tickets to the *Late Show*, call the above number at 11am on the day of the show. Phones will be answered as long as tickets are available.

Live with Regis and Kelly – For advance tickets, send a postcard to Live with Regis and Kelly Tickets, Ansonia Station, PO Box 230-777, NY, NY 10023-077 (there is a 12-month wait); or try for same-day tickets at the corner of West 67th Street & Columbus Avenue at 7am. *http://regisandkelly. go.com.*

NBC Studio Show Tickets – For stand-by tickets to *Late Night with Jimmy Fallon (stand-by tickets distributed at 9am)* or *Saturday Night Live (stand-by tickets distributed at 7am),* arrive at the West 49th Street entrance of 30 Rockefeller Plaza (under the NBC Studios marquee) before the time shown above on the day of taping. Be aware that lines form much earlier than the distribution time. NBC does not accept ticket requests by mail. For advance tickets, call the ticket information line or check the website. *✆212-664-3056. www.nbc.com.*

No Tickets?
Several TV shows in New York City include the audiences gathered outside the windows of the studio. If you are not able to acquire tickets to be in the studio audience, you can still appear on television. Just arrive early outside one of these studios:

The Early Show – *767 Fifth Ave. at E.59th St; Mon–Sat 7am–9am. ✆212-975-2890. www.cbsnews.com/ earlyshow.*

Good Morning America – *Times Square at W. 44th St. & Broadway; Mon–Fri 7am–9am. ✆212-580-5176. www.abcnews.com.*

The Today Show – *49th St. & Rockefeller Plaza, between Fifth & Sixth Aves.; Mon–Fri 7am–11am. ✆212-664-3056. www.nbc.com.*

ACTIVITIES FOR KIDS 👪

Sights of particular interest to children in this guide are indicated by the 👪 symbol.

DISCOUNTS

Some attractions offer discount fees for children. *New York Family*, a free monthly magazine, includes articles of interest to parents as well as an extensive calendar of family-oriented events, and is available at major attractions and libraries throughout the area *(www.newyorkfamily.com).* Most attractions in New York offer discounted, if not free, admission to visitors under 18 years of age. In addition, many hotels make family discount packages available and some restaurants provide a children's menu.

THINGS TO DO

Manhattan: Downtown
Best for kids Downtown: the historic ships and live street performers at

SHOPPING FOR KIDS			
Disney Store	1540 Broadway	✆212-626-2910	www.disneystore.com
FAO Schwarz	767 Fifth Avenue	✆212-644-9400	www.fao.com
Scholastic Store	557 Broadway	✆212-343-6166	www.scholasticstore.com
Toys R Us	1514 Broadway	✆646-366-8800	www.toysrus.com

Sony Wonder Technology Lab

Sony Wonder Technology Lab

South Street Seaport, and the entertaining guides at the Lower East Side Tenement Museum. Break from sightseeing at Battery Park City's parks and playgrounds. Ferries to the Statue of Liberty and Ellis Island depart from the tip of Lower Manhattan.

Manhattan: Midtown
A trip to the top of the Empire State Building is an unmissable experience for kids in Midtown, especially on clear, sunny days.
Take a boat ride around Manhattan on the top deck of the Circle Line Boat Tour, and investigate the newly expanded Intrepid Sea, Air & Space Museum.
Sony Wonder Technology Lab – *E. 56th St. at Madison Ave. 212-833-8100. http://wondertechlab.sony.com.* Located in Sony Plaza, the lab is an interactive learning center that explores the world of electronics.

Central Midtown
At Rockefeller Center, head for the Top of the Rock for jaw-dropping Manhattan views, or browse through the NBC Experience store; the NBC Studio Tour is a fun experience for kids over 6. At holiday time, the high-kicking Rockettes headline the Radio City Christmas Spectacular, the ultimate kids' show in New York.

And don't forget the indoor Ferris wheel at Toys R Us in Times Square.

Central Park and Uptown
In fine weather, spend the day outdoors at Central Park's Wildlife Center and Children's Zoo, or snag a seat at the Swedish cottage Marionette Theater. If it's raining, head for the American Museum of Natural History to see the dinosaur skeletons, reptile hall, meteorites and minerals.
Central Park Carousel – *At 64th St. in Central Park. Year-round seven days a week, weather permitting. www. centralparknyc.org.* Carousels have been thrilling kids at Central Park since 1871. The carousel's 58 hand-carved and hand-painted horses are reputedly the largest ever made.

Children's Museum of Manhattan – *212 W. 83rd St. 212-721-1223. www. cmom.org.* Gods, Myths and Mortals: Discover Ancient Greece and other educational exhibits keep children happily occupied here for hours.

Boroughs
The Bronx, Brooklyn, Queens, Staten Island.
Catch a baseball game at the new Yankee Stadium, or head for the New York Aquarium, the New York Transit Museum, and the refurbished

Cyclone Rollercoaster, Coney Island

©Terraxplorer/iStockphoto.com/

Brooklyn Children's Museum. Or make an animated movie at the Museum of the Moving Image in Queens.

Big Apple Circus – *Cunningham Park in Queens. May–Jun. ℘212-268-2500. www.bigapplecircus.org.* Classical circus acts mix with puppets, parades and floats in this New York favorite.

Bronx Zoo – *Fordham Rd. & Bronx River Pkwy. ℘718-367-1010. www.bronxzoo.com.* This stellar zoo in Bronx Park features more than 1,800 mammals, 1,200 birds and 1,000 reptiles and amphibians.

Coney Island – *1208 Surf Ave., Brooklyn. ℘718-372-5159. www.coneyislandusa.com.* Coney Island's roller-coaster, aquarium and minor league baseball stadium are all kid-friendly and fun, and a hot dog from Nathan's is a local tradition.

New York Hall of Science – *47–01 111th St., Queens. ℘718-699-0005.*

Grizzly Bear, Bronx Zoo

©Sharon Kennedy/iStockphoto.com

www.nysci.org. A hands-on science museum with over 200 exhibits in Flushing Meadows Corona Park.

Staten Island Ferry – *www.siferry.com.* One of the few free things to do in NYC, the ferry passes right by Ellis Island, giving a nice view of the Statue of Liberty. On the return trip, passengers enjoy a beautiful view of the New York City skyline.

WHERE TO EAT

New York City offers a wide variety of kid-pleasing eateries, anything from a hot dog or a pretzel from a roadside vendor to lunch on Mars.

Ellen's Stardust Diner – *1650 Broadway & W. 51st St. ℘212-956-5151. www.ellensstardustdiner.com.* Enjoy this classic 50s diner along with its singing waitstaff.

Hard Rock Cafe – *1501 Broadway at W. 43rd St. ℘212-343-3355. www.hardrock.com.* Rock and roll memorabilia is served up with heaping hamburgers and ribs.

Jekyll & Hyde Club – *1409 Sixth Ave. between W. 57th & W. 58th Sts. ℘212-541-9505. www.jekyllandhyde club.com.* A real New York favorite, visitors line up for tasty pub-style dining with a haunted house atmosphere.

Mars 2112 – *Corner of W. 51st & Broadway. ℘212-582-2112. www.mars2112.com.* Take a ride on a UFO to the unknown world of Mars where you will find food, games and even aliens!

FILMS: NEW YORK IN THE MOVIES

King Kong (1933) Merrian C. Cooper

Miracle on 34th Street (1947) George Seaton

On the Town (1949) Stanley Donen, Gene Kelly

On the Waterfront (1954) Elia Kazan

Breakfast at Tiffany's (1961) Blake Edwards

West Side Story (1961) Robert Wise, Jerome Robbins

Funny Girl (1968) Williams Wyler

Midnight Cowboy (1968) John Schlesinger

Rosemary's Baby (1968) Roman Polanski

The French Connection (1971) William Friedkin

The Godfather (1972) Francis Ford Coppola

Taxi Driver (1976) Martin Scorsese

Saturday Night Fever (1977) John Badham

Manhattan (1979) Woody Allen

Arthur (1981) Steve Gordon

Ragtime (1981) Milos Forman

The Cotton Club (1984) Francis F. Coppola

Ghostbusters (1984) Ivan Reitman

After Hours (1985) Martin Scorsese

Broadway Danny Rose (1985) Woody Allen

Desperately Seeking Susan (1985) Susan Seidelman

Hannah and Her Sisters (1986) Woody Allen

Moonstruck (1987) Norman Jewison

Wall Street (1987) Oliver Stone

Bright Lights, Big City (1988) James Bridges

Crimes and Misdemeanors (1989) Woody Allen

Do the Right Thing (1989) Spike Lee

New York Stories (1989) Francis Ford Coppola, Woody Allen, Martin Scorsese

When Harry Met Sally (1989) Rob Reiner

Goodfellas (1990) Martin Scorsese

The Fisher King (1991) Terry Gilliam

Jungle Fever (1991) Spike Lee

The Wedding Banquet (1993) Ang Lee

City Hall (1995) Harold Becker

Smoke (1995) Wayne Wang

The Mirror Has Two Faces (1996) Barbra Streisand

As Good as It Gets (1997) James L. Brooks

Men in Black (1997) Barry Sonnenfeld

The Siege (1998) Edward Zwick

You've Got Mail (1998) Nora Ephron

Pollock (2000) Ed Harris

Gangs of New York (2002) Martin Scorsese

Day After Tomorrow (2004) Roland Emmerich

The Interpreter (2005) Sydney Pollack

The Devil Wears Prada (2006) David Frankel

Nick and Norah's Infinite Playlist (2008) Peter Sollett

Mickey Mantle's – *42 Central Park South.* ℰ*212-688-7777. www.mickey mantles.com.* Check out the sports memorabilia museum, watch games on the numerous televisions and enjoy a plate of hickory-smoked ribs at this restaurant named after a famous New York Yankee.

Planet Hollywood – *1540 Broadway at W. 45th St.* ℰ*212-333-7827. www. planethollywood.com.* Dine by your favorite heartthrob's belongings. **Serendipity3** – *225 E. 60th St.* ℰ*212-838-3531. www.serendipity3.com.* Frozen hot chocolate satisfies young and old at this Upper East Side institution.

Calendar of Events

The following is a selection of New York's most popular annual events. Dates can vary each year. For more information consult periodicals, or contact NYC & Company (℘212-484-1222; http://nycgo.com).

JANUARY–FEBRUARY

MID–LATE JAN

New York National Boat Show
Jacob K. Javits Center
www.newyorkboatshow.com
℘212-984-7000

Winter Antiques Show
Park Avenue Armory, 67th St. &
Park Ave. www.winterantiques
show.com. ℘718-292-7392

LATE JAN–FEB

Chinese New Year Celebrations
Chinatown.
www.explorechinatown.com

EARLY FEB

Empire State Building Run-Up
350 Fifth Ave. www.nyrr.org.
℘212-860-4455

ALL FEB

Black History Month

MID-FEB

Westminster Dog Show
Madison Square Garden.
www.westminsterkennelclub.org.
℘212-465-6741

MARCH–APRIL

EARLY MAR

International Artexpo New York
Pier 94 on the Hudson River.
http://artexponewyork.com.
℘888-608-5300

MAR 17

St. Patrick's Day Parade
Fifth Ave. from 44th to 86th Sts.
www.nycstpatricksparade.org

MAR–APR

Macy's Spring Flower Show
Macy's (Herald Sq.). ℘212-
494-4495

MAR–JUN

Biennial Exhibit
Whitney Museum of American Art
(every two years). ℘212-570-3676

LATE MAR–APR

NY International Auto Show
Jacob K. Javits Center.
www.autoshowny.com.
℘800-282-3336

**Ringling Bros. and Barnum
& Bailey Circus**
Meadowlands and Long Island.
www.ringling.com

EASTER SUNDAY

Easter Sunday Parade
Fifth Ave. from 49th to 57th Sts.

LATE APR

Cherry Blossom Festival
Brooklyn Botanic Garden.
www.bbg.org. ℘718-623-7200

St. Patrick's Day Parade

©Yulia Ivanova/Dreamstime.com

July 4th Fireworks Over Brooklyn Bridge

©iStockphoto.com/Michal Besser.

MAY–JUNE

EARLY MAY
TriBeCa Film Festival
www.tribecafilmfestival.org.
☎ 212-941-2400

MID-MAY
Ninth Ave. Intl. Food Festival
Ninth Ave. from 37th to 57th Sts.
www.ninthavenuefoodfestival.
com. ☎ 212-581-7217

LATE MAY–EARLY JUN
Big Apple Circus
Cunningham Park, Queens.
www.bigapplecircus.org.
☎ 212-268-2500

LATE MAY–EARLY JUN, EARLY SEPT
**Washington Square
Outdoor Art Exhibit**
Greenwich Village. www.
washingtonsquareoutdoorart.
exhibit.org. ☎ 212-982-6255

EARLY JUN
Museum Mile Festival
www.museummilefestival.org.
☎ 212-606-2296

National Puerto Rican Day Parade
Fifth Ave. from 44th to 79th Sts.
www.nationalpuertoricanday
parade.org. ☎ 718-401-0404

JUN–JUL
Metropolitan Opera Parks Concerts
Various locations.
☎ 212-362-6000

Midsummer-Night Swing
Damrosch Park, Lincoln Center.
www.lincolncenter.org.
☎ 212-875-5766

**NY Philharmonic
Concerts in the Parks**
www.nyphil.org.
☎ 212-875-5709

JUN–AUG
**Street Performers and
Evening Concerts**
South Street Seaport.
www.southstreetseaport.com.
☎ 212-732-7678

SummerStage in Central Park
Rumsey Playfield.
www.summerstage.org.
☎ 212-360-2777

MID–LATE JUN
JVC Jazz Festival New York
Carnegie Hall, Lincoln Center
and other venues.
www.festivalnetwork.com

LATE JUN
LGBT Pride Week Celebrations
various locations.
www.nycpride.org.
☎ 212-807-7433

Mermaid Parade
Coney Island, Brooklyn.
www.coneyislandusa.com.
☎ 718-372-5159

JULY–AUGUST

JUL
Lincoln Center Festival
Alice Tully Hall.
www.lincolncenter.org.
☎ 212-875-5050

NYC Tap Festival
Citywide. www.atdf.org.
☏ 646-230-9564

JULY 4
Macy's Fireworks Celebration
www.macys.com/fireworks.
☏ 212-494-4495

AUG
Harlem Week
Harlem.
www.harlemweek.com

Lincoln Center Out-of-Doors
Damrosch Park, Lincoln Center.
www.lincolncenter.org.
☏ 212-721-6500

Mostly Mozart Festival
Lincoln Center.
www.lincolncenter.org.
☏ 212-721-6500

Race for Mayor's Cup
79th St. Boat Basin.
www.nymayorscup.com

SEPTEMBER–OCTOBER

LABOR DAY
West Indian-American Day
Carnival Parade
Eastern Pkwy. from Utica Ave. to
Grand Army Plaza, Brooklyn.
www.wiadca.com. ☏ 718-467-
1797

EARLY SEPT
US Open Tennis Tournament
USTA National Tennis Center,
Flushing.
www.usopen.org.
☏ 718-760-6200

MID-SEPT
Feast of San Gennaro
Mulberry St., Little Italy.
www.sangennaro.org.
☏ 212-768-9320

LATE SEPT–OCT
New York Film Festival
Lincoln Center.
www.filmlinc.com.
☏ 212-875-5050

OCT
The New Yorker Festival
Various Midtown locations.
www.festival.newyorker.com

MID-OCT
Columbus Day Parade
Fifth Ave. from 47th to 72nd Sts.
www.columbuscitizensfd.org.
☏ 212-249-9923

OCT 31
Halloween Parade
Greenwich Village.
www.halloween-nyc.com

NOVEMBER–DECEMBER

EARLY NOV
New York City Marathon
Verrazano-Narrows Bridge
to Central Park.
www.nycmarathon.org.
☏ 212-423-2249

NOV–DEC
Macy's Thanksgiving Day Parade
Central Park West to Herald Sq.
☏ 212-494-4495

Radio City Christmas Spectacular
Radio City Music Hall.
www.radiocitychristmas.com.
☏ 800-982-2787

LATE NOV–DEC
The Chorus Tree
South Street Seaport.
www.southstreetseaport.com.
☏ 212-732-7678

LATE NOV–EARLY JAN
Christmas Tree and 18C Neapolitan
Baroque Crèche
Metropolitan Museum of Art.
www.metmuseum.org.
☏ 212-535-7710

The Nutcracker NY
David H. Koch Theater, Lincoln
Center. www.lincolncenter.org.
☏ 212-870-5570

EARLY DEC
Christmas Tree Lighting Ceremony
Rockefeller Center.
www.rockefellercenter.com.
☏ 212-632-3975

Lighting of the Giant Chanukah
Menorah
Grand Army Plaza, Brooklyn;
Fifth Ave. at 59th St.

DEC 31
New Year's Eve Ball Drop
Times Sq.
www.timessquarenyc.org

Know Before You Go

USEFUL WEBSITES

http://nycgo.com
The official city tourism organization's website is packed with up-to-date information on New York City events, hotels, restaurants, shopping, etc.

http://nytimes.com
The online version of *The New York Times* has a New York City travel guide that includes articles focusing on city life, as well as information on hotels, restaurants, events and shows.

http://newyork.citysearch.com
Allows users to access a directory of services and find specific nightclubs, spas, hotels, restaurants and more. Also movies, events and shopping.

http://nymag.com
An online version of *New York Magazine* filled with articles on the city's movers and shakers as well as news, events, fashion and shopping.

http://ny.com
Information on trip planning, music, shopping, entertainment, sports, real estate and transportation. Includes links to maps and weather forecasts.

www.wheretraveler.com
Links to the website of *IN-New York Magazine*, featuring art and collectibles, Broadway shows, museums, shopping, musical events and a neighborhood guide.

www.citidex.com
An online telephone and information directory covering all points in Manhattan, with quick access to interactive maps, parking and transportation information.

www.cityguideny.com
Event-oriented site with up-to-date listings of shows, exhibitions, concerts, performances and activities. Includes an interactive activity planner and shopping and dining information.

www.nyc.gov
Official city government website with up-to-the-minute news and information. Includes a section for visitors with links to transportation, lodging, dining and sightseeing information.

www.downtownny.com
The website for the Downtown Alliance features dining, lodging, event and sightseeing information for Lower Manhattan. Includes listings of Wi-Fi hotspots in the area.

VISITOR INFORMATION

To obtain maps and information on points of interest, accommodations and seasonal events, contact the agencies below. NYC & Company, the city's official marketing and tourism organization, also publishes the annually updated *Official NYC Guide*, which is available free of charge.

NYC & Company
   ☎212-484-1200
   810 Seventh Avenue
   New York, NY 10019
   http://nycgo.com

New York State Division of Tourism
   ☎518-474-4116 or 800-225-5697
   1 Commerce Plaza
   Albany, NY 12245
   www.iloveny.com

Four free publications, *City Guide Magazine* (www.cityguideny.com), *IN-New York Magazine* (www.innewyork.com), *Where New York* and the *Official City Guide*, offer information on events, attractions, shopping and dining. They are available at hotels and visitor information kiosks. The **Official NYC Guide** is available free of charge from NYC & Company (*☎212-484-1200; http://nycgo.com*).

Volunteer New Yorkers take out-of-towners on two- to four-hour visits of city neighborhoods as part of a unique free service called **Big Apple Greeter**. Particular emphasis is placed on matching interests and language requirements of visitors and volunteers (*advance reservations required; ☎212-669-8159; www.bigapplegreeter.org*).

Consider purchasing a **CityPass** ticket booklet (*$79 adult, $59 youth 6–17; ☎888-330-5008; www.citypass.com*) that includes discounted admission to six major sights in New York (Empire

State Building Observatory; Museum of Modern Art; American Museum of Natural History; Metropolitan Museum of Art; and choice of Circle Line sightseeing cruises or the Statue of Liberty/Ellis Island and Guggenheim Museum or Top of the Rock at Rockefeller Center) and allows you to skip most ticket lines. Buy your CityPass online or at any of the participating attractions.

LOCAL TOURISM OFFICES
NYC & Company Official Visitor Information Center
810 Seventh Ave. between W. 52nd & W. 53rd Sts. 212-484-1200. http://nycgo.com. Open year-round Mon–Fri 8.30am–6pm, Sat–Sun 9am–5pm, holidays 9am–3pm.

Chinatown
Information kiosk at the triangle of Canal, Walker & Baxter Sts. Open year-round daily 10am–6pm, holidays 10am–3pm.

City Hall Park
Information kiosk at the southern tip of City Hall Park on the Broadway sidewalk at Park Row. Open year-round Mon–Fri 9am–6pm, Sat–Sun 10am–5pm, holidays 9am–3pm.

Financial District
Information center at Federal Hall National Memorial, 26 Wall St. Open year-round Mon–Fri 9am–5pm. Closed federal holidays.

Harlem
Information center at the Studio Museum in Harlem, 144 W. 125th St. between Lenox St. & Adam Clayton Powell Blvd. Open year-round Mon–Fri noon–6pm, Sat–Sun 10am–6pm. Closed holidays.

Times Square
Times Square Visitor Center at 1560 Broadway between W. 46th & W. 47th Sts. 212-484-1222. www.timessquarenyc.org. Open year-round Mon-Fri 9am–8pm, Sat–Sun 8am–8pm. Closed Jan 1 & Dec 25.

INTERNATIONAL VISITORS
Visitors from outside the US can obtain information from the multilingual staff at NYC & Company (212-484-1200; http://nycgo.com), or from the US embassy in their country.

EMBASSIES AND CONSULATES
In New York international visitors can contact the consulate of their country of residence. See chart below.

FOREIGN CONSULATES

Country	Address	Website	
Australia	150 E. 42nd St.	www.newyork.usa.embassy.gov.au	212-351-6500
Belgium	1065 Ave. of the Americas	www.diplomatie.be/newyork	212-586-5110
Canada	1251 Ave. of the Americas	www.newyork.gc.ca	212-596-1628
China	520 Twelfth Ave.	www.nyconsulate.prchina.org	212-244-9456
France	934 Fifth Ave.	www.consulfrance-newyork.org	212-606-3600
India	3 E. 64th St.	www.indiacgny.org	212-774-0600
Italy	690 Park Ave.	www.consnewyork.esteri.it	212-737-9100
Mexico	27 E. 39th St.	consulmex.sre.gob.mx/nuevayork	212-217-6400
Netherlands	1 Rockefeller Plaza	ny.the-netherlands.org	877-388-2443
Spain	150 E. 58th St.	www.maec.es/consulados/nuevayork	212-355-4080
Switzerland	633 Third Ave.	www.eda.admin.ch/newyork	212-599-5700
United Kingdom	845 Third Ave.	ukinusa.fco.gov.uk	212-745-0200

ENTRY REQUIREMENTS

Citizens of countries participating in the **Visa Waiver Program (VWP)** must apply for authorization online through the Electronic System of Travel Authorization *(www.cbp.gov)* and present a machine-readable passport to enter the US for general business or tourist purposes for a maximum of 90 days; otherwise a US nonimmigrant visa is required. For a list of countries participating in the VWP, contact the US consulate in your country of residence or check the official Visa Services website *(http://travel.state.gov)*. Citizens of nonparticipating countries must have a nonimmigrant visa. US citizens entering the US from countries participating in the **Western Hemisphere Travel Initiative** (Canada, Mexico, Bermuda and the Caribbean nations) must present a passport if traveling by air; a passport, passport card or other WHTI-compliant document if traveling by land or sea. Children age 16 and under entering from WHTI countries by land or sea must present proof of citizenship. Naturalized Canadian citizens should carry their citizenship papers. Inoculations are generally not required.

CUSTOMS REGULATIONS

All articles brought into the US must be declared at the time of entry. **Exempt** from customs regulations: personal effects; one liter (33.8 fl. oz) of alcoholic beverages per traveler over age 21; either 200 cigarettes, 50 cigars or 2 kilograms of smoking tobacco; and gifts that do not exceed $100 in value. **Prohibited items** include plant material; firearms and ammunition; meat or poultry products. For other prohibited items, exemptions and information, contact the US embassy or consulate before departing, or the US Customs Service (*877-227-5511; www.cbp.gov*).

HEALTH

The US does not have a national health program. Visitors should check with their insurer to determine if their medical insurance covers medical care in the US. Prescription drugs should be properly identified, and accompanied by a copy of the prescription.

ACCESSIBILITY &

In this guide wheelchair access is indicated with a & symbol. Most public buildings and attractions provide wheelchair access. All MTA buses and some subway stations are wheelchair-accessible; discounted fares are available. MTA also operates a door-to-door service for people with disabilities who are unable to use public transport; for information, contact MTA Accessible Line (*877-337-2017 or www.mta. info*). Hospital Audiences, Inc. provides information about cultural offerings in New York (*548 Broadway, 3rd floor, New York, NY 10012; 212-575-7676; www.hainyc.org*).

Getting There

BY AIR

New York City is served by three airports, two in the borough of Queens and one in New Jersey. They are all run by the Port Authority of New York & New Jersey. In all three airports, ground transportation and information booths are located on the baggage claim level. Plan to arrive at the airport at least two hours before flight departure time for domestic flights and three hours ahead for international flights. Due to increased security measures, it takes longer to get through airline security checkpoints. Carry-on restrictions vary somewhat, so be sure to check with your airline well in advance of your flight.

JOHN F. KENNEDY AIRPORT (JFK)

In Queens, 15mi/24km SE of Midtown Manhattan (allow 1hr driving time). 718-244-4444 or 800-247-7433. www.panynj.gov.

23

Most international flights arrive and depart from Kennedy. Airport information counters are located in all terminals. Departing passengers should allow themselves the maximum amount of time recommended by their airline. Restaurants with sit-down service are located in all terminals. Most modes of transportation depart outside each terminal. JFK Medport, a 24hr full-service medical clinic, is located in Cargo Area A (℘718-656-1245).

LAGUARDIA AIRPORT (LGA)

In Queens, 8mi/12.8km NE of Midtown Manhattan (allow 30min driving time). ℘718-533-3400 or 800-247-7433. www.panynj.gov.
LaGuardia is serviced by most domestic and North American air carriers. The airport information counter is located between concourses C and D on the departure level. Fast-food and full-service restaurants are located in all terminals. Most modes of transportation depart outside each terminal.

NEWARK LIBERTY INTL. AIRPORT (EWR)

In Newark, New Jersey, 16mi/25.7km SW of Midtown Manhattan (allow 45min driving time). ℘973-961-6000. www.panynj.gov.
Many travelers find this airport easier to navigate; flights include both international and domestic air carriers. Concierge counters are located in Terminals B and C. Restaurants with sit-down service are located on the concourse level of all terminals. Intra-airport monorail stations are available at each terminal. Most modes of ground transportation depart outside each terminal.

AIRPORT TRANSFERS

Contact ground-transportation information counters for listings of authorized agents and avoid solicitations from unauthorized drivers. For additional information contact the Port Authority of New York & New Jersey (℘212-435-7000 or 800-247-7433; www.panynj.gov).

😊 A Bit of Advice 😊

Always note the medallion number (on the roof of the taxi) and driver's six-digit license number (inside on the passenger-driver partition) of the taxi you ride in, in case there's a problem or you mistakenly leave a belonging in the cab. Dial 311 to complain or report lost property.

BUS

Buses travel frequently between the Airport Bus Center at the **Port Authority Bus Terminal** *(W. 42nd St. & Eighth Ave.; ℘800-221-9903)* and JFK Airport *(approx. 1hr; 🚌$15.75; every 30min)*; LaGuardia Airport *(approx. 45min; 🚌$12.75; every 30min)*; and Newark Airport *(approx. 30min; 🚌$15; every 15min)*.

TAXIS

Taxi service is available outside each terminal. Only yellow taxi cabs with roof medallions showing the taxi number are authorized by the New York City Taxi & Limousine Commission to pick up passengers on the street. Passengers at Kennedy and LaGuardia Airports should wait in line and allow a uniformed dispatcher to hail the next available cab. Fares to Manhattan: from JFK, $45 flat rate to any point in Manhattan *(tolls not included)*; from LGA, $28–$35 *(average metered rate plus tolls if applicable)*; from EWR, $50–$75 *(average metered rate plus tolls)* plus a $15 surcharge. A 50¢ surcharge is added to all metered fares nightly 8pm–6am; and a $1.00 peak-time surcharge weekdays 4pm–8pm. A 50¢ New York State Tax Surcharge is charged at all times. www.nyc.gov/taxi.

RAIL SERVICE

The **Air Train JFK** light-rail system connects JFK's terminals and parking lots to each other and to subway, bus and commuter rail lines to New York City and Long Island *(operates daily 24hrs; 🚌$5 off-airport connection, free within airport; ℘877-535-2478; www.*

airtrainjfk.com). **Air Train Newark** provides rail connection from terminals and parking lots of Newark Airport to Amtrak and New Jersey Transit rail lines *(operates daily 24hrs; fare depends on destination; ℘888-397-4636; www.airtrainnewark.com).*

SHUTTLES AND LIMOUSINES

Super Shuttle offers inter-airport service as well as service to and from Manhattan by van *(shared ride)* 24hrs daily *(☞$15–$23; ℘212-258-3826; www.supershuttle.com).* **New York Airport Service** express bus runs between Kennedy and LaGuardia Airports and Grand Central Railroad Terminal *(free transfer to Midtown hotels)*, and between Penn Station and Port Authority Bus Terminal daily *(call or go online for schedules and fares: ℘212-875-8200; www.nyairportservice. com).* **Olympia Trails Newark Airport Express Bus** *(call or go online for schedules and fares: ℘877-863-9275; www.newarkairportexpress.com)* runs from Newark to Bryant Park, Grand Central Terminal and Port Authority Bus Terminal. **Carey Limousine** *(reservations required; ℘202-895-1200 or 800-336-4646; www.ecarey.com)* offers chauffeur-driven cars at fixed rates between Manhattan and Kennedy *(☞$160–$250),* LaGuardia *(☞$140–$180)* and Newark *(☞$185–$280)* Airports *(rates are approximate and do not include tolls).* Other chauffeur-driven car services are available at the airport transportation counter via self-service telephones.

RENTAL CARS

See Getting Around.
Major rental-car agencies have counters on the arrivals level of the airport terminals. Free shuttle buses or Air Train serve the agency parking lots.

PUBLIC TRANSPORTATION

See Getting Around.
From Kennedy to Manhattan:
MTA A train from Howard Beach station; E, J or Z trains from Sutphin Blvd-Archer Ave-JFK station from

the airport *(see Rail Service above).* From LaGuardia: MTA M60 bus to Manhattan.

BY TRAIN
AMTRAK

℘800-872-7245, accessible in North America only; outside North America, contact your local travel agent. www.amtrak.com.
The US rail network, Amtrak offers daily service to Manhattan's **Pennsylvania Station** *(Seventh Ave. & W. 32nd St.)* on the *Adirondack* (originating in Montreal), the *Maple Leaf* (from Toronto), the *Silver Service* (from Miami), the *Lake Shore Limited* (from Chicago), the *Pennsylvanian* (from Pittsburgh), the *Ethan Allen Express* (from Rutland, VT) and the *Crescent* (from New Orleans). Overnight trains offer sleeping accommodations. The *Acela Express* and *Northeast Regional* lines (reservations required) connect Washington and Boston with New York City. Travelers from Canada should inquire with their local travel agents about Amtrak/VIA Rail connections. **USA RailPass** offers travel on the Amtrak network at discounted rates; passes are available for 15, 30 and 45 days.

LOCAL SERVICE

Rail service into Manhattan's **Grand Central Terminal** *(E. 42nd St. & Park Ave.)* is provided by **Metro-North** *(℘212-532-4900; www.mta.info/mnr),* which runs between Manhattan and New Haven, CT, Wassaic, NY and Poughkeepsie, NY. Both the **Long Island Railroad** *(℘718-217-5477; www.mta.info/lirr)* and **New Jersey Transit** *(℘973-275-5555 or 800-772-2287; www.njtransit.com)* operate out of Pennsylvania Railroad Station. **PATH (Port Authority Trans-Hudson)** rail lines *(℘800-234-7284; www. panynj.gov/path)* connect Manhattan with Newark and Hudson County, NJ.

BY CAR

See Access Roads map p38. Visitors bearing valid driver's licenses issued by their country of residence are not required to obtain an Inter-national Driver's License to drive in the US. Drivers must carry vehicle registration and/or rental contract, and proof of automobile insurance at all times. Rental cars in the US are usually equipped with automatic transmission, and rental rates tend to be less expensive than overseas. **Gasoline** is sold by the gallon *(1 gallon = 3.8 liters)* and is cheaper than in other countries. Most self-service gas stations do not offer car repair, although many sell standard maintenance items. Road regulations in the US require that vehicles be driven on the right side of the road. Distances are posted in miles *(1 mile = 1.6 kilometers)*.

BY BUS

Long-distance bus fares in the US are generally lower than other forms of public transportation. Buses do not offer sleeping accommodations. **Greyhound** *(advance reservations suggested; ☎800-231-2222; www. greyhound.com)* provides access to New York City at a leisurely pace; its Discovery Pass allows unlimited travel throughout the US and Canada for 7, 15, 30 or 60 days. **Peter Pan** *(☎800-343-9999; www.peterpanbus. com)* offers service throughout the Northeastern US.

Getting Around

LAY OF THE LAND

Manhattan's streets are laid out in a grid pattern. Streets run east–west and avenues run north–south. Fifth Avenue is the dividing line between east and west addresses. Though Avenue of the Americas is the official name, New Yorkers prefer to call it by its original name, Sixth Avenue. Generally, even-numbered streets are eastbound; odd-numbered streets are westbound. In Lower Manhattan (below 14th St.) most streets have names rather than numbers. North of Houston (HOW-stun) Street (with the exception of Greenwich Village), blocks are generally short and wide. To locate a particular address, check the Manhattan Address Locator *(www. ny.com/locator)* or in the Yellow Pages of the telephone directory.

PUBLIC TRANSPORTATION

The **Metropolitan Transportation Authority (MTA)** oversees an extensive network of buses, subway and commuter trains throughout the area. MTA New York City Transit runs the city bus and subway lines. Contact the

> ☺ **A Bit of Advice** ☺
>
> **Downtown** refers to the area south of 34th Street. **Midtown** stretches from 34th Street to 59th Street. Above 59th Street is referred to as **Uptown**. Uptown and downtown also refer to direction: if you're at 14th Street and your destination is 50th Street, you'll be traveling uptown to get to Midtown. If you're headed the other way, you'll be traveling downtown to get downtown.

agencies and companies listed under Local Service (☺ *see Getting There*) for route information and schedules to Long Island and upstate New York, New Jersey and Connecticut. The **MTA Travel Information Center** *(☎718-330-1234; www.mta.info)* provides route and fare information for subway and bus lines, plus online and voice-activated custom trip planners. System maps and timetables are available *(☞free)* on buses and at all subway stations, visitor information centers and most hotels. In this guide, subway and bus stops are indicated with the MTA symbol.

☺ **A Bit of Advice** ☺

Find **directions** for getting around
town by subway or on foot at:
www.511ny.org
www.mta.info
www.google.com

SUBWAY

Map inside back cover. The subway
system (24 lines and 468 stations) is
the most efficient way to navigate the
city. Subway entrances are indicated on
street level by a staircase descending (in some cases, ascending) to the
station. Large green or red globes
also herald the presence of a subway
station: a red globe indicates an exit
only. Virtually all lines run 24hrs/day
every 2–5min during rush hours, every
5–12min during the day and every
20min between midnight and 5am.
Platform signs indicate which trains
stop at the station (uptown trains are
northbound; downtown trains are
southbound). Signs on the side of
each train list the route number
or letter. Local trains stop at every
station; express trains do not.
Conductors announce each stop.
Because of ongoing track work, trains
may be rerouted, especially late at night
(midnight–5am); changes are usually
posted in stations near the turnstiles
—read them carefully. ☺*When riding
the subway late at night, avoid isolated
areas ("off-peak waiting areas" are
provided in stations), and ride in the car
carrying the train's conductor (located
in the fourth car of the train).*

BUSES

New York City Transit buses generally
operate daily 5.30am–2am. Some
routes on major corridors run 24hrs/
day. Weekend hours may be reduced
on some lines. During weekdays, most
buses run every 5–15min; frequency
varies at other times. Pick-up points
are recognizable by tall, round signs
bearing the bus emblem and route
number. Route maps are displayed
at most bus stops and shelters. Stops
are made at posted locations, two

to three blocks apart. Stops may be
made at other locations along regular
routes upon request between 10pm
and 5am. If you are unsure about the
route, verify your desired stop with the
driver. Route numbers are displayed
on the front and sides (sometimes
back) of each bus. Local bus routes are
indicated by a letter prefix indicating
the borough in which that line largely
operates (for example, M7):

M = Manhattan   **B** = Brooklyn
Bx = Bronx   **Q** = Queens
S = Staten Island

All buses are equipped with wide
doors, wheelchair lifts and related
accessibility features.

FARES

All system fares are $2.25 one way
with the exception of express bus fare,
which is $5.50. The **MetroCard** auto-
mated fare card is accepted on both
systems and includes a free transfer
for each fare, between subway and
bus, or bus to bus, within 2hrs of
paying the initial fare. Up to three
children *(under 44 inches tall)* may ride
free when accompanied by an adult.
MetroCard also offers unlimited ride
options: 7 days (✆$29) and 30 days
(✆$104). Reduced fares are available
for senior citizens and persons with
qualifying disabilities *(information:
✆718-330-1234)*.
MetroCards can be purchased (or value
added) at subway stations and retail
outlets. Discount passes are available
only from authorized merchants, the
Times Square Visitor Center, transit
museum stores (Grand Central Terminal
and downtown Brooklyn), and vending
machines that are located in many
stations.
Bus and subway travel information
is available 24hrs/day (✆718-330-1234).
Information can be obtained in 140
languages (✆718-330-4847). Maps and
schedules are also available online
(www.mta.info).

BY TAXI

Only yellow taxi cabs with roof medallions showing the taxi number are

😊 A Bit of Advice 😊

Twenty north–south blocks equal a mile; about seven east–west blocks equal a mile. Street addresses increase with their distance east and west from Fifth Avenue, usually by 100 per block.

authorized by the City of New York to pick up passengers on the street. All yellow medallion cabs are metered and share the same rate schedule (using other cabs may risk your personal safety): $2.50 upon entry, 40¢ each additional .2 mile. 40¢/minute is charged while the cab is stopped or in slow traffic. A 50¢ surcharge is added between 8pm and 6am, a $1.00 surcharge weekdays between 4pm and 8pm, and a New York State Tax Surcharge of 50¢ is applied at all times. There are no extra fees for additional riders, although taxis are able to accept only 4 or 5 passengers. In addition to the metered rates, passengers are responsible for toll fees, and drivers are usually tipped 15–20 percent. You can hail a taxi from the street in most areas in Manhattan; a taxi is available when its rooftop white number is lit. Taxi stands are located at most hotels, transportation terminals and entertainment centers (in other areas call for service). For more information, access the city's Taxi & Limousine Commission online (www.nyc.gov/taxi).

New York Water Taxi (℘212-742-1969; www.nywatertaxi.com) is another way to get around while avoiding city traffic. Water taxi pick-up and drop-off points are dotted around Lower Manhattan, Brooklyn and Queens. Routes and schedules vary by day and by season; check the website for a route map and fare information.

BY CAR

It's not necessary to have a car when visiting Manhattan. Public transportation is efficient and many sights can be reached easily on foot. Keep in mind that streets are usually congested, public parking lots expensive and street parking extremely difficult to find. **Rush hours**, the peak transit times for business commuters, occur weekdays between 7am–9am and 4.30pm–6pm. It's best to avoid driving during these times.

RENTAL CARS

Major car-rental companies have offices in Manhattan, in the outer boroughs, and at the three New York City area airports. Most agencies will only rent to persons at least 25 years old, although some will rent to younger drivers for

New York Water Taxi

Y. Kanazawa/MICHELIN

Alamo	✆800-462-5266 www.alamo.com
Avis	✆800-331-1212 www.avis.com
Budget	✆800-527-0700 www.budget.com
Dollar	✆866-434-2226 www.dollar.com
Enterprise	✆800-264-6350 www.enterprise.com
Hertz	✆800-654-3131 www.hertz.com
National	✆800-227-7368 www.nationalcar.com
Thrifty	✆800-847-4389 www.thrifty.com

a daily surcharge. A major credit card and valid driver's license are required (some agencies also require proof of insurance). Most rental companies offer seasonal discounts and accept membership privileges. The average daily weekday rate for a compact car, with unlimited mileage, ranges from $90 to 110. Weekly rates *(5 days)* for a compact car begin around $450. Note that rental cars are taxed 13.62 percent *(not included in the advertised rate)*. Many limousine and executive car-service companies offer transportation within the city and to the boroughs, and will customize an itinerary for a day to suit any visitor's needs. For a specific listing of companies, consult the *Official NYC Guide* (◔ *see Visitor Information in Know Before You Go*).

ROAD REGULATIONS

The maximum speed limit on major expressways is 65mph in rural areas and 55mph in and around cities. **Speed limits** in the city range from 25mph in residential areas to 30mph on major streets. Use of **seat belts** is mandatory for driver and passengers in the front seat of the car, and children under 16 years old in the back seat. Child safety seats are required for children under 4 years (seats are available from most rental-car agencies). In New York City,

unless otherwise posted, drivers are not permitted to turn right on a red traffic light. The majority of streets in Manhattan are one-way (traffic flows in one direction only). In New York it is illegal to drive with a cellphone in your hand; you must connect your phone to a hands-free device.

PARKING

If you are successful in finding street parking, pay close attention to signs indicating restrictions. Parking is prohibited during posted street-cleaning times. Parking in some residential areas is by permit only (restricted to area residents). Vehicles are systematically towed for violations. If you believe your car has been towed, dial ✆311 (the city government's information line), or ✆212-639-9675 (if you are outside the city), to find out.
The **Manhattan Tow Pound** is located at Pier 76 *(W. 38th St. at 12th Ave.; ✆212-971-0772; www.nyc.gov)*. For parking violations, call the city government's information line (✆311). Spaces identified with ♿ are reserved for people with disabilities only. Anyone parking in these spaces without proper identification is subject to a heavy fine. Privately operated parking lots and garages are abundant throughout the city; rates range from ✆$6 to $15/hr.

TOLL CROSSINGS

(for more information: www.www.mta.info/bandt)

Brooklyn-Battery Tunnel	$6.50
Cross Bay Memorial Bridge	$3.25
George Washington Bridge*	$8
Henry Hudson Bridge	$4
Holland Tunnel*	$8
Lincoln Tunnel*	$8
Marine Parkway Bridge	$3.25
Queens-Midtown Tunnel	$6.50
RFK/Triborough Bridge	$6.50
Throgs Neck Bridge	$6.50
Verrazano-Narrows Bridge	$13

*managed by the Port Authority
(🖥 www.panynj.gov)

Basic Information

BUSINESS HOURS

Most businesses operate Mon–Fri 9am–5pm. Banking institutions are generally open 9am–5pm; some offer Saturday service (9am–noon). Most retail stores and specialty shops are open Mon–Sat 10am–6pm (Thu until 9pm), Sun noon–6pm. Small, neighborhood convenience stores usually stay open past 10pm. Some stores on the Lower East Side and along Diamond and Jewelry Way *(47th St.)* close on Friday afternoon and all day Saturday for the Jewish Sabbath; stores keep normal hours on Sunday.

COMMUNICATIONS
AREA CODES

Manhattan	212, 646, 917
Bronx, Brooklyn, Queens, Staten Island	347, 718, 917, 929
Hudson River Valley	845, 914
Long Island	516, 631

Local calls from pay phones cost 50¢ for unlimited use (calls from Manhattan to the outer boroughs and vice versa are local but require dialing 1 and the area code). For long-distance calls, it is best to purchase a pre-paid phone card, which is available in most newsstands and drugstores. Some public telephones accept credit cards, and all will accept long-distance calling cards. Note that the rise in popularity of cellphones has resulted in a sharp decrease in the number of public pay telephones in Manhattan.

For **long-distance calls** in the US and Canada, dial 1 + area code + number. To place an **international call**, dial **011** + country code + area code + number. A list of country codes can be found in the front of the Yellow Pages. To place a collect call (person receiving call pays charges), dial 0 + area code + number and tell the operator you are calling collect. If it is an international call, ask for the overseas operator.

Most telephone numbers in this guide that start with **800**, 855, 866, **877** or **888** are toll-free (no charge) in the US and may not be accessible outside of North America. Dial **1** before dialing a toll-free number. The charge for numbers preceded by 900 can range from 50¢ to $15 per minute. Most hotels add a surcharge for local and long-distance calls. For further information, dial **0** for operator assistance.

You can send a **telegram** or money, or have money telegraphed to you, via the Western Union system (*☎800-325-6000; www.westernunion. com*).

SIM cards for GSM cellphones are available for purchase at T-Mobile and AT&T retail locations, as well as many electronics stores throughout Manhat-

IMPORTANT NUMBERS	
Emergency Police/Ambulance/Fire (24hrs)	☎911
Police (non-emergency, Mon–Fri 9am–6pm)	☎311 or 646-610-5000
Medical House Calls	☎212-327-1900
NY Hotel Urgent Medical Services	☎212-737-1212
Dental Emergencies NYU College of Dentistry (weekdays) Jan Linhart D.D.S., P.C. (24hrs)	☎212-998-9800 ☎212-682-5180
24hr Pharmacies CVS (10 locations in Manhattan) Duane Reade (7 locations in Manhattan) Rite Aid (2 locations in Manhattan) Poison Control Center (24hrs)	☎800-746-7287 ☎212-265-2101 ☎800-748-3243 ☎212-764-7667

SELECTED NYC POST OFFICES

Post Office	Street Address	Telephone Number	Section of Town
Canal Street Station	350 Canal St.	(800) 275-8777	Downtown
Chinatown	6 Doyers St.	(800) 275-8777	Downtown
Cooper Station	93 Fourth Ave.	(800) 275-8777	Downtown
James A. Farley	421 Eighth Ave.	(800) 275-8777	Downtown
Old Chelsea Station	217 W. 18th St.	(800) 275-8777	Downtown
Patchin	70 W. 10th St.	(800) 275-8777	Downtown
West Village	527 Hudson St.	(800) 275-8777	Downtown
Church Street Station	90 Church St.	(800) 275-8777	Downtown
Rockefeller Center	610 Fifth Ave.	(800) 275-8777	Midtown
Columbia University	534 W. 112th St.	(800) 275-8777	Uptown
Columbus Circle	27 W. 60th St.	(800) 275-8777	Uptown
Gracie	229 E. 85th St.	(800) 275-8777	Uptown
Lenox Hill Station	217 E. 70th St.	(800) 275-8777	Uptown
Planetarium	127 W. 83rd St.	(800) 275-8777	Uptown

tan. Note that GSM phones must be unlocked to use a SIM card for a North American network.

Free **internet access** is available at all branches of the New York Public Library, and many hotels provide internet access to their guests. Wi-Fi (wireless internet) hotspots abound in the city.

ELECTRICITY

Voltage in the US is 110 volts AC, 60 Hz. Foreign-made appliances may need AC adapters (available at specialty travel and electronics stores) and North American flat-blade plugs.

EMERGENCIES

In all major US cities you can telephone the police, ambulance or fire service, by dialing **911**. Another way to report an emergency is to dial 0 for the operator. *See chart on opposite page for important telephone numbers.*

LIQUOR LAW

The legal minimum age for purchase and consumption of alcoholic beverages is 21. Proof of age may be required. Most bars in New York City stay open until 4am. You can buy wine and liquor at liquor stores Monday to Saturday. Grocery and convenience stores sell beer anytime except Sunday 3am–noon.

MAIL

The main post office *(421 Eighth Ave. at W. 33rd St.; 800-275-8777)* is open Mon–Fri 7am–10pm, Sat 9am–9pm and Sun 11am–7pm. Branch offices are located in all five boroughs; for locations and phone numbers, check the phone directory under US Government or visit www.usps.com.

The chart above contains a selection of post offices in Manhattan.

Some sample rates for first-class mail: letter 44¢ (1oz), postcard 28¢; overseas letter 98¢ (1oz), postcard 94¢. Letters and small packages can be mailed from most hotels. Stamps and packing material may be purchased at many convenience stores, drugstores and post offices. Businesses offering postal and express shipping services are located throughout the city *(see Yellow Pages under Mailing Services).* For additional information, contact the US Postal Customer Assistance Center *(800-275-8777; www.usps.com).*

MONEY

The American dollar is divided into 100 cents.

A penny	1 cent;
A nickel	5 cents;
A dime	10 cents;
A quarter	25 cents.

CREDIT CARDS AND TRAVELER'S CHECKS

Rental-car agencies and many hotels require credit cards. **American Express Travel** is located at 200 Vesey Street (*212-640-5130)*. Most banks will cash brand-name traveler's checks and give cash advances on major credit cards, with proper identification. To report a lost or stolen credit card: American Express (*800-528-4800)*; Diners Club (*800-234-6377)*; MasterCard/Euro-card (*800-627-8372 or the issuing bank)*; Visa (*800-847-2911)*.

CURRENCY EXCHANGE

Currency exchange offices can be found at Kennedy, LaGuardia and Newark Liberty Airports. Some larger bank chains also offer currency exchange service. Private companies that offer currency exchange include **Travelex** *(1578 Broadway; 212-265-6063; www.travelex.com)*. Banks charge a small fee for this service; private companies generally charge higher fees.

The New York Times Buidling

© Chhobi/Dreamstime.com

Most banks are members of the network of **Automated Teller Machines (ATMs)** allowing visitors from overseas to withdraw cash using bank cards and major credit cards. ATMs can usually be found in banks, airports, grocery stores and shopping malls. Networks serviced by the ATM are indicated on the machine. To inquire about ATM service, locations and transaction fees, contact your local bank, MasterCard/Maestro/Cirrus (*800-424-7787)* or Plus *(www.visa.com)*. **Traveler's checks** are accepted in banks, most stores, restaurants and hotels.

TAXES

Prices displayed or quoted in the US do not generally include **sales tax** *(8.875 percent in New York City)*. Sales tax is added at the time of purchase and is not reimbursable (it can sometimes be avoided if purchased items are shipped overseas by the seller). In addition to city and state sales taxes, the city levies a 5.875 percent hotel occupancy tax plus $3.50 per night for rooms costing $40 or more. Since hotel rates do not reflect taxes, travelers should be aware of these added charges. An 18.375 percent parking garage tax is charged in the city. Tax percentages in areas beyond the city limits may vary.

MEDIA

The city's leading newspaper is *The New York Times (www.nytimes.com)*; check the Sunday Arts & Leisure and the Friday Weekend sections for entertainment information. Other dailies are the *Daily News (www. nydailynews.com)*, the *New York Post (www.nypost.com)* and *Newsday (www. newsday.com)*. The business-oriented *Wall Street Journal (www.wsj.com)* is published Monday through Saturday. New York also supports numerous daily and weekly foreign-language papers, ranging from *El Diario* to *Sing Tao*.
Several weekly publications provide listings of museum exhibits, art galleries, movies, concerts, restaurants, readings and special events. In magazine format,

The New Yorker (www.newyorker.com) and *Time Out New York (http://newyork. timeout.com)* can be purchased at newsstands. In newsprint, *L Magazine (www.thelmagazine.com)* and the *Village Voice (www.villagevoice.com)*, both free, can be found in curbside news-racks and in some bookstores. The *Official NYC Guide (http://nycgo. com)* and *NYC Arts*, free at city visitor centers, contains seasonal listings. *Next (www.nextmagazine.com)* caters to the gay community and is free at downtown cafes and bookstores.

PUBLIC HOLIDAYS

Most banks and government offices in the New York City area are closed on the legal holidays shown on the chart (many retail stores and restaurants remain open on days indicated with *):

New Year's Day	January 1
Martin Luther King Jr. Day*	3rd Monday in January
Presidents' Day	3rd Monday in February
Memorial Day*	Last Monday in May
Independence Day*	July 4
Labor Day*	1st Monday in September
Columbus Day*	2nd Monday in October
Veterans Day*	November 11
Thanksgiving Day	4th Thursday in November
Christmas Day	December 25

SMOKING

Smoking is prohibited throughout the state of New York in bars, restaurants, clubs and workplaces.

TIPPING

In the US it is customary to give a tip (a small gift of money) for services received from waiters/waitresses, porters, hotel maids and taxi drivers. In restaurants it is customary to tip the server 15–20 per cent of the bill (an easy way to calculate is to double the sales tax). Taxi drivers are generally tipped 15 per cent of the fare, hotel bellhops $1 per bag ($2 in luxury hotels), hotel doormen $1 per taxi, and hotel maids $2 per day.

MEASUREMENTS

In the US temperatures are measured in degrees Fahrenheit and measure-ments are expressed according to the US Customary System of weights and measures. Distances are given in miles.

TIME

New York City is located in the Eastern Standard Time (EST) zone, 5hrs behind Greenwich Mean Time. Daylight Sav-ing Time is observed from the second Sunday in March *(clocks are advanced 1hr)* to the first Sunday in November.

☺ A Bit of Advice ☺

SAFETY TIPS

☺ The best way to explore New York City is on foot. Use common sense, stay alert and avoid deserted streets and park areas after dark.

☺ Avoid carrying large sums of money, and don't let strangers see how much money you are carrying.

☺ Hold purses and knapsacks firmly, carry your wallet in your front pocket, and avoid wearing expensive jewelry.

☺ Stay awake when riding on public transportation, and keep packages close to you. MTA vehicles are equipped with devices that enable riders to notify personnel of emergencies. Exercise caution in the subway after 11pm. Ride in the conductor's car (usually in the middle of the train) if you are alone.

☺ Always park your car in a well-lit area. Close windows, lock doors and place valuables in the trunk.

*Abby Aldrich Rockefeller Sculpture Garden and The David and
Peggy Rockefeller Building, Museum of Modern Art*

The City of New York

By far the most populous city in the US, New York is a world unto itself by virtue of its size, the density and diversity of its population, its dynamic economic activity and its vibrant cultural life. The New York area has the largest concentration of people, income, finance, industry and transportation of any urban area in the US. New York streets have long been synonymous with some of the city's key industries: Wall Street with finance, Broadway with entertainment, Madison Avenue with advertising and Seventh Avenue with fashion. Today some 8.2 million people live in New York City, twice as many as in any other American city.

LOCATION

Situated on the East Coast of the US at 40° north latitude and 74° west longitude, New York City is bordered by the Hudson River, Long Island Sound and the Atlantic Ocean. The city occupies the western end of Long Island, all of two smaller islands (Manhattan and Staten Island) and a piece of the mainland to the north, adjacent to the Hudson River. The islands provide protection for one of the largest and safest harbors in the world, ideal for ocean-going vessels. Access to

the ocean is through the Narrows, a passage between Staten Island and Long Island. More than 578mi/930km of coastline, including some 14mi/22.5km of beaches, rim the city. New York City also encompasses several small islands, notably Liberty Island, home of the Statue of Liberty; Ellis Island, once the nation's leading immigration center; Riker's Island (located north of LaGuardia Airport), site of a large municipal prison; Governor's Island, a former US Coast Guard site; and Roosevelt Island, once home to public health institutions, now middle-income residential.

The total area of the five boroughs (*see below*) that make up New York City is about 305sq. mi/461sq. km; the longest distance between its boundaries, from the northeast to the southwest, is about 35mi/56.3km. New York City's height above sea level varies from 5ft (Battery Park, at the southern tip of Manhattan) to 410ft (Todt Hill on Staten Island). Its climate is continental *(for information about seasonal climates, see Planning Your Trip)*.

THE FIVE BOROUGHS

New York City as it exists today was created in 1898 when, under state charter, the city was expanded from its original confines of Manhattan to incorporate Brooklyn (Kings County), Queens (Queens County), The Bronx (Bronx County) and Staten Island (Richmond County).

Manhattan viewed from over Brooklyn Bridge

©Matt Tilghman/iStockphoto.com

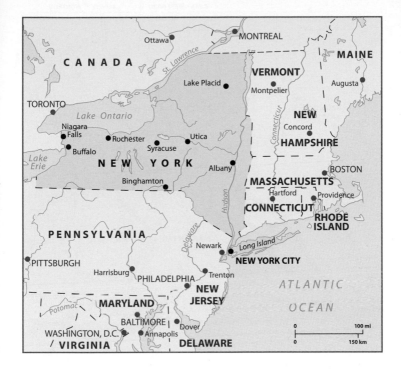

The counties correspond to the original colonial administrative divisions, and the names still designate judicial districts. The five boroughs are not developed to the same extent: a few open spaces exist on the fringes of Brooklyn and Queens, and Staten Island, despite much construction recently, remains the least urbanized.

Brooklyn, on the southwest tip of Long Island, is today the most populous of the five boroughs. Queens, to the northeast of it, is the largest and fastest growing. The heavily developed Bronx, the only borough that is part of the mainland, forms the gateway from the city to the affluent suburbs in the north. Although it remains the least populated borough, Staten Island has been growing since the completion of the Verrazano-Narrows Bridge from Brooklyn in 1964. Manhattan, the smallest of the boroughs with an area of 22.7sq. mi/36.5 sq. km, constitutes the heart of the city. With a population of 1,585,873 (2010), it is the most densely populated county in the US. This tongue-shaped island is the center for much of New York's cultural, financial and retail activity. Although the consolidation of the five boroughs took place over a century ago, residents of the so-called outer boroughs traveling to Manhattan still say they are "going to the city."

METROPOLITAN AREA

The city's vast metropolitan area, home to about 19 million residents, encompasses 23 counties and planning regions and extends more than 7,000sq. mi/11,265 sq. km.

Ten of these counties are in New York State, twelve in New Jersey and one in Pennsylvania. In addition to New York City, the area includes Newark, New Jersey (pop. approx. 280,000) and 10 other cities with more than 100,000 people. Organizations responsible for operating regional transportation facilities are the Port Authority of New York and New Jersey, which oversees bridges, airports and shipping ports (and the World Trade Center site) in the 17-county area in those two states, and the Triborough Bridge and Tunnel Authority.

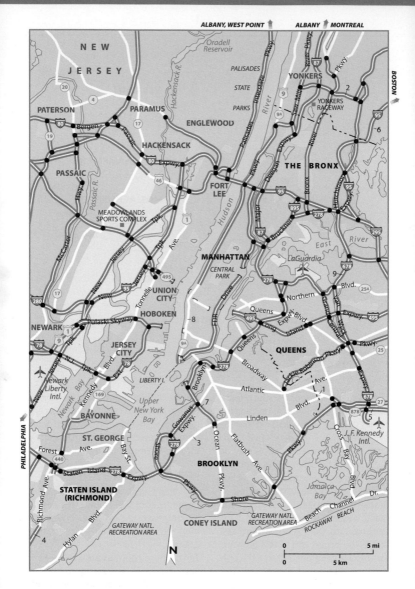

THE STATE OF NEW YORK

The city gave its name to the state (the 11th of the original 13 states of the Union), which, by virtue of its economic expansion and political influence, became known as the "Empire State." New York State extends from east of the Hudson River to the Great Lakes and Niagara Falls, and borders Canada on the north. The state is divided into counties, and its capital is Albany (New York City was the capital from 1784 to 1797).

ECONOMY

New York's $1.1 trillion economy would rank in the top 20 among the nations of the world. The powerful economy employs more than 3.7 million people, and local real estate is worth more than $800 billion. The city is home to the headquarters of 42 Fortune 500 companies.

SHIPPING

New York's sheltered, ice-free harbor and 500mi/806.5km of shoreline are easily accessible to the Atlantic. The port is the nation's third largest, although the advent of containership technology has forced most active piers from crowded Manhattan to roomier sites in Brooklyn, Staten Island and New Jersey, where one of the country's largest container terminals is at Port Newark/Elizabeth. Dozens of shipping lines serve the port. In 2009 the harbor handled $146 billion worth of cargo.

The Port Authority of New York and New Jersey manages the harbor's general cargo and containership terminals; six tunnels and bridges connecting the city with New Jersey; the region's major bus terminal on West 42nd Street; the Port Authority Trans-Hudson (PATH) rapid-transit rail system; three major airports; and a heliport. The Port Authority built and owned the World Trade Center; it retains ownership of the site and is playing an important role in determining its future.

FINANCE

New York is one of the world's preeminent financial centers. Domestic and foreign financial institutions maintaining a presence here include 199 foreign banks, many of them the top foreign branches of international banks.

More than 85 percent of US-based stock trades are conducted here, notably on Wall Street's New York Stock Exchange, the largest stock exchange in the world by dollar volume. The more than 8,000 companies listed by the NYSE had a combined value of $13.4 trillion in December 2010.

With hundreds of thousands of people employed in the financial services sector, New York was particularly hard hit by the global economic downturn of 2008, which brought the demise of several industry titans and the US government bailout of others. As commercial and investment banks, insurance companies, personal finance firms and brokerage houses all retool for economic recovery, industry analysts predict that, at least in the near future, a smaller percentage of the city's jobs will relate directly or indirectly to the financial industry.

TRANSPORTATION

New York is the only US city accessible by three major airports (John F. Kennedy, LaGuardia and Newark Liberty), which annually handle more than 100 million passengers. Travelers also arrive via a rail and bus network that brings in a million people daily, mostly commuters.

The streets of New York are served by some 13,000 taxicabs and more than 6,000 buses. The subway system, stretching from Coney Island to the North Bronx, with 468 stations and 24 lines, ranks among the largest in the world and serves over four million passengers a day. The free Staten Island Ferry takes more than 100 trips a day, conveying 65,000 passengers.

MEDIA

New York also reaches out to the world through communications. The city is home to four major television networks (ABC, NBC, CBS and Fox) and numerous cable channels (MTV, HBO, Food Network). Its film industry is the largest in the US after Hollywood, employing more than 100,000 people and generating $5 billion for the city's economy each year.

The city is also the nation's print capital. New York churns out some 350 consumer magazines and is home to Time/Life, Hearst and Condé Nast, among other Midtown magazine empires.

Major publishing houses McGraw-Hill and Random House also have headquarters in the area. Four of the ten largest newspapers in the United States are based in New York: *The New York Times, Post, Daily News* and the *Wall Street Journal*. Madison Avenue is still the nation's advertising capital.

HIGH-TECH

The area's high-tech industry grew rapidly during the 2000s: today, telecom and cable companies, together with internet service providers and publishers, employ more people in the region than California's Silicon Valley.

In 2006 Google chose New York's Chelsea neighborhood for the home of its largest engineering complex outside of its California headquarters, and further validated New York's high-tech image. Today more than two thousand people are employed by Google in New York.

MANUFACTURING

Manufacturing's share of the economy has long been declining—from 900,000 jobs in 1950 to fewer than 300,000 today; first-generation immigrants account for the majority of these workers. Still, New York's highly diverse industrial sector base comprises nearly 10,000 establishments, many relying on a reservoir of specialized labor skills. Food processing is a multi-billion dollar industry that employs thousands. Apparel manufacturing, employing tens of thousands, generates about $3 billion annually.

TOURISM AND CULTURE

Visitors to New York are drawn by the city's glamour, fine dining, shopping, and culture. In 2010, it welcomed nearly 48.7 million visitors, who spent more than $31 billion. Internationally, Great Britain sends the most visitors to the city, followed by Canada and Germany.

Broadway theater attendance reached nearly 12 million during 2010, with ticket sales of over $1 billion. Fine art in New York is both an attraction to visitors and an industry in itself. Some 500 art galleries can be found in the city with hundreds in Chelsea alone, and smaller clusters of galleries in SoHo and TriBeCa, as well as in Williamsburg and DUMBO (Down Under the Manhattan Bridge Overpass) in Brooklyn. Dozens of museums make their home in New York.

POPULATION

In the 19C and at the beginning of the 20C, recent immigrants, referred to as "hyphenated citizens" (such as Irish-Americans, Italian-Americans, German-Americans and so on), were often denied social status by the "aristocracy" of British and Dutch origin.

However, the pyramid of New York society was unable to withstand the forces of change, and today these multicultural strands, together with the more recent waves of immigrants, make up the very fabric of New York's population; more than one-third of the city's population was born elsewhere.

IRISH

Nearly half a million New Yorkers are of Irish descent, many emigrating to the US during the Irish potato famine in 1846. From the beginning the Irish were drawn to public affairs and city government. Carrying on the religious tradition of their homeland, they have contributed significantly to the influence of the Roman Catholic Church in the US. Irish-Americans are famous for their exuberant celebration of St. Patrick's Day, March 17, to honor their patron saint.

ITALIAN

New York's nearly 700,000 Italians make up the second-largest ethnic group in the city. Large-scale immigration, mainly of laborers and peasants from southern Italy and Sicily, started only after 1870. Many Italian immigrants started in the building industry, where they worked under the heavy hands of padroni (construction bosses); hard-working, enterprising newcomers tended to establish small family businesses, especially in restaurants, contracting and trucking. Italian convivial spirit and love of great food can still be found in Manhattan's Little Italy and on Arthur Avenue in The Bronx.

GERMAN

More than 250,000 New Yorkers claim German ancestry. More than six million Germans arrived in New York between the failed 1848–49 Revolution in Germany and World War I. Many settled mostly around Tompkins Square in the East Village, later moving farther uptown. Most Germans rapidly assimilated into New York society, but some German atmosphere can still be found in Yorkville on the Upper East Side.

CHINESE AND SOUTH ASIAN

Coming to the US in the mid-19C to work on railroad lines and in mines, Chinese

POPULATION FROM 1626 TO 2010		
1626	200	The first boatload of settlers brought by the Dutch to Nieuw Amsterdam consists primarily of French Huguenots.
1656	1,000	The first immigrants are followed by English, Scots, Germans and Scandinavians.
1800	60,000	Half of New York's population is of English origin.
1850s	630,000	Germans, Irish and Scandinavians arrive in large numbers.
1880	1,911,700	Eastern Europeans and southern Italians immigrate in great waves; this influx continues until 1924.
1900	3,437,200	This figure includes residents of all five boroughs, which were consolidated in 1898.
1920	5,620,000	After World War I, black migration increases both from the American South and from the West Indies.
1924		Immigration laws limit foreign immigration.
1930	6,930,500	City grows, but growth rate declines.
1950	7,892,000	After World War II many Puerto Ricans settle in New York, topping a million in 1957.
1960	7,782,000	From 1950 to 1960, the city loses more than 100,000 residents to the suburbs.
1970	7,896,000	Out-migration of New York's population from the city to the suburbs continues but is offset by immigration.
1980	7,071,639	Hard times in the 1970s cause many to flee the city.
1990	7,322,600	New York's foreign-born population of two million reflects the great influx of immigrants from Asia, Latin America and the Caribbean since 1965.
1995	7,312,000	Population declines slightly.
1999	7,428,162	Newcomers from the former Soviet Union, China, South Asia and Central and South America arrive at a rate of 100,000 a year in the 1990s, offsetting other population losses.
2000	8,008,278	In the new millennium, the city's population tops eight million.
2003	8,019,033	New York City's Jewish population dips below a million for first time in a century.
2010	8,175,133	Population reaches new high and is expected to reach 9.4 million by 2025.

immigrants hailed mainly from Canton. The most recent newcomers, primarily from Hong Kong, Shanghai and Taiwan, have swelled their numbers to nearly 500,000, with the greatest concentration living in Manhattan and the steadily expanding Chinatown in Flushing, Queens. In addition, there are over 300,000 South Asian immigrants from India, Pakistan, Bangladesh and Sri Lanka living in New York, nearly four percent of the total population.

EASTERN EUROPEAN

Before World War I, the massive waves of immigrants from the old Russian empire were not made up of Russians, but mostly of members of various minority nationalities – Ukrainians, Poles, Lithuanians and others. The 1917 Revolution brought only a trickle of so-called White Russians to New York as compared to the large numbers who immigrated to European capitals. Many Ukrainians and Russians, however, were among the displaced persons who settled in New York in the wake of World War II. The former Soviet Union has been a major source of new immigrants to New York. The city's Romanian community is the largest in North America, numbering about 160,000.

JEWISH

New York City's population of nearly a million Jews is the largest Jewish population outside of Israel, though only half

41

of what it was in 1957, when one-fourth of New Yorkers were Jewish. The decline is mainly attributed to the dispersion of the population to the suburbs but has been tempered by the influx in the 1990s of Jewish immigrants from the former Soviet Union. Sephardic Jews, originally from Spain and Portugal, had come to New York in the 17C, mostly via Holland and Latin America, though today most New York Jews are of Ashkenazi descent. Manhattan's Lower East Side was the first home for 1.5 million Jews who entered America between 1880 and 1910; a great number also settled in Brooklyn communities.

AFRICAN AMERICAN

New York has more African Americans than any other US city, totaling about two million. Initial black migration came from the American South. In the past two decades, migration from the Caribbean has resulted in a new Caribbean community in Upper Manhattan and Brooklyn. The black community has produced distinguished writers, playwrights and performers, and the influence of "rhythm and blues" and jazz has greatly impacted the American musical scene. During recent decades many black people have availed themselves of educational and economic opportunities offered in New York, though the disparity between black and white New Yorkers in almost all indices—education, income, health and infant mortality—is still striking.

LATINO

New York City's Puerto Rican population once numbered over a million; now at approximately 800,000, it is still the largest outside of Puerto Rico. All told, the Latino population, including Puerto Ricans, Dominicans, Mexicans, Cubans, Colombians and Ecuadorians, forms more than one-fourth of the city's population, numbering an estimated 2.5 million in 2009. The major concentration of the Puerto Rican population is in The Bronx, but the heart of New York's Puerto Rican community is East Harlem, better known as El Barrio. Mindful of their culture, Latinos have emerged as a vital community, lending a distinctive flavor to the city.

History

NIEUW AMSTERDAM TO NEW YORK

Before the arrival of Europeans, Algonquin- and Iroquoian-speaking Indians inhabited the island of Manhattan. The Algonquin tribe is credited for naming the island Manhattan, meaning "island of the hills." Following Henry Hudson's exploratory journey, the Dutch East India Company founded the colony of New Netherland on the site of present-day New York City in 1614. In 1625 the company established the trading post of Nieuw Amsterdam. Unlike other American colonies, New York was not founded by a religious group, but for purely commercial purposes, and it became the private property of the Dutch West India Company. This fact, combined with the difficulty of attracting immigrants from a generally content Dutch populace, gave New York a cosmopolitan makeup from the very start, attracting French Huguenots and non-Dutch immigrants from Holland. A fort and rondout batteries were constructed at the southern tip of Manhattan Island, controlling the entrance to the Hudson River. A city grew up to the south of a defensive wall, while farms and estates, called *bouweries*, were established farther north on Manhattan Island, as well as in Brooklyn, Queens, Staten Island and The Bronx. Initially ruled by a director-general, the town attained some form of self-government in 1653. The British, already established in New England to the north, took control of the colony in the late 17C, accepting the surrender of Director-General Peter Stuyvesant in 1664.

1524 – **Giovanni da Verrazano**, an Italian explorer in the service of the French king François I, is the first European to land on Manhattan.

1609 **Henry Hudson** sails up the river (now bearing his name) in his ship, the *Half Moon*, while on a voyage for the Dutch East India Company.

1614 The name New Netherland, given to the newly founded Dutch colony, designates the area around present-day New York City. The territory north of New York is called New England.

1625 The first permanent European settlement is established on Manhattan. The trading post is named **Nieuw Amsterdam** and includes a fort and 30 houses.

1626 **Peter Minuit** of the Dutch West India Company buys Manhattan from the Algonquin Indians in exchange for trinkets valued at 60 guilders, the equivalent of $24.

1647 **Peter Stuyvesant** (1592–1672) is appointed director-general of New Netherland, serving until 1664.

1653 The city of Nieuw Amsterdam receives a charter and municipal rule. Stuyvesant erects a protective wall along present-day Wall Street.

1664 As a repercussion of the English and Dutch trading rivalries in Europe, the English take Nieuw Amsterdam without a struggle and rename it **New York** after the Duke of York, brother of the English king Charles II.

BRITISH RULE

New York blossomed as an important trading post in the colonies of North America, second only to Boston in the trade of furs and farm products. By 1700 the tip of Manhattan claimed some 4,000 residents and had grown north beyond the Dutch palisade fortifications at Wall Street. The city began its passionate embrace of journalism with the cre-

ation of several newspapers. Columbia University and the city's first library were founded. Dutch language and culture began to wane in the century following Stuyvesant's surrender, although numerous Dutch families remained important in local society, government and business. New York's pivotal role as a commercial port for the American colonies placed the city in the center of the taxation controversies leading up to the American Revolution. The city was one of the first targets of the British Army, which occupied New York throughout the War for Independence.

1667 The Treaty of Breda, ending the second Anglo-Dutch War, confirms English control over the province of New Netherland. The city of New York passes under the English system of municipal government, and English replaces Dutch as the official language.

1673 The Dutch retake New York without a fight and rename it New Orange.

1674 By the Treaty of Westminster in 1674, the province of New Netherland becomes permanently English.

1720 With 7,000 inhabitants, New York is the third-largest city in the colonies.

1725 The city's first newspaper, the *New-York Gazette*, is founded by William Bradford.

1733 **John Peter Zenger** founds the *New York Weekly Journal*, in which he attacks the governor. A year later Zenger is imprisoned for slander. His acquittal marks the beginning of a free press.

1754 The city's first college, **King's College**, now Columbia University, opens. The New York Society Library is founded.

1763 Marking the end of the French and Indian War, or **Seven Years' War** (1756–63), the Treaty of Paris confirms English control of the North American continent.

1765 The Stamp Act Congress meets in New York, and representatives from nine colonies denounce the English colonial policy of taxation without re-presentation.

1766 Repeal of the Stamp Act. A statue is erected to **William Pitt**, the British statesman who did most to obtain the repeal.

1767 Parliament passes the Townshend Acts, a series of four acts that increase taxation and threaten the already established traditions of colonial self-government. The repeal three years later coincides with the Boston Massacre.

1776 The **Declaration of Independence** (July 4) is adopted and New Yorkers pull down the statue of George III at Bowling Green. On November 17, Fort Washington in northern Manhattan falls and the British occupy all of present-day New York City until 1783.

1783 The **Treaty of Paris** (September 3) ends the American Revolution and England recognizes the independence of the 13 colonies. The last British troops evacuate New York, and George Washington returns to the city in triumph before bidding farewell to his troops at Fraunces Tavern on December 4.

EMPIRE CITY

After briefly serving as US capital, New York established the commercial links and financial institutions that led the new nation into the Industrial Age. As the population of New York exploded beyond all predictions—despite outbreaks of yellow fever and cholera—the island of Manhattan grew northward along the gridiron plan established in the early 19C.

Broadway, a poplar-lined residential boulevard in 1790, became a commercial thoroughfare by 1820. Following the opening of the Erie Canal in 1825, the city handled more trade than all other US ports combined and became a leading shipbuilding center. The population doubled in the 1820s as immigrants arrived by the thousands from Germany, Ireland and Scandinavia.

1784 New York City becomes the capital of New York State and a year later is named US capital under the Articles of Confederation.

1789 **George Washington**, elected first president, takes the oath of office at Federal Hall.

1790 The first official census counts 33,000 people in Manhattan. The federal capital moves to Philadelphia.

1792 The forerunner to the New York Stock Exchange is founded.

1804 Vice President Aaron Burr mortally wounds political rival Alexander Hamilton in a duel on the Hudson River.

1812 **War of 1812**: the US declares war on Britain and the Port of New York suffers from the ensuing blockade until the war ends in 1814. Present City Hall opens.

1820 New York is the most populous city in the nation with 123,705 inhabitants. Growth brings disease, including a severe yellow fever epidemic in 1822.

1825 Opening of the **Erie Canal**. New York becomes the gateway to the Great Lakes and the West as 500 new mercantile businesses open.

1832 Cholera epidemic kills 4,000 citizens.

1835 The Great Fire destroys an extensive area in the business district.

1845 Another fire levels 300 buildings in Lower Manhattan. The first telegraph line connects the city to Philadelphia. The first baseball club, the New York Knickerbockers, is organized.

GROWTH AND GREENING

Large waves of immigration from Europe and the Americas spurred commercial and industrial growth, which led to a doubling of the city's population every 20 years, exceeding a million people by 1875. Shantytowns developed on vacant land to the north of the growing city, while aging neighborhoods became slums, including the infamous "Five Points" district north of City Hall.

The massive immigrant population fed a political machine based at Tammany Hall that established new heights of public graft and corruption in the 1860s and 70s by bilking taxpayers of tens of millions of dollars—more than $9 million during construction of the "Tweed Courthouse" alone.

The adjacent city of Brooklyn blossomed with residences and factories. Following the success of America's first World's Fair here in 1853, New York established itself as the cultural capital of America with the creation of Central Park, the American Museum of Natural History and the Metropolitan Museum of Art.

1849   Astor Place Riot: 31 die and 150 are wounded in a theater riot protesting British actor William Macready.

1851   The New York Times is published for the first time.

1853   The World's Fair opens at the Crystal Palace. Modeled on London's Great Exhibition of 1851, the fair is an early showplace for iron and glass architecture and the technological advances of the Industrial Revolution.

1857   Construction of **Central Park** begins in the wake of a depression brought on by financial panic; the park is officially completed in 1876.

1860   New York City counts 813,660 inhabitants, as immigration from Ireland, Germany and other European countries continues. Brooklyn counts 279,000 residents, double the number it had 10 years earlier.

1863   The city is rocked by the Draft Riots. Opposition by the poor to the rich man's practice of hiring a substitute to fight the Civil War spreads to encompass general discontent and racism, leaving 1,200 dead and 8,000 injured.

1865   The Civil War ends. After President Abraham Lincoln is assassinated, his body lies in state at New York's City Hall.

1868   Opening of **the El**, the first elevated railroad in Lower Manhattan.

1869   On September 24, financier Jay Gould, who had tried to corner the gold market with his associate James Fisk, sells out and brings about the financial panic known as "Black Friday." The American Museum of Natural History is founded.

1871   The New York Times finally exposes Boss Tweed's Tammany Hall ring of corrupt city officials. Tweed goes to prison, where he dies in 1878.

1872   The **Metropolitan Museum of Art** opens, moving to its present location in 1880.

A CITY OF IMMIGRANTS

Wall Street became the center of banking, finance and insurance in the US, and by the second decade of the 20C it began occupying its key position in the world economy. Immigration not only continued but increased dramatically as the 19C waned, bringing new groups from Southern and Eastern Europe.

New York became home to the largest Jewish community in the world as millions fled Russian persecution. Italian immigrants created Little Italy next to Chinatown, which was established in the 1870s but stunted by the Chinese Exclusion Act of 1882. Beginning in the late 1880s, **Jacob Riis** took his camera to New York's dark streets to expose the social ills of the tenement districts, ushering in the Progressive Era. Tammany Hall was exposed by an 1894 investigation, led by New York native **Theodore**

Immigrants arriving in New York in 1907

©Antique Research Centre/Tips Images

Roosevelt, of police corruption, thus launching a political career that would take him to the presidency. William Randolph Hearst's purchase of the *New York Journal* in 1895 and subsequent circulation battle with Joseph Pulitzer's *New York World* instigated the era of yellow journalism—largely responsible for the Spanish–American War.

1880–84 Some two million people arrive in New York City. Tenements and sweatshops proliferate, exploiting the new residents.

1882 Electricity is first offered for general use by Thomas Edison's plant in Lower Manhattan.

1886 Inauguration of the **Statue of Liberty**.

1889 The first telephone exchange opens on Nassau Street two years after Alexander Graham Bell demonstrated his invention in New York.

1891 Carnegie Hall opens with Tchaikovsky's American conducting debut.

1892 Ongoing rush of immigration leads to the completion of the Ellis Island facility—more than 12 million persons processed here by the mid-1920s.

1898 **Greater New York City** is created, comprising five boroughs: Manhattan, The Bronx, Brooklyn, Queens and Staten Island. With a population of more than three million, New York is the world's largest city.

1902 One of the city's first skyscrapers, the **Flatiron Building**, is completed.

1904 The first subway line opens.

CULTURE AND CRASH

New York served as the major US transshipment point for Allied equipment during World War I. Immigration began to slow following exclusionary legislation in the 1920s, but the city's population still increased from 4.8 million in 1910 to almost 7 million in 1930. Prohibition began in 1920, doubling the number of illegal liquor outlets in the city to 32,000 and providing the backdrop for bootlegging gangs and underworld influence in politics and government. **Greenwich Village** became an intellectual and artistic bohemia and the Algonquin Hotel's Round Table hosted the likes of the witty writers of the fledgling *New Yorker* magazine. The Harlem Renaissance in African-American arts and letters introduced writers like Zora Neale Hurston and Langston Hughes, and jazz legends like Duke Ellington and Cab Calloway. A host of new theaters along 42nd Street perfected the Broadway musical with tunes written in Tin Pan Alley. The Armory Show and the Ashcan school promoted modern art in America in the 1910s, and the following decades saw the founding of the **Museum of Modern Art**, the Whitney Museum of American Art and the Solomon R. Guggenheim Museum. The gaiety of the Roaring 20s came to an end with the Wall Street stock market crash on Black Tuesday, October 29, 1929, signaling the Great Depression.

1908 First celebration of New Year's Eve at Times Square.

1911 The Triangle Shirtwaist Company fire kills 145 sweatshop employees.

1913 The **Armory Show** introduces modern art to America.

1920 On September 16, a bombing on Wall Street takes 38 lives.

1925 The *New Yorker* magazine is founded. Alain Locke's anthology *The New Negro: An Interpretation* marks the heyday of the Harlem Renaissance.

1929 Stock market crash (financial panic of October) signals the start of the Great Depression.

1931 The Empire State Building is completed after almost two years of work.

1932 Mayor Jimmy Walker resigns from office in another Tammany Hall scandal.

BUST AND BOOM

The Great Depression prompted the closing of manufacturing plants in the city—thousands of homeless people slept in subway tunnels and waited in breadlines. Construction of **Rockefeller Center** and two World's Fairs buoyed New York as reform mayor Fiorello La Guardia—"the Little Flower"—led the city through the trials of the Depression, arresting gangsters like "Lucky" Luciano and supervising huge public works projects. The first US public housing project—First Houses—was built in 1935 and followed by a dozen more in the next decade. World War II made New York the busiest port in the world and solidified its international position in industry, commerce and finance. The United Nations established its headquarters

in Manhattan following the war as the city began building again. The 1950s brought new immigrants, with large numbers arriving from Puerto Rico and Asia. A haven for refugee intelligentsia from Europe, New York made its bid for international cultural capital in the 1950s and 60s, welcoming painters Piet Mondrian, Jacques Lipchitz, Fernand Léger and others, while fostering a new generation of avant-garde artists such as Jackson Pollock, Willem de Kooning, Louise Nevelson and Andy Warhol. Off-Broadway theaters enlivened the cultural scene and New York became a center for film and television.

1934 **Fiorello H. La Guardia** becomes mayor of New York City, serving until 1945.

1935 Harlem Riot exposes the effects of the Depression on African Americans.

1939–40 World's Fair at Flushing Meadows attracts more than 44 million visitors to preview postwar advances in domestic technology.

1945 **United Nations** charter is drafted in San Francisco, and the organization announces it will locate in New York City.

1959 Construction of Lincoln Center begins.

TERRORIST STRIKES

Racial and labor tensions beset the city in the 1960s, and in 1975 the city government defaulted into bankruptcy. The setbacks only stimulated New Yorker pluck, though, and by 1981, the city's budget was balanced. Despite the 1987 stock market crash, by the late 1980s an upswing in the world economy led to a massive expansion on Wall Street that continued straight through the Bull Market of the late 1990s. Presaged by a truck-bomb explosion at the World Trade Center in 1993, the attack on the World Trade Center on September 11, 2001, signaled the end of the stock market boom and brought the city into the international spotlight as residents banded together to mourn the dead.

1964 – The longest suspension bridge in the US, the Verrazano-Narrows Bridge opens between Brooklyn and Staten Island. The **Harlem Uprising** is the first major manifestation of Northern black unrest in the Civil Rights era.

1964–65 – **World's Fair** held on the same site as the 1939–40 fair features the 140ft-tall Unisphere model of the earth.

1965 – Malcolm X is assassinated at the Audubon Ballroom.

1973 – The **World Trade Center** opens.

1977 – Ed Koch becomes mayor.

1980 – John Lennon is assassinated in front of his New York City residence, The Dakota.

1989 – New York City's first African-American mayor, **David Dinkins**, is elected.

1993 – Terrorist bomb rocks the World Trade Center, injuring hundreds. **Rudy Giuliani** is elected mayor.

1996 – New York endures its worst blizzard in a century.

1999 – Two million people fill Times Square for a 24-hour-long New Year's Eve celebration to welcome the new millennium.

2000 – Yankees win Subway Series against Mets.

2001 – On the morning of September 11, in the worst terrorist attack in US history, hijackers crash two passenger planes into the Twin Towers, destroying the World Trade Center and resulting in the loss of over 2,750 lives.

STANDING TALL

In the wake of September 11, 2001, New Yorkers banded together with resolve. Cleanup was completed on schedule, but design, safety and cost issues held up new construction at the site for five years. Forced out of office by term limits, Rudy Giuliani ceded the mayor's office to billionaire **Michael Bloomberg**, who put the city on a stable financial footing and passed a raft of legislation in an effort to make New Yorkers healthier.

2002 – Billionaire financial-data baron Michael Bloomberg is sworn in as mayor. Cleanup crews remove 1.5 million tons of debris from the World Trade Center site.

2003 – A cascading power outage leaves New York City in the dark for 29 hours beginning at 4pm on Thursday, August 14. The New York legislature enacts a law banning smoking in virtually all bars, clubs and restaurants statewide.

2004 – Marking its 75th anniversary, the Museum of Modern Art reopens its Midtown location after two and a half years of renovation and expansion. Bloomberg is elected to a second term and bans trans fats from city restaurants.

2005 – For 16 days in February, Central Park is transformed by artists Christo and Jeanne-Claude's *The Gates*: 7,500 orange-fabric panels mounted on poles placed over walkways throughout the park. The installation attracts hundreds of thousands of visitors.

2006 – Work begins on the Freedom Tower, a 1,776ft skyscraper on the former World Trade Center site. The city welcomes a record 43.8 million visitors, up from 33.1 million in 1998, and ends the fiscal year with a $6 billion surplus.

2007 – Mayor Bloomberg drops out of the Republican Party and declares himself an independent. In October he announces a plan to plant 650,000 trees by 2017, five times the number planted the preceding decade.

2008 – Collapse of New York-based Bear Stearns and Lehman Brothers, leading investment services firms, creates shock waves in global financial markets and accelerates economic downturn.

2009 – City Council lifts term-limit laws to allow Mayor Bloomberg to run for a third term. Yankees win 27th World Series.

2011 – 2010 Census figures are released and New York City's population reaches an all-time high of 8,175,133.

Art and Culture

ARCHITECTURE

A stunning showcase for contemporary architecture, New York is first and foremost a city of skyscrapers. Yet beyond the skyline's perennially changing profile of steel and glass lies an architectural landscape remarkably rich in history and variety; indeed, the city leads the nation in preservation, encompassing thousands of buildings and historic districts that illustrate its development. From the elegant and elemental New York City brownstone to the dramatic ziggurat towers of the Roaring 20s, architecture is both stage and player in the drama of New York City.

FROM COMMERCIAL COLONY TO DEMOCRATIC REPUBLIC

Engineer Cryn Fredericksz laid out the fort and town of Nieuw Amsterdam in 1625. The earliest views of the colony depict narrow, irregular streets (still seen in lower Manhattan) and quaint homes sporting sloping gambrel roofs and columned porches (◎ see illustration p55). The English takeover of Manhattan in 1664 brought the Georgian style, whose symmetrical, solid facades typified the next phase of development, pushing north of Wall Street by 1700. Building in New York City halted during the British occupation, but renewed as the young Republic came into its own from 1790 to 1820, adopting a modified Roman Classical architecture known as the **Federal style**. The style defined not only grand public edifices and mansions, but also commercial warehouses and shops that were fast replacing their Dutch antecedents (as seen at South Street Seaport).

In the 1830s Americans turned to ancient **Greek architecture** as a symbol of the new nation. Public buildings and homes across the nation displayed Greek temple entrances in a new, confident show of democracy. Upper-class residential communities north of Houston Street saw the erection of "the Row" at Washington Square North (1831, Town & Davis) and Colonnade Row on Lafayette Street (1831, Seth Greer), wherein dwelt Delanos, Astors and Vanderbilts. The Federal Hall National Memorial, with its Doric temple facade of Westchester County marble, is a landmark example of the style.

MANHATTAN MARCHES NORTH

As New York rebounded from the Revolutionary War and grew in prosperity, it expanded to the north. City Engineer John Randel released the Randel Plan in 1811, which laid out a grid of streets from Houston Street all the way north to 155th Street and divided the city into narrow east–west blocks with 100ft-deep lots. The plan was criticized for ignoring the island's topography and extending so far north. The scale would prove prescient, but Manhattan's hills and outcroppings were methodically flattened over time.

Throughout the 19C, new residential areas were erected and then replaced with shops, hotels, restaurants and offices 10 or 20 years later. A serious fire in 1835 leveled 700 buildings in lower Manhattan, and another in 1845 consumed 300 structures, accelerating the process of building and rebuilding. New development reached Houston Street in 1820, 14th Street by 1840, 23rd Street by 1850 and 42nd Street by 1860. The improvement of public transportation from horse-drawn omnibuses in the 1830s to street railroads in the 1850s helped make the growth possible. Slums grew along with the city, as "rear buildings" and **tenements** proliferated in the

1840s and 50s and shantytowns filled the vacant lands in Central Park and upper Manhattan.

Broadway became the barometer of Manhattan's urban and architectural development. By the 1830s hotels on Broadway had pushed residential uses into Washington Square and Greenwich Village. Union Square became a fashionable address by mid-century. In 1862 George William Curtis lamented Broadway's changes in *Harper's Magazine*: "Twenty years ago it was a street of three-story red brick houses. Now it is a highway of stone, and iron, and marble buildings." The Randel Plan had not provided for open space, and existing private parks like the Elgin Botanic Garden and St. John's soon became lucrative building sites. The development of Central Park in mid-century created much-needed open space and enhanced the prospect of real estate development around it.

MID-CENTURY ECLECTICISM

Gothic Revival architecture, inspired by John Ruskin in England and suited especially to churches, was popular in the US from 1840. Richard Upjohn's landmark Trinity Church, built in 1846, epitomized the style and the **Romantic movement** that fostered it, with its dark, dramatic central spire and atmospheric cemetery. Withers and Vaux used the style for the Jefferson Market Library in 1874 and the first Metropolitan Museum of Art building in 1880. Peter B. Wight's National Academy of Design (1865, demolished) at East 23rd Street and Park Avenue was an important example of "Ruskinian" Gothic, as is the surviving National Arts Club (1884, Calvert Vaux) at 15 Gramercy Park South.

By mid-century the vertical, rectangular facades of the Italianate style proved ideal for the narrow lots of the booming city. Easily adapted to row houses, storefronts or warehouses, this decorative style first appeared with the 1846 A.T. Stewart's department store (280 Broadway). Italianate became the preferred style for row houses, as witnessed in the brownstones of Brooklyn Heights, Gramercy Park and Harlem. Anglo-Italianate row houses, with lower entrance stairs and narrow facades, filled the streets of Chelsea.

The **Italianate style** was the basis for cast-iron commercial loft buildings constructed throughout Lower Manhattan in the 1850s. The new "fireproof" material was easily detailed with ornamental flourishes, and the rhythm of round-arched window arcades separated by attached columns could be repeated on multiple floors as buildings grew taller in an era of skyrocketing land values. The facades were often marbleized or painted like stone to reassure a public distrustful of the new glass-and-iron architecture. By 1872 there were almost three miles of cast-iron facades in lower Manhattan, including the elegant **E.V. Haughwout Building**.

Baron Haussmann's redesign of Paris in the 1850s and 60s spawned a brief but intense affection for Parisian **Second Empire** architecture. Distinguished by the double-pitched mansard roof, the style befitted the extravagance of the Gilded Age and coincided with the 1870s development of the "Ladies Mile" along Fifth Avenue and Broadway from 10th Street to Madison Square. Former row houses sprouted mansard roofs punctuated by elaborate dormer windows as they were converted to retail uses, while new shops and department stores were designed in the style.

R. Corbel/MICHELIN

Haughwout Building

Brownstones

In *A Backward Glance*, Edith Wharton, who was born in a brownstone in 1862, decried "this little low-studded rectangular New York, cursed with its universal chocolate-colored coating of the most hideous stone ever quarried." Despite such claims, the brownstone has become the quintessential symbol of the New York neighborhood, a legacy of various speculative booms of the 19C, when row after rhythmic row of identical town houses appeared along the city's long residential blocks.

R. Corbel/MICHELIN

Characterized by high stoops, elegant cornices and large plate-glass windows, the four- and five-story buildings adopted many popular architectural stylings; initially the Italianate style (with heavy cornice and brackets) predominated, giving way to Renaissance Revival, Romanesque and Queen Anne designs. Builders first used cheap brown sandstone in the 1820s and 30s as a substitute for limestone or marble. Over time, the term "brownstone" came to refer to the entire category of 19C town houses; be they faced with stone or brick.

Originally built to house a single family in grand style, the edifices were subdivided into apartments as neighborhoods declined, and rapidly came to symbolize inner-city decay. In recent years, however, brownstones have become fashionable as preservation enthusiasts reconvert many into single-family homes, restoring their original function and cachet. Found in Greenwich Village, Murray Hill, Gramercy Park, Harlem, and the Upper East and West Sides of Manhattan, brownstones are also the dominant architectural feature in many parts of Brooklyn, including Park Slope and Brooklyn Heights.

BADLANDS AND BEYOND— MANHATTAN FILLS UP

By 1875 New York counted a million residents, and its neighboring boroughs were growing as well. The new elevated railroads, built from 1868, connected Downtown with once-distant areas around Central Park, leading to their rapid development.

The Sixth Avenue El began operating in 1877, followed by the Third Avenue El in 1878, offering service all the way to 129th Street. Within two years elevated lines opened on Second and Ninth Avenues. The year 1883 saw the completion of the Brooklyn Bridge, a dazzling display of structural supremacy that ushered in the era of **skyscrapers**. Elevated railroads transformed the city's streetscapes, as did telegraph, telephone and electric lines, causing the city to require that such lines be buried after 1884.

As immigration expanded in the late 19C, slums grew as well, presenting new challenges for architecture and city planning. New York passed its first tenement law in 1867, with a much stricter version following in 1879. In 1880 the Improved Dwellings Assn. built a model tenement on First Avenue north of 71st Street designed by Vaux and Radford, but design did not solve social ills. Urban reform efforts in the 1890s demolished some slums to make way for Columbus and Seward Parks.

The continuing growth of Manhattan led to the first **apartment buildings**, beginning with Richard Morris Hunt's 1869 Stuyvesant (demolished) on East 18th Street. Old Fifth Avenue mansions were razed for retail landmarks such as Tiffany & Co., and the entertainment district at Union Square was replaced in the 1880s by the "Rialto" along Broadway from Madison Square to 42nd Street.

The Upper West Side grew less rapidly than the Upper East Side, even though Riverside Drive had been laid out in 1865. Upper-class apartment housing designed for Singer sewing-machine magnate Edward S. Clark was derided for being so far uptown it might as well be in the Dakotas. The assessment proved flawed, as buildings sprouted up along the Ninth Avenue El line, but the name stuck to Clark's Dakota Apartments (1884, Henry J. Hardenbergh), a triumph of Victorian eclecticism. By the end of the century, the last farms and fields in northern Manhattan had been developed.

ARCHITECTURE FOR AN INDUSTRIAL AGE

Homes erected in the 1880s sported late Victorian styles, including the **Queen Anne**, with its picturesque, asymmetrical compositions; the **Romanesque Revival**, with its rusticated sense of repose and strength; and the **Beaux-Arts**, with its connotations of continental sophistication and elegance.

West End Avenue and Park Slope in Brooklyn included elegant examples of Queen Anne town houses and mansions, as did several apartment buildings on Gramercy Square. Romanesque Revival architecture came into national vogue with the career of Henry Hobson Richardson, who lived on Staten Island. The semicircular arches and heavy masonry of the style defined the City of Brooklyn Fire Headquarters (1892, Frank Freeman) and religious buildings such as the Eldridge Street Synagogue (1887, Herter Bros.), with its Moorish and Gothic elements. The **Richardsonian Romanesque** style found robust expression in the DeVinne Press Building (1885, Babb, Cook & Willard) at 399 Lafayette Street.

The success of the Chicago World's Columbian Exposition of 1893 created a rage for Neoclassical architecture, and the New York firm of McKim, Mead and White was among its best practitioners, designing grand public edifices as embodied in the US Custom House (1907) at Bowling Green, and retail establishments like the original Tiffany's (1906) at 409 Fifth Avenue. The architects' work at Columbia University and New York University in the 1890s epitomized Beaux-Arts planning and design, and their incomparable Pennsylvania Railroad Station (demolished) of 1910 was modeled on the ancient Baths of Caracalla in Rome.

Richard Morris Hunt designed the Neoclassical facade of the Metropolitan Museum of Art between 1895 and 1902. Several apartment buildings on Broadway, such as the richly encrusted Ansonia Hotel (1904) and the Apthorp (1908), adopted elegant Beaux-Arts ornaments. The style was well suited to a mercantile capital like New York City and characterized the new residential areas on the Upper East and West Sides. Grand Central Terminal (1913, Warren & Wetmore) and the New York Public Library (1911, Carrère and Hastings) are considered the height of Beaux-Arts design in New York City.

The early 20C was a period of historical revival in architecture, as the Beaux-Arts style was joined by Dutch Colonial, **Georgian**, **Tudor** and **Gothic** Revival. A wealth of terracotta ornament made the various mimicries all the more effective. Eclectic revivals reached their height in vaudeville movie palaces like the Apollo (1914, George Keister) and the many theaters on Broadway.

SKYSCRAPERS AND SETBACKS

Rapid growth in Manhattan helped pave the way for the skyscraper. James Bogardus erected the first **cast-iron building** at Washington and Murray Streets (reconstructed) in 1848, and Elisha Graves Otis installed the first safety elevator in E.V. Haughwout's building in 1857, an innovation that made taller buildings practical. Iron beams—a predecessor to the skeletal steel frames of skyscrapers—were used for the Cooper Union of 1859. The first true skyscraper—supported entirely by a steel frame—appeared in Chicago in 1884. Chicago school architect Louis Sullivan designed the Bayard-Condict Building in 1894, but New York preferred a more eclectic design approach, from the 1899 Neoclassical Park Row Building by R.H. Robertson to Daniel H. Burnham's epochal Flatiron Building of 1902. The tradition of enveloping new architecture in historical forms reached its literal height in Cass Gilbert's stunning Gothic Revival **Woolworth Building** of 1913, which at 792ft remained the world's tallest building for a generation.

In 1916 New York City passed the nation's first zoning law to ensure adequate light and air into the canyonlike streets of the metropolis. Zoning required buildings to set their facades back from the street as they grew higher, and soon towers shaped like ancient ziggurats dotted the Manhattan skyline. This form, combined with new technologies and the streamlined aesthetics of modern art, led to the art deco skyscraper, which achieved its greatest expressions in New York. By the late 1920s vertical stone panels with expressionistic ornament and recessed windows marked the emergence of **art deco** architecture in landmarks like the Chrysler Building, with its zigzag steel conical crown, and the expressive General Electric Building, with its complex brick and terracotta skin. The **Empire State Building** is a muscular example of art deco refinement; it was the tallest building on earth for more than 40 years.

BUILDING UP AND OUT

By the 1930s development could no longer march north in Manhattan to vacant land—areas had to be found where structures could be demolished and rebuilt, or built higher. The Financial District at the southern end of the island and Fifth Avenue near 42nd Street became high-rise office districts, and high-rise residential buildings appeared near Central Park. Park commissioner and city construction coordinator **Robert Moses** began a rapid park expansion program under Mayor **Fiorello La Guardia** in 1934, increasing park space by a third in two years and planning the 1939 World's Fair at Flushing Meadows. La Guardia and Moses brought New York City into the automobile age with the

Woolworth Building

R. Corbel/MICHELIN

construction of the Triborough Bridge; they approved the submergence of the last of the old elevated railroads and oversaw construction of LaGuardia Airport, one of the larger WPA projects in the country.

The Great Depression put a halt to most development for 20 years, but Rockefeller Center was built throughout the 1930s, proving that New York would continue to be the commercial capital of the world.

POSTWAR PROSPERITY AND PRESERVATION

Real estate awoke from its Depression-induced slumber in the late 1940s and New York began to build skyscrapers in the new **International style**, which eschewed ornament and setbacks for a boxlike slab set in an open plaza. Appropriately, one of these skyscrapers was the United Nations Headquarters, designed in 1947 by an international committee. The 1952 Lever House by **Skidmore, Owings & Merrill** introduced both the slab-plaza form and the new technol-

Lever House

R. Corbel/MICHELIN

ogy of the glass curtain wall, which soon achieved its clearest expression in the 1956 **Seagram Building** by **Ludwig Mies van der Rohe**. The style defined 1960s prosperity in buildings like the Marine Midland Bank (1967, Skidmore, Owings & Merrill).

Fulfilling its growing role as a world cultural mecca, Manhattan played host to innovative designs like Frank Lloyd Wright's spiraling study in white concrete, the Solomon R. Guggenheim Museum, a landmark of **Modernism**. The Whitney Museum of American Art (1966, Marcel Breuer) employed concrete in the very different vocabulary of a menacing **Brutalist** overhang, while the sensuous curves of Eero Saarinen's 1962 TWA Terminal at John F. Kennedy Airport were an international sensation.

Robert Moses continued to rebuild the city under a succession of mayors, creating a ring of expressways around the city, demolishing "slum" areas in urban renewal efforts and constructing tunnels and bridges that were later blamed for inducing blight.

The continued rebuilding finally provoked public outcry against the demolition of Penn Station in 1962. Although the station was destroyed, the city passed one of the nation's strongest landmarks laws in 1965. Grand Central Terminal's attempt to demolish its landmark building led to the 1978 Supreme Court case upholding landmarks laws throughout the US.

MODERNISM AND BEYOND

Modernism reached its Manhattan apogee with the twin towers of the World Trade Center (1973), encompassing an unprecedented 10 million square feet of office space. **Post-Modernism** arrived with the dramatic roofline of the 1978 Citicorp (now Citigroup) Center (Hugh Stubbins & Assocs.) and **Philip Johnson**'s 1984 AT&T Headquarters (now Sony Plaza), with its famous Chippendale top. Other notable post-Modern building features include the mirror-glass facades of the Jacob Javits Convention Center (1986, I.M. Pei & Partners) and the varied roof designs of Cesar Pelli's several World Financial Center buildings (1985–88).

The late 1990s have ushered in an era of **Entertainment Architecture**, an eclectic post-Modernism that revels in layered facades, dramatic lighting and signage that seems to explode from the traditional wall plane. Not surprisingly, Times Square, where lights and signs are the rule, features numerous examples of this architectural playfulness. Office buildings in the area have been growing more playful, too, as seen in the collage of styles and geometries that make up Fox and Fowle's Condé Nast Building (1999) and Reuters Building (2001). Sir Norman Foster's 42-story, accordion-like Hearst Tower (2006) combines post-Modern style with "green" building principles: 90 percent of the steel used in construction was recycled, the roof collects and distributes rainwater to area trees and the glass-paneled walls let in natural light while blocking solar radiation.

ARCHITECTURAL GLOSSARY
DUTCH COLONIAL (1620–1700)

Colonial architectural styles were imitations of their European contemporaries, modified slightly in deference to materials and climate. Dutch architecture during the 17C and 18C was characterized by tall, narrow buildings with stepped-gable rooflines, familiar from the streets and *grachten* (canals) of Amsterdam and other port cities, where homes were taxed on their frontage. Farm *(bouwerie)*

R. Corbel/MICHELIN

Dutch Colonial House

estates took their cues from the Dutch countryside, with sloping gambrel roofs and columned porches, as seen in the surviving Dyckman House in Manhattan and Wyckoff House in Brooklyn.

GEORGIAN (1720–90)

English Colonial architecture adopted the Renaissance interpretations of Classical architecture popular in the England of George I and George II, which emphasized symmetry and decorum. Frame, brick and stone houses featured hipped or sloping roofs with the gable end on the side, symmetrical window openings and a prominent central entrance, often ornamented with sidelights and a transom. The Van Cortlandt House is a good example. In larger public buildings, the style adopted more of the columns and pediments of its Classical ancestors, as seen in St. Paul's Chapel.

FEDERAL (1780–1830)

Federal is the term used to describe the more robust and Roman interpretation of Georgian architecture adopted by the newly freed colonies at the end of the 18C. These buildings saw a more liberal use of Classical columns and pediments, especially on entrance doorways, which often sported fanlights, and an occasional balustrade rimming the roofline. New York's City Hall of 1811 represents a lovely example of the style.

GREEK REVIVAL (1820–50)

The dramatic expansion of American democracy across the continent led to an architecture based on the pedimented, symmetrical orders of Classical Greek temples. Large public buildings often sported a lantern or cupola, with a two-story colonnaded facade. Vernacular versions included a low attic story; shallow roof; Doric, Ionic or Corinthian columns; and a pediment over the entrance. The Federal Hall National Memorial on Wall Street is a textbook Greek temple.

GOTHIC REVIVAL (1840–80)

Popular in England from the beginning of the 19C, the picturesque, asymmetrical forms of Gothic Revival facades often included towers, battlements and pointed-arch windows and gables. Linked to the Romantic movement, the style laid the basis for later picturesque movements like the Queen Anne. Smaller homes had intricately detailed bargeboards at the eaves and vertical siding, while larger homes and commercial buildings might include battlements, spires and gargoyles. Derived principally from medieval European cathedrals, the style was used for churches to great effect, as seen in Richard Upjohn's Trinity Church.

ITALIANATE (1840–80)

By mid-century, the Italianate style—with its heavy cornices and large brackets, decorated window lintels and convenient, rectangular massing—became

Allison Simpson/MICHELIN

St. Paul's Chapel

Flatiron Building

Peter Wrenn/MICHELIN

the American standard for homes and commercial buildings.

Based on more ornamental Renaissance forms than its staid Georgian cousin, the style featured tall, narrow windows with rounded arches often including incised or relief ornament, and high-stooped entrances accentuating the vertical rhythm of the style. Lower stoops typified the Anglo-Italianate style, adapted to Manhattan's narrow building lots. Executed in frame, brick and stone, the style is the basis for both New York brownstones and the typical cast-iron commercial facades, seen clearly in the E.V. Haughwout Building in Lower Manhattan. More elaborate homes adopted the Italian-villa variant, with a Classical cupola, rusticated corner quoins, pediments and paired or arcaded windows.

SECOND EMPIRE (1860–80)

Inspired by Baron Haussmann's redesign of Paris in the 1850s, this grandiose style is characterized by a short, steeply pitched mansard roof pierced by dormer windows. Generally symmetrical facades include quoined corners, projecting bays, windows flanked by pilasters, balustrades and an abundance of Classical decoration. Often mansard roofs were added to Italianate buildings in a close approximation of the style. Good examples include the former Arnold Constable and Lord & Taylor stores on Broadway.

ROMANESQUE REVIVAL (1860–1900)

Suggestive of medieval castles, the round arches, deeply inset window and door openings, and rough stone finishes of the Romanesque style inspired architects attempting to create a sense of permanence in the rapidly changing landscape of industrial America. The style was refined by Boston architect H.H. Richardson and helped define American architecture. The original City of Brooklyn Firehouse on Jay Street and the American Museum of Natural History are excellent examples of the style.

QUEEN ANNE (1880–1905)

This style is the one most commonly identified as "Victorian," with its asymmetrical composition, exuberant ornamentation and picturesque design marked by conical towers, projecting bays and elaborately decorated dormers and gables. The style is seen primarily in residential architecture like the Henderson Place Historic District.

CHICAGO SCHOOL (1885–1905)

The new structural technology of the steel frame allowed for the development of the first skyscrapers in Chicago in the 1880s. The design of these buildings celebrated their engineering and purpose, summed up by Louis Sullivan's phrase "Form follows function" and expressed in a gridlike facade of brick or terracotta, pierced by large panes of glass. The earliest skyscrapers adopted elements of Queen Anne and Romanesque design, and by the late 1890s incorporated the Beaux-Arts as well. Sullivan's 12-story Bayard-Condict Building (1899) on Bleecker Street bears the architect's characteristic foliate ornamentation.

NEOCLASSICAL OR BEAUX-ARTS (1890–1920)

As architecture became an established profession in the 19C, a study of Classical orders at Paris' famous École des Beaux-Arts became de rigueur. At the same time, the success of Chicago's 1893 World's Columbian Exposition popularized the monumental forms of the Roman Republic. Unlike the simpler Greek Revival style, Beaux-Arts architecture is more ornamental and sumptuous. Arched and arcaded windows, balustrades at every level, grand staircases, applied columns, decorative swags, garlands and even statuary embellish the edifices. The New York Public Library (1911), Grand Central Terminal (1913) and US Custom House (1907) at Bowling Green are premier examples of the style. Daniel Burnham's 1902 Flatiron Building made the style popular for skyscrapers.

ECLECTIC REVIVALS (1900–25)

The plasticity of terracotta and the search for appropriate forms to herald the dawn of the American empire made a wide range of historical styles achievable and popular in the first three decades of the 20C. The Beaux-Arts evolved into Georgian Revival and Renaissance Revival styles used for clubs, town houses, hotels and apartment buildings. Gothic Revival distinguished schools like Hunter College and came to be called Collegiate Gothic. Colonial Revival was the preferred suburban house style, and Moorish, Tudor, Egyptian and Chinese designs encrusted numerous buildings, especially theaters. The increasing eclecticism of skyscraper design literally reached a new height with Cass Gilbert's Gothic-inspired Woolworth Building.

*Sculpture for Living building
Astor Place*

Peter Wrenn/MICHELIN

ART DECO/MODERNE (1925–40)

Rejecting the historical ornament applied to commercial buildings in the 1910s, art deco first appeared as a style of decoration during the 1925 Exposition Internationale des Arts Décoratifs et Industriels Modernes in Paris. New York's 1916 zoning law, which called for skyscrapers to "step back" to provide light and air to the street, helped define the architectural aspects of art deco, which utilized setbacks, recessed windows and spandrels, and continuous piers to emphasize verticality. Designed in smooth stone or shiny terracotta surfaces, edifices featured highly stylized decorative and sculptural elements in low relief with a pronounced muscularity and abstraction. The Chrysler Building, Empire State Building and Rockefeller Center are landmark examples.

INTERNATIONAL STYLE (1930–70)

Applied ornament was abandoned altogether for sleek, sculptural lines in buildings, furniture and other designed objects, summarized by Mies van der Rohe's dictum "Less is more." Concrete, glass and steel were celebrated in buildings with boxlike massing set in open plazas. Exterior walls of glass and steel

Catskill Creek *(1845)*
by Thomas Cole

derived their design from proportion and materials alone, allowing the structures to express their function. The Lever House by Skidmore, Owings & Merrill (1952) and the Seagram Building by Mies van der Rohe (1958) are famous early International-style high rises.

POST-MODERN (1975–PRESENT)

This style is recognizable by its cavalier application of historical references and materials to modern steel-frame buildings. Surfaces of stone and mirrored glass are generally more colorful and modulated than their rigid and severe International-style predecessors, and elements of Classical architecture reappear on a grand scale. The AT&T Headquarters (1984, Johnson & Burgee)—now Sony Plaza—introduced post-Modernism to the nation with its whimsical "Chippendale" roofline, which resembles the top of a colonial cupboard. Philip Johnson and John Burgee's elliptical pink tower at 995 Third Avenue (1986)—the so-called Lipstick Building—captures the playfulness of post-Modernism.

The newest trend is to blend post-Modern design with "green" building principles. Sir Norman Foster's 42-story accordion-like Hearst Tower (2006) does that marvelously, using recycled steel, natural light and energy-efficient heating and cooling systems without sacrificing aesthetic appeal.

VISUAL ARTS

Preoccupied with settling their new nation, colonial New Yorkers had little time to spend painting or sculpting for other than the most practical reasons. The art of portraiture, though popular, was more a craft, practiced by itinerants and painters who had other livelihoods. In the decorative and household arts, ethnic custom and functionality reigned. Because of such practicality, New York became a center of cabinet- and silver making long before its fairly recent ascent as a hub of the visual arts. Silversmith Cornelius Kierstede and furniture maker Duncan Phyfe stand out among early New York's finest artisans.

HUDSON RIVER SCHOOL

The painters of the first distinctly American school of painting (1825–75) took their main inspiration from the dramatic scenery of the Hudson River Valley north of New York City. Artists **Thomas Cole** (1801–48), Asher B. Durand, Albert Bierstadt and Frederic E. Church embraced a romantic vision of nature and art, and imbued epic portrayals of America's grandiose landscapes with moral and transcendental meaning. These painters were among the many artists who swelled the ranks of the new art academies established in the city during the period, including the National Academy of Design (1825) and the Art Students League (1875).

EMERGENCE OF MODERN ART

Founded in 1908, the artistic group "The Eight" sought to rebel against the conservatism of the New York academic establishment. Dubbed the **Ashcan school** in derisive reference to its bald urban realism, "The Eight" (particularly its most prominent members Robert Henri, George Luks and John Sloan) produced vivid, sympathetic portrayals of the rough edges of urban life, which inspired a rich tradition of 20C American Realism (George Bellows and Edward Hopper) and found parallels in Jacob Riis' and Lewis W. Hine's documentary photographs of the immigrant population.

Photographer Alfred Stieglitz exhibited avant-garde European art in his Little Galleries of the Photo Secession from 1905 to 1917. Also known as "291," Stieglitz' gallery served as a launching pad for New York's first Modernist painters Arthur Dove, John Marin and Georgia O'Keeffe.

The watershed event in the history of modern art in America was New York's 1913 **Armory Show**, or International Exhibition of Modern Art, which displayed more than 1,300 objects—including works by European post-Impressionists, Fauvists and Cubists—and introduced the most recent European art to a largely unprepared and bewildered American public. Marcel Duchamp's Cubist-inspired *Nude Descending a Staircase* provoked particular controversy. Despite the hostile public response, the exhibit attracted important collectors and can be credited with encouraging the tradition of patronage, which culminated in the founding of the Museum of Modern Art in 1929, the Whitney Museum of American Art in 1931 and the Guggenheim Foundation in 1937.

After World War I, aspects of abstraction were explored by Stuart Davis, Patrick Henry Bruce and Charles Sheeler. The Great Depression brought an insular mood and public programs that fostered the social realism of Reginald Marsh and the mural painting of Thomas Hart Benton.

THE BALANCE SHIFTS

Prior to the 1930s many American artists traveled abroad to study and observe the latest developments in experimental art. However, as war fermented and the Great Depression lingered in Europe, foreign artists fled to New York. The arrival of Frenchmen Fernand Léger and André Masson, Spaniard Joan Miró, and Germans Josef Albers and Max Ernst brought an unprecedented opportunity for direct contact with Surrealist and Abstract art. In the decade after World War II, a true American avant-garde flowered, and New York emerged as a cultural mecca and world leader in the production and promotion of modern art. This period of fertile artistic activity culminated in the first radical American artistic movement, **Abstract Expressionism** (1946–late 1950s). Also known

One: Number 31, 1950 *(1950) by Jackson Pollock, Museum of Modern Art*

as the New York school, the Abstract Expressionists were divided among Action or Gesture painters (Jackson Pollock, Willem de Kooning, Franz Kline, Robert Motherwell and Clyfford Still), who emphasized the use of thick, sweeping brush strokes or dripped paint in the spontaneous, intuitive act of painting; and Color Field painters (Mark Rothko, Barnett Newman), who employed equally large but color-saturated canvases to envelop the spectator in meditative calm. As the Abstract Expressionists received international recognition, postwar American affluence prompted collecting and gallery activity. New York gradually came to the fore, replacing Paris as the epicenter of the art world. The late 1950s saw new artistic developments inspired by Abstract Expressionists: the brilliantly colored canvases of Stain Painting (Helen Frankenthaler), the simplified color fields of Hard Edge Painting (Al Held, Kenneth Noland) and the dramatic, shaped canvases of Frank Stella. In the 1960s, artists Roy Lichtenstein, Robert Rauschenberg, Andy Warhol and Claes Oldenburg debunked the high-art notions of Abstract Expressionism and irreverently employed comic-strip subjects and billboard painting techniques in the production of **Pop Art**.

Also emerging in reaction to Abstract Expressionism, 1960s **Minimalist** sculptors (Donald Judd, Carl Andre) used non-referential, geometric industrial forms to produce works of immediate and bold impact. The 1970s witnessed **Conceptual art**, whose adherents—environmental sculptors and performance artists—proposed ideas rather than the collectible object as the essence of art, and the revival of Realism (Chuck Close, Alex Katz and George Segal).

A CHANGING SCENE

The richly pluralistic artistic atmosphere of the 1980s and 90s embraced the post-Modern movements of neo-Expressionism (Julian Schnabel, David Salle), Graffiti art (Keith Haring, Jean-Michel Basquiat) and neo-Conceptualism (Barbara Kruger, Jenny Holzer), along with long-standing traditions of representation and painterly abstraction. In recent years, subjects anatomical, political and environmental have inspired artists on the leading edge—among them Damien Hirst and the "young British artists" who invaded New York in the Brooklyn Museum's Sensation show in 1999. Contemporary art can be viewed today in the galleries of SoHo, the East and the West Villages, West Chelsea and TriBeCa, as well as in New York's many museums.

LITERATURE

In the rich literary life of contemporary America, New York is no doubt the most vital force. Indeed, the Naked City is home to many notable figures in fiction and journalism, from Walt Whitman to Norman Mailer, each celebrating the city's enduring vibrancy.

EARLY LITERATI

Two kinds of writers have left an indelible mark on New York's literary scene: those who were born here and those who came here as to a cultural mecca, adopting the city as their own with an almost religious fervor.

The first of the latter group was probably "Common Sense" author and patriot Thomas Paine, who spent his last years in Greenwich Village at the dawn of the 19C. New York City typified the confidence and spunk of the young Republic at the time, although literary themes remained pastoral rather than urban. One of America's first literary giants was New York City-born **Washington Irving** (1783–1859). In his 1807 satirical essay collection *Salmagundi*, he referred to New York City as Gotham—the 13C English village where the inhabitants acted like madmen to prevent King John from residing there. Irving also wrote the parodic *A History of New York from the Beginning of the World to the End of the Dutch Dynasty* (1809) under the name Diedrich Knickerbocker, translated as "baker of marbles." He achieved lasting fame in America with *Rip Van Winkle* (1819) and *The Legend of Sleepy Hollow* (1820).

Best known for his work *The Last of the Mohicans*, contemporary **James Feni-**

Outdoor Sculpture

Manhattan's plazas, courtyards and open spaces have long been used as showcases for the city's monumental sculpture. In fact, some of the world's greatest sculptors have been called upon to adorn the city's public places with their works of art. As you visit Manhattan, be on the lookout for the works appearing on the list (⌖ *see chart below*), which represent only a selection of 20C outdoor sculpture gracing New York City's streetscapes.

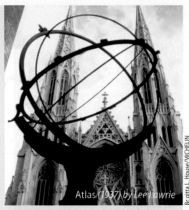

Atlas *(1937) by Lee Lawrie*

Brigitta L. House/MICHELIN

DOWNTOWN

The Red Cube (1967)	Isamu Noguchi	Plaza in front of HSBC Bank
Group of Four Trees (1972)	Jean Dubuffet	Plaza in front of Chase Bank
East-West Gate (1973)	Yu Yu Yang	Plaza in front of Wall Street Plaza
American Merchant Mariners' Memorial (1991)	Marisol	Battery Park
Shadows and Flags (1977)	Louise Nevelson	Louise Nevelson Plaza, intersection of Maiden Lane, William & Liberty Sts.
Gay Liberation (1980)	George Segal	Christopher Park at Christopher St. & Sheridan Sq.
Alamo (1967)	Tony Rosenthal	Astor Pl., Lafayette & W. 8th Sts.

MIDTOWN

Eye of Fashion (1976)	Robert M. Cronbach	Fashion Institute of Technology Plaza at W. 27th St. & Seventh Ave.
The Garment Worker (1984)	Judith Weller	Plaza at 555 Seventh Ave., at W. 39th St.
Prometheus (1934)	Paul Manship	Lower Plaza, Rockefeller Center
Atlas (1937)	Lee Lawrie	In front of International Building, Rockefeller Center
News (1940)	Isamu Noguchi	Associated Press Building, Rockefeller Center
Lapstrake (1987)	Jésus Bautista Moroles	Plaza in front of 31 W. 52nd St.
Looking Toward the Avenue (1989)	Jim Dine	Calyon Building Plaza, Sixth Ave. between 52nd & 53rd Sts.
Saurien (1975)	Alexander Calder	590 Madison Avenue, Madison Ave. & 57th St.
Peace Form One (1980)	Daniel LaRue Johnson	Ralph J. Bunche Park, United Nations
N0.9 (1974)	Ivan Chermayeff	9 W. 57th St.
Moonbird (1966)	Joan Miró	58th St. plaza of 9 W. 57th St.

UPTOWN

Reclining Figure (1965)	Henry Moore	Plaza Pool, Lincoln Center
Romeo and Juliet (1977)	Milton Hebald	Central Park, near entrance to Delacorte Theater at W. 81st St.
Night Presence IV (1972)	Louise Nevelson	Park Ave. & 92nd St.

61

Portrait of Washington Irving *(1809)* by John Wesley Jarvis, Sunnyside

Historic Hudson Valley

more **Cooper** (1789–1851) lived in the city in the 1820s and wrote *The Pioneers* and *The Pilot* here, finding adventure not in the city but at sea and in the wilds of the frontier.

Herman Melville (1819–91) was born and lived most of his life in New York, writing his great seafaring saga *Moby-Dick* here and continuing the literary tradition of the early 19C that focused on wilderness and adventure.

Melville also set pieces in and around the city, including "Bartleby the Scrivener," an early perspective on the commercial metropolis. **Clement Clarke Moore** (1779–1863) resided south of 23rd Street in Chelsea, where he wrote the famous poem "A Visit from St. Nicholas," that defined the modern image of Santa Claus.

LATE 19TH-CENTURY NEW YORK

By the mid-1800s, Americans had grown aware of their distinct national character, defined in part by the frontier but also by the energy generated through booming economic and technological growth. The Industrial Revolution brought about a transformation in the circumstances of life, changing forever the importance of the city, culture and morality.

The new morality of the modern world was epitomized by one of America's greatest poets, **Walt Whitman** (1819–92). Born in New York City, Whitman worked as reporter and editor for the *Brooklyn Eagle* in the 1840s, developing his forceful physical style and path-breaking sensuality in the bustling metropolis. Shortly after the first edition of *Leaves of Grass* in 1855, he served as editor for the *Brooklyn Times* and continued to capture the lusty spirit of his city in works like the classic *Crossing Brooklyn Ferry*.

Henry James (1843–1916) reversed the traditional role of writers coming to New York seeking fame. Born in the city, he set several novels and stories in New York, including *Washington Square* (1880), but spent most of his literary career as an expatriate in London, where he published his most famous work, *The Turn of the Screw*, in 1898. He returned to write *The American Scene* in 1907 but died a British subject in 1916.

New York native **Edith Wharton** (1862–1937) berated and celebrated the Gilded Age of her hometown in novels like *The Age of Innocence*, which won the Pulitzer prize. The great romantic Gothicist **Edgar Allan Poe** (1809–49) lived in The Bronx in the 1840s as well as in Greenwich Village and wrote several of his poems and stories here, including "The Raven," first published in the *New York Evening Mirror* in 1845. A former *New York Tribune* reporter, **Stephen Crane** (1871–1900), helped bring the American novel into the big city with *New York City Sketches* and *Maggie: A Girl of the Streets* (1893), gaining his greatest fame with *The Red Badge of Courage* (1894). **Mark Twain** (Samuel Clemens, 1835–1910) reported on the city for several Western newspapers, residing in the Village during his sojourns here. **William Dean Howells** (1837–1920), the "dean of American letters," came to New York in 1889 to serve as a *Harper's* magazine editor. By the late 19C, the city had become the literary capital of the US, surpassing Boston and Philadelphia.

The lure was so strong that English poet laureate John Masefield scrubbed floors in a saloon to support his New York address in the 1890s.

BOHEMIAN ENCLAVE

By the 1910s, Greenwich Village had become the country's bohemia, attracting avant-garde writers, artists and thespians, including playwright **Eugene O'Neill** (1888–1953), poet **Edna St. Vincent Millay** (1892–1950), author **Theodore Dreiser** (1871–1945) and poet **Edwin Arlington Robinson** (1869–1935). O'Neill based *The Iceman Cometh* and his 1921 Pulitzer prize-winning *Anna Christie* on his 1916 forays in the Village, while Millay used the neighborhood as the setting for *Second April* and *Renascence*. The radical aspects of Village life included the socialist magazines *Seven Arts* and *The Masses*, the latter involving revolutionaries Max Eastman, Art Young, John Reed and Floyd Dell. Poet **Marianne Moore** (1887–1972) arrived in the city in 1921, becoming editor of the *Dial* in 1925 and living out her life in Brooklyn. She was followed in 1923 by North Carolina transplant **Thomas Wolfe** (1900–38), who wrote *Look Homeward, Angel* in 1929 and *You Can't Go Home Again* (1940). F. Scott Fitzgerald (1896–1940) brought his party to town on more than one occasion as the city cemented its cultural position in the late 1920s.

As the Village continued its ferment, the Midtown Algonquin Hotel became host to the Thanatopsis, Literary Inside Straight and **Round Table** clubs. The latter group became an institution, led by drama critic and raconteur Alexander Woolcott, columnist Franklin P. Adams, and three figures associated with **The New Yorker** magazine: editor Harold Ross, author Dorothy Parker and humorist **Robert Benchley**. Established in 1925, *The New Yorker* elevated the standard of American discourse to a new, articulate and sophisticated level. For three generations its writing and criticism have attracted a nationwide audience, and its list of contributors includes many of the greatest 20C American writers, including essayists E.B. White and Edmund Wilson; novelists J.D. Salinger, Saul Bellow, John O'Hara and John Updike; film critic Pauline Kael; humorists James Thurber and Calvin Trillin; and musicologist Whitney Baillett.

> *"There is no place like [New York], no place with an atom of its glory, pride, and exultancy. It lays its hand upon a man's bowels; he grows drunk with ecstasy; he grows young and full of glory, he feels that he can never die."*
> **Thomas Wolfe**
> from *Death to Morning* (1935)

AFRICAN-AMERICAN LETTERS

The concentration of African Americans in Manhattan's Harlem neighborhood after the turn of the century created an atmosphere of independence and cultural pride that fostered the 1920s awakening known as the Harlem Renaissance. Even earlier, pioneering poet and author **Paul Laurence Dunbar** (1872–1906), living in the African-American bohemia of the Tenderloin, had celebrated the black spirit in his 1902 *Sport of the Gods*. **W.E.B. DuBois**' *The Souls of Black Folk* (1903) brought recognition to the problem of the "color line"; he formed the NAACP in New York in 1909.

But it was the rapid growth and sometime prosperity of Harlem after 1910 that nurtured the greatest flowering of African-American arts and literature in the 1920s. **Alain Locke**'s 1925 *The New Negro: An Interpretation* summarized the attitude and expectations of a community that found, in New York City, the support and freedom to express itself. **Langston Hughes** (1902–67) captured the streets of Harlem in *The Weary Blues* (1926) and recognized that Harlem was no longer simply a place but a symbol of African-American identity. Other important poets included Countee Cullen (1903–46), with *One Way to Heaven* (1932), and James Weldon Johnson (1871–1938), who released *The Book of American Negro Poetry* in 1922. Novelists included Jean Toomer (1894–1967), author of *Cane* (1923); West Indian native Claude McKay (1890–1948), who wrote *Home to Harlem* (1928); and **Zora Neale Hurston** (1891–1960), whose *Their Eyes Were Watching God* was published in 1937, when the stark realities of the Great Depression and racism had eclipsed the optimism of the Harlem Renaissance.

W.E.B. DuBois

©Oscar White/Corbis

COMING OUT OF THE DEPRESSION

The Great Depression marked a respite in New York's literary history as the city's urban atmosphere provided the backdrop for Ellery Queen mysteries and for sophisticated sleuths Nick and Nora Charles in Dashiell Hammett's *The Thin Man*. New York-born **Henry Miller** (1891–1980) went bumming around Paris in the 1930s, where he wrote the path-breaking *Tropic of Cancer* before returning to the city in 1940 and then relocating to the West Coast. New Yorker **John Dos Passos** (1896–1970) served up his critique of the nation in the novels *USA* and *Manhattan Transfer*. *Day of the Locust* author **Nathanael West** (1903–40) was born Nathan Weinstein in New York City before moving on to Hollywood. Others continued to make the pilgrimage, including Spanish poet and playwright Federico García Lorca *(Poet in New York)* and Russian poet Vladimir Mayakovsky *(Brooklyn Bridge)*.

POSTWAR PENMANSHIP

New York emerged from World War II more powerful, attractive and determined than ever as it sought to become the world's cultural capital. The hard-bitten, macho New York style of **Norman Mailer** (1923–2007) rocked the world in 1948 with his sensational novel *The Naked and the Dead*. Mailer still serves as a literary native son for an increasingly cosmopolitan metropolis. Playwright **Arthur Miller** (1915–2005) wrote the epochal *Death of a Salesman* in 1949. The 1950s saw the great Welsh poet **Dylan Thomas** (1914–53) succumb to the lure of New York City and an excess of drink at the White Horse Tavern.

In the 1950s and 60s, New York evolved into the cultural capital of the Jet Age, as writers, artists and aesthetes gathered in Cedar Tavern, fostering the experimentation of New York-school poets like Frank O'Hara and Barbara Guest and beats like **Allen Ginsberg** (1926–97), Jack Kerouac and Gregory Corso.

The period marked a resurgence of African-American literature in New York, with poet **Amiri Baraka** (LeRoi Jones) and author **James Baldwin**, whose important novels *Go Tell It on the Mountain* (1952) and *Another Country* (1962) are set in the city. Langston Hughes achieved new levels of poetry and commentary with *Shakespeare in Harlem* (1942) and *Montage of a Dream Deferred* (1951), while **Ralph Ellison** (1914–94) fired an early Civil Rights salvo in 1952's *Invisible Man*.

A LIVING TRADITION

During a 1963 newspaper strike, editors Robert E. Silver and Barbara Epstein founded one of the most important literary publications of the 20C, the *New York Review of Books*, now a biweekly that is indispensable to the serious and amateur critic alike. New York City is often the centerpiece for American comedies and slice-of-life dramas, as exemplified by comic playwrights **Neil Simon** and **Wendy Wasserstein**, and film directors **Woody Allen** and **Spike Lee**. The Black Arts movement of the 1960s brought **Nikki Giovanni**, **Maya Angelou** and **Gil Scott-Heron** to a growing audience that had become national in scope by the 1980s. **E.L. Doctorow** captured modern Gotham in a series of tragic and violent novels, including *Ragtime* (1978) and *Billy Bathgate* (1989).

The moral vacuity of the 1980s provided the setting for **Tom Wolfe**'s searing *Bonfire of the Vanities* (1987), while Oscar

Hijuelos' Pulitzer prize-winning *The Mambo Kings Play Songs of Love* (1989) captured the rhythms of the Cuban community. In *Underworld* (1997), Don De-Lillo weaves the Bronx of the 1950s and 90s into a complex tapestry of the post-war era. Other leading New York authors include Gore Vidal, Paul Auster and the late Susan Sontag. The Nuyorican Poets Café in Alphabet City, propelled by its weekly poetry slams, has in recent years become a mecca for an exuberant, multicultural spoken-word movement.

The city continues to draw literary pilgrims from across America and the globe, seeking critical approval, publishing opportunities and the manifold inspiration presented by the city's ongoing human drama.

SPECTATOR SPORTS

Since the 1920s New York's teams and its athletes have played in the limelight of the world's media capital. First there was **Babe Ruth** (1895–1948), who came to the city in 1920 as a great ballplayer and in a few years became an immortal. The Babe's Yankees are, of course, the prime symbol of the city's dominance, but are only one of a total of nine professional sports teams in the four major sports—baseball, basketball, football and hockey.

BASEBALL

The very first baseball games were played in Manhattan in the 1840s by players such as Alexander Joy Cartwright who formalized the layout of the diamond and the rules of the game. In October 1845, he and others organized themselves as the New York Knickerbockers, the game's first team. The city entered the big leagues for good with the formation of the New York Giants in 1883, and by 1924 the team had won 10 pennants in 20 years under manager John McGraw.

The Polo Grounds, their horseshoe-shaped home in Upper Manhattan (shared with the Yankees until Babe Ruth's popularity led McGraw to evict them), was the site of one of baseball's enduring moments: "the Catch," made by **Willie Mays**, running full speed, back turned to the plate, in the 1954 World Series. The Giants' nemesis, the Brooklyn Dodgers, lost when they were bad and lost in heartbreaking fashion when they were good. No matter.

Brooklynites flocked to Ebbets Field to root for "dem bums." In 1947 **Jackie Robinson** (1919–72) broke baseball's color line, heralding the Civil Rights movement. Robinson, Duke Snider and the Boys of Summer were the class of the league in the 1950s.

Yankee Stadium

©Rich Pilling/MLB Photos/Getty Images

The Subway Series

From 1947 to 1956, coinciding with the city's postwar golden era, the Yankees played seven (and won six) Subway Series (World Series matches involving only NYC teams) against the Dodgers and Giants. In 1951 no fan was left out: Giant Bobby Thomson's "shot heard round the world" off Dodger Ralph Branca decided a three-game playoff for the pennant. Then, in the World Series, with Brooklyn fans' approval, the Yankees beat the Giants.

The Dodgers' 1955 victory over the Yankees marked Brooklyn's brightest moment, a mood captured by the *Daily News'* front page: a drawing of an ecstatic hobo under the headline "Who's a Bum?" The Yankees won the 1956 rematch, and a year later, the Giants and Dodgers moved west, prompting, fans presume, the city's decline. New York's recent resurgence seemed to augur the Subway Series' return. And in 2000 it came to be. The Mets assumed the Dodgers' role of outer-borough underdog, and fans hoped for miracles.

Fiery Mets manager Bobby Valentine, son-in-law of Ralph Branca, faced off against his stoic counterpart, onetime Mets manager Joe Torre, a Brooklyn kid who saw Don Larsen's perfect game against the Dodgers in the 1956 Series. The city turned inward. A base hit or clean stop cheered on the Grand Concourse was met with stony silence in Astoria and Bensonhurst. And vice versa. The old days had returned to New York. Predictably, the Yankees won in five games.

Noted for their succession of strong arms (Tom Seaver, Jerry Koosman, Dwight Gooden) at pitcher-friendly Shea Stadium (⚑ *see Queens*), the expansion Mets are loved less for their dominance than for their underdog spirit.

The Yankees (who were, like Babe Ruth, born in Baltimore) moved to New York in 1903, their third season. In nearly 110 years the team has won 40 American League pennants and 27 World Series. The team's pantheon of sluggers—the Babe, **Lou Gehrig**, **Joe DiMaggio**, **Mickey Mantle**, **Yogi Berra**, **Reggie Jackson**—have all achieved a fame that transcends the game. The 1996 season marked the debut of manager Joe Torre and shortstop Derek Jeter, the core of the Yankees team that won six pennants and four World Series between 1996 and 2003. In 2005, 2006 and 2007 the team made it to the playoffs, only to lose in the first round. The Yankees ended their 85-year run at historic Yankee Stadium in 2008, moving to a new state-of-the-art facility adjacent to the old stadium (⚑ *see The Bronx*). In 2009 the Yankees returned to greatness, earning their 27th World Series win behind strong performances from future Hall of Famers Alex Rodriguez and Andy Pettitte.

FOOTBALL

New Yorkers didn't catch football fever until 1925, when Tim Mara started the New York Giants in the fledgling National Football League. That year, 70,000 filled the Polo Grounds to see the team take on Red Grange and the Chicago Bears. Although the Giants suffered an embarrassing loss in the 2001 Super Bowl to the Baltimore Ravens, the team bounced back in 2007, when quarterback Eli Manning led the underdog Giants to a stunning come-from-behind win over a previously undefeated New England Patriots team.

The perennial underdog New York Jets, behind the outsized personality of head coach Rex Ryan, have been stealing much of the New York limelight as of late. Ryan, along with young quarterback Mark Sanchez, is resurrecting the spirit of flamboyant quarterback "Broadway" **Joe Namath**, who became famous for "guaranteeing" a Super Bowl win over the Baltimore Colts back in 1969 (and in the process helped legitimize the upstart American Football League and pave the way for the eventual merger of the rival AFL and NFL).

BASKETBALL

New York basketball is first and foremost a street game. Only blizzards interrupt half-court games of "21." Not surprisingly, New York has sent a stream of flashy point guards to the pros, from Bob Cousy to Stephon Marbury. Atop the city's hoops world sits the Knicks, an original NBA franchise whose legendary early-1970s squad, led by Willis Reed, Walt "Clyde" Frazier and "Dollar" **Bill Bradley**, twice won championships. After a period of decline, the team rebounded with the hiring of Pat Riley as coach in 1991; fans flocked to Madison Square Garden to cheer (and boo) center Pat Ewing and the intimidating, defense-oriented Knicks.

Born with the ABA in 1967, the Nets, featuring the gravity-defying **"Dr. J," Julius Erving**, enjoyed early success and a few ABA titles. The team entered the NBA in 1976, then moved to New Jersey, where they remained on the periphery of the city's sports consciousness until 2002, when they rocketed to the NBA finals as the Knicks team disintegrated. The Nets returned to the NBA finals in 2003, losing to the San Antonio Spurs. The team has announced plans to move from New Jersey to Brooklyn by 2012.

HOCKEY

One of the NHL's "original six" teams, the Rangers, and the team's intensely loyal fans, had suffered through a 54-year drought between championships when **Mark Messier**, exiled from Edmonton, led the squad to a Stanley Cup in 1994. The Islanders, an expansion team formed in 1972, quickly assembled a nucleus of eventual Hall of Famers **(Bryan Trottier, Mike Bossy, Denis Potvin)** whose graceful play won four straight Stanley Cups in the early 1980s and helped transform the game's roughhouse image. The Islanders made it to the playoffs in 2007, but the New Jersey Devils, who arrived from Colorado in 1982, are generally regarded as the area's best team. Their tenacious defense, spearheaded by goalie Martin Brodeur, brought them three Stanley Cups—in 1995, 2000 and 2003—and a sizable following.

BOXING

John L. Sullivan (1858–1918) fought at the first Madison Square Garden, located in, yes, Madison Square, in 1883. In subsequent years and incarnations, the Garden became the country's boxing mecca. The current Garden was the site of the famous 1971 Ali–Frazier fight. Yankee Stadium also hosted key bouts, including **Joe Louis**' (1914–81) victory over German Max Schmeling, before 70,000 fans. The ascendance of Las Vegas and Atlantic City as boxing locales spelled the end of the city's preeminence.

OTHER

The **Belmont Stakes**, the third leg of thoroughbred racing's Triple Crown, is held at Belmont Park, on Long Island. The National Tennis Center in Flushing Meadows hosts the US Open, a grand slam event. Lifelong New Yorker **John McEnroe**, famous for his big mouth, short fuse and brilliant play, won the tournament four times, to the delight of local fans. Brazilian soccer legend Pelé, playing for the Cosmos, electrified New York in the mid-1970s, though local enthusiasm, and the league itself, petered out a few years later. The famed **New York City Marathon**, held the first Sunday in November, draws nearly 45,000 runners and more than two million spectators.

New York City Marathon

Y. Saito/MICHELIN

South Street Seaport
Peter Wrenn/MICHELIN

Manhattan is the heart of New York City. The smallest of the city's five boroughs, it's a tongue-shaped island bordered by the Hudson River on the west and the Harlem and East Rivers on the east. The island measures only 13.4mi long—about half the distance of a marathon race—and just 2.3mi at its widest point. The Dutch were the first Europeans to settle here, on the southern tip, calling their new territory Nieuw Amsterdam. Blame the colonial powers for the irregular street patterns found downtown—the neat grid of numbered streets throughout most of the island was not invented until 1811.

Downtown New York is New York at its most vital. So many disparate neighborhoods are crowded together, with so much to offer. At the toe of the island lies the **Financial District**, where the city was born in 1625. Today skyscrapers loom over a maze of colonial streets—most famously **Wall Street**—and ferries depart for the **Statue of Liberty** and

Ellis Island. The World Trade Center once stood here; out of its ashes, New York will see some exciting new buildings rise in coming years.

Directly north of the Financial District stands **Civic Center**, seat of city government. **TriBeCa**, to the west, is a warehouse district known for its chi-chi restaurants, design galleries and film festival, spearheaded by actor Robert De Niro. There are still a few rowdy red-sauce joints on Mulberry Street, but for the most part **Little Italy** has been engulfed by sprawling **Chinatown**, where every conceivable kind of jade statue, noodle, fish, dumpling, lantern and, on Canal Street, knock-off handbag can be found. For the real McCoy (handbag, that is), venture north to **SoHo**, where stores from Armani to Zara have pushed out most (but not all)

Union Square

© Patrick Frilet/hemis.fr

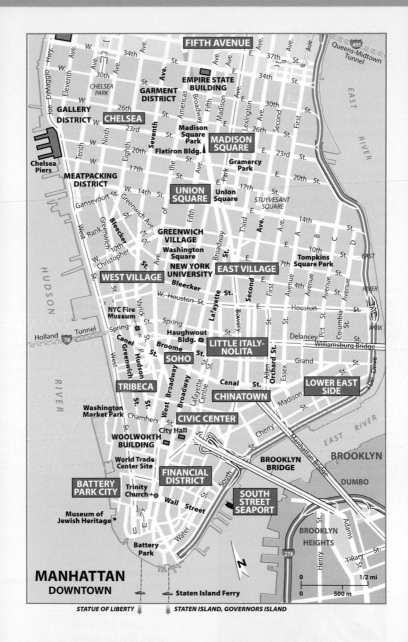

MANHATTAN
DOWNTOWN

STATUE OF LIBERTY   STATEN ISLAND, GOVERNORS ISLAND

of the art galleries (roomier **Chelsea** is now New York's prime gallery district). The historic brownstones of **Greenwich Village**, arranged along picture-perfect streets, are a wonder to behold but home to few artists (aside from movie stars): the city's bohemia has shifted to the grittier **Lower East Side** and East Village, where Old-World immigrants rub shoulders with heavily pierced hipsters. The **Lower East Side** has a hot nightlife scene. From **Union Square** to Madison Square, things get more sedate, especially around Gramercy Park. Midtown begins at 34th Street. Uptown is considered north of 59th Street.

Statue of Liberty★★★

The Statue of Liberty is one of New York City's most popular (and free) attractions. Nothing can compare with standing in front of the colossal statue—her arm raised high with a torch in her hand and broken shackles at her feet. A visit to the Ellis Island Immigration Museum on neighboring Ellis Island should be part of your trip. Some 12 million people gained permanent entry to the US between 1892 and 1954 at this federal "processing center," now restored. East of Liberty Island, Governors Island is home to historic military installations.

A BIT OF HISTORY

Birth of a Notion – The friendship between France and the US dates back to the American Revolution. In 1865 French law professor Édouard-René de Laboulaye came up with the idea to present the American people with a memorial commemorating this friendship. Six years later, the committee he formed to make the idea a reality selected Alsatian sculptor **Frédéric-Auguste Bartholdi** (1834–1904), who then traveled to America to study and promote the project.

Statue of Liberty
©iStockphoto.com/Tom Hall

Subway: 4, 5 train to Bowling Green, R train to Whitehall St. or 1 train to South Ferry.

Info: National Park Service: ✆212-363-3200. www.nps.gov/stli. Statue Cruises: ✆877-523-9849. www.statuecruises.com.

Location: Liberty Island and Ellis Island are accessible only by Statue Cruises ferries; the statue itself is accessible only with a Crown Ticket or Pedestal/Museum Ticket (reservations advised). All ferries stop at both islands (*$13 round-trip*). From Manhattan, ferries depart every 20–25min Jun–Aug 8.30am–4.30pm (rest of the year every 30–45min 9.30am–3.30pm) from **Battery Park**; the trip to Liberty Island takes about 15min. Purchase same-day tickets at Castle Clinton National Monument in Battery Park, or buy advance ferry tickets by phone or online (*see sidebar opposite*). From New Jersey, ferries depart every 40min in summer 8.30am–4.30pm from **Liberty State Park** (*PATH subway to Hoboken; then Light Rail to Liberty State Park; park open year-round daily 6am–10pm; ✆201-915-3440; www.state.nj.us/dep/parksandforests*). All ferries are boarded on a first-come, first-served basis. No ferry service Dec 25.

Timing: Allow a full day to visit both islands. Lines to buy tickets and pass through checkpoints can be extremely long on holidays and in summer.

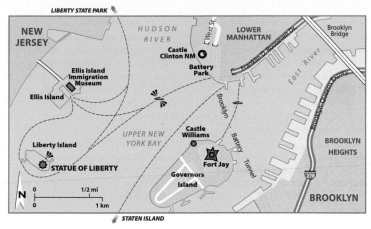

In 1869 Bartholdi had attended the opening ceremonies of the Suez Canal in hopes of getting a commission for a huge statue-lighthouse at the entrance to the new canal. Unsuccessful in nabbing the contract, he turned his energy to creating a similar monument in the US. When he entered New York Harbor, he was overwhelmed by the grandeur of the scene before him, and its significance as the main gateway to the New World. Then and there he knew that de Laboulaye's monument would be a figure of Liberty, and that one of the tiny harbor islands in this breathtaking setting would be an ideal site for it.

To raise funds and coordinate matters, a Franco-American union was established, with de Laboulaye as president. The project was to be a joint effort—the French would underwrite the statue itself, and the Americans, the pedestal.

Liberty on the Rise – As work on the statue progressed, the cost of construction almost doubled. To reach their goal, the French launched a massive fund drive, and by 1884 Liberty Enlightening the World was complete. At a ceremony held July 4, 1884, in Paris, the statue was presented to the ambassador of the US as a gift from the people of France. Following the festivities, Liberty was dismantled and packed in 220 crates, in preparation for the Atlantic voyage. In the meantime little progress had been made in the US in raising funds for the pedestal. Benefit balls, theatrical and sporting events, even a poetry contest were held, and in 1884 Liberty's arm, complete with torch, was exhibited in Madison Square. By 1885 the statue was ready for shipment, but funds were still lacking. Due largely to the fund-raising campaign of **Joseph Pulitzer** (1847–1911), the publisher of the *New York World*, donations were forthcoming. In front-page editorials, he criticized the rich for not providing funds, and encouraged all Americans to contribute as the

Buy Your Tickets in Advance

It's best to buy ferry tickets by phone or online at least 2 days (up to 60 days) in advance. Advance tickets may be picked up at the Prepaid Tickets window, and allow you to reserve a Crown Ticket or Pedestal/Museum Ticket (◐ *see Visit*). Be aware that long lines form at the ferry security checkpoint; the wait can exceed 2hrs, especially during summer and holiday seasons; advance tickets allow priority access to the security checkpoint. If you're not sure exactly which day you'll be visiting, you can buy a Flex Ticket valid for one-time use over three days (◉ *note: Crown or Pedestal/Museum Tickets are not available with Flex ticket, but a limited number are available daily first-come first-served at the Prepaid Tickets window*).

French had. He promised to publish in his newspaper the name of every donor, no matter how minor. Contributions began to pour in.

The Dedication – In May 1885 the French ship *Isère*, carrying its precious cargo, set sail from Rouen and about a month later dropped anchor in New York Harbor. Bartholdi traveled once more to New York to confer with the engineers and the architect chosen to design the pedestal, **Richard Morris Hunt**, one of the leading American architects of the day. Hunt's final design blended in character and scale to form an integrated unit with the statue. October 28, 1886—the day the festivities took place—was declared an official holiday in New York City. US president **Grover Cleveland** presided over the unveiling on Bedloe's Island (renamed Liberty Island in 1956). When the statue was unveiled, foghorns bellowed and a 21-gun salute sounded from nearby batteries. Liberty's crown was illuminated simultaneously, symbolizing prophetically the beacon of hope she would be to the millions who would flock to these shores.

Modern Liberty – Today the monument falls under the aegis of the National Park Service. For the most part Lady Liberty appears as she did at her dedication. In 1956 Congress approved plans to expand the base of the statue to make room for a museum; the American Museum of Immigration was dedicated in 1972. Between 1984 and 1986 individuals and corporations donated $150 million to repair the statue (the exterior had suffered degradation in the salty air) and to re-landscape the grounds in time for Liberty's centennial bash. Following the attacks of September 11, 2001, the statue was closed to visitors for three years. The pedestal and observation deck were reopened in late 2004. The crown has reopened for limited visits. Owing to weakening in Lady Liberty's upraised arm, the torch has not been accessible since 1916.

VISIT

There is no entrance fee to the national park grounds, which are open year-round daily 8.30am–5.15pm.
Closed Dec 25. National Park Service ℘212-363-3200. www.nps.gov/stli. Reserve Crown Ticket or Pedestal/ Museum Ticket in advance by calling the ferry company at ℘877-523-9849, or by visiting www.statuecruises.com.

Ferry Crossing

The *(15min)* ferry crossing offers great **views**★★★ of the Lower Manhattan skyline gradually receding into the background, and of the majestic and massive Statue of Liberty standing at the eastern end of the island, above the 11-point-star-shaped Fort Wood (1808–11). To your left, you'll see Governors Island, which can be toured in the summer.

Lady Liberty's Stats

Lady Liberty contains 125 tons of steel. The verdigrised sheets of copper that form her skin are a mere .1in thick, but all told they weigh 31 tons. Her concrete foundation weighs 27,000 tons. There are 25 windows in her crown, symbolizing the gemstones found on earth. The seven points of the crown signify liberty radiating to the seven continents and the seven seas. The tablet (23.5ft long, 2ft thick) in her left hand represents the Declaration of Independence and is printed with the year of its proclamation in roman numerals: july iv mdcclxxvi.

Other mind-boggling measurements:
Height from head to toe – 111ft   Right arm – 42ft long
Height from tip of torch to her toes – 151ft   Nose – 4ft long
Height from the tip of torch to the water – 395ft   Eyes – each 2.5ft wide
Right hand – 16.5ft long   Head – 17ft tall, 10ft wide
Index finger – 8ft long   Waist – 35ft across

How Bartholdi Built It

Frédéric-Auguste Bartholdi began work on the sculpture in 1874. He first made a clay figure 4ft high, and then three successively larger working models in plaster, which were corrected and refined before final dimensions were achieved. Turning his attention to the framework that would support the statue, Bartholdi called upon the skill and knowledge of the inventive French engineer **Gustave Eiffel** (1832–1923), who was later to build the Eiffel Tower. Employing construction techniques similar to the ones used for the skyscrapers of the 1880s, Eiffel created an intricate iron and steel skeletal frame to which 300 copper plates—each .1in thick and forming the skin of Liberty—were applied.

Liberty Island

Ranger-guided tours of the island's grounds are free of charge, scheduled through the day (staff permitting). Tours begin at the flagpole on the island; program listings are posted at the island's Administration/Information building. Audio tours (⊚$8) in Arabic, English, French, German, Italian, Japanese, Mandarin, Russian and Spanish may be rented from the ferry company or at the food and gift shop on the island.

Originally known as Bedloe's Island, after Isaac Bedloe, a French-born merchant whose family owned it until 1732, the island was chosen as a site, along with Governors Island and Ellis Island, for a land battery in 1800. Begun in 1806, Fort Wood was finished five years later; its zigzagging walls formed an 11-point star. For years the fort lay abandoned; in 1877 its site was chosen as the future home of the Statue of Liberty. You can still see the fortifications.

Bordering the walkway near the Statue of Liberty's pedestal are six slender sculptures by Phillip Ratner of key figures in the history of the statue: de Laboulaye, Bartholdi, Eiffel, Hunt, Pulitzer and Lazarus.

The waterfront promenade skirting the edge of the island affords terrific views. As you glance across the harbor, note the contrast between Manhattan's striking high-rises and the older, smaller-scale buildings in Brooklyn.

Inside the Monument

Access by Crown Ticket or Pedestal/Museum Ticket only.

Located on the second floor in the pedestal, the **Statue of Liberty Exhibit** traces the history and symbolism of the Statue of Liberty through museum objects, photographs, prints, videos and oral histories. In addition to historical artifacts and descriptive text, you'll also see full-scale replicas of the statue's face and foot. There's a section on the techniques used by Bartholdi to form the structure's copper exterior, and models the sculptor created as his ideas for the statue evolved.

The **Torch Exhibit** includes the original 1886 torch and flame. On the second-floor balcony overlooking this torch is a display on the history of the torch and flame, including diagrams, photographs, drawings and cartoons.

Observation Deck

Rising 10 stories above ground level at the top of the pedestal, the four-sided **observation deck** provides spectacular **views**★★★ of the New York Harbor, Lower Manhattan and the Financial District, the Verrazano-Narrows Bridge and New Jersey. From here you can also peer up into the statue's interior to see the crisscrossing framework overlaid by copper sheathing.

Crown

Not for the claustrophobic, acrophobic or vertigo sufferers, the climb to the crown—354 steps in a cramped, un-air-conditioned stairwell (temperatures can be 20 degrees higher than outside)—should only be attempted by those able to make it up to the top and back. Children must be at least 4ft tall. Head clearance is only 6ft 2in. At the top is a stunning view of New York Harbor and Lower Manhattan in the distance.

Ellis Island★★

Ellis Island is situated about halfway between Lower Manhattan and the Statue of Liberty in New York Harbor. Its grandly refurbished processing center stands as a testament to what it means to start life over in a new land. Between 1892 and 1954 Ellis Island received more than 12 million immigrants, one of the greatest mass migrations in history. Today more than 100 million Americans, some 30 percent of the country's population, can trace their ancestry in the US to one of the men, women or children who passed from a steamship to a ferry to the inspection lines in the great Registry Room at Ellis Island.

🛈 **Info:** National Park Service. ✆ 212-363-3200. www.ellisisland.org or www.nps.gov/elis.

◖ **Location:** Ellis Island is accessible by ferry only. Ferries (*$13 round-trip*) leave every 20–25min from Battery Park in Manhattan and every 40–45min from Liberty State Park in New Jersey daily 8.30am–4.30pm (*last ferry leaves Ellis Island at 6.30pm*). All ferries make a circuit including Liberty Island and Ellis Island.

◷ **Timing:** Visit Ellis Island after visiting the Statue of Liberty.

A BIT OF HISTORY

The Island – During the 1700s, the island was irreverently known as Gibbet Island, thanks to the fact that state criminals were executed here by means of hanging them from a "gibbet," or gallows tree. Samuel Ellis bought the land in 1785, and his heirs sold it to the state of New York in 1808. Like Governors Island and Bedloe's (now Liberty) Island, it held a fort to defend the harbor. In 1890 the island was chosen as a site for a federal immigrant processing center.

America's Great Immigrant Gateway – Inaugurated in 1892, Ellis Island quickly became the main port of entry for newcomers to America, replacing the old Immigrant Landing Station at Castle Garden, now known as **Castle Clinton**, which had operated from 1855 to 1890. From 1900 to 1924, an average of 5,000 new arrivals were processed daily, the majority in less than eight hours (only 2 percent of hopefuls were denied entry and shipped back to their country of origin, mainly for health reasons). Once cleared, immigrants took a ferry to the Battery in Manhattan. One-third of them

Ellis Island

©Ron Chapple Studios/Dreamstime.com

An Island Divided

Who owns Ellis Island: New York or New Jersey? The answer, according to the Supreme Court, is both. Blame it on the landfill. In 1834 the two states agreed to give New York the 3-acre island and New Jersey the waters around it, but as the tide of immigration increased in the early 20C, so did the island itself: by 1936 Ellis Island measured 27.5 acres and held more than 30 buildings. For half a century New York assumed that it owned the whole thing. Then New Jersey sued, claiming that Ellis Island's landfill was actually in the waters that it owned. In 1998 the High Court agreed, granting New Jersey 24.2 acres of as-yet-unde- veloped Ellis Island landfill and New York the original 3.3 acres, which hold the museum and the ferry slip. Predictably, both states declared victory.

settled in or near New York City; the rest traveled on to other parts of the country, often to meet relatives.

The Complex – The wooden buildings first used to house the immigration center were destroyed by fire in 1897, only five years after opening. A fireproof replacement, designed in the Beaux-Arts style by the local firm of Boring and Til- ton, opened in December 1900. Despite its massive proportions, that building quickly proved too small, prompting the addition of wings and a third floor, as well as the expansion of the island, with landfill, from 3 acres to 27.5 acres. Thirty-three additional buildings were ultimately constructed. Most remain standing, but shuttered. Restrictive laws and quotas passed in the 1920s diminished Ellis Island's importance as a reception site, and by 1953 the facil- ity was deemed too expensive to keep open: the island's staff numbered 250 to oversee a population of about 230 detained immigrants.

In 1954 the last detainee, a seaman who had overstayed his shore leave, was fer- ried back to the mainland, and the doors were closed. Shortly afterward, the gov- ernment tried to sell the site as surplus federal property, but no bid was judged high enough.

Decades of Neglect – For 10 years Ellis Island stood vacant, subject to vandals and looters who made off with anything they could carry, from doorknobs to fil- ing cabinets. The building's Beaux-Arts copper ornamentation deteriorated. Snow swirled through broken win- dows, roofs leaked, and weeds sprang up in corridors. Upon seeing the island's dilapidated state, Stewart Udall, Secre- tary of the Interior for President Lyndon Johnson, urged President Johnson to place the island in the permanent care of the National Park Service. Johnson complied, and Ellis Island became part of the Statue of Liberty National Monu- ment in 1965.

A New Beginning – Restoration of the Main Building began in earnest in the 1980s. Often compared to the refurbish- ment of the Palace of Versailles in France, the project took eight years to complete, at a cost of $156 million. The building reopened its doors in September 1990 as the Ellis Island Immigration Museum.

ELLIS ISLAND IMMIGRATION MUSEUM★★

Free ranger-guided tours (45min) of the museum are offered throughout the day; the schedule is posted at the information desk in the first-floor baggage room. Recorded audio tours of the museum are available in Arabic, English, French, German, Italian, Japanese, Mandarin, Russian and Spanish; headsets ⊚$8. ◷Open year- round daily 9.30am–5.15pm. ◷Closed Dec 25. ✆212-363-3200. www.ellis island.org or www.nps.gov/elis.

Crowned by four copper-domed towers, the former processing center (1900) has been restored to reflect its appearance from 1918 to 1924, the years of peak immigration. Five thousand artifacts spread throughout the museum's 30 galleries, along with recordings, films and live performances, tell the story of the building's role in the Great Migration to America.

First Floor

Visitors enter the baggage room, where immigrants were separated, sometimes forever, from their precious belongings. The old railroad office, to the north, houses the **Peopling of America** exhibit, which uses statistical displays to chronicle the history of immigration and ethnicity in the US from the 17C to the present.

Highlights include a 6ft globe that traces worldwide migration patterns since the 18C; and the Word Tree, which explains the origin of many American words. A poignant 30min film titled *Island of Hope/Island of Tears* portrays the human face of migration; it is screened in the two theaters located in the eastern wing (*pick up free tickets to the film at the Information Desk as soon as you enter the museum; shows fill up quickly*). The western wing houses the **American Family Immigration History Center**, where visitors can research their family heritage via a computerized database (*see sidebar below*).

Second Floor

The sweeping two-story **Registry Room/Great Hall**★★ was the site of the initial inspection of immigrants, who awaited their fate while queuing behind metal pens. The hall that once accommodated thousands has been left empty, save for a few scattered benches, to serve as a grand, quiet memorial. The pride of the 17,300sq-ft hall is its impressive vaulted ceiling. After a fire, the ceiling was rebuilt in 1917 by Spaniard Rafael Guastavino and his son with interlocking tiles; only 17 of the 28,000 tiles had to be replaced during restoration.

Third Floor

The highlight of this floor, Treasures from Home, presents objects donated by immigrants and their families, from a teddy bear to an elaborate wedding gown. In **Silent Voices**, large photographs taken before the restoration evoke the eerie feeling of an abandoned place, while furnishings recall the daily routine of processing, registering and caring for immigrants. Another exhibit, tracing 300 years of the island's history, displays five detailed models showing the evolving site plans of the island between 1897 and 1940.

Along the north wall of the mezzanine, a narrow **dorm room** has been furnished to reflect the cramped living conditions experienced by some of the detainees.

Ellis Island Living Theater

Professional theater pieces dramatizing the immigration experience and aspects of life in the New World are staged at the museum Apr–Labor Day. Plays are based on information from passenger

Manifest Destiny

Think you might have a relative who passed through Ellis Island? Check and see at the museum's **American Family Immigration History Center** or online at www.ellisisland.org. Developed and administered by the Statue of Liberty–Ellis Island Foundation, the center provides easy access to the ships' passenger manifest records of the 12 million people who entered America through the Port of New York and Ellis Island between 1892 and 1954. The database is searchable by immigrant name, but it is helpful if you also know the approximate age at arrival and date of arrival, as well as the port of departure. If you do get a "hit," you will be provided with the following information: immigrant's given name and surname, ethnicity, last residence (town and country), date of arrival, age at arrival, gender, marital status, ship of travel, port of departure, and line number on the manifest. Visitors can also obtain a reproduction of the original ship's manifest as well as a picture of the ship of passage. For further information call ☎212-561-4500.

Great Hall, Ellis Island Immigration Museum

©PhotoDisc

manifests, and feature professional actors. Recent shows have included *Liberty Dance*, *Irving Berlin's America*, *Bela Lugosi and the Legend of Dracula* and *The Titanic: A Survivor's Story*. Show times are posted at the Information Desk, where tickets (☞$6) may be purchased.

Grounds

Facing Manhattan, the **American Immigrant Wall of Honor** serves as a memorial to the nation's immigrant heritage. The 652.5ft-long, double-sided, semicircular wall contains the names of more than 600,000 individuals and families whose descendants have honored them by donating to the Ellis Island restoration project *(for more information on how to add a name, call ✆212-561-4500)*. The terrace offers breathtaking **views**★★ of the Manhattan skyline.

ADDITIONAL SIGHT
Governors Island

Accessible by ferry. ◷*The island is open for visits and programs June–mid-Oct Fri 10am–5pm, Sat–Sun 10am–7pm. Ferries (free; 7min one-way) depart every hour Fri and every 30mins Sat–Sun from the Battery Maritime Building (10 South St. at Whitehall St.) and from Brooklyn (Brooklyn Bridge Park).* ☞*Walking tours (90min) available; check website for details. Governors*

Island Preservation & Educational Corporation: ✆212-440-2202. www.govisland.com. Walking tours: ✆212-825-3045 or 212-440-2202. www. govisland.com or www.nps.gov/gois. Known in Dutch times as Nutten's Island, because of the many nut trees that grew here, the 150-acre island affords spectacular views of Manhattan and Brooklyn. It is the site of two pre-1800 structures: the **Governor's House** and **Fort Jay**. Another fort, **Castle Williams**, was built on the island at the beginning of the 19C, at the same time as **Castle Clinton**. For two centuries the island was a military reservation, most recently home to the Coast Guard.

In 2001, the two forts were designated national monuments and in early 2003 the federal government sold part of the island back to the state of New York for $1. The Governors Island Preservation and Educational Corporation has announced plans to create new parks, public spaces, a 2.2mi bike and pedestrian promenade on the island, and to rejuvenate areas of the historic district. National Park Service walking tours *(summer only)* explore the residential, administrative and historic structures to illustrate the history and development of the island. You can also rent bikes, play mini-golf, picnic or take in a free cultural program or concert.

Financial District★★

Widely considered the financial center of the world, the southern tip of Manhattan Isn't as buttoned-up as you might expect. Its U-shaped waterfront, lined with parks, draws hordes of visitors to view New York Harbor and catch ferries to Staten Island or the Statue of Liberty. Cradled within are the narrow streets laid out by New York's first Dutch settlers in the 17C. Nearly all of those original structures were destroyed, but developers left largely intact the curvy street plan when they built their gargantuan office towers. Two of those 'scrapers were the World Trade Center towers. People you'll see in the Financial District may have witnessed the events of September 11, 2001, firsthand. But fears that the neighborhood would always be marred by that day turned out to be unfounded: several of the district's attractions, including a number of museums, have undergone renovations and more improvements are in the works.

A BIT OF HISTORY

New York City was born in what is now the Financial District in 1625. The Dutch West India Company's trade was flourishing, and the town of Nieuw Amsterdam quickly developed as the center of Dutch influence in the colonies. The small town was defended to the south by a fort and to the north by a wall of thick wooden planks constructed in 1653 between the Hudson and East Rivers. A canal dug in the middle of Broad Street as well as a windmill attested to the town's Dutch heritage. About 1,000 persons lived here in wood and brick houses topped with Dutch gables and tile roofs. The inhabitants, though, were of varied origins; in 1642, when the first Stadt Huys (City Hall) was built at 71 Pearl Street, no fewer than 18 languages were spoken in Nieuw Amsterdam. A commercial agent of the Dutch West India Company first

MTA Subway: 4, 5 train to Fulton St.

Map: Following pages.

Info: *See sidebar, p84.*

Location: Use the map to locate St. Paul's first, then walk south from there on Broadway to Trinity Church before heading east on Wall Street. Detour north on William Street to tour the Federal Reserve Bank and its gold vault. Then head south to Battery Park for a relaxing stroll along the Promenade.

Parking: Don't even try. Finding a parking space here is like searching for the proverbial needle in the haystack. Free shuttle buses run along the waterfront between historic South Street Seaport and Battery Park City, stopping at Financial District attractions in between *(for more information, call 212-566-6700 or visit www.downtownNY.com/ DowntownConnection).*

Timing: With the exception of Wall Street, the sights selected here are described in descending star order, rather than geographically, so you'll know which attractions to see first, especially if you are short on time. Allow at least 4hrs to do justice to all the sights in the district.

Kids: The new Museum of American Finance is an entrancing look at how our money systems work. The bronze bull—the preeminent symbol of Wall Street—on Bowling Green comes in a close second.

Don't Miss: A free ride on the Staten Island Ferry.

governed the town, followed by a succession of governors, including **Peter Stuyvesant**. In 1664 the British took over Nieuw Amsterdam. During the 18C, colonial Georgian houses began to replace the narrow Dutch dwellings.

SIGHTS
Federal Reserve Bank of New York★★

&. *33 Liberty St.* ⏲ *Coin exhibit open year-round Mon–Fri 10am–4pm, except on bank holidays.* ✆ *Gold vault may be viewed by free guided tour (1hr) only, Mon–Fri 9.30am, 10.30am, 11.30am, 1.30pm, 2.30pm, 3.30pm;* ☺*one-week advance reservations required.* ℘*212-720-6130. www.newyorkfed.org.*

One of 12 US reserve banks in the country, the New York "Fed," as it is somewhat affectionately known, occupies an entire city block. It's meant to look imposing. Indeed, it's the most heavily fortified building in the city. But behind this gruff exterior lies a surprisingly soft heart. Through its gold-vault tour, its History of Money exhibit and its delightful publications (including hilarious comic books), the Fed makes the world financial system seem not only logical, but surprisingly interesting.

The Federal Reserve Bank of New York was completed in 1924 and expanded in 1935. Distinguished by massive rusticated walls of Indiana limestone and Ohio sandstone, it influenced bank architecture around the country. Architect Phillip Sawyer based his design on that of several 15C Italian Renaissance palazzos that were built to house the wealthiest banking and merchant families in Florence.

Visit – The New York Fed ceded its cash-collecting and cash-disbursing functions in 1992 to a New Jersey facility, largely because the Brinks trucks were constantly getting snarled in traffic. But there's still plenty of riches here. Inside the building, 80ft below street level (and 50ft below sea level), lies the Federal Reserve's **gold vault**★★. The vault was actually excavated in 1921 and the building was then built on top of it. Today it contains about $90 billion worth of gold bullion, most belonging to foreign governments (most of the gold belonging to the US is stored in Kentucky's Fort Knox). As visitors gaze at a sparkling wall of gold bars—some rectangular, some trapezoidal, all utterly fake-looking—a tour guide details the astounding security measures taken to protect them: hidden cameras, motion detectors, combination and time locks, a revolving 90-ton "door" that lowers three-eighths of an inch into the concrete floor, thus forming an airtight and watertight seal. Finally, among the New York Fed's 3,000 employees are several dozen expert marksmen, who

Gold vault, Federal Reserve Bank of New York

Federal Reserve Bank of New York

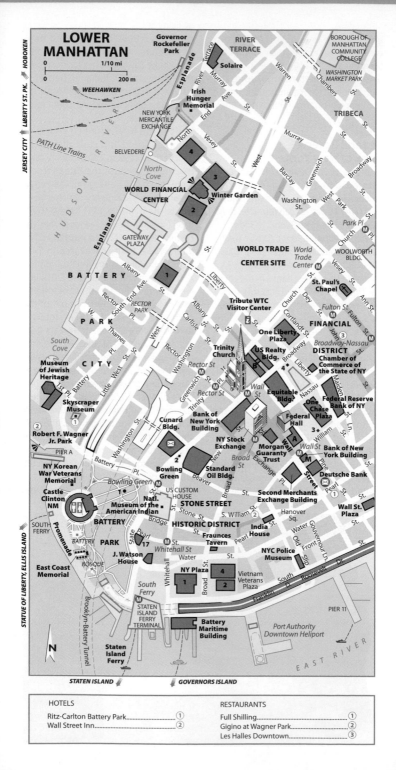

LOWER MANHATTAN

How the Federal Reserve System Works

President Woodrow Wilson brought the Fed into being on December 23, 1913, with the signing of the Federal Reserve Act. The aim of the law was to prevent a repeat of the liquidity crises and financial panics that occurred sporadically in the US throughout the 19C. The Fed is composed of 12 regional reserve banks spread across the country and a board of governors in Washington, DC. The system's function is twofold: the banks themselves handle the flow of coin and currency to and from local banks, and the board of governors sets US monetary policy, including all-important interest rates. By raising or lowering interest rates, the chairman of the Federal Reserve tries to keep the economy from either sagging or going into overdrive and then crashing, as it did in 2000. In performing this single task, the Fed chairman may be the most influential person in America.

regularly hone their skills on the second-floor shooting range.

Visitors who did not reserve a space on the tour can view the excellent **Drachmas, Doubloons and Dollars: The History of Money exhibit**★, co-curated by the American Numismatic Society. Here, hundreds of artifacts illustrate the many forms money can take: coins, cowrie shells, salt, tokens, gold, paper money and credit cards, for example. Take special note of the 1933 gold "**double eagle**," designed by Auguste Saint-Gaudens, and read about the fascinating history of this $20 coin. Also be sure to see the interactive, multimedia exhibit **Fed Works: Money, Banking and the Federal Reserve System**, an economic education in itself.

National Museum of the American Indian★★

1 Bowling Green.
♿ *See Major Manhattan Museums.*

Saint Paul's Chapel★★

♿ *Broadway, between Fulton & Vesey Sts.* ○ *Open year-round Mon–Fri 10am–6pm, Sat 10am–4pm, Sun 7am–3pm.* ○ *Closed major holidays.* ☏ *212-233-4164. www.saintpaulschapel.org.*
Belonging to the Trinity Church parish, this small chapel opposite the World Trade Center site is the oldest public building in continuous use in Manhattan. In the weeks following the attacks of September 11, 2001, it served as an aid station for rescue workers and a pilgrimage site for mourners. That history is recounted in the permanent exhibit

Unwavering Spirit: Hope and Healing at Ground Zero.

A Bit of History – Completed in 1766, St. Paul's Chapel resembles the Church of St.-Martin-in-the-Fields in Trafalgar Square, London. That is no coincidence: its architect, Thomas McBean, studied under James Gibbs, who designed St. Martin's. St. Paul's is constructed of native stone: Manhattan mica-schist with quoins of brownstone. In its early days, the church stood in a field outside the city proper. **George Washington** prayed here in 1789, after his inauguration as the first president of the US (the inauguration ceremony itself took place at the site of today's Federal Hall). Washington continued to worship here for the two years that New York City was the nation's capital.

Visit – The chapel stands in its own cemetery, a delightful spot full of trees and 18C tombstones, most of which are cracker-thin and illegible due to age. The **Bell of Hope** standing in front of the chapel entrance is a gift to New Yorkers from the Lord Mayor of the City of London on the first anniversary of the 9/11 attacks. It was cast in the same foundry as the Liberty Bell and Big Ben.

Inside the Georgian chapel, notice the woodwork, carving and door hinges; all were handmade under the direction of master craftsman Andrew Gautier. The ornamental design over the altar is the work of Pierre Charles L'Enfant, the French architect who designed the city of Washington, DC. Above **George Washington's pew** in the north aisle hangs an 18C oil painting of the Great Seal of the

For More Information

For information about **free concerts**, **exhibits** and **performances**, contact: the **Alliance for Downtown New York** ✆212-566-6700 www.downtownNY.com or the **Lower Manhattan Cultural Council** ✆212-219-9401. For **brochures** and **maps**, visit the **information kiosk** at **Federal Hall National Memorial** (🕑Mon–Fri 9am–5pm) or the **bookstore** at **Castle Clinton**, which keeps its supply well stocked.

Free shuttle buses run along the waterfront between South Street Seaport and Battery Park City, with stops at attractions in between.

🛈 For more information, call ✆212-566-6700 or visit www.downtownNY.com/DowntownConnection.

US, adopted in 1782. The elegant interior is visually overwhelmed, however, with the profusion of Ground Zero paraphernalia making up the **Unwavering Spirit exhibit**. Handmade banners, letters to missing relatives, photographs and documentary oral history stations surround the pews, an evocative re-creation of how the chapel looked and felt in the emotionally wrenching days following the attacks.

Staten Island Ferry★

Whitehall Ferry Terminal in Manhattan at southern tip of Battery Park.
♿ *See Staten Island.*

Trinity Church★★

♿*74 Trinity Pl. (corner of Broadway at Wall St.).* 🕑*Open year-round Mon–Fri 7am–6pm (churchyard until 4pm, 5pm during spring/summer), Sat 8am–4pm, Sun 7am–4pm.* 🚶*Guided tours daily 2pm. Classical music concerts Mon & Thu 1pm.* ✆*212-602-0800. www.trinitywallstreet.org.*

To appreciate how quickly and relatively recently New York City has grown, consider the fact that Trinity Church, upon its completion in 1846, was the tallest building in Manhattan. Today its graceful Gothic spire appears quaint, framed as it is by the tunnel of Wall Street skyscrapers that extend to the East River. Yet a feeling of tranquility continues to reign here, in the cool vaulted interior of the church and in its gated churchyard, where lie the remains of New Yorkers dating back to 1681.

A Bit of History – An Episcopal church, Trinity was founded by a charter granted by King William III in 1697. Among the influential locals who contributed to its construction was **William Kidd** (the legendary Captain Kidd), who lived nearby at Hanover Square before being hanged for piracy in London in 1701.

The first church building, completed in 1698, was devoured in the great fire of 1776. The second building's roof collapsed in 1839. The present edifice, designed by Richard Upjohn, has fared better, surviving even the September 11, 2001, attacks (just a block away) with only the loss of some of its mortar.

Visit – The building is made of red sandstone. Its spire rises 280ft and contains 10 bells, three of which date to 1797. The elaborately wrought bronze doors were designed by **Richard Morris Hunt**, architect of the Metropolitan Museum

Trinity Church from Wall Street

Allison Simpson/MICHELIN

and the pedestal of the Statue of Liberty. Inside, note the stained-glass windows behind the marble altar; they were designed by Upjohn. A small **museum** presents exhibits on Trinity Church's history and its relationship to the city (🕐 *open year-round Mon–Fri 9am–5.30pm, Sat–Sun 9am–3.45pm*).

Though seemingly frozen in time, Trinity's **cemetery** is in fact Manhattan's only remaining active interment site. Fortunately, you don't need a reservation to browse. It's a lovely space, with dozens of crooked and eroded tombstones shaded by 100-year-old oaks and elms. Famous internees include Alexander Hamilton and John Jacob Astor.

WALL STREET★★

New York has always been a magnet for capitalists, but not even the most optimistic Dutchman could have conceived the amount of money exchanged over the years on Wall Street.

A Bit of History – Running for less than a mile between Broadway and the East River, Wall Street derives its name from the short wooden wall built along its path by the Dutch in 1653. The wall marked the northern boundary of the fledgling trading post Nieuw Amsterdam and was meant to protect the residents from Indian attack. It was never tested in battle, however; in fact, colonists considered it a handy source of firewood. In 1699 the British, who had taken over the colony in 1664, dismantled the wall for good and replaced it with a street lined with houses and administrative buildings, including the colony's second city hall, at Broad and Wall Streets, site of today's Federal Hall National Memorial. (The first city hall, or Stadt Huys, was founded in a tavern on Pearl Street in 1653.) After the Revolution, the east end of Wall Street harbored a number of coffeehouses and taverns, earning the area around Wall and Water Streets the nickname "Coffeehouse Slip." The famous Tontine Coffee House, built in 1792 at that corner, served as the first home of the New York Stock Exchange.

Visit – What you'll find on Wall Street today depends entirely on when you see it and from what vantage point. On weekdays when the Exchange is open (stocks are traded between 9.30am and 4pm), it is full of frenetic bankers, traders and other office workers. During business hours, you're most likely to be allowed to step into the lobbies of some of the more historic buildings, though don't be surprised if you're refused; security all over the district has been drum-tight since 9/11 and will likely remain that way indefinitely. On weekends and holidays the street is dominated by tourists. At night it is practically deserted. Also note it's impossible to see the tops of many of Wall Street's tallest buildings from the street itself. Your best bet is to take the Circle Line boat tour and let the tour guide point them out to you.

Sights on Wall Street are ordered west to east by street numbers (not star order), beginning with 1 Wall Street.

Bank of New York Building

1 Wall St. Originally completed for Irving Trust Company in 1932, the 50-story white limestone tower rises 20 stories without a setback, then tapers into a graceful spire. It makes a fitting companion to neighboring Trinity Church. If you can get in, take a peek at the art deco lobby.

New York Stock Exchange

8–18 Broad St. at Wall St. Formerly one of New York's top tourist attractions (visitors were treated to a bird's-eye view of the gigantic trading floor), the stock exchange was closed to the public following the September 11, 2001, attacks. The eight-story building (1903, George B. Post), which remains surrounded by guarded barricades, resembles a Roman temple with its majestic facade of Corinthian columns, each crowned by an elaborate pediment with sculptures representing commerce. Yet the exchange itself far predates this structure. New York had an active securities market by 1790, when Alexander Hamilton, US secretary of the Treasury, first issued

Stone Street Historic District

Peter Wrenn/MICHELIN

Thanks to its 1996 landmark designation, once-dingy Stone Street between Hanover Square and Coenties Slip has become one of the Financial District's most charming thoroughfares. On warm days its cobblestone expanse is festooned with umbrella tables, courtesy of eight new restaurants and pubs. On cool and rainy days, these self-same joints provide a cozy respite from the concrete jungle. Stone Street is reputed to be New York's first paved street. Because of its proximity to the East River, it bustled with commercial activity for more than 200 years, rebounding quickly even after the 1835 fire razed 700 commercial buildings in the area. But when port activity began shifting to the west side in the early 20C, the street started a slow decline. Its recent resurrection comes courtesy of civic boosters and entrepreneurs led by Peter Poulakakos, who owns and operates the excellent **Financier** patisserie *(no. 62; ℘212-344-5600; www.financierpastries.com)* and its neighbor, **Ulysses' Bar** *(no. 58; ℘212-482-0400; www.ulyssesfolkhouse.com)*, which serves up lobster every Monday night and "cobblestone brunch" on Sundays *(11am–4pm).*

bonds to consolidate and refund debts incurred during the American Revolution. The small buttonwood tree (better known as a sycamore) to the left of the Broad Street entrance memorializes the legendary "buttonwood agreement." Though perhaps more fiction than fact, the story goes that in 1792 a group of 24 brokers met at the corner of Wall and Williams Streets, beneath a similar tree, and founded the stock exchange. The New York Stock Exchange wasn't formally organized, however, until 1817. Despite the predictable boom and bust cycles, it grew exponentially, fueled by railroad securities, war bonds and ever-present speculators. By 1865, when it took possession of the current site, it had had 10 homes of increasing size. Today, the Classical facade hides one of the most technically sophisticated financial operations on the globe, where about $67 billion worth of shares are exchanged daily.

Morgan Guaranty Trust Company

23 Wall St. at Broad St. This austere white marble building (1913, Trowbridge & Livingston) is better known for its history than its architecture. On September 16, 1920, just as the Trinity Church bells chimed noon, an anarchist ignited a wagonload of explosives outside its Wall Street facade. John Pierpont Morgan Jr., the target of the attack, was unharmed, but 33 civilians were killed and 400 were injured. Look closely at the area around the fourth window from the corner and you can still see pockmarks in the marble from the explosion.

Federal Hall National Memorial★

♿ *26 Wall St. at Broad St.* ◷*Open year-round Mon–Fri 9am–5pm.* ◷*Closed holidays.* ⟵*Guided tours available Mon–Fri 10am, 11am, 1pm, 2pm, 3pm.* ℘*212-825-6888. www.nps.gov/feha.* Grand though it may be, this structure itself is not among the most historic in the city, but the site certainly is. It was initially occupied by New York's first official city hall, on land donated by wealthy Dutch merchant Abraham de Peyster, whose statue you can admire in nearby Hanover Square; in 1702 the city government, then British, moved in. Also used as a debtors' prison, the site later became a staging ground for the American Revolution. In October 1765 the building hosted the Stamp Act Congress to protest "taxation without representation," a slogan that ended up driving the war for independence.

After ratification of the Constitution in 1788, Pierre Charles L'Enfant (who laid out Washington, DC's radial street grid) was hired to remodel the city hall for use as the nation's capitol. Though Federal Hall hosted the first congress and the swearing-in of George Washington in 1789, its time in the national limelight was short-lived. After the capitol moved to Philadelphia in 1790, the building housed city offices and in 1812 it was demolished and sold as salvage for $425.

Visit – The present building was designed by the firm Town and Davis and completed in 1842. It held the custom house, the US Subtreasury and various government offices, before being designated a historic site in 1939 and a national memorial in 1955. The towering bronze statue of George Washington (1883, John A.Q. Ward) at the top of its wide steps is a popular place for photos. Inside the memorial, 16 marble Corinthian columns support a splendid central rotunda rimmed with balconies.

Trump Building (A *on map*)
40 Wall St. Though this 1930s building bears The Donald's signature gold imprimatur, "TRUMP," above its revolving doors, the architectural highlight, a pyramidal crown, can be seen only at a distance.

Bank of New York Building

48 Wall St. Designed in 1927 by Benjamin Wistar Morris, who's better known for his exuberant Cunard Building at 25 Broadway, 48 Wall Street is topped by a Corinthian-columned temple and mounted bronze eagle.

As with the Trump Building, it's visible only from afar, but if you step inside, Morris' original pen-and-ink architectural drawings, on display in the lobby, will give you a sense of its upper reaches. Housed within the building, the Smithsonian-affiliated **Museum of American Finance**★ (👤♿🕑*open Tue–Sat 10am–4pm;* 🕑*closed holidays;* ✆*$8, $5 children;* 📞*212-908-4110; www.moaf.org*) has touch screens, tactile displays and other high-tech exhibits focusing on Wall Street's history, investing, US banking systems, financial markets and the country's top entrepreneurs. Don't miss the display of historical piggy banks, and the room devoted to Alexander Hamilton, the first US Treasury Secretary.

Nineteenth-Century Titans

The business activities and interests of the Morgans, Vanderbilts, Goulds and their descendants helped shape New York as a financial capital. After 1860, speculation flourished. On September 24, 1869, financier **Jay Gould** (1836–92), who had tried to corner the gold market with his associate James Fisk, sold out and brought about the financial panic known as Black Friday. **Cornelius Vanderbilt** (1794–1877), nicknamed "The Commodore" because of his interests in the shipping industry, began to extend his activities to the railroads in 1862. First the owner of small lines, he launched the famous New York–Buffalo line in 1873. At the same time, banker **J. Pierpont Morgan** (1837–1913) financed the great new industries: steel, oil and railroads. Generous, but a ruthless businessman, the founder of the famous Pierpont Morgan Library (now the Morgan Library) was succeeded by his son, John Pierpont Morgan Jr., the target of the assassination attempt in 1920 mentioned in this chapter.

Second Merchants Exchange Building

55 Wall St. A double colonnade of Ionic and Corinthian columns fronts this unusual structure, currently refurbished with apartment residences and not open to the public. In 1841 Isaiah Rogers designed a three-story building with a central domed trading hall to replace the original merchants exchange, which burned down in the Great Fire of 1835. When it was converted to use as the Custom House in 1907, the prolific architectural team of McKim, Mead and White added the upper tier of columns (and three more floors), doubling the building's volume.

The magnificent **Great Hall**, with its 72ft coffered ceiling, was deemed "unequaled in America" by the American Institute of Architects.

Deutsche Bank

60 Wall St. With its curious pairing of reflective glass and granite pilasters, the 47-floor office tower (1988, Roche, Dinkeloo and Assocs.) is one of the tallest in the district. On the ground floor is a public space that, despite its mirrored ceiling and potted palms, feels like a slightly seedy bus station.

WORLD TRADE CENTER SITE★★

Bounded by Church, Liberty, West & Barclay Sts. www.renewnyc.com and www.lowermanhattan.info.

The world's largest commercial complex stood here from 1970 until the morning of September 11, 2001, when two hijacked planes were flown into the Twin Towers, killing more than 2,750 people and bringing the 110-story structures—in which 50,000 people had worked—to the ground. It was the deadliest terrorist attack in US history. Fires burned for weeks, sending acrid smoke across the city. In all, eight buildings were destroyed. Workers carted off 1.5 million tons of steel and debris until the site was cleared in May 2002, well ahead of schedule. Rebuilding the site has proved far more difficult, thanks to the vast size of the project and the number of parties (politicians, developers, victims' families, architects and the police) with strong and often conflicting visions of its future.

The Master Plan

Ultimately, the site will contain an assortment of office buildings, memorials, parks and cultural venues, arranged roughly according to a master plan created by Polish-born architect Daniel Libeskind and a revised design released by the Lower Manhattan Development Corp. mid-2005. The centerpiece of the plan is a 1,776ft-tall structure (half building, half sculpture) called the Freedom Tower, which will combine underground retail shops and above-ground office and retail space. An observation deck will sit at 1,362ft. The cornerstone for the tower was put in place in fall 2004; completion is expected in late 2013.

The Memorial and Museum – The design that beat 5,000 other entries in the World Trade Center memorial design competition honors the request by some victims' families that the footprints of the towers not be built upon. *Reflecting Absence*, by architects Michael Arad and Peter Walker, features a one-and-a-half-acre grove of oak trees and preserves, as multilevel reflecting pools, the two square voids where the towers once stood. Construction began in 2006 on a revised plan that scaled back the cost to $500 million.

In addition to the memorial, a museum complex and visitor center are planned that will relate the events of September 11. In 2006 construction began on the National September 11 Memorial and Museum, as it is now named. The memorial officially opened to the public on September 12, 2011, and the museum should open on September 11, 2012.

The Transportation Hub – The Spanish architect Santiago Calatrava was given the green light to build a soaring $3.4 billion, four-level transport hub at the northeast corner of the World Trade Center site *(Church & Vesey Sts)*. The station will consist of two curved, intersecting planes of glass and steel, a design that was inspired by the image of a child

Tribute WTC Visitor Center

©Alan Klein/Tribute WTC Visitor Center

opening her hands to let a bird free, Calatrava has said. Projected cost over-runs have delayed the hub's completion, slated for 2014.

Visiting the Site

Shortly after the debris was cleared in 2002, city officials opened a viewing platform on Church Street so that visitors could see where the World Trade Center had stood, pay respects to the dead and watch the progress of rebuilding. The platform has been taken down, but the **Tribute WTC Visitor Center** *(120 Liberty St.;* ○*open year-round daily Mon & Wed–Sat 10am–6pm, Tue noon–6pm, Sun noon–5pm;* ☏*212-393-9160; www. tributewtc.org)* has visitor information and five exhibit galleries *(*○*$10)* devoted to the events of September 11. **Walking tours** of the site, led by volunteer guides (all of whom are survivors of the attacks or have personal links to the events of September 11) depart daily from the center *(*○*1hr 15min; Sun–Fri 11am, noon, 1pm, 3pm, Sat 11am, noon, 1pm, 2pm, 3pm, 4pm;* ○*$10)*. The **Winter Garden** provides a view of the World Trade Center site.

Battery Park★

On the southwestern tip of Manhattan, the maze of stone and steel suddenly gives way to an expanse of greenery, perfect for strolling along the waterfront promenade and enjoying up close views of the Statue of Liberty and the harbor islands.

Battery Park gets its name from two artillery stations built by the US military in anticipation of a British attack during the war of 1812. One of the structures, East Battery (Castle Williams), is located on Governors Island; the other, West Battery (Castle Clinton), was originally 300ft offshore.

Neither was ever used in combat, and in 1870 the area between Castle Clinton and the shoreline (which ran along State Street) was filled in, creating the park you see today. It contains a number of memorials and sculptures: most striking is the 15ft-diameter, 22-ton **Sphere**★★ (**1** *on map*) by Fritz Koenig, salvaged from the World Trade Center Plaza. Once a glimmering ball, it now resembles a battered suit of armor (located just inside Bowling Green entrance). The eternal flame was added, and lit, on September 11, 2002.

A recent restoration (2005) created new paths, a fountain, gardens, lights and a carousel to the *bosque* (Spanish for grove of trees) at the southernmost tip of the park. At the north end stands Pier A, the last Victorian pier shed in Manhattan. Restoration plans for the dilapidated pier are in the works, calling for a new visitor center, shops and restaurants, as well as moorings for historic vessels.

Promenade, Battery Park City

©Abraham Nowitz/Apa Publications

Promenade★★

Between Pier A & Whitehall Ferry Terminal.

The waterfront path offers great views of New York Harbor. Among the points of interest that visitors can spot are the Colgate clock and, beside it, Goldman Sachs' glimmering headquarters in Jersey City; Ellis Island's Beaux-Arts processing center; the Statue of Liberty; the docks at the foot of **Brooklyn Heights★★**; the red-brick buildings on Governors Island; and the cables of the **Verrazano-Narrows Bridge★★**, linking Staten Island and Brooklyn.

You'll notice two prominent memorials: the **East Coast Memorial** (near the South Ferry terminal) was dedicated in 1963. Eight stark granite walls are engraved with the name, rank and home state of 4,601 US servicemen who lost their lives in the Atlantic Ocean during World War II.

A bronze art deco-style eagle stands at the head of the monument. The **New York Korean War Veterans Memorial** (near the West St. entrance) is a 15ft-tall granite stela (1991) containing within it the carved-out silhouette of an infantryman who represents the "universal soldier." If you look through the cutout toward the water, you can see the Statue of Liberty.

Castle Clinton National Monument★

&♿🕐*Open year-round daily 8.30am– 5pm.* 🕐*Closed Dec 25.* ✆*212-344-7220. www.nps.gov/cacl.*

Most people know Castle Clinton merely as the place where they go to buy tickets to the Statue of Liberty and Ellis Island; indeed, it is the main visitor center for all of the national parks in New York City, and contains an excellent array of free brochures and maps, as well as a public restroom. But the structure itself—a round fort with 8ft-thick walls pierced with gun ports—has a long and interesting history.

As noted above, it was built between 1808 and 1811 on what was then an island 300ft offshore. Known as West Battery, it was designed to protect New York during the war of 1812, but was never fired upon. In 1824, the structure was remodeled into an entertainment venue called Castle Garden. Initially the site of hot-air balloon launchings and fireworks, it hosted, after a roof was added in the 1840s, operas and performances by such superstars as Jenny Lind, "the Swedish nightingale," brought to the US by none other than circus impresario P.T. Barnum.

Between 1855 and 1892, prior to the opening of Ellis Island, the structure served as an immigrant landing depot; then, from 1898 to 1942, it was home to the New York Aquarium. Today, unfortunately, not much of this history can be seen with the naked eye; the structure has been completely gutted. But if you're like most visitors, you'll have plenty of time waiting in line for Statue of Liberty tickets to imagine it.

ADDITIONAL SIGHTS
Bowling Green★

For the low, low price of one peppercorn per annum, gentlemen of the mid-19C were permitted to bowl on this egg-shaped park at the foot of Broadway. In 1776 independence-minded New Yorkers toppled a statue of King George III that stood here. Today the park is one of the Financial District's most pleasant public spaces, its fountain ringed with benches and historic plantings; the fence dates from 1771.

Standard Oil Building

28 Broadway at Beaver St. John D. Rockefeller's historic office tower (1928, Carrère and Hastings) is distinguished by the sweeping curve of its Broadway facade, which complements the Cunard Building across Bowling Green. Interestingly, its 480ft-high pyramidal tower is aligned with the Uptown grid, not with the street below—a siting done supposedly to keep the city's skyline geometrical. Previously, Alexander Hamilton's law offices stood here.

Fraunces Tavern

♿54 Pearl St. ◑Museum open year-round Mon–Sat noon–5pm. ◑Closed major holidays. ⊜$10. ℘212-425-1778. www.frauncestavernmuseum.org.
With its tile roof and cream-colored portico, this handsome brick house gives visitors a sense of New York City as it might have appeared during the American Revolution. In 1719 Etienne de Lancey, who later gave his family name to Delancey Street, built a home here. Samuel Fraunces bought it in 1762 and turned it into a tavern. For 10 days in 1783 Fraunces Tavern served as George Washington's last residence as general, and on December 4 of that year, he bade

farewell to his troops here before returning to his estate at Mount Vernon.
The authenticity of the building you see today is open to debate. In 1904 the Sons of the Revolution in the State of New York bought the structure, which by then had been significantly altered, and tried to restore it to what they believed the original might have looked like. It was opened to the public in 1907. Parts of the original walls were incorporated, but history and architecture buffs don't think that's enough to justify the museum's claim that Fraunces Tavern is the real McCoy.
Today the ground floor is used as a bar/restaurant (*℘212-968-1776*), and the upper floors display early American decorative arts in period rooms.

New York City Police Museum

♿100 Old Slip (between Water St. & South St.). ◑Open year-round Mon–Sat 10am–5pm, Sun noon–5pm. ⊜$8. ℘212-480-3100. www.nycpolicemuseum.org.
Just a stone's throw from the East River, a solid neo-Renaissance building built in 1911 for the NYPD's First Precinct house was reopened in 2002 as the home of this museum. The collection, which the police department began to assemble in the 19C, is a trove of official police equipment and artifacts.

Brigitta L. House/MICHELIN

A Bull for Black Monday

Guarding the northern entrance to Bowling Green, the 3.5-ton, 16ft-long bronze ♟♟ **statue** (*2 on map*) of a charging bull—the symbol of the stock market on the rise—may be the most photographed public artwork in the city. It may also be the most controversial. New York City artist Arturo Di Modica decided to create the bull after the worst day in Wall Street history, so-called Black Monday (October 19, 1987), when the Dow Jones lost 22.6 percent of its value. On the night of December 15, 1989, he and his friends carried it on a flatbed truck to the New York Stock Exchange and left it there beside a 60ft-tall Christmas tree. The police were called in to haul the bull away, but public outcry was such that the New York City Department of Parks & Recreation made room for it here, where it remains a "temporary" installation.

17 State Street

© Juan Antonio Alonso/age fotostock

Architecture Buffs

Notable Buildings

Spanning some 200 years, the architecture of the Financial District is some of the most noteworthy in the city. In the 19C, the Beaux-Arts and Classical Revival styles dominated. The name of the game in the 20C was skyscrapers, big skyscrapers. Some of the largest are on Water Street *(between Dover & Fulton Sts.)*, Manhattan's street of million-sq-ft towers. Indeed, to fully appreciate their vastness, you need to get off the island; the Brooklyn Heights Esplanade and the Circle Line boat offer the best vantage points. But there are quite a few you can admire from the street as you make your tour of the neighborhood. Here's a sampling:

17 State Street

This sleek mirrored office tower is like an ultra-tall quarter-slice of pie. Completed in 1989, it was designed by Emery Roth & Sons. On August 1, 1819, *Moby-Dick* author **Herman Melville** was born in a house on this site; there's an archaeological exhibit at the base of the building, New York Unearthed, run by the South Street Seaport Museum (◔*open by appointment only; ☏212-748-8786).*

Battery Maritime Building

11 South St. at the foot of Whitehall St.
The art nouveau ferry terminal (1909, Walker and Morris) next to the newly renovated Whitehall Ferry Terminal

has a brightly painted cast facade, a 55,000sq-ft waiting area, a stained-glass skylight and Guastavino tile vaults under its porch roofs. In 2006 a $60 million renovation of the building was completed. It already serves as the terminus of the ferry to **Governors Island**. Development plans include a future food market, restaurant and boutique hotel.

Chamber of Commerce of the State of New York

65 Liberty St. between Nassau St. & Broadway.
The International Commercial Bank of China occupies this wedding cake of a building (1901, James B. Baker), which sports an Ionic colonnade, a mansard roof and porthole windows. The building's ornate facade is preserved as a historic landmark.

One Chase Plaza

Pine St. between Nassau & William Sts.
David Rockefeller took a risk when commissioning Skidmore, Owings & Merrill to build this massive tower in Lower Manhattan for the bank he chaired. At the time of its completion in 1961 there was nothing like it; the bank vault was reputed to be among the world's largest: longer than a football field, it weighed 985 tons and had 6 doors, each 20in thick. The building might have stood out like a sore thumb for decades, but the World Trade Center and other behemoths came soon after, and it melded in nicely. The building is made of glass and aluminum and rises 813ft without a setback. Jean Dubuffet's black-and-white sculpture **The Group of Four Trees**★ (**3** *on map*) (1961) enlivens the concrete plaza.

Cunard Building

25 Broadway on Bowling Green.
In the old days you could buy passage on such ocean liners as the *Queen Elizabeth* and the *Queen Mary* in the grand **lobby**★ of this Renaissance-style structure (1921, Benjamin Wistar Morris); now you

can buy stamps—it's a post office. The 68ft rotunda is glorious. Note, too, how well the exterior facade complements the Standard Oil Building opposite.

Equitable Building
120 Broadway between Pine & Cedar Sts.

Like the Trinity and US Realty Buildings across the street, this immense Beaux-Arts edifice (1915) comprises twin towers connected by a recessed central section. Protests over the building's bulk (it encompasses 1.2 million sq ft of office space on less than an acre, or a floor area almost 30 times as big as the site itself) gave rise to the city's first zoning resolution, passed in 1916.

India House
1 Hanover Sq. between Pearl & Stone Sts.

At the foot of the Stone Street Historic District, this 1853 Italianate brownstone fronts Hanover Square, a quiet little plaza dotted with trees. The building is home to India House Club, an ultra-exclusive private club catering to Wall Street executives.

James Watson House
7 State St. between Pearl & Water Sts.

Now the rectory of the Shrine of St. Elizabeth Ann Bayley Seton, the brick house dates from 1792, and the graceful Ionic colonnade was completed in 1806. It is the only surviving residential structure from the Federal period. Seton (1774–1821), who was born on Staten Island, was canonized as America's first saint in 1975.

One Liberty Plaza
Liberty St. between Church St. & Broadway.

Skidmore, Owings & Merrill designed this dark, forbidding structure (1974), a 54-story monolith "decorated" with thick, horizontal steel beams and tinted gray windows. The bleak plaza across the street (Broadway)

is brightened by sculptor Isamu Noguchi's 28ft reddish-orange cube (**4** *on map*) (1967).

Trinity (B *on map*) and US Realty Buildings
111 & 115 Broadway at Thames St.

Connected by a pedestrian walkway on the top floor, these twin limestone structures (1907) were designed in an elaborate Gothic style to harmonize with neighboring Trinity Church.

Wall Street Plaza
Corner of Water & Pine Sts.

This elegant glass and aluminum tower was designed by James Ingo Freed and completed in 1973. Highlighting the building's plaza is Yu Yu Yang's tantalizing two-part sculpture, consisting of a pierced slab and a disk. Just beside, a plaque commemorates the ocean liner *Queen Elizabeth I*, whose last proprietor was also a former owner of Wall Street Plaza.

New York Plaza
Foot of Broad St.

The three buildings of this complex form a varied ensemble, linked by plazas and a ground-level concourse. Note in particular the 22-story Brutalist-style red-brick building of 4 New York Plaza, punctuated by narrow slit windows.

James Watson House

©Paul Knivett/Alamy

Battery Park City★

Most visitors to this vast commercial/residential complex come to enjoy its 35 acres of parks and the 1.2mi riverfront esplanade, a flower- and art-studded path along the Hudson River. (It is part of the 5mi-long Hudson River Park, which runs from Battery Park to 59th Street.) Also in Battery Park City are the Museum of Jewish Heritage, the Skyscraper Museum, the Irish Hunger Memorial and the World Financial Center's Winter Garden.

A BIT OF HISTORY

Well into the 1950s, Lower Manhattan's western shoreline was crammed with piers, wharves and ferry slips, around which longshoremen bustled to load and unload ships from all parts of the world. But in the 1960s, the advent of containership technology forced most active piers to move to roomier sites in Brooklyn, Staten Island and New Jersey. The idea to create Battery Park City was first conceived by Governor Nelson Rockefeller in the late 1960s. Under his leadership, engineers extended Lower Manhattan with 92 acres of landfill, most of which came, conveniently, from the neighboring World Trade Center site when it was excavated

MTA **Subway:** 4, 5 train to Bowling Green or 1 train to Rector St.
Map: See Financial District
Kids: Skyscraper Museum.

for construction of the Twin Towers. In the mid-1970s, the site was ready for development, but the city's shaky finances stalled construction. In 1979, during the administrations of Mayor Ed Koch and Governor Hugh Carey, the original plan was scrapped in favor of a new one calling for the extension of Manhattan's street grid into the complex, as well as the public parks and esplanade. In 1982 the first tenants moved into the Gateway Plaza apartment complex. Construction and improvements have proceeded apace ever since.

In 2004 what is touted as the world's first "green" high rise, the **Solaire**, was opened at 20 River Terrace. Designed by Cesar Pelli and Assocs., the 27-story residence has its own water treatment system, photovoltaic panels to reduce electricity use and a rooftop garden.

ESPLANADE AND PARKS★★

The esplanade is anchored on its south end by pleasant **Robert F. Wagner Jr. Park**. A raised observation deck here

---

᧬ Biking in the City ᧬

While New York's streets remain far from bike-friendly, the city's waterfront has become tantalizingly so. In fall 2003 the Department of Parks & Recreation unveiled a 32mi circuit that takes cyclists from the Battery up the West Side, past the George Washington Bridge almost to the northern tip of Manhattan, then down the Harlem and East Rivers and back to the Battery. There are gaps that require a little street maneuvering—around the United Nations on the East Side, for example—but it is a vast improvement over the days of yore. In any case, most visitors are content to bicycle up and down the West Side, which sports the smoothest paths and best views of, and around, Central Park. Battery Park City is as good a place as any to hop on. Friendly bike store **Gotham Bikes** can set you up with a pair of wheels, a helmet and a map *(112 W. Broadway between Duane & Reade Sts.;* ○*open year-round Mon–Wed & Fri–Sat 10am–6.30pm, Thu 10am– 7.30pm, Sun 10.30am–5pm;* ᧬ *rentals $30/day, including helmet;* ☎*212-732-2453; www.gothambikes.com).* Arrive early on warm weekends since bikes are available on a first-come, first-served basis only. For more information on cycling in New York, contact Transportation Alternatives *(*☎*212-629-8080; www.transalt.org).*

affords sweeping **views**★★ of New York Harbor. Underneath you'll find public restrooms, and **Gigino at Wagner Park**, an Italian restaurant with a large waterfront patio *(20 Battery Pl.; ⏂ see Where to Eat)*. On the north end of the esplanade lies 7-acre **Governor Rockefeller Park**, which has a playground, basketball and volleyball courts, a grass lawn (which turns into a de facto beach in summertime) and a Greek temple pavilion.

ADDITIONAL SIGHTS

Museum of Jewish Heritage★★
⏂ See Major Manhattan Museums.

🏛 Skyscraper Museum★
♿ 39 Battery Pl. 🕐 Open year-round Wed–Sun noon–6pm. 💲$5. 📞212-968-1961. www.skyscraper.org.

High-rise construction past, present and future is the focus of this enthusiastic newcomer to New York's museum scene, a must for architecture buffs. It opened its doors on April 2, 2004, in a 38-story tower standing opposite the Museum of Jewish Heritage at the southern tip of Battery Park City.

Roger Duffy of Skidmore, Owings & Merrill visually elongated the small, bi-level space by sheathing both floors and ceiling in polished steel—an appropriate gesture for a museum that celebrates verticality. Recent exhibits have focused on Frank Lloyd Wright's skyscraper designs and Lower Manhattan's development, featuring the original 9ft-tall model of the World Trade Center. The museum's bookstore stocks a wide array of New York architecture books and guides, and its award-winning website offers "virtual tours" of Manhattan.

Irish Hunger Memorial
North End Ave. & Vesey St.

Artist Brian Tolle created this striking memorial in 2002 to commemorate the Great Hunger of 1845–52, during which a million Irish died of starvation. The tragedy prompted many to emigrate, and between 1847 and 1851, more than a million Irish arrived in New York City. The site re-creates a rural Irish landscape with its abandoned stone cottage, fieldstone walls, fallow potato fields and thick green flora from the north Connacht wetlands. The memorial rests 25ft above the sidewalk on a titled limestone plinth with views of Liberty and Ellis Islands.

World Financial Center

The commercial heart of Battery Park City was designed by Cesar Pelli & Assocs. It consists of four towers sheathed in granite and glass, ranging in height from 33 to 51 stories. Linked by glassed-in bridges, each has a copper roof of a different geometric shape: mastaba, dome, pyramid and stepped pyramid. Together the complex encompasses 8 million sq ft of office and retail space, including the world headquarters of American Express. The **Winter Garden**★ is the highlight. This 10-story barrel-vaulted atrium is nestled between towers 2 and 3, providing a warm indoor venue for sixteen 43ft-tall palm trees and hundreds of office workers on their lunch hours (if they can find a seat—there's a woeful lack here of benches). The Winter Garden affords great **views**★ of both the water and the ongoing construction at the neighboring World Trade Center site. The space is used for free lunchtime music or dance performances about once a week *(for a schedule: 📞212-417-7050; www.artsworldfinancialcenter.com)*.

World Financial Center

Peter Wrenn/MICHELIN

South Street Seaport★★

This waterfront historic district and shopping hub ranks as New York's third-largest tourist attraction. Its cobblestone streets and wide-plank wharves are packed with sightseers, peddlers and street performers on warm days. But that's only part of the picture. Spread throughout the district are half a dozen first-rate historic sites maintained by the South Street Seaport Museum.

A BIT OF HISTORY

Historians call the seaport district the birthplace of New York City's economy. Founded in the 1600s as a small port, it underwent a period of rapid growth in the early 19C with the rise of international maritime trade. It was boosted by the inauguration of Fulton's Brooklyn ferry service in 1814 and the establishment of Fulton Market in 1822 (the fish market moved to the Bronx in 2005). With the opening of the **Erie Canal** in 1825, goods from the Midwest poured into the harbor. South Street became known to the world as the "Street of Ships" as China clippers, trans-Atlantic packets and other boats crowded the teeming wharves. In the 1960s Manhat-

MTA **Subway:** A, C train to Broadway-Nassau St. or 2, 3, 4, 5, J, Z train to Fulton St.

Map: Opposite.

Location: The seaport consists of 12 square blocks of cobblestone streets, with shops, historic vessels and a maritime museum. Most of the outdoor restaurants and bars are on Pier 17, but **Bridge Cafe**, on Water Street (see Where to Eat), is also a good choice.

P **Parking:** It's best to arrive by subway, but if you come by car, several paid lots lie within a six-block radius. Free shuttle buses run along the waterfront between historic South Street Seaport and Battery Park City (for information, call ☎212-566-6700 or visit www.downtownNY.com/DowntownConnection).

Don't Miss: The old-fashioned **print shop** at Bowne & Co. Stationers.

Kids: The museum offers **activities** for children (see sidebar opposite).

South Street Seaport

Peter Wrenn/MICHELIN

👨‍👧 The Seaport – JUST for Kids

Lest the next generation forgets that, yes, there used to be activity here at the seaport other than shopping and eating, the **South Street Seaport Museum** has a raft of educational family programs on weekends (🕐*year-round Sat–Sun noon–4pm*). On Saturdays kids make **arts**, **crafts** and **music** on an educational theme such as archaeology or the Chinese New Year. On Super Story Sundays, children can gather around to listen to **tales of the sea** (among other subjects); then they get to embark on a writing adventure of their own. Family programs are free with museum admission and are designed for children 4 years of age and older. Toddlers are welcome to join in with an adult.

tan lost out to more sophisticated piers in Brooklyn and New Jersey. In 1967 efforts to preserve the port's historic buildings, piers and vessels culminated in the founding of the South Street Seaport Museum. Today the seaport draws some 12 million people annually.

VISIT
South Street Seaport Museum★★

👨‍👧👍🕐*Open Apr–Dec Tue–Sun 10am–6pm; rest of year Thu–Sun 10am–5pm (ships noon–4pm).* 🕐*Closed Jan 1, Thanksgiving Day & Dec 25.* 📞*212-748-8725. www.seany.org.*

Museum sites are scattered throughout the district, which extends from Water Street to the East River between John Street and Peck Slip. Admission to the district is free; to visit museum sites, purchase a ticket (👝*$15, $10 ships only*) at the **visitor center** on Pier 16 or at the Schermerhorn Row Galleries at 12 Fulton Street.

Street of Ships★

Visitors to the museum are encouraged to climb aboard and explore several of the historic vessels moored on Piers 15 and 16. The **Peking** (*1 on map*) is a square-rigged, four-masted barque built in 1911 in Hamburg, Germany; informative panels within describe the history of the ship and its features. When all 32 sails were set, she presented an amazing acre of canvas to the wind. The **Ambrose** (*2 on map*) may also be boarded. She was the first lightship to serve as a guide to vessels approaching the entrance to

Ambrose Channel in New York Harbor. The **Wavertree** (*3 on map*) is an 1885 square-rigger built for the jute trade between India and Europe.

SHOPS AND GALLERIES
Schermerhorn Row Galleries★★

12 Fulton St. between Front & South Sts. Ship chandler and developer Peter Schermerhorn built these handsome brick structures between 1811 and 1813 during the seaport's heyday; they were used as countinghouses and warehouses. Today they hold the South Street Seaport's formidable collection of maritime art and artifacts. As part of a $21 million interior restoration completed in 2003, Schermerhorn Row was linked internally to the 1850 A.A. Low

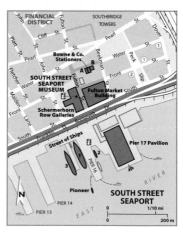

HOTEL	RESTAURANTS
Best Western Seaport Inn............①	Bridge Cafe.....................①
	Nelson Blue...................②

Going, Going, Gone

After a run of 170 years, the **Fulton Fish Market** finally closed its doors in the summer of 2005—a year after the original departure date—and moved 12 miles uptown to Hunts Point in the Bronx. There, instead of selling fish on ice in the city streets, it occupies a larger, enclosed refrigerated building designed to meet today's food handling standards. It's the end not only of the ever-present smell of fish here, but also of an era. For decades it was a real "New York experience" to venture to the docks at the crack of dawn and watch local chefs and grocers pick out the best catch of the day.

Building, which fronts John Street, to create 30,000sq. ft of gallery space. On exhibit is **Soundings: Treasures of the Collections of the South Street Seaport Museum**, which includes paintings by maritime artist James Buttersworth; prisoner-of-war ship models made from bones; scrimshaw (whalebone carvings); a print of the *Titanic* signed by survivors; and a collection of ivory, lacquer and silk souvenirs from the China trade. Another permanent exhibit, **Monarchs of the Sea: Celebrating the Ocean Liner Era**, recalls the glory days of the luxury liners, through models, artifacts and plans. The museum's core permanent exhibit, **World Port New York**, is a sweeping survey of the seaport and its economic, commercial and cultural impact on the city, region and country.

Bowne & Company Stationers

211 Water St. between Fulton & Beekman Sts. Museum ticket not required. ⏱*Open daily 10am–6pm.*
This charming 19C print shop, which still turns out wedding invitations and book plates on foot-powered presses, has the name and the financial support of the oldest company listed on the New York Stock Exchange.
Robert Bowne founded his original stationery store on Queen Street (now Pearl Street) in 1775. Today Bowne and Co. specializes in financial printing and has seven state-of-the-art printing plants across the country and in Canada. At this creaky old throwback, you can watch (and, if you're lucky, help) one of the two printers produce a Walt Whitman book on a treadle-operated press dating from 1901.

Walter Lord and Port Life and Melville Library Galleries

209 & 213 Water St. between Fulton & Beekman Sts. Temporary and permanent exhibits on waterfront and New York history are mounted in these two galleries flanking Bowne & Co. Stationers. Don't miss the massive scale model (¼in = 1ft) of the **Queen Mary**★ near the back of the Walter Lord Gallery.

PIER 17 PAVILION★

Jutting 400ft into the East River, Pier 17 is the shopping, dining and entertainment hub of South Street Seaport. The three-story glass and steel structure (1984, Benjamin Thompson & Assocs.) contains a huge indoor mall. Stroll to the end of the pier to drink in **views**★ of the Brooklyn Bridge and the East River.

Fulton Market Building

This brick and granite structure, also a Thompson & Assocs. creation (1982), is the fourth market to be built on this site. It holds a convention space as well as shops and restaurants.

Harbor Cruises

Both the South Street Seaport Museum and the **Circle Line Tour Company** offer boat tours of the harbor, departing from Pier 16. The museum takes visitors out on its 1885 schooner **Pioneer** for 2hr sails (⏱*May–Sept Tue–Fri 3pm, 7pm, Sat–Sun 1pm, 4pm, 7pm; 24hr advance reservations recommended;* ∞*$25–$30;* ✆*212-748-8786).* The Circle Line's vessels of choice are the catamaran *Zephyr*, which takes passengers past the Empire State Building, the Chrysler Building, the Brooklyn Bridge *(1hr;* ⏱*Apr–Dec daily*

10am, 11.15am, 12.30pm, 2pm, 3.30pm, additional tour 5pm May–Oct; ⊚$27) or the high-speed *Shark*, a thrill-oriented speedboat *(30min; ⏱May & Sept Sat–Sun*

only, hourly noon–5pm, Jun–Aug daily on the hour noon–7pm; ⊚$23; ☎866-977-6998; www.circlelinedowntown.com).

Civic Center★

The thumping heart of government bureaucracy, Civic Center teems with federal, state and local employees on weekdays. You'll want to plan your visit during normal business hours to peek inside the richly ornamented Surrogates Court and the New York State Supreme Court lobbies, as well as to see the New York African Burial Ground Project at the US General Services Administration Building; all three are closed evenings and weekends. A glorious exception is the Brooklyn Bridge; its pedestrian path is open 24/7.

BROOKLYN BRIDGE★★★

The pedestrian walkway runs along the north side of the bridge. In Manhattan it begins near the south corner of the Municipal Building on Centre Street across from City Hall Park. In Brooklyn it begins near the High Street–Brooklyn Bridge subway stop on the A/C line. Allow 30min to cross the bridge on foot. If walking from Manhattan to Brooklyn, continue on to nearby **Brooklyn Heights**★★.

MTA Subway: R train to City Hall or 4, 5, 6 train to Brooklyn Bridge-City Hall.
Map: Following pages.
Info: Stop by the Official NYC Information Kiosk at Barclay Street and Broadway, directly across from the Woolworth Building *(open Mon–Fri 9am–6pm, Sat–Sun 10am–5pm; brochures and maps are available after hours).* The center is the sign-up point for guided tours of City Hall *(1hr; Wed, noon).*
Timing: Allow 3hrs to visit the area, including 30min to cross the Brooklyn Bridge on foot.

The first bridge to link Manhattan and Brooklyn, this famed structure was one of the great engineering triumphs of the 19C and the world's longest suspension bridge for 20 years. Its graceful silhouette set against the New York

Brooklyn Bridge and Lower Manhattan

©Mario Savoia/Fotolia.com

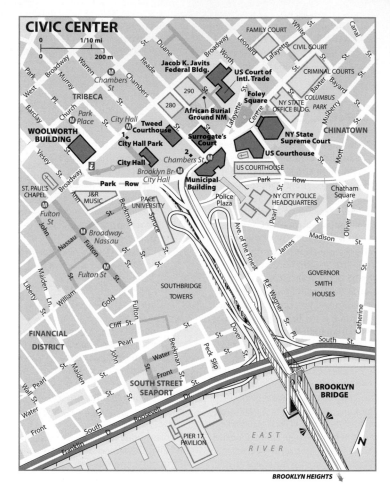

CIVIC CENTER

0 — 1/10 mi
0 — 200 m

FAMILY COURT
White St.
Canal St.
Leonard
Lafayette
CIVIL COURT
Duane St.
Broadway
Worth
Reade
CRIMINAL COURTS
Baxter
Bayard
Jacob K. Javits Federal Bldg.
US Court of Intl. Trade
Mulberry
290
Foley Square
COLUMBUS PARK
280
African Burial Ground NM
NY STATE OFFICE BLDG.
Cetre
CHINATOWN
TRIBECA
Chambers St.
Chambers
Park
Park
Murray
Warren
Broadway
West
Church
Pl.
Barclay
Vesey
WOOLWORTH BUILDING
Park Place
City Hall
Tweed Courthouse
1
City Hall Park
Surrogate's Court
2
NY State Supreme Court
US Courthouse
Mott
Chambers St.
City Hall
Brooklyn Br
City Hall
Municipal Building
US COURTHOUSE
Park Row
Chatham Square
ST. PAUL'S CHAPEL
Broadway
Park Row
J&R MUSIC
PACE UNIVERSITY
Police Plaza
NY CITY POLICE HEADQUARTERS
Fulton St
Ann
Beekman
Spruce
Pearl
John
Nassau
Broadway-Nassau
Fulton
Fulton St
Ave. of the Finest
St. James
Madison
GOVERNOR SMITH HOUSES
Oliver
Catherine
Liberty
Maiden Ln.
William
SOUTHBRIDGE TOWERS
Gold
Cliff St.
FINANCIAL DISTRICT
Pearl
John
Water
Beekman
Peck Slip
South St.
R.F. Wagner Sr.
Dover St.
Wall St.
Pearl
Maiden
Front
SOUTH STREET SEAPORT
Front St.
Roosevelt Dr.
BROOKLYN BRIDGE
Water
Front
South
Franklin
PIER 17 PAVILION
EAST RIVER
N

BROOKLYN HEIGHTS

Just the Facts

Brooklyn Bridge has a total length of 3,455ft with a maximum clearance above water of 133ft. The central suspended span between the two stone towers is 1,595ft long. The span is made of steel—the first time this metal was used for such a mammoth undertaking—and it is supported by four huge cables (15.75in thick) interconnected by a vast network of wires.

City skyline has inspired many artists, writers and poets. The stroll across the bridge is one of the most dramatic walks in New York.

The **view**★★ of the city and harbor through the filigree of cables is magnificent, especially as the sun sets.

Construction – In 1869 German-born John Augustus Roebling, a pioneer bridge builder responsible for the Niagara Falls and Cincinnati, Ohio suspension bridges, was commissioned to design a bridge linking Manhattan and Brooklyn. Shortly after the plans were approved, Roebling's foot was crushed while he was taking measurements for the piers. Despite an amputation, gangrene set in and he died three weeks later. His son, Washington Roebling, carried on the work, adopting new methods in pneumatic foundations, which he had studied in Europe.

To construct the foundations, workers used caissons immersed in water and then filled with compressed air to prevent water infiltration. To adapt to the air pressure, the workmen underwent periods of gradual compression before going down to work, and decompression afterward.

Despite these precautions, a few had burst eardrums or developed the "bends," which causes convulsions and can bring on partial or total paralysis. Washington Roebling himself was stricken with the bends. Confined to his sickbed, he nevertheless continued to direct the operation from his window overlooking the bridge. Finished in 1883, the bridge cost $25 million. With its intricate web of suspension cables and its majestic, pointed arches, the bridge represents an aesthetic and technical masterpiece. In 1972 the cables and piers were repainted in their original colors—beige and light brown. The walkway was rebuilt in 1983. The cables undergo regular maintenance.

History and Inspiration – The bridge immediately became the busy thoroughfare its planners had foreseen. On opening day, 150,000 people walked across it. Yet, less than a week after its inauguration by President Chester Arthur, tragedy struck. A woman fell on the stairway and her screams set off a panic, killing 12 people and injuring many more.

Fifteen years after the inauguration of the bridge, the city of Brooklyn was incorporated into New York. The bridge played a significant role in the development and growth of Brooklyn, the city's most populous borough.

Monumental and awe-inspiring, the Brooklyn Bridge has fascinated, obsessed and haunted New Yorkers. Immortalized in the works of Walt Whitman, it has also been painted on canvas by numerous artists. Colorful Cubist renditions of the bridge, created in the 1920s by Joseph Stella, are among the best-known depictions of the monument.

Woolworth Building

©Christian Hesse/Dreamstime.com

ADDITIONAL SIGHTS
Woolworth Building★★★
233 Broadway between Park Pl. & Barclay St. ⚬━ *Lobby closed to public.*

This 1913 skyscraper, the tallest in the world for 17 years, has been called a cathedral to commerce, and it's no wonder. Standing 792ft 1in in height, the tower is ornamented with the gargoyles, pinnacles, flying buttresses and finials more typical of ecclesiastical architecture and highly atypical of office buildings. In commissioning Cass Gilbert to design it, F.W. Woolworth, founder of the now-defunct five- and ten-cent store chain, got a true masterpiece.

A Bit of History – In November 1910, plans called for the building to be only 625ft tall, at a projected cost of $5 million. But after the caissons were sunk, Woolworth decided he wanted the structure to be the tallest in the world, which meant it had to top the 700ft Metropolitan Life Insurance Tower, completed in 1909. Gilbert happily revised his design, and the existing structure is the result. The final cost of the building was $13.5 million, which Woolworth paid in cash.

At the opening ceremony, President Woodrow Wilson pressed a button in Washington that lit up 80,000 light bulbs in the building, an awesome spectacle at the time. In 1930 the title of world's tallest passed to **40 Wall Street** (now the Trump Building), but the Woolworth Building continues to stand out in the relatively (for New York) low-rise environment of Civic Center.

Visit– The granite and limestone base of the building rises 27 stories without a setback. On top of the building's mansard roof, facing Broadway, is a 27-story, terracotta-clad tower capped in copper. Byzantine-style mosaics and frescoes cover the three-story barrel-vaulted lobby. Among the lobby sculptures are caricatures of Gilbert clutching a model of the building and Woolworth counting his nickels.

City Hall Park★★

Bounded by Chambers St., Park Row & Broadway. While much of the green expanse that surrounds City Hall and the Tweed Courthouse is off-limits to visitors, a 1999 renovation made the publicly accessible corner cupped by Park Row and Broadway a very pleasant hangout. Here wooden benches encircle a spiffy fountain, anchored by old-fashioned gas lamps. Magnolia trees and well-maintained plantings abound. The small plaza is also one of the best places to view the gilded 25ft statue *Civic Fame* on top of the Municipal Building in the distance, as well as adjacent Park Row.

A Bit of History – Before the Revolutionary War, the area was a common planted with apple trees on the northern edge of the budding city. Liberty poles were erected by the Sons of Liberty, and in July 1776, the Declaration of Independence was read in the presence of General George Washington, his troops and other patriots. Afterward, the crowd rushed down to **Bowling Green**★ to topple the statue of British monarch George III.

Visit – Today a statue (1893) of **Nathan Hale** (**1** *on map*) (1755–76) stands in the park facing City Hall; Frederick MacMonnies was the sculptor, and Stanford White built the base. Hale's famous last words, of course, were: "I only regret that I have but one life to lose for my country." **Horace Greeley** (**2** *on map*) (1811–72), the crusading founder of the *New York Tribune*, is comfortably seated across from the Municipal Building. The statue was designed by J.Q.A. Ward and completed in 1890.

City Hall★★

Visited by guided tour (1hr) only, year-round Wed noon, departing from Official NYC Information Kiosk (south end of City Hall Park, Broadway at Barclay St.). For a tour of City Hall and Tweed Courthouse, see Tweed Courthouse, below.
This is New York's second official City Hall (if you don't count the former tavern on Pearl Street that the Dutch used as a government seat). The first City

City Hall Park

Peter Wrenn/MICHELIN

"Boss" Tweed

Though he wasn't the only corrupt political leader in New York history, "Boss" William M. Tweed (1823–78) is the most notorious. His infamy is due in no small part to the large figure he cut: a jovial man standing 6ft tall and weighing nearly 300 pounds, he was popular among the immigrant groups who helped get him elected to the US House of Representatives and later, to the state senate. But it was his role in the Tammany Hall political machine that really made his reputation. From 1866 to 1871 the group who became known as the "Tweed Ring" essentially controlled all city spending; which is to say, they diverted it into their own pockets. Tweed and his crooked cronies illegally gained an estimated $30 million to $200 million in their dealings with the city. When Tweed died of pneumonia in prison, then-mayor Smith Ely refused to fly the city flag at half-staff.

Hall was opened at the corner of Wall and Broad Streets in 1702, where the Federal Hall National Memorial now stands. Distinguished by a Neoclassical facade and a Georgian interior, the building you see here was completed in 1811 at a cost of about $500,000. It is the work of architects Joseph F. Mangin and John McComb Jr., who won a competition for the design and a prize of $350. To cut costs, politicians had the northern facade faced with brownstone, not marble, figuring that the city would never grow large enough for anyone to notice. By 1956 it had become clear that they had erred in their prediction, and the entire building was refaced with Alabama limestone.

The tour takes in the rotunda and the coffered dome, which evokes Rome's Pantheon; the City Council Chamber, and the Governor's Room; and a museum and reception room, with period furnishings and 19C American portraiture.

Tweed Courthouse★

Visit by guided tour (1hr 30min) only, year-round Fri noon; reservations required (dial 311 or visit www.nyc. gov/designcommission).

A whopping $13 million was appropriated for the construction of this courthouse between 1862 and 1870, and still the building wasn't finished (*see sidebar on "Boss" Tweed, above)*! After years of neglect, the Old New York County Courthouse (1872, Kellum and Little) was treated to an $85 million restoration (2001). Its grand colonnade facing

Chambers Street now gleams like a fresh set of teeth.

The edifice, whose style has been described as "Anglo-Italianate," contains one of the city's finest 19C interiors. Of particular interest are the iron staircases and the Gothic-style courtroom, which is now the headquarters of the city's Department of Education. The tour includes a visit to the octagonal rotunda, site of Roy Lichtenstein's sculpture entitled *Element #E* (1984).

African Burial Ground National Monument★

At the southwest corner of Duane & Elk Sts. Interpretive center at 290 Broadway. 212-637-2019. www.nps.gov/afbg. Interpretive Center open Tue–Sat 10am–4pm. Burial ground open year-round daily 9am–4pm. Closed major holidays.

Archaeologists happened upon this major historical site by chance in 1991. They'd been hired to do field testing in preparation for the construction of a new 34-story federal office building. Soon they discovered the first human remains from an 18C African burial ground that had been all but forgotten. Called "the Negroes Burying Ground" on maps from the period, it was a desolate 5.5-acre plot outside city limits.

Until 1794, an estimated 20,000 people were buried here, stacked layer upon layer in unmarked graves, a testament to colonial New Yorkers' often-overlooked participation in the slave trade. Archaeologists ultimately unearthed more than

400 skeletal remains as well as burial artifacts from the site, and a small plot of land was set aside for a memorial, interpretive center and "new" burial ground. The site was declared a National Historic Landmark in 1993. In 2003, the remains were placed in handmade coffins from West Africa and lowered back into the ground in a ceremony of prayers, tributes, speeches, dance and song.

Visit – Several powerful artworks are on permanent display here. Artist Roger Brown's stunning 140sq-ft **mosaic**★ shows a honeycomb of skulls buried beneath a soil–like layer of gaunt faces, topped by New York icons like the Brooklyn Bridge, the Twin Towers and the Empire State Building. Similarly striking is Barbara Chase-Riboud's bronze sculpture *Africa Rising*.

Municipal Building★

1 Centre St. at Chambers St. Looming over the foot of Chambers Street is one of Civic Center's most striking buildings. McKim, Mead and White's first skyscraper (1914), it features a recessed central tower flanked by two protruding wings. The facade is distinguished by a monumental Neoclassical colonnade. Above the arch, Roman numerals mark the date of the founding of New Amsterdam (1626) and New York (1664). Also note the Guastavino tiles under the arcaded south wing (above the subway entrance). The gilded finial *Civic Fame*, by sculptor Adolph A. Weinman, stands at the top of the 40-story building, a barefoot female figure in a flowing dress, balancing on a copper ball. A five-pointed crown in her left hand symbolizes the five boroughs.

Across the street, the **Surrogate's Court** *(31 Chambers St. at Centre St.;* 🕐*open year-round Mon–Fri 9am–5pm;* 🚫*closed major holidays)* is architect John Thomas's Beaux-Arts masterpiece. Composed of Maine granite, it rises seven stories, took seven years to build, and cost $7 million. The exterior is embellished with mythical figures and famous New Yorkers, and its **central hall**★ boasts marble walls and mosaic ceilings.

Foley Square

Bounded by Centre, Lafayette & Worth Sts. This wedge-shaped plaza, named after city alderman Thomas F. Foley (1852–1925), once lay beneath a large pond, which was drained, and covered over in 1811. Houses built on the site began to sink due to inadequate drainage and poor foundations, and were abandoned. In the early 20C, the land was cleared for the New York State Supreme Court and other government offices.

A fountain, *Triumph of the Human Spirit* (2000), by Brooklyn sculptor Lorenzo Pace, stands at the southern tip of the square. The 50ft-tall black granite monument at its center was inspired by the art of Mali's Bambara tribe. The boatlike base evokes the slave trade. At the northern tip of Foley Square sits a treeshaded park.

On the west side stands the **Jacob K. Javits Federal Building**, a 1967 highrise faced with a checkerboard pattern of white concrete and black glass. It is attached to a bridge to the glass-box **US Court of International Trade**, suspended from concrete beams.

On the east side sits the **New York State Supreme Court**★ *(60 Centre St. between Worth & Pearl Sts.;* 🕐*open year-round Mon–Fri 9am–5pm;* 🚫*closed major holidays)*. Distinguished by a monumental Corinthian colonnade, the Classical Revival structure (1927) is faced with granite on its six sides. Inside, an elaborate central rotunda is covered with 1930s murals, and a polychrome marble floor is embedded with the signs of the zodiac.

Next door, the **Thurgood Marshall United States Courthouse** *(40 Centre St.)*, designed by Cass Gilbert, was completed in 1936. It presents a curious blend of architectural elements—a square, 32-story tower capped by a pyramidal top bursts through the roof of a Classical Revival temple.

Park Row

So named because it faces City Hall Park, this stretch of road between **St. Paul's Chapel**★★ and the foot of the Brooklyn Bridge was a fashionable promenade in the 19C. It eventually became the center of journalism in the city: the *Times*, *Tribune*, *Herald*, *World* and *Sun* all had offices here. The intersection with Nassau Street was called Printing-House Square. Today the block is occupied by the electronics emporium J&R Music. On the opposite side of City Hall, view the four-faced **brass clock** at 280 Broadway (at Chambers St.), which bears the *Sun*'s motto: "The Sun: It shines for all."

Chinatown★★

The narrow streets at the heart of Chinatown feel utterly unlike the rest of New York City. Densely packed markets stock everything from lychee to lipstick, while storefront restaurants serve up all manner of Asian cuisine. Especially crowded on weekends, the area bursts its seams at Chinese New Year (first full moon after Jan 19), when dragons dance down the streets accompanied by banner-carrying attendants and fireworks.

MTA **Subway:** B, D train to Grand St. or 6, J, N, Q, R, Z train to Canal St.

Map: Following pages.

Info: A staffed visitor information booth on Canal at Walker & Baxter Sts. is open year-round daily 10am–6pm. www. explorechinatown.com.

Timing: Allow 2hrs to visit Chinatown.

A BIT OF HISTORY

Just Visiting – The first Chinese in New York came in the 1870s from the California goldfields or from jobs building the transcontinental railroad in the western US. Most were men who, unlike other immigrants, had no intention of staying: they just wished to make their fortunes and return to a comfortable life in China. By the 1880s the community numbered about 10,000.

Then restrictive legislation (the Chinese Exclusion Act) was passed to stop further immigration, and growth was effectively halted. Unable to earn passage back to China, many "temporary" residents stayed. In part because single

Chinatown
© José Fuste Raga/age fotostock

☺ A Bit of Advice ☺

When you're shopping in Chinatown, try bargaining. It might work with some vendors.

men continued to make up the majority of the population, the neighborhood took on a rough-and-tumble character in the late 19C and early 20C.

Opium dens, brothels and gambling parlors sprang up, as did social clubs called tongs. While many of the tongs' activities were peaceful, turf wars occasionally broke out. All too often they were resolved with revolvers or hatchets, the latter giving rise to the term *hatchet men*.

Here to Stay – Following the 1943 repeal of the Chinese Exclusion Act, a new influx of immigrants arrived in New York from Taiwan and Hong Kong, as well as from mainland China. Garment factories, Chinese laundries, shops and restaurants appeared in the quarter, which has inexorably spread out from its dense core into neighboring Little Italy and the Lower East Side.

The present-day Asian community of New York has been estimated at 1,165,000. Manhattan's Chinatown now holds the largest Chinese immigrant community outside Asia. The majority of Manhattan's 195,000 Asians live in Chinatown.

VISIT

The heart of Chinatown lies in the area bounded by Worth, Baxter & Canal Streets, and the Bowery. **Mulberry** and **Mott** Streets are lined with shops piled high with displays of bamboo plants, tea sets, silk dresses, Chinese lanterns,

fans and the like. **Ten Ren Tea and Gin-seng** *(75 Mott St.; ☎212-349-2286)* is a lovely spot for tea lovers: the proprietors measure out a stunning range of teas, from $125-a-pound hand-picked green oolong to more affordable jasmine tea from beautiful old canisters. Neighboring **Ten Ren's Tea Time** *(79 Mott St.; ☎212-732-7178)* serves up freshly steeped hot cups as well as sweet tapioca iced tea ("bubble tea"), which is hugely popular with young Chinese.

NOTABLE STREETS
Pell, Doyers and Bayard Streets

These, the most atmospheric streets in the district, are so narrow that they are almost always in the shade. Note the red-painted brick structure on the southwest corner of Pell and the Bowery *(18 Bowery)*. Built in 1785 by **Edward Mooney**, a butcher, this structure is reputed to be the earliest surviving row house in Manhattan. Formerly a tavern, a store, a hotel, a pool parlor, a restaurant and a social club, it is now a community bank. **Doyers Street** makes a sharp 90-degree turn in the middle: legend has it that merchants built it that way so that flying ghosts could move through it. Later it became known as "the bloody angle" for the tong wars that were fought here between 1880 and 1926.

Canal Street, between Broadway and Mulberry Street, is world-famous for being crammed full of tiny stalls selling knock-off designer goods, especially handbags and scarves. Word has it that a network of secret passages and hidden rooms connects some of the stores, allowing proprietors to hide merchan-

Walking Tours

Get the inside look at the neighborhood on one of the Museum of Chinese in America's **Experience Chinatown** walking tours. Docents with family ties to the neighborhood will guide you around the streets, pointing out historic and personal landmarks. Tours (☜$15) are held every Saturday between May and December, 1pm–2.30pm. MoCA also offers specialty tours on such topics as cuisine and religion. Call the museum or visit www.mocanyc.org for a schedule and to make a reservation (required) (☎212-619-4785).

dise from the detectives hired to nab them for copyright infringement.

Two structures on Canal Street incorporate some of the more festive elements of Chinese architecture: the red-lacquered, pagoda-roofed Hong Kong Bank Building at **No. 241 Canal Street** *(at Centre St.)*, completed in 1983; and the Mahayana Buddhist Temple at **133 Canal Street** *(between the Bowery & Chrystie St.)*, whose entrance is flanked by gilded lions. Step inside the temple for a strong whiff of incense and to see the 10ft golden Buddha seated on a lotus; tiny fortune scrolls are available for $1. Across the street, the **Manhattan Bridge arch** and horseshoe-shaped **colonnade** (1913, Carrère and Hastings) were spruced up by the Department of Transportation recently, after decades of neglect.

A newly opened pedestrian path leads over the bridge to the hip DUMBO neighborhood in Brooklyn.

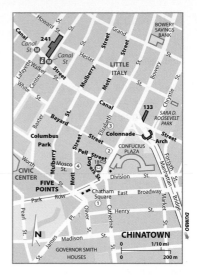

RESTAURANTS

Dim Sum Go Go..................(1)   Oriental Garden..........(3)
Great N.Y. Noodletown.......(2)   Peking Duck House....(4)

ADDITIONAL SIGHTS
Columbus Park

Chinatown's largest park recently underwent a massive renovation. New benches, paths, picnic tables, plantings and lights were installed on the north end, which is now a great place to enjoy a takeout order from **Tasty Dumpling** across the street or to watch Chinese men play intensely competitive games of checkers. A pleasant children's playground occupies the south end, which, ironically, used to be one of the most violent parts of the city. Known as **Five Points**, after the streets that intersected here in the early 19C—Mulberry Street, Anthony (now Worth) Street, Cross (now Park) Street, Orange (now Baxter) Street and Little Water Street (paved over)—it was a fetid, foul-smelling swampland where decaying houses, taverns and shacks stood shakily side by side in the shadow of an immense brewery.

Many of the residents were destitute Irish immigrants, whose notoriously violent gangs (the Plug Uglies, the Dead Rabbits, the Roach Guards) were featured in Martin Scorsese's 2002 film *Gangs of New York*. So infamous was the neighborhood that Charles Dickens came to write about it in 1842. What he saw appalled him (alleys knee-deep in mud; women sleeping on floors). The city leveled the whole area in the late 1880s.

Museum of Chinese in America (MoCA)

215 Centre St. between Grand & Howard Sts. ○*Open year-round Mon & Fri 11am–5pm, Thu 11am–9pm, Sat–Sun 10am–5pm.* ○*Closed major holidays.* ☞*$7; free Thu.* ☏*212-619-4785. www.mocanyc.org.*

Relocated in 2009 to a dramatic new building designed by Maya Lin (architect of the Vietnam Veterans Memorial in Washington, DC), the museum serves as a cultural and historical focal point in modern-day Chinatown.

The permanent exhibit **The Chinese American Experience** draws artifacts and photographs from the museum's collection to illustrate a chronological presentation of Chinese-American immigration history from the 17C to the present. Temporary exhibits of Chinese art and history are mounted in an adjacent gallery.

ADDRESSES

⏵ EAT

Chanoodle – *79 Mulberry St.* ✆*212-349-1495*. Peking duck is a specialty.

Dim Sum Go Go – *5 E. Broadway.* ⏺*See Where to Eat.*

Joe's Shanghai – *9 Pell St. Open daily 11am–11pm.* ✆*212-233-8888*. There's often a line out the door.

New Tu Do – *102 Bowery.* ✆*212-966-2666.* Vietnamese. Spring rolls, pho (soup), etc.

Oriental Garden – *14 Elizabeth St.* ⏺*See Where to Eat*. Fresh-from-the-tank seafood. A Chinatown favorite.

Tasty Dumpling – *54 Mulberry St. Open daily 9am–9pm.* ✆*212-349-0700*. Extremely cheap and fresh. Good for takeout and eating at Columbus Park.

Teariffic – *51 Mott St.* ✆*212-393-9009*. Tapioca tea plus shakes and appetizers. Very popular.

Vegetarian Dim Sum House – *24 Pell St.* ✆*212-577-7176*. All-veggie dim sum, plus a lot of vegetable dishes and imitation meat dishes.

Little Italy★
Nolita★

Little Italy, which once ran from Canal Street north to Houston and from Lafayette Street east to the Bowery, may now be more aptly termed Micro Italy. There are still 700,000 Italian Americans in New York City, but the commercial heart of their onetime stronghold in Manhattan has dwindled to a corridor: Mulberry Street. Between Canal and Broome Streets, this thoroughfare caters mainly to hungry tourists, though there are still some authentic delis, bakeries and gelaterias to be found. Little Italy's uber-fashionable sister, so-called Nolita (for North of Little Italy), sits within the neighborhood's former boundaries: four blocks by three blocks, it stretches from Broome to Houston Streets on Mulberry, Mott and Elizabeth Streets. The moniker "Nolita" came courtesy of real-estate developers who, in the 1990s, wanted to distinguish it from the red-sauce joints of the old neighborhood. And they did. Today Nolita is packed with trendy cafes and boutiques.

A BIT OF HISTORY

Italians have played a powerful role in shaping New York even before there was a city to shape. The Italian explorer

[MTA]**Subway:** 6, J, N, Q, R, Z train to Canal St.
⏺**Map:** Opposite.

Giovanni da Verrazano, working under the auspices of French king François I, was the first European to set foot on the island of Manhattan, in 1524. Italians didn't cross the Great Pond en masse until the late 1800s, however. Fleeing rural poverty in southern Italy, many initially settled in the notorious **Five Points** slum, which stood on what is now a corner of Chinatown. As families got on their feet, however, they moved north to SoHo, Greenwich Village and Little Italy. In 1880 fewer than 20,000 Italians lived in the city. That number rose to 220,000 by 1900, to 545,000 by 1910 and to more than a million by 1930. Women worked in the garment trade and men worked in construction, or started their own businesses as tailors, barbers, grocers or restaurateurs, bringing their native dishes into the melting pot of American cuisine.

La Cosa Nostra – Italians were no different from other immigrants, including the Irish and the Chinese, in organizing around their own interests—helping each other get jobs, for instance, and fostering their heritage. But with the onset of Prohibition in 1919, Italian social clubs gelled into unprecedented crime syndicates that together made up La Cosa Nostra. **Lucky Luciano** and

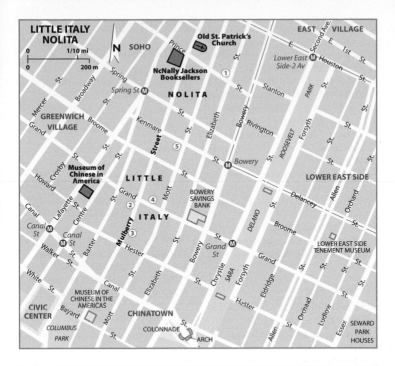

LITTLE ITALY
NOLITA

0   1/10 mi
0   200 m

N

SOHO

Prince

Old St. Patrick's
Church

NcNally Jackson
Booksellers

Lower East
Side-2 Av

EAST VILLAGE

SOHO

Spring

Spring St

NOLITA

Stanton

GREENWICH
VILLAGE

Broome

Kenmare

Street

Rivington

LOWER EAST SIDE

Museum of
Chinese in
America

LITTLE

Grand

Mott

BOWERY
SAVINGS
BANK

Bowery

ITALY

Delancey

Canal
St

Canal
St

Hester

Mulberry

Grand
St

Broome

LOWER EAST SIDE
TENEMENT MUSEUM

MUSEUM OF
CHINESE IN THE
AMERICAS

CIVIC
CENTER

Bayard

Mott

CHINATOWN

COLONNADE

SEWARD
PARK
HOUSES

COLUMBUS
PARK

ARCH

RESTAURANTS

Café Habana.. ①
Il Palazzo.. ②

Pellegrino's... ③
Nyonya.. ④
Lombardi's... ⑤

Al Capone were two of the New York City Mafia's earliest celebrities. They pioneered bootlegging operations during Prohibition; then, after that law was repealed, they moved into illegal gambling, loan sharking, pornography, drug smuggling and labor racketeering. Internecine battles occasionally burst into the public eye, as when **"Crazy" Joey Gallo** was gunned down during his 43rd birthday dinner at the original Umberto's Clam House on Mulberry Street in 1972 (then at 129 Mulberry; the restaurant has since moved to no. 178). **Proud Italians** – Despite such lively (or deadly, as it were) characters, many

Delicatessen window in Little Italy

©W. Zerla/Tips/Photononstop

109

local Italian Americans point out that they've contributed far more to the city, particularly in the political arena, than what you'll see on the HBO series *The Sopranos* or in Francis Ford Coppola's *Godfather* trilogy. **Fiorello La Guardia**, who was born at 177 Sullivan Street in 1882, served three terms as New York City mayor (1933–45). **Mario Cuomo** of Queens was a three-term New York State governor (1982–94). **Geraldine Ferraro**, also from Queens, became the first woman nominated by a major party (the Democrats) for national office (vice president) in 1984.

Finally, **Rudolph Giuliani** of Brooklyn made his name as a mob-busting federal attorney before serving as mayor from 1994 to 2002.

LITTLE ITALY

A visit to **Little Italy** basically consists of a **Mulberry Street**★ stroll. The stretch between Canal and Grand Streets is a veritable restaurant row, with white-aproned waiters sweet-talking diners into choosing their linguine over all others. On weekends from May to mid-October Mulberry Street is closed to vehicular traffic, making Little Italy one big alfresco party; the Feast of San Gennaro in mid-September is especially raucous. Try a scoop of gelato, served up in a cone or cup by sidewalk vendors.

NOLITA

Nolita is a boutique lover's paradise, a place where young designers sell funky home furnishings, one-of-a-kind neck-laces, accessories and clothes from tiny storefronts. Shopkeepers tend to be friendlier here than in SoHo, making Nolita a great place to browse.

The cafes are likewise ideal for people-watching. **Old St. Patrick's Church** (1815, Joseph F. Magnin), at the corner of Prince and Mulberry Streets, was New York's Roman Catholic cathedral until 1879, when it was replaced by a larger and grander structure in what is now Midtown. If the church is open, you can step inside and view the solemn Gothic interior.

ADDRESSES

🍴 TAKING A BREAK

$ Caffe Roma – *385 Broome St. at Mulberry St. Open daily 8am–midnight.* ✆*212-226-8413.* Tile floors, tin ceilings and ice-cream parlor chairs make this the most appealing of Little Italy's cafes. Sit outdoors and watch the world go by.

$ Ferrara – *195 Grand St. between Mott & Mulberry Sts. Open Sun–Fri 8am–midnight, Sat 8am–1am.* ✆*212-226-6150. www.ferraracafe.com.* Tucked around the corner from the bustling main drag of Mulberry Street, Ferrara is the place for cannoli, tiramisu, sorbet and gelato—all made on-site.

$ La Mela – *167 Mulberry St. between Broome & Grand Sts. Open Sun–Thu 11.30am–2am, Fri–Sat 11.30am–3am.* ✆*212-431-9493. www.lamelarestaurant.com.* Portions are fittingly humongous at this sprawling Little Italy landmark, which seats 500 at a time now that it has two kitchens. Photos of famous and not-so-famous revelers paper the walls.

Alleva Dairy – *188 Grand St. at Mulberry St. Open Mon–Sat 8.30am–6pm, Sun 8.30am–3pm.* ✆*212-226-7990. www.allevadairy.com.* Here's where you'll want to get your prosciutto, mozzarella and roasted-pepper sandwich, the deli's specialty. It was founded in 1892 and still has a friendly family feel.

NOLITA BONITA

$$ Cafe Gitane – *242 Mott St. between Prince & Houston Sts.* ✆*212-334-9552. www.cafegitanenyc.com.* This is Nolita's most popular hangout. Moroccan couscous, focaccia sandwiches, cheese plates, beer and cappuccino, all with a French accent. Open late.

🛒 SHOPPING

NOLITA BONITA

Bio – *29 Prince St. between Mott & Elizabeth Sts.* ✆*212-334-3006. www.bio-nyc.com.* Up-and-coming clothing designers display their latest collections in this vast gallery space. It's often featured in fashion magazines as a breeding ground for new talent.

Irregular Choice – *276 Lafayette St. between Prince & Jersey Sts. ℘212-334-3404. www.irregularchoice.com.* Rare among purveyors of New York style, this fun shop with its fantasy atmosphere sells fashion-forward footwear crafted for comfort.

McNally Jackson Booksellers – *52 Prince St. between Lafayette & Mulberry Sts. Open Mon–Sat 10am–10pm, Sun 10am–9pm. ℘212-274-1160. http://mcnallyjackson.com.* This bright, fairly new independent professes to offer "every book you could possibly want, and not a single book more." Order up a Japanese cherry or Moroccan mint brew in the newly remodeled cafe.

Lower East Side★

Despite being one of New York's hippest 'hoods, the Lower East Side has, for the most part, a refreshing lack of attitude and an astounding amount of local pride. "Come one, come all" has been its message to visitors since the 1880s, when it became the quintessential American melting pot. Though today's immigrants tend to be young artists, musicians, designers and restaurateurs, history lives on in the district's one-of-a-kind tenement museum and many famous ethnic eateries.

A BIT OF HISTORY

The Governor's Farm – Bounded by Houston Street, the East River, East Broadway and the Bowery, Lower East Side was rural long after southern Manhattan was developed. **Peter Stuyvesant**, the last Dutch governor of Nieuw Amsterdam, bought much of the land in 1651 from the Indians. To facilitate transport between his farm, or *bouwerie*, and the urban market, he laid out a broad, straight road, now known as the **Bowery**. Delancey Street was named for James de Lancey, an English landowner whose farm was confiscated after the American Revolution. Free blacks cultivated the soil here until around 1800, when development encroached agriculture.

The Gateway to America – The first mass migration to the Lower East Side occurred with the arrival of Irish immigrants fleeing the Great Hunger of 1845–52. From the 1880s until World

MTA **Subway:** F train to 2nd Ave., F, J, M, Z train to Delancey St.-Essex St. or B, D train to Grand St.

Map: Following pages.

Info: Visitor Center, 70 Orchard St. ℘212-226-9010. www.lowereastside ny.com.

Location: Start at the Visitor Center at address above (*open Mon–Fri 9.30am–5.30pm, Sat–Sun 9.30am–4pm; closed major holidays*). Here you'll find friendly staff to answer any questions, as well as brochures, shopping maps of the Lower East Side (some with a discount card), citywide bus maps and information on walking tours.

Parking: The Historic Orchard Street Shopping District offers 3hrs of **free parking** to visitors at its lot on Broome Street between Norfolk and Suffolk Streets (*open daily year-round*).

War I, millions of Southern and Eastern Europeans arrived via Ellis Island and were diverted to the Lower East Side, where they could meet other immigrants. The neighborhood became the most densely populated in the country. So overcrowded were some of the "railroad flats" (lots were 25ft wide and 100ft long, like railroad cars) that

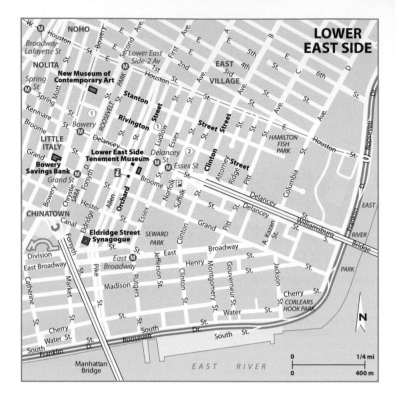

LOWER EAST SIDE

HOTEL		RESTAURANT	
Off SoHo Suites Hotel	①	'inoteca	①
		Schiller's Liquor Bar	②

family members took turns sleeping. In 1890 **Jacob Riis** documented the conditions in his now-classic book on urban poverty *How the Other Half Lives: Studies Among the Tenements of New York*. Eastern European Jews set down some of the strongest roots here, building nearly 500 houses of worship and schools; publishing Yiddish newspapers; and opening vaudeville theaters on the **Bowery**, otherwise known as the "poor man's Broadway." Some of the biggest names

Don't Forget the Bus!

So mammoth is the New York City subway system that many people (locals and visitors alike) forget that there is, as well, an extensive network of buses that are not only convenient, but free with unlimited-ride metro cards *(or $2.25 per ride for single rides, but you must have a MetroCard in advance; ☙ see Planning Your Trip)*. To get to and from the Lower East Side, consider taking the **M15** bus, which runs all the way up the east side of Manhattan between the **Whitehall Ferry Terminal** and **East Harlem** on First and Second Avenues; from the Lower East Side, you can pick it up at the corner of Allen and Delancey Streets. The **M14A** bus also serves the neighborhood, traveling along Grand and Essex Streets (the latter turns into Avenue A in **East Village**), then proceeding west to **Chelsea Piers** via 14th Street. Pick up a bus map at the Lower East Side Visitor Center.

Russ & Daughters

Courtesy of Russ & Daughters

A Nosher's Paradise

Though Zabar's on the Upper West Side is arguably *the* gourmet Jewish marketplace in New York, the Lower East Side was the original nosher's paradise; it remains just that. (Fittingly, the Yiddish word nosh means "to eat on the sly.") Since opening in 1914, **Russ & Daughters** *(179 E. Houston St.;* ◷ *open Mon–Fri 8am–8pm, Sat 9am–7pm, Sun 8am–5.30pm;* ✆ *212-475-4880; www.russanddaughters. com)* has been winning awards for its Caspian Sea caviar and just about everything else. Come in and put together a sampler of homemade salads (Romanian-style eggplant or whitefish and baked salmon), bagels, bialys, lox, roasted almonds or pistachios and homemade raspberry nut rugelach. The guys behind the counter are very friendly.

Katz's Delicatessen

Yeva Dashevsky/Katz's Delicatessen

The oldest Jewish (but not kosher) deli, **Katz's Delicatessen** *(205 E. Houston St. at Ludlow St.;* ◷ *open Wed–Thu & Sun 8am–10.45pm, Mon–Tue 8am–9.45pm, Fri–Sat 8am–2.45am;* ✆ *212-254-2246; www.katzdeli.com)*, has been curing and hand carving its own pastrami (ask for moist) since 1888 when it was often the first stop for Eastern European immigrants right off the boat. Pastrami-on-rye sandwiches, a local tradition, are tasty and unbelievably filling, so go with an appetite. To top it off, head over to the **Sweet Life** *(63 Hester St. at Ludlow St.;* ◷ *open Mon–Fri 10am–6.30pm, Sat–Sun 11am–6pm;* ✆ *212-598-0092; www. sweetlifeny.com)*, the Lower East Side's preeminent candy shop since 1982, which carries an awesome array of kosher treats, including dried fruits and nuts, hand-dipped chocolates, and macaroons, as well as jelly beans, gummy bears, licorice and hard candies.

in showbiz were raised on the Lower East Side (the **Marx Brothers**, **Jimmy Durante**, **Eddie Cantor**, **Al Jolson**, **Irving Berlin** and **George Gershwin** among them). The tide of immigration was halted in the 1920s with the passage of restrictive legislation. Many Jewish families moved to the Upper West Side and after World War II, thousands of African Americans and Puerto Ricans moved in. Afterward came the Beat poets, then, after neglect in the 1970s and '80s, a new generation of artists and musicians.

Lower East Side Today – Today only 10 per cent of Lower East Side residents are Jewish. The southern edge of the district is largely Chinese. Latinos still have a presence; their nickname for the quarter, "Loisaida," is still heard in some parts. But more prevalent, or at least visible, are the hordes of young Anglos who've transformed the gritty neighborhood into an urban village.

VISIT

Orchard Street★ between Canal and Houston Streets is the district's spine: to the south it is lined with bargain stores specializing in luggage, underwear and coats; farther north (around Broome Street), the trendy boutiques start. It is home to the **Lower East Side Tenement Museum**★★ *(nos. 90 and 97;* ⓖ *see Major Manhattan Museums).*

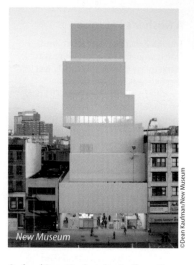

New Museum

©Dean Kaufman/New Museum

Orchard Street is closed to traffic on Sundays, when shopkeepers turn it into an outdoor mall.

Stanton Street and **Rivington Street** all the way east to **Clinton Street** are good places to find galleries, shops and cafes. A carnival atmosphere prevails at night around Ludlow Street between Houston and Delancey Streets; bars, restaurants and clubs here are full to the wee hours (*see Your Stay in New York City*).

NEIGHBORHOOD TOURS
Walking Tours

The Lower East Side Business Improvement District, which runs the Visitor Center, sponsors a walking tour at 11am every Sunday *(Apr–Nov)*; meet at Katz's Deli *(Houston & Ludlow Sts.)*. A **podcast walking tour** available (*free*) for download from the Lower East Side Business Improvement District website *(www.lowereastsideny.com)* directs you on a route starting from the Eldridge Street Synagogue and ending at the Essex Street Market, with vivid descriptions of the neighborhood's historical and cultural icons. The tenement museum and citywide walking tour companies, such as **Big Onion Walking Tours** *(2 hrs; $15; 212-439-1090; www.bigonion. com)*, conduct tours of this rich neighborhood as well.

During third Thursdays, neighborhood artists open their studios and galleries to the public *(6–9pm)*. The Lower East Side Visitor Information Center stays open until 9pm on third Thursdays and offers a free neighborhood guide for dining and nightlife options afterward.

ADDITIONAL SIGHTS
Eldridge Street Synagogue★

12 Eldridge St. between Canal & Division Sts. Museum open year-round Sun–Thu 10am–5pm, Fri 10am–3pm. Closed Jewish & major holidays. Guided tours offered (call or visit website for schedule). $10. 212-219-0888. www.eldridgestreet.org.

Completed in 1887, this was the first synagogue built by Eastern European Jews. In the late 1800s, as many as 1,000 people attended services here. Membership began to dwindle in the 1920s, and the sanctuary was closed in the 1950s. A preservation campaign launched in the 1980s restored the structure to its former glory. The building displays a striking rose window set against an ornate Moorish facade. Inside, hand-stenciled walls rise to a 70ft vaulted ceiling. The Museum at Eldridge Street features interactive exhibits on Lower East Side history, the architecture of the synagogue, and Jewish migration to America.

Bowery Savings Bank

130 Bowery between Grand & Broome Sts. Designed in 1895 by McKim, Mead and White, this Beaux-Arts gem is distinguished by imposing Corinthian columns and opulent detailing. The interior features an ornate, coffered vault with a large opaque skylight at its center.

New Museum★

235 Bowery at Prince St. Open Wed & Fri–Sun 11am–6pm, Thu 11am–9pm. Closed major holidays. $12 (free Thu 7–9pm). 212-219-1222. www.newmuseum.org.

Opened in late 2007, the striking new home of this edgy contemporary art museum punctuates the low-slung streetscape of the Lower East Side. Sheathed in glittering aluminum mesh, the building, by Tokyo architects Sejima + Nishizawa/SAANA, resembles a tower of messily stacked rectangular boxes looming brightly over the gritty Bowery. The museum keeps its permanent collections relatively small, focusing instead on temporary shows of resolutely contemporary paintings, sculptures, collages, videos, internet media and installation art, many by less well-known artists on the cusp of fame. Jeff Koons, Keith Haring, Bruce Nauman and Richard Prince were all the subject of New Museum exhibitions early in their careers.

ADDRESSES

⊕ NIGHTLIFE
⊕ See back of guide

Arlene Grocery – 95 Stanton St. between Ludlow & Orchard Sts.
Bowery Ballroom – 6 Delancey St. between Bowery & Chrystie Sts.
Mercury Lounge – 217 E. Houston St. between Ludlow & Essex Sts.
Pianos – 158 Ludlow St. at Stanton St.
Rockwood Music Hall – 196 Allen St.
TUTS – 196 Orchard St.

SoHo★

The heart of the Downtown fashion scene, SoHo—short for South of Houston (pronounced HOW-stun)—is New York at its trendiest and most colorful. Visitors throng the district on weekends, making even walking down the sidewalk difficult, especially given the proliferation of sidewalk tables full of purses and jewelry, sunglasses, scarves and amateurish (or more politely speaking, "outsider") art. For more serious art appreciators, there are still some top-notch galleries here, though many in the past decade have decamped for Chelsea, where rents are (or were) slightly cheaper. SoHo's cast-iron architecture gives the neighborhood a look all its own.

🚇 **Subway:** R train to Prince St. or C, E train to Spring St.
⊙ **Map:** Following pages.
▷ **Location:** SoHo is bounded roughly by Sullivan, West Houston, Lafayette and Canal Streets and is best experienced on foot (balance style with sense when it comes to shoes).
🕐 **Timing:** Saturdays tend to be the most crowded, especially on warm days and during the holiday shopping season. Many galleries are closed on Sundays and Mondays.
👪 **Kids:** New York City Fire Museum: the real McCoy, particularly for youngsters.

A BIT OF HISTORY

The site of the first free black community in Manhattan, SoHo was settled in 1644 by former slaves of the Dutch West India Company, who were granted land for farms. In the early 19C, Broadway was paved and a number of prominent citizens, including *Last of the Mohicans* author James Fenimore Cooper, moved in, bringing considerable cachet to the district. By 1825 it was the most densely populated neighborhood in Manhattan. In the late 1850s, large stores such as Tiffany & Co. and Lord & Taylor were joined on Broadway by grand hotels.

Theaters, casinos and brothels entertained visitors—and drove respectable middle-class families uptown. The exodus made room for new warehouses and factories, many built with ornamented cast-iron facades. The area thrived as a commercial center until the 1890s, when fashionable businesses began relocating to Fifth Avenue.

Art Brings a New Start – By the late 1950s, the neighborhood was a slum known as "Hell's Hundred Acres," and city planners slated it for demolition to make room for an expressway. Locals

Colorful buildings in SoHo

©Jose Antonio Sanchez/iStockphoto.com

fought the proposal and the area soon showed new signs of life. Often in violation of building codes, painters and sculptors converted vacant warehouses into studios, galleries and living quarters. An exciting underground art scene took root and thrived until the early 1980s, when Uptown galleries, boutiques and

affluent professionals began to push out the very artists who'd made the neighborhood so desirable in the first place.

SoHo Today – Today, few artists can afford to live or work in SoHo, and art museums haven't fared much better: the Guggenheim SoHo, the New Museum of Contemporary Art and the Alternative Museum have all moved out. Meanwhile, the migration of galleries northward to Chelsea continues. Locally owned boutiques have been largely supplanted by international couturiers such as Chanel and Prada. Indeed, SoHo has become a mecca for fashion-obsessed celebrities. That said, several excellent galleries remain in the neighborhood, as do a number of cafes and restaurants. As for shopping, sidewalk vendors offer up some good bargains, and despite what some haughty clerks might lead you to believe, browsing in even the most expensive stores is free.

Sullivan Street

Just as Little Italy has been gobbled up by Chinatown, so has the South Village, a onetime Italian stronghold, been gobbled up by SoHo. For a literal and figurative taste of what has been lost, head over to Sullivan Street. On the block between West Houston and Prince Streets stands **St. Anthony of Padua Roman Catholic Church** (no. 155), dedicated in 1888. Across the street sits **Joe's Dairy** (no. 156; ℘212-677-8780), an old-school cheese and salami shop that specializes in fresh and smoked mozzarella. **Pepe Rosso to Go** (no. 149; ℘212-677-4555) actually does have four tiny tables; snag one for a delectably cheap plate of pasta and a tumbler of red wine. Nearby, **Arturo's Pizzeria** (106 W. Houston St.; ℘212-677-3820) is a rowdy dive that wins praise, even among local pizza snobs, for its coal-fired-oven pies.

BROADWAY★

Overflowing with traffic, pedestrians and sidewalk vendors, this is SoHo at its most commercial. Most of the stores are bargain clothing and shoe outlets and national chains, but there are several happy exceptions: **Pearl River Mart**, once crammed into fourth-floor rooms on Canal Street, has spread out in style at no. 477 between Grand and Broome Streets. The bi-level Asian emporium carries a vivid array of slippers, silk jack-

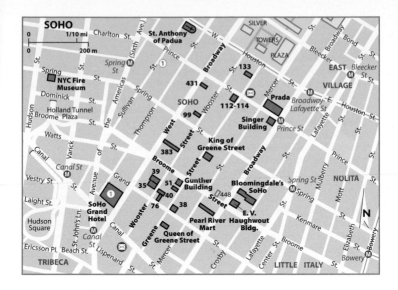

SOHO

HOTEL		RESTAURANT	
SoHo Grand Hotel	①	Blue Ribbon Sushi	①

ets, kimonos, paper lanterns, incense, ceramics and jade figurines. At no. 504 *(between Broome & Spring Sts.)* stands **Bloomingdale's SoHo**, a small-scale version of the Uptown department store. Opened in 2004, it has the same languid grace as the original. Finally there is **Prada** *(no. 575 at Prince St.)*, a retail fun house designed by Dutch architect Rem Koolhaas. Inside, a cylindrical glass elevator moves silently between floors, which are joined as well by a zebrawood slide and two grand facing staircases. Broadway is also home to the two most famous buildings in the district. The 1903 **Singer Building**★ *(nos. 561–563)*, designed by Ernest Flagg, ushered in a new era of skyscraper design. Delicate wrought-iron tracery and wide expanses of recessed glass keep the 12-story building from looming heavily over the street. Though the street-level facade of the **E.V. Haughwout Building**★ *(nos. 488–492)* now sports the garish red awnings of an office-supply chain, one need only lift one's eyes to see what all the fuss is about. This 1857 "Venetian palace," patterned with arched windows, balustrades and Corinthian columns, has

the oldest cast-iron facade in the city. Built for Eder V. Haughwout, a clock and chandelier merchant, the structure also housed the first safety passenger elevator, installed by **Elisha Graves Otis**.

BROOME STREET★

At Broome and Greene Streets, the 1873 **Gunther Building** *(nos. 469–475)* is a standout in cast-iron design. English-born architect **Calvert Vaux** designed the delicate cast-iron building at no. 448. **Gourmet Garage** *(no. 453)* has baked goods, sandwiches and salads. You can eat them outside on benches.

GREENE STREET★

This narrow cobblestone gulch is flanked by the richest collection of cast-iron building facades in the district. The two that are most impressive are known as the **King and Queen of Greene Street**, designed by Isaac F. Duckworth in 1872. The "queen" *(nos. 28–30)* sports a mansard roof, projecting bays and ornate dormer—all hallmarks of the Second Empire style. The cream-colored "king" *(nos. 72–76)* has a grandiose porch supported by Corinthian columns. Farther

Construction in Cast Iron

In the late 1700s, English designers began using cast iron to build textile mills. Iron frames were not only strong enough to hold up walls and ceilings, they were also much less bulky than brick and stone, thus allowing for more windows—crucial in the days before electricity. New York got its first cast-iron building in 1848, courtesy of ironmonger James Bogardus. It stood in TriBeCa until 1970, when the building was torn down. SoHo's cast-iron structures have fared better, in large part because, in 1973, most of the area was designated a historic district. The neighborhood contains the greatest concentration of buildings with cast-iron facades in the country. Architects in the 19C designed buildings with balustrades, cornices and columns. Then they commissioned ironmongers like Bogardus to render those facades in cast iron, which was fitted to a building. Once a mold was made, a design could be reproduced over and over again, allowing architects to mix and match elements as they saw fit. The technique flourished through the 1890s, when the development of steel framing and elevators made possible much taller commercial structures, and residential tastes turned back to brick and stone.

north on Greene, at 112–114 Prince Street, you'll find a building whose facade looks like cast iron but is actually a trompe l'oeil design painted on brick by artist Richard Haas in 1975. Notable galleries on Greene Street include the **Artists Space Gallery** *(no. 38)*, **Arcadia Gallery** *(no. 51)* and **Pomegranate Gallery** *(no. 133)*. Notable stores on Greene Street include **Anna Sui** *(no. 113)* and the dazzling **Moss** *(no. 150)*.

WEST BROADWAY★

SoHo's premier corridor for fashion, art and dining is anchored on its southern end by the **SoHo Grand Hotel** *(no. 310)*, built in the 1990s. **Bob & Kenn's Broome Street Bar** *(no. 363)*, housed in an 1825 structure, is a pleasant neighborhood pub. By contrast, the extremely swank **Downtown Cipriani** *(no. 376)* caters mainly to those with tans and jewels. **OK Harris Works of Art** *(no. 383)* pioneered SoHo's gallery district in 1969. **Franklin Bowles** *(no. 431)* gallery deals in contemporary art. Shoppers flock to stores like **Hilfiger** *(no. 372)*, **Anthropologie** *(no. 375)* and **D&G** *(no. 434)*.

WOOSTER STREET

The tranquil block between Canal and Grand streets is what SoHo was once like: everything has an elegant utility. The structure at nos. 28–30 dates from 1879; half its facade (on its Grand Street side) was made of cast-iron in 1888. Between Canal and Broome are two important galleries: the nonprofit **Drawing Center** *(nos. 35 & 40)*, which champions historical and contemporary drawings; and contemporary **Spencer Brownstone** *(no. 33)*. You'll also find emerging artists' work at **Peter Blum Gallery** *(no. 99)*. Local designers sell jewelry and clothes at the corner of Wooster and Spring Streets. Big-name stores include **Barney's Co-op** *(no. 116)* and **BCBG Max Azria** *(no. 120)*.

MUSEUM

New York City Fire Museum

👥👤 ♿ *278 Spring St.* 🕐*Open year-round Tue–Sat 10am–5pm, Sun 10am–4pm.* 🚫*Closed major holidays.* 💲*$7.* ☎*212-691-1303. www.nycfire museum.org.*

Located in a 1904 firehouse, this colorful museum displays fire-related art and artifacts—from the mid-18C to the present. A memorial wall commemorates the 343 firefighters who lost their lives in the aftermath of the 2001 attack on the World Trade Center.

TriBeCa★

An intriguing district of warehouses, loft residences, art galleries and chic restaurants, TriBeCa was named in the 1970s by a real estate agent hoping to create an identity as hip as SoHo's for the area. The acronym, which stands for Triangle Below Canal, stuck and, indeed, it's become a very trendy place. So far TriBeCa has not been commercialized nearly to the extent that SoHo has, despite being home to dozens of celebrities. For paparazzi-dodging starlets, that is precisely its appeal.

A BIT OF HISTORY

Once used as farmland by Dutch settlers, the area known as TriBeCa was included in a large tract granted in 1705 to Trinity Church. In the ensuing century, wealthy families built elegant residences around Hudson Square (now the Holland Tunnel traffic rotary).

A produce market opened in 1813 at the western edge of the neighborhood, but the quarter remained primarily residential until the mid-19C, when the shipping and warehousing industries formerly located at the South Street Seaport moved to deepwater piers on the Hudson River. Five- and six-story "store and loft" buildings, many with cast-iron or terracotta facades, were built around TriBeCa to accommodate the new

MTA **Subway:** 6, N, Q, R train to Canal St. or 1 train to Franklin St.

Map: Following pages.

Location: Technically TriBeCa is not a triangle but a trapezoid. Its boundaries are (clockwise from north) **Canal Street**, **Broadway**, **Barclay Street** and the **Hudson River**. Greenwich and Hudson Streets are the main thoroughfares for dining and nightlife; art and design stores are scattered throughout the district, especially on Duane, Franklin and White Streets.

Don't Miss: The TriBeCa Film Festival in late Apr–early May.

trade. By 1939 Washington Market, as the area along Greenwich Street came to be known, had a greater volume of business than all the other markets in the city combined.

In the 1960s, urban renewal projects called for the demolition of many old buildings along the waterfront. Their replacements (like the Borough of Manhattan Community College on West Street) are regarded as misbegot-

West Broadway

P. Orain/MICHELIN

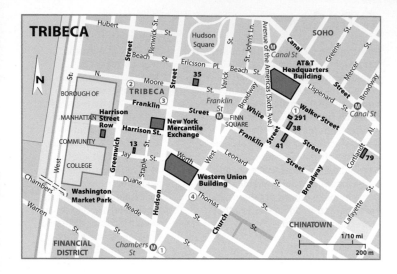

HOTEL		RESTAURANTS	
Cosmopolitan Hotel	①	Bread Tribeca	①
		Locanda Verde	②
		Nobu Next Door	③
		Odeon	④

ten eyesores. Luckily, enough of the old inland warehouse stock remained to attract artists pushed out of SoHo and others seeking industrial living space. The population grew from a mere 243 in 1970 to about 10,000 today. Loft apartments start at around $1 million.

Special Events – In late April and early May, about 300,000 film fans flock to screenings at the **TriBeCa Film Festival** (*☎646-502-5296; www.tribeca film.com/festival*). In the last weekend of the festival, TOAST, the **TriBeCa Open Artist Studio Tour**, invites visitors into the working spaces of over 70 established and emerging artists.

Art events are held concurrently at neighborhood galleries, art spaces and restaurants (*www.toastartwalk.com*).

CHURCH STREET

The nonprofit **Apexart gallery** (*no. 291; ☎212-431-5270; www.apexart.org*) shows cutting-edge art and architecture.

FRANKLIN STREET

Interior design stores such as **Urban Archaeology** (*no. 143*) line the block between Varick and Hudson Streets.

GREENWICH STREET

Thanks to this street's proximity to the Borough of Manhattan Community College and the waterfront, you'll find most of TriBeCa's foot traffic here, between Chambers and Moore streets. At its southern end sits **Washington Market Park**, with flower gardens, a large children's playground and a Victorian-style gazebo.

HARRISON STREET

Just off Greenwich Street, the so-called **Harrison Street Row** (*nos. 37–41*) is a group of restored 19C Federal-style row houses dating from 1796 to 1828. Such residences used to be common in TriBeCa, but sadly no longer. These structures (some were moved here from elsewhere in the district) are now private residences.

"Let's Do Lunch"

Near the 1 train subway station at Franklin Street and West Broadway sits **Pécan** *(130 Franklin St.; 646-613-8293)*, a gourmet-sandwich-and-salad shop where aspiring screenwriters come to kvetch. **Cosmopolitan Café** *(95 West Broadway; 212-766-3787; www.cosmopolitancafetribeca.com)* serves tasty focaccia sandwiches in a cozy setting. **Bread Tribeca** *(301 Church St.; www.breadtribeca.com; see Where to Eat)* is an industrial-chic, nouveau Italian restaurant; its half-sandwich-and-soup combo is good value. Try **Bubby's** *(120 Hudson St. at White St.; 212-219-0666; www.bubbys.com)* for homemade meatloaf, salads and pies.

HUDSON STREET

The brick and granite **New York Mercantile Exchange** *(2–6 Harrison St. at Hudson St.)* dates to 1884. The building once housed the offices of food brokers for the Washington Market. At no. 60 Hudson stands the **Western Union Building** (1930, Voorhees, Gmelin & Walker), clad with 19 shades of brick. Its vaulted lobby ceiling also features many tons of bricks. On North Moore St. just off Hudson sits **Cheryl Hazan Gallery** *(no. 35; www.cherylhazan.com)*, focusing on abstract work by emerging artists. Continue down North Moore Street to see FDNY Hook & Ladder No. 8 *(no. 14)*, otherwise known as the location that served as the Ghostbusters home base in the 1980s films.

WALKER STREET

At the corner of Walker Street and Avenue of the Americas rises the **AT&T Headquarters building** *(32 Ave. of the Americas)*, an ornate art deco tower designed by Ralph Walker in 1918. In the lobby, the original terrazzo floor and intricate wall and ceiling mosaics have been beautifully preserved. On the block between Lafayette Street and Broadway, just east of TriBeCa proper, stands **Art in General** *(no. 79; 212-219-0473; www.artingeneral.org)*, one of New York's leading nonprofit galleries since 1981.

WHITE STREET

The brick-paved stretch between Broadway and West Broadway is typically TriBeCa; many of its hulking 19C warehouses have been taken over by Downtown artists. Crowned by a mansard roof, the cast-iron structure at nos. 13–17 now contains several galleries. **Let There Be Neon Gallery** *(no. 38; www.lettherebeneon.com)* features the creations of founder Rudi Stern and other American neon artists. Launched in 1996, **The Flea** *(no. 41; 212-226-2407; www.theflea.org)* has become an acclaimed space for experimental theater artists. Its two spaces host up to four performances a week. Some are fledgling works in process; others, like *The Guys*, by Ann Nelson, are topical (often political) plays with revolving casts of A-list stars such as Sigourney Weaver, Bill Murray, Susan Sarandon and Tim Robbins. The unusual bulbous building at no. 49 is the **Synagogue for the Arts**, built in 1967 to plans by William H. Breger *(open year-round Mon & Wed–Thu 1–5pm, Tue 1–7pm; 212-966-7141; www.synagogueforthearts.org)*. It features a distinctive flame-shaped, sky-lit sanctuary, an outdoor sculpture plaza and a large gallery for events.

The Flea Theater

The Flea Theater/Spin Cycle PR

West Village★★

New York's historic bohemia contains several distinct areas. Washington Square is surrounded by classrooms and libraries of New York University. North of the square lies the village's "Gold Coast," a genteel quarter of churches, town houses and apartment buildings, most with uniformed doormen. Picturesque Greenwich Village, reaching west from Avenue of the Americas (Sixth Ave.) is lined with Federal and Greek Revival row houses. In the northwest corner, the Meatpacking District holds chic bistros and nightclubs.

MTA Subway: A, B, C, D, E, F, M train to West 4th St.-Washington Sq. or 1 train to Christopher St.

Map: Opposite.

Location: West Village stretches from Houston (pronounced HOW-stun) Street to 14th Street and from Broadway to the Hudson River.

Timing: Allow at least 4hrs to visit the West Village.

A BIT OF HISTORY

A Country Village – The area once sheltered an Algonquin Indian settlement. In 1696 British colonists founded a hamlet here called Greenwich after the town in England, now part of London.

After America won its independence from England, six parallel streets south of the area that became Washington Square Park (MacDougal, Sullivan, Thompson, Wooster, Greene and Mercer) were named for Revolutionary officers. The population of the village quadrupled in the early 19C when residents of "the city" (today's Financial District) came here seeking refuge from yellow fever and cholera, and then decided to stay.

Poets and Pagans – In the 1830s prominent families constructed elegant town houses on Fifth Avenue, north of Washington Square—today's Gold Coast. Meanwhile, homes on the Hudson River lost value as piers, markets, shipping offices and storage spaces proliferated there. In the late 19C, Irish, Italian and Chinese immigrants, and free blacks, came to live in the village, driving the "old money" uptown and creating an ethnically diverse bohemia.

Edgar Allan Poe (1809–49) was among the first writers to take advantage of the cheap rents and cultural diversions of the Village. During the early 1900s intellectuals, social reformers, artists and radicals came in droves, making the neighborhood the nexus of the American avant-garde. **Upton Sinclair** and other political rebels organized lectures, debates and all-night dances called "Pagan Routs" at the Liberal Club on MacDougal Street. A group of painters dubbed "The Eight"—or the **Ashcan school**—challenged established academic concepts and helped organize the revolutionary 1913 Armory show. Literary salons attracted such writers as **Walt Whitman**, **Mark Twain** and **Henry James**. Dozens of small theaters took root, nurturing the talents of playwrights like **Eugene O'Neill**. In the 1940s nearly all the Abstract Expressionists, including **Robert Motherwell**, **Jackson Pollock** and **Mark Rothko**, lived here.

Greenwich Village
©Jean-Marie Lanlo/Fotolia.com

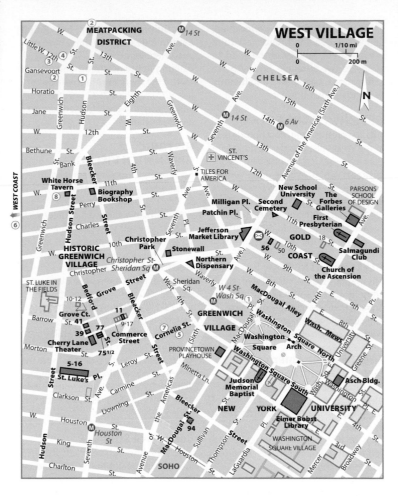

In the 1950s beat writers **Allen Ginsberg** and **Jack Kerouac** hung out and gave public readings in the Village. In the 1960s folk musicians like **Bob Dylan** made the coffeehouses and bars on MacDougal Street their second homes. **From Stonewall to Today** – Greenwich Village's ethos of tolerance has long made it a magnet for gay men and lesbians—a fact that not all New Yorkers have appreciated. A confrontation between the police and patrons of the Stonewall Inn on Christopher Street in 1969 culminated in a riot that is widely regarded as the start of the movement for gay and lesbian rights. Christopher Street's cabaret clubs, shops and bars continue to cater to a predominantly gay clientele; farther west, on Hudson, are a couple of bars with all-women clienteles. Many of those with "alternative" lifestyles have moved elsewhere, as Greenwich Village rents skyrocketed. Still, a creative and friendly attitude prevails here, largely unshackled to a nine-to-five schedule. Enjoying the cafes, shops, bars, parks and historic buildings is a full-time job.

GREENWICH VILLAGE★★

This, the prettiest and most historic part of the West Village, is the best place in the city to get lost: the skewed layout of streets west of Avenue of the Americas (Sixth Ave.) even sends locals' inner compasses spinning. For example, West 4th and West 10th Streets cross, a phenomenon unheard of in other parts of the city, where the 1811 grid prevails.

BLEECKER STREET★★

The heart of New York University's student ghetto south of Washington Square, Bleecker Street grows increasingly upscale as it makes its way northwest toward the Meatpacking District.

Avenue of the Americas to Seventh Avenue South

More Italian than Little Italy, this strip of Bleecker was called "the breadbasket of the Village" in the early 20C for its profusion of bread and pastry vendors. Today it's lined with delis, bakeries, cafes and restaurants (see Eat on Bleecker Street addresses p130).

bookbook (no. 266; ℘212-807-8655; www.bookbooknyc.com) carries books of every genre, including New York City history books and racks of half-price "remainders" (publishers' overstock).

Seventh Avenue South to Bank Street

The commercial spine of Greenwich Village is especially charming north of Grove Street, where most of the structures were built between 1820 and 1855; many have shops and restaurants on their lower floors. As a sign of the area's growing cachet, New York native **Marc Jacobs** opened six boutiques in the area, including his women's ready-to-wear and accessories lines at no. 403 (at Perry St.; ℘212-924-0026; www.marcjacobs.com). British handbag maker

Lulu Guinness and Bronx-born **Ralph Lauren** (née Ralph Lifshitz) have outposts here (nos. 394 & 381 respectively). Catering to the neighborhood's sweet tooth is the charming **Magnolia Bakery** (no. 401; ℘212-462-2572; www.magnoliabakery.com). Heavily frosted cupcakes are its specialty.

HISTORIC GREENWICH VILLAGE★★

Bounded by (clockwise from north) Christopher St., Seventh Ave. S., St. Luke's Pl. & Hudson St.
Within this area, the heart of Greenwich Village, crooked streets are lined with town houses and old trees.

Bedford Street★

This street holds three particularly noteworthy structures. Dating from 1873, **no. 75-1/2** measures only 9.5ft across, making it the narrowest house in the city; poet **Edna St. Vincent Millay** lived in it from 1923 to 1924. **No. 77**, built in 1799, is said to be the oldest house in the Village; it was originally a freestanding Federal-style frame house with its own yard. The Greek Revival brick facade was added in 1836.

Commerce Street★★

This tree-lined street feels a world apart from the hubbub of Manhattan. The group of small houses at nos. 9–17 suggests the scale of the Village in the early 19C. **Washington Irving** reputedly wrote The Legend of Sleepy Hollow while staying at **no. 11**, the home of his sister. The **Cherry Lane Theater** occupies the old barn at no. 38. A venue for Off-Broadway productions since the 1920s, it has hosted the American premieres of plays by **Samuel Beckett**, **Edward Albee** and **Eugene Ionesco**. The "twin sisters" at **nos. 39** and **41**, dating from 1831 and 1832 respectively, had their mansard roofs added in 1873. Legend has it that they were built by a sea captain for his two daughters—one for each, because they didn't get along.

Saint Luke's Place

Shaded by gingko trees and fragrant wisteria, the brick and brownstone Italianate residences at **nos. 5–16** form a stately row. They also are redolent with village literary history: poet **Marianne Moore** lived at no. 14 from 1918 to 1929; **Sherwood Anderson**, author of the interconnected stories in *Winesburg, Ohio*, lived at no. 12 in 1923. No. 16 was the home of novelist **Theodore Dreiser**.

Grove Street★

Like Bedford, Grove Street is a peaceful byway that seems miles away from feverish Manhattan. At nos. 10–12, peek through the gate of **Grove Court★**, a private alley lined with brick-fronted, white-shuttered Federal houses of the 1850s. Known as the **West Coast**, the western edge of the Village has been newly built up with celebrity-occupied glass-box apartment towers, including two by New York architect **Richard Meier**. His award-winning 16-story glass-and-steel towers overlooking the Hudson at 173–176 Perry Street at West Street (hence their name, Perry West) have a distinct international flavor; they are constructed around concrete cores to maximize views.

Christopher Park★

Christopher & Grove Sts. at Seventh Ave. S.
Established in 1837, this wedge-shaped park shelters a statue of Civil War General Philip Sheridan and sculptures of two gay couples (dedicated 1992) by George Segal. On the north side stands the **Stonewall Inn** (53 Christopher St.; 212-488-2705; www.thestonewall-innnyc.com), a popular gay bar that is situated in the original (now renovated) Stonewall Inn, site of the 1969 rebellion. The triangular **Northern Dispensary** at the east end was built in 1831 by local citizens to provide health care for the poor; it stood at the northern end of the city, hence the name. Edgar Allan Poe was treated here for a head cold in 1837. It is the only building in New York with one side on two streets (Grove &

Christopher) and two sides on one street *(Waverly Pl.)*.

Hudson Street★

This wide thoroughfare runs the length of the Village from TriBeCa on its southern end all the way up to the Meatpacking District. The stretch between Christopher and Bank Streets is lined with restaurants and cafes, most notably the **White Horse Tavern** (no. 567 at 11th St; 646-783-8979; www.whitehorsetavern nyc.com). Though largely known as the place where Welsh poet **Dylan Thomas** drank himself to death, the tavern is a landmark in its own right: built in 1880, the building is one of the few wood-framed structures remaining in the city. It's also remarkably authentic: tarnished brass chandeliers, white horse figurines, a carved oak bar, outdoor picnic tables and a neighborhood crowd make it a great spot to quaff a pint.

THE "GOLD COAST"★

The area from 9th to 13th Streets between University Place and Avenue of the Americas (Sixth Ave.) is sometimes trumpeted by realtors as the Village's "Gold Coast." Though few locals use that term, it derives from the differences between this quarter and the one south of Washington Square. In the mid-19C, it was populated by native-born, well-to-do New Yorkers.

Today much of the neighborhood lies within the Greenwich Village historic district. Note especially the remarkably preserved streetscapes on 10th, 11th and 12th Streets between Fifth Avenue and Avenue of the Americas (Sixth Ave.). Standouts on West 10th Street include **no. 56**; dating from 1832, it's one of the oldest houses in this part of the Village and retains much of its original detail, including pineapple newel posts. The playwright **Edward Albee** lived at 50 West 10th Sreet. On West 11th Street, note the structure with the angled steps at no. 18—no mere renovation, it replaced a brownstone that was blown up on March 6, 1970, when several members of the radical group the **Weathermen** accidentally detonated their cache

Tower and turrets of Jefferson Market Library

©Vladimir Korostyshevsky/Dreamstime.com

of dynamite. Three people were killed; the actor **Dustin Hoffman**, who lived next door at the time, witnessed the explosion. At nos. 72–76 lies the **Second Cemetery of the Spanish and Portuguese Synagogue**. The tiny triangular patch with a few eroded headstones is the only remnant of what was a larger square plot; burials took place here from 1805 to 1829. The composer **Charles Ives** lived next door from 1908 to 1911.

The Forbes Galleries★

62 Fifth Ave. at W. 12th St. Open year-round Tue–Wed & Fri–Sat 10am–4pm. Closed major holidays. 212-206-5548. www.forbesgalleries.com.

In seven small rooms on the ground floor of the Forbes Building, home of the well-known business magazine, thousands of toys, paintings and historical objects attest to the collecting enthusiasms of three generations of the Forbes family. Due to the fact that architect Thomas Hastings died midway through the project, the grand building was jointly designed by Carrère and Hastings (New York Public Library) and Shreve and Lamb (Empire State Building); it was completed in 1925. The galleries were the repository of the largest collection of Fabergé Easter eggs in the world (9 of 50) until February 2004,

when Forbes sold the eggs for more than $100 million. Many interesting collections remain here, however, among them: 12,000 **toy soldiers** arranged in battle scenes; more than 500 **miniature boats**, ranging from Noah's ark to ocean liners; Abraham Lincoln's opera glasses; and the bill for Paul Revere's ride.

Jefferson Market Library★

425 Sixth Ave. at W. 10th St. Open Mon & Wed 10am–8pm, Tue & Thu 10am–6pm, Fri–Sat 10am–5pm. Closed major holidays. 212-243-4334.

A profusion of pinnacles, gables, Gothic arches, turrets and traceried windows makes this red-brick building a cherished landmark. Charged with designing a courthouse, architects Frederick Clarke Withers and Calvert Vaux found inspiration in King Ludwig II's Neuschwanstein Castle in Bavaria, Germany. The completed courthouse (1877) now houses a branch of the New York Public Library. Behind it lies a formal garden managed by volunteers from the community (*open May–Oct Tue–Sun afternoons only*).

Across the street from the library there are two secret little enclaves: **Patchin Place** and **Milligan Place**. On the north side of West 10th Street, between Avenue of the Americas (Sixth Ave.) and Greenwich Avenue, sits Patchin Place. Theodore Dreiser and **e.e. cummings** once lived in these 1848 boardinghouses. Behind an iron gate on Avenue of the Americas (Sixth Ave.), between West 10th and West 11th Streets, the houses of Milligan Place date from 1852.

Church of the Ascension

36–38 Fifth Ave. at W. 10th St. Open year-round Mon–Fri noon–1pm & 5.30–6pm, Sun for services only. 212-254-8620. www.ascensionnyc.org.

Built of local brownstone, this Gothic Revival Episcopal church (1841) was designed by Richard Upjohn. Of particular interest in the soaring interior, remodeled by Stanford White in 1888, is John La Farge's superb mural of the

Ascension above the altar; the stained-glass windows, some of which were also designed by La Farge (they are illuminated at night); and the box pews.

First Presbyterian Church of New York

12 W. 12th St. ⏰*Open year-round Mon, Wed & Fri noon–12.30pm, Sun for services only.* ☎*212-675-6150. www.fpcnyc.org.*
Designed by Joseph C. Wells, this brownstone church was modeled after the Church of St. Saviour in Bath, England, with its tower inspired by that of Magdalen College, Oxford University. It was completed in 1846 for a congregation that formed in 1716. It now hosts a preschool as well as an active senior center.

New School University

66 W. 12th St. between Fifth & Sixth Aves. ☎*212-229-5488 (box office). www.newschool.edu.*
Originally founded in 1919, the New School for Social Research became known as the "university in exile" when intelligentsia fleeing Hitler's Germany took posts here in the 1930s. It merged with the Parsons School of Design *(66 Fifth Ave. between W. 12th & W. 13th Sts.)* in 1970 and with the Mannes College of Music in 1989. Today 9,400 students are enrolled in graduate and undergraduate programs here. Designed by Joseph Urban in 1930, the building, with its black-and-white-striped facade, is an early example of modern architecture in Manhattan. Its stunning **auditorium** is the setting for readings and literature forums, many open to the public.

Salmagundi Club

47 Fifth Ave. between E. 11th & E. 12th Sts. ⏰*Open year-round Mon–Fri 1–6pm, Sat–Sun 1–5pm.* ☎*212-255-7740. www.salmagundi.org.*
Built in 1852, this brownstone is the last survivor of what used to be a row of similarly grand private residences lining lower Fifth Avenue. Since 1917 it has been home to the Salmagundi Club, the oldest artists' club in the country.

Famous members include John La Farge, Louis Comfort Tiffany and Stanford White. Today's members of the club take painting and art appreciation classes and display their work in first-floor galleries, which are open to the public.

WASHINGTON SQUARE AREA★

The chunk of the Village bounded by West 8th Street, Broadway, Houston Street and Avenue of the Americas (Sixth Ave.) is anchored by Washington Square. Though architecturally disparate, the area is largely defined by the presence of **New York University**★ **(NYU)** founded in 1831 by Albert Gallatin, secretary of the Treasury under Thomas Jefferson. One of the largest private universities in the country, NYU has a student population of more than 40,000 and a steadily rising reputation among high school seniors. Applications to this so-called "dream school" increased by 300 per cent in the 1990s, and today its academic standing rivals that of some Ivy League schools.
NYU's Tisch film school is especially prestigious, having spawned directors **Spike Lee**, **Martin Scorsese** and **Oliver Stone**.

WASHINGTON SQUARE★

Originally a marshland and a favorite hunting ground of the colonists, the site was purchased by the city in 1788 for use as a potter's field and public gallows. (A large tree in the northwest corner of the park is the infamous Hanging Elm, thought to be one of the oldest trees in the city.)
In 1826 the square was officially designated as the Washington Military Parade Ground, and a fashionable residential enclave grew up around it.
Today the square is a haven for skateboarders, students, street musicians, hot-dog vendors, "speed chess" players (in the southwest corner of the park; hold on to your wallet) and in late May and early September, visual artists who come for the annual **Washington Square Outdoor Art Exhibit**.

Washington Arch★

Designed by architect Stanford White and fabricated with Tuckahoe marble, the 30ft-wide, 77ft-high triumphal arch commemorates the centennial of George Washington's inauguration as the first US president. Gracing its north face are two sculptures of Washington—as a soldier (by Herman MacNeil) and as a civilian (by A. Sterling Calder, father of the renowned 20C sculptor Alexander Calder). On the south side, note the frieze with the American eagle, the W for Washington at the center, and the trumpet-blowing statues. The arch underwent a $3 million restoration in 2003–04, and in 2005 the city allocated $16 million to redesign the park entirely. The controversial plan recentered the park's central fountain and included a perimeter fence that can be locked at night. Renovations eventually moved forward over the protests of some in the community who felt the plans would compromise the park's freewheeling character.

Washington Square North★

Often referred to as "the Row" for its concentration of 1830s Greek Revival town houses, this is the most attractive side of the square. The oldest structure (no. 20) was built in 1828–29, widened in 1859, and had a fourth story added in 1880. Nos. 7–13 and nos. 21–26 make up

Washington Arch
©Blaney Photo/iStockphoto.com

the rest of the Row. **Henry James'** novel *Washington Square*, written in 1881, was set in his grandmother's house, which once stood at no. 18. Famous residents include the painter **Edward Hopper**; architect **Richard Morris Hunt**; and **John Dos Passos**, who wrote *Manhattan Transfer* while living at no. 3.

Washington Mews

This quaint alley, with its cobblestone pavement, contained stables and servants' quarters for the town houses on Washington Square North. The structures now house NYU offices. Similarly picturesque, **MacDougal Alley** (*just off MacDougal St. between Washington Sq. West & W. 8th Sts.)* has been home to sculptor **Gertrude Vanderbilt Whitney**, whose gallery at 151/2–171/2 was the precursor to the **Whitney Museum of American Art**; painter **Jackson Pollock**, who stayed at no. 9 in 1949–50; and poet **Edwin Arlington Robinson**, who wrote his Pulitzer Prize-winning book *Tristram* in 1927 at no. 1.

Asch Building

29 Washington Pl. E. at Greene St.
Located just a block east of Washington Square, this is the site of the worst factory fire in New York City history. The top three floors were occupied by the Triangle Shirtwaist Company when, on March 25, 1911, a blaze broke out in the eighth-floor cutting room. Fed by thousands of pounds of fabric, the fire spread rapidly, sending panicked workers (the vast majority of whom were young Jewish women and girls) to fire exits that had been locked by proprietors and fire escapes that collapsed with the weight of escapees. A total of 146 workers died, dozens by jumping to their deaths in Washington Place. The tragedy sparked protests against unsafe working conditions throughout the country, and prodded the government to enforce workplace safety standards.

Washington Square South

The farrago of buildings here ranges in style from NYU's **Elmer Bobst Library** (*no. 70)*, a stark, red-sandstone cube de-

Evening in the Meatpacking District

©Age/Photononstop

signed by Philip Johnson and Richard Foster in 1972, to **Judson Memorial Baptist Church**★ *(no. 55)*, designed by Stanford White in 1893. The latter structure is clad in yellow brick, limestone and terra-cotta and adorned with elaborate Greco-Romanesque and Renaissance details. Ring the bell at 239 Thompson Street during business hours *(☾open Mon–Fri 10am–6pm)* and someone might let you in to see the superb stained-glass windows by John La Farge.

ADDITIONAL SIGHTS
MacDougal Street
Vestiges of Little Italy remain on the stretch between Houston and Bleecker Streets, where you'll find a few famous Italian cafes – **Caffe Reggio** *(no. 119; ☎212-475-9557; www.cafereggio.com)* and **Caffe Dante** *(no. 79; ☎866-681-0299; www.caffe-dante.com)*. Both have sidewalk tables and serve espresso, beer and wine, and Italian pastries and sandwiches late into the night. **Bob Dylan** owned and occupied the brownstone at **94 MacDougal Street** for a short period in the 1960s.

MEATPACKING DISTRICT
A Bit of History
Bounded by West 15th, Hudson Street, Gansevoort Street and the Hudson River, the northwest corner of the West Village

has blossomed into an uber-hip shopping, dining and clubbing destination. In the 1850s New York was the largest center of beef production in the country; slaughterhouses, meatpacking plants and storage facilities lined both its east and west sides.

For 19 years, **Herman Melville** worked in the Meatpacking District as an outdoor customs inspector. But as refrigeration technology improved, many of the big meat companies moved their facilities to the Midwest, closer to where the cattle were. Not that New York residents minded: the industry was increasingly seen as a public health hazard, especially after **Upton Sinclair** published *The Jungle* in 1906. In the late 1940s, the slaughtering district on the east side was cleared to make way for the United Nations, and later the practice was banned from the city altogether. The Meatpacking District was a rather dangerous place until the 1990s: after meat wholesalers would close for the day, drug dealers and prostitutes would prowl its cobblestoned streets.

The booming economy, along with Mayor **Rudy Giuliani**'s effective, yet controversial, crime policy in the early 1990s, cleaned up the neighborhood, and though some meat companies remain in business, its grit is for the most part a fashion accessory.

©David Brabyn/Corbis

The High Line

Paralleling the Hudson River between Gansevoort and 34th Streets, a 1930s elevated railroad bed looms 35ft above the bustling thoroughfares. Climb on up and you'll find one of Manhattan's unique public spaces: a pleasant, airy corridor of gardens, benches, water features and paths bending gently among the surrounding buildings with views of the river and the cityscape. It's a great place for a stroll. Plans call for the park eventually to extend all the way from the Meatpacking District to Penn Station. (🅘 *For more information, call* ✆ *212-206-9922 or go online to www.thehighline.org.*)

Restaurants, Clubs and Shops

Hotspots come and go with headspinning frequency here. Enduring restaurants include **Pastis** (🕭 *See Where to Eat*) and **Spice Market** *(403 W. 13th St. between Washington St. & Ninth Ave.;* ✆ *225-675-2322; www.spicemarketnewyork.com)*. Both are packed to the rafters at night; be sure to reserve ahead to avoid spending your evening in line. As a clubbing district, the Meatpacking District seems to have some staying power. Be ready to stay up late; some spots don't even start cranking until the wee hours (and music continues to thump in the not-so-wee hours). And dress to impress: the doormen can be highly selective about who gets in.

A few nightspots to look into: **Kiss & Fly** *(409 W. 13th St. between Ninth Ave. & Washington St.;* ✆ *212-255-1933; www.kissandflyclub.com)* and **Cielo** *(18 Little West 12th St.;* ✆ *212-645-5700; www.cieloclub.com)*.

That both **Stella McCartney** and the late **Alexander McQueen** chose to open their first boutiques on West 14th Street *(between Ninth & Tenth Aves.)* in 2002 says a lot about the sizzle of the district. Check out their clothing-as-art

at nos. 429 and 417 respectively. **Jeffrey New York** *(no. 449)* is a mini-mall of ultra-expensive togs run by a former shoe buyer for Barneys. The inside of **Diane von Furstenberg**'s shop *(874 Washington Ave. at 14th St.)* resembles a glittering jewel box.

ADDRESSES

🍷 EAT

BLEECKER STREET

Murray's Cheese Shop *(no. 254;* ✆ *212-243-3289; www.murrayscheese. com)* stocks more than 250 cheeses from countries all over the world. On hand are home-made bread, imported olive oil, and sausage. Murray's makes a mean panino.

Pasticceria Rocco *(no. 243;* ✆ *212-242-6031; www.roccospastry.com)* serves up delicious Italian ice. Relative newcomer **Amy's Bread** *(no. 250;* ✆ *212-675-7802; www.amysbread.com)* is a bright, friendly corner cafe, where you can get inventive sandwiches such as roast turkey on semolina, raisin and fennel bread, as well as all manner of cakes, cookies and muffins.

East Village★

This village is the center of alternative culture in New York: rock concerts, poetry readings and Off-Off Broadway theater productions take place here nightly. It's also one of the best places in the city to shop for books, records and vintage clothes.

A BIT OF HISTORY

The Beginnings – In 1651 Peter Stuyvesant, the Dutch-born director-general of the New Netherland colony, purchased the land bounded by today's 17th Street, 5th Street, Fourth Avenue and the East River—virtually the entire East Village—from the Indians for use as a farm. Though he lived Downtown while the colony was under Dutch rule, Stuyvesant withdrew from public affairs in 1664 after surrendering to the English, and moved to his manor house on what is now Stuyvesant Street.

In Transition – Briefly in the early 1800s, the district west of Second Avenue boasted fashionable town houses; the working-class neighborhoods farther east were home to Polish, Ukrainian and German immigrants until the early 20C. In the 1950s the area's low rents attracted writers and artists such as **Jack Kerouac** and bebop saxophonist **Charlie Parker** (they lived at 501 East 11th Street and 151 Avenue B respectively). The term "East Village" was coined in the early 1960s to distinguish the neighborhood from the rest of the

Subway: 6 train to Astor Pl. or F train to Second Ave.

Map: Following pages.

Location: This neighborhood is bounded by 14th Street, Avenue D, Houston Street and Broadway.

Timing: Allow at least 2hrs; more for browsing bookstores.

Lower East Side, of which it had previously been considered a part. The new name also linked this bohemia with the longer-lived artistic community in **Greenwich Village** across town. The glory days of the East Village were the 1980s, when rock bands like the **B-52s**, **Talking Heads** and the **Ramones** made names for themselves at the (former) legendary club **CBGB & OMFUG (Country, Bluegrass, Blues and Other Music for Uplifting Gourmandizers)**.

Today's East Village – The East Village today contains vestiges of almost all chapters of its history. Most of its side streets are lined by pretty 19C brownstones, spiffed-up tenements and lush trees; boutiques are scattered about on ground floors throughout the district. **St. Mark's Place**★ is the most densely commercial street (this is the name East 8th Street goes by between Avenue A and Third Avenue) in the East Village, drawing hordes of students and hippies with its sushi bars, jewelry and

St. Mark's Place

©Bertrand Gardel/hemis.fr

sunglass stalls, music stores and head shops. **Second Avenue**★ is really the district's spine, though. Here you'll find an astounding variety of ethnic eateries: Italian, Russian, Korean, Thai, Jewish and Mexican among them; First Avenue at East 11th Street is home to several traditional Italian places. Sixth Street between First and Second Avenues is known as **Little India**★ for the many festive and super-cheap Indian and Bangladeshi restaurants that line the block.

McSorley's Old Ale House *(15 E. 7th St. between Second & Third Aves.; ℘212-473-9148; www.mcsorleysnewyork. com)*, founded in 1854, is a storied dive. Celebrated in the writings of Joseph Mitchell and the paintings of John Sloan, the pub continues to offer tastes of "Old New York" as well as two types of homemade ale: light and dark. But in general the East Village attracts a very young crowd—almost all the cafes, bars, record stores and boutiques cater to patrons in their twenties and thirties who, if they are not living on a limited budget, like to pretend they are.

SIGHTS
Merchant's House Museum★
29 E. 4th St. between Lafayette St. & Bowery. ⊙*Open Thu–Mon noon–5pm.* ⊙*Closed major holidays.* ⬚$10. ℘212-777-1089. www.merchantshouse.org.
Constructed in 1832, this red-brick town house, with its Greek Revival doorway, has been transformed into a museum that illustrates the lifestyle of an affluent 19C family. Indeed, it is the only fully intact house museum in New York that provides a window on that period. Seabury Tredwell, a prosperous merchant, bought the structure in 1835. It remained in the family for 100 years. Today, three of its five stories are open to the public: the basement, which has a beehive oven and a gallery holding temporary exhibits (often drawn from the museum's collection of 19C costumes and textiles); the main floor, which has a spacious double parlor filled with Empire-style furnishings; and the second floor, which contains two bedrooms and a writing

nook. There's also a lovely 19C garden at the rear of the house.

St. Mark's Historic District★
A small historic district centers on Stuyvesant Street, which cuts across East 9th and 10th Streets between Second and Third Avenues. However "crooked" it may appear, it runs in fact almost in a true east and west direction. Peter Stuyvesant laid it out that way in the 1600s. It served as the driveway to his country house, which sat roughly at the intersection of East 10th and Stuyvesant Streets (burned down in 1778).

The Georgian-style Episcopal **St. Mark's Church-in-the-Bowery** *(131 E. 10th St. at Second Ave; ℘212-674-6377; www. stmarksbowery.org)* was built in 1799 on the site of Peter Stuyvesant's 1660 family chapel. Its Greek Revival steeple (1828) and cast-iron portico (1854) are both additions. The cast-iron fence dates from 1836. The church became heavily involved in the arts starting in 1919, when the poet Kahlil Gibran was appointed to the St. Mark's Arts Committee. Over the years Isadora Duncan, William Carlos Williams, W.H. Auden, Ben Hecht, Amy Lowell, Martha Graham and others performed. Sam Shepard had his first two plays produced here in 1964. In 1978 fire devoured the building, leaving only its stone shell. The church was rebuilt in a utilitarian fashion and continues to host many poetry readings and performances (ⓒsee *East Village Book Nooks panel, p134*). Seven generations of Stuyvesants, including Peter himself, are buried under the building. The lovely **graveyard**★ out back is paved with undulating cobblestones.

Renwick Triangle
The ivy-covered town houses hugged by East 10th Street *(nos. 114–128)* and Stuyvesant Street *(nos. 23–35)* were designed in 1861 by James Renwick, architect of St. Patrick's Cathedral.

Federal Town Houses
Two rare and well-preserved town houses from the Federal period stand on Stuyvesant Street. At **no. 21** is the

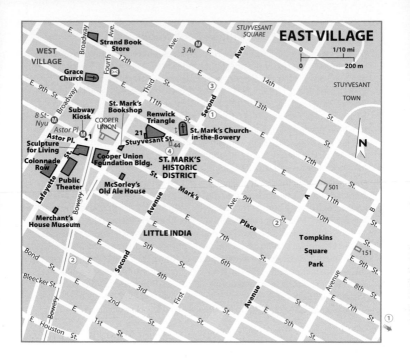

WEST VILLAGE

EAST VILLAGE

STUYVESANT SQUARE

STUYVESANT TOWN

Strand Book Store

Grace Church

St. Mark's Bookshop

Subway Kiosk

COOPER UNION

Renwick Triangle

St. Mark's Church-in-the-Bowery

Astor Pl.

21 Stuyvesant St.

Sculpture for Living

Cooper Union Foundation Bldg.

ST. MARK'S HISTORIC DISTRICT

Colonnade Row

Public Theater

McSorley's Old Ale House

Merchant's House Museum

LITTLE INDIA

Tompkins Square Park

N

HOTELS

East Village Bed & Coffee............................ ①
The Bowery Hotel.. ②

RESTAURANTS

Angelica Kitchen.. ①
Itzocan.. ②
Momofuku Ssäm Bar.................................... ③
Soba-Ya.. ④

Stuyvesant-Fish House, which was built in 1804 by Governor Stuyvesant's great-grandson Nicholas William Stuyvesant as a wedding gift for his daughter, who married one Nicholas Fish. The intent was apparently to keep an eye on the young couple: Nicholas William Stuyvesant lived at no. 44, which dates from 1795.

Tompkins Square Park★
Bounded by Aves. A & B and
E. 7th & E. 10th Sts.
Originally laid out in 1834, this 10-acre park, filled with 150-year-old elms, two dog parks, benches, flowers and fountains, is one of Downtown Manhattan's most attractive public spaces. This state of affairs is relatively recent. The park was a concert venue in the 1970s, hosting performers such as Jimi Hendrix. In the 1980s it was known as a haven for

drug dealers and homeless people. Riots broke out when the city closed the park in 1990 and tore down the bandshell, but most residents supported the move. Ongoing restoration, along with rising

Tompkins Square Park

©Jason Todd/Getty Images

133

East Village Book Nooks

Literary types love the East Village. Not only does it have a highly developed cafe culture; it has two of the finest bookstores in town. Boasting "16 miles of books" on its iconic red awning, newly expanded **Strand Book Store** *(828 Broadway at E. 12th St.; ☎212-473-1452; www.strandbooks.com)* carries thousands of used books, half-price reviewers' copies, publishers' overstock, books-on tape, and dozens of $1-a-book racks. Unlike most used bookstores, its whole inventory is online. **St. Mark's Bookshop** *(31 Third Ave. between E. 8th & E. 9th Sts.; ☎212-260-7853; www.stmarksbookshop.com)* draws arty academics with its stock of literary theory, photography books, rare 'zines and subversive fiction. It's open—and crowded—until midnight.

Local writers strut their stuff at a number of East Village haunts as well. **KGB Bar** *(85 E. 4th St. between Second & Third Aves., 2nd floor; ☎212-505-3360; www.kgbbar.com)* usually lands at the top of the heap for its A-list fiction readers, including Rick Moody and Mary Gaitskill. **The Poetry Project** *(131 E. 10th St.; ☎212-674-0910; www.poetryproject.org)* has had an all-star lineup of readers since its inception in 1966, including Allen Ginsberg; work tends toward the experimental. The **Howl! Festival**, named for Ginsberg's most famous poem, takes place in the East Village the third week in August and is chock-a-block with literary performances and events *(☎212-274-1111; www.howlfestival.com)*. **Nuyorican Poets Cafe** *(236 E. 3rd St. between Aves. B & C; ☎212-505-8183; www.nuyorican.org)* is the place to go for streetwise poetry slams.

real estate prices and plummeting crime rates, has brought back its original luster. Bars and restaurants line the west edge of the park on **Avenue A**.

Astor Place

This two-block-long street linking Broadway and Third Avenue got its name from **John Jacob Astor**, the fur-trade and real-estate magnate who helped develop the surrounding neighborhood starting in 1825. The restored

Cooper Union Foundation Building

©Tetra Images/Photoshot

1904 Astor Place **subway kiosk**, made of cast iron, stands on Astor Place between 4th Avenue and Lafayette Street (uptown trains only). Nearby is Bernard (Tony) Rosenthal's 1966 sculpture *Alamo*, a black cube rotating on one corner, which is a popular skateboard hangout.

Cooper Union Foundation Building★

Completed in 1859, this massive brownstone is the oldest extant steel-framed structure in America. It is the headquarters of **Cooper Union for the Advancement of Science and Art**, a free educational institution founded by Peter Cooper (1791–1883), a self-made industrialist, to provide formal schooling to working-class people who otherwise couldn't afford it. Its three colleges focus on architecture, engineering and art.

Sculpture for Living

Architect Charles Gwathmey intended his undulating green-glass skyscraper (2005) to stand out from its brick and brownstone neighbors, as would a piece of public art. He succeeded. Apartments from $2 million.

Grace Church

802 Broadway at E. 10th St.
🕐*Open Mon–Sat noon–5pm, Sun for services only.* 📞*212-254-2000.*
www.gracechurchnyc.org.

James Renwick, architect of the much larger **St. Patrick's Cathedral** in Midtown, designed this Episcopal church in 1846. Its recently restored spire is an elegant example of the Gothic Revival style. In 1863 circus impresario **P.T. Barnum** arranged for the rector to marry two midgets from his company: Charles S. Stratton, better known as Tom Thumb, and Lavinia Warren. Today the church hosts a regular concert series *(Tue–Fri 12.20pm; 📞212-254-2000 for schedule).* The church offers free guided tours every Sunday at 1pm.

Lafayette Street

Originally called La Grange Terrace, after Revolutionary War general Marquis de Lafayette's country estate near Paris, this stretch between Astor Place and East 4th Street was home to a social elite that included "Commodore" **Cornelius Vanderbilt** and **Warren Delano** (grandfather of President **Franklin Delano Roosevelt**) in the 19C. The remnants of four magnificent Greek Revival manses constructed in 1833 stand at nos. 428–434. They're known as **Colonnade Row** for their shared Corinthian colonnade.

John Jacob Astor had the monumental red-brick and brownstone building across the street *(no. 425)* built in 1854 to contain New York's first free library. Astor's 100,000-volume collection formed the nucleus of the New York Public Library 40 years later. The Off-Broadway **Public Theater** now occupies the building (and, it should be noted, perpetuates Astor's populist inclinations by sponsoring **Shakespeare in the Park**, a summer-long series of free plays in Central Park).

Chelsea★★

Chelsea is the center of New York's art world and gay community. It's a place of rich contrasts: busy commercial avenues intersect with quiet residential side streets, and tiny neighborhood cafes abut gargantuan dance clubs. Be sure to check out the ever-evolving waterfront area, home to the mammoth Chelsea Piers recreation complex, the Hudson River Greenway and several historic ships.

🚇 **Subway:** 1 train to 23rd St. (at Seventh Ave.) or C, E train to 23rd St. (at Eighth Ave.).
♿ **Map:** Following pages.
▶ **Location:** Chelsea is situated west of Avenue of the Americas (Sixth Ave.) between West 14th and 30th Streets.
🕐 **Timing:** Allow 3hrs to do Chelsea justice.

A BIT OF HISTORY

London Namesake – Chelsea got its name in 1750, when British army captain Thomas Clarke bought a farm bounded by West 21st and 24th Streets, Eighth Avenue and the Hudson River and named it after his London neighborhood. In 1813 the property passed to Clarke's grandson **Clement Clarke Moore** (1779–1863), an erudite scholar and literary figure who nevertheless remains best known for writing *A Visit from St. Nicholas* (also known as **The Night Before Christmas**). In the 1820s Moore helped shape the development of the district by donating a large chunk of land for the building of the General Theological Seminary, where he would later teach, and by specifying that residences had to be set back from the street behind spacious front yards. Moore also set aside land for park-like squares, giving the neighborhood a distinctly English feel, even as

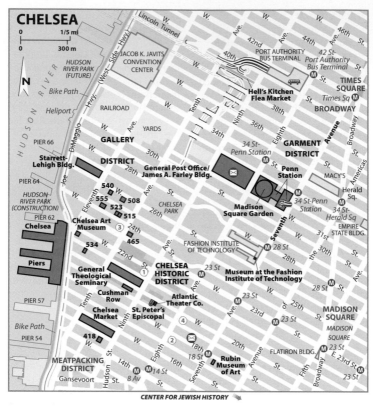

its population increasingly hailed from Germany, Italy, Scotland and Ireland. The **Hudson River Railroad** opened along Eleventh Avenue in 1851, spawning slaughterhouses, breweries and tenements. In 1871 about 50 people were killed near the intersection of West 24th Street and Eighth Avenue during a riot between Irish Catholics and Irish Protestants. From about 1905 to 1915, several motion picture studios operated here; many visiting performers stayed at the 1884 Chelsea Hotel. Hudson River dock activity began to decline in the 1960s, opening up warehouses and industrial spaces for new uses. Slowly artists moved in, and town houses began to be refurbished.

Contemporary Chelsea – More than 300 world-class **galleries** now occupy garages and lofts on the district's western flank, offering museum-quality exhibitions alongside up-and-coming group shows. On West 20th, 21st and 22nd Streets, a lovely historic district preserves Clement Clarke Moore's vision of elegant city living. For bars, diners and cafes, check out Eighth Avenue above West 16th Street.

There are two French cafes on Ninth Avenue above West 20th Street; try **La Bergamote**, a delectable French patisserie *(177 Ninth Ave. at W. 20th St.; ✆212-627-9010; www.labergamotenyc.com)*. Farther west, at Tenth Avenue, is the **Half King**, a snazzy bar and bistro co-owned by *Perfect Storm* author Sebastian Junger, and thus the sponsor of many literary events *(505 W. 23rd St. at Tenth Ave.; ☏212-462-4300; www.thehalfking.com).*

GALLERY DISTRICT★★★

⊙*Note that most galleries are closed Sun–Mon year-round; in the summer, many are open Mon–Fri only.*
For selected galleries, ☖ *see Addresses.*
Chelsea's many galleries are concentrated between West 20th and 30th Streets west of Tenth Avenue. Many visitors simply wander around, drifting in and out of street-level spaces that look interesting, but if you prefer a more organized approach, you can find comprehensive gallery listings and maps online at West Chelsea Arts *(www.westchelseaarts.com)* or oneartworld.com (the latter features various gallery districts in Manhattan). The sites also list opening receptions, which can be a fun and festive way to drink in the scene.

Chelsea Art Museum★

556 W. 22nd St. at Eleventh Ave.
☖⊙*Open year-round Tue–Wed & Fri–Sat 11am–6pm, Thu 11am–8pm).*
☜*$8.* ☏ *212-255-0719.*
www.chelseaartmuseum.org.
Housed in a three-story red-brick warehouse dating from 1850, the museum mounts a broad range of shows—from a traveling exhibition of 80 etchings by Francisco de Goya to a group show exploring the concept of the bogeyman. It is also home of the Miotte Foundation, which is dedicated to archiving and conserving the work of the French painter Jean Miotte (b.1926), an early proponent of so-called Art Informel, a school related to Abstract Expressionism that seeks to strip art of all reference to representation.

Starrett-Lehigh Building★

601 W. 26th St., between Eleventh & Twelfth Aves.
Wrapped in about nine miles of glass, this 1931 factory-warehouse is a stunning example of architecture for the machine age. Freight cars were ferried across the Hudson River from New Jersey on barges, rode the elevated High

☺ **A Bit of Advice** ☺

The closest subway stop *(C, E train to 23rd St.)* will leave you two long blocks away from most of the galleries, but the crosstown M23 *(23rd St.)* bus will take you all the way through the heart of the district and on to the waterfront and Chelsea Piers.

Line railroad into the building, and then, fully loaded, were hoisted to the upper floors by super-powered elevators. The structure was converted into offices (Martha Stewart Omnimedia and Hugo Boss are both leaseholders) and galleries in the 1990s.

Rubin Museum of Art★★

150 W. 17th St. at Seventh Ave.
☖ *See Major Manhattan Museums.*

CHELSEA HISTORIC DISTRICT★

On West 20th, 21st and 22nd Streets be-tween Ninth and Tenth Avenues stand some of Chelsea's loveliest brownstones. The well-preserved Greek Revival houses that make up **Cushman Row** *(406–418 W. 20th St.)* typify Clement Clarke Moore's vision for the neighborhood with their 10ft-deep front yards and cast-iron railings. They were

Cushman Row

built in 1840 by Moore's friend Alonzo Cushman, a merchant and banker. The pretty, green quadrangle of the **General Theological Seminary** stands across the street from the row, behind a high iron fence. The seminary and its grounds occupy the entire block bounded by West 20th and 21st Streets and Ninth and Tenth Avenues *(entrance at 175 Ninth Ave.;* ○*open year-round Mon–Fri noon–3pm, Sat 11am–4pm;* ℘ *212-243-5150; www.gts.edu)*. Note especially the 1836 fieldstone **West Building**, one of the oldest Gothic Revival structures in New York. A half-block east of the seminary sits **St. Peter's Episcopal Church** *(346 W. 20th St.; www.stpeterschelsea.com)*, which also dates from 1836 and is also in the Gothic Revival style. It was designed by Clement Clarke Moore for a congregation that outgrew its 1832 Greek Revival building (now the rectory). The hall east of the church was constructed as the church parish house in 1854; it's now home to the **Atlantic Theater Company** *(336 W. 20th St.;* ℘ *212-645-8015; www.atlantictheater. org)*, founded in 1985 by playwright **David Mamet** and actor **William H. Macy**. The theater company presents a full schedule of Off-Broadway plays.

ADDITIONAL SIGHTS
Chelsea Piers★
Pier 62 (West Side Hwy. at W. 23rd St). ℘ *212-336-6666. www.chelseapiers.com.* There is little that this gargantuan facility, a prime example of adaptive reuse, can't offer sports enthusiasts. In 1995 four long-neglected piers were turned into a sports complex that contains an ice-skating rink, a bowling alley, a pool, batting cages, a full-service health club (New York's largest), a toddler gym, a rock climbing wall, indoor soccer and basketball courts, beach volleyball courts, a kayak launch and even a driving range at which more than 100 million golf balls have been hit. Call or consult the website for information on specific sports and activities.

Center for Jewish History
15 W. 16th St. between Fifth & Sixth Aves. ○*Open Mon & Wed 9.30am–8pm, Tue & Thu 9.30am–5pm, Fri 9.30am–3pm, Sun 11am–5pm.* ○*Yeshiva University Museum galleries (⊜$8) open Tue, Thu & Sun 11am–5pm, Wed 11am–8pm (⊜free 5–8pm), Mon 3.30–8pm (⊜free), Fri 11am–2.30pm (⊜free).* ○*Closed Jewish & major holidays.* ℘ *212-294-8301. www.cjh.org.* This facility, the result of the artful merging and reconfiguration of four Chelsea brownstones, opened in 2000. Home to five organizations—the YIVO Institute for Jewish Research, the Yeshiva University Museum, the Leo Baeck Institute, the American Jewish Historical Society and the American Sephardi Federation—the center contains the largest collection of Jewish cultural and historical material outside Israel. Some 100 million archival documents, manuscripts and photos; 500,000 library volumes; and tens of thousands of artifacts, works of art and

Chelsea Piers

Peter Wrenn/MICHELIN

Flea Market

On weekends, scores of amateur dealers gather at **Hell's Kitchen Flea Market** near the Lincoln Tunnel *(West 39th St. between Ninth & Tenth Aves.)* to display an amazing collection of junk, antiques, and odds and ends. Joined by the Annex Market (formerly of Chelsea), the outdoor market is one of the city's largest, drawing an eclectic crowd. Try your luck and look for a silver frame or a vintage hat, but be sure to bargain and check the merchandise before paying *(☎212-243-5343; www.hellskitchenfleamarket.com).*

Hell's Kitchen Flea Market
Hell's Kitchen Flea Market

ritual objects are available to scholars and displayed on a rotating basis in the attractive central atrium and in galleries throughout the center. Also on the premises are a reading room, a kosher cafe and a theater.

Chelsea Market

75 Ninth Ave. between W. 15th & W. 16th Sts. A canny example of adaptive reuse, this 1898 Nabisco factory (where, in 1912, the Oreo cookie was first made) was reopened in 1997 as an urban food market *(☉open year-round Mon–Sat 7am–9pm, Sun 8am–7pm; www.chelseamarket.com).* Interspersed with stores selling flowers, meat, cheese and other gourmet essentials are cafes and bakeries, a Thai food restaurant and several soup-and-sandwich shops that are perfect for a quick bite. Free wireless internet access is available throughout the building.

GARMENT DISTRICT

Just north of Chelsea lies the Garment District, a somewhat dank, largely commercial area that runs roughly from West 30th Street to West 40th Street between Broadway and Eighth Avenue. The main drag is **Seventh Avenue**, also known as Fashion Avenue.

Though very little manufacturing is done in the district, fabric and notions stores abound, especially on West 38th and 39th Streets. To best appreciate the area's history, go to the **Museum at the Fashion Institute of Technology** *(Seventh Ave. at W. 27th St.; ☉open*

year-round Tue–Fri noon–8pm, Sat 10am–5pm; ☉closed major holidays; ☎212-217-4558; www.fitnyc.edu/museum), where student and expert work alike (Calvin Klein is an alumni) is on display in several large galleries. Also in the beautification business, wholesale potted-plant and flower vendors line both sides of West 28th Street *(between Sixth & Seventh Aves).* A few blocks north, between West 31st and 33rd Streets, stands **Madison Square Garden** and, underneath it, **Penn Station**—a vast entertainment and retail complex that is widely regarded as the worst architectural disaster in New York history.

The concrete cylinder, which seats 20,000 spectators above a cramped, airless train depot, replaced the original 1906 Penn Station, designed by McKim, Mead and White. Considered the firm's greatest local work, the cast-iron and glass structure was torn down in 1963 and replaced by the current eyesore, which hosts the New York Knicks, the Westminster Dog Show and arena rock shows *(☎212-465-6741 box office; www.thegarden.com).* In 1999 plans were announced to right this historic wrong by converting the nearby **General Post Office/James A. Farley Building** *(421 Eighth Ave. between W. 31st & 33rd Sts.; ☎212-967-8585)*—a companion McKim, Mead and White structure completed in 1908—into a new rail hub. But to date, little progress has been made on the project, other than a new funding initiative in mid-2007.

ADDRESSES

🎭 CHELSEA GALLERIES

Gagosian – *555 W. 24th St. between Tenth & Eleventh Aves. ☎212-741-1111. www.gagosian.com.* Larry Gagosian's 20,000sq-ft gallery was inaugurated in 1999 in a Richard Serra show. Other A-listers (Damien Hirst, Anselm Kiefer, Ed Ruscha) have since been featured.

Gladstone Gallery – *515 W. 24th St. between Tenth & Eleventh Aves. ☎212-206-9300. www.gladstonegallery.com.* This SoHo émigré shows work by top video and conceptual artists, including Matthew Barney.

Greene Naftali – *508 W. 26th St., 8th floor. ☎212-463-7770. www.greene naftaligallery.com.* The light-drenched eighth-floor gallery showcases international conceptual art.

Lehmann Maupin – *540 W. 26th St. between Tenth & Eleventh Aves. ☎212-255-2923. www.lehmannmaupin.com.*

Rem Koolhaas designed this simple gallery space, where you'll find a range of up-and-coming works.

Matthew Marks – *523 W. 24th St. between Tenth & Eleventh Aves. ☎212-243-0200. www.matthewmarks.com.* Arguably the most famous of Chelsea's galleries, Matthew Marks has shown work by Lucian Freud, Nan Goldin, Willem de Kooning, Jasper Johns, Weegee and others.

Paula Cooper – *534 W. 21st St. & 465 W. 23rd St. ☎212-255-1105. www.paulacoopergallery.com.* Long a champion of conceptual and minimalist art, Cooper has three spaces in Chelsea. The work of Zoe Leonard, Andres Serrano, Donald Judd and Sherrie Levine have shown here.

Wooster Projects – *418 W. 15th St. between Ninth & Tenth Aves. ☎212-871-6700. www.woosterprojects.com.* This Pop and contemporary art gallery has had museum-quality exhibitions of work by Andy Warhol and others.

Union Square★
Madison Square★

Large 19C and early 20C buildings, both brick and cast iron, line Broadway, Fifth Avenue and Avenue of the Americas. Originally built as department stores, many of them now house national chains selling clothing or furniture. A few blocks east sits the quiet Gramercy Park neighborhood, with its lovely brownstones and big drooping trees. It centers on an idyllic private square for which you need a key to get in. In Madison Square, at the north edge of the district, you'll begin to feel the thrum of Midtown, especially on weekday afternoons, when office workers, dog-walkers and tourists alike line up for hot dogs and ice cream at the art deco Shake Shack and enjoy them on the outdoor terrace.

🚇 **Subway:** L, N, Q, R, 4, 5, 6 train to Union Sq. or N, R train to 23rd St.

♿ **Map:** Following pages.

▶ **Location:** The area that stretches from 14th to 26th Streets between Third and Avenue of the Americas (Sixth Ave.) is primarily a retail district linking Downtown and Midtown.

▶ **Timing:** Gramercy Park is great for strolling and, in its vicinity, lunch; good cafes abound around Irving Place. At East 14th Street, on the south edge of the district, Union Square offers bountiful local produce and homemade foods (cheese, honey, baked goods) four days a week at its popular farmers' market, the city's largest.

SIGHTS
The sights below are arranged from south to north.

UNION SQUARE★
Bounded by East 14th and East 17th Streets, Union Square East (Park Avenue) and Union Square West (University Place), Union Square is a pleasant park, crisscrossed with bench- and tree-lined paths. It got its name in the early 19C because it marked the intersection (union) of two streets: Broadway and Fourth Avenue. The park opened in 1831 and by the mid-19C, it formed the groomed and gated centerpiece of an elegant residential and entertainment district. In the late 19C **Tiffany's** jewelry store, Brentano's books, and the restaurant **Delmonico's** (now located near Wall Street) faced the square.

As the city spread northward, so did the rich (into sprawling palaces on Fifth Avenue). In the early 20C Union Square became a popular place for rallies and demonstrations, thanks to the fact that several labor unions and radical publications had offices nearby. In the early 1960s **Andy Warhol** established his pop-cultural "Factory" (site of many of his movies and parties) in the ornate **Decker Building** (1893) at 33 Union Square West; it has since been converted into condos and a wine store.

The Park Today – Several statues grace Union Square, most notably **George Washington** (south) and **Abraham Lincoln** (north), both by Henry Kirke Brown, and the **Marquis de Lafayette** (east), by Frédéric-Auguste Bartholdi, better known as the sculptor of the Statue of Liberty. The tiered plaza on the southern end of the park still serves as a stage for protesters, who often have to share space with break-dancers and other performers. It can be quite a spectacle, a point not lost on the dozens of young people who sit on the steps on sunny days. Artists often display (and try to sell their work) near the renovated subway kiosk at the southwest corner of the park.

The north end of the park was renovated in 2008, adding new playspaces and

Union Square Greenmarket
Peter Wrenn/MICHELIN

public areas and spiffing up the public plaza and historic bandshell pavilion. Plans have been announced to open a restaurant in the pavilion.

Union Square Greenmarket★
Farmers, bakers, flower growers, ranchers and artisanal food makers from all over New York, Pennsylvania, New Jersey and even New England bring their bounty to the south plaza of Union Square every Monday, Wednesday, Friday and Saturday year-round (*stalls open 8am–6pm, weather permitting; www.grownyc.org*). Each season has its charms: in the spring come flatbed trucks full of perennials, herbs and tomato plants for rooftop gardens; in the summer, abundant produce; in the fall, apples galore, as well as hot cider and fresh doughnuts. A few farmers even show up in the winter to sell cheese, meat, pies and potatoes.

GRAMERCY PARK★
New York City's only private park anchors this tranquil, old-fashioned neighborhood known for its lovely architecture and good cafes and restaurants. The area was laid out in 1831 by developer Samuel B. Ruggles, who drained an old marsh (the word Gramercy is a corruption of a Dutch phrase meaning "little crooked swamp") to build a new residential enclave. Patterning the area after London's residential squares, he sold more than 60 lots with the promise that owners would have exclusive access to the park at its center, between 20th

and 21st Streets a half-block east of Park Avenue South—indeed, they still do. The city's elite built grand homes on the square beginning in the 1840s; apartment buildings catering to the middle classes went up in the 1870s. By the early 20C artists and intellectuals, including **Eugene O'Neill** and **Nathanael West**, moved in. Their presence was short-lived; the **West Village** soon beckoned, but their legacy remains in two of the city's oldest bars. O. Henry supposedly wrote his classic 1905 short story "The Gift of the Magi" in **Pete's Tavern** *(129 E. 18th St. at Irving Pl.; ☎212-473-7676; www.petestavern.com)*, a cozy pub that has been in continuous operation since 1864. Dating from 1892, the **Old Town Bar** *(45 E. 18th St. between Broadway & Park Ave. South; ☎212-529-6713; www.oldtownbar.com)* is a local favorite, with its high tin ceiling, long mahogany bar and juicy hamburgers.

Gramercy Park★

Enclosed by an 8ft-high cast-iron fence to which only local residents have keys, Gramercy Park consists of formal gardens, paths, benches and trees dating back to Ruggles' time; in the center stands a statue (1916, Edmont Quinn) of Shakespearean actor Edwin Booth (brother of John Wilkes Booth, President Lincoln's assassin), dressed to play his favorite role, Hamlet. Around the park are several notable buildings:

Gramercy Park West★ presents a harmonious front of red-brick town houses. **Nos. 3** and **4**, designed by Alexander Jackson Davis in 1846, boast elaborate cast-iron porches, reminiscent of those found in New Orleans. No. 4, the former home of **James Harper**, mayor of New York in 1844 and one of the founders of Harper & Bros. (now HarperCollins) publishers, is flanked by a pair of iron lanterns called "mayor's lamps": the mayor could request to have such lamps installed in front of his house to facilitate locating him in case of nighttime emergencies.

Gramercy Park South is home to two distinguished private clubs. At no. 15 stands the **National Arts Club★** *(www.*

nationalartsclub.org)*, which occupies the former home of **Samuel Tilden**, New York's governor from 1874 to 1876 and US presidential candidate in 1876. The mansion originally consisted of side-by-side 1840s brownstones, but in the 1870s Tilden had them overhauled and linked by **Calvert Vaux**, the co-designer of Central Park and the Metropolitan Museum of Art.

The result is a stunning example of 19C architecture and design, complete with bay windows, Gothic ornamentation, Victorian furniture and exquisite stained-glass ceilings (by **John La Farge** and **Donald MacDonald**). The club, which moved into the house in 1906 and has more than 2,000 elected members in all branches of the arts, sponsors some 200 events a year here *(☉open Sept–Jun)*; visual artists are represented in the basement galleries *(call ☎212-475-3424 for hours)*. Next door, at no. 16, is **The Players**, a club for thespians founded in 1888 by Edwin Booth in what was then his home. The 1845 brownstone *(☛closed to the public)* was renovated in the Greek Revival style by **Stanford White**.

On **Gramercy Park East** are two fancy apartment buildings. Dating from 1883, no. 34 is a red-brick Queen Anne-style tower with an octagonal turret corner. The entrance to the white terracotta Gothic Revival building at no. 36 (1910) is flanked by two concrete knights.

Theodore Roosevelt Birthplace National Historic Site★

28 E. 20th St. ☉Open year-round Tue–Sat 9am–5pm. ☉Closed major holidays. ☛Period rooms by guided tour (30min) only, on the hour 10am–4pm, except noon. ☎212-260-1616. www.nps.gov/thrb.

This 1920s brownstone was built to reproduce as closely as possible Teddy Roosevelt's childhood home, an 1848 brownstone that stood on the site until 1916.

32nd President of the US – A driving force in US politics for 40 years, **Teddy Roosevelt** (1858–1919) was vice president of the US in 1901 when President

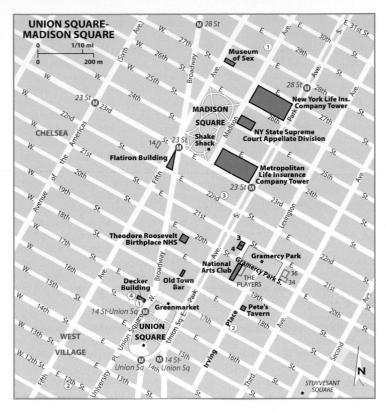

UNION SQUARE-MADISON SQUARE

0 — 1/10 mi
0 — 200 m

Museum of Sex ①

MADISON SQUARE

New York Life Ins. Company Tower

NY State Supreme Court Appellate Division

Shake Shack

CHELSEA

Flatiron Building

Metropolitan Life Insurance Company Tower

Theodore Roosevelt Birthplace NHS

Gramercy Park

National Arts Club

Decker Building

Old Town Bar

THE PLAYERS

14 St-Union Sq

Greenmarket

Pete's Tavern

UNION SQUARE

WEST VILLAGE

Union Sq 14th Union Sq

STUYVESANT SQUARE

N

HOTELS		RESTAURANTS	
The Carlton Hotel	①	Blue Water Grill	①
Inn at Irving Place	②	Gotham Bar and Grill	②
		Tamarind	③
		Union Square Cafe	④

William McKinley was assassinated by an anarchist in Buffalo, New York. Teddy succeeded to the Oval Office and won himself a second term in 1904. In 1908 he backed William Taft for the top job but, unhappy with Taft's performance, ran against his onetime friend in 1912. Taft and Roosevelt split the progressive vote, handing victory to Woodrow Wilson. But politics was only one of Roosevelt's passions: a hunter-naturalist, he gathered a large collection of wildlife specimens, which he later donated to the American Museum of Natural History and other institutions. He also gave his name to the **teddy bear** and won the Nobel Peace Prize for his mediating efforts between Russia and Japan.

His Boyhood Home – Teddy Roosevelt's parents, Theodore Sr. and Martha Bulloch, moved into the original house in 1854, and in 1858 Teddy was born. The Roosevelts were members of the city's elite; at the time, Gramercy Park was New York's most fashionable neighborhood. But by the 1870s high society began moving northward, and after a year in Europe in 1872, the Roosevelts, too, moved uptown, to a new house at 6 West 50th Street. The Gramercy Park brownstone was torn down in 1916 to make way for a commercial building, but after the former president died three years later, a citizens group raised money to purchase the site and rebuild it. Teddy's two sisters, as well as his niece

143

Quick Bite

The coffee at **71 Irving Place Coffee and Tea Bar** (*☎212-995-5252; www.irvingfarm.com*) was voted the best in the city by *New York Magazine*, thanks no doubt to the fact that the beans are roasted in small batches upstate. Home-made quiche, waffles, sandwiches, soups and cookies are also served in the inviting garden-level space, which is open both early (*🕐7am on weekdays, 8am on weekends*) and late (*🕐daily until 11pm*).

Eleanor Roosevelt, consulted with the architects on the color schemes, floor plan and other details to make the house appear as it did in 1865–72, Teddy's formative years.

Visit – Nearly 40 per cent of the furnishings are original to the house; another 20 per cent belonged to other family members. Tour guides bring visitors through five period rooms.

MADISON SQUARE★

This lovely 6-acre park has been transformed in the new millennium into one of Downtown's most inviting public spaces. Bounded by East 23rd and 26th Streets and Madison and Fifth Avenues, it was once part of a military parade ground. It was named after President **James Madison** in 1814, and in 1845 served as the playing field for the city's first baseball club, the New York Knickerbockers. From the 1850s to the 1870s the park was the center of an aristocratic neighborhood; author **Edith Wharton** was born at 14 West 23rd Street in 1862. From the 1870s to 1925 a succession of entertainment venues stood on the north end of the square, including the first two (of four) arenas called Madison Square Garden. Stanford White designed the second one in 1890 and was killed in a duel on its roof in 1906; the 8,000-seater was demolished in 1925 to make room for the New York Life Insurance Company building. Today Madison Square Garden stands 10 blocks north of Madison Square, in the Garment District.

Madison Square Park Today – Thanks to the efforts of the Madison Square Park Conservancy, the park is now a popular gathering place for people who live and work in the area. Old-fashioned benches and well-tended plantings line curving paths. In 2002 a children's playground opened on the east side of the square. The conservancy also commissions installations by prominent artists such as **Sol LeWitt**, whose *Curved Wall with Towers* graced the park in 2005. The most popular newcomer, however, is the

Madison Square

Allison Simpson/MICHELIN

Shake Shack (2004, James Wines), an ivy-covered, zinc-clad food kiosk at the park's south end that serves up burgers, ice-cream sundaes, shakes and cones as well as hot dogs, wine and beer (*open daily 11am–11pm; 212-889-6600; www. shakeshacknyc.com*). Surrounding the park are several landmark buildings.

Flatiron Building★★

Even if you've never been to New York City, you've likely seen this building before—it's a popular backdrop in television shows and movies. Viewed from the north side (the side that faces Madison Square Park), it looks like an iron (hence the name), the acute angle of its facade formed by Broadway and Fifth Avenue. Though it's only 6ft wide on this sharp corner, the building rises 22 stories straight up from the sidewalk. Famed Chicago architect Daniel Burnham designed the structure, which was finished in 1902. It features limestone at the bottom, then brick and terra-cotta on the upper floors. The Flatiron Building's enormous cornice makes its looming presence above the street even more pronounced.

Flatiron Building

©E. Riege/hemis.fr

Metropolitan Life Insurance Company Tower★

Madison Ave. between E. 23rd & E. 24th Sts.

LeBrun & Sons designed this tapered 700ft tower to resemble the campanile of St. Mark's in Venice, Italy. It was the tallest building in the world upon its completion in 1909. Today the tower is a fixture on the skyline, especially at night, when it looks like a glowing lantern. Note the enormous four-sided clock; its hour hand weighs 700 pounds.

New York State Supreme Court Appellate Division★

Madison Ave. at E. 25th St.

A Corinthian colonnade and about 30 figures by 16 sculptors—the most sculptors to work on a single building in the US—deck the exterior of this white marble building (1899, James Brown Lord). The marble sculptures, which weren't finished until 1901, represent allegorical figures such as Wisdom, Peace and Justice, as well as figures in legal history, such as Moses, Confucius and Justinian. Daniel Chester French, best known for his seated Abraham Lincoln in Washington, DC, created Justice (fourth from left on 25th Street).

New York Life Insurance Company Tower★

51 Madison Ave. between E. 26th & E. 27th Sts.

Woolworth Building architect Cass Gilbert designed this 40-story Gothic Revival tower (1928), which stands on the site of Stanford White's Madison Square Garden. Its pyramidal crown is prominently in the nighttime skyline.

Museum of Sex

233 Fifth Ave. at E. 27th St. Open Fri–Sat 10am–9pm, Sun–Thur 10am–8pm. Closed Thanksgiving Day & Dec 25. $16.75. Minimum age 18. 212-689-6337. www.museumofsex.com.
The graphic nature of this collection may come as a shock. Past exhibits, which occupy three nondescript galleries, have traced the history of the sex industry in New York City.

Midtown Manhattan is the New York City you probably pictured as a kid—big and glitzy, full of fast-walking, fast-talking business people, spangled showgirls and towering skyscrapers with postcard views. But that's not all there is. You'll also find quiet side streets, pleasant parks and world-class art, if you know where to look. Stretching from 34th Street to 59th Street from the Hudson River to the East River (the entire width of Manhattan), Midtown is made up of several very distinct areas.

How Manhattan Is Divided

- **Downtown**
  South of 34th Street

- **Midtown**
  34th Street to 59th Street

- **Uptown**
  North of 59th Street

- **East Side, West Side**
  Fifth Avenue marks the dividing line

Fifth Avenue is New York's most elegant thoroughfare. Famous for its upscale department stores and fancy boutiques, it's also home to the **Empire State Building** *(at 34th St.)* and **St. Patrick's Cathedral** *(at 50th St.)*. Brash **Times Square**, at Broadway and 42nd Street, is just the opposite: everything here, from the peanut vendors to the taxis to the billboards, competes for a piece of your senses. As you proceed north on Broadway, you'll find yourself in the heart of the country's largest **Theater District**, where the curtain rises on up to 40 live shows every night. Be sure to catch one.

Avenue of the Americas, also known as Sixth Avenue, is the spine of **Central Midtown**, which changes from block to block. At its southern end stands **Macy's** department store, a New York institution, and famous for its Thanksgiving Day parade.

Between 40th and 42nd Streets spreads picturesque **Bryant Park** (the de facto backyard of the **New York Public Library**). Between 48th and 51st Streets stands **Rockefeller Center**, a masterpiece of urban planning that's also home to NBC studios and the city's most famous skating rink. Keep heading

Fifth Avenue

©Vladi Sytnik/New York Image

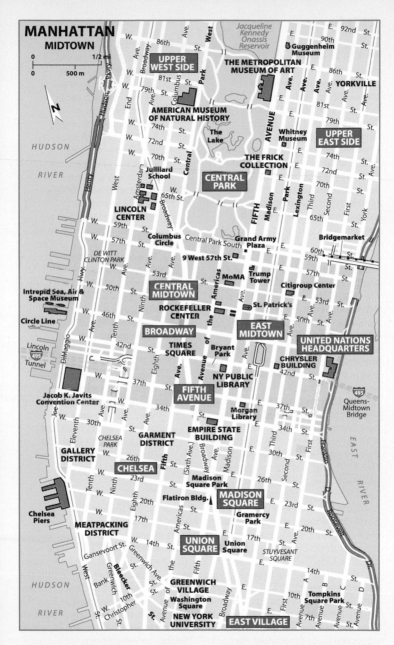

MANHATTAN
MIDTOWN

0   1/2 mi
0   500 m

N

HUDSON RIVER

Jacqueline Kennedy Onassis Reservoir

Guggenheim Museum

UPPER WEST SIDE

THE METROPOLITAN MUSEUM OF ART

YORKVILLE

AMERICAN MUSEUM OF NATURAL HISTORY

The Lake

Whitney Museum

UPPER EAST SIDE

THE FRICK COLLECTION

Julliard School

CENTRAL PARK

LINCOLN CENTER

Columbus Circle

Central Park South

Grand Army Plaza

Bridgemarket

9 West 57th St.

DE WITT CLINTON PARK

MoMA

Trump Tower

Citigroup Center

Intrepid Sea, Air & Space Museum

CENTRAL MIDTOWN

St. Patrick's

Circle Line

ROCKEFELLER CENTER

EAST MIDTOWN

Lincoln Tunnel

BROADWAY

TIMES SQUARE

Bryant Park

UNITED NATIONS HEADQUARTERS

CHRYSLER BUILDING

Jacob K. Javits Convention Center

NY PUBLIC LIBRARY

Queens-Midtown Bridge

FIFTH AVENUE

Morgan Library

EMPIRE STATE BUILDING

EAST RIVER

GALLERY DISTRICT

CHELSEA PARK

GARMENT DISTRICT

CHELSEA

Madison Square Park

MADISON SQUARE

Chelsea Piers

Flatiron Bldg.

MEATPACKING DISTRICT

Gramercy Park

UNION SQUARE

Union Square

STUYVESANT SQUARE

HUDSON RIVER

Gansevoort St.

GREENWICH VILLAGE

Washington Square

Tompkins Square Park

NEW YORK UNIVERSITY

EAST VILLAGE

---

north and you'll hit the new and vastly expanded **Museum of Modern Art**. East of Fifth Avenue, the area known as **East Midtown** contains some of the city's finest office buildings, from the art deco **Chrysler Building** to the Modernist **Lever House**, as well as the

spectacular Beaux-Arts **Grand Central Terminal**.

Finally, all the way at the East River, you'll find the headquarters of the **United Nations**, where some 5,500 people from 192 countries work to create a more peaceful world.

Fifth Avenue★★★

New York's most prestigious thoroughfare, Fifth Avenue between 34th Street and 57th Street is studded with striking landmark skyscrapers and churches, exclusive boutiques and grand public buildings. Elaborate department-store window displays at Christmastime make this well-traveled stretch even more festive, as do some of the city's grandest parades.

MTA Subway: B, D, F, M, N, Q, R train to 34th St.-Herald Sq.

Map: Following pages.

Location: Despite the presence of such mass-market ventures as American Girl Place and NikeTown, Fifth Avenue remains quite soigné, especially as you approach 57th Street, where the most expensive boutiques, as well as a number of top-notch art galleries, are clustered. It also tends to be crowded.

Timing: If you're short on time, visit Saks, Tiffany, Bergdorf Goodman and the New York Public Library during the day; and save the Empire State Building until evening. Otherwise start at the Empire State Building and walk north. To escape the clangorous daytime activity, retreat to one of the peaceful church sanctuaries, or duck into one of the area's posh hotel bars, such as the King Cole Bar in the St. Regis or TY in the Four Seasons.

A BIT OF HISTORY

Millionaires' Row – This part of Fifth Avenue has always been a magnet for the rich. In the 1860s the Irish-born department-store mogul **A.T. Stewart**, New York's wealthiest resident at the time, erected a splendid marble mansion at Fifth Avenue and 34th Street. The opposite corner—the site now occupied by the Empire State Building—was dominated by the huge brownstone of hotelier **William Astor**. The American railroad tycoon **Jay Gould** built a residence on the corner of Fifth Avenue and 47th Street, while the rival **Vanderbilt** dynasty established itself around 50th Street. So great was the concentration of wealth along Fifth Avenue that it became known as Millionaires' Row. Gradually through the 1880s, however, horse-drawn buses made the avenue more accessible to the masses—and thus less desirable to the elite. After **Caroline Astor** (William's wife and the self-appointed leader of New York high society) relocated to 65th Street in 1893, the city's movers and shakers followed suit, their mansions filled by, or demolished to make room for, high-end boutiques and fancy department stores.

34TH TO 51ST STREETS

Empire State Building★★★

350 Fifth Ave. between W. 33rd & W. 34th Sts. &⚪*Observatory open year-round daily 8am–2am (last elevator up at 1.15am).* ✆*$21 (*⚪*see A Bit of Advice box, p150).* ✆*212-736-3100. www.esbnyc.com.*

Strength and grace combine to make this the most famous skyscraper in the world and the quintessential New York landmark. Topping out at 1,454ft, it is the city's tallest building, and one of the few you can actually experience. Visit the tower's 86th-floor, 360-degree open-air observatory for the stomach-dropping height and jaw-dropping view.

A Bit of History

A Prestigious Site – From 1857 to 1893 the site was home to two mansions belonging to William and Caroline Astor. After the couple left in the 1890s, their son and nephew tore these down and built the jointly run Waldorf and Astoria hotels on the property. In October 1929, the hotels were demolished to make way for the Empire State Building. (The "new" Waldorf-Astoria Hotel opened two years later on Park Avenue.)

Up in a Jiffy – Building the Empire State Building was a purely speculative venture. In the 1920s New York City was experiencing a real-estate boom, and former New York State governor Al Smith, along with two investors, wanted to get in on the action. Unfortunately, their timing was off: contracts were signed just weeks before Black Tuesday, the start of the Great Depression. Nonetheless, construction went forward, sometimes at a furious pace. At the peak of operations, 3,500 workers added more than a story a day to the building's steel frame. The job was com-

Empire State Building

Peter Wrenn/MICHELIN

Empire State Building Q&A

Who designed it?
Shreve, Lamb, & Harmon Assocs., a local architectural firm.

Where does the name come from?
From George Washington, who allegedly referred to New York as the Empire State (for its economic strength) in 1784.

How tall is it?
86 stories to the top of the tower, 102 stories to the top of the "mooring mast," 124 stories to the top of the antenna.

How many elevators are there?
73, including 6 freight elevators, operating at speeds from 600ft to 1,400ft per minute. It is possible to ride from the lobby to the 80th floor in 45 seconds.

How many steps?
1,860, though the 100 or so participants in the annual Empire State Building Run-Up, held in early February, climb "only" 1,576 of them. The record was set in 2003 by Paul Crake, who made it to the top in just nine minutes and 33 seconds.

Do the colors of the lights on the tower at night have any significance?
Yes. The top 30 stories are illuminated from dusk to midnight in three tiers of color to reflect the day or the season. It's easy to guess what some colors mean (red, white and blue on July 4, green on Saint Patrick's Day), but much harder to guess others (red, yellow and green for Portuguese Independence Day, purple and white for Alzheimer's awareness). The Empire State Building's website has a complete schedule.

Is the Empire State Building ever struck by lightning?
Yes, about 100 times a year; its 22-story antenna acts as a lightning rod.

Does anyone ever get married on top of the Empire State Building?
Yes. The building hosts weddings once a year, on Valentine's Day. On February 14, 2009, 13 couples were married there.

😊 A Bit of Advice 😊

Queues for the observatory tend to be shortest first thing in the morning. Note that even if you have a **CityPass**, you will still have to wait in line twice: first to get through the security checkpoint and then for an elevator. If you don't have a CityPass, you will have to stand in line to buy tickets as well. The only way to avoid all lines is to buy a $45 express pass in advance from the Empire State Building ticket office.

"mooring mast," and the 86th floor was set aside as a ticket office and waiting room, but after one precarious trial run in 1932, the scheme was abandoned. In 1933 the building was scaled by a giant gorilla and his blond sweetheart in the movie *King Kong*. Then In 1945 an errant bomber plane crashed into the 79th floor, killing 14 people, including the crew (the building was structurally unharmed). A TV antenna was added to the mooring mast in 1953. At its tip is a flashing beacon that serves as a warning signal for aircraft.

pleted 45 days ahead of schedule and $5 million under budget.

The Best-Laid Plans – At the opening ceremonies on May 1, 1931, Smith bragged that the building would help usher in the age of the blimp. The distinctive 16-story spire atop the building was intended to be a dirigible

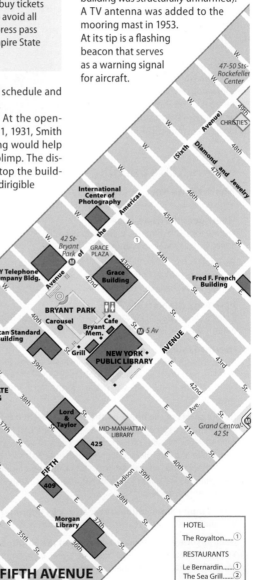

FIFTH AVENUE

HOTEL	
The Royalton......①	
RESTAURANTS	
Le Bernardin......①	
The Sea Grill......②	

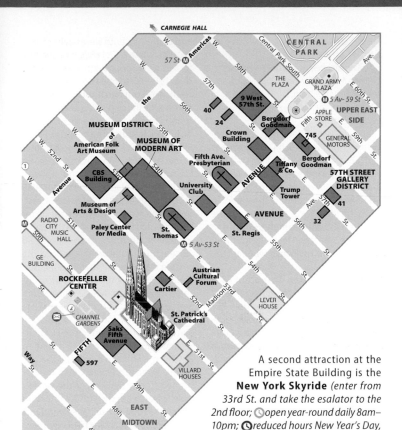

A second attraction at the Empire State Building is the **New York Skyride** *(enter from 33rd St. and take the esalator to the 2nd floor; ☉open year-round daily 8am–10pm; ☉reduced hours New Year's Day, Thanksgiving & Dec 25; ✍$41, $52 combined ticket includes Empire State Building Observatory; ☎212-279-9777; www.skyride.com)*, a 30min virtual-reality aerial tour of famous New York City landmarks guided by famous actors.

Lord & Taylor

424–434 Fifth Ave. between W. 38th & W. 39th Sts. ☎212-391-3344. www.lordandtaylor.com.

New York's oldest department store—the flagship of a national chain—was founded in 1826 by Samuel Lord and George Washington Taylor as a dry-goods store in Chinatown. After a brief stint on the Lower East Side, the store expanded (in 1860) into a five-story marble building on **Ladies' Mile**. Lord & Taylor moved to its present location in 1914. The Fifth Avenue store is particularly cherished for its elaborate holiday window displays on view during November and December.

To get to the **86th-floor observatory**★★★, enter the EmpireState Building from Fifth Avenue. There will be a sign inside the entrance indicating the total wait time and the visibility level. The highest visibility level posted is 25 miles, and it is said that on clear days the **views**★★★ extend 80 miles, all the way to the Berkshire Mountains in Massachusetts.

On overcast days the view can be less than a mile. If you decide to proceed, take the escalator to the second floor and get in line. Bags larger than an airline carry-on are not allowed, and there is no coat check, so pack lightly. Enjoy the view!

New York Public Library★★★

Fifth Ave. between W. 40th & W. 42nd Sts.
⟲Open Mon & Thu–Sat 10am–6pm,
Tue–Wed 10am–8pm, Sun 1–5pm.
⟲Closed major holidays. ✆917-275-
6975. www.nypl.org.

The crown jewel of New York City's library system, this Beaux-Arts masterpiece (1911) by Carrère and Hastings contains some of the most spectacular interiors in the city, as well as one of the largest research collections in the world. In 2008 the library was rechristened the **Stephen A. Schwarzman Building** to honor the Wall Street heavyweight who committed $100 million to renovate the landmark.

In the mid-19C, when this part of Fifth Avenue was known as "Millionaires' Row," New York didn't have a single public library. Instead, there were two private libraries that were accessible to the public free of charge. One was the **Astor Library**, a reference collection opened in 1849 with funds bequeathed by **John Jacob Astor** (1763–1848), a self-taught German immigrant who at the time of his death was the wealthiest man in America. The other was the **Lenox Library**, which consisted mainly of rare books, manuscripts and Americana. Neither institution allowed patrons to check out books and by the end of the 19C, both were having financial difficulties. A $2.4 million bequest by former New York governor **Samuel Tilden** (1814–86) to open a free library and reading room in the city made it possible to combine the collections and to build a grand structure to house them.

The NYPL Is Born – The New York Public Library's (NYPL) first director, a former army surgeon and librarian named Dr. John Shaw Billings, came up with the basic floor plan for the library: seven stories of stacks directly below a vast, light-filled reading room. Requests for books would be sent down to the stacks via pneumatic tubes; the books would be sent up on dumbwaiters (indeed, the system is so efficient that it is still used today). Carrère and Hastings incorporated Billings' demands into their exquisite design. Shortly after the cornerstone was laid in 1901, industrialist **Andrew Carnegie**, a champion of public libraries nationwide, offered $5.2 million to establish 65 branch libraries if the city would agree to maintain them. The city agreed. Today the NYPL is the world's only research library with a circulating branch system (there are currently 85 neighborhood branches). The NYPL also has more cardholders (2.32 million) and more materials (10.5 million items in circulation; more than 50 million total) than

Lion sculpture at the entrance of the New York Public Library

any other public library in the nation. Holdings range from well-thumbed pot-boilers to a Gutenberg Bible.

Exterior – Sculptor Edward Clark Potter created the two marble lions that flank the library's grand staircase. Sometimes referred to as Patience and Fortitude, they quickly became the library's mascots; a lion's head features prominently on most NYPL publications. In warm weather, the vast front **terrace** is dotted with folding chairs and food vendors. This is but a taste, as it were, of glorious **Bryant Park**, which unfolds behind the library toward Avenue of the Americas (Sixth Ave.) and which is especially popular at lunchtime in good weather.

Interior – The library's grand white-marble lobby, **Astor Hall**, contains a staffed information desk. Pick up a floor plan and inquire about the day's events (readings, lectures, performances). Major exhibitions on historical and literary themes are held in **Gottesman Hall**, which stands directly behind Astor Hall. The richly paneled **DeWitt Wallace Periodical Room**, with its 13 murals by Richard Haas, lies at the end of the corridor to your left. This is where Wallace, the founder of *Reader's Digest*, spent countless hours condensing articles for his legendary magazine. Climb the main staircase (or take the elevator) to the third floor. The soaring **McGraw Rotunda** at the top of the steps is adorned with murals depicting the recorded word. It is flanked by the **Salomon Room**, a 19C picture gallery that presents small rotating exhibits, and the Bill Blass Public Catalog Room. Proceed through the catalog room to the **Rose Main Reading Room**, which is arguably the most enchanted public space in the city. Nearly two city blocks long, it has intricately carved woodwork, 51ft ceilings covered with cerulean murals, and long oak tables dotted with brass reading lamps. You can also request to see any of the collection's 431,000 maps in the ornate Beaux-Arts **Map Division**; the collection specializes in cities, with a particular focus on New York.

Saks Fifth Avenue, Saint Patrick's Cathedral in the background

©Colin Paterson/Pictures Colour Library

Saks Fifth Avenue

611 Fifth Ave. between E. 49th & E. 50th Sts. 212-753 4000. www.saks.com.

Though now the epitome of Fifth Avenue luxe, Saks has humble roots. The original store was founded in 1902 by Andrew Saks (1847–1912), a former peddler, near Herald Square. His son Horace opened this store, Saks Fifth Avenue's flagship, in 1924. Today there are 46 Saks stores in 22 states. In December of each year, the Fifth Avenue store's holiday window displays are a popular complement to the nine-story Christmas tree across the street at **Rockefeller Center**.

Saint Patrick's Cathedral★★

Fifth Ave. between E. 50th & E. 51st Sts. Open year-round daily 6.30am–8.45pm. 212-753-2261. www.saintpatrickscathedral.org.

St. Patrick's Cathedral looks positively quaint amid the skyscrapers of Midtown today, but when the site was chosen in the 1850s, New Yorkers complained that it was too far out in the country. At the time, of course, the city's population was clustered downtown, but church officials correctly predicted the general migration northward.

Native New Yorker **James Renwick** (1818–95) was chosen to design the new cathedral in large part because his design for Grace Church in the East Village, completed in 1846, was so well received. Construction on St. Patrick's began in 1859 and was supposed to take eight years. Instead, thanks to the intrusion of the Civil War, it took twenty. The church was dedicated in 1879 but was still not complete. The 330ft spires were added in 1888. St. Patrick's is reminiscent of the cathedral of Cologne, Germany. Missing, however, are the extensive stone carvings (owing partially to the use of granite, a hard stone) and the flying buttresses, hallmarks of Gothic architecture.

Inside, the cathedral follows a typical cruciform plan. Three portals with intricately sculpted bronze doors open into the spacious nave, which is illuminated by stained-glass Gothic windows. A series of slender marble pillars supports the cross-ribbed vaults, which rise 110ft above the nave. Note also the graceful baldachin over the high altar, by Renwick, and the monumental organ. Located behind the apse, the Lady Chapel was added in 1906. The cathedral hosts a series of free organ, chamber music and choir concerts yearly *(check the website for schedule)*.

52ND TO 57TH STREETS
Austrian Cultural Forum
11 E. 52nd St. Open year-round Mon–Sat 10am–6pm. 212-319-5300. www.acfny.org.

This severe sliver of a building (2002, Raimund Abraham) asserts Austria's presence in the New York cultural scene. The 24-story tower presents a jagged edge to the street, its sloped, glass-wall facade marked by protruding beams and overlapping setbacks. The interior is stark but serene. Three levels of galleries and a 90-seat theater present multimedia work by Austrian artists.

Saint Thomas Church★
1 W. 53rd St. at Fifth Ave. Open year-round Mon–Fri 7.30am–6.30pm, Sat 9am–3pm, Sun 7am–6pm. Guided tours (1hr) Sun 12.30pm. 212-757-7013. www.saintthomaschurch.org.

Topped by a single tower, this Episcopal church by Cram, Goodhue and Ferguson was completed in 1913. Gothic Revival in style, it was the fourth building to house the congregation, which was formed in 1823 in what is now SoHo. Today the church is well known for its all-male choir, which performs at Sunday services and in concerts both at the church and worldwide. The church also offers a series of organ recitals *(check website for concert schedules and tickets)*.

A wealth of statues and delicate tracery adorns the facade on Fifth Avenue. In the center of the main portal, Saint Thomas, flanked by six of the apostles, welcomes worshippers. The remaining apostles are arrayed overhead in the tympanum.

Detail of the facade, St. Thomas Church

Architecture Buffs

As you saunter up Fifth Avenue, take special note of these Fifth Avenue architectural gems:

Former Tiffany's store
no. 409, at E. 37th St. Tiffany & Co. occupied this Renaissance Revival corner building from 1905 (the year the structure was completed) until 1940, when the jeweler moved to its present location at 727 Fifth Avenue *(at E. 57th St.)*. Architect Stanford White based his design on the Palazzo Grimani in Venice.

No. 425 Fifth Avenue
Famed post-Modernist architect Michael Graves was the force behind this slender tower (2003). Faced with yellow brick and white limestone, it tapers up 55 stories.

Fred F. French Building
no. 551, at E. 45th St. The real-estate developer had his 1927 headquarters built with typical art deco pizzazz. From the polished-bronze entrance, the structure rises 38 stories in a series of massed setbacks, culminating in colorful friezes.

Former Scribner's Bookstore
no. 597, between E. 48th & E. 49th Sts. A vast wall of iron and glass lets copious light into a two-story vaulted store, once full of books. It was designed in 1913 by Ernest Flagg, architect of the Singer Building in SoHo.

Cartier
no. 651, at E. 52nd St. A century ago Fifth Avenue was lined with Renaissance Revival mansions like this one, built in 1905. The French jeweler Cartier acquired the building and turned it into a shop in 1917.

University Club
1 W. 54th St. at Fifth Ave. Charles McKim of McKim, Mead and White designed the 1900 headquarters of this private social club in the Italian Renaissance style. Adorning the building's three-tiered granite exterior are the shields of major American universities, all carved by Daniel Chester French, creator of the Lincoln statue in Washington, DC's Lincoln Memorial.

St. Regis Hotel
2 E. 55th St. at Fifth Ave. The Beaux-Arts-style St. Regis (1904) was commissioned by John Jacob Astor IV as one of the first luxury hotels in the city. Note the Maxfield Parrish mural in the swank King Cole Bar, transported here after the Knickerbocker Hotel in Times Square closed in 1921.

Trump Tower
no. 725, at E. 56th St. This flamboyant glass-sheathed tower, designed by the firm Der Scutt, is most interesting for the steep setbacks on its Fifth Avenue facade, which are lushly planted with trees and shrubs (☞ *no longer accessible to the public, unfortunately*). Several levels of upscale shops surround the pink marble lobby.

Crown Building
no. 730, at W. 57th St. The chateau-like crown of this French Renaissance tower (1921, Warren & Wetmore)

©Erick Nguyen/BigStockPhoto.com

Trump Tower

9 West 57th Street, with the "9" sculpture

©Peter Foley/epa/Corbis

is richly embellished in 23-carat gold leaf. The Museum of Modern Art opened its first gallery here, on the 12th floor, in 1929 and later housed the headquarters of Playboy Enterprises.

9 West 57th Street★
9 W. 57th St. A twin to the Grace Building at the corner of Avenue of the Americas (Sixth Ave.) and West 42nd Street, this striking high rise of dark glass and white travertine (1974, Skidmore, Owings & Merrill) swoops up from a broad base to become a flat panel topping out at 50 stories. The chunky red "9" sculpture on 57th Street is the work of graphic designer Ivan Chermayeff.

57TH STREET GALLERY DISTRICT
Midtown anchor of the New York art world, 57th Street is home to more than 60 high-end galleries, many of which contain museum-caliber work. Here's a sampling of the more celebrated dealers:

Mary Boone
745 Fifth Ave., 4th floor. ☏212-752-2929. www.maryboonegallery.com. The doyenne of the SoHo gallery scene of the 1980s puts on strong shows by young artists, often women, in her gallery above Bergdorf's.

Her blockbusters show in her larger space in Chelsea.

David Findlay Jr. Fine Art
41 E. 57th St., 11th floor. ☏212-486-7660. www.davidfindlayjr.com. Specializes in American 19C and 20C masters, American modernists from 1910 to 1950 (the Ashcan school, the Steiglitz Group) and American contemporary art.

Marian Goodman
24 W. 57th St., 4th floor. ☏212-977-7160. www.mariangoodman.com. Carries a slate of well-known artists, including Jeff Wall, Dan Graham, Gerhard Richter, Lawrence Wiener, William Kentridge and Thomas Struth.

Marlborough Gallery
40 W. 57th St., 2nd floor. ☏212-541-4900. www.marlboroughgallery.com. Handles a number of important estates, such as those of James Rosati and Jacques Lipchitz, as well as the work of Fernando Botero, Red Grooms and Tom Otterness.

The Pace Gallery
32 E. 57th St., 2nd floor. ☏212-421-3292. www.thepacegallery.com. Represents contemporary heavy hitters like Sol LeWitt, Chuck Close and Kiki Smith. The gallery recently hosted a major retrospective of the drawings of Louise Nevelson.

Michael Rosenfeld
24 W. 57th St., 7th floor. ☏212-247-0082. www.michaelrosenfeldart.com. Shows 20C American art in all media. The gallery specializes in WPA (1930s–40s) Realists and Modernists.

Edwynn Houk
745 Fifth Ave. ☏212-750-7070. www.houkgallery.com. Specializes in 20C photography, with an emphasis on the 1920s and 30s. Dorothea Lange (estate), Annie Leibovitz, Elena Dorfman and Robert Polidori are represented here.

Below the sculptures, bas-reliefs depict the legend of Saint Thomas. Step to the left of the main portal to admire the narrow "Brides' Entrance," decorated with symbolically joined hands.

On entering the nave, note the lovely **reredos** of Dunville stone that rises to a height of 80ft above the altar. Numerous recesses shelter statues of Christ, the Virgin Mary, the apostles and other saints, carved by **Lee Lawrie**, sculptor of the monumental bronze *Atlas* at Rockefeller Center. Also of interest are the stained-glass windows in deep reds and blues, the pulpit and the sculptured organ case. *The Adoration of the Magi* at the end of the narthex is attributed to Peter Paul Rubens.

Fifth Avenue Presbyterian Church

7 W. 55th St. ◐*Open Jun–Sept Mon–Fri 9am–5pm, Sat–Sun 8am–4pm; rest of year Mon–Fri 9am–5pm, Sat 8am–5pm, Sun 8am–4pm.* ◑*Closed holidays.* ℘*212-247-0490. www.fapc.org.*

This Gothic Revival church (1875) is one of the last churches built in brownstone in the city. The sanctuary, with a seating capacity of 1,800, is notable for its magnificent organ casing and an intricately carved ashwood pulpit.

Tiffany & Co.

727 Fifth Ave. at E. 57th St. ℘*212-755-8000. www.tiffany.com.*

Stop to gaze at the sparkling window displays at the legendary jewelry store, Tiffany & Co. It was founded as a stationery store by New Yorkers Charles L. Tiffany and John B. Young in 1837. Charles' son **Louis Comfort Tiffany**, the famous stained-glass artist, took over the business upon his father's death in 1902 and sold his jewelry and enamels here. The store's international reputation was sealed by Truman Capote in his novella *Breakfast at Tiffany's* and the subsequent movie starring Audrey Hepburn. It remains the place for watches, engagement rings and silver.

Bergdorf Goodman

745 & 754 Fifth Ave. at 58th St. ℘*800-558-1855. www.bergdorfgoodman.com.*

Considered the most elegant and understated of Fifth Avenue's department stores, Bergdorf was founded in 1894 as a tailor and furrier, gradually moving into elite women's fashion in the first part of the 20C. It acquired the present site *(no. 754)* in 1928, and in 1990 bumped its popular men's department across the street *(to no. 745)*.

Like many of the other major Fifth Avenue stores, Bergdorf is noted for its eye-catching window displays.

Bergdorf Goodman

©Ellen Rooney/Axiom/age fotostock

Broadway★★

Times Square★★
and Theater District★

Broadway–Times Square is quintessential New York—sensory overload, in which car horns blare, sidewalks overflow with pedestrians, giant billboards glow and spin, and megastores lure shoppers not just with products but with retail "experiences." Intermingled with such global commercialism is a 100-year-old tradition of local, live entertainment. Jammed shoulder to shoulder in the Theater District are nearly 40 historic venues where you can catch everything from a Shakespeare play with a Hollywood cast to a musical performed by life-size puppets.

TIMES SQUARE★★

Throughout the 19C, Times Square was known as Longacre Square and was a center for horse trading and harness making. But when the **The New York Times** decided to build a new headquarters in the trapezoidal plot formed by Broadway and Seventh Avenue between 42nd and 43rd Streets, publisher Adolph Ochs asked that the name of the area be changed accordingly. The city granted his wish, and the new building, at One Times Square, was grandly christened on December 31, 1904. As part of the festivities, Ochs arranged for a brightly lit "time ball" to be lowered from atop the building precisely at midnight, a tradition that continues to this day. Roughly a million revelers converge on the square each **New Year's Eve** to count down as the ball drops, and nearly a billion more watch the spectacle on television.

The Great White Way – In the first decade of the 20C, Times Square overtook the Bowery as the city's entertainment district. **Vaudeville houses** sprung up around the square, which was newly accessible via subway by 1904 and train by 1913, the year of Grand Central Terminal's completion. In 1916 a city zoning bill encouraged the construction

MTA **Subway:** 1, 2, 3, 7, A, C, E, N, Q, R train to 42nd St.-Times Sq. or B, D, F, M train to 42nd St-Bryant Park.

Map: Following pages.

Info: Visitor Center. Seventh Ave. between 46th & 47th Sts. ℘212-869-1890. www.timessquarenyc.org.

Location: Though Broadway runs the entire length of Manhattan (13.4 mi) and The Bronx (4 mi), it is the street's half-mile between 40th and 50th Streets that is regarded as Broadway. Times Square (which extends from Times Square proper onto the surrounding side streets) is not a square at all but rather an elongated X formed by the intersection of Seventh Avenue and Broadway.

Timing: Reserve an entire evening to best experience Broadway–Times Square, unquestionably more vibrant after dark, when neon lights and glittering marquees assault the senses. Though pricey, definitely take in a play or musical in the Theater District (*see Duffy Square, where* **TKTS** *sells half-price tickets the day of the show*).

of large electric signs in Times Square, and the Great White Way was officially born. The number of hotels, restaurants, dance halls and theaters steadily increased until the stock market crash of 1929, after which point legitimate theater gave way to burlesque shows in some venues and to cinema in others. The descent continued, and by the 1970s, Times Square was a shadowy world of X-rated bookstores, porn shops and prostitution. For some, the seediness had a romantic appeal—indeed,

Times Square Information Center

The lobby of the 1926 Embassy movie theater on the east side of Seventh Avenue, between 46th and 47th Streets, has been turned into a well-organized visitor center covering sights citywide. Open year-round daily from 9am to 8pm, it contains exhibits, a staffed information desk, plentiful brochures, several computer terminals with free internet access, a US Post Office, a Broadway ticketing service, public restrooms and free newspapers known for their cultural events listings: *Village Voice (www.villagevoice.com)* and *The L Magazine (www.thelmagazine.com)*. The center's website *(www.timessquarenyc.org)* is also chock-full of news and advice.

those New Yorkers wax nostalgic for the bad old days depicted in John Schlesinger's *Midnight Cowboy* (1968) and Martin Scorsese's *Taxi Driver* (1976)—but civic leaders generally saw the area as a blight on the landscape.

Attempts to clean up Times Square began as early as the 1950s, but not until the 1990s was significant progress made. Prodded by Mayor **Rudolph Giuliani**, the city and state commissioned architect **Robert A.M. Stern** and graphic artist **Tibor Kallmann** headed up a revitalization plan for West 42nd Street. Giuliani, meanwhile, used the city's powers of eminent domain to push out the sleaze factor and offered gener-

ous tax abatements to persuade giant corporations such as Disney, MTV and Condé Nast to purchase and develop real estate in the area. The strategy worked. Now well into its third decade, the "new" Times Square bustles at every hour, a family-friendly, larger-than-life spectacle not to be missed.

Though most of the advertising in Times Square touts products totally unrelated to the place itself (Cup of Noodles, anyone?), some retailers have linked blaring signage to actual shopping experiences. They call it "retailtainment," though the awkwardness of the word ensures that no one else will. **M&M's World** *(1600 Broadway at W. 48th St.; ℘212-295-3850;*

Times Square crossover by night

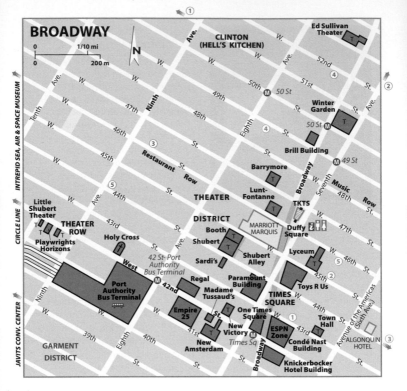

BROADWAY

HOTELS		RESTAURANTS	
Casablanca Hotel	①	Azuri Café	①
Hotel Grace	②	Carnegie Delicatessen	②
Iroquois	③	Firebird	③
Mayfair New York	④	Gallagher's	④
Muse Hotel	⑤	Marseille	⑤

www.mymms.com) takes the concept of "candy store" to a new extreme, filling multiple levels of prime real estate with all things associated with the brand. **Toys R Us** *(1514 Broadway at W. 44th St.; ☎646-366-8800; www.toysrus.com)* is both a toy store and a small amusement park, with an indoor Ferris wheel and an animatronic dinosaur.

Sights with greater historical significance along Broadway include the following (listed from south to north):

Knickerbocker Hotel Building

1462–1470 Broadway at W. 42nd St. (southeast corner).

Now surrounded by shimmering skyscrapers, this Classical brick pile with the mansard roof recalls Times Square's first heyday. Financed by **John Jacob Astor**, the 556-room hotel was home to the opera superstar **Enrico Caruso** from the time of its opening in 1907 until Caruso's death in 1921. Here, in 1912, is where an immigrant bartender named **Martini di Arma di Taggia** perfected the drink that bears his name; one of its first champions was **John D. Rockefeller**. On Armistice Day 1918, Caruso stepped out on his balcony and led the crowd of revelers in Times Square in singing the "Star-Spangled Banner," followed by the French and Italian national anthems. The hotel closed in 1921 and was converted to offices.

From 1940 to 1959 the most famous tenant was **Newsweek** magazine, which was owned by John Jacob's great-great-grandson Vincent Astor until 1961. The building was converted to residential lofts in 1980 and has since undergone a $10 million renovation.

One Times Square

Bounded by W. 42nd & W. 43rd Sts., Broadway & Seventh Ave.

This 25-story building, barely visible beneath its mammoth signage (especially on the video-screen-laden north face), was the home of *The New York Times* from 1904 to 1913 and remains the centerpiece of New Year's Eve celebrations. In 1928 it became the site of the world's first **"zipper" sign**: 14,800 bulbs were arrayed in a 5ft-tall, 360ft-long ribbon that wrapped all the way around the building. By flashing bulbs on and off, messages were moved ("zipped") past stationary viewers. Today a modified version of the sign is run by **Dow Jones**; amber light-emitting diodes (LEDs) have replaced the old incandescent bulbs.

Condé Nast Building

4 Times Sq. (Broadway at W. 42nd St.).

Completed in 1999, this glimmering 48-story skyscraper by the firm Fox & Fowle was the first of a cluster of office buildings that now stand at the south end of the square. Its unusual crown features a jumble of elements, most prominently giant billboards with the address: 4 Times Square. The largest in the world, **NASDAQ**'s 120ft-high LED display curves around the northwest corner of the building above a ground-floor TV studio. On upper stories are the offices of *The New Yorker*, *Vanity Fair*, *Vogue* and other Condé Nast publications *(www. condenast.com).*

Paramount Building

1501 Broadway (west side) between W. 43rd & W. 44th Sts.

This gracefully stepped building, which culminates in a clock tower topped with a (once-illuminated) glass ball, held offices and the Paramount movie theater upon its completion in 1926. And what a theater it was. The lobby was modeled after the Paris Opera House, with white marble columns, balustrades and a grand staircase. Inside were red-velvet curtains, gilt ceilings, brass railings, Greek statues in wall niches and 3,600 plush seats. The theater was gutted in the 1950s, but the building got back a replica of its marquee courtesy of World Wrestling Entertainment, a recent tenant. The Hard Rock Cafe took over the space in 2005.

Duffy Square

The sliver of concrete bounded by Broadway, Seventh Avenue and West 47th Street has been home to the ever-popular TKTS booth, where half-price theater tickets are sold on the day of the show. The square was named after **Francis P. Duffy** (1871–1932), the nationally revered "fighting chaplain" of New York's 69th Regiment in World War I. After the war Duffy befriended actors and playwrights as the pastor of **Holy Cross Church** *(333 W. 42nd St. between Eighth & Ninth Aves.).* In 2008 a $19 million renovation of Duffy Square spiffed up the terrain and added striking, illuminated red steps to the north end. The staircase structure enclosing the new **TKTS** booth *(℘212-912-9770; www.tdf.org)* is a great place to have a seat, gaze out over Times Square, and plan your evening's entertainment. The overhaul of Duffy Square was the first of several initiatives to make Times Square the most pedestrian-friendly spot in Midtown; in 2009 Broadway from 47th to 42nd Streets was closed to vehicular traffic, making it a perfect spot for an evening stroll.

Brill Building

1619 Broadway between W. 49th & W. 50th Sts.

Completed in 1931, the Brill Building was the epicenter of the country's pop music industry for several decades; at its peak in 1962, the 11-story structure contained a whopping 165 music businesses: publishers, producers, agents, songwriters, singers and musicians, everyone madly trying to come up with the next big hit. **Carole King**, **Paul Anka**, **Bobby Vee** and **Neal Sedaka** all regularly did busi-

New York CityPass

If you plan on doing serious sightseeing, consider buying a **New York CityPass** (≈$79, children 6–17 $59; ☏888-330-5008; www.citypass.com). This handy ticket booklet gets you into the American Museum of Natural History, the Empire State Building observatory, the Metropolitan Museum of Art, the Museum of Modern Art and your choice of the Guggenheim Museum or the Top of the Rock at Rockefeller Center, and the Circle Line sightseeing cruise or Statue of Liberty/Ellis Island cruise at half the price you would pay for separate admissions. What's more, once you have your pass, you get to skip ticket-purchasing lines, which can be depressingly long. Buy it online or at any of the participating institutions.

ness here. (Movie buffs will also note that the building's art deco brass facade and foyer featured prominently in the 1957 classic film *Sweet Smell of Success*, starring Tony Curtis and Burt Lancaster.)

A block south, on West 48th Street between Avenue of the Americas (Sixth Ave.) and Seventh Avenue, stretches **Music Row**, where at one time you could find the world's largest selection of musical instruments, particularly guitars. Visiting rock musicians still come here to shop, although several long-standing music shops have relocated elsewhere.

THEATER DISTRICT★

New York's historic theater district spans the blocks between West 42nd Street northward to roughly 53rd Street, fanning out on both sides of Broadway. At one time more than 80 theaters were built in the district. Some 40 remain, still offering a wide variety of entertainment.

Though theater in New York dates back to the time of the colonists, the Times Square theater district was not inaugurated until 1895, when **Oscar Hammerstein** opened the Olympia theater complex at Broadway and 45th Street. In the subsequent three decades, about 85 theaters were built between Avenue of the Americas (Sixth Ave.) and Eighth Avenue in Midtown.

Early on, many specialized in vaudeville or burlesque. Elaborate dance revues like **Florenz Ziegfeld**'s *Follies* were also tremendously popular. But in the 1920s, Broadway theaters began staging more serious fare: classic dramas (Ibsen, Shaw, Chekhov, Pirandello) as well as work

by local playwrights, such as **Eugene O'Neill** and **Clifford Odets**. Rising musical talents like **George Gershwin**, **Cole Porter** and **Oscar Hammerstein II** (the Olympia founder's grandson) turned their attention to the stage around this time too, giving rise to a new art form: the **American musical**—still Broadway's main attraction.

Yet not all theaters in the theater district hosted live performance. Some of the grandest venues in fact were devoted to the **cinema**. The mother of them all, the **Roxy Theater** at Broadway and 50th Street, was called "the cathedral of the motion picture": it had 6,300 seats and a power plant large enough to light a city of 250,000. (Sadly, it was razed in 1961.)

Live theater waned during the Depression due to its high cost, but the coup d'état for the Theater District came during World War II, when the Great White Way was darkened for two long seasons. Many venues did not reopen, or did so as second-run or adult movie houses. Not until the 1990s were they returned en masse, both architecturally and artistically, to the mainstream. Today the roughly 40 theaters here constitute the densest grouping of live-performance venues in the US.

West 42nd Street★★
Between Broadway & Eighth Ave.
Packed cheek by jowl on this bright, frenetic block are some of the most touristic attractions in Times Square, as well as some of the most historic. At no.214, the long-neglected **New Amsterdam Theater**, commissioned in 1903 by Florenz Ziegfeld and host to such stars

Winter Garden Theater

© Bertrand Rieger/hemis.fr

Historic Theaters

As you stroll through the Theater District, take note of these particularly historic structures:

Town Hall
113–123 W. 43rd St. between Broadway & Ave. of the Americas.

Designed by McKim, Mead and White in 1921, the hall isn't fancy outside, but the acoustics have been deemed ideal by everyone from Winston Churchill to Laurie Anderson. Check online for a calendar of events (*www.the-townhall-nyc.org*).

Lyceum Theater
149–157 W. 45th St. between Broadway & Ave. of the Americas.

This 1903 structure boasts a grand Beaux-Arts facade and undulating marquee. It is the oldest New York theater still used for legitimate productions and was first to be landmarked.

Lunt-Fontanne Theater
205 W. 46th St. between Broadway & Eighth Ave.

The palazzo-style building was designed in 1910 by Carrère and Hastings. *The Sound of Music* premiered here, and the Disney musical *Beauty and the Beast* played at the theater for nine years out of its thirteen-year run.

Barrymore Theater
243–251 W. 47th St. between Broadway & Eighth Ave.

The marquee of this 1928 theater is held up by stunningly ornate ironwork. *A Streetcar Named Desire* had its Broadway debut here in 1947.

Winter Garden Theater
1634 Broadway between W. 50th & W. 51st Sts.

The theater stands on the former site of the American Horse Exchange, which was built in the early 1800s by William K. Vanderbilt. The Winter Garden is now home to *Mamma Mia!*, the hit musical based on the songs of Swedish pop group ABBA.

Ed Sullivan Theater
1697 Broadway at W. 53rd St.

Comedian **David Letterman** films his nightly TV show here. CBS named the theater after celebrity TV host (and native New Yorker) Ed Sullivan in 1967.

Booth Theater
222 W. 45th St. between Broadway & Eighth Ave.

Built in 1913 with a Renaissance-style facade, the theater was named for actor Edwin Booth and shares its facade with the **Shubert Theater** next door. The two are linked by Shubert Alley.

as French legend Maurice Chevalier and Italian actress Eleonora Duse, has been restored to its art deco splendor by the Walt Disney Corp. *The Lion King* ran here for nearly 10 years.

Across the street stands the **New Victory Theatre** *(no. 209)*. Originally built in 1899 by Oscar Hammerstein, it reopened as a children's performance space in December 1995 after a much-acclaimed $12 million renovation. Down the block, **Madame Tussaud's** *(no. 234;* 👥👤 🕐*open year-round Fri–Sat 10am–10pm, Sun–Thu 10am–8pm;* ✆*800-246-8872; www.nycwax.com;* 🎟*$35.50, children $28.50)* packs more than 200 wax celebrities into its nine-story, 85,000sq-ft digs. Two cineplexes face off down the block: **Regal** *(nos. 243–247)*, in Robert A. M. Stern's mall-like E-Walk Complex, and **Empire 25** *(no. 234)*, a five-floor movie house whose 1912 facade and lobby (by architect Charles Lamb) used to stand down the block (they were lifted and moved to this more spacious locale). Behind the crisscrossed steel girders on the southwest corner of Eighth Avenue and 42nd Street stands the **Port Authority Bus Terminal**, in which you can kill time at the resident bowling alley before your bus ride.

Theatre Row, a complex of five small Off-Broadway and Off-Off Broadway houses (88 to 199 seats), opened in spring 2002 at 410 West 42nd Street *(between Ninth & Tenth Aves.; www.theatrerow.org)*. Neighbors include **Playwrights Horizons** *(no. 416)*, whose two theaters (99 and 198 seats) opened in January 2003 after a $32 million renovation, and the 499-seat **Little Shubert Theater** *(no. 422)*, new as of November 2002.

Intrepid Facts and Figures

Length: 900 feet
Displacement: 41,434 tons
Beam: 103 ft 4.25 in
Width (Flight Deck): 192 feet
Forward Draft: 29 feet
Aft Draft: 27 feet
Propellers: 4

Restaurant Row
W. 46th St. between Eighth & Ninth Aves. Flanking both sides of this block are restaurants that cater to theatergoers with prix-fixe dinner specials and service that is timed precisely to the 8pm curtain. In other words, you can enjoy your dinner without having to constantly check your watch.

For more adventurous fare, however, you might want to explore **Ninth Avenue**; a trendy new restaurant opens here practically every week. This is the main drag of the neighborhood called **Clinton** (by developers) or **Hell's Kitchen** (by locals).

Shubert Alley
From W. 44th to W. 45th Sts. between Broadway & Eighth Ave.
"Stagedoor Annies" line up in this pedestrian alley (one of several in the area) to get the autographs of stars going to, or coming from, performances. At intermission or after shows, many theatergoers, performers, writers and critics drop in to famous **Sardi's** restaurant, at the alley's south end *(234 W. 44th St.;* ✆*212-221-8440; www.sardis.com)*, for a meal or a drink. Well known for the caricatures of celebrated theatrical personalities lining the walls, Sardi's has been a fixture in the Theater District since 1921.

ADDITIONAL SIGHTS
Just four blocks west of bustling Times Square flows the wide Hudson River and alongside it lie several points of interest. To get to the river, either walk or take the M42 bus west along 42nd Street.

The Island by Boat★★ 🚢
Taking a narrated boat ride is one of the best ways to learn about the city—Manhattan is an island, after all. And on a **Circle Line Boat Tour** *(departs from Pier 83, W. 42nd St. at the West Side Hwy.;* ✆*212-563-3200; www.circleline42.com)*, the guides know their stuff, peppering running historical commentary with the latest New York gossip. The full island tour takes three hours but there are shorter tours too. Look online or check at the ticket counter for options, sched-

ules and prices. (The Circle Line operates boats from South Street Seaport, and to and from the Statue of Liberty as well.)

Intrepid Sea, Air & Space Museum★

Pier 86, W. 46th St. & Twelfth Ave.
Open Apr–Oct Mon–Fri 10am–5pm, Sat–Sun & holidays 10am–6pm; Oct–Mar Tue–Sun 10am–5pm. Closed Thanksgiving Day & Dec 25. $22; youth 3–17 $17; children under 3 & military free. 212-245-0072. www.intrepidmuseum.org.

Lying at berth on the Hudson River at the edge of Midtown, the aircraft carrier USS *Intrepid* today forms the heart of a state-of-the-art museum complex celebrating the history of US achievements in the sky, on the seas and in outer space.

USS *Intrepid*

©Dantang/iStockphoto.com

The Intrepid – Commissioned in 1943 for service in World War II, the Essex-class carrier executed several campaigns in the Pacific Theater (surviving two kamikaze attacks) and during the Cold War and the Vietnam War. During the 1960s she participated in recovery operations for the US space program, plucking both Mercury and Gemini capsules from the water after their return to earth. Decommissioned and retired from active service in 1974, the *Intrepid* was established here as a museum in 1982. Following extensive renovations and upgrading of museum facilities, she was reopened to the public in 2008.

Measuring 900ft long and weighing over 41,000 tons, the vast aircraft carrier was a veritable floating city to its 3,388-man crew during its years of active service. Many areas of the vessel are open for exploration, so visitors can see what life was like on board, from the decidedly minimal crew's berths (and slightly more spacious officers' quarters), to the dining halls and recreation areas. You can also climb up to the bridge, command center for the ship, and down to the Anchor Room. Videos highlight the ship's history, and the mechanisms that handled aircraft takeoff and landing. Topside on the Flight Deck and below on the Hangar Deck you'll find 30 aircraft

from all branches of service displayed, including a Lockheed **A-12 Blackbird** spy plane, capable of Mach-3 speeds. The supersonic passenger airliner **Concorde** is displayed on the pier; climb aboard to imagine yourself crossing the Atlantic in under three hours.

The Growler – On the north side of Pier 86, this SSG-577 submarine offers visitors a rare opportunity to climb aboard a Cold War-era nuclear submarine. The command center, which managed the launch of the sub's 56ft Regulus cruise missiles, is open for viewing, as are the tiny living and working quarters.

Jacob K. Javits Convention Center

Eleventh Ave. between W. 34th & W. 39th Sts. 212-216-2000. www.javitscenter.com.

I.M. Pei designed this huge black-glass complex in 1986—enclosing 1.8 million square feet. The center accommodates up to 85,000 conventioneers as well as massive exhibits. An enormous exposed-steel frame of 76,000 tubes and 19,000 nodes serves as the beams, walls and roof of the hall and is supported by columns rising 90ft.

Central Midtown★★

Although Fifth Avenue officially separates the east and west sides of Manhattan, in Midtown it is Avenue of the Americas (aka Sixth Ave.) that actually feels like the dividing line. In part, that is because its neighbors are so distinct. One block west, the Theater District is a rowdy quarter of blazing marquees and chain restaurants. One block east, the department stores of Fifth Avenue are the height of gentility. Avenue of the Americas and the swath around it are more eclectic. Macy's department store ("the world's largest") anchors a frenetic shopping hub at its southern end (34th St). The Museum of Modern Art dominates a lively museum district at its northern end (53rd St.). In between you'll find Bryant Park and Rockefeller Center.

A BIT OF HISTORY

In the colonial era, this slice of Midtown belonged to the city but was actually the country, as New York's population was concentrated well below Canal Street. Then in 1801 **David Hosack** (1769–1835), a professor of botany and medicine at **Columbia University** (and, interestingly, the surgeon in attendance at the 1804 duel between **Alexander Hamilton** and **Aaron Burr**), purchased the land now occupied by Rockefeller Center to establish a teaching garden in which Hosack explored the medicinal properties of native plants. After 10 years, Hosack shuttered his greenhouse and sold the land to the State of New York. The state then turned it over to Columbia University with the understanding that the school would move its campus here. Instead, the university rented out parcels to farmers for $100 a year.

By the mid-19C, the area was covered with brownstone town houses, home to upper-middle-class families who couldn't afford a mansion on Fifth Ave-

MTA Subway: B, D, F, M train to 47th-50th Sts./Rockefeller Center.

Location: Centered on Avenue of the Americas (Sixth Ave.), Central Midtown lies a block west of Fifth Avenue. Macy's anchors the lower extremity, the Museum District the upper reaches. Rockefeller Center serves as its centerpiece.

Kids: Ice skating at Rockefeller Center; the carousel at Bryant Park.

nue but were nonetheless members of high society. But upon the completion of the Sixth Avenue "El" (elevated railroad) in 1878, a majority of these residents began moving farther uptown, leaving their fine houses to poorer tenants. Later, during the Prohibition era (1920–33), the district became known as the **"speakeasy belt"** for its concentration of semi-secret nightclubs. Following Prohibition's repeal, many speakeasies reopened as legitimate jazz clubs.

The construction of Rockefeller Center changed the character of the neighborhood. More than 225 buildings were demolished to make room for the original 12 buildings of the complex, and the residential population was dispersed to other parts of the city. But with that loss came significant gain. The center was hailed as an architectural triumph. Rockefeller's insistence that early tenants be affiliated with the television and radio industries paid off as well: other media outlets soon gravitated to the district, boosting its worldwide visibility and local cachet. The 1939 opening of the Museum of Modern Art at 11 West 53rd Street (a project championed by John D. Rockefeller Jr.'s wife, **Abby Aldrich Rockefeller**) was similarly prescient: the institution now anchors one of the city's most vital museum districts.

Cleaned up in the mid-1990s by a restoration corporation founded by the Rockefeller Brothers Fund, the Bryant Park is Midtown Manhattan's only large public green space, and a lovely one at that.

ROCKEFELLER CENTER★★★

Between Fifth & Sixth Aves. and W. 48th & W. 51st Sts. ☎212-332-6868. www.rockefellercenter.com. For tours, ☙see Things to Do at Rockefeller Center panel, p172.

Located in the heart of Midtown Manhattan, this "city within a city" encompasses more than a dozen harmoniously designed skyscrapers, a formal garden, 100 works of public art, a world-famous skating rink, the headquarters of the television giant NBC and the art deco masterpiece Radio City Music Hall.

The Center Evolves – Rockefeller Center had its start in 1926, with a proposal to build a new concert hall for the Metropolitan Opera in the heart of Midtown. Opera administrators turned to Standard Oil chairman and philanthropist **John D. Rockefeller Jr.** for help. Rockefeller was ideally suited for the job. Unlike most other New York City moguls, who had mansions on upper Fifth Avenue, "John D.," as he was known, had spent most of his childhood and adulthood on West 54th Street, and was eager to see

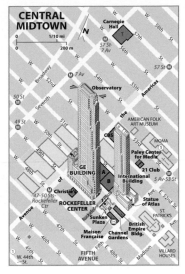

HOTEL	RESTAURANT
City Club.....................①	The Modern.....................①

the neighborhood improved. Far more important, he was one of the richest men in the world, with a fortune of about $1 billion ($10 billion in today's dollars). Rockefeller's plan was to replace the down-at-the-heels neighborhood with a new opera house and tall office buildings around a plaza. The stock market crash of 1929 forced the opera to back out of

21 Club

21 W. 52nd St. ☎212-582-7200. www.21club.com.

During Prohibition New York City abounded with illegal watering holes, but none was more famous, more elegant, or more ingenious than Jack and Charlie's 21, a subterranean club on West 52nd Street. Opened in 1922, it catered to New York's smart set, in particular the hard-drinking, wise-cracking members of the **Algonquin Round Table**. Jack and Charlie's had good food, good liquor and a dance floor with a full orchestra.

Most importantly, it was equipped with a chute through which alcohol could be quickly disposed of in the event of a raid, as well as a secret basement wine cellar with a two-ton door and an address that actually put it next door, at no. 19. After Prohibition the speakeasy reemerged as the legendary 21 Club, a favorite haunt of **Humphrey Bogart**, **Richard Nixon** and, apparently, rich equestrians, who donated the 33 painted jockey statues that adorn the building's exterior. The club opened a second-floor restaurant in 2002 to rave reviews. The barroom, lined with framed cartoons by famous artists, remains a classic piece of old New York. Drop in for a drink or dinner (☙*jacket & tie required; reservations recommended*).

View over to Central Park from the GE Building's Top of the Rock

C. Ochterbeck/MICHELIN

the deal for lack of funds, but Rockefeller pushed forward with the project.

"Radio City" Is Born – Rockefeller assembled a team of architects from three firms (one of whom was Wallace K. Harrison, designer of the United Nations Headquarters and Lincoln Center) to design a city-within-a-city for the emerging radio and television industries. The architects preserved the original blueprint's central plaza; around it would be 13 art deco office buildings linked by underground concourses and street-level promenades.

Bas-relief and glass screen by Lee Lawrie, GE Building

C. Ochterbeck/MICHELIN

Buoyed by Rockefeller's optimism and dollars, construction began in 1931 and continued through the Depression. The project employed 4,000 New Yorkers at a time when other developers were cautiously waiting for the economic situation to improve. Between 1947 and 1973, seven additional buildings were added to the complex (1939). Today, Rockefeller Center is generally acknowledged to be a jewel of urban design.

GE Building★★★

30 Rockefeller Plaza.

This lithe 70-story skyscraper (originally the RCA Building) is Rockefeller Center's tallest and finest structure. John D. celebrated its completion in 1933 by moving the family offices here from 26 Broadway near Bowling Green. The building is made of limestone with glass and aluminum details. Its strong vertical lines, softened with staggered setbacks in the upper stories, are considered a triumph of art deco design. The National Broadcasting Co. (NBC), a General Electric subsidiary, is headquartered here.

Above the entrance to the GE Building is a bas-relief and glass screen (1933) by the sculptor **Lee Lawrie**.

The figure represents Wisdom, shown grasping a drafting compass whose points are directed toward the light and sound waves carved into the cast glass below. The quotation is taken from the Bible.

Step inside the **lobby** to view the immense ceiling and wall murals by the Spanish artist **José María Sert**. The *American Progress* murals are the second series executed on this site. The first, by Mexican muralist **Diego Rivera**, depicted a May Day workers' demonstration led by Vladimir Lenin. When Rivera refused to remove Lenin from the scene, Rockefeller destroyed the painting. (By contrast, when a fresco Rivera completed for **Henry Ford** incited similar controversy just months earlier in Detroit, Henry's son Edsel defended it, and today the painting is regarded as Rivera's most significant work in the US.) The GE Building's **Top of the Rock**★★ contains exhibits on the history of the building as well as an open-air platform on the 70th floor with 360-degree **views**★★★ of the city.

On the 65th floor the famed **Rainbow Room** was once the spot for drinks, dancing and great views of the sparkling city at night. The space closed in 2009 following a tenant–landlord dispute; no new operator has been named but the historic venue can't stay vacant for long *(www.rainbowroom.com)*.

Channel Gardens★★

This long, flower-bedecked passage was named in 1936 by a clever journalist who observed that it separated the **Maison Française** (1933) and the **Brit-**

ish Empire Building (1932) just as the English Channel separates France and Great Britain. The plantings change seasonally, beginning with Easter lilies on Good Friday. From the Fifth Avenue side of the gardens, take in the **view**★★ of the GE Building towering over the complex; the symmetrical framing is typical of the City Beautiful movement.

The **sunken plaza** lies at the heart of Rockefeller Center. Here, at the top of the steps leading to the lower plaza, is a plaque citing John D.'s personal creed. On the far side of the plaza floats Rockefeller Plaza's best-known artwork, a massive gold-leaf bronze statue of **Prometheus** (**1** *on map*) (1934, Paul Manship), shown stealing fire from the gods as a gift for humankind. The floor of the plaza has been frozen into an ▲▲**ice-skating rink** every winter since 1936. It is particularly festive in December, when the street-level plaza is decked with holiday decorations, including a huge Christmas tree. In warmer weather the rink holds an outdoor bar and restaurant.

Radio City Music Hall★★

1260 Ave. of the Americas. ☎*212-247-4777. www.radiocity.com.*
A treasured New York landmark, Radio City Music Hall is one of the city's most grandiose art deco creations and a spectacular entertainment venue.

Channel Gardens

C. Ochterbeck/MICHELIN

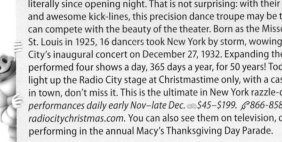

Radio City Christmas Spectacular

...5-6-7-8. Radio City Music Hall and **The Rockettes** have been intertwined literally since opening night. That is not surprising: with their sparkly costumes and awesome kick-lines, this precision dance troupe may be the only group that can compete with the beauty of the theater. Born as the Missouri Rockets in St. Louis in 1925, 16 dancers took New York by storm, wowing crowds at Radio City's inaugural concert on December 27, 1932. Expanding their ranks to 36, they performed four shows a day, 365 days a year, for 50 years! Today The Rockettes light up the Radio City stage at Christmastime only, with a cast of 140. If you're in town, don't miss it. This is the ultimate in New York razzle-dazzle. *Two to five performances daily early Nov–late Dec.* $45–$199. *866-858-0007. www. radiocitychristmas.com.* You can also see them on television, once a year, performing in the annual Macy's Thanksgiving Day Parade.

The music hall opened its doors to the public in 1932, under the direction of **Samuel "Roxy" Rothafel**, to present variety shows. To become more profitable, the hall began operating as a movie house and soon hosted great movie premieres. When the movie business became unprofitable, plans were made to tear the building down. Public outcry put an end to the plan and the building was completely renovated in 1979. Today it is famed for its musical spectaculars and for concerts by top performing artists. Visit the interior by attending a show or by taking the **Radio City Stage Door Tour** (*year-round daily 11am–3pm, every half-hour, departs from the main lobby, 1hr;* $19.25, tickets available at

the *Radio City Sweets & Gifts Shop, Ave. of the Americas between 50th & 51st Sts. or through Ticketmaster 800-745-3000).* All concert tickets are available on a first-come, first-served basis from the box office (*open year-round Mon–Sat 11.30am–6pm)* or through Ticketmaster (*800-745-3000; service fee applied).*

The Interior★★★
As you enter the Grand Foyer, designed by Donald Deskey, your eyes rise from the plush carpet, featuring a geometric pattern representing six musical instruments, up to the sweeping Grand Staircase and three mezzanine levels. Ezra Winter's enormous 60ft-by-40ft mural *Fountain of Youth* adorns the wall behind the staircase. Magnificent chandeliers emit a suffused light overhead. Each weighs two tons and can be lowered for cleaning by pushing a button. Immense wall mirrors extend up to the sparkling ceiling, covered in gold leaf.

In the auditorium, note the curved wall-and-ceiling design and the huge proscenium arch (60ft high), the most striking feature of the 5,882-seat theater. The stage itself is equipped with complex machinery: three elevators, a three-section turntable and an orchestra elevator. The musicians in the orchestra and the two electric organs (with pipes up to 32ft high) and their organists, can be whisked away behind the walls or below the floor when necessary, without interrupting their playing. Lower-level rooms form a striking art deco ensemble.

Radio City Music Hall

C. Ochterbeck/MICHELIN

International Building★

*630 Fifth Ave. between W. 50th &
W. 51st Sts.*

In front of the Fifth Avenue entrance of the 41-story International Building (1939) rises a spectacular two-ton bronze statue of **Atlas**★★ (1937, Lee Lawrie and René Chamballan) carrying the world as a punishment for defying Zeus.

On the building's south facade on 50th Street is an elaborate **sculptural relief** (Lee Lawrie), installed in 1935. The bottom panel portrays "the four races of mankind" in their symbolic habitats. The four outer panels at the bottom depict the old age of imperialism and the new age of republics. The relief is crowned by a sunburst and clock.

Inside, the **lobby** features columns and walls made of marble from the Greek island of Tinos; the ceiling is covered with gold leaf.

Above the escalators stands a bust of **Charles Lindbergh**, a donation from the Air Mail Pioneers of America, and above the East 50th Street exit is a bronze globular clock.

Associated Press Building

*(**B** on map) 50 Rockefeller Plaza
between W. 50th & W. 51st Sts.*

This 1937 building is most notable for the dynamic stainless-steel relief **panel**★★ above its entrance. Created by sculptor **Isamu Noguchi** in 1940, the panel, titled *News*, captures figures carrying tools of the journalist's trade: a camera, a notepad, a typewriter and a telephone.

MUSEUM DISTRICT★★

*W. 52nd & W. 53rd Sts. between Fifth &
Sixth Aves. Subway: E, M trains to Fifth
Ave.-53rd St.*

The world-famous and recently expanded Museum of Modern Art (MoMA) on West 53rd Street may be the biggest museum in Midtown, but it isn't the only museum in Midtown. It's not even the only museum on West 53rd Street. In recent years a small and evolving museum district has cropped up around it, offering excellent exhibits in more manageable settings (and for

less than half the ticket price of MoMA, and with no waiting in line). The American Folk Art Museum, housed in a stunning 2001 building by Matthew Baird of the local firm Tod Williams and Billie Tsien, is particularly worth a visit: about 150 pieces from the permanent collection are always on exhibit, showing the skill and creativity of self-taught artists. A showcase of two nationwide—and increasingly worldwide—fixtures, the Paley Center for Media seeks to preserve the history of television and radio and their contributions to American culture.

Museum of Modern Art★★★

*11 W. 53rd St. See Major
Manhattan Museums.*

American Folk Art Museum★★

*45 W. 53rd St. See Major
Manhattan Museums.*

The Paley Center for Media

*25 W. 52nd St. between Fifth & Sixth
Aves. Open year-round Wed &
Fri–Sun noon–6pm, Thu noon–8pm.
Closed Jan 1, Jul 4, Thanksgiving Day
& Dec 25. Guided tours available
(ask at the front desk for schedule)
$10. 212-621-6800.
www.paleycenter.org.*

The massive TV and radio archive of the former Museum of Television & Radio (MTR) was created by former CBS chairman **William S. Paley** with a view toward preserving two increasingly popular but ephemeral fixtures of American culture: radio and television. The museum was opened in 1975 and was the only one of its kind until 1996, when a sister museum built by Richard Meier in Beverly Hills was inaugurated. The New York location is housed in a 17-story building (the William S. Paley Building) designed by John Burgee with Philip Johnson in 1989. In June 2007 MTR announced a name change (for both locations) to The Paley Center for Media to better convey the expanded nature of its functions. The center is broadening its focus to include all media. Likewise, it is increasing the number of its public

Y. Kanazawa/MICHELIN

Things to Do at Rockefeller Center

Unlike most attractions in New York City, Rockefeller Center really sparkles in winter. If you happen to be here at that time of year, take a whirl around the sunken **skating rink** (⊙*open Oct–Apr; call* ℘*212-332-7654 for schedule and rates*), gawk at the six- to ten-story decorated **Christmas tree** *(early Dec–early Jan)*, view the elaborate holiday window displays at adjacent Saks Fifth Avenue and other department stores, and get tickets to The Rockettes' dazzling **Christmas Spectacular** at Radio City Music Hall (ⓒ*see sidebar p170*). That said, there's plenty to do here at other times of year as well. Start your visit at the **GE Building** *(30 Rockefeller Plaza)*. At the information desk in the lobby, you can pick up a self-guided **walking-tour map** of the complex and a directory of shops and get answers to your questions (the center's website, www.rockefellercenter.com, is also a good resource). **Rockefeller Center walking tours** (60min) led by Rockefeller Center historians (who use closed-circuit headsets to speak to tour participants) are available daily (☞*hourly from 10am;* ⬱*$15;* ℘*212-698-2000*) and focus on the history of the Rockefellers and the art and architecture of the complex. Meet at the tour desk inside the **NBC Experience Store** (*W. 49th St. & Rockefeller Plaza*). **NBC Studio Tours** (☞*70min ,departs from the Experience Store*) take visitors through the studios where various shows, including **Today**, **NBC Nightly News** and **Saturday Night Live**, are taped; television technology such as the weather screen is also demonstrated (⊙*year-round Mon–Sat 8.30am–5.30pm, Sun 9.15am–5.30pm, departs every 15–30min;* ⊙*no tours Thanksgiving Day & Dec 25;* ⬱*$19.25; reservations recommended, children under 6 not permitted;* ℘*212-664-3700; www.nbcstudiotour.com*). For a look at Rockefeller Center both above and below decks, try the Art and Observation tour, which covers most public areas and artworks, ending with a trip to the Top of the Rock observation deck (☞*90min, daily, hourly from 10am;* ⬱*$30* (☺*reservations recommended;* ℘*212-698-2000*).

You can attend a **live taping** of **Late Night with Jimmy Fallon** or Saturday Night Live, both headquartered at the GE Building *(30 Rockefeller Plaza;* ☺*children must be at least 16 years of age for SNL and 17 for Jimmy Fallon;* ℘*212-664-3056*). In both cases, your best bet is to get tickets well in advance, but there are also same-day standby tickets available in the morning for afternoon or evening tapings. Show up at the corner of 49th Street and Rockefeller Plaza no later than 9am on mornings of tapings for Jimmy Fallon—to say "hi" to mom and dad on SNL, show up around 6am and sit tight for an hour. The **Today Show** is taped inside and outside the studio *(weather permitting)* daily from 7am to 11am. The earlier you arrive, the more likely it is you'll be in the front row.

Finally, for more upscale entertainment, consider attending an auction at the world-famous fine-art auction house **Christie's** at 20 Rockefeller Plaza. Most auctions are free and open to the public. *For a schedule and information, call* ℘*212-636-2000 or go to www.christies.com.*

discussions about today's media and media's impact on culture.

Visitors to the center can browse the permanent archive of more than 140,000 radio and television broadcasts, then view their selections in individual screening areas. The collection includes defining moments in history (Neil Armstrong walking on the moon) and sports (Joe Namath and the New York Jets upsetting the Baltimore Colts in Super Bowl III), along with episodes of popular television programs long off the air.

You can also request and view documentaries, news broadcasts, political coverage and broadcast advertising. The center hosts a full slate of panel discussions featuring newsmakers and performers *(check the website for schedule).*

AVENUE OF THE AMERICAS (SIXTH AVENUE)★
Subway: B, D, F, M, N, Q, R train to 34th St.-Herald Sq.

This is the spine of Central Midtown. Lined mainly with large office buildings, it has attractions of its own, most notably Macy's and Bryant Park. As you proceed north up the avenue, you'll see Rockefeller Center and the Museum District.

Macy's★
151 W. 34th St. between Broadway & Seventh Ave. ✆212-695-4400. www.macys.com.

Since 1924, Macy's has boasted that it is "the world's largest store." Ten stories tall and a city block long, this is the mother ship of department stores. Macy's started in 1858 as a dry-goods store at the corner of 14th Street and Sixth Avenue. Founder Rowland H. Macy was the first to introduce colored bath towels, tea bags and Idaho baked potatoes. The shop moved to its present location in 1902 and opened an addition in 1931. Today there are more than 800 Macy's stores in 45 states.

Macy's sponsors the annual Macy's **Thanksgiving Day Parade**, spearheaded in 1924 by company employees. Best known for its performances by elite high-school marching bands from all around the US, its massive helium-filled balloons shaped like cartoon characters, and the final float bearing Santa Claus to ring in the holiday season in New York, the parade is attended by millions of New Yorkers and watched by an estimated 50 million Americans on television.

Bryant Park★★
Ave. of the Americas between W. 40th & W. 42nd Sts. www.bryantpark.org.

With its green folding chairs, pebble allées, used-book stalls, outdoor restaurants and London plane trees, this formal park behind the New York Public Library is one of the loveliest outdoor spots in the city.

Macy's Department Store

©Macy's

HBO Bryant Park Summer Film Festival

On Monday nights in the summer, Bryant Park becomes a massive drive-in without the cars. At 5pm, movie lovers arrive (on foot) with blankets, lawn chairs and picnic dinners. There they soak up the atmosphere, chatting with fellow cinephiles, and wait until dark, when a free movie is projected onto a giant screen.

The programming darts all over film history, with a good mix of sci-fi camp classics (like *The Fly* from 1958), Alfred Hitchcock thrillers, crowd-pleasing musicals, and blockbusters (like *Jaws*).

Schedules available at the park or online. ✆212-512-5700. *www.bryantpark.org.*

A Bit of History – Built on a site once occupied by a potter's field (in 1823) and the short-lived glass-and-steel Crystal Palace (1853–58), Bryant Park was named for the poet, civic leader and firebrand newspaper editor **William Cullen Bryant** (1784–1878) in 1884. Parks Commissioner **Robert Moses** supervised a major renovation in 1934, at which time the large sunken lawn was laid out, the balustrade around the perimeter was added and the plane trees were planted. Still,

the park became a haven for homeless people and drug dealers in the 1960s and 70s, and fell into rapid decline. In the 1980s the Rockefeller Brothers Fund spearheaded a nonprofit corporation to revive the park, providing maintenance beyond what the city offered, installing food kiosks and sponsoring public events. In seven years crime dropped 92 per cent and the number of park users doubled. A lavish and sensitive renovation, unveiled in 1992, made Bryant Park more beautiful than it had ever been, with new lights, entrances, plantings and other amenities.

Visit – More than 5,000 office workers come to the park for lunch on warm weekdays. Many bring their laptops: in 2002 the entire park was set up with free wireless internet access. On the south side of the park there's a small 🚻 **carousel**. Among the sculptures dotting the landscaped alleys, note the 1911 bronze **statue** of William Cullen Bryant.

The skyscrapers around the park include the **American Standard Building** (1924, Raymond Hood) on the south side, made of black brick with gold terracotta trim. Formerly the Radiator Building, it was the subject of a painting by **Georgia O'Keeffe** done in a sharp art deco style in 1927 *(Radiator Building—Night, New York)*. West of the park, at 1095 Sixth Avenue, rises the streamlined form of the **New York Telephone Company Building** (now Verizon), completed in

Bryant Park

1970. But most dramatic is the building sweeping upward on the north side of the park: the **Grace Building** (1974, Skidmore, Owings and Merrill), made of travertine and tinted glass.

A nearly identical building, by the same architects and built the same year, stands at **9 West 57th Street**★.

International Center of Photography

1133 Sixth Ave. at 43rd St. ◷*Open year-round Tue–Thur & Sat–Sun 10am–6pm, Fri 10am–8pm.* ◷*Closed major holidays.* ◷*$12.* ☏*212-857-0000.* *www.icp.org.*

Founded by Cornell Capa in 1974, the International Center of Photography (ICP) mounts major exhibits of work by photographers and photojournalists who engage in "concerned photography," as well as those exploring the relationship between photographic representation and politics, memory or popular culture.

The Midtown gallery space was opened in 1989 as a satellite of the original museum at Fifth Avenue and 94th Street, but it became the ICP's sole exhibition area after a major renovation and expansion in 2000 and the closing of the Uptown site in 2001. Today it boasts more display space than the two sites formerly did combined, as well as a cafe and a well-stocked gift shop. About 20 exhibitions are mounted per year, some of which are drawn from the museum's collection of 100,000 prints, as well as from holdings of other museums and partner facilities like the eminent George Eastman House in Rochester, New York. Recent shows included a retrospective of the fashion photography of Edward Steichen during his years as a contributor to *Vogue* and *Vanity Fair* magazines; and an intriguing exhibition of 19C tintypes, a popular method of image making in the decades following the Civil War.

Diamond and Jewelry Way

W. 47th St. between Fifth & Sixth Aves. ☏*212-302-5739.* *www.diamonddistrict.org.*

Nearly 90 per cent of the diamonds that enter the US make a pit stop on this 750ft-long block, the world's largest shopping district for diamonds and other precious stones, both set and loose. The diamond business in New York began in the late 19C when merchants opened stores downtown. By the 1920s the Canal Street diamond district was well established, but the diamond retailers slowly gravitated uptown along with their wealthy customers. The present district took shape in the 1940s.

Today a whopping 2,600 businesses are registered in the neighborhood, the vast majority devoted to the diamond trade. Some merchants have their own jewelry shops, but most have small booths in the district's 25 jewelry "exchanges." Each exchange contains up to 100 shops, and each of those has a specialty (pearls, wedding rings, watches, gold). You'll hear carat, cut, colors and clarity discussed in Spanish, Yiddish, Armenian, Russian, Arabic. Also notice the plainclothes security guards and sophisticated security systems that protect the dealers.

CBS Building

51 W. 52nd St. at Sixth Ave.

Known as the "Black Rock," this 38-story monolith is Finnish-born architect Eero Saarinen's only high-rise building; in fact, he was working on its design at the time of his death in 1961. The structure was completed in 1965. Massive Canadian black granite columns adorn the exterior (most of the weight of the building is carried by a central core), their corners pointed out for dramatic

🙂 Good to Know 🙂

Two restaurants are situated on the terrace of the library: the casual outdoor **Bryant Park Cafe**, a great place for an alfresco burger and beer; and the more upscale **Bryant Park Grill**, which serves American food indoors and on its seasonal rooftop patio. Tom Colicchio's **'wichcraft** is a takeout option along Sixth Ave.

Carnegie Hall

©Clive Sawyer/Pictures Colour Library

effect. The sunken plaza at the building's base is one of the most pleasant in the neighborhood.

CARNEGIE HALL

156 W. 57th St. at Seventh Ave. Visit the interior by attending a concert, or taking a 1hr guided tour (Oct–May Mon–Fri 11.30am, 12.30pm, 2pm, 3pm, Sat 11.30am, 12.30pm, Sun 12.30pm; $10; 212-903-9765). Tickets may be purchased at the box office (open Mon–Sat 11am–6pm, Sun noon–6pm, box office remains open 30min past start time on performance days; closed major holidays). 212-247-7800. www.carnegiehall.org.

Majestic Carnegie Hall is one of the world's most prestigious concert venues, a fact that its namesake and fiscal sponsor, the steel magnate **Andrew Carnegie**, foresaw when he laid the cornerstone in 1890. Indeed, since its completion in 1891, Carnegie Hall has been graced by American luminaries Woodrow Wilson, Dr. Martin Luther King, Duke Ellington, Judy Garland, George Gershwin, Bob Dylan and many others. In every language and culture, to debut at Carnegie Hall is to have "made it."

The idea for Carnegie Hall came about in 1887 on an ocean liner bound from New York to London. On the ship Andrew Carnegie and his wife, Louise Whitfield, a singer, met a young conductor, **Walter Damrosch**, who had been crusading to get a world-class concert hall built in New York. Damrosch made his case to

the Scottish-born millionaire, and four years later the dream was realized when Louise cemented the final stone with a silver trowel from Tiffany's. Architect and cellist William B. Tuthill designed the structure in the Italian Renaissance style, cladding its exterior with iron-spotted brick and terracotta. So it wouldn't need support beams, Carnegie Hall's walls were made several feet thick—a major contribution to the hall's excellent acoustics.

Carnegie Hall has three performance spaces. The largest is the **Isaac Stern Auditorium**, with 2,804 seats, named after the Ukrainian-born violinist who made his debut here in 1943. The third-floor **Weill Recital Hall** (originally known as the Chamber Music Hall) seats 268 and was designed by Tuthill in the Belle Époque style. Situated on the south side of the building and accessed from Seventh Avenue, **Zankel Hall** reopened in 2003 after a strikingly modern redesign. It seats 599. You don't have to take a tour to visit Carnegie Hall's museum.

Rose Museum at Carnegie Hall

154 W. 57th St., 2nd floor. Open Sept–Jun daily 11am–4.30pm. Closed major holidays.

Inaugurated in 1991, the Rose Museum chronicles Carnegie Hall's history (both the building and the performances that have taken place here) and exhibits its archival treasures, which include Benny Goodman's clarinet and Arturo Toscanini's conducting baton.

East Midtown★★

East Midtown contains some of the city's finest 20C architecture, from the Beaux-Arts Grand Central Terminal and the art deco Chrysler Building to the post-Modern Sony Plaza. Betwixt and between are posh apartment buildings, historic churches and luxurious hotels, including the Waldorf-Astoria.

A BIT OF HISTORY

In the early 19C, steam-powered locomotives chugged down Park Avenue all the way to a depot on 23rd Street, bringing with them noise and dirt. Residents complained, and in 1854 an ordinance was passed banning trains south of 42nd Street. That helped pave the way for Downtown development, but did nothing to improve the lot of those in East Midtown, whose tenements surrounded an open, sooty rail yard that spread from 42nd to 56th Streets. (The tracks were roofed over from 56th Street to a tunnel at 96th Street.)

MTA **Subway:** 4, 5, 6, 7 train to Grand Central-42nd St.

Map: Following pages.

Location: East Midtown is the designation for the area roughly bounded by Madison and Third Avenues between East 34th and 57th Streets.

Timing: Allow 4hrs to do East Midtown justice, excluding visits to the museums. To enjoy the cafes, shops and the museums, reserve a full day.

Kids: Sony Wonder Lab.

Underground Railroad – Railroad magnate "Commodore" **Cornelius Vanderbilt** (1794–1877) opened the first Grand Central depot, a vast glass-and-iron shed, in 1871, on the present site of the Grand Central Terminal. Shortly thereafter, he began lowering the tracks feeding into it below street level, reducing some of the noise pollution. But it was not enough to make the area habitable;

View over East Midtown

©P. Helger/Fotolia.com

Pinnacle of Chrysler Building

Y. Saito/MICHELIN

smoke was still a big problem, and in 1889 the city demanded that the railroad (now run by the Commodore's offspring) either electrify the trains or leave the city. To finance the electrification process, the Vanderbilts sank the entire rail yard fronting the depot below ground and sold the land above it to developers, who soon lined Madison and Park Avenues with exclusive apartment buildings. The Grand Central Terminal you see today was completed in 1913.

After World War II, many apartment houses along Madison, Park and Lexington Avenues in Midtown were replaced by high-rise office towers: it was here that the "glass box" style of corporate architecture was pioneered. Interestingly, because the railroad tracks are so close underground, many of these skyscrapers are built on stilts.

Today the area has an eclectic mix of old and new. **Park Avenue**★★ is suited for a stroll: here, alongside the remaining apartment buildings, with uniformed doormen, and banks, are the Waldorf-Astoria Hotel, St. Bartholomew's Church and the Lever House. Upscale shops line **Madison Avenue**★ (especially north of 53rd St.) and **57th Street**★.

SIGHTS
Chrysler Building★★★
405 Lexington Ave. at E. 42nd St.
This famous New York landmark pays homage to the car. Automobile magnate Walter P. Chrysler commissioned architect William Van Alen to design the tallest building in the world. Completed in 1930, it was the tallest, rising to 1,048ft (77 stories)—until the Empire State Building opened in 1931. One of the first buildings to feature exposed metal as part of its design, the Chrysler Building is topped by a distinctive spire of radiant stainless steel arches that glimmers in sunlight and glows in the nighttime illuminations. The pinnacle resembles a radiator cap from a 1930 Chrysler car. Abundant automotive decorations adorning the setbacks under the spire include silver hood ornaments, stylized racing cars and the huge radiator-cap gargoyles at the fourth level, modeled after a 1929 Chrysler. (Chrysler no longer has offices in the building.)
The **lobby**, a superb example of art deco, is faced with red African marble. The elevator cabs feature ornate doors and richly paneled interiors. Note also the elaborate ceiling mural by Edward Trumbull.

Grand Central Terminal★★★
Park Ave. & E. 42nd St.
Often referred to as the "gateway to the nation," this world-famous railroad terminal is a masterpiece of urban architecture. Today, more than 150,000 commuters a day pass through the terminal, which is a veritable city within a city.

A Bit of History
A Group Effort – In 1903 several prominent architectural firms were invited to submit proposals for a new train station. The winners were Reed and Stem, from St. Paul, Minnesota. Soon after the deal was made, the New York firm Warren & Wetmore submitted a different proposal. Allegedly, because Warren was a cousin of New York Central Railroad chairman William K. Vanderbilt, the second proposal was accepted as well, and the two firms were forced to collaborate on the final design. Ten years later, when the

Grand Central Terminal

©Mario Savoia/iStockphoto.com

building was inaugurated, it was hailed as a great success.

Landmark Law Tested – In the heyday of rail travel, Grand Central was hopping day and night. In 1947 more than 65 million people traveled the rails via Grand Central Terminal. In the 1950s, though, subsidized highways and parkways made driving convenient and affordable, and railroad usage plummeted. At the same time, the price of real estate in Midtown was skyrocketing. The railroad sold its office building behind the terminal in 1958 to make room for the 59-story Pan Am Building (now the MetLife Building). In 1968 the railroad wanted to demolish the terminal itself (but keep the facade) and build a 55-story tower on the site. The city's landmark commission, established in response to the destruction of Pennsylvania Station

in 1967, rejected the proposal and was sued by the railroad as a result. The case went all the way to the Supreme Court, where in 1978 the city prevailed in a 6–3 decision, a true landmark ruling. Still, Grand Central was in dire need of repair. In 1990 a $425 million master plan was adopted to bring the terminal back to its 1913 splendor. Eight years later the grandly restored Grand Central was rededicated.

Visit

🕐*Open year-round daily 5.30am–2am (shops and restaurants have shorter hours). www.grandcentralterminal.com.* To take a **self-guided tour** of the station, go to the "I LOVE NEW YORK" information window and pick up a map and directory. You can also print out the walking tour information from the web-

---

Grand Central Terminal: Shops to Single Out

Among the main-floor concourse shops (there are nearly 50), keep these in mind: under the West Balcony, the **New York Transit Museum Gallery and Store** (🕐*open Mon–Fri 8am–8pm, Sat–Sun 10am–6pm; ☏212-878-0106; www.mta.info/museum*), an annex of the main museum in Brooklyn Heights, mounts changing exhibits on transportation history and sells transit-related merchandise, such as wallet-size subway maps. Under the East Balcony, the **Grand Central Market** (🕐*open Mon–Fri 7am–9pm, Sat 10am–7pm, Sun 11am–6pm*) is a fresh-foods bazaar, with outposts of local gourmet companies such as Oren's Daily Roast coffee and Murray's Cheese, as well as a butcher, a fishmonger and several produce stalls.

Grand Central Oyster Bar and Restaurant

Richard B. Levine/Photoshot

Grand Central Terminal, lower level. ☎212-490-6650. www.oysterbarny.com.
The Guastavino-tiled ceiling, so low you can practically touch it, hovers over this famed restaurant, where New Yorkers, not just travelers, come for the best selection of fresh seafood in the city. Settle in at the counter and order oysters Rockefeller and clam chowder—it's a tradition. The shellfish stews are also divine. The extensive wine list of some 400 bottles features many available by the glass.

site. Guided tours are offered Wednesdays and Fridays. The Wednesday tour is led by the **Municipal Arts Society** (*☞$10 suggested donation; ☎212-935-3960)*: meet at the information booth in the center of the main concourse at 12.30pm. The Friday tour is led by the **Grand Central Partnership** (*☞free; ☎212-883-2420;)*: meet in the sculpture court of 120 Park Avenue at the southwest corner of Park Avenue and 42nd Street at 12.30pm.

Cleaned and renovated in 2005, the 42nd Street granite **facade** is pierced by three massive arched windows separated by an order of double columns. Surmounting the windows are the immense 13ft clock and Jules-Félix Coutan's sculpture *Transportation* (1914), which incorporates the figure of Mercury (commerce) flanked by Hercules (strength) and Minerva (intellect). Below the sculpture stands a bronze statue (1869) of Cornelius Vanderbilt.

Grand Central Terminal's 12,000sq-ft **Main Concourse** is one of the most spectacular spaces in the city. In the center stands a brass and onyx clock atop an information booth, a traditional New York City rendezvous point. On each end of the hall, balconies, approached by grand staircases, hold shops and restaurants. But it is the 12-story-high turquoise **vaulted ceiling**, decorated

with electrified constellations of the zodiac, that makes Grand Central grand: not only is it gorgeous to look at, but its height causes sounds in the concourse to be pleasantly muffled, as they would be in a cathedral. One of the city's least-known oddities is that the zodiac was created backward in 1913; terminal representatives say it will probably never be corrected.

Beneath the Main Concourse is a sprawling **Dining Concourse** (*☉open Mon–Sat 7am–9pm, Sun 11am–6pm)*, a food court featuring locally owned restaurants. Here you'll find the best quick bites in the area, especially on weekends, when lunch spots catering to the office crowd are closed. Try Two Boots' pizza, Pepe Rosso's panini or Hale & Hearty's soup, and don't miss the Oyster Bar (*☞see box above)*.

The Morgan Library★★
225 Madison Ave. at E. 36th St.
☞See Major Manhattan Museums.

Saint Bartholomew's Church★
325 Park Ave. at E. 51st St. ☉Open year-round Mon–Wed & Fri–Sat 8am–6pm, Thu 8am–7pm, Sun 8am–7.30pm.
☞Art & architecture tour following Sun service, approximately 12.15pm (☞$7 suggested donation). ☎212-378-0222. www.stbarts.org.

😋 A Bit of Advice 😋

Hands-down, the best place in Midtown for an outdoor meal or glass of wine on a warm day is Inside Park, the cafe at St. Bart's. The food is great: gourmet burgers, grilled fish, delectable pastas all using organic or sustainably produced ingredients—and the atmosphere is even better. Umbrella-shaped tables cover the church's historic terrace (🕐open spring–fall), which is elevated enough from the street to provide a soothing respite from traffic but is still very much part of the neighborhood. It offers great views of the adjoining church and nearby skyscrapers. *109 E. 50th St. at Park Ave. 🕐Open Apr–Oct daily for breakfast & lunch, Mon–Sat for dinner; rest of year Mon–Fri for breakfast & lunch. 🕾212-593-3333. www.insideparknyc.com.*

Considered one of architect Bertram G. Goodhue's most successful constructions, this Episcopal church (1919) expertly blends Romanesque style with Byzantine details. Its multicolored dome and terraced garden provide a soothing contrast to a neighborhood that abounds in sharp angles, metal and glass.

The eclectic front **portal** (1903), donated by the Vanderbilts, was moved here from the original St. Bartholomew's Church, which stood on Madison Avenue from 1872 to 1918. Its three pairs of sculptured bronze doors depict scenes from the Bible.

Sony Wonder Technology Lab

Sony Wonder Technology Lab

Immediately upon entering the **narthex**, look up: the mosaic ceiling is fantastic. In the baptistery stands the statue of a kneeling angel, the work of 19C English sculptor James Redfern. The church's Aeolian organ is the largest in the city. The church's cafe, Inside Park, is quite popular (ᵇsee box above).

Scandinavia House★

58 Park Ave. at E. 38th St. 🕐Open year-round Tue–Sat noon–6pm. 🕐Closed major holidays. ∾Free. 🕾212-779-3587. www.scandinaviahouse.org.

Uncompromisingly modern, this zinc, glass and spruce structure houses the American-Scandinavian Foundation, the cultural headquarters for the five Nordic countries in the US. The building (2000, Polshek Partners) rises six stories and contains a wood-paneled theater, light-filled galleries, a glass-enclosed gift shop and the Smörgås Chef restaurant (🕐open Mon–Sat 11am–10pm, Sun 11am–5pm; 🕾212-847-9745), an elegant, smörgåsbord-style cafe serving Scan-

dinavian specialties. Major exhibits on Scandinavian art and design rotate through the spacious galleries; there are also frequent film screenings, concerts, children's programs, lectures and programs such as a recent retrospective of the life and work of Victor Borge.

👥 Sony Wonder Technology Lab★

Sony Plaza Bldg., 550 Madison Ave. at E. 56th St. 🕐Open year-round Tue–Sat 10am–5pm, Sun noon–5pm. 🕐Closed major holidays. ∾Free; entry tickets required; ☞reservations recommended. 🕾212-833-8100. www.sonywondertechlab.com.

Sprawling over four floors of the Sony Plaza Building, this high-tech wonderland encourages kids (eight and older) to explore electronics through structured-play environments. Interactive exhibits include using digital instruments to create a song, editing a music video and assisting a doctor with an ultrasound examination and performing virtual

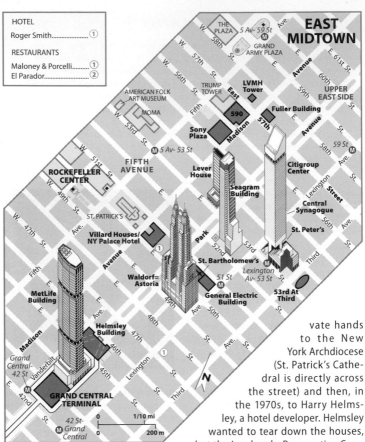

EAST MIDTOWN

UPPER EAST SIDE

FIFTH AVENUE

CRYSLER BUILDING ✈ ②

open-heart surgery. For tech-minded children it's great fun, but call in advance to make a reservation, especially on weekdays, when it fills with school groups.

Villard Houses★
(New York Palace Hotel)

451–457 Madison Ave. at E. 50th St.

In 1881 Henry Villard, a Bavarian immigrant who founded the *New York Evening Post*, hired McKim, Mead and White to design a group of six town houses: one for himself and the others for sale. The architects looked to the Palazzo della Cancelleria in Rome for inspiration, setting the brownstones in a U-shape around a central courtyard. Villard moved in with his family in 1883, but declared bankruptcy shortly afterward and had to sell the complex. It passed from pri-

vate hands to the New York Archdiocese (St. Patrick's Cathedral is directly across the street) and then, in the 1970s, to Harry Helmsley, a hotel developer. Helmsley wanted to tear down the houses, but the Landmarks Preservation Commission stopped him. His solution? Build a 55-story skyscraper directly on top of the houses.

To get a sense of the grandeur of the original homes, enter the courtyard—formerly a carriage yard—through the wrought-iron gates fronting Madison Avenue, and step inside the central mansion. Appointed in an ornate, Italian Renaissance style, this is the lobby of the luxurious **New York Palace Hotel**. On the second level, the red Verona fireplace, original to the Villard Houses, was crafted by Augustus Saint-Gaudens.

Waldorf-Astoria Hotel★

301 Park Ave. between E. 49th & E. 50th Sts. ✆212-355-3000. www.waldorfastoria.com.

This world-famous hotel (1931, Schultze and Weaver) occupies an entire city

Park Avenue Lobby, Waldorf-Astoria Hotel

Waldorf-Astoria

block. Distinguished by its twin chrome-capped towers rising 47 stories from an 18-story granite base, it replaced two separate hotels (the Waldorf and the Astoria) that were demolished to make way for the Empire State Building. The lush apartments in the north tower *(accessible via a private entrance on 50th St.)* have been occupied by such notables as Herbert Hoover, Henry Kissinger, John F. Kennedy and Cary Grant. According to long-standing protocol, certain dignitaries who stay at the Waldorf are entitled to see their national flags flying in front of the hotel.

The elegant main **lobby** has an eclectic mix of art deco ornamentation and Second Empire furnishings. Its marble floor is embellished by an intricate mosaic known as the *Wheel of Life*. The bronze clock in the east lobby was crafted in London in 1893.

Central Synagogue

652 Lexington Ave. at E. 55th St.
Sanctuary tour Wed 12.45pm. Free. 212-838-5122. *www.centralsynagogue.org.*
Distinguished by its bronze onion domes, this landmark structure was designed in 1870 by the German architect Henry Fernbach for a Reform congregation that traces its roots back to 1838. It is the oldest synagogue in continuous use in the city. The masonry exterior is dominated by two octagonal towers rising 122 feet and topped with onion domes of green copper. Following a devastating 1998 fire that collapsed the roof and required removal of nearly all the interior surfaces, the **sanctuary**★ has been fully restored, with elaborate new stenciling, woodwork and stained glass.

ADDRESSES

FULLER BUILDING GALLERIES

The historic Fuller Building (41 E. 57th St.) hosts a trove of art galleries, making it a little hive of Uptown artistic commerce. A few not to miss:

Bonni Benrubi Gallery – *13th floor* 212-888-6007. *www.bonnibenrubi. com.* Opened in 1987, Bonni Benrubi brings up-and-coming photographers to the fore, including Matthew Pillsbury and Massimo Vitali.

David Findlay Gallery – *11th floor.* 212-486-7660. *www.davidfindlayjr. com.* You'll find 20C contemporary and estate works here by Howard Daum, Robert Henri and Alfrend Henry Maurer, among others.

Howard Greenberg Gallery – *14th floor.* 212-334-0010. *www. howardgreenberg.com.* Long a leading light in the market for 20C fine art photography, Greenberg maintains an illustrious roster including Edward Steichen, Diane Arbus, Robert Capa, Dorothea Lange and Alfred Stieglitz.

Lever House

©Mark Fiennes/Arcaid/Corbis

Architecture Buffs

East Midtown contains some of New York's most distinctive high-rises. Here are some of the most famous—and infamous.

Lever House★★ – *390 Park Ave. between E. 53rd & E. 54th Sts.* When it opened in 1952, the green-glass Lever House, designed by Skidmore, Owings and Merrill, was considered avant-garde. Indeed, it stood in sharp contrast to the stone and brick apartment buildings of Park Avenue. But the Lever House would have many international-style imitators on Park Avenue and throughout the city. The 21-story vertical slab of green glass and stainless steel seems to float above a two-story horizontal base.

Seagram Building

©Richard E. Levine/UPPA/Photoshot

Seagram Building★★ – *375 Park Ave. between E. 52nd & E. 53rd Sts.* New York City's only creation by German-born Ludwig Mies van der Rohe (with Philip Johnson), this bronze glass-and-steel tower (1958) is widely regarded as one of the finest International-style skyscrapers ever made. Less than half of its "zoning envelope" was used; Mies opted instead to set the slender, 38-story tower on pillars in a vast granite plaza—a radical gesture considering the price of real estate.

53rd At Third★ – *885 Third Ave. between E. 53rd & E. 54th Sts.* It should be obvious at a glance why people call this otherwise nameless skyscraper the "lipstick building." Rising in tiers from tall columns, the elliptical tower of reddish-brown and pink stone and glass was designed by post-Modernists Philip Johnson and John Burgee and completed in 1986.

Chanin Building★ – *122 E. 42nd St. at Lexington Ave.* A prime example of the art deco style, this 56-story building (1929, Irwin Chanin) is wrapped with a terracotta frieze of floral bas-reliefs by Edward Trumbell on its bottom four floors. Inside the intricately detailed lobby, look at the door frames, grilles and mailboxes.

Citigroup Center★ – *153 E. 53rd St. at Lexington Ave.* This 915ft aluminum-and-glass-sheathed tower (1978) is best known for its top, which slopes at a 45-degree angle and is visible in most pictures of the New York City skyline. The tower stands on four colossal pillars—each 9 stories, or 115ft high, and 22ft square—set at the center of each side, rather than at the corners of the building. Beneath these cantilevered corners, which extend 72ft from the central columns, nestles **St. Peter's Church** *(access on E. 54th St.)*, an evangelical Lutheran church that sold its land to Citicorp on the condition that a new church would be in the complex.

Daily News Building★

– *220 E. 42nd St. at Second Ave.* Abandoning the Gothic style popular at the time, the Daily News Building (1930) features white-brick piers alternating with patterned red-and-black-brick spandrels, giving the tower a vertical striped look and an illusion of height greater than its actual 37 stories. The lobby is famed for its huge revolving **globe** (12ft in diameter) and the clock that gives readings in 17 time zones. The floor is laid out as a giant compass indicating most of the principal cities of the world and their distance from New York City.

Fuller Building★

– *41 E. 57th St. at Madison Ave.* Art deco from top to bottom, this black granite building (1929) is topped by a limestone tower. In the richly ornamented **lobby**, bronze elevator doors chronicle the building's construction and the mosaic floor displays other Fuller Construction Co. commissions, notably the Flatiron Building. The Fuller Building is home to many galleries.

General Electric Building★

– *570 Lexington Ave. at E. 51st St.* Its reddish-orange spire topped by a spiky crown, this marvelous, 51-story art deco creation (1931, Cross & Cross) was designed to be viewed in conjunction with its western neighbor, St. Bartholomew's Church. Decorative features include rays, flashes and lightning bolts, which are particularly appropriate to the building's principal tenant.

Helmsley Building★

– *230 Park Ave. at E. 46th St.* Once the headquarters of Cornelius Vanderbilt's New York Central Railroad Co., this 1929 tower is pierced by two tunnels reserved for Park Avenue motor traffic and two street-level arcades for pedestrians. The Renaissance Revival building was designed by Warren & Wetmore, the firm responsible for Grand Central Terminal's imposing exterior. Step inside the opulent lobby to admire the travertine walls and bronze detailing.

Step back, way back, perhaps to 50th Street, to admire the building's gilded cupola.

LVMH Tower★

– *17–21 E. 57th St. between Fifth & Madison Aves.* Slender, multifaceted, the 23-story Louis Vuitton–Moët Hennessey building (1999, Christian de Portzamparc) looks as if it were chipped out of crystal, especially when illuminated at night. It houses retail space on the first two levels and LVMH's offices on the upper floors. The Louis Vuitton store, the world's largest, stands a few doors down, on the corner of Fifth Avenue *(1 E. 57th St.)*. Japanese architect Jun Aoki added the intriguing glass facade in 2004.

Sony Plaza★ (former AT&T headquarters)

– *550 Madison Ave. between E. 55th & E. 56th Sts.* The "lipstick building" (885 Third Ave.) isn't the only Philip Johnson–John Burgee skyscraper with a nickname. This one, completed in 1984, is called the "Chippendale building" for its unusual roofline, which looks like the top of a colonial cupboard (a triangle split at the peak by a semicircular hollow). To conserve energy, only a third of the 40-story structure's pink-granite exterior is covered with windows.

590 Madison Avenue (former IBM Building)

– *590 Madison Ave. at E. 56th St.* A 17ft flame-red stabile by Alexander Calder stands sentinel at the doorway of this polished black granite, 43-story high-rise (1983, Edward Larrabee Barnes). Note the imposing cut-corner overhang above its entrance, a common feature of 1980s skyscrapers. The building's greenhouse-like public **atrium**★ is one of the most pleasant in the district.

MetLife Building (former Pan Am Building)

– *200 Park Ave. at E. 45th St.* Towering 59 stories over Grand Central Terminal, this octagonal 'scraper (1963) was conceived by a group of architects that included Walter Gropius of the Bauhaus school.

United Nations Headquarters★★★

The United Nations (UN) complex in New York enjoys extraterritorial status. And it really does feel like a world unto itself. It's abuzz with diplomats from all corners of the world—some in the native dress of their home countries—when the General Assembly is in session (Sept–Dec). Even if you don't plan on taking a guided tour (the only way to gain access to the inner chambers), it's worth sending your bag through the metal detector to see the artwork and exhibits inside the General Assembly building and learn about this renowned institution.

A BIT OF HISTORY

An Ambitious Goal – The United Nations is essentially a town hall for global affairs. Its basic structure was established in 1944 at a series of conferences held at the Dumbarton Oaks mansion in Washington, DC.

The point of those meetings, which were attended by representatives from the US, Great Britain, China and the Soviet Union, was to create an international body more capable of maintaining world peace than the League of Nations, the organization created by US president Woodrow Wilson after World War I.

The UN officially came into existence on October 24, 1945, when its charter—which had been signed in San Francisco on June 26 of that year—was ratified by a majority of the 51 founding members. The UN Charter's ambitious goals include fostering international cooperation to solve economic, social, cultural and humanitarian problems; resolving international disputes peacefully; and ending threats or use of force against any nation.

Unlike its predecessor, the League of Nations, the United Nations has a security council that can approve the use of force against a country that is deemed to have infringed on the rights of another country.

MTA Subway: 4, 5, 6, 7 train to Grand Central Terminal.

Map: Following pages.

Location: The UN complex is situated on 18 acres of land along the East River, between East 42nd and East 48th Streets. The General Assembly Hall and Conference Building are accessible only by guided tour. The Secretariat Building and the Library are closed to the public.

Timing: To avoid long lines, arrive at the UN when it opens at 9am. Be prepared for a **security screening** and a waiting period until you are called for your 1hr tour. All large parcels must be checked before entering, so go to the UN with as little as possible. The only **place to eat** is the coffee shop in the basement of the General Assembly Building.

Building the UN – The decision to build the UN headquarters in New York City was made in London by the General Assembly at its first session, on February 14, 1946, after offers for permanent sites had been received from many parts of the world. One reason New York was chosen over other US cities is that the Soviet Union threatened to boycott the organization if it was on the West Coast. In December 1946 John D. Rockefeller Jr. offered the United Nations a gift of $8.5 million to acquire the present site on the East River. At the time, this area consisted mainly of slaughterhouses and breweries. The construction program, costing more than $67 million, was financed in large part by the US government, which made available an interest-free loan of $65 million—a sum that has been entirely reimbursed.

American architect Wallace K. Harrison, who would later design Lincoln Center, oversaw a team of architects from 10

United Nations Headquarters

©JTB/Photoshot

countries—including **Charles E. Le Corbusier** of France and **Oscar Niemeyer** of Brazil. They came up with a master plan of four buildings on grounds that are, at their eastern edge, cantilevered over Frankin D. Roosevelt (FDR) Drive to take advantage of the riverfront.

The 39-story Secretariat Building was inaugurated in 1950; the sloping General Assembly Building and the boxy Conference Building came next, in 1952; and the marble, glass and aluminum Dag Hammarskjöld Memorial Library was completed in 1961. Today, five of the six main organs of the UN are housed here. The sixth—the International Court of Justice—is located at The Hague in the Netherlands. A nearly $2 billion renovation of the complex began in 2009, with a projected completion date of 2013.

THE GROUNDS

Entrance on First Ave. between E. 45th & E. 46th Sts.

The United Nations flies the flags of its 192 member states on an arc of flag-poles along First Avenue. The flags are arranged north to south in English alphabetical order, from Afghanistan to Zimbabwe. (Delegations seated in the General Assembly follow the same order, although the starting point in the alphabet varies from year to year, depending on which member state is randomly selected to take the first seat.)

Two striking sculptures stand near the visitor entrance. A gift from the country of Luxembourg, **Non-Violence**★, the giant revolver with the knotted barrel, was created by the artist Carl Fredrik Reutersward in 1988. Italy donated **Sphere Within a Sphere**★, by Italian sculptor Arnaldo Pomodoro, to the UN in 1996.

The promenade along the north end of the General Assembly Building affords a view of the gardens (⊶ *closed to the public*), which are dotted with outdoor sculpture. The bronze equestrian statue, *Peace* (1954, Anton Augustincic), was a gift from Yugoslavia.

THE BUILDINGS
General Assembly Building★★

Public Areas: ◷*Open year-round daily 9am–4.45pm.* ◷*Closed major holidays.* ☛*Other parts of the UN complex accessible by guided tour (45min) only, every 30–60min Mon–Fri 9am–4.45pm, Sat–Sun 10am–4.15pm;* ☛*limited schedule in effect during the general debate (mid-Sept–mid-Oct), check the website for details. Children under 5 not permitted on tours. For tours in lan-*

The UN's Top Dog

The secretary-general, the UN's highest-ranking official, is appointed by the General Assembly on the recommendation of the Security Council for a five-year term, and is charged with carrying out the decisions made by the six organs of the UN. He or she may bring to the General Assembly any matter that appears to threaten international peace. Since 1946, eight men held this coveted and controversial title: Trygve Lie of Norway (1946–52), Dag Hammarskjöld of Sweden (1953–61), U Thant of Burma (1961–71), Kurt Waldheim of Austria (1972–81), Javier Pérez de Cuéllar of Peru (1982–91), Boutros Boutros-Ghali of Egypt (1992–96), Kofi Annan of Ghana (1997–2006) and currently Ban Ki-moon of Korea.

guages other than English, call ℘212-963-7539 on the day you would like to visit. ☜$16. ℘212-963-4475 (inquiries); ℘212-963-8687 (tour information). http://visit.un.org.

The heart of the United Nations, this long, low-lying structure, marked by a sloping roof and bowed sides, contains the vaulted Assembly Hall. The vast **lobby** is a fascinating space full of historic objects (a model of Sputnik I, a Foucault pendulum and a statue of Poseidon) as well as three rotating **art exhibits**, usually centered on international themes. On the west side of the lobby is a dramatic, 15ft-by-12ft **stained-glass window** by Marc Chagall, symbolic of humankind's struggle for peace. Unveiled in 1964 as a memorial to former UN secretary-general Dag Hammarskjöld, the window was contributed by members of the UN staff and the artist. Beside the window is a small **meditation room**, whose focal point is a massive block of iron ore dimly spotlit from above. The **basement**, accessed by a curving staircase to the left of the entrance, contains the UN post office, which has its own postmark and stamps, as well as an old-fashioned coffee shop, a public inquiries office, a bookstore, a gift shop and public restrooms.

General Assembly Hall

☜Visit by guided tour only. Decorated in blue, green and gold, this oval hall is situated above the lobby. It is 165ft long and 115ft wide, with a ceiling that rises 75ft to an oval skylight. Some 1,321 seats on stepped platforms form an arc around the raised podium on which the president of the General Assembly, the UN secretary-general and a high-ranking UN official sit. Above the podium, the emblem of the United Nations hangs between the illuminated boards indicating members' votes. On either side are glass-enclosed booths for the interpreters who work in the six official UN languages (Arabic, Chinese, English, French, Russian and Spanish). All 1,898 seats in the hall (several hundred are reserved for the news media, for alternate delegates and for the public) are equipped with earphones that allow the listener to tune in to a translation of the proceedings in any of the six official languages. The side walls are decorated with **murals** by Fernand Léger of France. The General Assembly meets every year in regular session, which starts in September. Special sessions and emergency sessions may be called at the request of the Security Council or by a majority of the member states. The assembly may discuss any matters within the scope of the UN Charter, except those under consideration by the Security Council.

Secretariat Building★★

⊶Closed to the public. This tall, thin slab of glass and marble is one of the city's most distinctive structures. Rising 39 stories without a setback, it presents broad rectangular faces of green-tinted glass to both the city and the river. In contrast, its narrow north and south facades are capped with 2,000 tons of white Vermont marble. In front of the building stands a circular marble pool that contains Single Form (**1** on map), an abstract sculpture (1964) by Barbara Hepworth.

Conference Building

☛*Closed for renovation. Projected reopening: 2013.* This five-story building extends 400ft along the East River on land cantilevered over FDR Drive. As its name suggests, the structure contains a number of meeting rooms as well as darkrooms, printing presses and recording studios. Its narrow top floor contains the delegates' dining room, private dining rooms, a staff cafe and a kitchen. The three main conference rooms, each 72ft wide, 135ft long and 24ft high, contain the chambers for the Security Council, the Trusteeship Council and the Economic and Social Council.

Security Council Chamber – Donated by Norway, this chamber is decorated with gold-and-blue wall hangings and a mural by Norwegian artist Per Krohg symbolizing Peace and Liberty, Equality and Fraternity. The Security Council has primary responsibility for the maintenance of international peace and can be convened at any time members feel that peace is threatened. The council is made up of 15 member states: a representative from each of the five permanent member states (China, France, the Russian Federation, Great Britain and the US) and a representative from each of 10 nonpermanent members chosen by the General Assembly for two-year terms.

Trusteeship Council – The furnishings in this room were donated by Denmark. Precious woods sheathe the walls and provide the backdrop for a large teak statue of a woman releasing a bluebird, which symbolizes Hope and Independence. The Trusteeship Council was created with the goal of helping nonautonomous colonies exercise their right to self-determination. Between 1946 and 1994, when the council formally suspended regular meetings, more than 70 former colonial territories, including all of the original 11 trust territories, exercised self-determination.

Economic and Social Council – This room was designed by Sven Markelius of Sweden with funds contributed by Sweden. It features exposed pipes and ducts, dark-paneled walls, a dropped ceiling and a brightly lit meeting area at the center. The 54-member council coordinates the efforts and resources of various UN and affiliated organizations

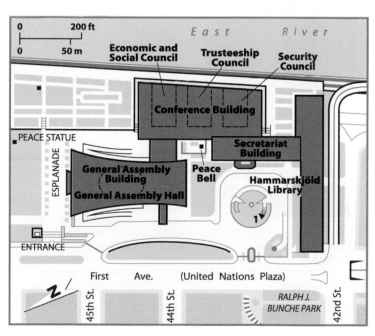

toward the alleviation of economic and social problems.

Garden – o—*Closed to the public.* In the garden just west of the Conference Building between the Secretariat and Assembly buildings stands a pagoda sheltering a Japanese **peace bell** made of copper coins and metal donated by the children of 60 countries, as well as a **sculpture** by Henry Moore titled *Reclining Figure: Hand.*

Hammarskjöld Library

o—*Closed to the public.* Located on the southwest corner of the complex, the library, a gift of the Ford Foundation, is dedicated to the memory of the second secretary-general, Dag Hammarskjöld, killed in 1961 in a plane crash during a peacekeeping mission to the Congo. Its marble walls enclose 380,000 volumes for the use of UN delegates, Secretariat staff members and scholars. In addition, there are newspapers, reading rooms, a collection of 80,000 maps and an auditorium.

ADDITIONAL SIGHTS
Dag Hammarskjöld Plaza
E. 47th St. between First & Second Aves. www.hammarskjoldplaza.org.
This block-long promenade serves as an informal gateway to the UN. Once mainly a staging area for demonstrations, it was redesigned in the mid-1990s with help from local volunteers. Today it's the site of a woodland sanctuary known as the Katharine Hepburn Garden (Hepburn was a longtime resident of the neighborhood), a Holocaust memorial wall and a **farmers' market** (◷*Mar–Nov Wed*).

Japan Society
333 E. 47th St. ◷*Special exhibitions only, Tue–Thu 11am–6pm, Fri 1 1am–9pm, Sat–Sun 11am–5pm.*

The Trump in Trump World Tower

Trump World Tower
©Jeff Gynane/BigStockPhoto.com

Born in Queens in 1946, Donald Trump began perfecting the "Art of the Deal" at a young age. After graduating from Wharton, the University of Pennsylvania's prestigious school of business, he entered the world of real estate under his father's tutelage. Before long, he was on his own in Manhattan, beginning a steady acquisition of the properties and constructing the buildings that constitute his New York City empire today. Most renowned is Trump Tower, completed in 1983, which receives over 2.5 million visitors a year. The equally impressive Trump World Tower, rising high above the neighboring United Nations Headquarters, was completed in 2001. Among his many other buildings in Manhattan are Trump Place, Trump International Hotel and Tower, Trump Parc, Trump Park Avenue, Trump Plaza, Trump Palace, and 610 Park Avenue. In 2004 "The Donald"—a title bestowed by his former wife Ivana—became a television star with the instant success of his NBC business-reality show *The Apprentice*. As a result, the already famous Trump has increased his pop-culture notoriety to epic proportions. His trademark hairstyle is more recognizable than ever, as is his contribution to the American lexicon: "You're fired."

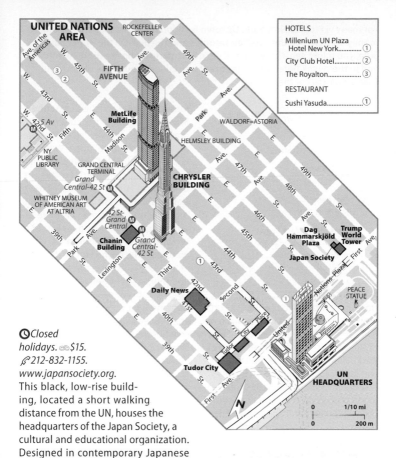

UNITED NATIONS AREA

ROCKEFELLER CENTER

FIFTH AVENUE

MetLife Building

NY PUBLIC LIBRARY

GRAND CENTRAL TERMINAL

Grand Central-42 St

WHITNEY MUSEUM OF AMERICAN ART AT ALTRIA

42 St-Grand Central

Chanin Building

Grand Central-42 St

WALDORF=ASTORIA

HELMSLEY BUILDING

CHRYSLER BUILDING

Dag Hammarskjöld Plaza

Trump World Tower

Japan Society

Daily News

Tudor City

PEACE STATUE

UN HEADQUARTERS

N

0   1/10 mi
0   200 m

HOTELS

Millenium UN Plaza Hotel New York............... ①

City Club Hotel.............. ②

The Royalton.................. ③

RESTAURANT

Sushi Yasuda..................... ①

🕐 *Closed holidays.* 💲*$15.* 📞*212-832-1155. www.japansociety.org.*
This black, low-rise building, located a short walking distance from the UN, houses the headquarters of the Japan Society, a cultural and educational organization. Designed in contemporary Japanese style, the interior contains a bamboo pool, exhibit gallery, auditorium, library, language center, conference rooms and garden, all of which blend together to create a tranquil effect. The center sponsors two major art installations a year, as well as ongoing film series, lectures and performances.

Trump World Tower

845 United Nations Plaza.
Soaring 881ft over the United Nations is **Donald Trump**'s latest contribution to the New York skyline: the world's tallest residential building. The 72-story bronze-glass box (2001, Costas Kondylis and Partners) represents a return to Modernist simplicity; inside, though, more is more. A deal to sell the four top-floor co-ops as a single $38 million, 20,000sq-ft duplex penthouse fell through. Undeterred, Trump raised the asking price to $56 million. Yankees shortstop Derek Jeter and Microsoft founder Bill Gates are among owners of more modestly priced apartments.

Tudor City

Tudor City Pl. at E. 42nd St. (access via stairs in Ralph J. Bunche Park at corner of First Ave. & 42nd St.).
When you step into this little oasis of Tudor Gothic apartment buildings and quaint parks, it's easy to forget you're in New York City. That was precisely developer Fred F. French's point. Around 1925 he began buying up dilapidated houses on the bluff-top site to replace them with housing affordable to the middle class. He had the structures face inward to a pleasant central courtyard and left the riverfront facades nearly windowless.

For many visitors to New York, Uptown is synonymous with upscale—old money, designer clothes, coiffed poodles and the like. On the Upper East Side, you might see a little bit of that, particularly along Madison Avenue and in the swank hotels and restaurants sprinkled around the district. But that is only part of the picture.

How Manhattan Is Divided

♦ **Downtown**
South of 34th Street

♦ **Midtown**
34th Street to 59th Street

♦ **Uptown**
North of 59th Street

♦ **East Side, West Side**
Fifth Avenue marks the dividing line

A Bit of History

Uptown Manhattan comprises, in short, everything north of 59th Street—a very large and diverse area. The focal point of Uptown is the aptly named **Central Park**. Though far from central when it was landscaped in the 1860s, this 843-acre greensward, arguably the greatest urban park in the world, now anchors Uptown Manhattan. To the east, on **Fifth Avenue**, you'll find the **Metropolitan Museum of Art** and the **Guggenheim Museum**, among other cultural treasures on Museum Mile. To the west lies the historically liberal Upper West Side, home to the **Lincoln Center** performing arts complex, the **American Museum of Natural History** and well-known **Columbia University**. Strange though it may sound, this area was once the ugly little sister of the Upper East Side: brownstone, the predominant building material, was frowned on by the social elite, whose members preferred bricks and mortar (or better yet, marble and gold leaf). In any case, that time is long past and the Upper West Side's brownstone-lined side streets are considered some of the city's prettiest.

North of Central Park, there's a sharp divide on either side of the park both racially and economically. Above 106th Street on the east side lies Spanish Harlem, or El Barrio, home to many of the city's Puerto Ricans; on the west side, Columbia University edges **Harlem**

Gondola on the lake in Central Park

Peter Wrenn/MICHELIN

GEORGE WASHINGTON BRIDGE

MANHATTAN
UPTOWN

THE BRONX

Strivers Row

W. 138th St.

Renaissance Ballroom and Casino

Abyssinian Baptist

W. 135th St.

Mother A.M.E. Zion

African American Walk of Fame

Schomburg Center

Florence Mills Home

Harlem YMCA

CITY COLLEGE OF NY

Broadway

Amsterdam Ave.

Convent Ave.

138th St.

Bruckner Blvd.

Willis Ave.

Third Ave.

W. 127th St.

HARLEM

Apollo Theater

Harlem USA

W. 122nd St.

Powell Jr. Blvd.

Douglass Blvd.

Studio Museum in Harlem

125th St.

General Grant National Memorial

MORNINGSIDE PARK

COLUMBIA UNIVERSITY

120th

St.

MARCUS GARVEY PARK

Riverside

Park

Riverside Drive

Cathedral of St. John the Divine

Frederick

116th

Nicholas

St.

Lenox (Malcolm X)

120th

EL BARRIO

HUDSON

RIVER

Cathedral Pkwy.

Adam

Central Park North

Malcolm Shabazz Harlem Market

MASJID MALCOLM SHABAZZ MOSQUE

116th

Fifth

Lexington

Third

Second

First

JEFFERSON PARK

106th

St.

Museum for African Art

Dana Discovery Center

Harlem Meer

Madison

110th

HARLEM RIVER

FIREMEN'S MEMORIAL

Conservatory Garden

El Museo del Barrio

106th

Riverside

West

Amsterdam Ave.

Manhattan Ave.

West

100th St.

Museum of the City of New York

WARDS ISLAND

Park

W. 96th St.

CENTRAL PARK

102nd

St.

Hell Gate

MILL ROCK

Islamic Cultural Center of New York

96th

St.

UPPER WEST SIDE

W. 92nd

St.

W. 90th

St.

W. 86th

St.

Jacqueline Kennedy Onassis Reservoir

Columbus

Park

FIFTH

Jewish Museum

Cooper-Hewitt, National Design Museum

Guggenheim Museum

90th

St.

Gracie Mansion

Carl Schurz Park

AMERICAN MUSEUM OF NATURAL HISTORY

THE METROPOLITAN MUSEUM OF ART

86th

Ave.

YORKVILLE

East End

New-York Historical Society

W. 79th St.

W. 74th

St.

81st

St.

UPPER EAST SIDE

79th

St.

Henry

Broadway

West End

W. 72nd

St.

W. 70th

St.

The Lake

Whitney Museum

Roosevelt

74th

St.

Ave.

Central

THE FRICK COLLECTION

72nd

St.

70th

St.

York

Island

Juilliard School

Amsterdam

65th St.

CENTRAL PARK

FIFTH

Madison

Park

Lexington

Third

First

BLACKWELL FARM HOUSE

Lincoln Center

Broadway

Columbus

W. 59th

St.

W. 57th

St.

W. 53rd

St.

Tenth Ave.

Eighth Ave.

63rd

Columbus Circle

9 W. 57th St.

CENTRAL MIDTOWN

Central Park South

Grand Army Plaza

Trump Tower

Bridgemarket

60th

59th St.

E. 57th St.

Tramway

Queensboro Bridge

WEST CHANNEL

EAST CHANNEL

FRANKLIN

0   1/2 mi

0   500 m

N

around 125th Street. The capital of African-American culture, Harlem was the birthplace of jazz in the 1920s and still has a number of cool live clubs. Still farther north, the island of Manhattan slims down to a narrow spit and rises up into rocky bluffs. Atop one of these,

you'll find **The Cloisters**, a castle constructed from the pieces of five French monasteries dating back to the 12C. The Metropolitan Museum displays some of its medieval collection here, including the legendary and mysterious Unicorn tapestries.

Central Park★★★

Manhattan's beloved backyard, this 843-acre haven of greenery, light and air draws more than 25 million people each year. Situated in the island's geographical center, Central Park measures 2.5mi long by .5mi wide, extending from 59th to 110th Streets, and Fifth Avenue to Central Park West. Framed by the enchanting silhouettes of surrounding buildings, the man-made park offers a quiet oasis in the heart of bustling Manhattan, and many opportunities for recreation.

MTA Subway: N, Q, R train to Fifth Ave.-59th St.

Map: Following pages.

Info: For public programs, go online or call 📞212-310-6600; for sports and recreation facilities 📞212-348-4867; www.centralparknyc.org. See visitor centers in the panel opposite.

Location: Use the map on the following pages to familiarize yourself with the park and for the walking tour.

Kids: See the Just for Kids sidebar, p198, for ideas.

A BIT OF HISTORY

An Idea Takes Shape – Editor and poet **William Cullen Bryant** launched the idea of Central Park in 1844 in his newspaper, the *New York Evening Post*. Bryant and other public-minded New Yorkers urged the city to acquire a "waste land" beyond 42nd Street. Some 750 acres of rock and swamp (from 59th to 106th Sts.) were purchased for $5 million. **Frederick Law Olmsted** (1822–1903) and **Calvert Vaux** (1824–95) won the competition for the park's design.

Years in the Making – Clearing began in 1858 with a labor force of 3,000 mostly Irish workers. After 19 years of extensive drainage, planting, road and

bridge building and ingenious landscaping, the park emerged essentially as we now know it. Olmsted and Vaux blended natural and man-made elements to create a park inspired by the Romantic style highly favored in the mid-19C. Over 185 acres were set aside for lakes and ponds. A public–private partnership between the Central Park Conservancy and the city's Department of Parks & Recreation, created in 1980, oversees the park's maintenance.

Central Park, looking south

©Terraxplorer/iStockphoto.com

VISITING CENTRAL PARK

Area code: 212

SAFETY Central Park is patrolled by the police and park rangers in vehicles, on horseback and on skates. Direct-line emergency call boxes are located throughout the park.
Explore the park in daylight hours. Avoid visiting at night, especially alone or in the Ramble.

VISITOR INFORMATION See **Information** at the beginning of the chapter. The park visitor centers are *(call for seasonal hours):* **The Dairy** *(65th St.)*, **Belvedere Castle** *(79th St.),* **North Chess & Checkers House** *(64th St.)*, **Tavern on the Green** *(67th St.)* and the **Charles A. Dana Discovery Center** *(Central Park North & Fifth Ave.)*. For additional information, contact the **Central Park Conservancy** *(℘310-6600; www.centralparknyc.org).*

RECREATION The **NY Road Runners Club** *℘860-4455. www.nyrrc.org.* Baseball/softball fields are converted for soccer/football in fall and winter *(use by permit only; ℘408-0209; www.nyc.gov/parks)*; **tennis courts** are located mid-park at 94th & 96th Streets and require a permit to use *(open Apr–Nov; ℘360-8133).*

Ice-skating lessons and skate rentals in season at **Wollman Rink** *(east side between 62nd & 63rd Sts.; $10.50 Mon–Fri, $15 Sat–Sun; ℘439-6900; www.wollmanskatingrink.com)* and **Lasker Rink** *(mid-park between 106th & 108th Sts.; $6.50; ℘917-492-3857).* Loeb Boathouse rents **bicycles** *(Apr–Nov daily 10am–6pm; $9–$15/hr; ℘517-2233)* and **rowboats** *(Apr–Nov daily 10am–dusk; $12/hr);* **gondola rides** are also offered on the lake *(May–Sept Mon–Fri 5–9pm, Sat–Sun 2–9pm; $30/30min, reservations required; ℘517-2233).*

TOURS Free walking tours by the **Central Park Conservancy** *(for schedule, call ℘360-2726 or visit www.centralparknyc.org).* **Bike tours** *(Apr–Nov daily 10am, 1pm, 4pm, Sat–Sun also at 11am; $49, includes bike rental & tour guide; ℘541-8759; www.centralparkbiketours.com).*

Horse-drawn-carriage rides available at Central Park South near the Plaza Hotel and at Tavern on the Green *(year-round daily 24hrs/day unless temperature is below 18°F or above 89°F; 1–4 passengers; $50/per carriage for 20min).*

WALKING TOUR

Enter Central Park South at Fifth Ave. & E. 60th St. from Grand Army Plaza. Walk north to the Wildlife Center.
The first two digits of number plates on lampposts throughout the park indicate which cross street you are nearest. Just before the Wildlife Center, look west to see Wollman Memorial Rink, a popular spot for ice-skating in winter. To the south a crescent-shaped **pond**, surrounded by luxuriant vegetation, borders the Hallett Nature Sanctuary on a rocky outcrop.

Central Park Zoo

East side between 63rd & 66th Sts. Map available at entrance. Open daily 10am–4.30pm (winter), 5pm (summer), 5.30pm (summer weekends). $12;
$7 children (includes admission to Children's Zoo). ℘212-439-6500. www.centralparkzoo.com.
This 5.5-acre zoo houses more than 450 animals in a habitat that represents three climatic regions: the tropical zone, the temperate regions and the polar circle. Kids can feed the domesticated animals in the Children's Zoo (feed available for purchase). Notice the Delacorte Clock over the entrance arch, with its moving bronze animal figures.

▶ *Exit the Children's Zoo at the north end and walk under 65th St. Bear left at the fork, then left again to take the wide steps to cross East Dr. Enter the southern end of The Mall at the statue of Shakespeare.*

The Mall, lined with benches

Peter Wrenn/MICHELIN

The Mall

This straight, wide path is lined with elms and sculptures of famous writers. At the north end, the Naumburg Bandshell is still used for performances. Summer evening events are staged at SummerStage at the Rumsey Playfield, east of the band shell. Lying west of the Mall, the Sheep Meadow attracts throngs of people to its green lawn, which also offers superb views of the city skyline. To the far west of the Sheep Meadow stands Tavern on the Green (*see sidebar below*), housed in a former sheep barn (1870).

▷ *From The Mall, take the steps down to Bethesda Terrace.*

Bethesda Terrace

Considered the centerpiece of the park, this lovely sandstone plaza resembles a Spanish courtyard with its sweeping stairs and central fountain. Crowning the fountain is a statue by Emma Stebbins titled *Angel of the Waters* (1868).

▷ *From the fountain, take the pathway to the left.*

The Lake

A graceful iron bridge, Bow Bridge has been the subject of many a photograph. To the west lie the **Strawberry Fields** and the International Garden of Peace honoring musician John Lennon, one of the famous Beatles. It lies steps away from the Dakota apartment building, where Lennon lived and was murdered. To the east sits the Loeb Boathouse, a popular eating spot in summer. Between the lake and Fifth Avenue, Conservatory Water attracts mariners of all ages with model sailboats.

▷ *Enter the Ramble. ☻To reduce your chances of getting lost, stay on paths on the west side of the Ramble, keeping the lake in view as much as possible.*

The Ramble

Interrupted by a meandering brook, this 38-acre wooded hill north of the lake is threaded with paths that wind among large boulders.

▷ *You will cross two bridges before you reach West Dr. Then turn northward on West Dr.*

Swedish Cottage

This log structure, a model of a Swedish schoolhouse, was built in Central Park in 1877. It now serves as home to the 👤👤 **Marionette Theatre**, which presents puppet shows throughout the year (*see Just for Kids sidebar above for*

Tavern on the Green

Edging the west side of Central Park, the famed **Tavern on the Green** restaurant has been the site of innumerable film and television scenes and serves as the finish line for the New York Marathon. In 2010 the building was reconceived as the **Tavern on the Green Visitor Center & Gift Shop**, one of the Central Park Conservancy's five visitor centers in the park. You can still get a bite to eat, but now it will be at one of four upscale mobile food trucks that set up there daily. Future plans are up in the air, but for the time being the space is open for all to experience (*at W. 67th St; www.centralparknyc.org*).

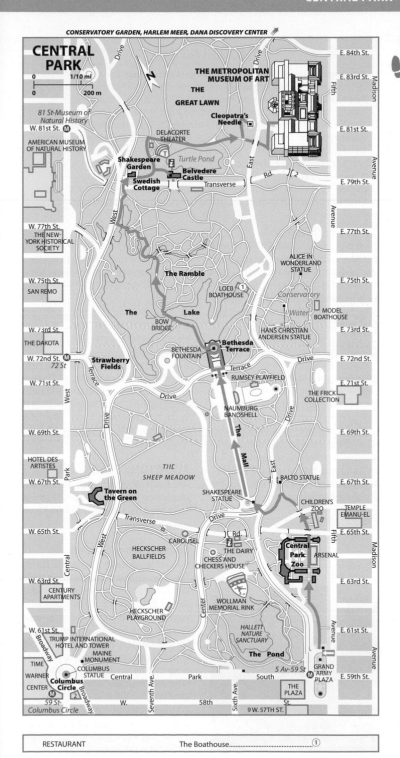

CONSERVATORY GARDEN, HARLEM MEER, DANA DISCOVERY CENTER

RESTAURANT — The Boathouse..................... ①

👥 Just For Kids

Popular destinations for children include the **Central Park Zoo** (☜*$7 for children ages 3–12*), the **Carousel** *(weather permitting;* ☜*$1.25/ride)* and the **Swedish Cottage Marionette Theatre** *(W. 79th St. & West Dr.; performances year-round Mon–Fri 10.30am, noon, Wed also 2.30pm, Sat–Sun 1pm;* ☜*$8 adults, $5 children, reservations required;* ✆*212-988-9093).* Educational field day kits (games and sports equipment) are available at the **North Meadow Recreation Center**, where wall climbing, challenge courses and adventure programs for youth are offered year-round *(mid-park at 97th St.;* ✆*212-348-4867).* There's ⌇ swimming at Lasker Pool *(*◷*daily in season 11am–3pm, 4–7pm),* catch-and-release ⌇ fishing at Harlem Meer (bamboo poles and bait available at the Dana Discovery Center) and storytelling at the Hans Christian Andersen statue.

hours and prices). In the **Shakespeare Garden**, adjacent to the cottage, flowers, herbs, trees and shrubs that are mentioned in the works of the Bard can be seen. Small plaques display quotes from the playwright pertinent to a garden setting.

▷ *Go up the stairs to Belvedere Castle.*

Belvedere Castle

Complete with merlons and crenels, Belvedere Castle was designed by Vaux as an imitation medieval Scottish castle (1872). Its site atop Vista Rock permits views of the northern end of the park. Just north of Belvedere Castle lie Turtle Pond and the Delacorte Theater. Beyond, the **Great Lawn** occupies the site of the Receiving Reservoir, opened

in 1842 to supply the city water system. Today it is best known as the setting for performances by the Metropolitan Opera and the New York Philharmonic.

▷ *From Belvedere Castle, walk northeast toward the Metropolitan Museum of Art.*

Just before reaching the museum, note **Cleopatra's Needle**, a 77ft pink-granite obelisk (16C) from Heliopolis, given to the City of New York in 1880 by the Khedive Ismael Pasha. Translated hieroglyphs tell the story of Pharaoh Thutmose III.

ADDITIONAL SIGHTS

Just south of 96th Street, the 107-acre Jacqueline Kennedy Onassis Reservoir is rimmed by a popular running track and a bridle path.

Conservatory Garden

E. 103rd St, opposite El Museo del Barrio. This 6-acre garden was created in 1936. The ornate wrought-iron Vanderbilt Gate (1894) was crafted in Paris for the Vanderbilt Mansion on Fifth Avenue. Opposite the entrance is the half-acre Central Garden, flanked by two crab-apple allées and ending in a wisteria pergola. The South Garden, known as "The Secret Garden" after Frances Hodgson Burnett's children's classic, features 175 varieties of perennials. The French-style North Garden boasts two dazzling annual displays: 20,000 spring tulips and 5,000 chrysanthemums in fall.

Belvedere Castle

©Klaas Lingbeek-van Kranen/iStockphoto.com

Upper East Side★★

Known primarily as an enclave for New York City's "old money," the Upper East Side is full of posh town houses and ultra-expensive shops, especially between Madison Avenue and Central Park, the catalyst to the area's settlement. But not everything here is exclusive. In the early 20C many of the Gilded Age mansions along Fifth Avenue were donated to art institutions and opened to the public. The result is **Museum Mile**, an impressive stretch of cultural real estate.

A BIT OF HISTORY

The area now known as the Upper East Side was largely rural until the mid-19C. Prior to that it contained only a few scattered hamlets. In the mid-18C the village of **Yorkville** sprang up between the burgeoning town of New Amsterdam at the south tip of Manhattan and the small Dutch farming community of **New Harlem** 10mi north. In the late 18C several prominent families built large wood-frame country manors along the East River; of these, Gracie Mansion, dating from 1799, is one of the few survivors. In 1811 Hamilton Park was established near Park Avenue and 68th Street around two English-style residential squares.

But it wasn't until 1858, when 3,000 men started clearing the land for Central Park, that development of the Upper East Side started in earnest. Horsecar lines began running up Second, Third and Madison Avenues to 86th Street in the years after the Civil War. Elevated trains were installed on Second and Third Avenues in 1879, bringing with them German and Irish immigrants who settled into nearby brownstones and worked at newly established factories along the East River.

On Fifth Avenue, development took a different shape. The Metropolitan Museum of Art opened at 82nd Street in 1880. In the 1890s New York's high society, such as the **Astors** and the **Carne-gies**, began building palatial residences overlooking Central Park. Luxury apartment buildings soon followed, especially after the railroad tracks on Park Avenue were buried in 1902. By the 1920s, aging millionaires had begun donating their mansions to charity for use as cultural institutions as Gilded Age ostentation fell out of vogue.

Today some of the richest New Yorkers, such as billionaire Mayor **Michael Bloomberg**, live in town houses on the Upper East Side that, from the street, may not look too fancy. But they are. Most have at least four stories and stretch farther back than you'd imagine. Apartment buildings with the requisite white-gloved doormen also remain highly desirable, as do, for a very few, residence hotels like the Pierre. Celebrities who have made their way past the old guard into the neighborhood have included **Greta Garbo**, **Katharine Hepburn**, **Jacqueline Kennedy** and **Woody Allen**.

FIFTH AVENUE★★★

MTA *Subway: N, Q, R train to Fifth Ave.-59th St.* A hundred years ago, the strip of Fifth Avenue from East 59th Street to East 96th Street was called the **Gold**

- MTA **Subway:** N, Q, R train to Fifth Ave.-59th St.
- **Map:** Following pages.
- **Location:** The Upper East Side is bounded by East 59th Street, East 96th Street, Fifth Avenue and the East River. Its heart lies east of Fifth Avenue. See the map in this chapter to orient yourself.
- **Timing:** Allow a full day for the 2mi walking tour, excluding visits to the major museums, so you can enjoy morning and afternoon breaks as well as lunch along the way.
- **Don't Miss:** Shopping on Madison Avenue.

Coast for its grandiose mansions overlooking Central Park. Today's **Museum Mile** embraces the northern third of that stretch—from East 82nd Street (the Metropolitan Museum of Art) extending up to East 105th Street (El Museo del Barrio). The following walk embraces both the Gold Coast and the Museum Mile, making it a little over 2mi total.

◆●◆WALKING TOUR

Begin this 2mi tour at the intersection of 58th St. & Fifth Ave.

Grand Army Plaza★★

Fifth Ave. (E. 58th St. & E. 60th St.).
Cut in half by Central Park South, this oval plaza marks the end of Midtown's Fifth Avenue luxury shopping district and the start of the Upper East Side's "Gold Coast." On the southern end splashes the 1915 **Pulitzer Fountain**, by Carrère and Hastings (statue of the Roman goddess Pomona by Karl Bitter). A huge gold-leaf bronze sculpture of General William Tecumseh Sherman, by Augustus Saint-Gaudens (1903), stands on the north side. Nearby horse-drawn carriages are often waiting to take visitors for a ride around the south end of Central Park. Several significant buildings surround the plaza.

The Plaza★

Designed by Henry J. Hardenbergh in the French Renaissance style in 1907, the Plaza Hotel was a New York institution of status for nearly a century. Coming-out parties and charity balls drew the cream of New York society; overnight guests included the Duke and Duchess of Windsor and the Beatles. The structure itself was one of the first buildings in New York to be named a landmark, but the designation applied only to the exterior facade. Developer El-Ad Properties bought the hotel in 2004 and carried out a $400 million renovation that reconfigured many of its 800 guest rooms as condominiums and restored several of the majestic public rooms, including the Oak Room, the Grand Ballroom and the Palm Court, to their original grandeur.

Paris Theatre

4 W. 58th St. at Fifth Ave. ✆*212-688-3800. www.theparistheatre.com.*
Classic revivals and first-run foreign films (subtitled, not dubbed, of course) play at this charming cinema, one of the few left in Manhattan that hasn't been chopped up to house multiple screens. Its neon marquee is vintage 1960s.

General Motors Building

767 Fifth Ave. between E. 58th & E. 59th Sts.
This 50-story tower (1968) is articulated by white marble piers, alternating with black glass. In the forecourt plaza rises the stunning 32ft glass-cube of the **Apple Store** (2006), open 24/7. On the ground floor sits the beloved toy store FAO Schwarz, and the CBS television studio where *The Early Show* is broadcast each weekday morning: show up outside between 7am and 9am and you may get on camera (✆*212-975-2515; www. cbsnews.com*).

Sherry-Netherland★

781 Fifth Ave. at E. 59th St.
The hotel/apartment building (1927) rises 38 stories from a brick base to a

---

Museum Mile Festival

Once a year for the past 27 years, usually on a Tuesday evening in early June (rain or shine), Fifth Avenue from East 82nd Street to East 105th Street is the site of the best block party in the city. The street is closed to traffic, and admission to all the museums within Museum Mile is free. Many venues sponsor live entertainment—from accordion and klezmer music to Weimer-era cabaret singers, from full orchestras to salsa bands—and artist-led activities like chalk drawing. Roving the streets in between are magicians, jugglers, face painters and clowns. *For more information, go online to www.museummilefestival.org.*

French Chateau-style tower. Above the 24th floor each apartment takes up a full floor. The small lobby has marble mosaic floors; custom-made chandeliers; and hand-painted, wood-paneled elevators. The sidewalk clock outside was installed when the building opened in 1927.

Hotel Pierre
2 E. 61st St. at Fifth Ave.
Opened in 1930, the luxury hotel was named after its owner, the celebrated chef Charles Pierre, who built it with a group of Wall Street backers. Most of the 700 rooms were leased annually by a wealthy clientele, as either primary residences or pieds-à-terre. Today the hotel, which is owned by the Taj hotel group, holds a mix of condominium owners, full-time renters and overnight guests. The Pierre's most famous moment: In 1972 five men in tuxedoes tied up 16 hotel workers and looted the vault, which held an estimated $11 million in cash and jewels.

810 Fifth Avenue
This elegant limestone apartment house (1926) has only one unit on each of its 13 floors. Famous former residents include William Randolph Hearst, Nelson Rockefeller and Richard Nixon, who lived with his family on the fifth floor between 1963 and 1968.

New India House
3 E. 64th St. at Fifth Ave.
This Beaux-Arts mansion was originally built (by Warren & Westmore, architects of Grand Central Terminal) as a private residence for Mrs. Caroline Astor's daughter Carrie. It's now the headquarters of the Consulate of India and the Indian delegation to the UN.

Temple Emanu-El★
1 E. 65th St. at Fifth Ave. ◷*Open year-round Sun–Thu 10am–4.30pm. Services Fri 6pm, Sat 10.15am.* ✆*212-744-1400. www.emanuelnyc.org.*
Located on the site of Mrs. Astor's former mansion, this Byzantine Romanesque synagogue was completed in 1929. It is the leading Reform synagogue in New

---

Truman Capote's Black and White Ball

Among the thousands of parties held at the Plaza Hotel over the years, one stands out above all the rest: Truman Capote's Black and White Ball. Held in honor of *Washington Post* publisher **Katherine Graham**, the 1966 event was dubbed "the party of the century." Guests were required to dress in black and white and wear masks. **Candace Bergen**, for one, had Halston make her a fur-trimmed black strapless dress with a matching white fur mask topped with bunny ears. The elite guest list also included **Andy Warhol**, **Tennessee Williams**, **Frank Sinatra** and **Mia Farrow** (then husband and wife), **Norman Mailer** and dozens of others, as well as assorted **Rockefellers**, **Vanderbilts**, and **Rothschilds**. Afterward the *Breakfast at Tiffany's* author was fond of saying that he invited 500 friends (540 showed up) and made 15,000 enemies.

York and the largest in the world. The majestic main sanctuary, rising to 103ft, can hold 2,500 worshippers. The ceiling, the marble columns in low relief, and the great arch covered with mosaics are reminiscent of the basilicas of the Near East. The **sanctuary** harbors the Holy Ark, which contains the Torah scrolls.

The Frick Collection★★★
◷*See Major Manhattan Museums.*

7 East 72nd Street★
At Fifth Ave.
This building and its neighbor at 9 East 72nd Street were both designed as private residences. Flagg and Chambers designed no. 7, a five-story Renaissance Revival town house, for Oliver Gould and Mary Brewster Jennings in 1899. Carrère and Hastings designed the larger mansion at no. 9 for Henry T. Sloane, heir to the W. and J. Sloane home furnishing company, in 1896. The Lycée Français de

New York occupied both structures from 1964 until 2001, when the mansions were sold as single-family residences. Asking prices were $15 million and $25 million respectively. The emir of Qatar supposedly bought no. 9.

Harkness House
1 E. 75th St. at Fifth Ave.
An intricate wrought-iron fence protects this Italian-style palazzo (1900), built for Edward S. Harkness, son of a partner of John D. Rockefeller. Today the building houses the Commonwealth Fund, a major philanthropic organization founded by Harkness' wife Anna.

New York University Institute of Fine Arts
1 E. 78th St. at Fifth Ave.
This immense limestone town house (1912, Horace Trumbauer) was modeled after a Louis XV-style chateau in Bordeaux, France. In 1915 American Tobacco Co. founder James B. Duke, his wife Nanaline, their daughter, Doris, two other relatives and 13 servants lived here. Nanaline and Doris Duke gave the house to New York University in 1957.

Ukrainian Institute of America
2 E. 79th St. at Fifth Ave.
🕐*Open during exhibitions Tue–Sun noon–6pm.*
🎟️*$5.*

☎*212-288-8660. www.ukrainian institute.org.*
Architect C.P.H. Gilbert was renowned among the rich for his opulent French Gothic designs, of which this landmark 1897 castle is typical: it even has a (dry) moat. Financier Isaac D. Fletcher, its original owner, left the mansion, along with his art collection, to the Metropolitan Museum of Art in 1917. The Met in turn sold the house to oil tycoon Harry F. Sinclair, who later went to prison for contempt of court in the Teapot Dome scandal of the 1920s. The Ukrainian Institute of America bought the building in 1955. Step inside to view the magnificent **woodwork** and **chandeliers**; exhibits by Ukrainian artists on Ukrainian themes are mounted on three floors.

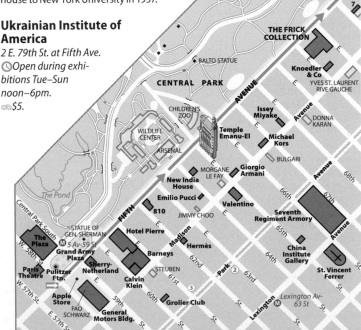

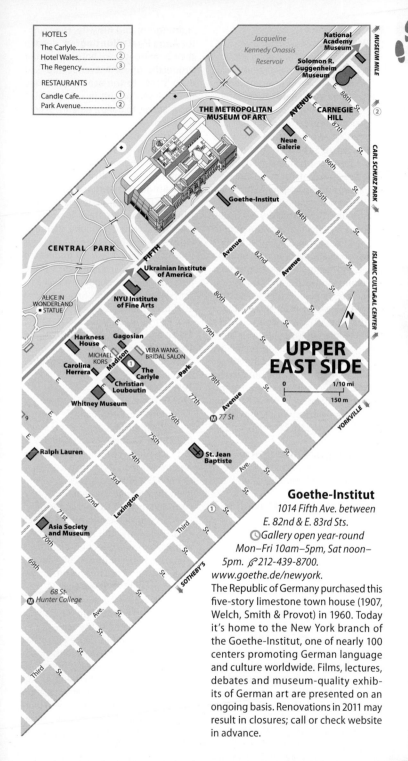

HOTELS

RESTAURANTS

Jacqueline Kennedy Onassis Reservoir

National Academy Museum

Solomon R. Guggenheim Museum

MUSEUM MILE

THE METROPOLITAN MUSEUM OF ART

FIFTH AVENUE

CARNEGIE HILL

Neue Galerie

CARL SCHURZ PARK

Goethe-Institut

CENTRAL PARK

ISLAMIC CULTURAL CENTER

Ukrainian Institute of America

ALICE IN WONDERLAND STATUE

NYU Institute of Fine Arts

N

UPPER EAST SIDE

Harkness House

Gagosian

MICHAEL KORS

VERA WANG BRIDAL SALON

Madison

Carolina Herrera

The Carlyle

Christian Louboutin

Whitney Museum

Park Avenue

0 ——— 1/10 mi
0 ——— 150 m

YORKVILLE

M 77 St

Ralph Lauren

St. Jean Baptiste

Lexington

Third St.

Asia Society and Museum

SOTHEBY'S

68 St-
M Hunter College

Goethe-Institut

1014 Fifth Ave. between E. 82nd & E. 83rd Sts.
Gallery open year-round Mon–Fri 10am–5pm, Sat noon–5pm. 212-439-8700.
www.goethe.de/newyork.

The Republic of Germany purchased this five-story limestone town house (1907, Welch, Smith & Provot) in 1960. Today it's home to the New York branch of the Goethe-Institut, one of nearly 100 centers promoting German language and culture worldwide. Films, lectures, debates and museum-quality exhibits of German art are presented on an ongoing basis. Renovations in 2011 may result in closures; call or check website in advance.

Neue Galerie★

1048 Fifth Ave. at E. 86th St.
Open year-round Thu–Mon 11am–6pm. Closed major holidays. $15.
212-628-6200. www.neuegalerie.org.

Cosmetics mogul **Ronald Lauder** established this museum in 2001 to house his own collection of early 20C Austrian and German art and that of his friend, art dealer **Serge Sabarsky**, who died in 1996. The museum's home, a Louis XIII-style Beaux-Arts mansion built in 1914 by Carrère and Hastings, was the home of Mrs. Cornelius Vanderbilt III.

In the lobby, **Cafe Sabarsky** re-creates a Viennese coffeehouse of the period; taking museum fare to a higher level, it offers tortes, strudels, smooth Viennese coffee, and Austro-Viennese staples such as herring sandwiches and goulash.

The second floor is devoted to Austrian art. Works by **Gustav Klimt** (*Black Feather Hat*, 1910) and **Egon Schiele** form the heart of the collection. There are also fine examples of decorative art and furniture by members of the Wiener Werkstaette. The third floor houses the German collection, focusing on members of the Blaue Reiter, Neue Sachlickkeit and the Bauhaus (Wassily Kandinsky, Paul Klee, George Grosz).

Guggenheim Museum★★

1071 Fifth Ave.at E. 88th St.
See Major Manhattan Museums.

National Academy Museum★

1083 Fifth Ave. at E. 89th St.
Open Wed–Thu noon–5pm, Fri–Sun 11am–6pm. Closed Jan 1, Thanksgiving Day & Dec 25. $10. 212-369-4880. www.nationalacademy.org.

This 1902 town house contains 10,000sq. ft of gallery space. Here, the museum displays rotating selections from its impressive collection of American art. American artists **Thomas Cole** (of the Hudson River school), **Samuel F. B. Morse** (who also invented the telegraph), **Rembrandt Peale** and others established the National Academy of Design in 1825. In 1940 **Archer Milton Huntington** (heir to the shipping and railroad fortune of his father, Collis P.

Huntington) and his wife, the sculptor **Anna Hyatt Huntington**, deeded their bow-front town house and other properties on Fifth Avenue and East 89th Street to the academy for one dollar. A second gift in 1955 enabled the academy to build a separate school next door.

Today displays rotating selections from its 5,000-piece permanent collection, which includes work by members and former members **Winslow Homer**, **John Singer Sargent**, **Isabel Bishop**, **Chuck Close**, **Jasper Johns** and **Jim Dine**, among others. Three floors of galleries are accessed through a charming wood-paneled bookstore, which leads to a marble entrance foyer dominated by a gracefully sweeping staircase and a statue of the Greek goddess Diana by Anna Hyatt Huntington. Renovations in 2011 may result in closures.

Cooper-Hewitt, National Design Museum★★

2 E. 91st St. at Fifth Ave. See Museums.

Jewish Museum★

1109 Fifth Ave. at E. 92nd St. Open year-round Thu 11am–8pm, Fri–Tue 11am–5.45pm. Closed Jewish & major holidays. Guided tours (45min) available Mon–Tue & Thu–Fri; check website for times. $12 (free Sat). 212-423-3200. www.thejewishmuseum.org.

Founded in 1904 as part of the Jewish Theological Seminary of America (*3080 Broadway*), this museum houses a 28,000-piece collection of Judaica that offers insight into 4,000 years of Jewish history. The French Gothic-style mansion, built in 1909 for Felix M. Warburg, a prominent Jewish banker who emigrated to the US from Germany in 1894, was donated to the seminary by his wife, Frieda, in 1947. Since 1993, it has undergone several renovations.

Large temporary shows are presented on the second floor. On the third and fourth floors is a permanent installation Culture and Continuity: The Jewish Journey, in which 800 works from the permanent collection are arranged to examine

Jewish identity from antiquity to the present. The media center *(3rd floor)* offers visitors access to the National Jewish Archive of Broadcasting.

Museum of the City of New York★★

1220 Fifth Ave. at E. 103rd St.
See Major Manhattan Museums.

El Museo del Barrio

1230 Fifth Ave. at E. 104th St. Open year-round Tue & Thu–Sat 11am–6pm, Wed 11am–9pm, Sun 1–5pm. Closed major holidays. $9; free Wed 6–9pm & third Sat of each month. 212-831-7272. www.elmuseo.org.

Housed on the ground floor of an imposing U-shaped building, this museum and cultural center presents art from the Caribbean and Latin America.

El Museo was founded in a public-school classroom in 1969 by Puerto Rican artists and activists from *el barrio* ("the neighborhood") of East Harlem *(96th St. to 125th St., Fifth Ave. to the East River)*. Today the museum works with other institutions to create major traveling exhibitions of Latin American art. It also presents rotating selections from its 8,000 piece permanent collection of artworks.

MADISON AVENUE★★ TO LEXINGTON AVENUE

Subway: 4, 5, 6, N, Q, R train to Lexington Ave.-59th St.

East of Fifth Avenue lies the heart of the Upper East Side. Here you'll find leafy side streets lined with town houses and broad avenues, each with a different character.

Madison Avenue★★, which cuts the block between Fifth and Park Avenues in half, is lined with elite boutiques and world-famous designer stores, as well as upscale galleries. Many are open by appointment only, but **Gagosian** *(no. 980 at E. 76th St.; 212-744-2313; www. gagosian.com)* and **Knoedler & Co** *(19 E. 70th St. between Fifth & Madison Aves.; 212-794-0550; www.knoedlergallery. com)* keep regular hours. **Park Avenue** is almost entirely residential, with large apartments facing off across the elegantly manicured median strip. **Lexington Avenue**, the most congested of the three streets, is packed with shops, though none are as exclusive as those on Madison.

The most famous landmark on Lexington is the art deco-style department store **Bloomingdale's** *(between E. 59th & E. 60th Sts.; 212-705-2000; www.bloomingdales.com).* The 54-story **Bloomberg Tower**, by Cesar Pelli & Assocs., bloomed just one block south *(E. 58th St.)* in 2005. Headquarters of Mayor Mike's media empire, it has received high marks for its graceful form and airy atrium.

Not all of the Upper East Side's treasures are on the avenues, however. As on Fifth Avenue, many former town houses have been given over to cultural institutions, consulates and clubs, some offering public access.

The **China Institute Gallery** *(125 E. 65th St. between Park & Lexington Aves.),* located in a stately row house across from the famous French hair salon **Yves Durif**, has presented critically acclaimed shows of Chinese art in various media since 1966 *(open Tue & Thu 10am–8pm, Fri–Mon & Wed 10am–5pm; closed major holidays & between exhibits: best to call ahead; $7, free Tue & Thu after 6pm; 212-744-8181; www. chinainstitute.org).* Likewise the **Grolier Club** occupies a 1917 town house at 47 East 60th Street *(between Madison & Park Aves.).* Founded in 1884 in honor of the 16C French bibliophile Jean Grolier, it houses 90,000 volumes. The books are for scholars only, but the club regularly mounts public shows related to the book arts in the first-floor exhibit hall *(library open Sept–Jul Mon–Fri 10am–5pm; closed major holidays; 212-838-6690; www.grolierclub.org).*

SIGHTS

Sights listed in descending star order.

Whitney Museum of American Art★★

945 Madison Ave. at E. 75th St.
See Major Manhattan Museums.

Madison Avenue Shopping

Though it has stiff competition from 57th Street and Fifth Avenue—and even SoHo and Chelsea nowadays—Madison Avenue between 59th and 78th Streets remains, inch for inch, the most luxurious shopping strip in the city.

Here are some of the brightest stars *(for a full list, see Your Stay in New York City)*. Native son **Calvin Klein** anchors the southern end with a palace showcasing clothing (only his couture line, of course) and home furnishings *(no. 654 at E. 60th St.; ℘212-292-9000; www.calvinklein.com)*.

Barneys *(no. 660 at E. 61st St.; ℘212-826-8900; www.barneys.com)* beckons the *Sex and the City* crowd with nine exuberant stories of ultra-chic brand names, from Manolo Blahnik to Comme des Garçons.

Impeccable French accessories designer **Hermès** has its only New York store at no. 691 *(at E. 62nd St.; ℘212-751-3181; www.hermes.com)*.

Emilio Pucci, popularized in the 1960s by Jacqueline Kennedy Onassis, is hip again with updated versions of the same wildly patterned clothes *(24 E. 64th St. between Fifth & Madison Aves.; ℘212-752-4777; www.emiliopucci.com)*.

Michael Kors has opened a new store in the space previously occupied by Ungaro *(no. 790 at E. 67th St.; ℘212-452-4685; www.michaelkors.com)*.

For Oscar-worthy gowns, check out **Valentino** *(no. 747 between E. 64th & E. 65th Sts.; ℘212-772-6969; www.valentino.com)*, and, farther north, **Carolina Herrera** *(no. 954 at E. 75th St.; ℘212-249-6552; www.carolinaherrera.com)*.

Men gravitate toward **Giorgio Armani** for European-style suits and torso-hugging T-shirts *(no. 760; ℘212-988-9191; www.giorgioarmani.com)*.

Bronx-born **Ralph Lauren** (née Ralph Lifschitz) displays his timeless fashions in the opulent 1895 Gertrude Rhinelander Waldo House *(no. 867 at E. 72nd St.; ℘212-606-2100; www.polo.com)*, replete with fresh-cut flowers and gilt-framed paintings. Farther north you'll find the super-luxe French shoe store **Christian Louboutin** *(no. 965 between E. 75th & E. 76th Sts.; ℘212-396-1884; www.christian louboutin.com)*.

Asia Society and Museum★

725 Park Ave. at E. 70th St. ◷*Open year-round Tue–Sun 11am–6pm (Fri until 9pm, except Jul–Labor Day).* ◷*Closed major holidays.* ☞*Guided tours Tue–Sun 2pm (also Fri 6.30pm except Jul–Labor Day).* ◔*$10.* ℘*212-288-6400. www.asiasociety.org.*

This artfully revamped museum and cultural center is New York's leading purveyor of Asian arts and culture. The society was founded in 1956 by John D. Rockefeller III, a noted collector of Asian art. In 1960 the first galleries were opened on this site, and in 1981 Edward Larrabee Barnes designed the present eight-story building in red granite and sandstone. A $30 million renovation, overseen by local architect Bartholomew Voorsanger (2001), doubled the size of the bookstore and galleries and added the glass-enclosed **Garden Café**, a popular lunch spot.

Voorsanger's white-steel **staircase** with blue-glass steps brings to mind the sun-bleached skeleton of a fish. The stairs link three levels of bamboo-floored galleries with the spacious lobby, set off from the museum shop by curved shoji screens. Third-floor galleries hold rotating masterworks from the Rockefeller Collection. Other galleries contain temporary shows of predominantly contemporary art. Films, lectures and performances are presented in the basement theater *(check the website for schedule)*.

The Carlyle★

35 E. 76th St. at Madison Ave. ℘212-744-1600. www.thecarlyle.com.

A slice of old New York, this classic art deco hotel was completed just before the 1929 stock market crash. It became a favorite of Presidents Truman and Kennedy, and still is one of the most

atmospheric places on the Upper East Side. Tucked on the ground floor is the incomparable **Bemelmans Bar** (*see sidebar, p209*), reputedly a favorite haunt of Jackie O (*open daily noon–11.30pm; live jazz each night*). Finally there is **Café Carlyle**, a 1930s-style supper club, where acts have included **Woody Allen**, **Eartha Kitt** and **Ute Lemper**.
(For entertainment schedules or to make reservations at either Café Carlyle or Bemelmans, call the main number or see the website.)

Church of St. Jean Baptiste★
184 E. 76th St. at Lexington Ave.
Open year-round Mon–Fri 7.30am–6.30pm, Sat–Sun 8am–6.30pm. 212-288-5082. www.sjbrcc.net.
Completed in 1913 for a parish then largely composed of French Canadians (now it is multiethnic), this Classical Revival church has an exquisitely painted barrel-vaulted ceiling, topped by a central dome 175ft above floor level. The 50ft-high altar consists of Italian marbles and mosaics. The stained-glass windows throughout the church were crafted in Chartres, France.

Church of St. Vincent Ferrer
869 Lexington Ave. at E. 66th St.
Open year-round daily 7.30am–6.30pm, holidays 7.30am–3pm. 212-744-2080. www.csvf.org.
Designed by Bertram G. Goodhue in the Gothic Revival style, this church—named after the patron saint of builders—was completed in 1918 for the Dominican Order. The granite facade has a rose window and limestone trim carved by Lee Lawrie, famed for his sculpture of Atlas at Rockefeller Center. Step inside to see the altar and stained glass.

Islamic Cultural Center of New York
1711 Third Ave. at E. 96th St. Open by appointment only. 212-722-5234. www.islamicculturalcenter-ny.org.
Women are requested to wear headscarves and long sleeves.
Completed in 1991 from designs by Skidmore, Owings & Merrill, this pink-

marble center for Muslim worship is the first major mosque built in New York City. The two-story domed prayer hall, where light streams through a curtain wall of windows distinguished with Eastern motifs, is particularly stunning. Designed to serve the city's Muslim population of more than half a million, the mosque is flanked by a 12-story minaret, from which the faithful are called to prayer.

Seventh Regiment Armory
643 Park Ave. between E. 66th & E. 67th Sts. 212-616-3930. www.armoryonpark.org.
Now serving as an arts organization hosting concerts, lectures, art exhibits and antiques shows, this massive red-brick fortress (1877) looms over Park Avenue. Step inside and gaze at the dark-paneled foyer with ornate iron fixtures and contemplate what lies beyond. Its robust architecture became a model for urban armories nationwide.
Charles W. Clinton, a veteran of the regiment and a student of architect Richard Upjohn, came up with the imposing medieval design, complete with square towers, crenellations, slits for crossbow arrows, and 6in-thick oak doors with spiked rivets. Because such armories doubled as men's clubs, quite a bit of thought went into its interior as well; the lavish appointment was overseen by **Louis Comfort Tiffany**.

SIGHTS ALONG THE EAST RIVER
M15 Bus; 4, 5, 6 train to 59th St. & 86th St.
The Upper East Side may be posh, but its waterfront generally is not. There's good reason for that. In the late 18C the area was rural, an ideal site for Archibald Gracie's country manor. But by the mid-19C, the riverfront up to 86th Street was lined with factories and stables, and Second and Third Avenues were overshadowed by rumbling elevated trains. Wealth, when it came to the neighborhood in the late 19C, gravitated toward Central Park. That remains largely the case, but there are a few notable excep-

Kitchen Arts & Letters

1435 Lexington Ave. at E. 94th St.
℘212-876-5550. www.kitchen
artsandletters.com.

An intriguing little spot, Kitchen Arts & Letters only stocks books on food and wine; some 13,000 titles, in fact, ranging from traditional recipe compilations to out-of-print rarities, antique food advertisements and cooking memorabilia. Foreign language titles are available as well.

tions to explore—especially around Gracie Mansion, the mayor's official residence. A pedestrian and bicycle path links the following sights, but because it is cut off from nearby businesses and residences by Franklin D. Roosevelt Drive, it can be quite secluded. Instead, consider taking the M15 bus (northbound on First Ave., southbound on Second Ave.) or the Lexington Avenue (4/5/6) subway.

Bridgemarket★

E. 59th St. near Queensboro Bridge.
A cathedral-like hall under the roadway to the Queensboro Bridge has been restored to its original grandeur after decades in oblivion. Until the 1930s, food vendors sold their goods in the vaulted arcade known as Bridgemarket. The city then used it for storage.

The impetus to salvage Bridgemarket came when British designer Terence Conran opened **The Conran Shop** houseware and modern design emporium in 1999. In a return to its roots, Bridgemarket's other major tenant became a Food Emporium supermarket, which filled in thousands more square feet of reclaimed space.

Under the soaring vaults of Bridgemarket's eastern (and higher) half is **Guastavino's** *(409 E. 59th St.; ℘212-980-2711; www.guastavinos.com)*, which opened as a chic American brasserie but which now serves as an event space. The restaurant's name pays homage to Spanish architect Rafael Guastavino and his son, Rafael, who designed the space. They built the 30ft by 30ft "Catalan Vaults" completely from layers of flat rectangular tiles and mortar. Each of the 36 vaults that form the arcade's canopy is faced with about 1,600 tiles. Their work can also be seen at the Oyster Bar in Grand Central Terminal and in the Registry Room at Ellis Island.

Roosevelt Island

MTA *Subway: F train from Lexington Ave.-63rd St. or tramway (departs from Second Ave. & E. 59th St. year-round Fri–Sat 6am–3.30am, Sun–Thu 6am–2am every 15min; $2.25 one-way, payable by MetroCard; ℘212-832-4555). www.rioc.com.*

Roosevelt Island Tram

© SVLuma/Fotolia.com

Just 300yds offshore from Manhattan in the East River sits the 2.5mi long Roosevelt Island, named for 32nd president Franklin Delano Roosevelt. It's linked to Manhattan by bridge, by subway and by an aerial tramway *(see A Bit of Advice, below)*. One of the oldest farmhouses still standing in New York City resides on the island: Blackwell Farm House (1796). The 147-acre island is also home to a residential "town-in-town," built in the 1970s, which includes mixed-income housing, retail shops, schools, hospitals and parks. A waterfront promenade on both sides of the community offers views of the river and the Manhattan skyline. In 2010 construction began on Four Freedoms Park at the island's southern tip, the name a reference to FDR's famous 1941 address *(www.fdr fourfreedomspark.org)*.

Gracie Mansion★

East End Ave. at E. 88th St.  *Visit by guided tour (45min) only, Wed 10am, 11am, 1pm, 2pm. Reservations required. $7. 311 (212-639-9675 outside New York City). www.nyc.gov.*

Located in the northern section of Carl Schurz Park, this 1799 country manor is the official residence of the city's mayor. The Federal-style mansion bears the name of Archibald Gracie, a merchant who entertained many dignitaries here, including Alexander Hamilton and John Quincy Adams. The house was eventually acquired by the city in 1896, falling into neglect until the Museum of the City of New York took it over in 1924. In 1942 it became the official home of the mayor (although the last few mayors have chosen to live elsewhere). The current restoration features a striking marbleized entry floor and fine Federal- and Empire-style furnishings.

Carl Schurz Park

Located along East End Ave. from E. 84th to E. 90th Sts.

Completed in 1891 and remodeled in 1938, this park stretches along East End Avenue, capturing East River views from the promenade. It is named for a famous 19C German immigrant who served as

---

> ### ☺ A Bit of Advice ☺
>
> Although Roosevelt Island is accessible by subway, take the $4.50 *(round-trip)*, 4min Roosevelt Island tram ride over the East River for great views of the city in each direction. It's an inexpensive way to get an elevated look at Manhattan and Queens. The tram parallels the Queensboro Bridge linking the two boroughs (see departure information above).

US senator and as secretary of the Interior under President Hayes. Gracie Mansion stands at the north end.

Fronting the park across East End Avenue at East 86th Street is the Henderson Place Historic District, comprising 24 Queen Anne-style turreted houses (1881).

Sotheby's

1334 York Ave. at E. 72nd St. 212-606-7070. www.sothebys.com.

Founded in London in 1744, this famous auction house has annual sales of more than $2 billion. Here at the New York branch, auctions are held year-round, with major sales of Impressionist, modern and contemporary art in the spring.

> ### Bemelmans Murals
>
> Bemelmans Bar is named after the artist **Ludwig Bemelmans**, who in addition to creating the *Madeleine* series of children's books, painted, in 1947, all four walls of the bar with murals of his characters frolicking in Central Park. In exchange for the work, Bemelmans and his family lived free of charge at **The Carlyle** hotel for a year and a half. No wonder he wanted his headstone to read "Tell them it was wonderful." The muted colors of the paintings perfectly complement the rich leather banquettes.

Upper West Side★★

Historically the seat of the city's intelligentsia, the Upper West Side remains an enclave of performing artists and literate liberals drawn to the area's world-famous cultural venues (Lincoln Center on the south end, Columbia University on the north) and parks (Central Park to the east and Riverside Park to the west). In between are dozens of side streets lined with picturesque brownstones and trees, making the neighborhood one of New York City's most appealing.

A BIT OF HISTORY

The neighborhood got its start in the mid-1600s, about the time that Governor Peter Stuyvesant established the village of Nieuw Haarlem around 125th Street (today's Harlem).

In the colonial era several well-to-do Englishmen, such as Colonel Roger Morris (ᕔ see Morris-Jumel Mansion), had hilltop manor houses on bluffs overlooking the Hudson River, bringing more traffic and expansion en route. In 1844 **Edgar Allan Poe**, for instance, lived in a farmhouse (long since demolished) on West 84th Street, just west of Amsterdam Avenue. This is the place where he

MTA Subway: 1, A, B, C, D train to 59th St.-Columbus Circle.

ᕔ **Map:** Opposite.

▶ **Location:** The Upper West Side reaches north from Columbus Circle to 125th Street between Central Park and the Hudson River. ᕔ See the map in this chapter to orient yourself.

🕐 **Timing:** Reserve a day to explore Central Park West, including the Time Warner Center, the American Museum of Natural History and neighboring sights. Allow a second day to visit Columbus University, St. John's Cathedral and Riverside Church. Take in Lincoln Center by attending a performance.

🞕 **Don't Miss:** Zabar's, and the view from the Mandarin Oriental hotel's 35th-floor Lobby Lounge.

wrote his famous poem "The Raven" ("… quoth the Raven, 'Nevermore' ").

As with other neighborhoods, transportation was key to the Upper West Side's urbanization. An elevated train up Ninth Avenue (today's Columbus Avenue)

The Dakota

©Steven Allan/iStockphoto.com

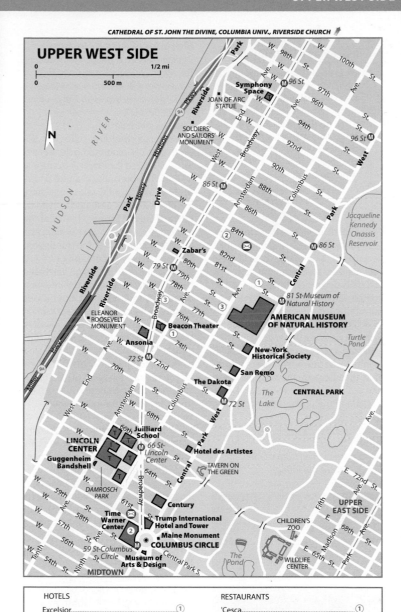

UPPER WEST SIDE

HOTELS	
Excelsior	①
Mandarin Oriental	②
On the Ave	③

RESTAURANTS	
'Cesca	①
Good Enough to Eat	②
Ocean Grill	③

brought with it a wave of brownstone and tenement construction in the 1880s. But high society considered the area remote, as even its early champions acknowledged. When Singer Sewing Machine president Edward Clark hired Plaza Hotel architect Henry Hardenbergh to design an ornate apartment building at 72nd Street and Central Park West, he dubbed it **The Dakota**, after the distant Dakota Territory.

Completed in 1884, it spurred a building boom of Beaux-Arts **apartment houses** catering to well-heeled professionals and celebrities. Middle-class Jewish families arrived from the congested

Broadway's Beginnings

To get to Nieuw Haarlem (now Harlem) from Nieuw Amsterdam (today's Financial District), 17C travelers often followed an Indian path that ran diagonally along a ridge up Manhattan. That road—long known as the Bloomingdale Road, after Bloemendael, a flower-growing community near Haarlem—is now simply Broadway.

Lower East Side in the 1930 and were soon joined by artists and intellectuals fleeing Hitler's Germany; some of these new denizens took positions at nearby Columbia University. Others pursued literature and music, both of which were nurtured in a district long known for its excellent bookstores and music schools. In recent years the Upper West Side has attracted a raft of young professionals —initially because rents were affordable, then because the neighborhood had a lively singles scene, and now because of the proliferation of family-friendly activities.

SIGHTS

Sights are described from south to north (not in order of star rating).

Time Warner Center

©Björg Magnea/Time Warner Center/MWW Group

Museum of Arts & Design★

2 Columbus Circle. ⏱*Open year-round Tue–Wed & Fri–Sun 11am–6pm, Thu 11am–9pm.* ⏱*Closed major holidays.* ☞*$15; pay-what-you-wish Thu 6–9pm.* ☏*212-299-7777.* *www.madmuseum.org.*

The unusual building rising on the south side of Columbus Circle was the focus of heated controversy from 2002 to 2005. The previous structure on the site—an almost windowless nine-story marble box—was designed in 1964 by **Edward Durell Stone** (creator of the Kennedy Center for the Performing Arts in Washington, DC) for the Huntington Hartford Gallery of Contemporary Art. The Museum of Arts & Design purchased the building in 2002 with the intention of radically redesigning it, but historic preservationists raised a fuss, claiming the building was an "icon of the Modern Movement." A court ruling in mid-2005 gave the museum the go-ahead, and work was completed in 2008. The new facade of gray glass and glazed terra-cotta has drawn both praise and pans from the architectural community.

The museum's primary mission is to show objects made from glass, ceramics, fiber, metal, wood and clay, or some combination thereof. An active schedule of temporary exhibitions is complemented by Permanently MAD, an ongoing exhibition of astonishingly beautiful works drawn from the museum's 250-piece permanent collection.

Columbus Circle

MTA *Subway: 1, A, B, C, D train to 59th St.-Columbus Circle.*

At the southwest corner of Central Park, three major arteries—Eighth Avenue, Broadway and Central Park South—all feed into one of New York's few traffic circles. This circle, Columbus Circle, is the gateway to the Upper West Side. The name comes from the 700-ton statue installed at its center in 1894: explorer **Christopher Columbus** stands atop a 70ft granite column. The three prows on the column represent his famous fleet: the *Niña*, the *Pinta* and the *Santa María*. At the base is a fountain with an angel holding a globe and seasonal plantings. Another sculpture, the **Maine Monument** (1913), is located at the entrance to Central Park.

This grand composition is dedicated to the 260 men who lost their lives when the battleship *Maine* was destroyed in Havana Harbor in 1898. Columbus Circle is surrounded by several noteworthy buildings.

Time Warner Center★

Cupping the west side of Columbus Circle with its vast semicircular facade, this huge mixed-use, twin-towered complex was inaugurated in 2004. It stands on the site of the former New York Coliseum, an unpopular structure built by the legendary parks commissioner **Robert Moses** for use as a convention center in the 1950s.

When the Javits Center was opened in 1986, the Coliseum's owner, the Metropolitan Transportation Authority, put the site on the market. Media mogul Mort Zuckerman and others drew up a plan to raze the Coliseum and replace it with a mixed-use facility that looked, on paper at least, much like the structure you see today. But the design by architect **Moishe Safdie** was savaged by the press. With Upper West Side residents prompting the backers, including Salomon Brothers, to pull out of the project, Safdie was replaced by Skidmore, Owings & Merrill's **David Childs**, whose blueprint drew less fire. The financing (some $1.7 billion) came together, and over the course of five years the Coliseum was replaced by the Time Warner Center.

Two sharply angled, 80-story glass towers rise from a seven-story curved base. The idea was reputedly to echo the twin-towered design of some of the art deco apartment buildings on Central Park West. The interior holds 2.8 million sq. ft of space. Only a fraction is taken up by the world headquarters of its signature tenant, **Time Warner**, and the studios of its subsidiary **CNN**. The rest has been chopped up into condos, shops, performance spaces, hotel rooms and restaurants.

Highlights of the Time Warner Center

Jazz at Lincoln Center★ – Though still affiliated with Lincoln Center, the organization, under the guidance of **Wynton Marsalis**, stages its jazz concerts here, in three facilities on the fifth floor: the Frederick P. Rose Hall, the Allen Room and Dizzy's Club Coca-Cola. The **box office** (◯open Mon–Sat 10am–6pm, Sun noon–6pm; ✆212-721-6500; reservations for Dizzy's Club ✆212-258-9595; www.jalc.org) is located outside the complex at Broadway and West 60th Street; look for the marquee.

Mandarin Oriental New York Hotel – Accessed through West 60th Street, the luxury hotel has its lobby on the 35th floor. There spreads the spectacular **Lobby Lounge**★★ (◯open Fri–Sat 9am–2am, Sun–Thu 9am–1am; ✆212-805-8876; www.mandarinoriental.com/newyork), widely regarded as the best feature of the Time Warner complex.

Shops and Restaurants – Roughly 40 shops are arrayed in mall-like fashion around a four-story atrium space at the heart of the Time Warner Center. The most popular (among locals) is the gargantuan Whole Foods supermarket in the basement. Above the shops, on the fourth floor, are restaurants, including chef Thomas Keller's ultra-exclusive dining spot **Per Se**.

Trump International Hotel and Tower

Dominating the north side of Columbus Circle, this glitzy high-rise contains luxury condominiums as well as 167 hotel rooms. The 52-story structure was originally designed in 1969 by Thomas E. Stanley as Gulf + Western Plaza. Donald Trump slapped his name on it in the 1990s and paid Philip Johnson and Costas Kondylis to reskin the structure in gold-tinted glass. A large hammered-steel globe sculpture was placed in front of it, a symbol of the Trump empire's international scope.

Lincoln Center Plaza

Allison Simpson/MICHELIN

Lincoln Center★★

MTA *Subway: 1, A, B, C, D train to 59th St.-Columbus Circle. Columbus Avenue between W. 62nd & W. 66th Sts. ℘212-546-2656. www.lincolncenter.org.*
Devoted to drama, music and dance, Lincoln Center for the Performing Arts is a 16-acre complex comprising five major theater and concert buildings, a library, a bandshell and two outdoor plazas *(free performances held in summer)*. It is home to 12 constituent companies, namely: the Metropolitan Opera, New York Philharmonic, New York City Ballet, New York City Opera, the Chamber Music Society of Lincoln Center, the Film Society of Lincoln Center, Jazz at Lincoln Center, the Juilliard School, Lincoln Center for the Performing Arts, Inc., Lincoln Center Theater, the New York Public Library for the Performing Arts and the School of American Ballet.

A Bit of History

The idea for such a grand cultural center, where operas, ballets, plays and concerts could take place simultaneously, originated in 1955, and two years later the city bought the necessary land in what was then a run-down neighborhood. John D. Rockefeller III chaired the building committee; the board of architects was headed by **Wallace K. Harrison**, who had helped design the United Nations and Rockefeller Center. Construction finally began in 1959 (nearly 188 buildings were razed to make way) and continued over the next 10 years, ending with the Juilliard School. In 1991 the multipurpose Samuel B. and David Rose Building was added northwest of the Juilliard School. In all, the sleek rectangular buildings of glass and Italian travertine marble can accommodate 13,666 spectators at a time.

In 2006, work began on the **Transforming Lincoln Center** project, a massive

Café des Artistes

1 W. 67th St. between Central Park West & Columbus Ave.

Two major changes occured in 2009 on West 67th Street when both Tavern on the Green and Café des Artistes announced closure. With one of the city's most romantic interiors and fashionable addresses (on the ground floor of the legendary Hotel des Artistes), Café des Artistes catered to the well-heeled and the famous. Designed by Howard Chandler Christy in 1934, the murals of female nudes are a must-see, and in fact there are plans to open another restaurant in the space; stay tuned for details.

renovation program to modernize and expand the campus' performance venues, educational facilities and public spaces. Cranes loomed, concrete mixers rumbled and streets were blocked as Alice Tully Hall, the David H. Koch Theater, Josie Robertson Plaza (and its spectacular fountain), West 65th Street and the Lincoln Center Promenade on Columbus Avenue all received splashy new upgrades. The end result modernized Lincoln Center's facilities and developed a more pedestrian-friendly integration between the complex and the surrounding streets.

Visit

Begin with a stop at the new **Visitor Center** *(between Broadway & Columbus Ave. at W. 62nd St.)*, an atrium complex housing a cafe, restrooms, information desk and a box office offering discounted tickets to same-day performances at Lincoln Center. Guided tours of the various venues depart from here, and the center also hosts free live performances. **Guided tours** explore Lincoln Center's largest performance spaces: the Metropolitan Opera House *(see below)*, the David H. Koch Theater and Avery Fisher Hall *(1hr; $15; call 212-875-5350 for schedule)*; there's also a tour of Jazz at Lincoln Center facilities on Columbus Circle *($15; call 212-875-5350 for schedule)*. Of course, you can also experience Lincoln Center by attending a performance *(schedules and ticket information 212-546-2656; www.lincolncenter.org)*.

Metropolitan Opera House

For backstage tours, see sidebar above. 212-362-6000. Distinguished by a 10-story colonnade, this opera house, which opened in 1966 with Samuel Barber's *Antony and Cleopatra*, forms the centerpiece of the main plaza. Designed by Wallace K. Harrison, the 3,800-seat hall was the successor to a large Italian Renaissance opera house (1883) at Broadway and 39th Street that was closed in 1966 and later demolished. The "new" Metropolitan Opera House hosts both the Metropolitan

Backstage Tours

Always wanted to know what goes on behind the scenes? Book a 90min tour of the Metropolitan Opera House, which covers areas of the opera house not included on the general tour of Lincoln Center. On the backstage tour, held on select days October through June, visitors get an overview of the process of making opera at the Met. You'll be led from the shops where artisans create, and work on, the sets, costumes and wigs; through the rehearsal spaces and dressing rooms; and finally to the vast stage and auditorium. For a tour schedule or to buy tickets call 212-769-7028 or visit www.metoperafamily.org ($16, reservations required).

Opera and the American Ballet Theater (ABT) and contains seven rehearsal halls and storage space for six opera sets. In the lobby hang large murals by Marc Chagall, *The Sources of Music* and *The Triumph of Music*. The red-carpeted double staircase is accentuated by crystal chandeliers, a gift from Austria *(for ABT tickets and information, 212-477-3030; www.abt.org)*.

Avery Fisher Hall

Originally called Philharmonic Hall, this concert hall, designed by Max Abramovitz and set to the right of the main plaza, was renamed in 1973 in recognition of a gift from Avery Fisher, the founder of Fisher Radio. The 2,738-seat auditorium is home to the New York Philharmonic, the country's oldest orchestra, which previously played at Carnegie Hall.

David H. Koch Theater

Designed by Philip Johnson, this theater is home to the New York City Opera and the New York City Ballet.
The City Center of Music and Drama, which oversees the two companies, operates the theater, owned by the City of New York. Completed in 1964, it seats 2,713 people.

Beacon Theatre

©Whitney Cox/MSG Entertainment

For Architecture Buffs: Notable Buildings

Pressed for space and for time, many New Yorkers "order in" or eat out more than they cook. Some even use their ovens as storage space. But few apartments lack kitchens altogether, as was the case with two of the Upper West Side's most famous and eye-catching buildings: the **Ansonia** *(2109 Broadway between W. 73rd & W. 74th St.)* and **Hotel des Artistes** *(1 W. 67th St. between Central Park West and Columbus Ave.).* Like a hotel suite, apartments had parlors, dining rooms, bedrooms and bathrooms. They also had room service—residents could order food from the main kitchen and have it delivered via a dumbwaiter. Onetime home to **Arturo Toscanini**, **Babe Ruth** and **Igor Stravinsky**, the Ansonia (1904, Paul E.M. Duboy) is an exuberant Beaux-Arts wedding cake of a building, sporting a corner turret, balconies, terracotta ornamentation and a dormered mansard roof. Hotel des Artistes (1918, George Mort Pollard) is more subtle, but has an equally impressive roster of former tenants, among them **Isadora Duncan**, **Norman Rockwell** and **Noël Coward**. Given the number of artists in the neighborhood, it's hardly surprising that it contains one of the city's most beautiful theaters, the **Beacon** *(2124 Broadway at W. 74th St.; ✆212-465-6500).* Designed by Rambusch Studio in 1929, the **interior**★★ is a marvel of ornately carved rococo swirls and red velvet that now serves as a stunning backdrop to singer-songwriters like **Lucinda Williams** and **Norah Jones**. Finally, about those apartment buildings on Central Park West: the Gothic **Dakota**, setting for the Roman Polanski film *Rosemary's Baby*, is the most famous. Well-known residents have included **Lauren Bacall**, **Leonard Bernstein**—and **John Lennon**, who was shot outside the West 72nd Street entrance in 1980. Central Park's Strawberry Fields are now dedicated to him. But other apartment buildings are taller and more visible. The two that are best known both have twin towers (to provide maximal light and air): the 1931 art deco **Century** *(25 Central Park West between W. 62nd & W. 63rd Sts.)* and the 1930 **San Remo**, whose towers are topped by Athenian temples *(145–146 Central Park West between W. 74th & W. 75th Sts.).*

Other Venues

The Lincoln Center complex also includes the **Guggenheim Bandshell** (in Damrosch Park, behind the opera house to the south), the site of free concerts. Behind the opera house to the north is the **New York Public Library for the Performing Arts** *(♿🕐open year-round Mon & Thu noon–8pm, Tue–Wed & Fri–Sat noon–6pm; 🕐closed major holidays; ✆917-275-6975; www.nypl.org/lpa).* This building (1965; Skidmore, Owings & Merrill) houses a museum of the performing arts, a 200-seat auditorium and a music library whose extensive collections include original manuscripts, diaries, recordings, photographs and costumes.

Founded in 1985, the not-for-profit **Lincoln Center Theater** mounts productions of new plays and classic revivals in two venues built next to the library according to plans by Eero Saarinen: the 1,050-seat **Vivian Beaumont Theater** and the 299-seat **Mitzi E. Newhouse Theater**. Across West 65th Street is the Juilliard Building (1968, Pietro Belluschi, Catalano and Westermann), which contains the elite **Juilliard School** for the arts and **Alice Tully Hall**, which hosts performances of the Chamber Music Society of Lincoln Center and others. Next door, on the plaza level of the **Rose Building** (1991), is the **Walter Reade Theater**, where the **Film Society of Lincoln Center** presents repertory films (both classics and new releases) throughout the year (*212-875-5600; www.filmlinc.com*). It's also one of the main venues for the prestigious New York Film Festival, sponsored by the film society each fall.

New-York Historical Society★★

170 Central Park West at 2 W. 77th St. See Major Manhattan Museums.

American Museum of Natural History★★★

Central Park West between W. 77th & W. 81st Sts. See Major Manhattan Museums.

Cathedral of St. John the Divine★★

MTA *Subway: 1 train to Cathedral Pkwy.-110th St. 1047 Amsterdam Ave. at W. 112th St.*

Seat of the Episcopal Diocese of New York, this is reputedly the largest cathedral in the world, built in the Gothic style. The massive stone edifice—begun in 1892 and still under construction—can welcome up to 3,000 worshipers at a time and is also the setting for frequent dance, music, film and drama performances, many of them free. The 13-acre area on Amsterdam Avenue between Cathedral Parkway and West 113th Street contains seven ancillary buildings and gardens.

In 1872 Horatio Potter, then bishop of New York, presented a proposal for a cathedral to the diocesan convention. Construction on this site in Morningside Heights did not begin until 1892, and some 25 years into the project, the original 1888 Romanesque design was scrapped for a revised plan in the Gothic style by Ralph Adams Cram. The choir and sanctuary were completed in 1911,

and the nave was begun in 1916. A century is needed to finish the cathedral.

Visit

Open year-round Mon–Sat 7am–6pm, Sun 7am–7pm. Highlight tours (1hr) Tue–Sat 11am, 1pm, Sun 1pm, $6; Vertical tours (roof access) Sat noon, 2pm, $15. 212-316-7540. www.stjohndivine.org.

Two square Gothic towers (to reach 266ft when completed) flank the symmetrical west facade, where the central **Portal of Paradise** features a double set of bronze doors bearing scenes from the Old *(left doors)* and New *(right doors)* Testaments. The doors, each weighing three tons, were produced in Paris by Ferdinand Barbedienne, who also cast the Statue of Liberty. Between the doors is the figure of St. John the Divine.

The portals open into the narthex, or vestibule, where stained-glass windows from the studio of Ernest W. Lakeman represent the Creation *(on the left)* and scenes from the Old Testament *(on the right)*. A semicircle of eight granite columns encloses the sanctuary, containing the great choir and the high altar. Niches in the marble parapet fronting the altar hold statues of notable figures, including St. Paul, Abraham Lincoln and George Washington; a stone block representing the 20C is carved with the images of Gandhi, Dr. Martin Luther King Jr., Albert Einstein and Susan B. Anthony.

The apse aisle, or ambulatory, contains seven chapels and, on the south side, displays paintings of the 16C Italian school, a glazed terracotta Annunciation (15C, Della Robbia school) and a 16C silk-embroidered cloth, representing the Adoration of the Magi.

The domed baptistery is decorated with niches holding figures associated with the early history of Nieuw Amsterdam, including Peter Stuyvesant, depicted with his wooden leg.

To the east of the south transept lies the small Biblical Garden, planted with flora mentioned in the Bible. The distinctive **Peace Fountain** (**1** *on map*), which celebrates the triumph of good over evil, was executed by Greg Wyatt. It domi-

Student Hangout

Since 1961 the **Hungarian Pastry Shop** (*1030 Amsterdam Ave. between W. 110th & W. 111th Sts.; ☎212-866-4230*) has been the place for Columbia University students to study, debate and hang out. The burgundy-walled interior of this bohemian, family-owned cafe evokes another era—you might even be inspired to deconstruct Kafka over that *caffé Viennese (☕ order it topped with whipped cream)*. Pastries includes brioches, strudel and an assortment of Eastern European standards. Outdoor tables offer a nice perspective on Morningside Park.

nates the children's sculpture garden to the south, where animal sculptures by local youths have been cast in bronze.

Columbia University★

🚇 *Subway: 1 train to 116th St.- Columbia University. W. 114th to W. 120th Sts. between Amsterdam Ave. & Broadway. Main entrance at W. 116th St. The visitor center (🕐open year-round Mon–Fri 9am–5pm; 🚫closed major holidays) is located in Low Memorial Library. 👣Guided tours (1hr) that access the interior of many of the buildings are available year-round (Mon–Fri 1pm). ☎212-854-4900. www.columbia.edu.*

The first college in New York and the fifth oldest in the nation, Columbia is one of the country's most distinguished universities and a member of the prestigious Ivy League.

Founded in 1754 by a charter from George II, King's College was first located in Lower Manhattan, where the original class of eight men met in the schoolhouse of Trinity Church. Among the early students at King's College were Alexander Hamilton, aide-de-camp to General Washington and later secretary of the Treasury; and John Jay, first chief justice of the US. After the Revolution, the school reopened in 1784 under a new name: Columbia College. In 1897 it moved to the present site after 40 years at Madison Avenue and East 49th Street. Today the coeducational university has an enrollment of some 25,000 students and an endowment of over $6 billion.

Columbia's historic **main campus** occupies 36 acres in Morningside Heights. Its formal axial arrangement is typical of the turn-of-the-19C Beaux-Arts movement. Charles McKim envisioned Low Memorial Library as the focus of his 1894 design, which encompasses the area north of West 116th Street. Added in 1934, Butler Library faces Low Library across a majestic mall, while handsome limestone and brick classroom buildings

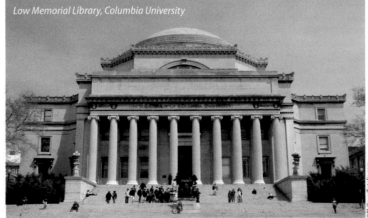

Low Memorial Library, Columbia University

©Philipus/Fotolia.com

define the quadrangles. The university began expanding in the early 20C, adding the 1926 Casa Italiana by McKim, Mead and White; and later the Law School building and School of International and Public Affairs, all on Amsterdam Avenue. Today the university continues to grow, with plans (not without controversy) to expand north of 125th Street into the Manhattanville neighborhood.

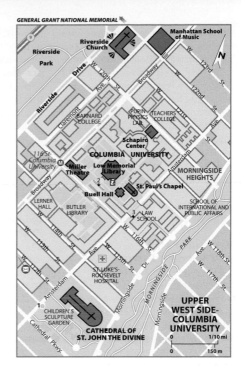

Low Memorial Library★

The gift of Seth Low, president of Columbia from 1890 to 1901, this Neoclassical building, completed in 1897, was the first major structure on the campus. Designer Charles McKim modeled the library on the Roman Pantheon. Since 1934 the building has served as an administrative center and exhibit hall. Step inside to view the marble rotunda, with its 130ft dome and 16 colossal columns.

Saint Paul's Chapel★

This 1907 building, a Northern Italian Renaissance design by Isaac Phelps Stokes, features a vaulted interior with salmon-colored Guastavino tiling and chancel windows by John La Farge. The carved pulpit, choir stalls and organ front recall those in the Church of Santa Croce in Florence, Italy. Because of the chapel's excellent acoustics, many concerts are held here.

Schapiro Center

Completed in 1992 for $62 million, this Neoclassical building was designed by Hellmuth, Obata and Kassabaum and contains state-of-the-art laboratories for research in microelectronics, video imaging and other technologies. A glass-enclosed skyway connects it to the 1927 Pupin Physics Laboratories, where the Manhattan Project, which pioneered the development of atomic energy in the US, originated.

Temple Hoyne Buell Hall

The only building remaining from the former Bloomingdale Insane Asylum, this 1878 edifice is the oldest structure on campus and now serves as a center for the study of American architecture. Frequent exhibits are mounted in the first-floor galleries. La Maison Française, the university's French cultural center, is located on the upper floor.

Outdoor Sculpture

A number of sculptures by European and American artists also distinguish the campus. Fronting Low Library is

🙂 A Bit of Advice 🙂

For a great **panorama** of Riverside Park, the Hudson River and the New Jersey shore, visit Riverside Church's observation deck (call in advance for hours open). Take the elevator to the 20th floor, but then you'll have to climb the final 147 steps. You'll pass the chambers of the 74-bell carillon.

the Neoclassical bronze figure—the university's emblem—*Alma Mater* (**2** *on map*) designed by Daniel Chester French in 1903. In front of Philosophy Hall *(east of Low Library)* is Rodin's famous bronze *The Thinker*, cast from the 1880 model in 1930. West of Low Library stands the *Great God Pan* (1899) by George Grey Barnard. Modern works include *Bellerophon Taming Pegasus* (**3** *on map*) by Jacques Lipchitz (1967), mounted over the entrance to the Law School; and *Tightrope Walker* (1979) by Kees Verkade and *Three Way Piece: Points* (1967) by Henry Moore, both on the Amsterdam Avenue overpass.

Riverside Park★ and Riverside Drive★

MTA *Subway: 1 train to 116th St.-Columbia University.*

Both Riverside Drive and Park take advantage of the beautiful views along the Hudson River. Frederick Law Olmsted designed them as a single entity in 1875. The curving drive, home to artists and musicians, boasts majestic elms, walkways and scenic overlooks, 19C row houses, turn-of-the-19C mansions and elegant early 20C apartment buildings. The park extends from West 72nd to West 155th Streets *(recommended area:*

below W. 100th St.) and contains some of the city's most important monuments such as the **Soldiers' and Sailors' Monument** *(W. 89th St.)* and the Firemen's Memorial *(W. 100th St.)*. The 91st Street garden, an English garden maintained by local residents, is worth seeing. Together, the park and drive are a designated New York City Historic Landmark.

Riverside Church★

490 Riverside Dr. between W. 120th & W. 122nd Sts. Entrance at 91 Claremont Ave. ⏰*Open year-round daily 7am–10pm.* 🎧*Free guided tours Sun 12.15pm.* ✆*212-870-6700.* *www.theriversidechurchny.org.*

With its soaring 400ft tower—containing reputedly the largest carillon in the world—this streamlined Gothic Revival building is a dominant Upper West Side landmark. It's also an important community center offering a broad range of social services and cultural programs. It was founded before 1850 as a small Baptist congregation in the Lower East Side.

John D. Rockefeller Jr. helped fund the present 1927 building of limestone, designed by Allen and Collens and

---

Upper West Side Delicacies

The Upper West Side is renowned for its purveyors of specialty foods. Among the most celebrated is **Zabar's** *(2245 Broadway at W. 80th St.; ✆212-496-1234; www.zabars.com)*, which features a stupendous selection of unusual food from around the globe as well as a fine selection of cookware. Zabar's has come a long way since its beginnings as a Jewish deli: today the store sells more than 1,000 pounds of smoked salmon per week.

The adjoining cafe may look plain, but it serves one of the best cappuccinos in town. Across the street is **H&H Bagels** *(2239 Broadway; ✆212-595-8000; www.hhbagels.com)*, which receives FedEx orders from around the globe and churns out more than 50,000 bagels a day.

For a wonderful selection of fresh produce, stop by **Fairway Market** *(2127 Broadway between W. 74th & W. 75th Sts.; ✆212-595-1888; www.fairwaymarket. com)*; the supply of mushrooms alone is worth the trip. **Citarella** *(2135 Broadway at W. 75th St.; ✆212-874-0383; www.citarella.com)* features a variety of seafood salads for take-out as well as an outstanding range of fish. Huge, delectable chocolate-chip cookies are baked by the ovenful at **Levain Bakery** *(167 W. 74th St. at Amsterdam Ave.; ✆212-874-6080; www.levainbakery.com)*. This cheerful basement bakery also turns out oatmeal-raisin cookies and scones, brioches and specialty sandwiches to gobble on the spot or take to go.

Music to Your Ears

Home to some of the country's most accomplished musicians, the Upper West Side offers a range of performances year-round. Though tickets are priced for a student budget, Columbia's **Miller Theatre** is a totally professional outfit. World-class musical performances range from Bach concertos to experimental work by living composers like Steve Reich and John Zorn, who are likely to be on hand for a Q&A *(2960 Broadway at W. 116th St.; ℘212-854-7799; www. millertheatre.com)*. To hear free classical music, go to a student recital at the **Juilliard School** *(60 Lincoln Center Plaza; ℘212-769-7406; www.juilliard.edu)* or the **Manhattan School of Music** *(120 Claremont Ave. at W. 122nd St.; ℘917-493-4428; www.msmnyc.edu)*. These institutions are among the country's best conservatories, so work is likely to be first rate. Another local institution worth a visit is **Symphony Space** *(2537 Broadway at W. 95th St.; ℘212-864-5400; www. symphonyspace.org)*. The programming here is extremely varied and includes the annual 12hr Wall to Wall, a celebration of works by a specific composer (Miles Davis, Joni Mitchell and Ravel have been featured in past years) as performed by a variety of musicians; and the literary performance series, where noted Broadway and Hollywood actors read classic and new short stories.

Henry C. Pelton (the south wing was added in 1960).

The west portal faces Riverside Drive and evokes the sculptures at Chartres Cathedral in France. Prophets from the Old Testament are carved into the columns on the left, with New Testament figures on the right. The tympanum above features a Christ in Glory and symbols of the Four Evangelists. In the narthex two **stained-glass windows** depict the life of Christ, made in the 16C for the Cathedral of Bruges in Belgium. From the narthex, enter the nave, which is 100ft high and 215ft long, with space for 2,500 worshipers. The clerestory windows are modeled after those at Chartres, while the chancel screen is notable for 80 panels illustrating figures whose lives embodied Christian ideals: among them Luther, Milton, Lincoln and Pasteur. A passage from the narthex leads to a small, Romanesque **chapel**.

If the observation deck is open (☽ see *A Bit of Advice box, p219*), you'll pass the chambers of the carillon on the final 147-step climb.

General Grant National Memorial★

Riverside Dr. at W. 122nd St. ☽*Open year-round daily 9am–5pm.* ☽*Closed Jan 1, Thanksgiving Day & Dec 25.* ℘*212-666-1640. www.nps.gov/gegr.*

☽*Free guided tours daily on the hour 10am–3pm.*

Popularly known as Grant's Tomb, this Neoclassical monument is the final resting place of **Ulysses S. Grant** (1822–85) and his wife, Julia Dent Grant (1826–1902). Grant was commander of the Union Army during the Civil War and president of the US from 1869 to 1877. The white granite mausoleum, topped by a stepped cone, was designed in 1890 by John H. Duncan and took six years to build.

The tablet above the Doric portico bears the words "Let us have peace"; the words were part of Grant's written reply to the Republican Party in 1868, in which he accepted his nomination as presidential candidate. Gold-tinted clerestory windows create a soft glow in the marble interior, which recalls Napoleon's tomb at the Invalides in Paris.

A dramatic coffered dome is suspended directly over the sunken crypt, where niches contain busts of Grant's comrades-in-arms: Sherman, Sheridan, Thomas, Ord and McPherson. Two small rooms display photographs illustrating Grant's life and achievements.

The free-form mosaic benches flanking the tomb outside were designed by Pedro Silva in the early 1970s as part of a community project to involve neighborhood youths with the monument.

Harlem★

Though only a fraction of the city's African Americans live in Harlem anymore, the neighborhood continues to nurture its history as a fulcrum of African-American culture. In the 1920s and 30s, jazz greats mingled in smoky bars with writers who proclaimed their African-American identity in novels and poetry that commanded the world's attention. That period was called the Harlem Renaissance. Now another renaissance is under way as some of the famous old landmarks are being restored, museums expanded and 19C brownstones renovated by both black and white Manhattanites.

A BIT OF HISTORY

Established in 1658 by the Dutch governor **Peter Stuyvesant** in northern Manhattan, Nieuw Haarlem was mostly farmland and remained largely rural until the New York and Harlem Railroad inaugurated service along Fourth Avenue (Park Avenue) in 1837. An even bigger wave of development occurred in the latter part of the 19C with the construction of the elevated rail lines in the western part of the valley. By the early 1890s, Harlem had become one of the most fashionable residential areas in New York City, replete with fine department stores, an opera house, a symphony hall and a yacht club.

Hopes that Harlem would continue to expand foundered in the beginning of the 20C, when brownstones built by enthusiastic developers could not be filled. Despite the racism that prevailed at the time, white landlords began to rent to middle-class black families—for

Subway: 2, 3, A, B, C, D train to 125th St.

Map: See Uptown map.

Info: Stop by the Harlem Visitor Information Kiosk in the lobby of the Studio Museum in Harlem *(144 W. 125th St.;* ℘*212-222-1014).*

Location: Harlem lies north of Central Park, bordered by Columbia University on the west and El Barrio and the Harlem River on the east. The majority of its attractions are found between 125th Street and 138th Street.

Timing: Allow half a day to visit Harlem plus time to have lunch in one of its restaurants. *See Addresses.*

a price. Often, African-American real-estate agents had to guarantee rent payment with their own money. By 1920 the black population of central Harlem was estimated at about 60,000.

Harlem Renaissance – Harlem experienced its heyday in the 1920s. As bootleg liquor flowed, popular nightspots—including the original **Cotton Club** on Lenox Avenue and **Small's Paradise**—drew nightly standing-room-only crowds (some, ironically, white-only as well) with performances by jazz greats **Duke Ellington**, **Count Basie** and **Cab Calloway**. Harlem became the undisputed Capital of Jazz. It was also a hotbed for emerging writers and artists such as **Langston Hughes** and **Zora Neale Hurston**, who celebrated their African-American identity in original, powerful language.

The Renaissance came to an end with the Great Depression, however. Though the jazz scene remained active with the arrival of innovators such as **Charlie Parker**, **Miles Davis** and **John Coltrane**, older jazz artists began gravitating to Greenwich Village or touring Europe. The middle classes also left as

125th Street Area

Settepani – *196 Lenox Ave. at W. 120th St.* ℘*917-492-4806. www.settepani.com.* This bakery offers pastries, cappuccino and ample sidewalk seating.

Brownstones in Harlem

©Thomas Pozzo di Borgo/Bigstockphoto.com

jobs were scarce. Abandoned housing deteriorated and crime soared. By the 1960s Harlem's celebrities were distinctly political.

Most famously, **Malcolm X** preached in the early 1960s at the Black Muslims' Temple of Islam (now the Masjid Malcolm Shabazz) at 116th Street and Lenox Avenue (he was assassinated in 1965 at the Audubon Ballroom on West 166th Street). Later, Harlem produced New York's only black mayor, **David Dinkins**. And after leaving office in 2000, former US president **Bill Clinton** established his office at 55 West 125th Street.

Harlem Today – Some of Harlem's landmark buildings, jazz clubs and brownstones have been lovingly restored in recent years.

There are also a number of recently built stores, restaurants and galleries. **Harlem USA**, smack dab in the center of Harlem on bustling West 125th Street and Frederick Douglass Boulevard, is the biggest of the new complexes; the glass-enclosed mall has multiple megastores, restaurants, a workout facility and a cineplex. But there's still a way to go, with such landmarks as the **Florence Mills Home** (220 W. 135th St.) and the crumbling **Renaissance Ballroom and Casino** (2341–2359 Adam Clayton Powell Jr. Blvd. between 137th & 138th Sts.); recent plans call for the ballroom to be razed and replaced with condominiums and retail and community space.

125TH STREET AREA

Also known as Martin Luther King Jr. Boulevard, 125th Street was the site of rallies, marches and protests during the Civil Rights movement. Today it's a bustling commercial artery of discount stores and street vendors, with several Harlem landmarks and cultural centers sprinkled in between.

Try to arrive before 10am to see self-taught artist Franco Gaskin's **murals***: they're painted on the retractable metal doors that are rolled over storefront windows at night.*

Then venture south to the **Mount Morris Park Historic District** (roughly bounded by W. 119th & W. 124th Sts., & by Mount Morris Park West & Lenox Ave.), where you'll find rows of stately houses and brownstones.

Studio Museum in Harlem★

144 W. 125th St. between Lenox Ave. & Adam Clayton Powell Jr. Blvd. Subway: 2, 3 train to 125th St. Open year-round Thu–Fri noon–9pm, Sat 10am–6pm, Sun noon–6pm. Closed major holidays. $7; Sunday free). Guided tours available by appointment. 212-864-4500. www.studiomuseum.org.

Established in 1968 to provide studio space for African-American artists, this museum has since grown into a major visual art and performance center hosting an active slate of public programs including lectures, workshops, gallery

The Studio Museum in Harlem

Adam Reich/The Studio Museum in Harlem

talks and book discussions, most centered on artists of African descent. Selection of the Studio Museum's 1,600-work permanent collection is always on view; Isaac Julien, Gwen Knight Lawrence, Julie Mehretu, James VanDerZee and Betye Saar are just a few of the artists represented. The vast majority of gallery space, however, is devoted to temporary shows in all media, ranging from folk art to watercolor to video. Recent exhibitions have included a retrospective of the works of Barkely L. Hendricks, and a first solo exhibit by Kehinde Wiley. The Project Space gallery hosts site-specific works created for that space by both emerging and well-known artists. There's also a full calendar of jazz, tap and other types of performance.

Apollo Theater

253 W. 125th St. between Frederick Douglass & Adam Clayton Powell Jr. Blvds. ◔*Box office open Mon–Fri 10am–6pm, Sat noon–5pm.* ☏*212-531-5305.* ☛*For backstage tours (1hr), call* ☏*212-531-5337 for schedule & reservations. www.apollotheater.org.*
Recently renovated to the tune of $12 million, the Apollo opened in 1914 as Hurtig & Seamon's New Burlesque Theater, where black audiences were excluded. Two decades later, under a new name and management, the

Apollo Theater became a mecca of black entertainment. The "Amateur Night at the Apollo" contest soon became world-famous for having given the nod to such music legends as **Ella Fitzgerald**, **Sarah Vaughan**, **James Brown** and the **Jackson Five**. After a hiatus, Amateur Night was revived in the 1980s. Held every Wednesday at 7.30pm, it's still considered one of the most prestigious performance opportunities in the US, with the audience voting on each week's winners.

Malcolm Shabazz Harlem Market

52–60 W. 116th St. between Fifth Ave. & Malcolm X Blvd. ◔*Open daily 10am–8pm winter; 10am–9pm summer.* ☏*212-987-8131.*
Located just down the hill from the silver-domed temple where Malcolm X (Shabazz) preached, this popular indoor–outdoor bazaar has about 80 stalls where vendors hawk everything from tube socks to African (or African-style) clothing, leather goods, masks, figurines, incense and art.
⌂*Though the market itself is open daily, many of the vendors don't operate on Sunday and the pickings can be pretty slim. You'll find the best selection Monday through Saturday, when the market is at its boisterous best.*

135TH STREET AREA

Central Harlem around 135th Street became active during the Harlem Renaissance as a cultural and social center; it's now the site of a historic district of 19C row houses, several noted restaurants and churches, and an important African-American cultural archive.

Schomburg Center for Research in Black Culture★

515 Malcolm X Blvd. at W. 135th St.
🕐*Exhibition hall open year-round Tue–Thu noon– 8pm, Fri–Sat 10am–6pm.*
🕐*Closed major holidays.* 📞*212-491-2200. www.schomburgcenter.org.*
This branch of the New York Public Library system contains one of the world's largest archives relating to black heritage and mounts temporary exhibits on African-American history.
Arthur Schomburg (1874–1938), a black Puerto Rican who was an influential cultural leader during the Harlem Renaissance of the 1920s, began the collection in an effort to discredit the contemporary belief that African Americans had no history. Today more than five million books, photographs, manuscripts, films, recordings and works of art are kept in the center, which is housed in a 1905 landmark library building designed by McKim, Mead and White (restored in 1990) and a modern 1980 annex. In the vestibule you'll find the Pietro Calvi bust of 19C actor **Ira Aldridge** in the role of Othello; and the art installation *Rivers*, a tribute to Langston Hughes and Arthur Schomburg. **Exhibits** such as a major photographic and audio exploration of the life of Malcolm X are located on the first floor.

Strivers Row★

W. 138th & W. 139th Sts. between Adam Clayton Powell Jr. & Frederick Douglass Blvds.
These two blocks of Georgian and Renaissance Revival houses were developed in 1891. Developer David H. King Jr. commissioned three architects, including Stanford White, to design a residential district here for the well-to-do. What you see here—two blocks of attractive houses on quiet tree-lined streets—is the result. Also known as the St. Nicholas Historic District, the area was dubbed Strivers Row in the 1920s when it became a haven for up-and-coming black professionals. More recent strivers have brought loving attention to the homes *(Stanford White's work is 203–267 W. 139th St.).* On the avenues capping the rows are a couple of boutiques selling African and African-American designs and the famous restaurant and jazz club Londel's.

Abyssinian Baptist Church

132 Odell Clark Pl. (formerly W. 138th St.). 🕐*Open Mon–Fri 10am–6pm, Sun 9am, 11am for services only.* 📞*212-862-7474. www.abyssinian.org.*
This large 1923 Gothic Revival church is home to New York's oldest black congregation, founded in 1808. It became prominent in the 1930s under the leadership of **Adam Clayton Powell Jr.** (1908–72), the flamboyant pastor and Civil Rights advocate who was elected to Congress in 1944, then stripped of his congressional office for financial improprieties in 1967; he was reinstated two years later. Clippings and photos in the memorial room trace his career.

African-American Walk of Fame

W. 135th St. between Adam Clayton Powell Jr. & Frederick Douglass Blvds.; located midblock.
Commissioned by the Harlem Chamber of Commerce in 1995 as part of the redesigning of the streetscape of 135th Street, the African-American Walk of Fame is a series of embedded bronze plaques crafted by New York sculptors Otto Neals and Ogundipe Fayoumi. The plaques honor people of African descent who have made significant contributions in music, science, the arts and community service. Start at 236 West 135th Street, walk west toward Frederick Douglass Boulevard, then cross the street. Plaques resume at 219 West 135th Street.

A Few Facts

The **George Washington Bridge** spans the Hudson River in one pure line 3,500ft long. The towers are 604ft high, and the supporting cables have a diameter of 36in. The upper level, 250ft above water, holds eight lanes; the lower level is divided into six lanes.

Harlem YMCA

180 & 181 W. 135th St. between Adam Clayton Powell Jr. & Malcolm X Blvds.
Literary greats **Langston Hughes**, **Richard Wright** and **Ralph Ellison** were only a few of the artists of the 20C to make a home at the Harlem YMCA. The building at 181 West 135th Street opened in 1919. By the late 1920s it had outgrown its new facility. A new imposing Colonial Revival building was constructed across the street and inaugurated in 1932.

Mother A.M.E. Zion

140–148 W. 137th St. between Adam Clayton Powell Jr. & Malcolm X Blvds.
℘ *212-234-1544.*
Mother Zion, as it is affectionately called, is the oldest black church in New York State, founded in 1796 by dissatisfied congregants of the John Street Methodist Church. (A.M.E. stands for African Methodist Episcopal.) As a center of strength for the community, Mother Zion established itself wherever the African-American community would migrate: from Leonard and Church Streets (now TriBeCa), to West 10th and Bleecker Streets in Greenwich Village, to its final home here on West 137th Street in Harlem, where it's been since 1925. The Gothic Revival structure was designed by **George W. Foster Jr.**, one of the first African-American architects to be registered in New York. During the 19C Mother Zion was a "freedom church"—a station on the Underground Railroad.

NORTH OF HARLEM

Several interesting sights lie north of Harlem in the hilly neighborhoods of Inwood, Hamilton Heights and Washington Heights. Since the following attractions are far-flung and generally not conducive to a walking tour, we have listed subway information.

George Washington Bridge★★

MTA *Subway: A train to 181st St.*
A tremendous feat of engineering, this toll bridge, which links 179th Street in Manhattan to Fort Lee in New Jersey, was, for a number of years, the longest bridge in the world and is still the only 14-lane suspension bridge. Designed by O.H. Amman (an American engineer of Swiss origin, who also conceived the Verrazano-Narrows Bridge) and

Touring Harlem

Although most parts of Harlem are safe, you may want to limit your visit to daylight hours. If you plan to go to a jazz club or restaurant after dark, take a taxi or car service. Also keep in mind that major avenues have been renamed for Harlem icons. Sixth Avenue above Central Park is known as **Malcolm X Boulevard**, Seventh Avenue as **Adam Clayton Powell Jr. Boulevard**, and Eighth Avenue as **Frederick Douglass Boulevard**.

To fully grasp Harlem's significance, many visitors take **guided tours** of Harlem. Two companies to consider: **Harlem Spirituals, Inc.** (℘ *212-391-0900; www. harlemspirituals.com*), which offers an evening visit of Harlem that includes soul food and jazz, a Sunday visit with a gospel and soul-food brunch, and a Wednesday-morning visit of Harlem with gospel *(all tours depart year-round from office at 690 Eighth Ave. between W. 43rd & 44th Sts.; reservations required)*. The **Municipal Art Society** also conducts walking and bus tours of the neighborhood on an occasional basis, as well as private tours by appointment (℘ *212-935-3960; recorded information ℘ 212-453-0050; www.mas.org*).

George Washington Bridge seen from New Jersey

©Jeremy Edwards/iStockphoto.com

architect **Cass Gilbert**, the bridge was opened in 1931, and cost about $59 million. In 1959 the growing volume of traffic required the construction of a lower level, opened in 1962. At the same time, an intricate system of interchanges was installed.

The best view of the George Washington Bridge may be had from the sightseeing boats (see Sightseeing in Planning Your Trip) that circle Manhattan, or from the Henry Hudson Parkway along the Hudson River.

Hispanic Society of America★

Broadway between W. 155th & W. 156th Sts. MTA *Subway: 1 train to 157th St. or B train to 155th St.* ○Open Tue–Sat 10am–4.30pm, Sun 1–4pm. Tours (45min) Sat 2pm. Free. 212-926-2234. www.hispanicsociety.org.

This small but fascinating museum offers a panorama of Spanish civilization from pre-Roman times to the present and has a collection of Old Masters considered by some to be second only to those found at the Prado in Madrid. Located opposite a bronze statue of El Cid (1927, Anna Hyatt Huntington), the two-story building is part of a cluster of cultural institutions known as **Audubon Terrace**, after naturalist James Audubon, who once had a country house on the site. Charles Pratt Huntington, nephew of railroad heir Archer M. Huntington, commissioned these

Harlem Open Artist Studio Tour

For two days in the fall, nearly 100 Harlem artists open their doors to the public, providing a window into the artistic process and a unique shopping opportunity; you can bypass dealers and retailers and purchase works directly from the artist. Both browsers and buyers are welcome. *For a schedule, event map, and other information, go to www.hoast.org.*

Neoclassical buildings in the early 20C. Today the American Academy of Arts and Letters—the country's most prestigious honor society for writers, artists, architects and composers—also has its headquarters here. The society exhibits public art and manuscripts twice a year *(call or go online for schedule : 212-368-5900; www.artsandletters.org).*

Designed as an interior courtyard in the Renaissance style, the society's first-floor gallery presents traditional and ritual objects such as choir stalls, exquisite silverware, Paleolithic tools, Renaissance tombstones, silk brocades and altar frontals. Upon entering, notice the two life-size portraits by 18C Spanish artist Francisco de Goya, including one of the Duchess of Alba. To the right, the 15C Mudéjar door is surrounded by colorful tiles. The Sorolla room (far right) features paintings by Sorolla y Bastida titled Provinces of Spain. A research library is located on the first floor.

The second-floor balustrade contains earthenware, ceramics, metalwork, porcelain, lusterware and jewelry displayed in glass cases. Portraits by renowned artists El Greco, Morales, Ribera, Velázquez and Goya line the walls.

Morris-Jumel Mansion★

65 Jumel Terrace between W. 160th St. & Edgecombe Ave. MTA *Subway: 1 train to 157th St. or C train to 163rd St.* ○*Open year-round Wed–Sun 10am–4pm.* ○*Closed major holidays.* ↝*Guided tours (*↝*$5) Sat noon.* ↝*$5.* ✆*212-923-8008. www.morrisjumel.org.*

Occupying a hilltop site with a view of the Harlem Valley, this Georgian mansion is the only colonial home to survive in northern Manhattan. Today it's part of a historic district that includes 20 wood-frame row houses built in the 1880s.

This mansion has an intriguing history. Col. **Roger Morris** of England built the house (originally known as Mount Morris) in 1765, but a decade later he was driven out by Patriots to England, where his Loyalist sentiments were better appreciated. During the Battle of Harlem Heights in 1776, the estate was General George Washington's headquarters; in 1810 it passed to **Stephen Jumel**, a wealthy French wine merchant. Jumel's wife, Eliza Bowen, was never fully accepted in New York society, and the Jumels set sail for France in 1815, where they traveled more comfortably in Napoleonic circles. Jumel died in 1832, and a year later his widow returned and married **Aaron Burr**, the third vice president of the US. After a year of marriage, the couple separated. Their divorce was granted on the day Burr died, in 1836. While constructed of brick, the mansion features wood facades, corner quoins and a two-story Federal-style portico. The **interior** is particularly noteworthy for the rear drawing room on the first floor, possibly the first octagonal room in the US. The front parlor contains Madame Jumel's fashionable Empire-style settee, chairs and French chandelier. On the second floor, Madame Jumel's bedroom and dressing room feature Empire furniture that once belonged to the Bonaparte family; note especially the 19C mahogany slipper chairs.

Hamilton Grange National Memorial

St. Nicholas Park at Convent Ave. & W. 141st St. MTA *Subway: 1, A train to 145th St.* ⚠*Closed for restoration; predicted reopening late 2011.* ✆*212-283-5154. www.nps.gov/hagr.*

Designed in 1801 by John McComb Jr. (architect of City Hall), this Federal-style clapboard house was **Alexander Hamilton**'s country estate and his principal residence when he was killed in a duel with Aaron Burr in 1804. In 1889 the house, which Hamilton fondly referred to as his "sweet project," was moved from its original location to Convent Avenue, where its facade was obscured by surrounding buildings; for a time it served as the rectory for St. Luke's Church. In June 2008 the entire structure

Spirituals

By the end of the 18C, spirituals, often referred to as slave songs, were becoming an integral part of the African-American worship experience and an important form of storytelling. Although the harmonies are based on Protestant hymns, the rhythms reflect ancestral African musical traditions such as the call and response, in which a primary singer's verses are echoed by a chorus. While text and harmonies are simple, emotion fills the core of every song; melodies are lined with "blue" notes (flat notes) that would later become an important part of blues and jazz compositions. Some of the best-known spirituals are "Nobody Knows the Trouble I've Seen," "Go Down, Moses" and "Joshua Fit the Battle of Jericho."

was jacked up and moved again to its current location in verdant St. Nicholas Park, a site that approximates its original rural setting. Restoration work by the National Park Service is returning the house to its original appearance.

Historic District

The picturesque gabled row houses on Hamilton Terrace and Convent Avenue include some unusual Dutch and Flemish Revival dwellings dating from the 1880s, when the district was developed as a suburb for prosperous New Yorkers. Note St. Luke's Episcopal Church *(285 Convent Ave.)*, designed in the Romanesque Revival style in 1892.

Just south of Hamilton Heights lies City College's campus, begun in 1897. The star pupil, architecturally, is the 1907 Shepard Hall *(W. 140th St between St. Nicholas Terrace & Convent Ave.)*, which resembles a Gothic cathedral. It is clad with Manhattan schist excavated when the subway was built.

Inwood Hill Park

MTA *Subway: A train to 207th St.*
Do not walk in the park alone.

Set at the northwestern tip of Manhattan, this park is separated from Fort Tryon Park by a ravine dotted with apartment houses. Wooded and hilly, the terrain seems to have altered very little since the Algonquins inhabited the area. During the Revolution, British and Hessian troops were quartered here. Today the park is quite empty, except for picnics on Sundays. East of the park stands **Dyckman Farmhouse Museum** *(between W. 204th St. & Broadway;* open year-round Wed–Sat 11am–4pm, Sun noon–4pm; closed major holidays; $1; 212-304-9422; www.dyckmanfarmhouse.org)*, the only extant 18C Dutch Colonial farmhouse in Manhattan. Appointed with period Dutch and French furniture, and bordered by a charming herb garden and a smokehouse, the structure illustrates life in colonial America.

ADDRESSES

EAT

Harlem has a number of excellent restaurants and cafes. Here are a few of the more established ones.

$ Miss Maude's Spoonbread Too – *547 Lenox Ave between W. 137th & W. 138th Sts. 212-690-3100. www.spoonbreadinc.com.* Baskets of fresh hot cornbread start things off at this budget-priced soul food mecca. The fried chicken draws admirers from all over Manhattan, accompanied by tender greens and tasty macaroni and cheese.

$$ The Cotton Club – *656 W. 125th St. between Twelfth Ave. & the West Side Hwy. 888-640-7980. www.cottonclub-newyork.com.* A slice of old Harlem, the Cotton Club hosted some of the biggest names in jazz in the 1920s: Duke Ellington's band, Lena Horne, Josephine Baker, Cab Calloway and Louis Armstrong and many others. Today in addition to its Monday-night swing dances, the club has jazz and blues shows with a buffet dinner Thursdays through Saturdays. Be sure to make a reservation.

$$ Sylvia's Soul Food Restaurant – *328 Lenox Ave. between W. 126th & W. 127th Sts. 212-996-0660. www.sylviasrestaurant.com.* Sylvia Woods has delighted diners with her Southern food and hospitality since 1962, and has seen her business grow immensely as a result (regulars' waistlines have likely done the same). Order the delicious greens, candied yams and Southern fried chicken, and take home some of Sylvia's famed cornbread mix or barbecue sauce. For a special treat, come for the Sunday gospel brunch *(12.30pm–4pm)*.

$$$ Londel's Supper Club – *2620 Frederick Douglass Blvd. between W. 139th & W. 140th Sts. 212-234-6114. www.londelsrestaurant.com.* Nestled in the Strivers Row area, this upscale Harlem restaurant has become a meeting place for local celebrities and political figures. Ask for the house specialty, pan seared salmon, or the delicious blackened catfish. Londel's has live jazz on tap on Friday and Saturday evenings, and hosts a gospel brunch on Sundays.

New York is unquestionably the cultural capital of the nation. Several of the city's venerated cultural institutions were founded in the latter half of the 19C, amassing glorious treasures from around the world in the intervening 150 years. Centers of academic research as well as repositories of art and artifacts, these museums both delight and educate the public. The following are Manhattan's cultural heavyweights, ordered alphabetically by three- and two-star ratings. For a listing of museums in the outer boroughs, as well as other museums in Manhattan, see the Index, under the heading Museums.

American Museum of Natural History★★★

Central Park West between W. 77th and W. 81st Sts.

One of New York's most illustrious establishments, this museum ranks among the largest of its kind in the world. Dealing with all facets of natural history, its outstanding collections range from minerals and gems to dinosaurs, and from Indian totem poles to Tibetan gowns.

A BIT OF HISTORY

The Building – Founded in 1869 by **Albert S. Bickmore**, the museum was initially installed in the Arsenal, in Central Park. Calvert Vaux designed the first building of the present structure to be built on a swampy area north of The Dakota. Construction of the colossus, today composed of 23 interconnected buildings, began in 1874 and was formally opened three years later.

Finally completed in the 1930s, the complex is a curious mixture of styles, the result of its being worked on by various architects at different periods. John Russell Pope's rotunda-topped hall (1836) is the state's memorial to **Theodore Roosevelt**. In 1996 the fourth-floor fossil halls were renovated, and 2000 saw the opening of the **Rose Center for Earth and Space**, a seven-story glass box containing a gargantuan sphere wherein the **Hayden Planetarium**'s turbo-charged space show is shown. Enjoy views of the center, Theodore Roosevelt Park and the old apartment buildings of 81st Street from the **Arthur Ross Terrace**, a vast public space built above a sunken park-

Subway: B, C train to 81st St. or 1 train to 79th St.

Map: See Upper West Side.

Location: Stop by the information desk to pick up the museum's detailed floor plan to get your bearings. Food service is available on three levels, and museum shops can be found on the first, second and fourth floors.

Timing: The two biggest attractions here are the fossil halls and the Hayden Planetarium at the adjoining Rose Center for Earth and Space. Buy tickets to the space show when you first arrive (they sell out, especially on weekends), allowing a couple of hours to check out the museum before the show begins. Once you're done with the fossil halls (if time allows) proceed to the Hall of Ocean Life and the Hall of Minerals and Gems.

Kids: Dinostore *(4th floor)* is particularly popular.

Don't Miss: Check the museum's website *(www.amnh.org)* for the schedule of shows in the Hayden Planetarium's Space Theater.

Barosaurus skeleton in the Theodore Roosevelt Rotunda

©AMNH/C. Chesek and D. Finnin

ing lot. To the west (Columbus Avenue) sits the **Weston Pavilion**, a glass-walled little sibling to the Rose Center, housing a suspended 18ft aluminum-and-steel spherical armillary that demonstrates New York's exact position in the cosmos on January 1, 2000. On West 77th Street an eight-story **library** holds the museum's 450,000 volumes.

The Collections – Culled from more than 1,000 expeditions since 1869, the museum's holdings include over 30 million artifacts and specimens, with only a small part on view in 45 exhibit halls. The displays include life-size dioramas of animals shown in their natural habitats: though some viewers find them dated, the ground and vegetation are faithfully reproduced, and the background scenes are effectively painted by artists using sketches made at the original sites. The latest scientific information and interpretive techniques inform the design of the new galleries.

VISIT

👥🚹♿🕐*Open year-round daily 10am–5.45pm.* 🕐*Closed Thanksgiving Day & Dec 25.* 👣*Guided tours available daily 10.15am–3.15pm.* 💰*$16 suggested donation; $9 children. Museum admission plus Rose Center and either space show, IMAX film or special exhibition $24; children $14. SuperSaver ticket includes admission to Rose Center, all special exhibitions, IMAX*

film and space show $32; children $20. 🍴. 📞*212-769-5100. www.amnh.org.* Below we present the highlights of each floor. Some halls may be devoted to temporary exhibits or closed for renovation; check at the information desk. Touch screens are located throughout the museum and provide directions to, and descriptions of, each exhibit.

THEODORE ROOSEVELT MEMORIAL HALL★★★

Main Entrance – On the Central Park side is the main entrance, which opens onto the main lobby of the museum (*2nd floor*), part of a majestic 800ft-long facade. Before entering, look at the Ionic colonnade of Theodore Roosevelt Memorial Hall bearing the statues of explorers and naturalists Daniel Boone, John James Audubon, and Lewis and Clark. An equestrian statue (1940, James Earle Fraser) featuring Roosevelt flanked by a Native American and an African American, stands sentinel at the entrance to the hall.

Second Floor – Posed with imagination, protecting its young from an allosaurus, a replica of a **barosaurus** looms over the Roosevelt rotunda. Rising to five stories (50ft), the skeleton of this Jurassic herbivore is a resin-and-foam replica of the original fossilized bones, which are too fragile to be mounted for display. Just west of the rotunda is the spectacular **Hall of African Mammals**★, dedicated to Carl Akeley, who revolutionized museum display with his realistic dioramas in the early 20C. Highlighted by a herd of African elephants on the alert, dioramas present zebras, antelopes, gorillas, lions and gazelles in their natural surroundings. In the galleries on the third-floor level of this hall, other dioramas depict various species of monkey, rhinoceros, leopard and hyena.

The **Hall of African Peoples** traces the development of complex human culture on the African continent. The **Hall of Mexico and Central America** displays an outstanding pre-Columbian collection. Of special interest are the exhibits related to the Aztec and Mayan civilizations, gold ornaments of the ancient Americas and stone and clay sculptures from central Veracruz.

The **Hall of South American Peoples** exhibits Andean and Amazonian treasures, including the 2,500-year-old Paracas mantle, that are testimony to the religious beliefs and social organization of the ancient, recently extinct and existing cultures of this continent.

The **Hall of Asian Peoples**★ features a comprehensive exhibit of life from prehistoric times to the late 19C, when Western technology began to influence the traditions of the Orient.

First Floor – A seagoing Haida war canoe from the Queen Charlotte Islands in British Columbia, Canada, dominates the foyer. Carved out of one piece of cedar in 1878, the watercraft can hold more than 30 passengers. The **Hall of Northwest Coast Indians**★ presents superb totem poles, American-Indian and Inuit tools and handicrafts. The **Hall of Human Origins**★ strives to place humans in the context of the natural world with displays on fossils and genomic research.

A 34-ton meteorite fragment found in Greenland, in 1895, forms the focal point of the **Hall of Meteorites**★. The hall incorporates more than 130 meteorite specimens in its investigation of the nature and history of meteorites and their role in unlocking the history of the solar system. Among the meteorite "greatest hits" documented are the one that produced a 185mi crater in the Yucatan peninsula some 65 million years ago and is credited by some with killing off the land dinosaurs.

In the **Halls of Minerals and Gems**★★, you may feast your eyes on more than 4,000 specimens of rocks, minerals and gems, including rubies, emeralds and diamonds. Here you'll find the Star of India, the world's largest star sapphire (weight: 563 carats).

On the opposite side of the building *(Central Park West)*, and still on the first floor, the **Hall of Biodiversity**★ bustles with an array of life-forms intended to convey the variety and interactivity of life on earth. The exhibit also communicates a strong environmental message about human impact on biodiversity worldwide. The west wall displays 1,500 specimens and models that illustrate the wonders of biodiversity. The heart of the exhibit, however, is the walk-through **diorama** of the Dzanga-Sangha rain forest in Africa. This lush setting includes 160 replica species and more than 500,000 carefully crafted leaves.

An immense (94ft-long) model of a blue whale, suspended in a dive position, dominates the two-story **Hall of Ocean Life**★. Shimmering lights and an underwater soundscape "immerse"

Taking a Break

Take a break for a meal at one of the museum's four eateries. The **Museum Food Court** *(lower level; ⏰ open daily 11am–4.45pm)* serves pizza, pasta, salads and classic sandwiches. The **Cafe on One** *(1st floor; ⏰ open daily 11am–4.45pm)* has gourmet fare like beet and goat cheese salad and focaccia sandwiches. The **Cafe on 4** *(4th floor; ⏰ open Sat–Sun 11am–4.45pm)* offers light fare along with coffee and soft drinks. Within the Food Court, the **Juice Bar** *(near subway entrance; ⏰ open daily 11am–4.45pm)* offers fresh fruit drinks, coffee, soda and sweets.

Hall of Biodiversity

©AMNH/D. Finnin

visitors in the whale's ocean home. Traditional dioramas—notably the two-story Andros Coral Reef—have been restored and im-proved. On the mezzanine you'll find eight high-tech exhibits that explore ocean ecosystems (such as estuaries, polar seas, the deep-sea floor). Films on different subjects are shown in the **IMAX Theater**, a 996-seat auditorium equipped with a gigantic movie screen four stories high and 66ft wide.

Third Floor – The **Hall of Reptiles and Amphibians** features the world's largest living lizard, the 10ft Komodo dragon. The **Hall of Primates** displays animals from the same biological order as man, beginning with the tree shrew. To the west of the primates, displays on the lifestyles of the Eastern Woodlands and Plains Indians include model houses, weapons, tools and utensils. In the **Hall of North American Birds**, you'll find a variety of birds from all corners of the country, including the wild turkey, which Benjamin Franklin wanted to designate America's national bird.

The **Hall of the Pacific Peoples**★, inspired by the work and ideas of Dr. Margaret Mead (1901–78), contains exhibits related to six cultural areas of the Pacific: Australia, Indonesia, the Philippines, Melanesia, Micronesia and Polynesia. A large display case near the center of the hall holds sacred masks, carved figures and boldly decorated shields illustrating the rich and diverse art of the peoples of the Sepik River basin.

Fourth Floor – *Begin your visit in the orientation center (see box below).* Completed in 1996, the six **fossil halls**★★ on the top floor represent a visual and intellectual tour de force, but visitors should be prepared for an overwhelming experience. Curators have attempted a stunning departure from the usual presentation of this type of material by arranging the familiar fossil remains and interpretive exhibits along a cladogram, or "branching evolutionary tree." Such an arrangement is intended to depict evolutionary relationships among contemporaneous creatures as well as through time.

Beginning with the **Hall of Vertebrate Origins**, you can navigate along the branches of the tree, following the

A Bit of Advice

When you visit the Fourth Floor, be sure to stop first at the **Wallach Orientation Center**. The fossil halls are dense with information, making a preliminary visit to the orientation center essential. At the center, you'll preview the layout of the halls and learn what the key concepts are within each. You can also view a video presentation, *The Evolution of Vertebrates (12min)*.

Rose Center for Earth and Space

©AMNH/D. Finnin

development of vertebrates from the earliest jawless fishes to dinosaurs and mammals. As the cladogram progresses, "advanced" features emerge (jaws, four limbs, grasping hands and so on) to create the branching effect that furthers evolution. Specimen alcoves on either side of the main branch explore groups of related animals in detail. The museum has the largest collection of fossil vertebrates in the world, and visitors scouting out skeletal remains will not be disappointed. In the **Hall of Saurischian Dinosaurs** (distinguished by grasping hands), huge apatosaurus and Tyrannosaurus rex tower over tiny Archaeopteryx lithographica. In the **Hall of Ornithischian Dinosaurs** (whose pubis bones point backward), note the "mummy," really a fossilized imprint of a duck-billed dinosaur carcass. Discovered in 1908, the fossil is so detailed that it has even preserved the texture of the animal's skin. Together the two dinosaur halls present more than 100 specimens, 85 per cent of which are real fossils. The final wing showcases Mammals and Their Extinct Relatives, including ancient mammoths, mastodons, saber-toothed cats and giant sloths.

ROSE CENTER FOR EARTH AND SPACE★★

W. 81st St., on the museum's north side. ⏱Same as the museum. Space show every 30min Mon–Fri 10.30am–4.30pm, *Sat–Sun 10.30am–5pm. 🔊Audio tours (75min; 🎧free with admission). 🎧Admission is included in museum ticket. 📞212-769-5200. www.amnh.org.* Accessible via the museum *(first and second floors)*, or through its own arched entrance on West 81st Street, the center blends cutting-edge science with high-impact visuals to describe the mysteries of the cosmos.

The thrilling 30min space **show**★★★, put on inside the Hayden Sphere, is not to be missed. The most advanced of its kind, it brilliantly combines education and entertainment in an eye-popping journey to the edge of the observable universe, using 3-D maps developed with the help of NASA.

Outside the theater, a 400ft-long display, Scales of the Universe, demonstrates the enormity of space with scale models, touch screens and text panels. Dangling from the ceiling above it are models of the planets of our solar system. A presentation *(2min)* on the Big Bang uses lasers and SurroundSound to conjure the birth of the universe. Upon exiting, visitors descend a spiral ramp to the first-floor **Hall of Planet Earth**★, where exhibits focus on geologic and climatic features of our own planet. Down on the lower-level, the **Hall of the Universe**★, hums with up-to-the-minute video from the Hubble Telescope, models of cosmic phenomena, and artifacts including the 15-ton Willamette Meteorite.

The Cloisters★★★

Isolated on a hill in Fort Tryon Park, The Cloisters re-creates a fortified monastery. Housed in four reconstructed medieval cloisters and part of a fifth, its collections, which include sculptures, tapestries and other objects spanning over centuries, enjoy an unrivaled reputation among lovers of medieval art.

A BIT OF HISTORY

The Collection – The core of the collection is made up of medieval sculptures and architectural remains assembled by the American sculptor **George Grey Barnard** (1863–1938), during his frequent trips to Europe. Opened to the public in 1914 in a brick building on Fort Washington Avenue, the collection included sections of the cloisters of Saint-Michel-de-Cuxa, Saint-Guilhem-le-Désert, Bonnefont-en-Comminges and Trie, all from southern France.

In 1925 **John D. Rockefeller Jr.** granted a large sum to the Metropolitan Museum of Art to purchase the Barnard collection. The Rockefellers also donated more than 40 sculptures from their collection. Five years later Rockefeller presented

Subway: A train to 190th St. or M4 bus to Fort Tryon Park-The Cloisters

Location: Though it looks far on a map, The Cloisters is only about a 30min subway ride from Midtown Manhattan. From the 190th Street subway station, it's a lovely 15min walk through Fort Tryon Park. You may also hop aboard the M4 bus at the traffic circle outside the subway station and take it one stop north to the museum.

Timing: 2hrs. Rent the audio guide (⊜$7), which provides valuable historical commentary.

Kids: Though The Cloisters is a bit dour for most kids, there's an enjoyable Family Tour option on the audio guide, offering medieval music and stories to go along with works in the museum.

Don't Miss: The world-famous Unicorn tapestries.

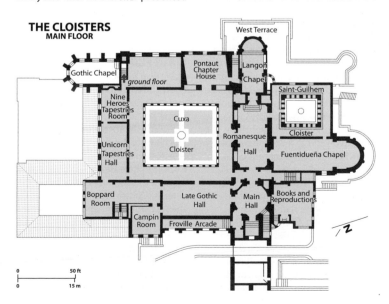

THE CLOISTERS
MAIN FLOOR

West Terrace

Gothic Chapel
ground floor
Pontaut Chapter House
Langon Chapel
Saint-Guilhem
Nine Heroes Tapestries Room
Cuxa Cloister
Romanesque Hall
Cloister
Unicorn Tapestries Hall
Fuentidueña Chapel
Boppard Room
Late Gothic Hall
Main Hall
Books and Reproductions
Campin Room
Froville Arcade

0   50 ft
0   15 m

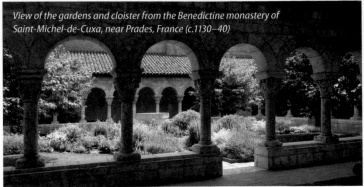

View of the gardens and cloister from the Benedictine monastery of Saint-Michel-de-Cuxa, near Prades, France (c.1130–40)

The Metropolitan Museum of Art, The Cloisters Collection, 1925

Medieval Music

The Fuentidueña Chapel hosts an occasional series of period music concerts *(tickets include museum admission)*; check the website for ticket information and schedule.

the City of New York with an estate he owned in what is now Fort Tryon Park, stipulating that the northern part be reserved for the new Cloisters. Designed by **Charles Collens** of Boston, also responsible for Riverside Church, the complex was completed in 1938. The museum remains administratively a part of the Metropolitan Museum of Art. **The Setting** – Covering 62 acres of wooded hills above the Hudson River, **Fort Tryon Park**★★ was landscaped by Frederick Law Olmsted Jr. If you're here on a temperate day, stop to visit the gorgeous **Heather Garden**★★ just south of the museum. The eponymous fort, since demolished, was the last fortification to resist the British invasion of Manhattan during the American Revolution. The fight involved the first woman soldier of the Revolution, Margaret Corbin.

VISIT

Open Mar–Oct Tue–Sun 9.30am–5.15pm; rest of the year Tue–Sun 9.30am–4.45pm. Closed Jan 1, Thanksgiving Day & Dec 25. Free guided tours available Tue–Fri & Sun 3pm; garden tours May–Oct Tue–Sun 1pm; self-guided audio tour available in four languages $7. $20 suggested

donation (includes same-day admission to the Main Building of the Metropolitan Museum of Art). 212-923-3700. *www.metmuseum.org /cloisters.*

The central structure, containing a group of cloisters, chapels and halls, is arranged around a square tower inspired by that of Saint-Michel-de-Cuxa in southern France. As you enter on the east side of the building, note the driveway paved with Belgian blocks—originally from New York streets—reminiscent of European cobblestones; a functional portcullis guards the staff parking lot.

To fully appreciate the treasures at The Cloisters, we highly recommend taking a guided tour or renting the self-guided audio tour. Following are a few highlights you should be sure not to miss.

MAIN FLOOR

See floor plans.

Fuentidueña Chapel★ – This "chapel" is largely devoted to Spanish Romanesque art. Suspended from the ceiling of the apse hangs a well-preserved 12C crucifix from the Convent of Santa Clara at Astudillo in Spain.

Romanesque Hall★ – The entrance features a round-arched doorway characteristic of the Romanesque style. On the left side, the capitals are carved with graceful birds feeding on acanthus plants. The capitals on the right bear carvings of imaginary animals surmounted by a delicate acanthus motif.

Saint-Guilhem Cloister★ – The covered walkway contains columns and

THE CLOISTERS
GROUND FLOOR

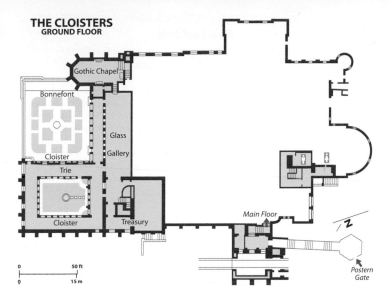

Gothic Chapel

Bonnefont

Glass
Gallery

Cloister

Trie

Cloister

Treasury

Main Floor

Postern
Gate

0 ___ 50 ft
0 ___ 15 m

capitals from the Benedictine abbey of Saint-Guilhem-le-Désert, near Montpellier, France. The fountain in the center of the cloister was once a Romanesque capital in the Church of Saint-Sauveur in the Auvergne region of France.

Cuxa Cloister★★ – Although this is the museum's largest cloister, it is only one-quarter the size of the original structure. The various elements came from the Benedictine monastery of Saint-Michel-de-Cuxa, near Prades, in the French Pyrenees. Abandoned during the French Revolution, the monastery was sold, but in 1913 Barnard was able to bring together about half of the original Romanesque capitals, 12 columns, 25 bases and 7 arches. Rose-colored Languedoc marble was cut from original quarries to complete the reconstruction. Both medieval and modern plants are grown in the garden. A lovely space.

Early Gothic Hall★ – This recently renovated room contains 13C–14C French stained glass and sculpture, including an imposing painted sandstone statue of the Virgin (c.1250) that once stood in the Strasbourg Cathedral.

Nine Heroes Tapestries Room★★ – Contained within this dimly lit room are several **tapestries** (1410) that are among the oldest in existence, along with the Apocalypse tapestries in Angers, France.

The theme of the Nine Heroes, very popular in the Middle Ages, includes three pagans (Hector, Alexander, Julius Caesar), three Hebrews (David, Joshua, Judas Maccabeus) and three Christians (Arthur, Charlemagne, Godfrey of Bouillon). Their feminine counterparts were the Nine Heroines.

Unicorn Tapestries Hall★★★ – The **Unicorn tapestries** are among the most exceptional of the golden age of tapestry, which flourished at the end of the 15C and the beginning of the 16C. The set of seven tapestries originally hung

Unicorn in Captivity (c.1495–1505)

New Leaf Café

1 Margaret Corbin Dr., in Fort Tryon Park. Open year-round Tue–Fri noon–3.30pm, 6–10pm, Sat 11am–3.30pm, Sun 11am–3.30pm, 5.30–9.30pm. ☎212-568-5323. www.newleafrestaurant.com.

Couple your visit to the Cloisters with a meal at this lovely restaurant just a short walk from the museum. Opened in 2001, it's housed in a 1930s-era stone park building that's been renovated to look both sleek and inviting, with high-arched windows and rustic furniture, though a seat at one of the patio tables, surrounded by the lush foliage of Fort Tryon Park, is irresistible on a summer day. Creative fare highlights local and seasonal ingredients and includes favorites like roasted house smoked venison, though the burger is always a good bet as well. All proceeds go to the New York Restoration Project, for the upkeep of public green spaces in northern Manhattan.

in the Château de Verteuil in Charente (southwestern France), the home of the well-known La Rochefoucauld family. Six of the tapestries were acquired by John D. Rockefeller Jr. in 1922; the seventh was added in 1938. Be sure to listen to all of the audio guide commentary on these tapestries; the story they tell is fascinating.

Boppard Room★★ – The six stained-glass panels you see here were created for the Carmelite church (late 15C) in the town of Boppard, Germany. There is also an ornate Spanish alabaster altarpiece (15C) and a striking brass eagle lectern (16C) from Belgium.

Campin Room★★ – This room contains the famous **Annunciation Triptych** by 15C Flemish artist Robert Campin. The central panel represents the Annunciation. The side panels depict the donors, on the left, and on the right, St. Joseph in his workshop; notice the mousetrap on St. Joseph's workbench and the painstakingly reproduced details of the town square in the background.

GROUND FLOOR

Gothic Chapel★★ – This structure provides a superb setting for a collection of tomb effigies and slabs. Notice the effigy of Jean d'Alluye (13C) and four monumental Catalan sarcophagi of the Counts of Urgel (14C). The tombs come from the Premonstratensian monastery of Santa Maria de Bellpuig de las Avellanas, north of Lérida in Spain. The apsidal windows are now glazed with 14C Austrian stained glass.

Bonnefont Cloister★★ – This pretty cloister, with views of the tower, the park and the Hudson River, contains elements (13C–14C) of the former Cistercian abbey at Bonnefont-en-Comminges in southern France as well as a herb garden with 250 species of plant cultivated in the Middle Ages.

Trie Cloister – Because of its small size, this cloister induces the serenity associated with a monastery. In the summer it hosts a small outdoor cafe serving sandwiches and snacks under the arcades.

Glass Gallery – This room is named for the roundels and panels of stained glass (15C–16C) representing scenes from the Old and New Testaments. Small works of art are displayed here; note especially the intricate lindenwood sculpture of a seated bishop by famed artist Tilman Riemenschneider.

Treasury – The Cloisters' collection of smaller objects of exceptionally fine quality is displayed in this recently updated gallery. The outstanding piece is a walrus-ivory cross from the 12C, the so-called Cloisters Cross, carved with great attention to detail.

Also of interest is a rosary bead of boxwood with a tiny representation of the Passion inside (16C, South Lowlands). Be sure to peer under the cloth covers over the glass cases in the anteroom, where you'll find two magnificent *Belles Heures (Books of Hours)* that once belonged to Jean, Duke of Berry, and an outstanding collection of hand-painted 15C playing cards.

The Frick Collection★★★

1 E. 70th St. between Fifth & Madison Aves.

One of the world's most distinguished small museums, The Frick Collection offers a unique opportunity to view an exceptional trove of Old Masters, furnishings and decorative arts in the luxurious confines of a sumptuous mansion. There are more than 1,100 works in all, ranging from the Renaissance to the 19C, most chosen by Henry Clay Frick himself.

A BIT OF HISTORY

Pittsburgh coke and steel industrialist **Henry Clay Frick** (1849–1919) began collecting works of art in 1880, when he took his first trip to Europe with his friend **Andrew Mellon**, the primary benefactor of the National Gallery of Art. First concentrating on 18C English paintings, Frick later ventured into sculpture —bronzes in particular—then furniture, enamels, porcelain and Old Masters. In 1913 he commissioned Thomas Hastings, architect of the New York Public Library, to design this 40-room mansion for his family and his art collection, with an eye toward opening it to the public after his death. Though Frick died in

Subway: 6 train to 68th St.

Location: Museum maps are available at the admission desk at the end of the Reception Hall. Pick up your free audio tour in the Entrance Hall; packed with insightful commentary on dozens of works throughout the museum, it's an absolutely essential part of a visit. An audiovisual presentation (22min), shown in the Music Room every hour on the half-hour, describes the arc of Frick's collecting career.

Timing: Allow several hours. There is no cafe, so you may want to eat first.

Don't Miss: Rembrandt's arresting *Self-Portrait* (West Gallery), Ingres' beguiling *Comtesse d'Haussonville* (North Hall), Fragonard's monumental *Progress of Love* (Fragonard Room) and Bellini's masterful *St Francis in the Desert* (Living Hall).

1919, the opening did not take place until 1935, four years after his wife's death. Today The Frick Collection contains works ranging from the 14C to

/Fragonard Room

©Michael Bodycomb/The Frick Collection, New York

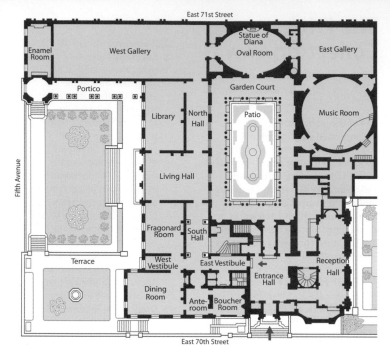

the 19C, many arranged in eclectic thematic ensembles, rather than by school or period, simply because Frick liked them this way. Such quirks are part of the grand institution's fusty genius.

VISIT

&.⊙*Open year-round Tue–Sat 10am–6pm, Sun 11am–5pm.* ⊙*Closed major holidays.* *Audio tours available at no charge.* *$18; pay-what-you-wish Sun before 1pm. Children under 10 not admitted.* *212-288-0700. www.frick.org.*

Highlights of the collection are listed below in clockwise fashion from the Entrance Hall.

Anteroom★ – This room features Jan van Eyck's *Virgin and Child with Saints and Donor* (1440–41), composed in the last year of the artist's life and completed by his assistants, and El Greco's *Purification of the Temple* (c.1600), a small canvas stuffed with action and intrigue.

Dining Room★ – The spacious room includes portraits by Hogarth, Romney and Reynolds, and a masterpiece by Gainsborough, *The Mall in St. James's Park* (1783).

Fragonard Room★★★ – Eleven decorative paintings by Jean-Honoré Fragonard (1732–1806) hang in this recently refurbished gallery. Four of the large panels were commissioned by Madame du Barry, a mistress of Louis XV. They recount the various stages of a romantic encounter: *The Pursuit, The Meeting, The Lover Crowned* and *Love Letters*. Exquisite furnishings add to the total effect.

South Hall★ – Jean-Henri Riesener, the premier cabinet maker during the reign of Louis XVI, designed the opulent drop-front secretary and chest of drawers seen here for Queen Marie Antoinette, possibly for her apartment in the Tuileries. Also note the two small canvases by the 17C Dutch master Vermeer; *Officer and Laughing Girl* (c.1655–60) is particularly remarkable for its radiant luminosity.

Living Hall★★ – Rich walnut paneling and elaborate plaster moldings complement the 16C masterpieces found here. Henry Clay Frick counted two of these among his three favorites: Giovanni Bellini's *St. Francis in the Desert* (c.1480), showing the saint awestruck amid a mysteriously lit, finely rendered landscape, and Hans Holbein the Younger's searing portrait of the great humanist scholar Sir Thomas More, beheaded for treason in 1535.

Library – Dominated by a portrait of Henry Clay Frick over the mantel, this wood-paneled room houses an array of books, as well as English paintings from the 18C and 19C. Tucked in a corner is one of Gilbert Stuart's many portraits of George Washington, likely purchased for patriotic rather than artistic reasons.

North Hall★★ – Above the superb blue marble side table by Belanger, one of the costliest works produced under Louis XVI, hangs Ingres' renowned portrait of the *Comtesse d'Haussonville* (1845), granddaughter of the great Madame de Stael. Pictured here in her twenties, the countess is already a mother of three yet still full of smoldering sensuality and ambition. Ingres worked on the portrait for three years, after seven false starts and countless preparatory sketches. Small works by Degas and Monet hang nearby.

Enamel Room★ – Several Italian Primitive and Renaissance works form an appropriate backdrop to the splendid collection of Limoges painted enamels of the 16C and 17C. The most striking painting is *St. John the Evangelist* by Piero della Francesca, the saint's jewel-encrusted robe contrasting sharply with his ashen face and bare feet.

West Gallery★★★ – The largest gallery in the house, a vast skylit hall, contains an astonishing mix of monumental landscapes and portraits from the 16C to the 19C. Rembrandt was only 52 when he painted this heart-stopping *Self-Portrait* (1658), yet he appears far older, even ageless, with his huge hands, godlike robes and unfathomable eyes. Vermeer's luminous *Mistress and Maid* (c.1665–70) shows a domestic moment full of mysterious import, highlighted by the artist's signature golden light. The painting was Frick's last purchase.

Oval Room – Renoir's delightful *Mother and Children*, displayed at the Second Impressionist Exhibition of 1876, hangs before a well-placed bench. Take a seat and enjoy it; the audio commentary on this one is particularly witty.

East Gallery – Works in this gallery rotate more frequently than do other works in the museum. It is fairly certain, however, that the four sumptuous full-length portraits by Whistler on either end of the hall will remain on long-term display.

Garden Court – One of the most delightful parts of the museum, the court provides a cool haven in summertime thanks to its marble floor, fountain and pool, tropical plants and flowers. Originally used as a carriage court, the space was redesigned by John Russell Pope during the 1935 renovation.

West Gallery

Metropolitan Museum of Art★★★

Fifth Ave. between E. 80th & E. 84th Sts.

Richly endowed and supported, the Metropolitan Museum of Art (informally called the Met) is the largest museum in the Western Hemisphere and the pride of New York. It houses a veritable encyclopedia of the visual arts, with works on display from prehistory to the present, and draws more than five million visitors a year.

A BIT OF HISTORY

In 1866 **John Jay**, grandson of America's first chief justice of the Supreme Court, conceived the idea for a grand, European-style art museum in New York. Firebrand newspaper editor William Cullen Bryant took up the charge and enticed the culturally sophisticated Union League Club to head up just such an institution.

The Met first opened in 1870 in the former Dodsworth's Dancing Academy at Fifth Avenue and 53rd Street. But already plans were in motion to build a permanent facility. Fortunately, Frederick Law Olmsted and Calvert Vaux had left room for a museum on the east side of Central Park, at 81st Street. Vaux and architect Jacob Wrey Mould designed for the site a Gothic-style, red-brick edifice that has long since been engulfed by major additions and expansions.

The Building – The Met's signature Beaux-Arts facade, designed by Richard Morris Hunt, was completed in 1902, while the north and south side wings, designed by McKim, Mead and White, were completed in 1911 and 1913 respectively. The architectural firm Roche, Dinkeloo & Assocs. designed many of the more recent additions, most notably the 1975 Robert Lehman Wing and the 1978 Sackler Wing, with its dramatic Temple of Dendur. The Petrie European Sculpture Court, a skylit, sun-drenched area dotted with benches, greenery and statuary, was inaugu-

MTA **Subway:** 4, 5, 6 train to 86th St.

▷ **Location:** The main entrance to the Met is on Fifth Avenue at East 82nd Street. You enter the Great Hall. In the center is an Information Desk stocked with literature, including a detailed floor plan and a schedule for the day's tours and events; volunteers are on hand to answer questions. There are admission booths and checkrooms on either side of the hall.

🕐 **Timing:** Allow at least 4hrs, more if you're a real art lover. To avoid the biggest crowds, visit on a weekday and arrive early. Audio Guides (◉$7) are highly recommended, with valuable commentary on hundreds of works, including special exhibitions. The Audio Guide desk is at the rear of the hall, to the left of the Grand Staircase.

👥 **Kids:** The Family Audio Guide, included in the regular Audio Guide, is a series of commentaries on artworks throughout the museum especially geared for children ages 6–12. Ask for a map of these selections at the Audio Guide desk. Programs for younger children—such as sketching and storytelling—are offered daily in the Uris Center.

😊 **Don't Miss:** The Temple of Dendur in the Egyptian Wing, the newly expanded Greek and Roman galleries, and the phenomenal trove of Dutch Masters in the European Paintings galleries, and the view from the Roof Garden.

rated in 1990. A three-part renovation and expansion of the Greek and Roman Art galleries was completed in April 2007, with the opening of a 40,000sq-ft Roman sculpture court and mezzanine gallery for Etruscan art. In all, the Met boasts about two million feet of exhibition space, with more being added all the time as the museum constantly reorganizes and expands to accommodate its growing collection.

The Collection – The seed of the Met's immense collection was planted in 1877 with Catherine L. Wolfe's donation of 143 paintings representing the Dutch and Flemish schools. Ten years later, railroad financier Henry Gurdon Marquand gave 37 European paintings to the museum, including Vermeer's masterpiece *Young Woman with a Water Pitcher*. Louisine Havemeyer's collection of French Impressionists was added in 1929 and Muriel Kallis Steinberg Newman's definitive collection of American Abstract Expressionist canvases arrived in 2005.

Thanks to such generous gifts, as well as a large endowment that allows the museum to purchase some of the most prized artworks in the world, the Met has built a cache of nearly three million objects, a fourth of which are on display at any given time. In addition, the Met regularly organizes blockbuster temporary shows exploring a single great artist's oeuvre. Among those who've recently received such royal treatment are Walker Evans, Jasper Johns, van Gogh and Pierre Bonnard.

VISIT

🚹♿🕐*Open year-round Tue–Thu & Sun 9.30–5.30pm, Fri–Sat 9.30am–9pm. Open holiday Mondays, Memorial Day & Labor Day.* 🕐*Closed Jan 1, Thanksgiving Day & Dec 25.* 🗣*Guided tours (1hr) available in 10 languages.* 💲 *$20 suggested donation $20 (includes same-day admission to The Cloisters).* ✖🅿. 📞*212-535-7710. www.metmuseum.org.*

The Metropolitan Museum of Art

The Metropolitan Museum of Art

EGYPTIAN ART★★★

First floor.

The Met's 36,000-piece Egyptian art collection is one of the finest and most comprehensive outside of Egypt, a true treasure trove of priceless art and artifacts. More than half of the holdings were provided by the museum's own archaeologists, who spent 30 years in Egypt at the beginning of the 20C excavating some of the richest sites. Today almost all of the Met's exquisitely painted coffins, figurines, jewelry, stelae and tombs are on view.

Some 69,000sq ft of gallery space is arranged chronologically from the Predynastic period (c.5000–3000 BC) through 30 dynasties (c.3100–342 BC) and the eras of foreign influence to late antiquity (c.AD 700). A walk through the galleries therefore provides an illustrated history of the ancient Egyptians. At the same time, the works stand on their own as magnificent examples of art and design. Begin your expedition in gallery 1, an orientation space that presents background information, a timeline and a wall map, along with Predynastic artifacts and sculpture, then proceed through the exhibition.

Temple of Dendur

©Brooks Walker/Metropolitan Museum of Art

Highlights

Mastaba of Perneb – Old Kingdom. While the pyramid is the best-known form of Egyptian tomb architecture, mastabas (offering chapels) like this one, which was the final resting place for a dignitary c.2381–2323 BC, were popular among the elite. Go inside to see the elaborate hieroglyphs.

Meketre Models – Dynasty 12. This cache of models from the tomb of Meketre at Thebes, one of the richest and most complete sets ever discovered, conveys in miniature a sense of the active bustle of daily life in ancient Egypt.

Jewelry – Dynasty 12. The royal jewels of Princess Sithathoryunet are considered among the finest examples of ancient Egyptian jewelry. The stunning pectoral, a gift from her father, and the gold cowrie-shell girdle are technical and aesthetic marvels.

Statues of Hatshepsut – Dynasty 18. One of the few queens to ascend the throne, Hatshepsut was depicted by sculptors in the full regalia of her office—including, occasionally, a beard—yet still retained her feminine qualities. She built her monumental funerary temple complex at Deir al Bahri, a true ancient wonder completed around 1500 BC.

Sarcophagus of Harkhebi – Dynasty 26. This chubby basalt sarcophagus is one of the most pristine in the museum's collection, the serene facial expression and hieroglyphs seemingly untouched

by time. It was found at the bottom of a 50ft-deep pit inside a limestone box.

Temple of Dendur★ – Early Roman period (c.23–10 BC). This three-room monument to the goddess Isis was among monuments rescued from submersion prior to the completion of the Aswan High Dam. A gift from Egypt, it came, piece by piece, to the US in 1967 and was assembled here in 1978.

Fayum Portraits – Roman period (c. AD 160). Made of pigment mixed with hot wax (known as encaustic), these lifelike portraits were crafted as mummy masks by Greeks living in Fayum. They represent the first introduction of European-style painting techniques into Egypt.

EUROPEAN PAINTINGS★★★

Second floor.

Arranged by national schools, these galleries showcase work by the European Old Masters. Religion, history, portraiture, mythology, still life and landscape fill these canvases, which together demonstrate the evolution of media and style from the early Renaissance to the Age of Reason.

The Italian Schools – As the Middle Ages waned after 1300, Europeans began to broaden their horizons beyond the Church, and the arts and sciences flourished. By the 15C, Florence teemed with artists cultivating new approaches to light, form and subject, and in 1504 three of the greatest and most fertile

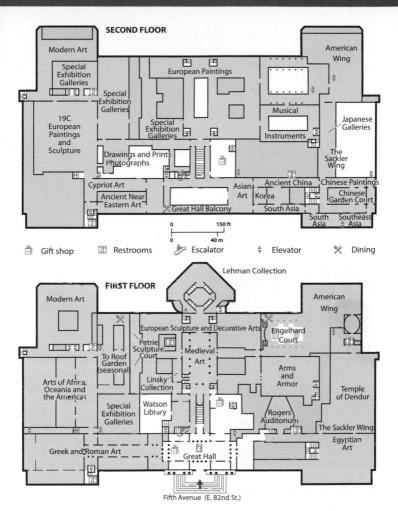

SECOND FLOOR

Modern Art

Special Exhibition Galleries

Special Exhibition Galleries

19C European Paintings and Sculpture

European Paintings

American Wing

Musical Instruments

Japanese Galleries

The Sackler Wing

Special Exhibition Galleries

Special Exhibition Galleries

Drawings and Prints Photographs

Cypriot Art

Ancient Near Eastern Art

Great Hall Balcony

Asian Art

Korea

Ancient China

South Asia

Chinese Paintings

Chinese Garden Court

South Asia

Southeast Asia

0 ____ 150 ft
0 ____ 40 m

🎁 Gift shop   🚻 Restrooms   🛝 Escalator   ↕ Elevator   ✕ Dining

Lehman Collection

FIRST FLOOR

Modern Art

European Sculpture and Decorative Arts

Petrie Sculpture Court

To Roof Garden (seasonal)

Linsky Collection

Medieval Art

Engelhard Court

Arms and Armor

American Wing

Temple of Dendur

Arts of Africa, Oceania and the Americas

Special Exhibition Galleries

Watson Library

Rogers Auditorium

The Sackler Wing

Egyptian Art

Greek and Roman Art

Great Hall

Fifth Avenue (E. 82nd St.)

Renaissance minds worked in that city: Leonardo da Vinci, Michelangelo and Raphael. Other cities around Italy hatched regional styles, borne along by the creative tide of the Renaissance, but by the high Renaissance in the 16C, Venice came to dominate. There, Titian, Tintoretto and Veronese composed huge, active canvases characterized by vivid colors, large foreground figures and realistic landscape backgrounds. Their work anticipated the Baroque sense of the picture as a whole, of surface versus line, of a continuous rhythm rather than objects set against a backdrop, as would later be seen in 18C Venetian master Giovanni Battista Tiepolo's luminous canvases.

Northern Europe – North of Italy, other artistic sensibilities stirred. The Catholic Church persisted in its influence over painters of the early Netherlandish school, and their work reflects that curious Gothic mixture of the devout and the macabre. A century later Peter Paul Rubens broke the Church's spell over artistic content and expression. In Holland, 17C painters celebrated their recent independence from Spain with landscapes, portraits and scenes of everyday life. Dark and quiet, Dutch (indeed European) painting reached its apex at the hand of Rembrandt van Rijn and Johannes Vermeer.

EUROPEAN PAINTINGS HIGHLIGHTS (ITALIAN SCHOOLS):

Giotto	*The Epiphany*, c.1320
Fra Filippo Lippi	*Man and Woman at a Casement*, c.1435
Sandro Botticelli	*The Last Communion of St. Jerome*, c.1491
Raphael	*The Agony in the Garden*, c.1505
Titian	*Venus and Adonis*, c.1565
Tiepolo	*A Dance in the Country*, c.1756

EUROPEAN PAINTINGS HIGHLIGHTS (NORTHERN EUROPE):

Jan van Eyck	*The Crucifixion and The Last Judgment*, c.1425
Pieter Brueghel	*The Harvesters*, 1565
Peter Paul Rubens	*Venus and Adonis*, c.1635
Rembrandt van Rijn	*Aristotle with a Bust of Homer*, 1653
Johannes Vermeer	*Young Woman with a Water Pitcher*, c.1662

The Metropolitan Museum of Art, Henry G. Marquand Collection

Young Woman with a Water Pitcher
(c.1662) by Johannes Vermeer

EUROPEAN SCULPTURE AND DECORATIVE ARTS★★★

First floor.

This is one of the museum's largest and broadest departments, its 50,000-piece collection spanning more than 500 years, from the Renaissance to the early 20C. The term "decorative arts" encompasses furniture, woodwork, ceramics, glass, metalwork, jewelry and textiles. These are presented alongside traditional sculpture in galleries and in meticulously re-created **period rooms**★. Italian Renaissance sculpture, French and English furniture, and French and German porcelain are the department's strong suits.

Gubbio Studiolo – The art of intarsia is on glorious display in this studiolo (small room), which was built in the 1470s as a personal retreat for the Italian duke Federico da Montefeltro. Thousands of pieces of walnut, beech, rosewood and oak are arranged mosaic-like on the walls to create startlingly realistic images of objects related to the duke's interests, including music and books.

Jack and Belle Linsky Collection – Opened in 1984, these galleries present the private art and artifacts compiled by the Linskys over a period of 40 years. Approximately 375 works of art—paintings by early European masters, Renaissance and Baroque bronzes, European porcelains, 18C French furniture, and jewelry—are displayed in seven rooms designed to create the intimate setting of a private residence.

Petrie European Sculpture Court – One of the museum's beautiful converted courtyards, this airy space displays monumental Italian and French sculpture, including Auguste Rodin's *Burghers of Calais*. Adjacent galleries in the Kravis Wing pick up the threads of European decorative arts with 19C and early 20C objects and furniture.

GREEK AND ROMAN ART★★★

First floor.

April 2007 marked the triumphant completion of a 15-year, $225 million plan to redesign and enlarge the museum's galleries for ancient Greek and Roman art, one of the finest collections of its kind in the world. Prior to the redesign, a mere 2,000 of the Met's 17,000 artifacts were on display; today more than 5,300 objects are on view without crowding.

Greek Art – The grand, barrel-vaulted Jaharis Gallery, just south of the Great Hall, was inaugurated in 2005. The gallery's soaring height, skylights and new limestone walls are a fitting backdrop for large-scale sculpture from ancient Greece, including oversize statues of a wounded Amazon and the Greek hero Protesilaos. Flanking this space are six smaller galleries presenting Greek works in roughly chronological progression from 6C–4C BC.

Roman Art – At the far end of the Jaharis Gallery, past the gargantuan capital and base of an Ionic column from the Temple of Artemis at Sardis, lies the beautiful Leon Levy and Shelby White Court for Roman and Etruscan Art, opened in 2007. The centerpiece of the sun-bathed atrium is a serene fountain surrounded by 20 Roman sculptures, almost all of which are copies of Greek originals, attesting to the Romans' intense admiration for Greek art. Two larger-than-life-size statues of Hercules—one young, one old, both from the 1C AD—face off from either side of the court. Etruscan art is shown on the mezzanine around the rim of the court. The highlight here is a spectacular bronze processional chariot dating from the mid-6C BC, with relief panels depicting the life of Achilles.

Cypriot Art – On the second floor above the Jaharis Gallery, four new art galleries presenting work from Cyprus were unveiled in 2000.

19C EUROPEAN PAINTINGS AND SCULPTURE★★★

Second floor.

Recently reconfigured and expanded by 8,000sq ft, these galleries are among the most important in the museum, holding within them one of the world's greatest collections of European art from the 19C and early 20C.

Here you'll find the museum's extensive collection of Romantic, Barbizon, Impressionist and post-Impressionist paintings and 19C European sculpture. Completed in 2007, the new arrangement includes work of the early modern era, with artists such as Bonnard, Modigliani, Matisse and Picasso shown in relation to their forebears.

Romanticism – Out of the humanitarian ideals of the Enlightenment grew two major schools of artistic thought: Neoclassicism and Romanticism. The Neoclassicists, preeminently Jacques-Louis David, turned to ancient Greece and Rome for new inspiration. Rejecting such precision, the painters of the Romantic movement reveled in a freer attitude toward brush stroke and color, relying on historic events and settings for their exoticism, drama and allegory. In a portent of Impressionism, Eugène Delacroix, master Romantic, declared, "I do not paint a sword but its sparkle."

Barbizon – The Barbizon school (c.1830–70)—named after the village of Barbizon near Fontainebleau Forest, France, where the artists gathered—was formed in reaction to Romanticism. For these painters—the most famous of whom were Jean-Baptiste Camille Corot, Théodore Rousseau and Jean-François

---

Taking a Break

Many galleries throughout the museum are furnished with benches, ideal for contemplating a particular painting or sculpture. But for more extended relaxation periods, or to stop for a chat, consider these pleasant spots. On the first floor, the Temple of Dendur and the Charles Engelhard Court are both glass-enclosed atriums with casual seating. There's also a secluded patio on the ground floor of the Lehman Pavilion. On the second floor, the Astor Court in the Chinese galleries makes a peaceful stop. Also keep in mind that you can leave the museum, take a stroll in Central Park and come back as long as you keep your admission tag.

19C EUROPEAN PAINTINGS AND SCULPTURE HIGHLIGHTS:

Eugène Delacroix—*The Abduction of Rebecca*, 1846
Jean-François Millet—*Calling the Cows Home*, c. 1872

Millet—nature was painted not merely as a backdrop for dramatic events but as a subject in and of itself.

Impressionism – The Impressionists took this idea further, painting nature and figures alike rapidly, with quick brush strokes, to give a spontaneous "impression" of a scene. So radical did these works seem in subject, palette and technique that they were refused admission to the annual exhibitions of the conservative Paris Salon. Undaunted, the Impressionists mounted eight of their own exhibitions between 1874 and 1886, eventually gaining critical acclaim.

Post-Impressionism – Because of its very nature and the diversity of its practitioners, the Impressionist phenomenon, though short-lived, opened the floodgates of artistic interpretation. Arising both out of and in opposition to its precepts, post-Impressionism pushed the formal aspects of painting in new emotional, compositional, coloristic, symbolic and scientific directions.

AMERICAN WING★★★

First and second floors and mezzanine.
Spanning three centuries, the collection of American paintings, sculpture and decorative arts can be found in the northwest corner of the museum.

Thanks to a major and much-needed renovation and expansion of these rooms, this is likely to be one of the museum's most exciting departments in coming years.

Decorative Arts – The Classical Galleries (first floor) display decorative arts created between 1810 and 1845. Americans enthusiastically embraced the ancient world in this period, patterning everything from vases to sofas after Greek, Roman and Egyptian models. Gothic and Renaissance elements began creeping in shortly thereafter. An American idiom reasserted itself in the late 19C with the onset of the Arts and Crafts Movement. A handsome oak-paneled stairwell by McKim, Mead and White (1884) has been installed near the entrance to the DeeDee Wigmore Galleries, where you'll find furniture by the Herter Brothers and Stickley, in addition to several gorgeous stained-glass windows by Louis Comfort Tiffany. Late Colonial-era decorative arts, including a fine selection of tall clocks, can be found on the second floor near the Colonial-era paintings.

Painting – The museum's impressive holdings of American paintings from the 18C to the early 20C reside en masse in spacious, light-filled galleries on the mezzanine and second floors. Usually less crowded than the more centrally located European painting galleries, these are some of the most pleasant galleries in the museum, with particularly large troves of work by John Singer

Madame X (Madame Pierre Gautreau) (1883–84) by John Singer Sargent

©The Metropolitan Museum of Art

Sargent, James McNeill Whistler, Thomas Eakins and Mary Cassatt on the mezzanine and John Singleton Copley, Charles Willson Peale and John Trumbull on the second floor.

Charles Engelhard Court – Monumental sculpture, stained glass and architectural elements occupy this glass-enclosed courtyard. On the lower level you'll find the facade of the United States Bank (1824, Martin E. Thompson), once on Wall Street, and on the main level the loggia designed by Louis Comfort Tiffany for his Long Island home.

ANCIENT NEAR EASTERN ART★★
Second floor.

The collections of this department number some 7,000 pieces covering a vast region of southwestern Asia, one that today reaches from Turkey to Afghanistan and the Indus Valley, and from the Caucasus Mountains in the north to the Arabian Peninsula. The sculpture, pottery and metalwork you see here date from 8000 BC to AD 651.

The profusion of cultures that inhabited this region produced finely wrought artifacts of great beauty and sophistication. One silver piece of particular note is the silver figurine of a kneeling bull holding a vase between his hooves, a Proto-Elamite work dating from around 2900 BC. A gold Iranian cup with four bas-relief gazelles from around 1000 BC is similarly striking.

The **Sackler Gallery★**, just east of the Great Hall Balcony, has been reconstructed to mimic the proportions of an audience hall of the palace built by Assyrian king Ashurnasirpal II at Nimrud (in what is now Iraq), in the 9C BC. Two human-headed winged lions, carved meticulously from limestone, guard the doorway, and extraordinary monumental reliefs and statuary from the palace line the gallery walls.

ARMS AND ARMOR★
First floor.

This encyclopedic collection comprises more than 15,000 arms, designed mainly for display rather than for actual military

AMERICAN WING HIGHLIGHTS:

John Singleton Copley—
Daniel Crommelin Verplanck, 1771

Gilbert Stuart—
George Washington, 1795

Emanuel Gottlieb Leutze—*Washington Crossing the Delaware,* 1851

Frederic Edwin Church—
The Heart of the Andes, 1859

Thomas Eakins—
Max Schmitt in a Single Scull, 1871

James McNeill Whistler—
Portrait of Theodore Duret, 1883

John Singer Sargent—
Madame X, 1883–84

Mary Cassatt—
Lady at the Tea Table, 1885

use. Flanking a vast **equestrian court★** containing parade armor from the 16C, four small western galleries present European arms—including rare pieces commissioned by various kings and rulers—while three eastern galleries focus on articles from China, Japan, India, Turkey and Iran.

Most of the works here are incredibly ornate. Sword hilts are embellished with tortoiseshell, cup hilts are encrusted with jewels and even the guns are made of gold. Late-15C helmets from Iran adopt the shape of a turban, and various sabers and their scabbards are intricately decorated with inlaid emeralds, diamonds and other precious stones.

A small gallery on the north side displays firearms from Europe and the United States, including an 1862 Colt police revolver, one of the most popular firearms during the Civil War.

ARTS OF AFRICA, OCEANIA AND THE AMERICAS★★
First floor.

Artworks from sub-Saharan Africa, the Pacific Islands, and North, Central and South America are located in the museum's south wing, which was named in honor of Nelson Rockefeller's son, Michael, who disappeared while on an expedition to the island of New Guinea in 1961. The core of the collection encompasses approximately 3,500 works donated to the museum by Nelson Rockefeller in the late 1970s. The department now owns about 11,000 objects spanning a period of 4,000 years.

Africa – Sculpture, primarily ritualistic masks and figures carved in wood, dominates the art of Africa. A collection of monumental sculpture by the Dogon of Mali fills one of the galleries. A terracotta seated figure recalls the work of Henri Matisse. Ferocious-looking Senufo helmet masks incorporate the jaws and teeth of a crocodile, the horns of an antelope and the tusks of a warthog. Note the richly detailed brass relief plaque from Nigeria (16C–17C), depicting a warrior chief, warriors and attendants in full battle regalia.

Oceania – Following an extensive three-year renovation and redesign, the galleries for Oceanic art—the collective term for the more than 25,000 islands of the Pacific—reopened in November 2007. The centerpiece of the new configuration is the spacious, sunlit gallery for Melanesian art. Highlights among the 300 works on view are a remarkable group of nine delicately carved poles, ranging up to 20ft in height, used by the Asmat people of New Guinea in ceremonies to cast death away from a community, along with the 48ft-long

Asmat canoe, which could hold 20 people. Also on display is a soaring, boldly colored ceiling from a ceremonial house of the Kwoma people of New Guinea, commissioned in the early 1970s.

Americas – A new gallery devoted to the art of the Native North American peoples was inaugurated in November 2007, with works arranged by region. The peoples of the Plains and the Northwest Coast Indians are particularly well represented, the former by clothing and a fascinating illustrated book known as the Maffet Ledger, the latter by colorful masks and rattles. Among the items you may see from South America are a pair of Mochica shell-and-stone-mosaic ear spools (3C–6C AD); a pendant (Colombia, 13C–16C AD) in the form of a figure wearing an elaborate headdress; and a boldly painted Sicán funerary mask (Peru, 11C–9C BC). As for the arts of Mesoamerica, note especially the Mayan seated figure (6C AD), one of the few extant three-dimensional Mayan pieces in wood.

ASIAN ART★★

Second floor.

The Met's Asian art collection—the largest of its kind in the West, with some 60,000 pieces—traces the development of Chinese, Japanese, Korean, Southeast Asian and South Asian art from the second millennium BC to the present. Ceramics, metalwork, paintings, sculptures, bronzes, jades and textiles are on display in expansive, well-appointed galleries.

China – Spanning the period from the Neolithic (early 2000 BC) through the Tang dynasty (10C AD), these galleries include jades, ceramics, bronze ritual vessels and tomb art. Just off the Great Hall Balcony, the Chinese Sculpture Court is dominated by a monumental standing boddhisattva (awakened one) (5C AD). In the center of the painting galleries is the tranquil glass-covered **Astor Court**★, a reproduction of a Ming dynasty courtyard and scholar's study in Soochow, China, containing traditional Chinese plantings, a moon-viewing terrace, and formal rock garden. The study, built with traditional mortise-and-tenon

Seated Couple (16C–19C) from Mali, Dogon peoples

©The Metropolitan Museum of Art

joining techniques, contains handsome furniture of the era.

On the third floor, several quiet rooms contain elegant Chinese decorative arts: textiles, ivory work, bamboo and box-wood items, red lacquerwork and jades.

Korea – The gallery surveying Korean art holds a collection that includes earthenware and Bronze Age pieces, scroll paintings and ceramics. Note the series of lacquered wood boxes with intricate inlay.

South and Southeast Asian Art – These 18 stunning galleries display some 1,300 works from Nepal to Burma. In the South Asian galleries, look for the ornate teak-wood dome of a late-16C Jain meeting hall, carved with figures of the eight cosmic rulers and their animal and human attendants. Among the rooms devoted to Southeast Asia (Cambodia, Thailand, Vietnam and Indonesia), a skylit gallery of monumental Khmer sculptures from the Angkor period (8C–14C AD) stands out.

Japan – The second-floor Sackler Wing galleries hold changing exhibits of Japanese paintings, sculpture, lacquer, wood-block prints, scrolls, screens and kimonos. Also on view are a shoin-style reception room modeled on a room in the Onoji temple (17C) outside Kyoto, and *Water Stone*, a sculpture by Isamu Noguchi (see the Noguchi Museum in Queens).

LEHMAN COLLECTION★★
Lehman Pavilion.

Considered one of the finest private art collections in the US, the Robert Lehman Collection was compiled by financier Philip Lehman and his son, Robert. Rather than being integrated into the museum's other departments, these works—predominantly European painting, sculpture and decorative arts from the 14C to the early 20C—are housed in a tinted-glass pavilion added to the west side of the museum in 1975. Some 3,000 works of art are displayed in 11 first-floor galleries, 7 of which are appointed to resemble rooms in Robert Lehman's residence on West 54th Street, and in additional ground-floor galleries. Strengths of the collection include Italian paint-

LEHMAN HIGHLIGHTS:

Petrus Christus—*Goldsmith in His Shop, possibly St. Eligius*, 1449

Sandro Botticelli— *The Annunciation*, c.1485

El Greco— *St. Jerome as a Scholar*, c.1614

Rembrandt—*The Last Supper, After Leonardo da Vinci*, 1635

J.A.D. Ingres—*Portrait of the Princesse de Broglie*, 1853

Pierre-Auguste Renoir—*Two Young Girls at the Piano*, 1892

Balthus—*Nude Before a Mirror*, 1955

ings of the 14C and 15C, masterworks of the 18C–19C Dutch and Spanish schools, and French Impressionist paintings of the 19C and 20C.

MEDIEVAL ART★★
First floor.

Tracing the development of art from the fall of Rome (4C) to the Renaissance (16C), the museum's extensive collection of medieval art comprises more than 6,000 works from the early Christian, Byzantine, Migration, Romanesque and Gothic periods. Among the treasures not to be missed are some exquisite pieces of Byzantine silver, Romanesque and Gothic metalwork, and Gothic stained glass and tapestries. Additional medieval art objects are exhibited at The Cloisters.

Byzantine Art – Secular and liturgical artworks from Constantinople, spanning the Byzantine Empire's 1000-plus-year reign, line the corridors flanking the main staircase and reclaimed space underneath and behind the stairs. The north corridor, to the right of the staircase, holds early secular art of the Byzantine Empire and works by the Franks, the Goths and other peoples at the fringes of the empire. The south corridor, dedicated to liturgical art of the Byzantine Church and middle- and late-Byzantine secular art, features among its devotional objects the Antioch Chalice, said to have been used by Christ in the Last Supper. Underneath the stairs, a crypt-like gallery features Byzantine Egyptian art under a series of low brick arches.

Medieval Tapestry Hall – Hung along the walls of this small hall is an ensemble of tapestries, dating from the 14C to the early 16C, woven principally in the workshops of Flanders (Arras, Brussels and Tournai). Dating from the late-Gothic period, large panels of stained glass from Cologne, Germany and England fill two walls of the gallery.

Medieval Sculpture Hall – This large hall was built to evoke the ambience of a church, with a nave separated from the side aisles by massive columns. Stretching between two columns, a splendid wrought-iron Baroque **choir screen**★ rises almost the full height of the hall. Begun in 1668 for the Cathedral of Valladolid, in Spain, it was completed in 1764.

Medieval Treasury – In addition to portable shrines, reliquary caskets and sacramental objects, the Treasury also contains two fine sculptural groups (early 16C) of the Entombment and Pietà, from the Périgord region of France.

MODERN ART★★

First and second floors, mezzanine and roof garden.

Paintings, sculptures, works on paper and decorative arts from 1900 to the present are on view in the Lila Acheson Wallace Wing, situated in the southwest corner of the building. Located on top of the wing, the **roof garden**★ offers a superb setting for contemporary sculpture while affording splendid **views** of Manhattan's Midtown and Uptown skylines; it also holds a cafe. The museum's collection of modern art is particularly strong in paintings of the School of Paris and in postwar art by such luminaries as Anselm Kiefer and Jasper Johns, but as space is limited, only a limited selection of works are on view. The 2005 receipt of the Muriel Kallis Steinberg Newman Collection of American Abstract Expressionist paintings—one of the most important gifts the museum has ever received—will likely prompt a reworking and expansion of the galleries here. For now, be sure to see the large-scale

contemporary works on the mezzanine, including two of Chuck Close's *Lucas*, Lucian Freud's *Naked Man, Back View* and Andy Warhol's silkscreen *Mao*.

COSTUME INSTITUTE★

Ground floor.

Established in 1937, the Costume Institute collects and preserves clothing from the 16C to the present. Today, the 31,000-article collection of regional garb includes apparel from five continents, ranging from the elegant wardrobes of ancient royalty to chic fashions by the most distinguished contemporary American and European couturiers. Owing to the fragility of the garments, the department has no permanent exhibit, but mounts two major exhibitions a year drawing items from the collection to explore topics related to fashion, history and society; a recent show featured a retrospective of the House of Chanel. There's also an intriguing Audio Guide tour, Costume: The Art of Dress, narrated by actress Sarah Jessica Parker, highlighting historic fashion in paintings and sculptures throughout the museum's galleries. The annual Costume Institute Gala *(in spring)* gives Hollywood starlets and fashion editors the opportunity to trot out the latest looks.

DRAWINGS, PRINTS AND PHOTOGRAPHS★

Second floor.

The museum has a formidable collection of drawings, prints and photographs. Drawings and prints are displayed in the Robert Wood Johnson Jr. Gallery, a long, thin hall extending from the top of the Great Staircase south toward the 19C European Paintings and Sculpture galleries, and photography can be found in the galleries that flank it.

Drawings – Some of the finest drawings in the museum's collection were gifts from railroad titan Cornelius Vanderbilt, who gave the Met 670 drawings by or attributed to European Old Masters. In 1935 the museum purchased an album of 50 sheets by Francisco Goya. Today the Met owns 11,000 drawings—some complete works, others studies for paint-

Eating and Drinking at the Met

There are several food and drink options at the Met. The most casual and the least expensive is the **cafeteria** *(ground floor, below Medieval Hall;* 🕐*open Tue–Thu 11.30am–4.30pm, Fri 11.30am–7pm, Sat 11am–7pm, Sun 11am–4.30pm)*. Here you'll find sandwiches, salads, hot entrées and desserts, with booster seats and a children's menu for kids.

A more formal option is the **Petrie Court Café** *(first floor, in European Sculpture and Decorative Arts;* 🕐*open Tue–Thu & Sun 9.30am–4.30pm, Fri–Sat 9.30am–10.30pm;* ☎*212-570-3964)*, at the back of the Petrie sculpture court overlooking Central Park; it has a full bar and a more extensive menu, including a popular daily afternoon tea and Sunday brunch. It becomes a swank wine bar on Friday and Saturday evenings. The **Roof Garden Café** *(access via first-floor elevator;* 🕐*open May–Oct, weather permitting, Tue–Thu & Sun 10am–4.30pm, Fri–Sat 10am–8pm)* serves up dazzling views of Central Park along with light fare such as packaged sandwiches, chips, cookies and fruit. Beverages include espresso, soft drinks, beer, wine and sangria, plus martinis on Friday and Saturday nights. You can get salads, sandwiches and desserts at the **Balcony Café**, overlooking the Great Hall *(*🕐*open Tue–Sun 11am–4.30pm)*; on weekend nights the space transforms into the **Balcony Bar** *(*🕐*open Fri–Sat 4–8.30pm)*, where cocktails are accompanied by live classical music.

ings—by such greats as Michelangelo, Leonardo da Vinci and Rembrandt.

Prints – The Met's impressive cache of 1.5 million prints includes woodcuts, lithographs and other works made from engravings by some of Europe's most gifted artists: Rembrandt, Albrecht Dürer, Hogarth, Fragonard and Toulouse-Lautrec among them.

Photographs – Opened in 2007, the sleek, high-ceilinged Joyce and Robert Menschel Hall for Modern Photography displays large-scale photographs made since 1960 to great effect; selections here change every six months. Photographs from earlier periods are shown across the hall in the Howard Gilman Galleries. In all, the museum owns about 20,000 photographic images, including large holdings of work by Alfred Stieglitz and Walker Evans.

ISLAMIC ART★
Second floor.

The Met's cache of Islamic art is one of the most comprehensive in the Western world. The department traces the development of Islamic art, beginning with the founding of Islam in the 7C and ending in the early 19C. Encompassing works from various geographical regions, including Mesopotamia, Persia, Morocco, Egypt, Syria and India, the collection is particularly well known for its glass- and metalwork, ceramics, miniatures and classical carpets. As part of ongoing renovations to the museum, in 2011 the rebranded **Galleries for the Art of the Arab Lands, Turkey, Iran, Central Asia, and Later South Asia** were reopened following an eight-year project to reorganize and enlarge the collection.

MUSICAL INSTRUMENTS★
Second floor.

This rare, original collection is more than 5,000 strong *(*🎧*the Audio Guide contains samples of music these instruments make).* The western galleries focus on European instruments, including the oldest extant piano (1720), three Stradivarius violins, two classical guitars of Andrés Segovia and keyboard instruments. The eastern galleries highlight instruments from the Near and Far East, the Americas and Africa, including seldom-seen pieces such as an Indonesian sesando, a type of zither made from palm leaves, and an Indian mayuri, or bowed sitar. Most of the instruments are in working order and are used for occasional concerts.

Museum of Modern Art★★★

11 W. 53rd St. between Fifth & Sixth Aves.

One of the world's preeminent cultural institutions, the Museum of Modern Art (MoMA) offers an unparalleled overview of the modern visual arts. The rich collection includes not only painting, drawing and sculpture but also photography, decorative arts, architectural plans and models, video and the US' most comprehensive film archive.

A BIT OF HISTORY

The founding of the museum dates back to 1929, when three wealthy and culturally sophisticated women—**Abby Aldrich Rockefeller**, **Lillie P. Bliss** and **Mary Quinn Sullivan**—led a campaign to promote the modern arts in the US. The first show, of the then little-known post-Impressionists, opened in temporary quarters that fall. Over the next decade, founding director **Alfred H. Barr Jr.** shaped the museum's philosophy, notably expanding the idea of what constitutes art. Among Barr's pioneering exhibits were shows of photography, design and architecture, none of which were acknowledged as legitimate art forms at the time. Today MoMA's holdings in all three disciplines—in addition to modern and contemporary painting and sculpture—are world-class.

The Museum of Modern Art's dramatic "new" building actually encompasses the work of several top-tier architects. The original 1939 marble-and-glass museum building, by **Philip Goodwin** and **Edward Durell Stone**, was one of the first examples of the International style in the US. The sculpture garden and east wing are 1964 additions by Philip Johnson. A 1979 renovation by **Cesar Pelli** more than doubled the gallery space and included the addition of the glass-faced Garden Hall and a 44-story residential tower to the west. In 2004 work was completed on the museum's

MTA Subway: E, M train to Fifth Ave.-53rd St.

Map: See Fifth Avenue.

Location: The admission desk is at the right, inside the entrance; if you have a CityPass, go to the desk on the left by the coat check. All large bags must be checked (no luggage or laptops). Free audio tours are available past the security guards on the right. Free gallery talks convene in the second-floor atrium at 11.30am and 1.30pm daily; arrive 10min early to ensure a spot.

Timing: Plan your visit for a weekday and arrive before 11am; MoMA gets uncomfortably crowded on weekends and late in the afternoon. You can buy tickets online in advance. If you choose not to take a guided tour, start with the Painting and Sculpture galleries on the fourth and fifth floors, home to most of the museum's most famous works, then pick a few other exhibits according to your interests. Don't try to see everything in one day.

Kids: The audio tour includes Modern Kids, a delightful series of recorded commentaries to help children appreciate the museum.

Don't Miss: Vincent van Gogh's *The Starry Night*, Pablo Picasso's *Desmoiselles d'Avignon*, Claude Monet's *Reflections of Clouds on the Water-Lily Pond*, Salvador Dalí's *Persistence of Memory*, Jackson Pollock's *One: Number 31*.

Dining at MoMA

MoMA has three attractive dining facilities. Overseen by chef Danny Meyer, the force behind the celebrated Union Square Cafe (🛈 *see Where to Eat*), they all serve food that far surpasses the usual museum fare. The **Modern** is the fanciest of the three, presenting French-American cuisine in a sleek, Bauhaus-inspired dining room overlooking the sculpture garden *(reservations recommended; ℘212-333-1220; www.themodernnyc.com)*. Open well past museum hours due to its separate entrance on West 53rd Street, the Modern also has a more casual **Bar Room** and seasonal terrace. On the second floor of the museum, **Cafe 2** is a stylish rustic Italian diner. Patrons order from a menu posted at the entrance (panini and hand-made pastas are specialties), then take a number and a seat; the food is brought to the table. In a small space overlooking the sculpture garden, **Terrace 5** serves sumptuous gourmet desserts and "savory bites" like marinated olives, smoked salmon and artisanal cheese, along with cocktails, wine and espresso drinks. Kids can order hot chocolate, chocolate milk or a root beer float.

most ambitious expansion and renovation to date, overseen by Japanese architect **Yoshio Taniguchi**. The redesigned building has nearly twice the capacity, including an appropriately dramatic lobby, as well as vastly improved screening rooms and food services.

VISIT

🕐*Open Wed–Thu & Sat–Sun 10.30am–5.30pm, Fri 10.30am–8pm (Thu 10.30am–8.45pm Jul–Aug).* 🕐*Closed Thanksgiving Day & Dec 25.* 💬*Guided gallery talks (1hr) daily 11.30am, 1.30pm.* ☞*$20; free Fri 4–8pm).* ℘*212-708-9400. www.moma.org.* The following text is an overview of the museum's permanent collections. Some works mentioned may not be on view, as the museum constantly rotates its collection. In addition to the permanent displays there are usually two or three major temporary shows at MoMA. Check local listings or the museum's website for details.

LOBBY

The lobby is the most stunning aspect of Taniguchi's redesign. A low, long space greets you as you enter from West 53rd Street. Once you buy your ticket and check your bag, you turn right toward the entrance to the galleries and are treated to a stunning view straight back through a wall of glass into the sculpture garden. Walking toward it you have a sense of release as the ceiling soars

skyward. From the back right corner, you can look up into the stairwell and see two levels of delicate pedestrian walkways crossing between galleries, as well as the kelly-green Bell 47D1 Helicopter (1945), by artist Arthur Young, suspended above you (the best view of the helicopter is from the third floor). Arrayed around the lobby are changing exhibits of large-scale paintings and sculptures.

SCULPTURE GARDEN

The sculpture garden is one of the museum's most enchanting spaces, its sleek marble patios punctuated by two rectangular pools and warmed by beech

Entrance at 53rd Street, Museum of Modern Art

©2009 Timothy Hursley/Museum of Modern Art

trees and seasonal plantings. Plenty of chairs make it a great place to relax in warm weather. The glass-walled Modern restaurant runs along the south side, while all around rise the buildings of Midtown: the International-style skyscraper visible at the east end of the garden is Ludwig Mies van der Rohe's Seagram Building.

The sculptures in the garden rotate, though large pieces are likely to remain in place for years at a time. A recent addition is *Broken Obelisk* (1963–69), by Barnett Newman, a monumental steel pyramid on which an upside-down obelisk seems to balance on its point. You'll also find Auguste Rodin's larger-than-life *Monument to Balzac* (1898, cast 1954), showing the author wrapped dramatically in the dressing gown he often wore while writing. A permanent fixture of the garden is Aristide Maillol's *The River* (1943) at the end of the far reflecting pool, originally designed in honor of a slain pacifist and cast after the artist's death.

SECOND FLOOR

Atrium – The Atrium serves as a meeting place for daily guided tours of the museum. Check the sign posted here for the day's topics. While the Highlights tours broadly examine the museum's most famous works, others are a bit esoteric, with themes like Feeling Minimalism: Exploring the Body through Minimalist Sculpture. Arrive at 11.20am or 1.20pm to ensure a spot, as the tours are limited to 25 people. The Atrium contains a rotating selection of large-scale painting and sculpture.

Prints and Illustrated Books★ – MoMA's collection of over 53,000 modern prints and illustrated books is the most comprehensive collection of its kind in the world. Works range from woodcuts, etchings and lithographs to digital prints and artist reproductions, dating from the 1880s to the present. Only a tiny fraction of the works are on view at any given time, in heady exhibits put together by the museum's curators. A recent show, Wunderkammer: A Century of Curiosities, reinterpreted a centuries-old tradition of organizing and showcasing various seemingly unrelated objects by means of a "cabinet of curiosities." Works from the museum's permanent collection (some previously never displayed) included pieces by Joseph Cornell, Claes Oldenburgh, Louise Bourgeios and Jim Dine; a special cabinet was custom-made for the show.

Media Gallery – This small gallery features selections from the museum's 1,200 video and media works. Selections from the museum's Department of Film archive of 20,000 films are shown in three state-of-the-art underground theaters (*$10 per day if not entering the museum; 212-708-9480*).

THIRD FLOOR

Architecture and Design★★ – These delightful galleries stem from Alfred Barr's original (and confirmed) conviction that modern art should embrace the design realm. Expect to see furniture from the Arts & Crafts and Bauhaus movements, stained-glass windows by Frank Lloyd Wright, drawings and plans by Mies van der Rohe, Eames chairs and other classic works, as well as common objects that curators believe to have particularly fetching designs, such as the Bic pen and the Apple iMac computer.

Drawings★ – Thematic exhibits in these intimate galleries are drawn from MoMA's collection of more than 10,000 works in pencil, ink, charcoal, watercolor, collage and mixed media. A recent show, Pipe, Glass, Bottle of Rum, examined the thought-provoking tradition of appropriation in fine art by means of some 100 works drawn from the museum's collection.

Photography★★ – MoMA devotes a large section of the third floor to photography shows, thanks to the breadth and depth of its 25,000-work collection. Nearly all the great photographers in the medium's history are represented, not just with one photograph but often with whole series. Eadweard J. Muybridge's studies in animal locomotion are often on display, as are works by Alfred Stieglitz, Man Ray, Diane Arbus and Walker Evans. These are complemented with expansive single-artist retrospectives or thematic exhibitions.

FOURTH FLOOR
Painting and Sculpture II ★★★ –
Along with Painting and Sculpture I galleries on the fifth floor, these galleries form the heart of the museum, with great modern works from the 1940s and the 1960s. The galleries are organized according to a rough chronology, spanning the period from early Abstract Expressionism to Abstract and Pop Art. (The museum's contemporary works are shown in special exhibits on the second and sixth floors.)

Works from the 1940s display a tremendous range of styles, though many share a feeling of alienation brought about by the horrors of World War II. Swiss sculptor Alberto Giacometti's attenuated animal and human figures have a decidedly morbid cast, while British painter Francis Bacon mined the newspaper for particularly disturbing and violent images to inspire his work. Jackson Pollock pioneered Abstract Expressionism in 1947 by laying his canvases on the floor and splattering them with paint, creating a sinuous web of color through free, expressive movements.

The term Color Field was used in the 1950s to describe work by such painters as Mark Rothko, Clyfford Still and Barnett Newman, whose lyrical canvases explored the subtle relationships of large planes of color.

The 1960s saw both the extension of Abstract Expressionism and the repudiation of it. Robert Rauschenberg and Jasper Johns (who had studios in the same New York loft building) continued the search for expression through the innovative use of surface textures, incorporating or drawing on familiar objects and symbols such as flags and license plates. Pop Artists also found inspiration in familiar objects—Warhol's Campbell's Soup cans being the prime example— but their playful, cartoonish style contrasted sharply with the seriousness of Abstract Expressionism.

FIFTH FLOOR
Painting and Sculpture I ★★★ – These
galleries contain the vast majority of the museum's most famous works, including many that are widely regarded as masterpieces.

You'll see a dazzling array of styles here, representing all the major schools and artists of the early modern period. Defining color through the interplay of

The Starry Night *(1889) by Vincent van Gogh*

MoMA's Gone Shopping

MoMA does a brisk business in modern-art-related items, from thick coffeetable books and tote bags to clothing. Across the street from the museum stands the popular **MoMA Design Store**, which teems with funky versions of ordinary objects (silverware, stationery) as well as handmade jewelry and gifts. (If you don't want to deal with museum crowds, scoot down to SoHo, where there's another location of the MoMA Design Store at 81 Spring Street.) **MoMA Books**, on the second floor of the museum, sells books on art, architecture and design *(access by museum admission only)*. You can also shop online at www.momastore.org.

reflecting light, Impressionists such as Claude Monet sought to create a naturalistic "impression" of their subject instead of a literal rendering; Monet's late-career, 50ft-long triptych *Reflections of Clouds on the Water-Lily Pond* is a perfect example, supplying "the illusion of an endless whole," according to the artist. By contrast, the post-Impressionists, including Paul Cézanne, Vincent van Gogh and Henri de Toulouse-Lautrec, emphasized form, rendered through simplified shapes and expressive line; van Gogh's *The Starry Night* (1889) is hands-down the most renowned painting in the museum, an evocative dreamlike landscape of thickly painted waves rolling above a sleeping town.

Pablo Picasso and Georges Braque pioneered Cubism in the early 20C, marking a radical departure from Western art by reducing their subjects to apparently abstract geometrics; Picasso's *Les Desmoiselles D'Avignon* is one of MoMA's cherished works of this period, an 8ft-by-7ft canvas showing five naked prostitutes, their bodies flat and angular, their eyes lopsided and spooky.

Other movements covered on this floor include Fauvism (Henri Matisse), Expressionism (Wassily Kandinsky), Futurism (Umberto Boccioni), Dada (Marcel Duchamp), Surrealism (Salvador Dalí) and De Stijl (Mondrian), with a few Americans (Hopper and Wyeth) thrown in for good measure.

American Folk Art Museum★★

45 W. 53rd St. between Fifth & Sixth Aves.

After years of bouncing from one place to the next, this first-rate museum found a permanent home in 2001 next door to the Museum of Modern Art. Though it would seem impossible to rival its illustrious neighbor, the American Folk Art Museum presents intelligent, provocative exhibits by self-trained artists in its new space.

A BIT OF HISTORY

The museum was founded in 1961 to preserve and display American folk art from 1961 to the present. Initially,

MTA **Subway:** E, M train to Fifth Ave.-53rd St.

it occupied various brownstones and then a ground-floor gallery near Lincoln Center before a plan for a new building finally materialized in the late 1990s. Architects Tod Williams and Billie Tsien replaced two brownstones with a seven-story structure that looks as forbidding from the outside as it is welcoming within.

VISIT

♿⏰*Open year-round Tue–Thu & Sat–Sun 10.30am–5.30pm, Fri 10.30am–7.30pm.* ⏰*Closed major holidays.* 🎟*$12; free Fri 5.30–7.30pm.* ✕. ✆*212-265-1040. www.folkartmuseum.org.*

The metal facade consists of tall, rectangular panels arranged like bricks. Above the entrance, one column of panels is set at a sharp angle to the rest, like a half-open door letting in a long shaft of light. Upon entering (a gift shop full of handmade crafts stands to your right), you'll feel a sense of compression, as the space narrows past the admissions desk. Then it opens into a vast atrium, around which the museum's formidable collections are arrayed, on the walls and in niches in the stairwells.

Collection – The bilevel permanent exhibit, Folk Art Revealed, displays 150 works from the 6,000-piece permanent collection in a particularly creative way. By juxtaposing aesthetically similar works crafted as much as two centuries apart, the curators challenge viewers to consider the function of folk art and the persistence of certain themes. Patriotic symbols are a mainstay of the form, ranging from a wooden gate painted with the American flag in 1876 to a red, white and blue "freedom quilt" made by an African-American artist facing racism in the South in the 1960s.

Other folk art is utilitarian yet beautiful: the massive wooden tooth that serves as a dentist's shingle; the ship's figurehead; the Shaker cupboard. But what really captures the imagination are the wildly idiosyncratic expressions that grow out of deprivation, such as the tall sculpture made entirely from bones and the feverishly romantic storybooks by recluse Henry Darger. Other floors hold temporary exhibits. One recent show, The Seduction of Light, juxtaposed works by 19C master Ammi Phillips against paintings by Mark Rothko (1903–70).

Cooper-Hewitt, National Design Museum★★

2 E. 91st St. at Fifth Ave.

Founded in 1897 by Sarah, Eleanor and Amy Hewitt (granddaughters of industrialist Peter Cooper) as part of the Cooper Union of New York, this eclectic museum explores design across continents and cultures. Visitors also get a de facto tour, as the museum is situated in the opulent 64-room Andrew Carnegie mansion.

A BIT OF HISTORY

The Complex – When it came to real estate, **Andrew Carnegie** was the boldest of the robber barons, having a luxurious Beaux-Arts mansion (1902) built on a parcel surrounded by farms and shanties. By the time Carnegie died in 1919, Fifth Avenue was filled with such palaces; Carnegie's wife Louise remained here until her death in 1946. After a major renovation, the museum opened in 1976 as the National Design Museum. It has been affiliated with the Smithsonian Institution since 1967.

MTA Subway: 4, 5, 6 train to 86th St.

The Collection – The Cooper-Hewitt owns more than 250,000 objects related to the art, craft and commerce of design. Some 24 centuries and all the world's continents are represented. The prints and drawings collection includes works by 15C Italian master Andrea Mantegna, Americans Frederic Church and Winslow Homer, and Italian Surrealist Giorgio de Chirico. Other highlights include an assortment of 18C and 19C birdcages; 10,000 wall coverings, from embossed leather to block-printed Arts & Crafts wallpaper; 45 pieces of Roman-Syrian glass; and 1,000 embroidery samplers dating from the 17C to the 19C.

VISIT

Closed for renovation at time of publication. The newly renovated and expanded gallery is due to open in late 2013. Consult website or call for details.

National Design Triennial

Following in the tradition of the famous (or infamous) Whitney Biennial, the Cooper-Hewitt now has a design triennial, featuring contemporary works in all media that the curators feel express the leading edge of design. The results are ingenious. Eighty-seven designers and firms were chosen to participate in the 2006 triennial, with works ranging from prefabricated houses to robots.

212-849-8400.
www.cooperhewitt.org.
Most of the museum's 9,000sq. ft is devoted to major temporary exhibitions; in 2007 only one small gallery—the former music room—was dedicated to works from the permanent collection. But change is in the air; in 2011 the museum began an ambitious expansion and renovation that will double the current exhibition space; afterward, many more treasures from the permanent collection will be on view. The new and improved museum will reopen in late 2013.

Guggenheim Museum★★

1071 Fifth Ave. at E. 89th St.

MTA Subway: 4, 5, 6
train to 86th St.

Officially named the Solomon R. Guggenheim Museum, this spiraling concrete monument to Modernism, located on Fifth Avenue between 88th and 89th Streets, is among the most original and widely recognized structures in the US. Visited more than any other building designed by Frank Lloyd Wright, it is as much a work of art as the sculptures and paintings it contains. The museum is the permanent home for a renowned collection of Impressionist and modern art.

A BIT OF HISTORY

Heir to a vast mining fortune, **Solomon R. Guggenheim** (1861–1949) and his wife, Irene Rothschild, began collecting Old Masters in the late 19C. But in the early 20C, at the urging of their artistic adviser, Hilla Rebay (an artist in her own right), they shifted their focus to non-representational, or "non-objective," works; especially those by Kandinsky, Mondrian and Moholy-Nagy. Guggenheim established a foundation to bring his collection to the public in 1937, and

Rebay commissioned Frank Lloyd Wright to design a building for it in 1943, but such was the resistance to Wright's design, and his reciprocal contempt for traditional New York architecture, that the project was held up for years, and Guggenheim died before construction finally began, in 1956.

"My Pantheon" – Calling it "my Pantheon," after the domed Roman monument, Wright considered the idiosyncratic building, based on a complex trigonometric spiral, his crowning achievement. From the start, however, the museum was controversial. It clashed with its surroundings, was a nightmare to construct and, with its interior ramp and sloping walls, proved a difficult place either to view or to display art. To top it all off, the smooth concrete facade began showing cracks almost as soon as it was completed in 1959.

As a result, there have been many alterations and rounds of restoration. Most recently, in 1992, a 10-story annex was added to accommodate offices and more galleries, and in 2005 12 layers of paint were removed from the facade to reveal and repair the cracks.

Solomon R. Guggenheim Museum

Photo by David Heald/©The Solomon R. Guggenheim Foundation, New York

VISIT

&🕐Open year-round Fri & Sun–Wed 10am–5.45pm, Sat 10am–7.45pm. 🕐Closed Dec 25. 🎧 Self-guided audio tours free with admission. 💷$18; pay-what-you-wish Sat after 5.45pm. 🍴. 📞212-423-3500. www.guggenheim.org.

Few public spaces in New York rival the drama of the main gallery, with its spiraling, quarter-mile-long ramp. Start your visit at the top or bottom; either way, it will be a journey of discovery. Additional galleries are in annexes.

As for the art, the museum owns some 6,000 works, but only a hundred or so are displayed at any given time. Selections from the **Thannhauser collection**★—75 Impressionist, post-Impressionist and early modern masterpieces—are shown in the second-

floor annex galleries. The earliest work in the collection is a pre-Impressionist landscape by Pissarro from around 1867. There are also canvases by Renoir, Manet, van Gogh and Toulouse-Lautrec, as well as still-lifes by Cézanne and small sculptures by Degas and Maillol. Picasso is especially well represented, with both early paintings (*Woman Ironing*, 1904) and late ones (*Woman with Yellow Hair*, 1931). On the third floor you're likely to see **paintings**★ by Wassily Kandinsky alongside other post-Impressionist, nonobjective works from the founding collection in the Kandinsky Gallery.

The rest of the museum is given over to large-scale temporary shows, some taking up virtually the whole museum, as did a recent overview of work created by Americans influenced by the arts of Asia, and a sweeping survey of Russian art.

Guggenheim Goes Global

The Guggenheim has seen the value in expanding. It has also learned the risks. After the museum opened its hugely successful Bilbao outpost in Spain, designed by Frank Gehry in 1997, other cities clamored for a Guggenheim of their own. Berlin, Venice and Las Vegas each got one; then the money dried up (the Las Vegas outpost closed after 15 months). In 2002 Guggenheim SoHo closed, and plans for a Gehry-designed pile on the southern tip of Manhattan were scrapped. In May 2003 there seemed to be a break in the clouds; the mayor of Rio de Janeiro, Brazil, signed on for a waterfront Guggenheim. But almost immediately the plan met with resistance, and by mid-2005 the project had bogged down in court. In June 2005, the museum announced the winner of a design competition for a Guggenheim in Guadalajara, Mexico, but funding challenges appear to have stalled that project as well. More promising plans are in the works for the largest Guggenheim yet, in Abu Dhabi, United Arab Emirates.

Lower East Side Tenement Museum★★

97 Orchard St. at Broome St.

If Ellis Island recounts chapter one of the American immigrant experience, this remarkable museum recounts chapter two—out loud and in person. Tour guides interpret several generations of immigrant life at 97 Orchard Street, a five-story tenement building (now a National Historic Landmark) in the heart of what was once the most densely populated neighborhood in the US.

A BIT OF HISTORY

Tenements, or multiple-family dwellings, often served as the first home for immigrants newly arrived in New York. Between 1863 and 1935, some 7,000 people lived in this single structure alone. Many worked long shifts in nearby factories and slept short ones on couches and in chairs, hoping to save enough for a bigger apartment uptown. Yet as overcrowded as the Lower East Side was at the time, there was also a powerful sense of community here, with lively markets, vaudeville theaters and social networks that helped these Americans build lives in a new land, dream of the future and feel at home.

MTA Subway: F train to Delancey St., J, M, Z train to Essex St. or B, D train to Grand St.

▷ **Location:** The museum may be viewed by guided tour only. Tours meet at the visitor center at 108 Orchard Street, at Delancey Street. Your tour guide will walk you down the block to the actual tenement building.

🕐 **Timing:** Tours last approximately 1hr and are limited to 15 people. Each tour is offered between 4 and 16 times per week, depending on the day and the season. Advance tickets are recommended. You may buy tickets through the museum's website or by calling ✆866-606-7232. Same-day tickets, if available, can be purchased at 108 Orchard Street.

👥 **Kids:** The Confino Living History Tour is geared for children 5 and over; other tours are appropriate for children 8 and older.

Levine Kitchen, Lower East Side Tenement Museum

Battman Studios/Lower East Side Tenement Museum

VISIT

🕐*Visitor center and gift shop (at 108 Orchard St.) open year-round daily 10am–6pm.* 🕐*Closed Jan 1, Thanksgiving Day & Dec 25.*
🔎*Tenement may be visited by 1hr guided tour only (call or check website for hours).* 👓*$20.* 📞*212-982-8420. www.tenement.org.*

Getting By – This tour brings visitors into the apartments of the German-Jewish Gumpertz family in the 1870s and the Sicilian-Catholic Baldizzi family in the 1930s. In addition to describing families' lives within the building, guides talk about what kinds of social-welfare services were available to them.

Piecing It Together – During this tour visitors get to know two Jewish families affiliated with the garment industry.

Visitors "meet" the Polish-born Levines in 1897 following a family birth and the Rogarshevskys in 1918 following a family death.

Confino Living History – 👪 *Sat–Sun*. Geared toward families with children, the tour explores the apartment once occupied by the Confinos, Sephardic Jews who emigrated to the US from what is now Greece in the 1900s. On hand to answer questions and tell stories is a guide acting as the family's sassy teenage daughter.

Moore Family – The museum's newest tour introduces visitors to a family of Irish immigrants who lost a child while living at 97 Orchard Street in 1869, and examines the health-care choices they and other immigrant families faced in the 19C.

Morgan Library and Museum★★

225 Madison Ave. at E. 36th St.

🚇**Subway:** 6 train to 33rd St.

A cultural treasure trove, this highly regarded institution houses an outstanding collection of rare books, manuscripts, drawings, prints, paintings, ancient seals and letters assembled by J. Pierpont Morgan (1837–1913) and augmented after his death. The recent expansion and renovation by architect Renzo Piano gives even more reason to visit.

A BIT OF HISTORY

The Collection – Son of financier Junius Spencer Morgan, **J. Pierpont Morgan** built his father's firm into the largest private bank in the US. The House of Morgan, as it was known, bailed out the US government to head off a depression in 1895, developed the railroad system, and helped form US Steel.

Morgan began collecting seriously in 1890, eventually amassing more than 3,000 objects, including 600 medieval and Renaissance manuscripts and 1,500 Old Master drawings. The collection has since expanded with purchases and

gifts, including the Pierre Matisse Gallery archives in 1998, containing letters from artists including Balthus, Chagall, Miró and others.

The Campus – In 1902 J. Pierpont Morgan commissioned the firm of **McKim, Mead and White** to build a permanent home for his collection that would be accessible to the public following his death. The Beaux-Arts main building *(33 E. 36th St.)* was completed in 1906 after several tempestuous tugs-of-war between Morgan and Charles McKim. A boxy annex on the corner of Madison Avenue and East 36th Street was added by Morgan's son in 1928. These two buildings were later joined to a large brownstone building on the corner of Madison Avenue and East 37th Street, the younger Morgan's former residence. By the turn of the 20C, however, the collection had outgrown the space, and the facilities needed modernizing and upgrading. Architect Renzo Piano saw a three-year, $100 million and expansion, linking the th

Lobby, Morgan Library and Museum

©2006 Todd Eberle/Morgan Library and Museum

ings with glass and steel pavilions and carving out space for a 280-seat theater underground. The new campus doubled the exhibition space.

VISIT

&.⏲Open Tue–Thu 10.30am–5pm, Fri 10.30–9pm), Sat 10am–6pm, Sun 11am–6pm. ⏲Closed Jan 1, Thanksgiving Day & Dec 25. ☞Guided tours offered daily; call for schedule. ⊙$15; free Fri 7–9pm. ✕. ☎212-685-0008. www.themorgan.org.

The most striking feature of Renzo Piano's design is the lobby, a soaring glass atrium off which the old buildings and new galleries radiate. At the rear of the lobby you'll find the casual Morgan Cafe, with the more formal Morgan Dining Room and gift shop in the brownstone to your left *(south side)*. To the right *(north)* and on the second floor are the exhibition areas.

Study and Library★★ – The opulence of Mr. Morgan's former **study** is enhanced by a painted and carved wood ceiling (16C), red damask hangings, 15C–17C stained-glass windows and massive black-wood furniture. It was in this study that Morgan gathered the top bankers and financiers of the day for a crisis meeting to avert a national financial panic in 1907.

Among the works of art here are Tintoretto's *Portrait of a Moor* (1570) and one of the museum's three Gutenberg Bibles. Lined with three-tiered, floor-to-ceiling bookshelves, Morgan's **library** showcases the financier's passion for the written word. A 16C Flemish tapestry representing the Triumph of Avarice hangs above the marble fireplace, and the carved ceiling sports a series of lunettes and painted spandrels featuring the signs of the zodiac.

Engelhard Gallery★★ – 2nd floor. This gallery contains rotating selections from the museum's permanent collection. Among the items you might discover here are drawings by Rembrandt, Leonardo, Degas and Dürer; original scores by Mahler (the world's largest collection of his manuscripts), Beethoven (the handwritten music for the Violin Sonata no. 10 in G major), Schubert, and Gilbert and Sullivan; and handwritten literary manuscripts, journals and letters by Charles Dickens (the manuscript of *A Christmas Carol*), Mark Twain, Jane Austen, Henry David Thoreau (the author's journals) and John Milton (the sole surviving manuscript of *Paradise Lost*). The museum also possesses a large number of letters and records of artists such as Marc Chagall, Alberto Giacometti and Joan Miró.

Morgan Stanley Galleries – Special exhibitions are mounted in these spacious galleries.

Thaw Gallery – This tiny gallery shows off the museum's store of medieval reliquaries, manuscripts and sculptures.

Museum of the City of New York★★

Fifth Ave. at E. 103rd St.

Founded in 1923 as America's first institution dedicated to the history of a city as well as its present and future, this museum chronicles the changing face of New York from a modest Dutch trading post to an international metropolis. The museum's rich collections, housed in a handsome Georgian Revival building overlooking Central Park, span three centuries of New York memorabilia, decorative arts, furnishings, silver, prints and paintings.

VISIT

Open Tue–Sun 10am–5pm, holiday Mondays. The museum will remain open during its ongoing renovation and reconfiguring program, though some galleries may be closed. Projected completion 2015. Closed Jan 1, Thanksgiving Day & Dec 25. Guided tours available. $10. 212-534-1672. www.mcny.org.
Start your visit by seeing *Timescapes*, a multimedia presentation *(22min)* of the story of New York City from its pre-European settlement period to its booming present. The museum's trove of 1.5 million objects encompasses paintings, sculptures, Broadway and performing arts artifacts, model ships, furniture and decorative arts. Costumes and textiles are a particular strength, and the museum's collection of photographs of New York is unrivaled anywhere in the city.
The New York silver collection encompasses nearly three centuries of **silver**, including tea services and monogrammed tankards. There's also an exquisite assortment of historic playthings, some 10,000 in all, ranging from plush teddy bears, mechanical banks to dollhouses, such as a rare 1769 Ann Anthony Pavilion noted for its "shadow box" style and primitive wax figures.

Subway: 6 train to 103rd St.

Location: A lofty rotunda bisects two long galleries displaying rotating exhibits. The information desk is located to the right of the entranceway and the museum shop to the left.

Timing: Plan about 2hrs to see the museum; a visit here makes an excellent first stop for a visit to New York. Begin by seeing the introductory video presentation *Timescapes*, then stroll the rotating exhibits.

Kids: The historic toy and model ship collections.

Also See: New-York Historical Society.

Much of the museum's display space is devoted to special exhibitions on a wide variety of topics ranging from New York history and architecture to fashion, politics, photography, performing arts and the environment. The museum recently hosted the first major retrospective of the works of Finnish architect Eero Saarinen.

Museum of the City of New York

Harry Zernike/Museum of the City of New York

Museum of Jewish Heritage★★

36 Battery Pl.
(in Battery Park City)

Like its eminent neighbors the Statue of Liberty and Ellis Island, this ever-evolving Jewish history museum, which titles itself "A Living Memorial to the Holocaust," celebrates freedom while remembering the stories of those who struggled to achieve it.

A BIT OF HISTORY

The museum is one of the most architecturally striking in New York. Not only does it command some of the finest views of the harbor, but its design (Roche, Dinkeloo and Assocs.) is steeped in significance. The main structure's six planar facades and six-tiered roof symbolize the six points of the Star of David and recall the six million people who died in the Holocaust. This section, holding 30,000sq ft of exhibition space, opened in 1997. Expansion followed almost immediately. The 80,000sq-ft Robert M. Morgenthau Wing—containing a theater, a lecture hall, more gallery space, a cafe and other features—was designed by the same architects and completed in 2003. Together the two structures form a graceful composite.

MTA Subway: 4, 5 train to Bowling Green.

🕐 **Timing:** Plan 2–3hrs to see the museum. Consider having lunch at the Heritage Cafe, an excellent onsite kosher restaurant with harbor views.

👫 **Kids:** The museum's family guide, available at the admissions desk, contains a tour of the first floor of the museum for children ages 7 to 11. 🚸Parents should use discretion in bringing children through the The War Against the Jews and Ours to Fight For exhibits, as both contain graphic material.

♿ **Also See:** The Jewish Museum.

VISIT

♿🕐*Open Fri 10am–5pm during daylight savings (rest of year & eve of Jewish holidays 10am–3pm), Sun–Tue & Thu 10am–5.45pm, Wed 10am–8pm.* 🕐*Closed Jewish holidays & Thanksgiving Day.* ⌨*$12; free Wed 4–8pm.* 🍴. 📞*646-437-4202. www.mjhnyc.org.*

The main, ziggurat-shaped building holds the museum's core exhibit of 2,000 historic photographs, 800 historical and cultural artifacts and 24 original docu-

Garden of Stones, Museum of Jewish Heritage

©Melanie Einzig/Museum of Jewish Heritage

mentary films. The objects are arranged on three floors, each of which is focused on a distinct theme. Storytelling is at the heart of the museum's mission. Jewish Life a Century Ago, on the first floor, recounts Jewish life and culture from the 1880s to the 1930s. The second floor's War Against the Jews deals with the Holocaust. Particularly poignant are the six **Klarsfeld pillars**, columns covered with photographs of some 2,000 French citizens deported to and killed at Auschwitz. Each picture is brought to life with a short biographical sketch. **Louis Bannet's trumpet** is also on display. Nicknamed the "Dutch Louis Armstrong," the Rotterdam native was sent to the Auschwitz-Birkenau camp but spared for his astounding musician-

ship; he was the personal bandleader for Dr. Josef Mengele. A massive Torah scroll ends the exhibit in the skylit galleries of the third floor, under the banner of "Jewish Renewal." Here visitors can also enjoy splendid **views**★★ of the harbor.

The galleries in the adjoining **Morgenthau Wing** hold special exhibitions.

In 2003 the museum inaugurated English sculptor Andy Goldsworthy's permanent outdoor installation **Garden of Stones**★. To represent life emerging from lifelessness, Goldsworthy hollowed out 18 boulders, filled them with soil, and planted a single dwarf oak in each. As the trees mature in the coming decades—it will take 50 years for them to reach maturity—the trees will become part of the stone.

National Museum of the American Indian★★

1 Bowling Green

The Smithsonian Institution opened this small but smartly curated museum in 1994, after Congress passed an act allotting funds to foster and protect Native arts and culture. For 10 years it was the Smithsonian's only such display space; then, in September 2004, a $199 million, 250,000sq-ft facility was opened on the Mall in Washington, DC, to great fanfare. Still, the New York branch has plenty to recommend it.

A BIT OF HISTORY

The museum's home is indeed a grand setting. The **Alexander Hamilton US Custom House**★★, overlooking Bowling Green, ranks among the finest Beaux-Arts structures in the city. Designed by Cass Gilbert and completed in 1907, the granite building rises seven stories and is embellished with 44 massive columns, each topped with the head of Mercury,

[MTA] **Subway:** 4, 5 train to Bowling Green.

the god of commerce. Daniel Chester French, sculptor of the Lincoln statue in Washington, DC's Lincoln Memorial, created the four female figures flanking the entrance: they represent Asia, Africa, Europe and America.

The Man Behind the Museum – The New York branch of the National Museum of the American Indian is known as the **George Gustav Heye Center** in honor of the man who founded the collection. **Heye** (1874–1957), a wealthy investment banker, gathered almost a million objects from indigenous peoples throughout the Western Hemisphere, buying pretty much everything he could lay his hands on, starting with a deerskin shirt in 1897. The collecting strategy succeeded in filling first his personal museum, then this one and now much of the new museum in Washington, DC.

VISIT

♿☉*Open year-round Thu 10am–8pm, Fri–Wed 10am–5pm.* ☉*Closed Dec 25.* ✆*Free.* ✆*212-514-3700. www.nmai.si.edu.*

Yup'ik mask, Good News Bay, Alaska (c.1910), Infinity of Nations exhibition

© Ernest Amoroso/National Museum of the America's Indian, Smithsonian Institution

Step inside to view the soaring oval **rotunda**, encircled with murals

painted by Reginald Marsh in 1936–37. The museum's galleries branch off from this central space and contain changing exhibits. One recent year-long show (2008–09) put a spotlight on Native American women's dresses and the relationship between these beautifully crafted textile objects and the identity of their wearers. The Diker Pavilion for Native Arts and Cultures was inaugurated in September 2006 with a four-year-long survey of 77 works from the permanent collection. Among the most eye-catching pieces were a hand-painted set of Apache playing cards dating from 1880; a 1910 Nez Perce basketry hat; a pair of Huron moccasins, embroidered with moose hair around 1820; and a 1940 Quechua girl's dancing outfit with matching hat and cape, from Peru.

New-York Historical Society★★

170 Central Park West at W. 77th St.

Housed in an imposing Neoclassical building fronting Central Park, the New-York Historical Society approaches its rich trove of material with a keenly modern curatorial eye. In addition to its antique treasures, including a number of prominent Hudson River school paintings, it has amassed the world's most comprehensive collection of artifacts related to the September 11, 2001, terrorist attacks.

A BIT OF HISTORY

The city's oldest museum, the New-York Historical Society was chartered in 1804 with a view to preserving the history of the US, and since then has amassed a 60,000-piece collection.

While most exhibits usually touch on some aspect of New York and its history, some have a national scope. One of the society's most cherished holdings is its

🚇 **Subway:** B, C train to 81st St. or 1 train to 79th St.

✈ **Don't Miss:** The Henry Luce III Center for the Study of American Culture, an engrossing display of art and arcana, highlights of which are expounded on by prominent New Yorkers.

♿ **Also See:** Museum of the City of New York.

set of 435 watercolors by John James Audubon, made in preparation for the plates illustrating his classic text *Birds of America* (1827–38).

Around 40 of these light-sensitive works are displayed each year roughly from mid-February to mid-March. In 2011 the New-York Historical Society underwent major renovations that will add new and updated exhibitions, permanent installations and galleries and an overhauled restaurant space (reopening November 2011, but call ahead to confirm).

VISIT

♿🕐 *Open year-round Tue–Thu & Sat 10am–6pm, Fri 10am–8pm), Sun 11am–*

View from Cozzens' Hotel Near West Point *(1863) by John Frederick Kensett*

New-York Historical Society

5.45pm. ⊚$10; free Fri 6–8pm). ✕.
☏*212-873-3400. www.nyhistory.org.*

First Floor – The galleries on the first floor hold large temporary exhibits of art and artifacts, many of which are culled from the society's archives. In 2009, New York Painting Begins displayed selections from the museum's outstanding collection of 18C portraits.

Second Floor – Thomas Cole's *The Course of the Empire* and other works from the **Hudson River school** are hung on a rotating basis alongside smaller landscapes and portraiture by Rembrandt Peale and others.

Third Floor – The society's renowned library of historic prints and photographs is open to researchers only.

Fourth Floor – The Henry Luce III Center for the Study of American Culture presents a mesmerizing array of nearly 40,000 objects, in what it calls a "working storage" format. Floor-to-ceiling glass cases are packed with board games, spectacles, Tiffany lamps, fire fighting equipment, clocks, busts, china, you name it, all organized according to type and described on the self-guided audio tour. Also on this floor is a permanent exhibit on slavery in New York.

Rubin Museum of Art★★

150 W. 17th St. at Seventh Ave.

Inaugurated in October 2004, this stunning museum is the first Western institution dedicated solely to presenting and interpreting the art of Bhutan, Tibet, Nepal and other parts of the Himalayas.

A BIT OF HISTORY

The museum is the brainchild of businessman Donald Rubin and his wife, Shelley, who, after amassing one of the world's largest private collections of Himalayan art, decided to share it with the public. First they founded the web-

🚇**Subway:** 1 train to 14th St.

site *(www.himalayanart.org)*, an online catalog of 25,000 works, and then they financed this lovingly curated facility in Chelsea. The space, which used to house Barney's department store, was transformed into a museum by Richard Blinder of Beyer Blinder Belle.

VISIT

♿🕐*Open year-round Mon & Thu 11am–5pm, Wed 11am–7pm, Fri 11am–10pm, Sat–Sun 11am–6pm.* 🕐*Closed Jan 1, Thanksgiving Day & Dec 25.* 👥*Guided tours (1hr) Mon–Fri 3pm, Sat–Sun 1pm, 3pm.* ✕. ⊚*$10; free*

Detail of 15C painting of Ushnishavijaya from Western Tibet

Rubin Museum of Art

Artistic Adventures

Recognizing that Western visitors may be unfamiliar with Himalayan art, the Rubin Museum has created an extensive education and outreach program to encourage understanding and appreciation of the works in its collection. A staff of enthusiastic guides offers daily tours that approach Himalayan art from different perspectives and themes, such as the artistic process or the significance of movement in the various works. If you can't attend one of the tours, don't miss the excellent "Gateway to Himalayan Art" introductory exhibit.

Fri 6–10pm. ✆ *212-620-5000. www.rmanyc.org.*
Cool stone floors and warm, polished-wood accents make the main floor of the museum both spacious and inviting. Upper levels, reached via elevator or the spiral staircase that remains from the original Barney's store, have a hushed quality appropriate to the art on display, much of which has a spiritual component.

Some 900 paintings, sculpture, textiles and ritual objects spanning two millennia are on display. Most pieces date from the 12C to the present and were made to inspire faith, explain religious concepts or tell sacred stories, though they can be equally appreciated on the grounds of technique, imagination and individual artistry. Curators encourage both modes of appreciation, providing informative wall texts, yet letting the beauty of the work speak for itself.

Of special interest are the permanent exhibits Gateway to Himalayan Art and Masterpieces of Himalayan Art, which together provide an in-depth introduction to first-time visitors. Galleries on the third and fifth floors take the viewer behind the scenes, answering questions about why and for whom the art was made. The museum also features thoughtfully curated special exhibits drawn from the permanent collection; recent shows included an examination of fine embroidery from India and Pakistan, and the role of the guru in Himalayan art.

Whitney Museum of American Art★★

945 Madison Ave. at E. 75th St.

Dedicated to the advancement of contemporary artists, this museum holds one of the world's foremost collections of 20C American art, housed in a stark granite building designed by Marcel Breuer and Hamilton Smith. Rising above a sunken sculpture garden in a series of inverted stairs, the cantilevered structure (1966) represents a striking example of the Brutalism style of architecture.

A BIT OF HISTORY

Founded in 1931, the museum grew out of the Greenwich Village studio of sculptor and art collector **Gertrude Vanderbilt Whitney** (1875–1942). After founding the Whitney Studio Club, Whitney began acquiring works by living American artists, creating the core of today's collection of more than 10,000 works by painters such as Edward Hopper, de Kooning, Kelly, Gorky, Prendergast, Demuth and Motherwell, and sculptors such as Calder, Nevelson, Noguchi and David Smith. The museum moved to the current building, its third

MTA Subway: 6 train to 77th St.

Don't Miss: If you're lucky enough to be in the city between March and June on an even-numbered year, be sure to stop by the **Whitney Biennial**, a survey of the contemporary American art scene that never fails to raise eyebrows.

home, in 1966. From its inception, the museum has provided a unique venue for American artists and played a special role in the development of contemporary art. The museum's frequently changing exhibit programs have been known to explore daring, innovative and often controversial topics. The film and video department presents works by independent American film and video artists. The museum is also known for its invitational biennials, held since 1932, which attempt to offer the public a representative cross-section of the current American art scene.

VISIT

Open year-round Wed–Thu & Sat–Sun 11am–6pm, Fri 1–9pm. Closed Thanksgiving Day & Dec 25. Free guided tours (1hr) available daily. $18; pay-what-you-wish Fri 6–9pm. 📞 *212-570-3600. www.whitney.org.*

The **permanent collection** is displayed on a rotating basis in galleries on the fifth floor. Masterworks of American art from the first half of the 20C are continuously on view, including paintings by Hopper, Marsden Hartley, Georgia O'Keeffe, Stuart Davis and Arshile Gorky. Also featured is a selection of postwar and contemporary works by such artists as Philip Guston, Jasper Johns, Alex Katz, Lee Krasner, Jackson Pollock, Kiki Smith and Andy Warhol. Large temporary exhibits fill up the other floors; recent shows included Protect Protect, a major retrospective of the work of sculptor Jenny Holzer.

Whitney Museum of American Art

Jerry L. Thompson, N.Y./Whitney Museum of American Art

271

THE BRONX

The only New York borough located on the mainland, The Bronx typifies the contradictions of a mature urban environment. Marked by run-down apartment buildings and massive housing projects, the south Bronx is inhabited mainly by low-income groups and a multibillion-dollar baseball franchise, the New York Yankees. The central Bronx holds the world-famous Bronx Zoo and the New York Botanical Garden. Grand mansions and lush gardens characterize prosperous sections of the north Bronx, such as Riverdale. To the east lies the largest park in New York City, Pelham Bay Park, with its popular sandy beach, Orchard Beach.

Area: 44 square miles
▶ **Population:**
1,385,108 (2010)

A Bit of History

The Bronx was named after Jonas Bronck, a Swedish émigré who arrived here in 1639. In the late 1800s the borough developed around the village of Morrisania (**AZ** *on large Bronx map*), which now forms the section of The Bronx centered on Third Avenue and 161st Street. The village was named after members of the Morris family, prominent during the Revolutionary period:

Lewis Morris, a signer of the Declaration of Independence, and Gouverneur Morris, a member of the US Constitutional Convention. As settlement of the Bronx blossomed, journalist John Mullaly led a movement to buy inexpensive land parcels and preserve them as parks. As a result, almost 25 per cent of the borough today consists of parkland. In 1891 New York University opened a campus near Morris Heights; Bronx Community College later acquired the campus. Today the borough is home to many colleges and universities, including Fordham University and the SUNY Maritime College, one of the leading maritime programs in the nation.

The Bronx was a part of Westchester County until 1898, when it was incorporated into New York City.

Arthur Avenue Retail Market

©Lauree Feldman/age fotostock

272

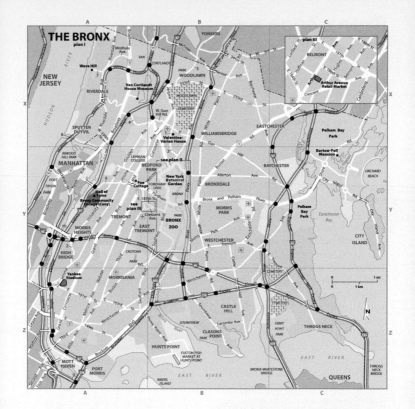

THE BRONX
plan I

NEW JERSEY

Famous Residents

Among the celebrities who have called The Bronx home are actors Tony Curtis, Anne Bancroft and Penny Marshall; athlete Lou Gehrig; writers Edgar Allan Poe, Mark Twain and Herman Wouk; statesmen John Adams, John F. Kennedy and Colin Powell; and fashion designers Calvin Klein and Ralph Lauren.

Van Cortlandt House Museum

© Britta Jaschinski/Apa Publications

In 1904 the first subway line connecting The Bronx to the island of Manhattan opened, causing significant migration to this outlying borough. Jews from Eastern and Central Europe settled here en masse, and by 1949 almost 50 per cent of Bronx residents were Jewish. That figure has declined precipitously in the years since; today Hispanics make up about half of The Bronx's population. Another third are African American. The latest addition to The Bronx is the Fulton Fish Market, which moved from Lower Manhattan in 2005 to acreage near Hunts Point Cooperative Market.

Bronx Zoo★★★

Covering 265 acres of woodland, this popular zoo is the largest urban wildlife park in the country, exhibiting more than 4,000 creatures in settings that replicate as closely as possible the animals' natural habitats.

A BIT OF HISTORY

The Bronx Zoo is located in Bronx Park, a vast expanse of land laid out in the late 19C on both banks of the Bronx River. Opened in 1899, it has expanded its mandate from merely presenting animals to the public to conserving them in the wild, a trend marked by the NY Zoological Society's name change to the Wildlife Conservation Society in 1993. Today the zoo exhibits some 2,000 mammals, 1,000 birds and 1,000 reptiles and amphibians, in addition to more than 2,000 invertebrates, in a series of realistic exhibits that make every effort to replicate the animals' natural habitats. It is ranked among the leading zoos in the country for its exhibit technology and captive management techniques.

VISIT

Bronx River Pkwy. at Fordham Rd.
👫♿🕙*Open Apr–Oct Mon–Fri 10am–5pm, Sat–Sun & holidays 10am–5.30pm; rest of year daily 10am–4.30pm. Many exhibits close 15–30min*

Siberian Tiger at Bronx Zoo

©Vladimir Korostyshevskiy/Dreamstime.com

MTA Subway: 2, 5 train to West Farms Square/E. Tremont Ave. to zoo's Asian entrance or the MTA BxM11 express bus (*$5.50*), which makes limited stops along Madison Ave.

▶ **Location:** When you buy your ticket, be sure to get a map and check the schedule for daily animal activities such as the Sea Lion feeding or the Tiger Enrichment show. The Dancing Crane Cafe is near the Zoo Center, across from the gift shop, and is open year-round; seasonal snack stands are dotted throughout the park.

🕐 **Timing:** Lines can be long at the most popular attractions, such as the Skyfari gondola ride, the Wild Asia exhibit, Congo Gorilla Forest, and the Bug Carousel, especially on weekends and as the afternoon draws on.

👫 **Kids:** The whole zoo is geared for kids, but the Bug Carousel and the Children's Zoo are particularly child-centric.

😊 **Don't Miss:** The Wild Asia Monorail and Congo Gorilla Forest, plus the zoo's newly opened Madagascar! exhibit, with fearsome hissing cockroaches.

Bronx Zoo Express

One of the easiest ways to get to the zoo is by bus. The MTA BxM11 express bus (*$5.50, exact change or MetroCard required, no unlimited-ride MetroCards*) runs every 20min, making limited stops along Madison Avenue in Manhattan, including at 26th, 54th and 99th Streets. The Bronx Zoo is the first stop after 99th Street.

before zoo closes. 🌐$16 ($12 children 3–12), plus extra fees for some exhibits; Wed by donation. Total Experience ticket 🌐$29.95 ($19.95 children) includes all extra fees. ✕. 🅿$13. ✆718-367-1010. www.bronxzoo.com.

The Bronx Zoo has more than 20 indoor and outdoor animal exhibits as well as a number of rides and attractions, from camel rides to the Bug Carousel (in lieu of carnival horses, the carousel has colorful insects). A few of the best.

Congo Gorilla Forest★★ – 🌐$5. This 6.5-acre, African rainforest habitat is the zoo's most thrilling exhibit. It provides a home to 400 animals of 55 species, including 20 lowland gorillas, one of the largest and most important breeding groups in North America. In addition to the gorillas, you'll find pygmy marmosets, okapi and mandrills, as well as DeBrazza's and black-and-white colobus monkeys.

Tiger Mountain★★ – The ingenious design of this exhibit—the viewing platform is tucked within the naturalistic enclosure, behind glass—lets viewers get within several yards of gorgeous Siberian tigers. Watch these royal creatures relax by the pool, prowl the forest or play with their toys. Demonstrations at 11.30am, 1.30pm and 3.30pm daily.

Wild Asia★★ – 🕐*Open May–Oct.* 🌐$4. Zookeepers will describe what you're seeing as you take a monorail ride *(20min)* through 38 acres of hilly, wooded land, home to Indochinese tigers, gaur cattle from Thailand, red pandas, Asian rhinoceroses and Mongolian wild horses.

Madagascar! – The world's fourth-largest island and its varied habitats come to life in the zoo's newest featured exhibit. The lemurs and their crazy antics are the stars of the show, but don't miss the chance to see Nile crocodiles and hissing cockroaches.

Children's Zoo★ – 🕐*Open Apr–Oct.* 🌐$4. This zoo-within-the-zoo houses some 500 animals and features a fun prairie dog exhibit, a rope spider web and a farmyard where kids can feed domestic animals.

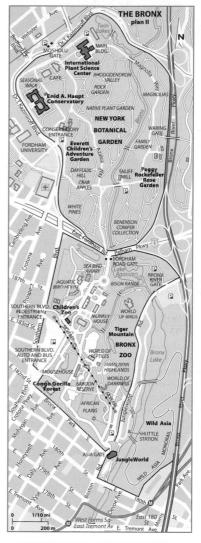

😊 A Bit of Advice 😊

While there are many concession stands throughout the zoo, most sell expensive and unhealthy food such as fried chicken, french fries, nachos, hot dogs, ice cream and soda. To save money and eat more healthily we recommend that you bring your lunch. You're free to use the tables clustered around the concession stands regardless of what's on your plate.

New York Botanical Garden★★

Located directly north of the Bronx Zoo, this is one of the largest and oldest gardens in the country. Walking trails wind through its 250 rolling acres, past thousands of flowering trees, shrubs and plants that reach their peak in spring and early summer. A large conservatory and a full slate of special exhibits make a visit rewarding in the fall and winter months as well.

A BIT OF HISTORY

The New York Botanical Garden was founded in 1891 after Columbia University botany professor Nathaniel Lord Britton and his wife, Elizabeth, visited England's Royal Botanic Gardens at Kew and decided New York should have a similar horticultural showpiece.

They chose this large tract in the north Bronx and forged a public–private partnership between the city and noted philanthropists such as Andrew Carnegie, Cornelius Vanderbilt and J. Pierpont Morgan to finance the buildings and build the collections. In 1896 the New York Botanical Garden appointed Nathaniel Lord Britton its first director, and

MTA Train/Subway: Metro-North Harlem Line local train from Grand Central Terminal to Botanical Garden Station (20min). Or take 4, B, D subway to Bedford Park Blvd. and transfer to Bx26 bus east to the Mosholu Gate entrance.

Location: At the entrance you can pick up a map and learn about the day's special events.

Kids: The Everett Children's Adventure Garden shows how plants live and function.

Don't Miss: The Enid A. Haupt Conservatory, beautiful in all seasons.

since then the garden has grown in its size and mission, displaying a wonderful array of plants and seasonal blooms and conducting important botanical research.

VISIT

200th St. & Kazimiroff Blvd. ♿ ⏰ Open year-round Tue–Sun 10am–6pm, holiday Mondays. ⏰ Closed Dec 25. ☙ Guided tours. 🎟 $20 includes all exhibits and seasonal shows; $6

Enid A. Haupt Conservatory, New York Botanical Garden

©Terraxplorer/iStockphoto.com

grounds-only pass; grounds-only admission free Wed all day, Sat 10am–noon. ✖. ▣ $12. ✆718-817-8700. www.nybg.org.

The New York Botanical Garden has more than 50 gardens to explore, from the lovely perennial and herb gardens, to the rock garden and forest. Here are a few favorites.

Enid A. Haupt Conservatory★★ – The nation's largest Victorian glasshouse, this magical conservatory opened to the public in 1902 and is now home to A World of Plants, a global ecotour that includes tropical rainforests, deserts, and the world's most comprehensive collection of palm trees under glass. The conservatory hosts the garden's popular seasonal flower shows, including the orchid show in March, bonsai show in October and model train show in December. Green thumbs can also get advice at the home gardening center.

Peggy Rockefeller Rose Garden★★ – Beautifully renovated in 2007, the garden dates back to 1916 and now features more than 3,000 rose plants, from antique roses to modern hybrid teas, floribundas and shrub roses. They're in fragrant bloom each spring (beginning in late May) and fall (beginning in early September).

Everett Children's Adventure Garden★ – This garden is full of hands-on activities that allow children to learn how plants live and function.

International Plant Science Center★ – Here you can visit the library's reading room and rare book room, an exhibition gallery and the orchid rotunda. A five-story addition to the center houses a herbarium containing seven million plant specimens, the largest such collection in the Western Hemisphere. Enjoy lunch or a snack in the Garden Cafe, bordering lush display gardens.

Around The Bronx

Grid letters in parentheses after each attraction's name refer to the map.

Yankee Stadium (AZ)

👥▲1 E. 161st St. & River Ave. ▐MTA▌4 ,B, D train to 161st St. ☚Guided tours (1hr) daily every 20min noon–1.40pm; home games may affect tour schedule. ✆646-977-8687. Tour and ticket information at www.yankees.com.

On April 16, 2009, the New York Yankees played their first regular-season home game in their gleaming new stadium, located just north of the site of the iconic old structure—"the house that Ruth built"—that had been their home since 1923. Behind a handsome granite-and-stone facade lies a state-of-the-art facility that incorporates historic touches from the old stadium alongside modern amenities.

The best way to experience the new Yankee Stadium's improved facilities and sight lines is to catch a home game. If your timing doesn't permit that, guided tours cover the monumental Great Hall, the Yankees museum, the batting cages, the Yankees dugout and Monument Park, where you'll find bronze plaques, monuments and retired jersey numbers of Yankee greats.

Valentine-Varian House (BX)

3266 Bainbridge Ave. at E. 208th St. ▐MTA▌*D train to 205th St. or 4 train to Mosholu Pkwy.* ☚*Visit by guided tour (30min) only, year-round Sat 10am–4pm, Sun 1–5pm.* ◷*Closed major holidays & Dec 25–Jan 1.* ⌕*$5.* ✆*718-881-8900. www.bronxhistorical society.org.*

This fieldstone house originally stood on the opposite side of the street, on land acquired in 1758 by Isaac Valentine. The scene of many skirmishes during the Revolution, the area was purchased in 1791 by Isaac Varian, a prosperous farmer whose son later became the 63rd mayor of New York City. Situated on its present site since 1965, the house now contains the **Museum of Bronx History**, which features changing exhibits on the history of the borough.

Poe Cottage (ABY)

E. Kingsbridge Rd. & Grand Concourse.
MTA *4, D train to Kingsbridge Rd.*
Visit by guided tour (30min) only, by appointment only during restoration work. Closed major holidays & *Dec 25–Jan 1.* $5. 718-881-8900. *www.bronxhistoricalsociety.org.*

From 1846 to 1849 this little wooden house (1812) was the home of author **Edgar Allan Poe** (1809–49), who wrote "Annabel Lee" and other poems during his stay here. Poe moved to this cottage and away from the noise and congestion of New York City in the hope of saving his wife, Virginia Clemm, from tuberculosis; she died, however, in 1847. The author died two years later in Baltimore, while on a return trip to the cottage from Virginia. The cottage was moved across the street in 1913 and transformed into a museum in 1917. Today the restored house contains displays of memorabilia and manuscripts, and an audiovisual slide show *(20min).*

Van Cortlandt House Museum★ (ABX)

Enter Van Cortlandt Park at Broadway & 246th St. MTA *1 train to 242nd St.-Van Cortlandt Park.* Open year-round *Tue–Fri 10am–3pm, Sat–Sun 11am–4pm.* Closed major holidays. $5; *free Wed.* 718-543-3344. *www.vancortlandthouse.org.*

Built in 1748, this colonial plantation house has been admirably preserved by the city and the National Society of Colonial Dames. It is believed that George Washington used the house as headquarters before making his triumphant entry into New York City in November 1783.

The manor, appointed with furnishings in the Colonial style, reflects a refinement and style of living typical of 18C and 19C New York gentry. Among the nine rooms open to the public, note the Dutch room, the kitchen and the nursery, which contains one of America's oldest dollhouses.

Bronx Community College (AY)

University Ave. & W. 181st St.
MTA *4 train to Burnside Ave.; walk 4 blocks west to University Ave., then north to campus.* Free guided tours *available.* . 718-289-5161. *www.bcc.cuny.edu.*

Founded in 1891 as the Bronx campus of New York University, the institution is now home to Bronx Community College. The 52-acre campus lines the banks of the Harlem River and boasts the **Hall of Fame for Great Americans**★ *(Hall of Fame Terrace at W. 181st St.).*

Completed by Stanford White in 1900, this Beaux-Arts complex, the first American pantheon, consists of an outdoor colonnade, 630ft in length, surrounding three buildings (Gould Memorial Library, the Language Hall and Philosophy Hall).

Arthur Avenue

This petite stretch of red-sauce joints and pungent food markets in the Belmont community, just west of Bronx Park, is known affectionately by New Yorkers as the real Little Italy, partly because it's still an Italian-American (and not Chinese) stronghold, and partly because it's not as touristy as Manhattan's version. Start out at the **Arthur Avenue Retail Market** *(no. 2344)*, which is crammed with stalls hawking everything from wheels of parmigiano reggiano to eggs and sliced veal. **Mike's Deli**, at the rear of the market, offers incredible sandwiches. For a meal you'll never forget, get in line at **Dominick's** *(no. 2335;* 718-733-2807)*, the legendary southern Italian joint where the waiters tabulate the bills in their heads (no menu, no checks) and the crowd is always lively. For seafood antipasto of mussels, squid and lobster in a spicy tomato sauce, settle in at the slightly fancier **Mario's** *(no. 2342;* 718-584-1188; www.mariosrestarthurave. com)*, a 1919 institution made famous in Mario Puzo's book *The Godfather*.

Gardens in Wave Hill

Mick Hales/Wave Hill

Bronze busts of 98 outstanding Americans in numerous fields—from Susan B. Anthony to the Wright brothers—line the niches of the colonnade.

Pelham Bay Park (CXY)

MTA *6 train to Pelham Bay Park.*
The largest park in the city at 2,766 acres offers a variety of outdoor activities including golfing, hiking, cycling, tennis, horseback riding, ball playing and fishing. Especially popular on hot summer days, Orchard Beach features one mile of sandy shore.

Bartow-Pell Mansion Museum★ (CY)

895 Shore Rd., within Pelham Bay Park. ◓*Open year-round Wed & Sat–Sun noon–4pm.* ◓*Closed major holidays.* ◞◞*Guided tours (*☞*$8) by appointment. .* ☞*$5.* 🅿. ☎*718-885-1461. www.bartowpellmansionmuseum.org.*
The history of this site dates to 1654, when Thomas Pell purchased the land from the Siwanoy Indians. Robert Bartow, a descendant of Pell's, built the Neoclassical stone mansion overlooking Long Island Sound between 1836 and 1842. The elegant interior contains Greek Revival detailing, including a freestanding elliptical staircase, and furnishings in the American Empire style.
The restored 1840s stone carriage house (◓*open Apr–Oct)* serves as an interpretive center.

Wave Hill★ (AX)

♿*W. 249th St. & Independence Ave.*
MTA *1 train to W. 242nd St.; free hourly shuttle from subway. Or Metro-North Hudson Line from Grand Central to Riverdale; wait for hourly shuttle or walk uphill up W. 245th St. and turn left on Independence Ave.* ◓*Open mid-Apr–mid-Oct Tue–Sun 9am–5.30pm; rest of year Tue–Sun 9am–4.30pm.* ◓*Closed major holidays.* ◞◞*Free garden and conservatory tours Sun 2pm.* ☞*$8; free Tue & Sat 9am–noon & all day Tue off-peak months).* ✕🅿. ☎*718-549-3200. www.wavehill.org.*
Opened to the public in 1965, this enchanting 28-acre estate comprises award-winning gardens and greenhouses, meadows and woodlands, all on a spectacular **site**★★ overlooking the Hudson River. Built as a country home by William Lewis Morris in the 1840s, the main mansion was later owned by publisher William Appleton. Theodore Roosevelt's family occupied it in 1870 and Mark Twain leased the estate in 1901. Other celebrity residents include conductor Arturo Toscanini and George Perkins, J.P. Morgan's business partner. The building was restored in the 1960s and now serves as a visitor center. Some 18 acres of landscaped gardens contain more than 3,000 species of plants and a variety of trees. Of special interest are the greenhouses, the lovely aquatic garden and fragrant herb garden.

New York's most populous borough, Brooklyn is situated on the western tip of Long Island and extends from the East River to Coney Island and from the Narrows to Jamaica Bay. Although almost half a million Brooklynites commute to Manhattan today, the borough is far from being a bedroom community. Long a haven for writers and artists, including poet Walt Whitman, it boasts cultural institutions that rival those in Manhattan and has an attitude to match. Brooklyn is the birthplace of Arthur Miller, Barbra Streisand and Woody Allen, among many others.

Area: 81 square miles
▸ **Population:**
2,504,700 (2010)

A Bit of History

A Dutch Settlement – Brooklyn was founded in 1636 by Dutch settlers, who named it Breuckelen ("broken land") after a small town near Utrecht. Other villages followed, spreading westward along the river, and by the late 18C regular ferry service to Manhattan was established. Brooklyn became an incorporated city with about 30,000 inhabitants in 1834, was connected to Manhattan via the Brooklyn Bridge in 1883, and was integrated into New York City in 1898.

A Mix of Neighborhoods – Brooklyn holds an impressive variety of neighborhoods. Just to name a few, there's Park Slope, a sedate enclave of brownstones bordering sylvan Prospect Park; Brooklyn Heights, home to much of Brooklyn's "old money" and the elegant harborfront promenade; DUMBO, with its dramatic bridge views and burgeoning gallery scene; Williamsburg, an extension of the East Village with its hip restaurants and shops; Brighton Beach, a thriving Russian neighborhood; and Fort Greene, known for its tightknit community of African-American professionals and block after block of pristine brownstones.

Cranberry Street, Brooklyn Heights

© Christian Heeb/hemis.fr

BROOKLYN HEIGHTS★★

MTA 2, 3 train to Clark St.

Heavily fortified during the Revolution, Brooklyn Heights was the site of General Washington's headquarters during the Battle of Long Island. In the mid-19C the neighborhood developed as a choice residential area, largely because of its proximity to Manhattan, and it remains an exclusive address, with brownstones and town houses representing almost every style of 19C American architecture lining its narrow, tree-shaded streets. The Heights' main commercial drag, home to most of its restaurants and shops, is Montague Street, though Atlantic Avenue has some good options too (see sidebar below).

✦WALKING TOUR

○ *Distance: 2.4mi. Begin at Monroe Pl.*

Leaving the subway station, walk toward Monroe Place. At the corner of Clark and Henry Streets stands the Hotel St. George, once the largest hotel in New York City. The building has since been converted into co-ops, luxury apartments and dormitories for area students.

○ *Turn onto Monroe Place.*

At **45 Monroe Place** stands the New York State Supreme Court's Appellate Division. The Classical Revival building dates from 1938 and has two huge Doric columns flanking the entrance.

○ *Turn left at Pierrepont St.*

The handsome 1881 Queen Anne-style brick building at no. 128 houses the **Brooklyn Historical Society**, the borough's only history museum, comprised of a few small art and history exhibits drawn from the society's extensive permanent collection (○open Wed–Fri & Sun noon–5pm, Sat 10am–5pm; ○closed Jan 1, Jul 4, Thanksgiving & Dec 25; ✆$6; ✆718-222-4111; www.brooklynhistory.org).

○ *Backtrack on Pierrepont St. and continue to the corner of Henry St.*

Atlantic Avenue

The main thoroughfare of Brooklyn's Lebanese and Middle Eastern populations has become one of New York's most popular culinary destinations. Sample delicacies like lamb kebabs and stuffed grape leaves, but try to resist snapping up little bags of every spice imaginable. Some of the avenue's highlights include **Tripoli** (no. 156; ✆718-596-5800; www.tripolirestaurant.com), a campy two-level restaurant (check out the sea mural on the main level) that serves up hummus, falafel and honeyed desserts. Visit **Sahadi's Importing Co.** (no. 187; ✆718-624-4550; www.sahadis. com) for Lebanese pistachios, feta, spices and coffee. End your walk at **Pete's Waterfront Ale House** (no. 155; ✆718-522-3794; www. waterfrontalehouse.com) for a restorative gulp of one of the 50 varieties of bottled beer.

82 Pierrepont Street represents a splendid example of the Richardsonian Romanesque style, with its bulky massing and its rough, unfinished masonry surfaces, rounded arches and bas-relief carving. Built in 1890 as a private residence, it was later enlarged and converted into apartments.

Turning onto Willow Street, note nos. **155**, **157** and **159**, three Federal-style houses sporting handsomely detailed entranceways. A skylight in the pavement in front of no. 157 allows daylight to filter down into a tunnel that connects no. 159 to no. **151**, formerly a stable and now an apartment.

Farther up the street, on the opposite side, nos. **108–112** illustrate the picturesque Queen Anne style, with their great variety of building materials and blend of elements of the Romanesque, Gothic and Renaissance.

○ *Continue on Willow St. and turn right onto Orange St.*

At the corner of Hicks and Orange Streets stands the 1914 parish house of the historically significant **Plymouth Church of the Pilgrims** down the block (*visit by 15–30min guided tour only, Mon–Fri 10am–4pm, Sun 12.15–2pm, stop in at 75 Hicks St., or in the church itself following 11am Sun service and ask for assistance, or call ahead; ☎718-624-4743; www.plymouthchurch.org*). The first Congregational Church in Brooklyn, this simple brick meetinghouse dating from 1846 served for 40 years as the pulpit for abolitionist Henry Ward Beecher and a stop on the Underground Railroad. President Lincoln worshiped here on two occasions in 1860; tour guides will point out his pew. The church is also well known for its large stained-glass windows by Tiffany.

▷ *Backtrack to Hicks St. and continue two blocks north; turn left onto Middagh St.*

Several Federal-style clapboard houses, built in the 1820s, line the street. Among the best preserved are the double-frame house at nos. **31–33** and the charming dwelling at no. **24**. To get to DUMBO, remain on Middagh and turn right on Columbia Heights. Otherwise, continue to the esplanade as described below.

▷ *Take Willow St. to Cranberry St. and continue toward the East River to the Brooklyn Heights Esplanade.*

Overlooking the harbor, the esplanade offers excellent **views**★★ of Manhattan's Financial District; the view is especially impressive in the early evening when the lights glimmer across the river. Behind the terrace lies a series of houses with lovely private gardens.

▷ *Walk along the esplanade; turn left onto Pierrepont St. and right onto Pierrepont Pl.*

Note the elegant brownstone mansions at **nos. 2** and **3 Pierrepont Place**.

▷ *Continue on Pierrepont Pl., which becomes Montague Terrace; turn left onto Remsen St. and right onto Hicks St.*

Off to the left is **Grace Court Alley**, a picturesque mews that was the stable alley for the fine homes on Remsen Street.

▷ *Continue along Hicks St. and turn left onto Joralemon St.*

The intersection of Hicks and Joralemon Streets was the location of the country home of Philip Livingston, a signer of the Declaration of Independence. It is reported that on August 29, 1776, General Washington met at Livingston's home with his chiefs of staff to plan the evacuation of his army.

▷ *Continue east on Joralemon St. to Court St.*

The Civic Center area presents a jarring contrast to the residential section, with its monumental public buildings such as Borough Hall (the former Brooklyn City Hall) and the massive Richardsonian Romanesque central post office.

▷ *Continue on Joralemon St. to Boerum Pl. and turn right.*

New York Transit Museum★

👥♿ *Boerum Pl. & Schermerhorn St. (**M** on map).* 🕐*Open year-round Tue–Fri 10am–4pm, Sat–Sun noon–5pm.* 🕐*Closed major holidays.* 💲*$6; $4 children 3–17.* ☎*718-694-1600. www.mta.info/mta/museum.*
Located in the refurbished 1930s Court Street shuttle station, the museum tells the story of New York's labyrinthine transit system with a fascinating collection of vintage subway cars and history exhibits. The story of the New York City subway is told in text, pictures and maps along the platform. At the working signal tower (near the end of the platform), flashing lights represent trains making their way under downtown Brooklyn on the connecting track. Exhibits include Steel, Stone and Backbone, a look at the building of the subways, and **On**

the **Streets**, which gives buses and trolleys their proper due. The intriguing **Fare Collection** exhibit lets you touch and handle the various fare devices (paper tickets, tokens, MetroCards) the transit system has used over its history. The walls of the R-46 Gallery are plastered with posters of films set in the subways. (☾ *See also the NY Transit Museum Gallery Annex and Store in Grand Central Terminal.*)

DUMBO

MTA *A, C train to High St or F train to York St.*

DUMBO—the acronym stands for "Down Under the Manhattan Bridge Overpass"—is one of the most vibrant new neighborhoods in Brooklyn, a place where moody cobblestone streets are lined with imposing warehouse buildings, many converted into loft apartments and galleries. A number of top-notch restaurants and gourmet stores opened here in the last 10 years, and the newly renovated Brooklyn Bridge Park is a great place to rest or picnic, especially if you've just walked over the legendary span.

A Bit of History – DUMBO, which stretches roughly from Fulton Street to Hudson Avenue, and from Prospect Street to the East River, used to be known as Fulton Landing after Robert Fulton, who in 1814 built a pier here for the steamships he ran to Manhattan, just 8 minutes away.

The completion of the Brooklyn Bridge in 1883 put an end to the ferry, and the neighborhood became an industrial district with virtually no residents until the 1980s, when artists began converting its abandoned warehouses into studios. Though today it has its share of multimillion-dollar condos, DUMBO still has an adventurous spirit to it, owing partly to its protected location and partly to the

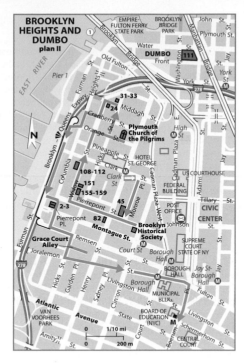

RESTAURANT
River Café..............................①

passion of its residents to keep it culturally rich and self-renewing.

Visit – The best time to visit DUMBO is on Saturday afternoon, when the majority of its galleries and shops are open and the restaurants and parks are full

Tom's Luncheonette

782 Washington Ave. at Sterling Pl. ☏*718-636-9738.* This Brooklyn institution—it's been here since 1936—is the great all-time breakfast spot. It's open from 6am to 4pm Monday through Saturday. It's also a family affair with Tom, his wife and their kids all tending shop. As son Gus says, "We don't have customers, we have friends." Stop in for a cherry-lime rickey or a real egg cream after your visit to the Brooklyn Museum of Art or the Botanic Garden.

Park Slope

Situated just west of Prospect Park, this neighborhood is one of the most desirable addresses in Brooklyn, thanks largely to the rows of handsome brownstones—two- to four-story brick town houses covered with a distinctive sandstone paste—that line most of its wide, shaded streets. Discovered by fixer-uppers in the late 1970s, they now routinely fetch upward of $2 million apiece; often much more. Some are single-family residences, and others are divided into apartments. The best have high stoops and rich Gothic, Italianate or Romanesque detailing. A few mansions are interspersed throughout the neighborhood. One is the **Montauk Club** *(northeast corner of Lincoln Pl. & 8th Ave.)*, constructed in 1891 in a style reminiscent of a Venetian palace. Of particular interest are the friezes, which depict historic scenes associated with the Montauk Indians. The main commercial artery of Park Slope is Seventh Avenue. It's home to quaint boutiques and bookstores, as well as a number of good restaurants and cafes.

of locals. The **DUMBO First Thursday Gallery Walk**—featuring open studios and gallery receptions, as well as live music, on the first Thursday of each month—is another lively option. A good place to start your visit is **111 Front Street**, where a dozen galleries occupy the second floor (the friendly Dumbo General Store cafe is on the first); for more art, check out **Powerhouse Arena** *(37 Main St.)*, an art book publisher that also puts on photography shows, performances and other events. Sweet tooths flock to **Jacques Torres Chocolate** *(66 Water St.)* for its ethereal truffles, cookies and European-style hot chocolate, all made onsite. If you're looking for a full meal, try **Bubby's** *(1 Main St.)*, a TriBeCa import that serves up homey staples like pie and chicken, or the upscale **River Cafe** *(1 Water St.)*. Barge-music is the most famous entertainment option in the neighborhood, though **St. Ann's Warehouse** *(38 Water St.; www. stannswarehouse.org)* runs a close second for its avant-garde theater performances.

PROSPECT PARK★

Map opposite. MTA *2, 3 train to Grand Army Plaza. www.prospectpark.org.*
Once part of an estate belonging to the Litchfield family, this 585-acre haven of woodlands and rolling hills is an outdoor oasis for Brooklynites.

A Bit of History

The land for Prospect Park was purchased by the city in piecemeal fashion in the 1850s and 60s and landscaped by Frederick Law Olmsted and Calvert Vaux, the architects of Central Park, in 1865. Construction was completed in 1873, but it wasn't until 20 years later that work began on the ornate triumphal arch that marks its entrance at Grand Army Plaza. John Duncan, architect of Grant's Tomb, designed the arch, which is dedicated to the fallen Union soldiers of the Civil War, and Stanford White, architect of Washington Square Arch, oversaw the placement of sculptures and bas-reliefs upon it. Cupping the southeast corner of the plaza is the main branch of the Brooklyn Public Library, whose Art Moderne facade was recently treated to a thorough cleaning.

Visit

Prospect Park thrums with activity year-round but is especially lively on summer weekends, when ballgames and barbecues fill up its vast grassy lawns and free outdoor concerts are held in its bandshell several evenings a week as part of the Celebrate Brooklyn! festival (see website for schedule). The park's visitor center is located in the Audubon Center, also home to the Songbird Cafe and many nature programs. The undulating 3.35mi loop road, Park Drive, is a favorite with runners, in-line skaters and

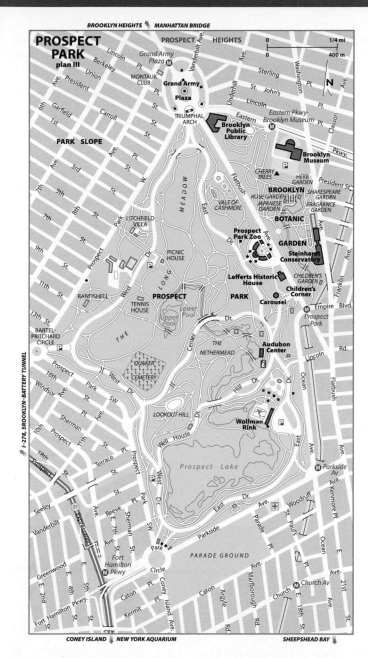

PROSPECT PARK
plan III

cyclists; it is open to vehicular traffic only during weekday rush hours.

Children's Corner – 👶🧑 MTA *B, Q, S train to Prospect Park.* A cluster of sights on the east side of the park is particularly appealing for children. The **Lefferts Historic House Museum** is a 1783 Dutch

farmhouse whose period rooms and programs interpret daily life in Brooklyn in the 1820s (♿ 🕐 *open Jan–Mar Sat–Sun noon–4pm, Apr–May Sat–Sun noon–5pm, Summer Thu–Sun noon–5pm, until 6pm Jul–Aug;* ☎*718-789-2822).* Just south of the house stands a 1912 **car-**

ousel with 51 fancifully carved horses and other animals (⏰operates Apr–Jun & Sept–Oct Thu–Sun & holidays noon–5pm, Jul–Aug noon–6pm; ⬛$2; ☎718-965-8999). To the north of the house is the nifty **Prospect Park Zoo**★ (♿⏰open Apr–Oct Mon–Fri 10am–5pm, Sat–Sun & holidays 10am–5.30pm, rest of year daily 10am–4.30pm; ⬛$8, $5 children 3–12; ☎718-399-7339). Run by the distinguished Wildlife Conservation Society, it contains more than 400 animals of some 80 species, including red pandas, sea lions, kangaroos, emus, porcupines and other creatures—all of which you can see at much closer range than you can at the zoo's much larger, busier and more expensive counterpart in the Bronx.

BROOKLYN BOTANIC GARDEN★★

♿900 Washington Ave. MTA 2, 3 train to Eastern Pkwy., or B, Q, S train to Prospect Park. ⏰Open mid-Mar–Oct Tue–Fri 8am–6pm, Sat–Sun 10am–6pm; rest of year Tue–Fri 8am–4.30pm, Sat–Sun 10am–4.30pm. Open holiday Mondays except Labor Day. ⏰Closed Jan 1, Thanksgiving Day & Dec 25. ⬛$10; free Tue & Sat 10am–noon & Mon–Fri mid-Nov–Feb ($18 combined ticket with Brooklyn Museum). ⏱Free guided tours Sat–Sun 1pm. ✕. 🅿$3 first hour; $2 each additional hour. ☎718-623-7200. www.bbg.org.

Located to the east of Prospect Park and to the south of the Brooklyn Museum, this outstanding botanical garden contains a great variety of vegetation, including one of the finest assemblages of roses in the country. Covering 52 acres, it invites visitors to explore its prim rows of cherry trees—site of the popular late-April Cherry Blossom Festival—and its many well-kept gardens: Shakespeare, Children's, Rose, Herb, Rock, Native Flora, Lily Pool Terrace, Japanese, Fragrance and Bluebell Wood, among others.

Built in 1988, the **Steinhardt Conservatory**★ contains a Tropical Pavilion, an aquatic exhibit and the country's largest bonsai collection, as well as a gallery that hosts consistently outstanding shows of botanical illustrations and art (⏰open every day the garden is open mid-Mar–Oct 10am–5.30pm, rest of year 10am–4pm).

BROOKLYN MUSEUM★★

200 Eastern Pkwy. MTA 2, 3 train to Eastern Pkwy. ⏰Open Wed & Sat–Sun 11am–6pm, Thu–Fri 11am–10pm (first Sat of month until 11pm). ⏰Closed Jan 1, Thanksgiving Day & Dec 25. ⬛$10 ($18 combined ticket with Brooklyn Botanic Garden). ⏱Audio tours, cellphone tours and iPod tours available. ✕. 🅿$3 first hour, $2 each additional hour. ☎718-638-5000. www.brooklynmuseum.org.

Cherry blossoms in Brooklyn Botanic Garden

©Patrick Cullina/Brooklyn Botanic Garden

Housed in a monumental Beaux-Arts building designed by McKim, Mead and White, the Brooklyn Museum is New York's second-largest art museum behind the Met, and well worth a visit if you happen to be in the borough. The collection contains a whopping 1.5 million works, ranging from one of the world's best troves of Egyptian antiquities to *The Dinner Party* by Judy Chicago, a hallmark of feminist art from the 1970s. A dramatic new glass entrance by Polshek Partnership Architects, unveiled in 2004, is just one of many recent improvements to this fine institution.

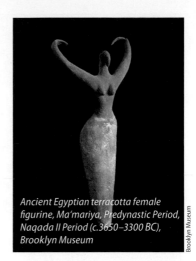

Ancient Egyptian terracotta female figurine, Ma'mariya, Predynastic Period, Naqada II Period (c.3650–3300 BC), Brooklyn Museum

Brooklyn Museum

Visit

As you enter the museum from Eastern Parkway, take a moment to explore the Rodin sculptures arranged in the front of the lobby. At the admission desk, pick up a museum map with cellphone tour stops, or rent an iPod to use *(☞$5)*—all with excellent commentary on *The Dinner Party*, the American Identities exhibit, the Egyptian collection and the African art galleries. These are generally regarded as the best departments in the museum, so if you're short on time, focus on them first. The temporary shows are also excellent.

First Floor – The Brooklyn Museum's collection of 5,000 works of **African art**★★ is the largest such collection in an American museum, with more than 100 cultures represented over a span of 2,500 years. Two long galleries contain a wealth of eye-catching works, including wooden statuettes, witch doctors' wands, masks and ceremonial shields, all nicely laid out and described in helpful wall texts.

Second Floor – Galleries here showcase art from China, Korea, Japan, Southeast Asia, India and the Islamic world. Of particular note is the museum's collection of **18C** and **19C Persian paintings and decorative arts**★, one of the finest groupings in the Western world. The colorful carpets and mosaics reveal astounding craftsmanship. Rarely seen works on paper are rotated through the Asian and Islamic galleries, includ-ing some striking watercolors. Don't miss the ferocious *Head of a Guardian* from 13C Japan or the lovely Chinese ceramics.

Third Floor – This floor presents the museum's **Egyptian collection**★★★, one of the finest in the world. To best appreciate the display of more than 1,100 works, start in the Kevorkian Gallery of ancient Middle Eastern art. Here you'll find impressive bas-reliefs from the palace of Assyrian king Ashur-nasir-pal II at Nimrud. This gallery opens onto an introductory gallery full of exhibits on Egyptian religion, culture and technology, stressing the theme of permanence and change. Flanking this gallery are two galleries full of artifacts, with earlier works (Old and Middle Kingdom) arrayed in the colorful room to the right

Arty Facts

👥 Sundays (Oct–May) at 11am and 1.30pm the Brooklyn Museum sponsors a 90min family program cleverly known as "Arty Facts." Guides introduce children ages 4–7 and their adult companions to work in a gallery, then use it as the basis for an art-making project. Meet in the main lobby; no reservations necessary *(☞$10 materials fee)*.

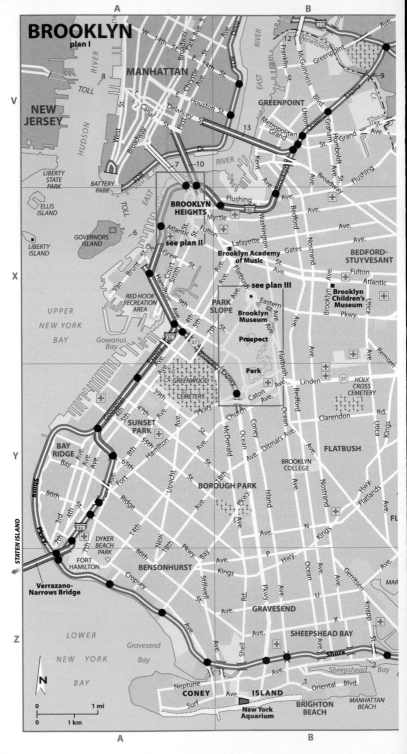

BROOKLYN
plan I

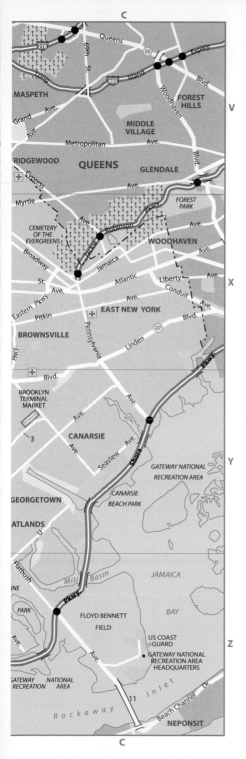

and later ancient works (New Kingdom) in the neutral-toned Rubin Gallery to the left; the latter is capped with a room displaying temple and tomb art, always some of the most fascinating ancient Egyptian works. Selections from the museum's collection of **European paintings** are hung on the four walls surrounding the Beaux-Arts Court, each wall addressing a theme: portraiture, landscape, narrative, and rural and urban life. Here, lesser-known works are interspersed with great ones, such as Millet's *The Shepherd Tending His Flock* (1886).

Fourth Floor – Devoted largely to the decorative arts, this floor presents a fascinating collection of **American period rooms**★ ranging from the 17C to the present. The most sumptuous is the Rockefeller smoking room from the 1880s, the sleekest is the art deco Wiel-Worgelt Study, and the simplest is the recently refurbished Jan Martense Schenck House (c.1625), moved here from the Flatlands section of Brooklyn. Also noteworthy are the tremendous Tiffany stained-glass windows outside the elevator and the art nouveau gates by Emile Robert down the hall.

Sharing the fourth floor is the **Elizabeth A. Sackler Center for Feminist Art**★, inaugurated in March 2007. Designed to highlight women's contribution to the art world in the past 40 years, the 8,300sq-ft space contains several large galleries for changing exhibits as well as the massive permanent installation of *The Dinner Party*★, constructed in 1974–79 by artist Judy Chicago and hundreds of volunteers.

The centerpiece of the work is a triangular table measuring 48ft on each side, with a total of 39 place settings for women

Heart of Brooklyn Shuttle

The **HOB Connection** is a free shuttle service linking the Brooklyn Museum with the surrounding neighborhoods during Target First Saturdays (5–11pm, first Saturday of each month). A convenient way to get more out of your visit to Brooklyn, the hop-on, hop-off service features tour guides and discounts and special deals at area restaurants and shops. Late First Saturday opening hours at the Brooklyn Museum make this an appealing evening option. Check the website for updates, and for other HOB Connection routes: www.heartofbrooklyn.org.

across the ages arranged chronologically around the periphery. Each setting is hand-crafted with embroidered runners, napkins, utensils, ceramic chalices and painted china plates sculpted into feminine forms. Among those honored with a place at the table are the Primordial Goddess, Sojourner Truth, Anne Hutchinson, Eleanor of Aquitane and Georgia O'Keeffe. Heritage Panels in an adjoining gallery show Chicago and her research team's effort to build a complete women's history (or *herstory*, as they call it).

Fifth Floor – The Brooklyn Museum has garnered international renown for its collection of **American painting**★★. Major works by almost all the heavyweights are here, from Copley, Cole, Eakins, Homer and Bierstadt to Sargent, Cassatt, Chase, Durand, Saint-Gaudens and Bellows. You'll also find modern works by such well-known artists as Georgia O'Keeffe, Max Weber, Stuart Davis and Marsden Hartley.

With the creation of the Luce Center for American Art in 2001, the museum completely reorganized its display of the collection. The installation American Identities integrates paintings with selected sculptures and decorative artworks to investigate eight themes, among them landscape, the Civil War, the modern world and daily life.

The wall texts explain the juxtapositions, but it's best to have the audio guide to fully appreciate the arrangement. The Visual Storage Study Center, completed in 2004, compactly displays some 1,500 objects from the museum's American collection, organized by type and medium.

AROUND BROOKLYN
Grid letters in parentheses after each attraction's name refer to the map.

Coney Island★ (ABZ)
👤👤 MTA *D, F, N, Q train to Stillwell Ave. (last stop). www.coneyislandusa.com.*
Located at the southern tip of Brooklyn and lapped by the Atlantic Ocean, Coney Island is the city's most famous beach, one that draws subway riders from all parts of the city not just for its plentiful sand but for its ramshackle charm.

Coney Island—the name comes from the Dutch words for Rabbit Island—has long been a place of honky-tonk entertainment, with seedy carnival games and a kitschy burlesque show, a rickety 1927 roller coaster (the Cyclone) and a super-size hot-dog stand (Nathan's Famous). Some are worried that its days are numbered: a developer bought Astroland in 2006 and closed the historic old amusement park at the end of the 2008 season, although The Cyclone roller coaster (a historic landmark) and some of the other attractions remain. The new owner has plans for a modern, year-round amusement park, and although the influx of money has altered the honky-tonk atmosphere to some degree, the Coney Island experience remains one of NYC's summer treasures.

👤👤 Coney Island is a summertime attraction, even if you have no intention of sunning yourself on the beach. The **Cyclone**★★ and the **Wonder Wheel**★★ Ferris wheel are open daily from Memorial Day to Labor Day (weekends only in spring and fall). Summer is also when the **Brooklyn Cyclones**★ minor league baseball team plays at the delightful, 7,500-seat KeySpan Park *(1904*

Coney Island—The Wonder Wheel

©Peter Wrenn/MICHELIN

Surf Ave.; ℘718-449-8497; www.brook lyncyclones.com). More than half a million spectators attend the colorful and risqué **Mermaid Parade**★★, held in late June each year; the **Nathan's Famous Fourth of July International Hot Dog Eating Contest**★ draws about 50,000 iron-stomached fans to see contestants scarf down upward of 60 hot dogs (and buns) in 12 minutes; it's a Coney Island tradition to try at least one for yourself. **Nathan's** *(1310 Surf Ave. at Stillwell Ave.)* and the **New York Aquarium**★★ *(☞see below)* are open year-round.

New York Aquarium★★ (BZ)

👪♿*W. 8th St. & Surf Ave.* 🚇*F, Q train to W 8th St.* 🕐*Open Jun–Aug Mon–Fri10am–6pm, Sat–Sun 10am–7pm; rest of year closing times vary from 4.30pm to 5.30pm. Last entry 45min before closing.* 💲*14.95; $10.95 children 3–12.* 🍴. 🅿*$13.* ℘*718-265-3474. www.nyaquarium.com.*
Opened in 1896 in what is now Castle Clinton National Monument, the aquarium was reputedly the first public aquarium in the US; it moved to the corner of the Coney Island Boardwalk and West 8th Street in 1957. As part of the Wildlife Conservation Society, the aquarium is a top-of-the-line facility that aims to educate as well as entertain in its exhibits and demonstrations.

When you enter, you'll be in the original 1957 Conservation Hall, home to the **Glover's Reef**★ exhibit, a 165,000-gallon tank containing marine life found around that reef in the Caribbean, including moray eels and sharks. Outside the hall is the **Sea Cliffs**★ exhibit, a 300ft-long rocky coast habitat for walrus, sea otters, fur seals and penguins (be sure to check out the underground viewing platform on your way out). Ever popular **sea lion shows**★★ are held in an amphitheater just across the path. **Explore the Shore**, a 20,000sq-ft educational center, features 65 exhibits

Sea turtle at the New York Aquarium

©Sandy Matzen/BigStockPhoto.com

including a 400-gallon wave tank showing subtidal, intertidal and upper tidal zones and a salt marsh simulating the nearby Jamaica Bay wetlands. Next to it is the mesmerizing and otherworldly **Alien Stingers Exhibit**★★, opened in 2002, showcasing dozens of species of sea jellies, corals and anemones from around the world. Consider planning time to see the excellent 4-D Experience attraction *(⊜included in $18.95 Total Experience Ticket or $6 when purchased separately).*

Brooklyn Children's Museum (BX)

👥 ⟨ *145 Brooklyn Ave.* MTA *3 train to Kingston Ave.; cross Eastern Parkway walking north on Kingston (with traffic) to St. Mark's Ave. (6 blocks); turn left on St. Mark's and walk one block to Brooklyn Ave. Museum is on corner.* ⏱*Open Tue–Sun 10am–5pm (call or visit website for seasonal updates).* ⏱*Closed major holidays.* ⊜*$7.50.* ✆*718-735-4400.*
www.brooklynkids.org.

Founded in 1899 in Brower Park, this institution was one of the first museums designed especially for children, and it recently completed an exciting expansion and renovation. Designed by renowned Uruguayan architect Rafael Viñoly, a bright yellow L-shaped addition wraps around the four-story building the museum has occupied since 1977, doubling exhibit space to 100,000sq ft.

In addition the entire structure was retrofitted with a geothermal heating and cooling system, as well as solar panels for energy, making it the first "green" museum in Brooklyn. Rare among children's museums, this one maintains a permanent collection of cultural and natural history objects, many of which appear in interactive, hands-on exhibits covering cultural and natural history, the sciences and the performing arts. The museum also offers a full slate of family workshops and special performances year-round.

Brooklyn Academy of Music★ (BX)

⟨ *30 Lafayette Ave. Check the website for a listing of events.* ✖. ⊡ ✆*718-636-4100. www.bam.org.*

The Brooklyn Academy of Music (BAM) is widely regarded as New York's premier venue for avant-garde performance, and a wealth of new programming in recent years ensures BAM's continued vibrancy. Founded in 1859, it is the city's oldest continually operating performing arts center. After its original Brooklyn Heights premises burned down in 1907, it moved to its Fort Greene home. Behind its imposing brick Beaux-Arts facade lies an elegant 1,100-seat opera house that has hosted Enrico Caruso, Isadora Duncan, Arturo Toscanini, Paul Robeson and, more recently, Philip Glass, Laurie Anderson, and the Merce Cunningham Dance Company; bely-

Brooklyn Children's Museum

©Ron Chapple Studios/Dreamstime.com

Just the Facts

The Verrazano-Narrows Bridge has a total length of 6,690ft. The main span between the towers rises 690ft above water, allowing the largest ocean liner to pass under it, and extends 4,260ft. The main cables are 3ft in diameter. The bridge supports two levels for car traffic—six lanes each—but no sidewalk for pedestrians. Ironically, its most famous moment each year is as the starting point of the New York City Marathon *(first Sun in Nov)*, when runners fill both levels of the bridge before setting off on their 26.2mi journey through the five boroughs.

ing its old-fashioned appearance, its technical capabilities and acoustics are first rate. A second venue, the 900-seat Harvey Theater (formerly the Majestic), is located a block and a half away at 651 Fulton Street and is home to the Brooklyn Philharmonic Orchestra. In addition to live performances, BAM has daily film screenings of classic and foreign films—part of its Cinematheque series—and new art-house fare.

Verrazano-Narrows Bridge★★ (AZ)

Toll: ☞$13 per car, paid only on westbound crossing.
The spiderweb silhouette of the Verrazano-Narrows Bridge, the longest suspension bridge in the US, links Brooklyn to Staten Island above the Narrows (the entrance to New York Harbor).
The bridge bears the name of Italian explorer Giovanni da Verrazano, a Florentine merchant in the service of French king François I who discovered the site of New York in 1524. At the

Brooklyn entrance to the bridge stands a monument composed in part of stones from the castle of Verrazzano in Tuscany, and from the beach of Dieppe, the French port from which the pilot sailed. The Triborough Bridge and Tunnel Authority began work on the bridge in January 1959, and on November 21, 1964, the bridge was inaugurated in the presence of Govenor Nelson Rockefeller and the bridge's engineer, O.H. Amman, who also designed the George Washington Bridge.

Shore Parkway★ (ACXZ)

This pleasant drive follows the shoreline from Bay Ridge all the way to Queens and John F. Kennedy Airport, affording successive views of the Verrazano-Narrows Bridge and Staten Island, the Rockaways and Jamaica Bay. On bright sunny days when clear visibility extends across the glittering water, Shore Parkway offers a refreshing respite from the bustle of Manhattan.

Named after the wife of Charles II of England, Catherine of Braganza (1630–85), Queens is the largest borough of New York City. Situated on Long Island north and east of Brooklyn, it extends from the East River in the north to Jamaica Bay and the Atlantic Ocean in the south, with a long east–west finger of land—the Rockaways—enclosing Jamaica Bay. Home to both of the city's major airports—JFK and LaGuardia—it is a borough in which nearly half of its residents are foreign-born. Hispanics and Asians are the fastest-growing ethnic groups in Queens.

Area: 112 square miles
▶ **Population:**
  2,230,722 (2010)

A Bit of History

In 1642 a Dutch settlement was founded at Maspeth, but it was not until 1645 that Queens' first permanent settlement, at Vlissingen (Flushing), was established. Clashes between English and Dutch settlers over freedom of worship marked the borough's early years. In 1662 the Dutch arrested John Bowne for allowing Quaker gatherings in his home. Bowne appealed his case, paving the way for religious freedom in the colonies.

Until the mid-19C, Queens remained a sparsely populated neighborhood of small villages and farms. As New York City blossomed, urbanization of Queens accelerated, attracting successive waves of German and Irish immigrants. By the end of the 19C, when Queens became incorporated into New York City as a borough, some 150,000 people lived here. In the 1920s Queens attracted the silent film industry, which operated some 20 studios in Astoria before relocating to sunny Hollywood. On the heels of the 1939 World's Fair, the borough developed a reputation as a haven for sports and recreation, an image it retains today as the home of the USTA Billie Jean King National Tennis Center and Citi Field, which replaced the Shea Stadium as the home of the New York Mets.

The 1970s witnessed the development of an active political machine; from its ranks rose Mario Cuomo, governor of New York from 1982 to 1994. In the past

Houses in Queens

The Noguchi Museum

Bill Taylor/The Noguchi Museum, New York

decade Queens has become the city's most ethnically diverse borough, with a sizable community of Indian and Pakistani immigrants in Jackson Heights, a large Chinatown in Flushing and growing numbers of Hispanics throughout. Culturally the borough is best known for the P.S.1 (a MoMA affiliate), the Museum of the Moving Image and The Noguchi, all in western Queens within easy access to Midtown Manhattan.

AROUND QUEENS

Grid letters in parentheses after each attraction's name refer to the map.

The Noguchi Museum★★ (AX)

9–01 33rd Rd. at Vernon Blvd. (♿entrance on 33rd Rd between 9th & 10th Sts.). **MTA** *N, Q train to Broadway station in Queens; walk 10 blocks west toward Manhattan; turn left on Vernon Blvd.; pass Socrates Sculpture Park office; walk 2 blocks to 33rd Rd. On Sun, a shuttle bus for the museum (👜$10 round-trip) departs from Park Ave. at 70th St. in Manhattan (in front of the Asia Society) at 12.30pm, 1.30pm, 2.30pm, 3.30pm; the trip takes 30min. ⏱Open year-round Wed–Fri 10am–5pm, Sat–Sun 11am–6pm. ⏱Closed Jan 1, Thanksgiving Day & Dec 25. 👜$10; pay-what-you -wish first Fri of each month). ✕. ☎718-204-7088. www.noguchi.org.*

Conflicting and harmonious relationships between nature and the man-

made are a recurrent theme in the sculpture of **Isamu Noguchi** (1904–88), the renowned Japanese-American artist whose works include public spaces (Detroit's Hart Plaza), playgrounds (Atlanta's Playscapes), gardens and fountains. In addition to works in stone, terracotta, wood and metal, Noguchi created ethereal-looking akari light sculptures; he also designed stage sets for choreographers Martha Graham and George Balanchine.

Founded in 1985 in a former warehouse space by Noguchi himself, the museum underwent extensive renovation in mid-2004. Today, the complex consists of an outdoor sculpture garden and a two-story, 27,000sq-ft building with 10 indoor galleries, an education center, a cafe and a museum shop. The ground floor displays a permanent presentation of Noguchi's works selected from his personal collection; the upper floor features rotating exhibits relating to his work. The museum shop showcases many of the artist's interior designs, including furniture and lamps.

Museum for African Art★ (AY)

36–01 43rd Ave. at 36th St. **MTA** *7 local train to 33rd St. Station; walk east to 36th St., then left one block to 43rd Ave. ⚠This exhibition space is closed; call or check the website for location and hours of traveling shows. ☎718-784-7700. www.africanart.org.*

295

Since opening as the Center for African Art in 1984, the museum has mounted dozens of major shows exploring Africa's artistic traditions and cultural heritage. And finally, after years of hopping from one neighborhood to the next, it is getting a permanent home.

Governor Eliot Spitzer and other notables were on hand on September 24, 2007, for the ground-breaking ceremony at 1280 Fifth Avenue (at E. 110th St.) in Manhattan, where the museum will set up shop inside a new condominium tower designed by Robert A.M. Stern (&see location on Upper Manhattan map, p192). Projected date of completion is late 2012. The museum is curating exhibitions in a variety of locations throughout the city in the meantime; check the website for schedule and construction updates.

Museum of the Moving Image★ (AX)

👥♿ 36–01 35th Ave. at 36th St. in Astoria. MTA M, R train to Steinway St.; walk south on Steinway St. to 35th Ave; turn right and proceed 3 blocks to museum (note: M train does not run on Sat–Sun). ⏰Open Tue–Thu 10.30am–5pm, Fri 10.30am–8pm, Sat–Sun 10.30am–7pm. ⏰Closed Jul 4, Thanksgiving Day & Dec 25. ⊛$10; free Fri 4–8pm. ✕. ☎718-777-6688. www.movingimage.us.

Located on the former site of the Astoria Film Studios (built by Paramount Pictures in the 1920s), this unique museum is devoted to the history, technology and the art of film, television and digital media. The 130,000-piece collection encompasses portrait and scene-still photographs, special effects materials and production equipment; costumes, props and memorabilia from the television and film industries; and clips from movies, videos and advertisements. The museum is especially fun for kids, as visitors are invited to make their own short animations, experiment with sound effects, or dub their voices into a famous movie.

Occupying 15,000sq-feet of the museum's second and third floors, the fascinating core exhibit **Behind the Screen** highlights the history of the moving image and features interactive exhibits detailing the creative and technical process of making film, television, and digital entertainment. A major three-year expansion and renovation of the museum was completed in 2011.

MoMA P.S.1★ (AY)

22–25 Jackson Ave. at 46th Ave. MTA 7 train to 45th Rd.-Court House Sq. ⏰Open year-round Thu–Mon noon–6pm. ⏰Closed Jan 1, Thanksgiving Day & Dec 25. ⊛$10 contribution requested; free with MoMA ticket if presented within 30 days of purchase. ✕. ☎718-784-2084. www.ps1.org.

Housed in a gigantic former public school building only 10min by subway

Lobby, Museum of the Moving Image

© Peter Aaron/Esto. Courtesy of Museum of the Moving Image

MoMA PS1

Matthew Septimus/MoMA PS1

from Manhattan, this MoMA affiliate is one of the city's most exciting contemporary art centers.

A kind of mega-gallery, the five-story facility can hold up to 10 shows at a time, with plenty of space for large-scale work. There are also a few interesting site-specific works scattered about, by artists such as James Turrell, Richard Serra and William Kentridge.

Summer's a particularly fun time to visit, as that's when the courtyard is filled by an installation by the winner of its Young Architects Program and when the popular **Warm-Up** dance party takes place (🕐 *open Jul–Aug Sat 2–9pm;* 💲*$15 admission includes exhibitions*).

Jamaica Bay Wildlife Refuge (CZ)

MTA *A train to Broad Channel. From the subway, take Noel Rd. to Cross Bay Blvd. and turn right (.8mi); a visitor center is on the left* (🕐 *open daily 9am–5pm;* 🕐 *closed Jan 1, Thanksgiving Day & Dec 25). Access also via Q53 bus (ask to be let off at visitor center).* 🕐 *Open year-round daily dawn–dusk.* 🅿️ . ☎*718-318-4340. www.nps.gov/gate.*

Located just south of JFK Airport, this peaceful wildlife refuge is a major migratory haven for birds, attracting a wide variety of waterfowl and land and shore birds. It forms part of the Gateway National Recreation Area, one of the nation's largest urban parks.

A self-guided **nature trail**★ through the marshes affords pleasant views of the skyline to the west *(1.8mi; 1.5hrs; request free permit at the visitor center).* Farther south on Cross Bay Boulevard, beachfront communities dot the five miles of **Rockaway Beach**★ *(access from* MTA *A train at stations between 25th & 116th Sts.).* On sunny days, you can stroll the boardwalk and enjoy the breeze. For great views, start at Beach 116th Street

Astoria

Though there aren't as many Greeks living in this friendly neighborhood as there were a few decades ago, Astoria is still well known throughout New York City for its Greek food. Dripping with honey and soaked in butter, the baklava at **Omonia** *(32–20 Broadway;* ☎*718-274-6650; www. omoniacafe.com)* is some of the freshest you'll ever taste.

A local institution, **Uncle George's** *(33–19 Broadway;* ☎*718-626-0593)* is a 24hr family-friendly Greek diner where you can get a huge meal—the rotisserie chicken with lemon potatoes is a specialty— with wine for well under $20.

Taverna Kyclades *(33–07 Ditmars Blvd.;* ☎*718-545-8666)* packs them in with its simply prepared grilled seafood and family-style portions.

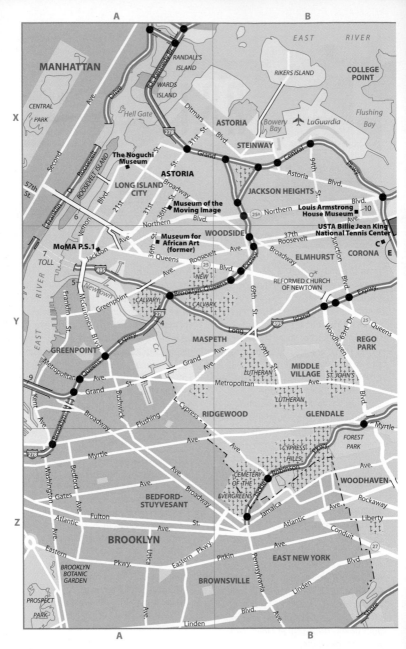

MANHATTAN

CENTRAL PARK

X

57th St.

The Noguchi Museum

LONG ISLAND CITY

MoMA P.S.1

Y

GREENPOINT

Z

BROOKLYN

BROOKLYN BOTANIC GARDEN

PROSPECT PARK

EAST RIVER

RANDALL'S ISLAND

WARDS ISLAND

Hell Gate

ROOSEVELT ISLAND

ASTORIA

Museum of the Moving Image

Museum for African Art (former)

NEW CALVARY

CALVARY

MASPETH

LUTHERAN

LUTHERAN

RIDGEWOOD

BEDFORD-STUYVESANT

EAST RIVER

RIKERS ISLAND

ASTORIA

STEINWAY

JACKSON HEIGHTS

WOODSIDE

Roosevelt

ELMHURST

REFORMED CHURCH OF NEWTOWN

MIDDLE VILLAGE

ST. JOHN'S

GLENDALE

CYPRESS HILLS

CEMETERY OF THE EVERGREENS

BROWNSVILLE

EAST NEW YORK

EAST RIVER

COLLEGE POINT

Flushing Bay

LaGuardia

Bowery Bay

Louis Armstrong House Museum

USTA Billie Jean King National Tennis Center

CORONA

REGO PARK

Queens

FOREST PARK

WOODHAVEN

Myrtle

(end of the Rockaway Park subway spur) and head in either direction.

Flushing (CX)

MTA 7 train to Main St.
Call or see websites for directions to sights listed below.

Now known for its enormous East Asian (predominantly Chinese and Korean) population, nearly half its residents, Flushing started in 1645 as a small Dutch settlement named Vlissingen.

In 1657 the town rejected Governor Peter Stuyvesant's demand that they

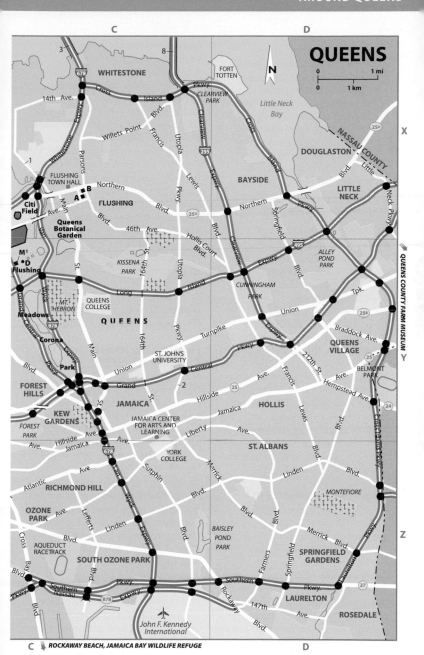

C   ROCKAWAY BEACH, JAMAICA BAY WILDLIFE REFUGE

expel "Quakers, Papists, Jews, Turks and other heretics," thus becoming the first US municipality to guarantee religious freedom to all residents and visitors.

At 137–15 Northern Boulevard stands the old **Flushing Town Hall**, a Romanesque Revival building (1862) that has been restored to its original appearance and now hosts art exhibits and concerts in the 308-seat theater on its first floor (*galleries open year-round Sat–Sun noon–5pm; $5 suggested admission;* 718-463-7700; www.flushingtownhall.com).

"Over the great bridge, with the sunlight through the girders making a constant flicker upon the moving cars, with the city rising up across the river in white heaps and sugar lumps all built with a wish out of non-olfactory money. The city seen from the Queensboro Bridge is always the city seen for the first time, in its first wild promise of all the mystery and the beauty in the world."

F. Scott Fitzgerald
from *The Great Gatsby* (1926)

Bowne House (CX A)

37–01 Bowne St. ⊘*Closed for renovation; call or check website for hours & updates.* ℘*718-359-0528. www.bownehouse.org.*

Though they were persecuted elsewhere, Quakers, or the Society of Friends, found a home in Flushing. But not without a struggle. John Bowne, an Englishman who settled in Flushing, was arrested for allowing Quakers to hold meetings in his home but was ultimately acquitted. The oldest structure in Queens, this house (1661) was inhabited by nine successive generations of Bownes and contains a collection of 17C and 18C furniture as well as pewter, paintings and documents.

Kingsland Homestead (CX B)

143–35 37th Ave. ⊙*Open Mon–Fri 9.30am–5.30pm.* ⟲ *Tour by appointment.* ⊘*Closed major holidays.* 🅿. ℘*718-939-0647. www.queens historicalsociety.org.*

Constructed in c.1785, this two-and-a-half-story edifice presents a mix of Dutch and English traditions; note in particular the divided front door and central chimney. The former farmhouse now serves as the headquarters of the Queens Historical Society and houses the local history museum (⊙*open year-round Tue & Sat–Sun 2.30–4.30pm;* ⊛*$3).* The homestead stands in a small park in Flushing next to the remains of a Weeping Beech tree that was planted in 1847; until its death in 1998 it was one of only two living official city landmarks.

Queens Botanical Garden (CXY)

43–50 Main St . ⊙*Open Apr–Oct Tue–Sun 8am–6pm; rest of year Tue–Sun 8am–4.30pm, holiday Mondays.* ⊘*Closed major holidays.* ⊛*$4; free Wed 3–6pm, Sun 4–6pm Apr–Oct & all times Nov–Mar.* 🅿*$5.* ℘*718-886-3800. www.queensbotanical.org.*

Literally growing out of a garden for the 1939–40 World's Fair, the Queens Botanical Garden now sprawls over 39 acres, comprising a bee garden, a rose garden, a fragrance garden, woodlands, a compost biotope and oak allée, and many other discrete sections, for an engaging look at the world of plants. In October 2007 a new visitor center opened, then the most environmentally friendly building in the city with its planted green roof, solar panels, geothermal heating and cooling system, and compost toilets.

Flushing Meadows Corona Park (BCXY)

www.nycparks.gov.

Once a swamp favored by ducks and then a sanitary landfill—F. Scott Fitzgerald famously called it a "valley of ashes" in *The Great Gatsby*— this 1,275-acre park was developed in the 1930s to accommodate New York's first World's Fair (1939–40).

Designs for the park included the creation of **Meadow Lake**, measuring .8mi in length, and the New York City Building, which housed the United Nations General Assembly between 1946 and 1949 and now contains the **Queens Museum of Art**.

A second World's Fair in 1964–65 brought the **New York Hall of Science** and Queens' most distinctive work of art, the **Unisphere (D)**, a 140ft-tall steel globe encircled with atomic-age rings. That said, the park's most popular attractions are no doubt **Citi Field**, home of the New York Mets baseball team, and the **USTA Billie Jean King National Tennis Center**, where the US Open tournament is held each year over the course of two weeks in late summer.

Queens Museum of Art (CY M1)

In the New York City Building (located next to the Unisphere). MTA 7 train to Willets Point; follow signs to museum. Open year-round Wed–Sun noon–6pm. Closed major holidays. $5 suggested donation. 718-592-9700. www.queensmuseum.org. Originally conceived as an arts center for the borough of Queens, the museum today features 20C and contemporary art exhibitions with a diverse global outlook. Don't miss the highlight—the **Panorama of New York City★★**, a spectacular architectural model of New York City built for the 1964–65 World's Fair at a scale of 1in to 100ft. The model was updated in 1992 and again in 2006. Covering more than 9,335sq ft, it contains an unbelievable 895,000 buildings in addition to parks and other features. The history of the New York City Building is recounted through photographs and other memorabilia. Another gallery in the museum presents a rotating selection of **Tiffany glass**.

New York Hall of Science (BY C)

47–01 111th St., western edge of park. Open Apr–Jun Mon–Thu 9.30am–2pm, Fri 9.30am–5pm, Sat–Sun 10am–6pm; Jul–Aug Mon–Fri 9.30am–5pm, Sat–Sun 10am–6pm; rest of year Tue–Thu 9.30am–2pm, Fri 9.30–5pm, Sat–Sun 10am–6pm. Closed Labor Day, Thanksgiving Day & Dec 25. $11; $8 children 2–17. $10;$14 during New York Mets home games. 718-699-0005. www.nysci.org. Though built for the 1964–65 World's Fair, this museum of science and technology has done a stand-up job of staying up to date, with 400 hands-on exhibits exploring all branches of science. Expanded in 2007, the 60,000sq-ft **Science Playground** now has plenty for preschool-age children to do, like playing in sandboxes, banging on drums and crawling through mazes. Other exhibits include The World of Microbes, where you can gawk at live organisms through a microscope, a hall full of interactive exhibits about the science behind sports and the massive new **Marvelous Molecules★**, which explores the shared chemistry of all living things.

Queens Zoo (BCY E)

53–51 111th St., adjacent to Hall of Science. Open Apr–Oct Mon–Fri 10am–5pm, Sat–Sun & holidays 10am–5.30pm; rest of year daily 10am–4.30pm. $8; $5 children 3–12. 718-271-1500. www.queenszoo.com. The Queens Zoo, formerly the Flushing Meadows Zoo, is run by the Wildlife Conservation Society, and as befits that esteemed organization (which also runs the Bronx Zoo, the New York Aquarium and two other city zoos), it is a clean, humane place for animals and an entertaining and informative place for children and adults. Unlike the other zoos in the city, here you'll find only creatures from the Americas, in naturalistic environments. From **North America**, you'll find American bison, mountain lions, California sea lions *(feedings daily at 11.15am, 2pm, 4pm)*, American bald eagles, Roosevelt elk and a coyote named Otis who was mysteriously discovered in and rescued from Central Park in 1999. From **South America**, you'll find spectacled bears and thick-billed parrots. There's also a **petting zoo** with domestic animals. The aviary, a geodesic dome, was designed by Buckminster Fuller and used in the 1964–65 World's Fair in Queens.

Citi Field (CX)

MTA 7 train to Mets-Willets Pt. 718-507-8499 (tickets). www.mets.com. The New York Mets' gleaming new stadium (2009) replaced beloved Shea Stadium, the team's home since 1964. A game ticket gets you past the red brick facade (intended to evoke historic Ebbets Field) to the sparkling new amenities and fun spots like the FanFest amusement area (open for games).

Louis Armstrong House Museum★ (BX)

34–56 107th St., Corona. MTA 7 train to 103rd St./Corona Plaza; walk north on 104th St., turn right onto 37th Ave (not Dr.) & left on 107th St. Visit

Living Room, Louis Armstrong House Museum

©Lisa Kahane/Louis Armstrong House Museum

by guided tour (40min) only, year-round Tue–Fri 10am–5pm, Sat–Sun noon–5pm. Tours begin on the hour and are limited to 8 people. Closed Jan 1, Thanksgiving Day, Dec 24, Dec 25 & Dec 31. $8. 212-478-8274. www. louisarmstronghouse.org.

Located in a residential section of Corona, Queens, not far from Citi Field, this two-story, red-brick house was home to jazz great Louis Armstrong from 1943 until his death in 1971. After the death of Armstrong's wife Lucille in 1983, the property came into the hands of the city. In September 2003, the house opened to the public as a museum.

The house—furnishings, personal effects and all—provides a window into the domestic life of Louis Armstrong and reveals one of America's most important musical artists as modest, fun-loving and unpretentious.

An extraordinary time capsule of post-World War II decoration, the interior represents the work and taste of Lucille and her decorator—who show a predilection for beiges, creams and textured wallpapers. Though Louis was on the road up to 300 days a year, his presence can be clearly felt here. He recorded more than 1,000 hours of his home life on his ever-present reel-to-reel tape players. Snippets from the tapes are played during the tour; in the dining room, you'll hear Armstrong riff on Brussels sprouts as he eats his dinner.

The museum's entrance and gift shop are built into the house's ground-level garage, as is a changing exhibit of items from the Louis Armstrong Archives.

Queens County Farm Museum (DY)

73–50 Little Neck Pkwy., Floral Park. Take Long Island Expwy. to Exit 32; continue south on Little Neck Pkwy. (10 blocks to museum entrance). MTA E, F train to Kew Gardens, then Q46 bus to Little Neck Pkwy.; walk north 3 blocks. Open year-round Mon–Fri 10am– 5pm (outdoor visits only), Sat–Sun 10am–5pm (farmhouse & greenhouse open). Closed major holidays. Free parking available. 718-347-3276. www.queensfarm.org.

This 47-acre farm—New York City's only historical farm—provides an informative glimpse of Queens County's agrarian origins and a welcome respite from the urban sprawl. Anchoring the property is an 18C Flemish-style farmhouse with its original furniture (*visit by 30min guided tour only, Sat–Sun 11am–4pm*). Greenhouses brim with plants, and farm implements are on display.

The museum is especially fun for children, with its petting zoo, hayrides *(Sat–Sun, weather permitting)* and fall corn maze *(Sept–Oct)*.

STATEN ISLAND

Measuring about 14mi long by 8mi wide, Staten Island still has a relatively rural look, with some 2,800 acres of forest, meadow and wetlands preserved as part of the Staten Island Greenbelt. Linked to Brooklyn by the Verrazano-Narrows Bridge, to New Jersey by no fewer than three bridges, and to Downtown Manhattan by the delightful (and free) Staten Island Ferry, the borough nonetheless stands apart from the urban hubbub with its decidedly suburban feel. It's home to a large number of the city's firefighters and municipal workers, and to several interesting attractions that merit a stop.

Staten Island's Alias

Dutch merchants passing through here in the early 1600s named Staten Island after the Dutch States General. But the island acquired another name: Richmond, which honors the Duke of Richmond, brother of Charles II, king of England. Be sure to visit Historic Richmond Town.

Area: 60 square miles
▶ **Population:** 481,613

A Bit of History

The first permanent settlement was established at Oude Dorp by Dutch and French Huguenot families in 1661. Over the next two centuries the island thrived on farming and agriculture, ferrying goods to Manhattan and New Jersey. After integration with the other boroughs in 1898, Staten Island grew considerably, attracting hardworking immigrants to its farms and factories and hard-playing society folk to its resort hotels. The boom went bust after World War I, when many residents left to make their fortunes on the mainland. The borough blossomed once again when the Verrazano-Narrows Bridge opened in 1964, bringing an influx of Manhattanites seeking to escape the bustle of New York. Today Staten Island is primarily a bedroom community, culturally and economically related more to New Jersey than to New York. But it does have a number of attractions—art, history and nature—that merit exploration if you have the time.

Staten Island Ferry

© Christian Heeb/hemis.fr

AROUND STATEN ISLAND

Map opposite. Grid letters in parentheses after each attraction's name refer to the map.

To visit the sights below, you can take buses from the ferry terminal at St. George or, in some cases, the Staten Island Rapid Transit (SIRT).

Staten Island Ferry★

👤🧍♿ *Ferry departs from Whitehall Terminal off Whitehall St. in Lower Manhattan for the St. George Ferry Terminal on Staten Island, year-round daily 24hrs/day about every 30min (hourly midnight–6am). 25min.* ✆*Free (no cars allowed on ferry).* ✖🅿. *For schedule, dial ☎311 (outside New York City, ☎212-NEW-YORK). www.siferry.com.*

Any visit to New York should include a ride on the Staten Island Ferry. On the windy voyage, which covers 5mi and takes about 25min, the ferry skirts the Statue of Liberty, giving passengers magnificent **views★★★** of Manhattan and the bay. The ferry that was the start of Cornelius "Commodore" Vanderbilt's fortune now runs night and day, transporting some 20 million passengers a year, many of them commuters.

St. George (BY)

Facing Lower Manhattan across the bay, this small town is surrounded by suburban homes and gardens. In the 1850s, in the waters near St. George, quarantine was imposed on ships arriving from overseas. St. George has been the seat of the county and borough government since 1920. In 2005, the St. George terminal building reopened after a two-year renovation, sporting a 40ft-tall glass viewing wall, shops and outdoor plaza.

Staten Island Museum (BY|)

👤🧍 *75 Stuyvesant Pl. From the Staten Island ferry terminal walk 1 block west to Wall St.; turn left on Wall St. and walk 2 blocks to the museum.* 🕐*Open Sun–Fri noon–5pm, Sat 10am–5pm.* 🕐*Closed major holidays.* ✆*$3; free children under 12. ☎718-727-1135. www.statenislandmuseum.org.*

Founded in 1881, the Staten Island Institute of Arts and Sciences, the island's oldest cultural institution, runs this museum exploring the history, art and ecology of the island. A small exhibit explores the history of the Staten Island ferry line through photographs, ships' wheels, whistles and other artifacts as well as elaborate scale models. Another describes the Lenape Indians, "the first Staten Islanders." You can buy ferry souvenirs and nautical art in the well-stocked museum store.

Alice Austen House Museum★ (BY; A)

♿ *2 Hylan Blvd. From the Staten Island ferry terminal take S51 bus to Hylan Blvd. (a 15min ride), then walk one block east to water and house.* 🕐*Open Mar–Dec Thu–Sun noon–5pm.* 🕐*Closed major holidays.* ✆*$2. ☎718-816-4506. www.aliceausten.org.*

One of the few accomplished woman photographers of her day, **Alice Austen** (1866–1952) captured turn-of-the-19C life in New York City, from exclusive society gatherings to poignant scenes of immigrant life. The picturesque Victorian cottage where Austen lived most of her life was constructed in 1690, and was dubbed "Clear Comfort" by her mother. The cottage fell into disrepair after Austen's death, but was restored according to her photographs, and today serves as a charming museum of her life and work. Changing exhibits feature prints from her glass-plate negatives, as well as shows of work by other photographers. Trimmed in gingerbread, the porch affords superb **views★★** of the harbor and Manhattan in the distance.

Snug Harbor Cultural Center & Botanical Garden★ (BY)

♿ *1000 Richmond Terrace. From the Staten Island ferry terminal take S40 bus to Snug Harbor (about a 10min ride).* 🕐*Grounds open daily dawn–dusk; see hours for individual sights below.* 🕐*Closed Jan 1, Thanksgiving Day & Dec 25.* 👥*Guided tours available.* ✆*$6 includes visitor center, Newhouse galleries and Chinese scholar's garden.* ✖🅿.

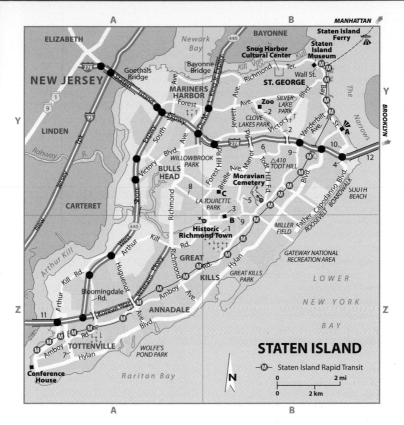

STATEN ISLAND

—Ⓜ— Staten Island Rapid Transit

0   2 mi

0   2 km

𝄞 718-448-2500. www.snug-harbor.org.
Founded in 1801 as the first maritime hospital and retired sailors' home in the US, the 83-acre park and its 28 buildings are being restored and converted to a center for the visual and performing arts. The complex also hosts a number of lovely gardens, a children's museum and performance spaces.

Eleanor Proske Visitors' Center –
♿Ⓒ*Open Wed–Sun noon–5pm.*
Snug Harbor's oldest building. A prime example of 1830s Greek Revival architecture with its restored ceiling mural, punctuated by a skylit dome.

Newhouse Center for Contemporary Art – *Main Hall, Building C.*
♿Ⓒ*Open Wed–Sun noon–5pm.* ⚌*$3.*
Staten Island's premier spot for contemporary art, the center mounts exhibits in 15,000sq. ft of gallery space as well as creating a home for 30 artists' studios.

Noble Maritime Collection –
Building D. ♿Ⓒ*Open Thu–Sun 1–5pm.*

Ⓒ*Closed major holidays.* ⚌*$5.* 𝄞*718-447-6490. www.noblemaritime.org.*
The museum examines the life and work of John A. Noble, a French-born maritime artist who established a floating houseboat studio in a "boneyard" of old boats nearby. Exhibits include examples of his writing and artwork, his houseboat studio, ship models and a model dormitory room.

Botanical Garden – ♿Ⓒ*Open winter Tue–Sun 10am–4pm; summer Tue–Sun 10am–5pm.* ⚌*$5.* ✕ 🄿. 𝄞*718-425-3500.*
A stroll through this lovely garden reveals a perennial garden, a herb and

---

😊 A Bit of Advice 😊

For the best views from the ferry from Manhattan to Staten Island, sit on the right side of the boat. You'll get a fairly close view of the Statue of Liberty and Ellis Island.

Old Bermuda Inn Restaurant

301 Veteran's Rd. West. ℰ718-948-7600. www.theoldbermudainn.com.
This stately 1830 Victorian mansion-turned-restaurant has five working fireplaces, museum-quality antiques, oil portraits of old Staten Island families and even a friendly ghost (allegedly the former mistress of the house, Martha Mesereau, waiting for her husband to return from the Civil War). Though it's better known for its atmosphere than for its cuisine, the Old Bermuda Inn does turn out a moist crab cake and hosts a popular Sunday buffet brunch. Call ahead: the place is sometimes fully booked for private parties, especially on weekends.

butterfly garden designed to attract these colorful insects, and a greenhouse sheltering orchids and other tropicals. The enclosed Chinese Scholar's garden captures the essence of Chinese landscape painting. A Secret Garden and the new Tuscan Garden round out the international approach.

Staten Island Children's Museum –
👥👶♿🕐*Open Jul–Aug Tue–Sun 10am–5pm; rest of year Tue–Sun noon–5pm (schedule follows public school calendar, open school holiday Mondays).* 🕐*Closed major holidays.* ⊛*$6 (check website for free days).* ✕🅿. ℰ*718-273-2060. www.statenislandkids.org.*
Interactive exhibits, creative workshops and field trips encourage children to learn by doing. Most activities are designed for children between the ages of 2 and 10.

Staten Island Zoo (BY)

👥👶♿*614 Broadway. From the Staten Island ferry terminal take S48 bus to Forest Ave. & Broadway. Turn left on Broadway and walk 3.5 blocks.* 🕐*Open year-round daily 10am–4.45pm.* 🕐*Closed Jan 1, Thanksgiving Day & Dec 25.* ⊛*$8; $5 children 3–14, free under 3 (free Wed after 2pm).* ✕🅿. ℰ*718-442-3100. www.statenislandzoo.org.*
Located in Barrett Park, this small zoo, is especially known for its comprehensive collection of snakes and reptiles, housed in new facilities. Other residents include leopard tortoise, mandrill, meerkat, ring-tailed lemur, red panda and North American river otter.

Jacques Marchais Museum of Tibetan Art★ (BZ; B)

338 Lighthouse Ave. From the Staten Island ferry terminal take S74 bus to Lighthouse Ave.; turn right and walk up the hill. 🕐*Open spring–summer Wed–Sun 1–5pm; fall–winter Thu–Sun, 1–5pm.* 🕐*Closed major holidays.* ☚*Guided tours available.* ⊛*$6. ℰ718-987-3500. www.tibetanmuseum.org.*
Laid out on Lighthouse Hill in enchanting terraced gardens, the museum displays a rare collection of art covering the culture, religion and mythology of Tibet, Nepal, China, Mongolia and India. The museum buildings were constructed to resemble a small Buddhist mountain temple. Highlights of the collection include an authentic three-tiered Buddhist altar and a large Tibetan thangka, or scroll painting, depicting the Green Tara, goddess of universal compassion. The thangka, which was painted in the 17C, has been painstakingly restored by Tibetan artist Pema Wangyal using only traditional techniques and materials.

Staten Island Greenbelt (BY; C)

Nature Center: 700 Rockland Ave. at Brielle Ave. From the Staten Island ferry terminal take S62 bus to Bradley Ave. Transfer to S57 bus, which will take you to the Brielle and Rockland Ave. stop. Cross the street at the light. 🕐*Open Apr–Oct Tue–Sun 10am–5pm; Nov–Mar Wed–Sun 11am–5pm.* 🅿. ℰ*718-351-3450. www.sigreenbelt.org.*
This 2,800-acre forest preserve is a secret gem for nature enthusiasts, with more than 30 miles of trails, including

some moderately difficult ones to the summit of Todt Hill, the highest point on the Atlantic coast south of Maine. Start your visit at the Greenbelt Nature Center; which has exhibits on the ecology of the park, trail maps, and restrooms, and sponsors a variety of special programs. You can also get maps and access trails at the High Rock Park office (200 Nevada Ave.), which anchors a 90-acre forest tract. An 18-hole golf course and a replica early-20C carousel round out the greenbelt's offerings.

Voorlezer's House

Staten Island Historical Society

Historic Richmond Town★ (ABZ)

👤🚻♿ 441 Clarke Ave. From the Staten Island ferry terminal, take S74 bus to Richmond Rd./St. Patrick's Pl. ⏰Open Jul–Aug Wed–Sun 11am–5pm; rest of year Wed–Sun 1–5pm. ⏰Closed Jan 1, Easter Sunday, Thanksgiving Day & Dec 25. 👥Guided tours available Wed–Fri 2.30pm , Sat–Sun 2pm, 3.30pm. ⚹$5; $3.50 children 5–17. ✕🅿. 🖉718-351-1611. www.historicrichmondtown.org.

Richmond was originally a crossroads settlement among the scattered farms of Staten Island. Interpreting life from the 17C to the 19C, this 25-acre living history museum is located on the site of one of the earliest settlements on Staten Island. Thirty original structures make up the town, including private dwellings, craft shops, a schoolhouse and municipal buildings. Staff members dressed in period costumes reenact everyday chores, and artisans occasionally demonstrate the crafts of yesteryear. You may buy tickets to the village at the visitor center, housed in the **County Courthouse**, an imposing Greek Revival structure from 1837. Highlights include the late-17C **Voorlezer's House**, reputedly the oldest elementary school in the US, and the mid-18C **Guyon-Lake-Tysen House**, where domestic skills such as spinning and weaving are demonstrated.

Moravian Cemetery (BY)

2205 Richmond Rd. From the Staten Island ferry terminal, take S74 bus to Richmond Rd./Todt Hill Rd. or SIRT to Grant City, then walk west down Greeley Ave. to Richmond Rd. ⏰Open daily 8am–6.30pm. 🖉718-351-0136. www.moraviancemetery.com.

This peaceful, garden-like cemetery is affiliated with the Moravian church. Adorned with a columned portico, the white church was built in 1845 by the Vanderbilt family, one of whose ancestors belonged to the sect in the 17C. The original 1763 Dutch Colonial-style church is now the cemetery office. Ascetic in its beliefs, the Moravian denomination was founded in the 15C as an evangelical community in Bohemia (Moravia), and adhered to strict observance of Biblical teachings.

Conference House (AZ)

7455 Hylan Blvd. From Staten Island ferry terminal take S78 bus to Craig. Ave.; walk 1 block south to Satterlee, cross street and enter park. ⏰Open Apr–mid-Dec Fri–Sun 1–4pm. ⚹$3. 🖉718-984-6046. www.conferencehouse.org.

Situated at the southwestern tip of Staten Island, the Conference House is named after the negotiations between the British and Americans (including John Adams and Benjamin Franklin) on September 11, 1776, in a futile attempt to end the emerging Revolutionary War. The handsome 17C fieldstone manor house has been restored and now contains a historic museum. The interior, furnished with 18C pieces, interprets the life and times of Col. Christopher Billop, the house's original owner.

Kykuit, Hudson River Valley
©John Hill/ Historic Hudson Valley/www.hudsonvalley.org

Hudson River Valley★★★

Along this famous waterway, you'll discover a storied landscape dotted with the eye-popping mansions of the Vanderbilts, Goulds and Rockefellers atop wooded bluffs above the river. You'll pass roadside fruit stands, wineries with a view and green pastures. And you'll behold the golden-hued scenes of the country's first literary and art movements; scenes that filled the canvases of Thomas Cole, Frederic Edwin Church and other painters of the Hudson River school, as well as the pages of Washington Irving and James Fenimore Cooper.

A BIT OF HISTORY

Originating high in the Adirondack mountains in upstate New York, the Hudson River flows 315mi to the sea. Navigable as far as Albany, it was linked in 1825 to the Great Lakes by the Erie Canal, once a busy waterway between Albany and Buffalo. On its journey south to New York City, the majestic Hudson flows between rocky crags and wooded peaks, still alluring despite encroaching industrial blight in some places.

🚗 DRIVING TOUR

Up and back, it's about 180mi of hills, hollows and history as you tour the southern part of the Hudson River Valley. Occasionally, from Route 9 heading north, and Route 9 West, for the return, you'll be able to glimpse the river.

EAST BANK

180mi round-trip. &See map p314.
▷ *Leave Manhattan via Henry Hudson Pkwy., which turns into the Saw Mill River Pkwy., heading north. Take Exit 9/ Executive Blvd. and continue to its end. Turn left on Broadway, then next right on Odell Ave. Follow Odell to the end and turn left on Warburton Ave. Continue south for 1.3mi.*

🗎 **Info:** ✆800-232-4782. www.travelhudson valley.com.
▷ **Timing:** The best time to visit the Hudson River Valley is the fall, when Indian summer gilds the forests lining the river banks. If you plan to stay overnight, be sure to reserve a room well in advance. If you have only one day for your visit, we recommend driving north on the east bank in the morning and returning on the west bank in the afternoon.

Hudson River Museum

&*511 Warburton Ave. in Yonkers.* ⊙*Open year-round Wed–Sun noon– 5pm.* ⊘*Closed major holidays.* ⊜*$5.* 🅿 ✕. ✆*914-963-4550. www.hrm.org.* There's something for everyone at this combination historic house, art and history museum, and planetarium. Glenview, the late-Victorian-style stone mansion (1876), features Eastlake and Gothic Revival-style interiors, including rooms restored to show off the lifestyle of an upper-class 19C family. Paintings by Hudson River school artists Asher B. Durand, Jasper Cropsey and George Inness are part of the permanent collection. Artist Red Grooms created the fanciful bookstore space in the New Wing in 1979. Stargazers should take in a show at the **Andrus Planetarium** (👤👤⊙*Sat–Sun 12.30pm, 2pm, 3.30pm;* ⊜*$2, $1 children).*

▷ *Past Yonkers, exit from Saw Mill River Pkwy. at Ashford Ave.-Dobbs Ferry. Go west on Ashford Ave., then turn right on Broadway (Rte. 9). Beyond Irvington, turn left on West Sunnyside Lane.*

Sunnyside★

West Sunnyside Lane, off Rte. 9 in Tarrytown. ➥*Visit of house by guided tour (1hr) only, Apr–Oct Wed–*

Washington Irving's Sunnyside

Mon 10am–5pm; Nov–Dec Sat–Sun only 10am–4pm (also day after Thanksgiving). ⊙Closed Thanksgiving Day & Dec 25. ⊛$12. 🅿.
🖉914-591-8763 or 914-631-8200. ww.hudsonvalley.org.
This wisteria-draped house on the east bank of the river was the home of author **Washington Irving** (1783–1859), chronicler of Rip van Winkle and Sleepy Hollow; now classic tales, peopled with characters of Dutch descent.
A fitting introduction to "knickerbocker" country from the man who invented the term, this Dutch- and Spanish-style "snuggery," as Irving called it, was built on an existing stone cottage he pur-chased in 1835. Inside, you'll see family belongings and furnishings; the library is appointed largely as Irving left it.
The surrounding 20-acre grounds are landscaped in the romantic style pop-ular during the mid-19C, and provide good views of the Hudson.

◐ *Continue north on Rte. 9.*

Lyndhurst★

635 South Broadway (Rte. 9) in Tarrytown. ⊙Open mid-Apr–Oct Tue–Sun 10am–5pm; rest of year Sat–Sun 10am–5pm. ⊙Closed major holidays, except holiday Mon.
👞Guided tours available. ⊛$12.

Stone Barns Center for Food and Agriculture

630 Bedford Rd., Pocantico Hills. ⊙Open year-round Wed–Sun 10am–5pm.
👞Guided and audio tours of the property available. Kids' programs offered.
🖉914-366-6200. www.stonebarnscenter.org.
Set on 80 rolling acres just down the road from Union Church and Kykuit, this lively educational complex, part of the former Rockefeller estate, encompasses gardens, pasture and woodlands, a 22,000sq-ft year-round greenhouse, a restaurant, a cafe and a terrific bookstore specializing in cookbooks and gardening titles. The place gets its name from the regal Norman-style stone barns that stand at its center, built for John D. Rockefeller in the 1930s and used to house cattle through the 1970s. Today, the hay barn is used for classes on a wide range of topics, from botanical drawing to the ABCs of fennel *(check the website for schedule)*, while the former dairy barn houses Blue Hill at Stone Barns, an award-winning gourmet restaurant featuring the farm's own Berkshire pigs, broad-breasted turkeys, heirloom tomatoes, exotic mushrooms and other seasonal products *(reservations required; 🖉914-366-9600; www. bluehillfarm.com).*

Antiquing in the Hudson River Valley

In the village of **Cold Spring**, two of the biggest stores here are Busy Bijou Galleries Ltd. *(50 Main St.; ☎845-265-4337; www.bijougalleries.com)*, which hosts about 25 dealers, and Downtown Gallery Ltd. *(40 Main St.; ☎845-265-2334; www.artantiquegallery.com)*, with 30-plus dealers. Farther north, **Rhinebeck** is known for the Beekman Arms Antique Market *(24 West Market St.; ☎845-876-3477; www.beekmandelamaterinn.com)*, with 30 dealers showing their wares in an old red stable behind the Beekman Arms Hotel. Finally, at the northern tip of the valley sits **Hudson**, boasting 70 top-tier antique and design stores, plus a number of galleries and boutiques, along its main drag, Warren Street. The term "antique" here stretches well into the 20C, with sleek and stylish mid-century modern pieces juxtaposed with more traditional 19C designs *(www.hudsonantiques.net)*.

✕ *May–Oct.* 🅿. *☎914-631-4481. www.lyndhurst.org.*
From a distance, this picturesque mansion looks like a baronial castle on the Rhine. The Gothic Revival-style house perches on a wooded bluff above the Hudson River. Originally a two-story villa (1838, Alexander Jackson Davis) designed for a mayor of New York City, the house was enlarged for a subsequent owner in 1865. In 1880 financier and railroad tycoon Jay Gould acquired the 67-acre estate, which remained in the family until the death of Gould's daughter in 1961. Peaks, pinnacles, porches and turrets embellish the exterior, accentuating the mansion's irregular shape. Inside, ribbed and vaulted ceilings, pointed arches, stained-glass windows and imposing furnishings reinforce the Gothic mood. In the din-

ing room, take note of the simulated marble colonnettes and leather wall coverings popular in the 19C. Walk or drive around the grounds to discover striking views of the mansion and its parklike 19C landscaping.

▷ *Continue north on Rte. 9 to Sleepy Hollow (formerly North Tarrytown).*

Philipsburg Manor★

On Rte. 9 in Sleepy Hollow. 🚶 *House visit by guided tour (1hr) only, Apr–Oct Wed–Mon 10am–5pm; Nov–Dec Sat–Sun only 10am–4pm (also day after Thanksgiving).* 🕐*Closed Thanksgiving Day & Dec 25.* 💲$12. ✕ 🅿. *☎914-631-3992. www.hudsonvalley.org.*
The site conveys a sense of the manor system under which much of the Hudson River Valley was settled.

Interior of the New World Dutch barn, Philipsburg Manor

Music Room, Kuykuit

At the height of its power, the influential Philips family controlled 52,000 acres of land along the river by royal charter. The family erected a stone manor by the Pocantico River to function as a business office, and a grist mill to grind the grains that tenant farmers brought as payment of their rent. Their three mills formed the basis of the successful trading network and shipping business that helped make them the richest family in the colonies. Today a working mill has been reconstructed on the site, and the house has been furnished with the help of a 1750 probate inventory. Be sure to see the barn and tenant farmhouse, which add to the ambience of the manor.

Kykuit★★

♿*On Rte. 9 North. Tours depart from the visitor center at Philipsburg Manor.*
🚶*Visit by guided tour (90min–2hrs 15min) only, early May–early Nov Wed–Mon 9am–3pm, Sat–Sun 9am–4pm.*
👓*$23–$40. Advance tickets suggested (no service charge for online purchases); see website for tour descriptions and prices.* ✕🅿. 📞*914-631-3992. www.hudsonvalley.org.*

Lords of the Manor

In 1629, to encourage the settlement of New Netherland with private rather than company money, the Dutch West India Company granted estates, each measuring 16mi along the river, to its shareholders. Called "patroons" (patrons), these landholders agreed to send 50 tenant farmers within four years to cultivate the land. Unique in America, this feudal system worked poorly as the absentee patroons mismanaged their estates and attracted few settlers. Even so, when the English took over in 1664, they converted the patroonships into manors and continued to grant lands up and down the river to wealthy families. As freehold lands grew scarcer, more farmers began to settle as tenants on the manors of such families as the Van Rensselaers, Beekmans and Livingstons, who formed the upper crust of the valley's "nobility." Violent tenant uprisings led to a new state constitution in 1846 outlawing "feudal tenures." Soon, however, new generations of American aristocracy—Vanderbilts, Goulds and Rockefellers among them—would flock to the river's edge to build their mansions amid those of the venerable families of the Hudson Valley. Today a remarkable concentration of historic homes and properties remains the lingering legacy of this centuries-old Dutch settlement pattern.

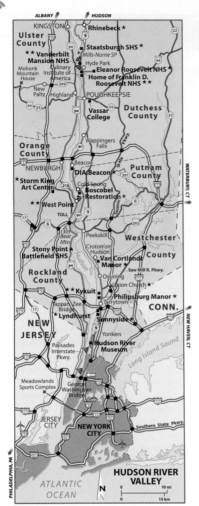

HUDSON RIVER VALLEY

brimmed with antique furniture, lovely Chinese porcelain of the Han, Tang and Ming dynasties, an assortment of china services and Nelson's burgeoning modern **art collection**★. He acquired his love of contemporary art, particularly sculpture, from his mother Abby Aldrich Rockefeller, a founder of the Museum of Modern Art in New York. His basement art galleries contain many treasures, including tapestries by Picasso.

The **gardens**★ and terraces of Kykuit, designed in the orderly, Beaux-Arts fashion by William Welles Bosworth (who also redesigned the facade), take their inspiration from Italian hilltop gardens. Nelson's careful siting of more than 70 modern sculptures around the grounds only enhances the beauty of the landscaping. Lovely **views**★ across the Hudson, particularly from the west porch, blend with gardens and art to form painterly tableaux.

Located just north of Kykuit on Bedford Road (Rte. 448) is the lovely **Union Church of Pocantico Hills**★, a nondenominational Protestant church built on Rockefeller lands in 1921 (&☉open Apr–Oct Mon & Wed–Fri 11am–5pm, Sat 10am–5pm, Sun 2–5pm; Nov–Dec Mon & Wed–Fri 11am–4pm, Sat 10am–4pm, Sun 2–4pm; ☉closed Thanksgiving Day & Dec 25; ◉$5; 🅿. ℘914-332-6659; www. hudsonvalley.org). It is best known for its **stained-glass windows**★, designed by Henri Matisse and Marc Chagall and commissioned by the Rockefellers. The Matisse rose window, completed two days before the artist's death, glows with shades of clear blue, bright yellow and deep green. Chagall designed the eight side panels, representing Old Testament themes, as well as the large window at the rear of the church. It is the only such assemblage created by Chagall in the US.

▷ *Return to Rte. 9 and continue northward toward Ossining.*

One of the last grand homes to be built in the Hudson River Valley, Kykuit (Dutch for "lookout," pronounced Kye-cut) offers a glimpse into the lives of four generations of Rockefellers. Built between 1906 and 1913 by **John D. Rockefeller Jr.** for his father, patriarch of Standard Oil, the estate sports a Beaux-Arts facade and interiors adorned in the Neoclassical style typical of English country homes.

Today, furnishings and room arrangements date to the residency of New York state governor **Nelson Rockefeller** and his wife, Happy, who moved into the house in 1963. By then the house

Up to Ossining, the scenery along Route 9 is quite pretty, somewhat reminiscent of northern New England. Trees arch over the road at various points, and stone walls, made from rocks once cleared from farms, flank the route. From Ossining and Peekskill northward to Hyde Park, Route 9 is lined with fast-food restaurants, gas stations and big-box chain stores. At Peekskill, our tour leaves Route 9 temporarily for a prettier route *(see below)*.

▶ *Pass through Ossining, site of the Ossining Correctional Facility, formerly known as "Sing Sing" prison. Take the Croton Point Ave. exit. Turn right, then right again on South Riverside Ave.*

Van Cortlandt Manor★

Off Rte. 9 on South Riverside Ave., in Croton-on-Hudson. Visit house by guided tour (1hr) only, late May–early Sept Thu–Sun & Mon holidays 10am–5pm; Nov–Dec Sat–Sun 10am–4pm (also day after Thanksgiving). Closed Thanksgiving Day & Dec 25. $12. 914-631-8200; 914-271-8981. www.hudsonvalley.org.

Legend has it that Benjamin Franklin, the Marquis de Lafayette, John Jay and other notable personalities visited this manor. Home to the Van Cortlandt family for 260 years, the house has been restored to its appearance during the tenure of Pierre Van Cortlandt, patriot and the first lieutenant-governor of New York State, who presided over 86,000 acres.

The house contains original family furnishings, paintings and pewter. Don't miss the large kitchen, with its original hearth, Dutch oven and cooking utensils. Fields, gardens and the ferry house evoke 18C life in the Hudson Valley.

▶ *Continue on Rte. 9 North to Peekskill; bear left onto Rte. 6/202 West; at Bear Mountain Bridge follow Rte. 9D (N).*

This drive offers beautiful **views** of the river and the New Jersey Palisades as the road dips into the valley and then rises into the hills.

Boscobel Restoration★★

On Rte. 9D, 4mi north of junction with Rte. 403, Garrison. Visit by guided tour (45min) only, Apr–Oct Wed–Mon 9.30am–5pm; Nov–Dec Wed–Mon 9.30am–4pm. Closed Thanksgiving Day & Dec 25. $16. 845-265-3638. www.boscobel.org.

Set back from the road and overlooking the Hudson River, Boscobel, a handsome example of Federal domestic architecture, was begun by States Morris Dyckman (1755–1806) in 1804 and completed after his death by his wife Elizabeth.

In the 1950s the property on which Boscobel originally stood was sold and the mansion was almost destroyed. Preservationists acquired the building and moved it piece by piece to Garrison, where it was reconstructed on grounds high above the Hudson. Rebuilt and refurbished, Boscobel opened in 1961.

Van Cortlandt Manor

The overall appearance is one of Federal elegance and refinement. The recessed central portion of the facade, with its slender columns and carved trim, contrasts with the otherwise unadorned exterior. The restored interior features graceful arches, fireplaces embellished with classical motifs, delicately carved woodwork and a freestanding central staircase lit by a tall Palladian window. Furnishings include many pieces by leading New York craftsman Duncan Phyfe.

◯ *Follow Rte. 9D North to Beacon.*

Dia:Beacon★

♿ *3 Beekman St., Beacon.* ◯ *Open mid-Apr–mid-Oct Thu–Mon 11am–6pm; mid-Nov–mid-Apr Fri–Mon 11am–4pm.* ◯ *Closed major holidays.* ◷ *$10.* ✕ ⊡. ☎ *845-440-0100. www.diabeacon.org.* This 240,000sq.-ft gallery, housed in what used to be a Nabisco factory, is the toast of the Hudson Valley contemporary art world. In addition to show-

ing selections from the Dia Foundation's permanent collection— which includes large-scale conceptual works by Andy Warhol, Joseph Beuys, Richard Serra, Donald Judd and others—Dia mounts vast retrospectives of noted artists such as Agnes Martin and Robert Smithson. The bookstore and cafe are both excellent.

◯ *Follow Rte. 9D North to Rte. 9 North and continue to Poughkeepsie. Head east on Rte. 44/55, then turn right onto Raymond Ave. (Rte. 376).*

Vassar College

Raymond Ave. in Poughkeepsie. ☎ *845-437-7000. www.vassar.edu.* Vassar is one of the best-known private liberal arts colleges in the US. Founded as a women's college in 1861, it became coeducational in 1969 and now has 2,400 students, 40 per cent of whom are men.
The buildings reflect traditional American and European styles, as well as mod-

---

Culinary Institute of America

Main Dining Room

Lorna Smith/CIA

1946 Campus Dr., Hyde Park. Reservations required. ☎ *845-471-6608. www.ciachef.edu.*

On the premises of a former Jesuit seminary reside the five restaurants of The Culinary Institute of America (CIA). Here, 2,400 chefs-in-training gain practical experience in preparation, cooking and serving under the watchful tutelage of CIA's world-renowned faculty. Each of the restaurants offers a different and excellent dining experience. Here you'll find the food and atmosphere are outstanding, and the students friendly and earnest. **St. Andrew's Café** *(Mon–Fri)* serves contemporary fare emphasizing fresh seasonal ingredients in a family-friendly setting; **American Bounty** *(Tue–Sat)* focuses on the bounty of the Hudson River Valley; the elegant **Escoffier** *(Tue–Sat)* will please the Francophile with its light take on classic French cuisine; and **Ristorante Caterina de Medici** *(Mon–Fri)* serves authentic regional Italian dishes. The casual **Apple Pie Bakery Café** *(Mon–Fri 7.30am–6.30pm)* offers soups, salads, sandwiches, artisanal breads and pastries (eat-in or takeout) prepared by CIA's baking and pastry arts majors. *All CIA restaurants are open for lunch and dinner (the Bakery Café is open for breakfast as well). Dress is business casual.*

Franklin D. Roosevelt National Historic Site

National Park Service, Hyde Park NY

ern trends in architecture: notice Ferry House (Marcel Breuer) and Noyes House (Eero Saarinen), dormitories erected in 1951 and 1958 respectively. The Thompson Library houses most of Vassar's more than one million print volumes.

Return to Rte. 9 and continue north to Hyde Park, where you'll find the following three sights tightly clustered.

Home of Franklin D. Roosevelt National Historic Site★★

On Rte. 9 in Hyde Park. Visit by guided tour (1hr) only, year-round daily 9am–5pm. Grounds (free) open dawn–dusk. Closed Jan 1, Thanksgiving Day & Dec 25. $14; free children under 15. 845-486-1966. www.nps.gov/hofr.

This vast estate—known as the "Summer White House" during FDR's presidency—is one of the most important historic sites in the Hudson Valley. It was acquired by the president's father in 1867; FDR was born here in 1882. The mansion, Springwood, dates back to the early 19C but has since been remodeled and enlarged, and more recently, refurbished. It is unique among historic homes for the exceedingly personal experience it offers. Memorabilia of the late president (1882–1945) and his family can be found in the house, library and museum.

Exhibits trace the transformation of a "charming New York socialite into one of America's great statesmen." In the rose garden, a simple monument of white Vermont marble marks the final resting place of Franklin and Eleanor Roosevelt.

Eleanor Roosevelt National Historic Site★

On Rte. 9G in Hyde Park. Visit by guided tour (45min) only, May–Oct daily 9am–5pm; rest of year Thu–Mon 9am–4.30pm (tours at 1pm, 3pm). Grounds (free) open dawn–dusk. Closed Jan 1, Thanksgiving Day & Dec 25. $8; free children under 15. 845-229-9422. www.nps.gov/elro.

The Roosevelts often came to this tranquil corner of the estate on the Fall Kill for family picnics. FDR built a stone cottage on the property in 1925, and a year later Eleanor Roosevelt (1884–1962) and her friends opened a furniture factory nearby. After the business folded in the mid-1930s, the building was remodeled and eventually became Eleanor's beloved Val-Kill cottage. Mrs. Roosevelt considered Val-Kill her only true home, and after the president's death, she chose to spend her remaining years here working, entertaining her friends and receiving foreign dignitaries.

Vanderbilt Mansion National Historic Site★

On Rte. 9 in Hyde Park, 2mi north of FDR National Historic Site. Visit by guided tour (45min) only, year-round daily 9am–5pm. Grounds (free) open dawn–dusk. ⏱*Closed Jan 1, Thanksgiving Day & Dec 25.* ☞*$8.* 🅿. 𝒫*845-229-7770. www.nps.gov/vama.* This sumptuous Beaux-Arts residence (1898) was designed by McKim, Mead and White for Frederick W. Vanderbilt and his wife Louise. Remarkably preserved and luxuriously appointed, it bears witness to a bygone age of opulence. Before the Vanderbilts bought the property in the early 19C, it belonged to famed botanist Dr. David Hosack. He and other earlier owners of the estate were exceedingly interested in landscaping; as a result, the grounds represent one of the greatest intact surviving examples of the Romantic style of landscape architecture in the US. The lavish interior contains art and furniture befitting America's "nobility" and ranging from Renaissance to rococo in style.

Walking trails along the river afford scenic views of the valley.

◗ *Continue north on Rte. 9 to Staatsburg.*

Staatsburgh State Historic Site★

Off Rte. 9 on Old Post Rd., in Staatsburg. *Visit by guided tour (1hr) only, Apr–Oct Wed–Sat 10am–5pm, Sun 11am–5pm; rest of year Sat–Sun 11am–5pm (call for special holiday hours).* ☞*$5.* 🅿. 𝒫*845-889-8851. www.staatsburgh.org.*

Built on land that had been in **Ruth Livingston Mills**' family since 1792, this 79-room Beaux-Arts mansion engulfs a Greek Revival home constructed in 1832. Ruth and Ogden Mills inherited the property in 1890, and hired architects McKim, Mead and White to transform the home into a "palace royale" fit for entertaining. Part English baronial hall (note the heavily wooded entryway), part French palace (the Louis XVI **dining room** rivals any in the Hudson River Valley for its scale, luster and view), the home boasted 14 bathrooms and accommodations, indoors and out, for weekend visitors.

Mrs. Mills' furnishings and personal touches reflect pride in her colonial and Revolutionary War heritage as a member of the Livingston family. She considered herself heiress, as well, to Mrs. Astor as queen of American society. Take advantage of the hiking trails on the grounds, since they offer rare access to the Hudson's edge.

◗ *Continue north on Rte. 9 to Rhinebeck.*

Rhinebeck★

Founded in 1686 by Dutch settlers, Rhinebeck is perhaps the quaintest and most upscale of all the Hudson River villages, replete with antique stores, boutiques, a picturesque inn and several tasty restaurants.

For an inexpensive breakfast or lunch, it's hard to beat **Bread Alone** *(45 East Market St.; 𝒫 845-876-3108; www. breadalone.com)*, known throughout the valley for its robust breads, muffins, soups and sandwiches. On Sundays *(*⏱*May–Nov 10am–2pm; www. rhinebeckfarmersmarket.com)*, a farmers' market on East Market Street (in the municipal parking lot) features fresh produce, local wines and honey, as well as gourmet foods made by local chefs. Be sure to check out what's happening at the Dutchess County Fairgrounds while you're in town; just north of downtown Rhinebeck on Route 9, the 168-acre site hosts a packed calendar of weekend events, from horse shows to arts and crafts fairs *(𝒫845-876-4001; www. dutchessfair.com)*. The **Old Rhinebeck Aerodrome** *(*⏱*open mid-May–mid-Oct daily 10am–5pm;* ☞*$10 Mon–Fri, $3 children 6–12, $20 Sat–Sun, $5 children 6–12; 𝒫845-752-3200; www.oldrhinebeck. org)* is known for its large collection of vintage cars, airplanes and motorbikes, as well as for its air shows *(*⏱*open mid-Jun–mid-Oct Sat–Sun 2pm)*; rides on a 1929 biplane *(*☞*$75 per person)* offer aerial views of the Hudson Valley; call for details.

WEST BANK

◗ *Return to Poughkeepsie, cross the Hudson River and continue south on Rte. 9 West.*

Storm King Art Center★

Take Rte. 9 West to the Cornwall Hospital Exit, then bear left onto Rte. 107; at the intersection turn right and follow Rte. 32 North over the bridge, turning left immediately after the bridge onto Orr's Mill Rd. Open Apr–Oct Wed–Sun 10am–5.30pm; early Nov–mid-Nov Wed–Sun 10am–5pm; Jun–Aug grounds open until 8pm Sat (admission fee applies). Guided tours (1hr) daily 2pm; Acoustiguide self-guided tour available ($5). $12; $8 children 5–18; free under 5. 845-534-3115. www.stormking.org.

This unique outdoor museum of contemporary sculpture covers 500 acres of meadow, hillsides, forest, lawns and terraces. Large-scale works by such artists as Alexander Calder (The Arch), Mark diSuvero, Alexander Liberman (Iliad), Henry Moore, Louise Nevelson, Isamu Noguchi (Momo Taro) and David Smith are installed on the grounds, most of them in settings that have been specially landscaped for the sculpture. Changing exhibits of paintings, graphics and smaller sculptures from the center's collection are presented in the Normandy-style museum building (1935), formerly a private residence.

West Point★★

10mi southeast of Storm King Art Center on Rte. 218 South.

Overlooking the Hudson River, West Point is renowned as the site of the United States Military Academy, the oldest of the nation's service academies. Fortress West Point was established in 1778 as a series of fortifications to protect the strategically important Hudson at this most defensible location. After the Revolutionary War the grounds became a repository for trophies and captured equipment. It was not until 1802 that the US Military Academy was established by Congress, and West Point selected as its site. In the academy's first year, five officers trained and instructed the ten students; there are now more than 4,400 men and women cadets. Among its graduates West Point counts generals MacArthur (1903), Patton (1909), Eisenhower (1915) and Schwartzkopf (1956); and astronauts Borman (1950), Aldrin (1951), Collins (1952), White (1952) and Scott (1954).

Visit

The campus may be visited by guided tour (1hr) only; you need not take a tour to see the visitor center and museum. Tours depart about every 45min from the visitor center Apr–Oct Mon–Sat & holidays 9.45am–3.30pm, Sun 11am–3.30pm; rest of year call or see website for schedule. 2hr tours also available; call or see website for details. Photo ID required for visitors ages 16 and older. No tours Jan 1, Thanksgiving Day, Dec 24 & Dec 25, on football Saturdays or during Graduation. $11. West Point Tours: 845-446-4724. www.westpointtours.com.

Acceptance Day Parade, West Point

U.S. Army Photo

In the **visitor center**, films and exhibits introduce visitors to the history and sights of West Point and the life of a cadet (*open year-round daily 9am–4.45pm; closed Jan 1, Thanksgiving Day & Dec 25; 845-938-2638; www.usma.edu*).

Near the visitor center, the **museum**★★ (*open year-round daily 10.30am–4.15pm; closed Jan 1, Thanksgiving Day & Dec 25; ; 845-938-3590*) thoroughly examines the history of the military, the academy, warfare and weapons using dioramas, print materials and artifacts, including Napoleon's sword and Goering's jewel-encrusted marshal's baton. Its collection of arms, which traces the development of automatic weapons from the Civil War to the present, began with ordnance captured at the Battle of Saratoga in 1777.

Buildings that are open to the public on the guided tour include the **Cadet Chapel**, an example of the "military Gothic" style, built in 1910; 18C **Fort Putnam**★ (*open for Saturday football games & during Graduation week only*), partially restored in 1907 and completed in 1976; the **Battle Monument**, commemorating victims of the Civil War; and **Trophy Point**. Among the Revolutionary War relics at Trophy Point are links of the great chain that was strung across the Hudson River to prevent British ships from passing.

The Parades – These famous reviews, known for their precision of movement, are held from early September through November and from late April through May (*for schedules: 845-938-2638; www.usma.edu*).

▶ *Continuing south, Rte. 9 West passes Bear Mountain, the highest point (1,305ft) in Palisades Interstate Park.*

Stony Point Battlefield State Historic Site

Park Rd., off Rte. 9 West. Grounds open mid-Apr–Oct Mon–Sat 10am–5pm, Sun noon–5pm; museum Wed–Sat 10am–4.30pm, Sun noon–4.30pm; rest of year grounds only Mon–Fri 10am–4pm. $5 on Sat–Sun. 845-786-2521. www.nysparks.com.

The British wrested this rocky, strategic promontory from the Americans in 1779, thereby gaining control of the entrance to the Hudson Highlands and safeguarding Kings Ferry, which connected the east and west banks at this narrow stretch of river. Anxious to retrieve it, General "Mad" Anthony Wayne mounted a surprise attack on the point in July of that year, fording the marshes below at midnight and overcoming the British in less than an hour. The battle would be the last in the north and a tremendous morale-builder for continental troops. Now a state historic site, the rugged, windswept terrain is studded with interpretive signs that describe the fighting and with picnic spots that afford fine views over the Hudson. In the **museum**, exhibits and a 12min video offer further details of the battle. The oldest **lighthouse** on the Hudson River, built in 1826 on the site of the central powder magazine, has been restored to working order with a 19C Fresnel lens (*open Apr–Oct most weekends; guided tours by appointment*).

▶ *Continue the drive south on Palisades Interstate Parkway—offering superb* **views**★★ *of Yonkers, The Bronx and Manhattan—to the George Washington Bridge, which leads back to Manhattan.*

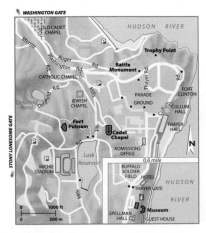

Long Island★★

Long Island is the largest island linked to the continental US. Only 20mi at its widest point, it is 118mi long, with dramatic shoreline all along its length. Because it's so close to New York City (indeed, both Brooklyn and Queens are on Long Island), the western part of the island has become heavily suburban, with the attendant traffic and strip malls, while the eastern part is more rural and serene.

NORTH SHORE

Facing Long Island Sound, the North Shore is a place of rocky necks and steep bluffs, thick woods and picturesque coves. Gilded Age robber barons so loved the landscape that they built great estates on some of the best waterfront lots.

Today several of these mansions are open to the public, offering a tantalizing glimpse into the lives of the superrich; other attractions include history museums—including Teddy Roosevelt's former home—and stunning gardens. Farther out, the North Fork, stretching from Riverhead to Orient Point, is increasingly known for its excellent wineries, bed-and-breakfast inns, quaint towns and great restaurants.

Info: ☎877-386-6654. www.licvb.com.
Location: Lying east of Manhattan, the island sweeps east-northeast from the mouth of the Hudson River into the Atlantic Ocean.

Sands Point Preserve★

127 Middleneck Rd., Port Washington.
Open year-round daily 8am–4pm.
$5 per car; $2 walk-in; free Wed. P.
☎516-571-7900. http://thesandspoint preserve.com.

This former Gold Coast estate, purchased by railroad tycoon Jay Gould in 1900, features two grandiose mansions, reflecting the styles and aspirations of New York society during the Gilded Age. **Castlegould**, originally planned as stables and servants' quarters, houses an information center and rotating exhibits. Built in 1912, the massive Tudor-style **Hempstead House** was Castlegould's main residence; it was sold by Gould to Daniel Guggenheim in 1917. The US Navy operated a naval training center here from 1946 to 1967; it's now used for special events, and guided tours are sometimes available *(check website for details)*. The Normandy-style manor

Sands Point Preserve

KKMPhotos/Long Island CVB

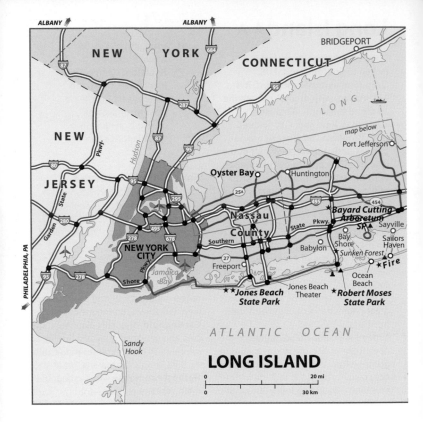

ALBANY · ALBANY

NEW YORK

CONNECTICUT

BRIDGEPORT

NEW JERSEY

Hudson

LONG

map below

Port Jefferson

Oyster Bay · Huntington

Nassau County

NEW YORK CITY

Southern · State Pkwy · Bayard Cutting Arboretum SP★

Sayville

Babylon · Bay Shore · Sailors Haven

Jamaica Bay

Freeport · Sunken Forest★

Ocean Beach

★★Jones Beach State Park · Jones Beach Theater · Fire

★Robert Moses State Park

Sandy Hook

ATLANTIC OCEAN

LONG ISLAND

0 — 20 mi
0 — 30 km

PHILADELPHIA, PA

house known as **Falaise**★ gets its name from the French for "cliff," due to its precarious seaside perch (⤳*visit by 1hr guided tour only, late May–Oct Thu–Sun noon, 1pm, 2pm, 3pm;* ⊘*$6).* The mansion was erected by Capt. Harry F. Guggenheim, son of Daniel, and now contains a collection of 16C and 17C French and Spanish artifacts. Step to the rear of the house for spectacular **views**★★ of the sound from the arcaded loggia.

Nassau County Museum of Art

M *on map. One Museum Dr., in Roslyn Harbor. Take Rte. 25A East, cross the Roslyn Viaduct and turn left on Museum Dr.* ◐*Open year-round Tue–Sun 11am–4.45pm.* ◐*Closed Dec 25 & for six weeks a year during exhibition changes; call for details.* ⊘*$10.* ✕ 🅿*$2 (charge on Sat–Sun).* ✆*516-484-9338. www.nassaumuseum.com.*
The museum is headquartered on the grounds of a late-19C estate built for

Lloyd Bryce, the paymaster-general of New York, and acquired in 1919 by Childs Frick, the son of Henry Clay Frick. Changing art exhibits covering all periods are presented in the elegant Georgian Revival mansion, which has been converted into eight galleries. The landscaped lawns, ponds and gardens encompass 145 acres, offering an ideal outdoor setting for sculpture shows. Also on the grounds is the **Art Space for Children**, featuring delightful exhibits geared toward children and family programming (◐*open Tue–Sun noon–4.30pm).*

Old Westbury Gardens★

71 Old Westbury Rd., Old Westbury. ◐*Open mid-Apr–Oct Wed–Mon 10am–5pm (no entry after 4pm).* ⤳*Guided tours (45min) available on the hour and the half-hour.* ⊘*$10.* ✕🅿. ✆*516-333-0048. www.oldwestburygardens.org.*

Occupying grounds formerly belonging to John S. Phipps, sportsman and financier, this 200-acre estate contains woods, meadows, lakes and formal gardens. The stately Charles II mansion has been preserved as it was during the family's occupancy in the early 20C. The interior features antique furnishings, paintings by Thomas Gainsborough and John Singer Sargent, gilded mirrors and objets d'art.

Oyster Bay

Famed as a vacation spot and for its sheltered pleasure-craft harbor, this picturesque town brims with historic landmarks, quaint shops and tree-shaded streets lined with Victorian and Colonial homes. Oyster Bay's most famous resident was **Theodore Roosevelt**, who spent 20 years at Sagamore Hill; his grave (**A** *on map*) is located in Young's Cemetery.

Planting Fields★★

&. *1395 Planting Fields Rd., Oyster Bay.* ⏱*Grounds open year-round daily 9am–5pm.* ⛔*Closed Dec 25.* ∞*$8/car May–Labor Day daily; Labor Day–Oct Sat–Sun; free rest of the year.* 🅿. ℘*516-922-9200. www.plantingfields.org.*

This former private estate of financier William Robertson Coe is now a state historic park.

The 409 acres of planting fields contain 160 acres that have been developed as an arboretum; the remaining land has been kept as a natural habitat. The plant collections include more than 600 rhododendron and azalea species (*in bloom May–Jun*); the Synoptic Garden, comprising approximately five acres of selected ornamental shrubs for Long Island gardens; the camellia collection, the oldest and largest of its kind under glass (*in bloom Feb–Mar*); and greenhouses filled with orchids, hibiscus, begonias and cacti. Amid these landscaped gardens

Planting Fields

KKMPhotos/Long Island CVB

and spacious lawns stands **Coe Hall**, a fine example of the Tudor Revival style (◷open Apr–Sept daily 11.30am–3.30pm; ◷closed Dec 25; ⌣1hr guided tour daily 12.30pm, 2.30pm; ⌷$3.50; 🅿; ✆516-922-9210).

Sagamore Hill National Historic Site★

🚹🚹Cove Neck Rd, Oyster Bay. ◷Open late May–Labor Day daily 9am–5pm; rest of year Wed–Sun 9am–5pm. ◷Closed holidays. ⌣Visit mansion by guided tour (1hr) only, 10am–4pm. ⌷$5; free children under 15. 🅿. ✆516-922-4788. www.nps.gov/sahi.

Located east of the village of Oyster Bay, this gracious mansion (1885) is maintained as it was during Theodore Roosevelt's presidency (1901–09). The 23-room Queen Anne structure retains more than 90 per cent of the family's original furnishings.

During the guided tour, you'll hear humorous anecdotes about Teddy's life and presidential pursuits. Be sure to note the rhinoceros-foot inkstand, a trophy of his hunting days, and the bronze *Paleolithic Man* by Frederic Remington in the library. After the tour, take a seat on the wide piazza and enjoy sweeping views of the grounds. In the **Old Orchard Museum** (◷open 10am–5pm), exhibits and a 20min biographical film trace Roosevelt's life.

Raynham Hall Museum

20 West Main St., Oyster Bay. ◷Open year-round Tue–Sun 1–5pm. ◷Closed major holidays. ⌷$5. Audio tour available ($1). ✆516-922-6808. www.raynhamhallmuseum.org.

This old farmhouse played an important role during the American Revolution. It was the home of Samuel Townsend, whose son, Robert, was George Washington's chief intelligence agent in New York City. Inside you'll see period furniture and memorabilia (1770s–1870s).

Cold Spring Harbor

From 1836 to 1862 the Cold Spring Harbor whaling fleet of nine ships sailed to every navigable ocean in search of whale oil and bone. The commanders of these vessels came from established whaling centers such as Sag Harbor.

Cold Spring Harbor Whaling Museum★

🚹🚹 ♿ 279 Main St. (Rte. 25A). ◷Open year-round Tue–Sun 11am–5pm. ⌷$6; $5 children 5–18; pay-what-you-wish Sun 11am–noon. ✆631-367-3418. www.cshwhalingmuseum.org.

Dedicated to the preservation of the town's history as a whaling port, this museum features several outstanding exhibits, including a fully equipped 19C whaleboat and a detailed diorama of Cold Spring Harbor, showing village houses, whaling company buildings and wharves as they appeared in the 1850s, the heyday of the whaling industry. Throughout the museum are examples of whalecraft: harpoons, navigational instruments and whaling-ship models. Note especially the extensive collection of scrimshaw (carvings of ivory tusks or whale bones), the whaler's folk art.

Old Bethpage Village Restoration★★

👤*1303 Round Swamp Rd., Old Bethpage.* 🕐*Open Apr–Dec Wed–Sat 10am–4pm, Sun 11am– 5pm.* ᎒*$10; $7 children 5–12.* 🅿. 🖉*516-572-8400. www.nassaucountyny.gov.*

Nestled in a 209-acre valley, Old Bethpage is an active farm community that re-creates a pre-Civil War American village. More than 55 historic buildings reflecting the architectural heritage of Long Island have been moved to the site of the former Powell Farm.

Take a leisurely stroll through the village to observe the weaver making cloth, the farm wife preparing a meal and farmers working their fields. Depending on the time of year, you can also watch sheep-shearing, cider making and other seasonal activities.

Vanderbilt Museum★

👤 *180 Little Neck Rd., Centerport.* *Visit of house by guided tour (1hr) only, year-round Tue & Fri noon–4pm, Sat 11am–5pm, Sun noon–5pm.* 🕐*Closed Jan 1, Thanksgiving Day & Dec 25.* ᎒*$12; $7 grounds only.* 🅿. 🖉*631-854-5555. www.vanderbilt museum.org.*

Overlooking Northport Harbor, this 43-acre estate holds the Vanderbilt Mansion, a marine museum and a planetarium. The 24-room Spanish Revival mansion belonged to William K. Vanderbilt Jr., great-grandson of railroad tycoon Cornelius Vanderbilt. Inside, you'll see elaborately carved marble and woodwork and original family furnishings, as well as natural history collections in the Habitat Wing.

Also on the grounds is the **Marine Museum**, a showcase for artifacts gathered by William during his travels, including ship models, arms and weaponry, and birds. The **planetarium** presents a variety of shows throughout the year *(for admission fees & schedule:* 🖉*631-854-5555).*

Sunken Meadow State Park★

♿ *Sunken Meadow Pkwy. at Rte. 25A, Kings Park.* 🕐*Open year-round daily dawn–dusk.* 🍴. 🅿 *($10 late May–mid-Sept; $8 mid-Sept–mid-Nov.* 🖉*631-269-4333. www.nysparks.com.*

Bordering Long Island Sound, this park offers a wide range of recreational activities, including golfing (27 holes), swimming, nature trails and bike paths. Sunken Meadow refers to the large, fine-sand beach lining the sound.

Stony Brook★

When you visit this pleasant hamlet, you'll think you've entered a Federal-style village from 18C or 19C America. It's also home to a branch of the State University of New York.

Long Island Museum of American Art, History and Carriages★

👤 ♿🕐*Open year-round Fri–Sat 10am–5pm, Sun noon–5pm (check schedule for Monday holiday hours).* 🕐*Closed major holidays.* ᎒*$9; $4 children 6–17.* 🖉*631-751-0066. www.longislandmuseum.org.*

A Smithsonian affiliate since 2006, this museum complex on 9 acres tells the story of Long Island. The **History Museum**, located inside a 19C lumber mill, has changing displays on American life from the 18C to the 1900s. Don't miss the antique wildfowl decoys and a gallery of **miniature period rooms** from colonial times to the 1930s. The two-story Carriage Museum houses an exceptional collection of horse-drawn carriages, some 250 of them. The show-stopper is the c.1880 "Grace Darling" omnibus, decorated with landscape paintings. The paintings and drawings of **William Sidney Mount** (1807–68), a local landscape painter, and other 19C and 20C artists are presented in changing exhibits in the Art Museum. Also on the grounds are a blacksmith shop and one-room schoolhouse.

North Fork★

🄸 *Tourist information:* ✆*631-298-5757.*
www.northfork.org.

Roughly 25mi east of Stony Brook, the Long Island Expressway ends and the island splits in two, like tines of a fork. As home to the upscale resort towns of the Hamptons and miles of white-sand beaches, the South Fork has always garnered the lion's share of the tourist trade, leaving the North Fork for the locals. That is changing, however: in recent years the rural North Fork has gained a strong reputation for its award-winning **wineries** and plush bed-and-breakfast inns. Strung out along 24mi of Route 25, its 11 quaint towns boast a number of new wine bars and restaurants. Along the coastal Route 48 you'll find beaches, parks and ocean views.

At the head of the Great Peconic Bay sits Riverhead, home to **Atlantis Marine World**, an Atlantis-themed aquarium with sharks, eels, stingrays, exotic fish and a living coral reef (👪♿ &🕙*open year-round daily 10am–5pm;* 🕙*closed Dec 25;* 👓*$21.50; $18.50 children 3–17;* ✕🅿; ✆*631-208-9200; www.atlant ismarineworld.com).* As you proceed east on Route 25 the landscape takes on a rural character, with rolling farmland, vineyards and orchards on both sides.

A good place to stop for an informal breakfast or lunch is **Love Lane Kitchen** *(240 Love Lane;* ✆*631-298-8989; www. lovelanekitchen.com)* in quaint Mattituck, where you can get homemade granola or gourmet sandwiches. A bit farther on, Cutchogue's village green sports the 1649 **Old House**, one of the oldest frame houses in the country. Also here are the 1840 Old School House and the 1890 Red Barn, both filled with period furnishings (☜*open by 1hr guided tour only, late Jun–Labor Day Sat–Mon 1–4pm;* ✆*631-734-7122).*

Wineries dot both sides of Route 25 between Jamesport and Southhold, the heart of Long Island's winery region. Most tasting rooms warmly welcome walk-ins with daily tastings for a modest fee. Check the Long Island Wine Council website for winery contact information and maps *(www.liwines.com).*

Southold is home to one of the area's best-kept secrets: the **Custer Institute Observatory**, where you can peer into the heavens through a high-powered Meade telescope at no charge every Saturday night from dusk to midnight *(off Rte. 25 on Main Bayview Rd.;* ✆*631-765-2626; www.custerobservatory.org).*

Greenport's marina is home to the **Bounty**, the schooner built as the floating set of the 1962 film *Mutiny on the Bounty* and used more recently in *Pirates of the Caribbean II.* From Greenport you can grab the ferry to scenic **Shelter Island** *(for ferry schedule call* ✆*631-749-0139 or visit www.northferry.com).* Finally, out at the tip of the island, in Orient, is **Orient Beach State Park** (✆*631-323-2440; www.nysparks.com),* with 45,000ft of frontage on Gardiners Bay and a rare maritime forest with red cedar, blackjack oak trees and prickly-pear cactus. Swimming season lasts only from late June through August, but nature trails are open year-round.

SOUTH SHORE

Long Island's famed beaches dot this scenic shoreline, where three long, thin barrier islands—including scenic, car-free Fire Island—front both the Atlantic Ocean and the Great South Bay. Farther east are the Hamptons resort communities, where multimillion-dollar second homes line the ocean and boutiques and restaurants cater to the tastes and pocketbooks of the wealthy. At the tip of the South Shore, laid-back Montauk sports beachside motels, a famous lighthouse, sprawling beaches and a ubiquitous bumper sticker: "Montauk: The End." Pick one up to show you've been there. Attractions below are presented west to east.

Jones Beach State Park★★

Off Wantagh Pkwy., Wantagh.
✆*516-785-1600. www.nysparks.com.*

Six and a half miles of sandy beaches are the highlight of this popular state park, with its double exposure to the ocean and bay. Other features include the massive open-air **Jones Beach Theater**, two swimming pools, sports fields, play areas, a 2mi wooden boardwalk and the Theodore Roosevelt Nature Center, which has a butterfly garden and an interpretive walk on the sand dunes, among other exhibits (*open Memorial Day–Labor Day Wed–Sun 10am–4pm, rest of year Sat–Sun 10am–4pm; 516-780-3295*).

Bayard Cutting Arboretum State Park★

Rte. 27A, Oakdale. Open Apr–Oct Tue–Sun 10am–5pm; rest of year Tue–Sun 10am–4pm. Closed major holidays. $6/vehicle (Apr–Oct). . *631-581-1002. www.bayardcuttingarboretum.com.*
Created in 1887 by William Cutting, according to plans by Frederick Law Olmsted, the arboretum covers 690 acres of woodlands and planted areas. Many of the specimens in the pinetum date back to the original plantings of fir, spruce, pine and other evergreens. Rhododendrons and azaleas *(in bloom May–Jun)* border the walks and drives; wildflowers add blazes of color throughout the park.

Fire Island★

A place to relax for weary New Yorkers, this 32mi-long, car-free barrier island varies in width from .5mi to less than 200yds and boasts more than 1,400 acres of the **Fire Island National Seashore**★★ (*631-687-4750; www.nps.gov/fiis*). While the island has experienced a real-estate boom in the past few years, it's still far more laid back than the Hamptons.

Ocean Beach is the largest and liveliest of the 17 communities on Fire Island, with a rowdy party scene on summer weekends. To soak up the sun and scene, grab a deck chair at **Matthew's Seafood House** (*935 Bay Walk; 631-583-8016; www.matthewsseafood.com*), a family-owned spot since 1974. It's your best bet for seafood in the area and just a 2min walk from the Ocean Beach ferry terminal.

Sailors Haven, across the Great South Bay from Sayville, is home to one of the best-known areas of Fire Island, the **Sunken Forest**★, a maritime woodland thick with oak and sassafras trees thought to be 200 to 300 years old. An interpretive boardwalk trail wends through its various ecosystems. There are wide sandy beaches nearby.

Robert Moses State Park★ (*631-669-0470; www.nysparks.com*), on the western part of Fire Island, is a shoreline park named for Robert Moses, the former superintendent of Long Island parks. The park's dunes and sea grasses provide refuge for various waterfowl. A .75mi boardwalk leads from Parking Lot 5 to iconic **Fire Island Lighthouse**★, completed in 1858. There's a visitor center in the keeper's quarters at its base, but the real fun (for those without a fear of heights) is climbing the 156 iron steps and two ladders to the top,

Beach on Fire Island, Long Island

©John Archer/iStockphoto.com

GETTING TO AND AROUND FIRE ISLAND

You may drive to the east and west ends of the island—including Robert Moses State Park—but there are no public roads on the island itself. Most people get to the island by ferry and then explore it on foot or by **water taxi** (631-665-8885; www.fireislandwatertaxi.com). From Patchogue, Long Island, you can take the **Davis Park Ferry** (631-475-1665; www.davisparkferry.com) to the eastern part of the island, including beautiful Watch Hill Beach. From Sayville, Long Island, you can take the **Sayville Ferry Service** (631-589-0810; www.sayvilleferry.com) to the central communities, including the Sunken Forest. From Bay Shore, take the **Fire Island Ferries** (631-665-3600; www.fireislandferries.com) to Ocean Beach. Ticket prices vary depending on route and time of day but generally cost $13–$17 per adult round-trip.

for spectacular panoramic **views**★★ (open Apr–Jun & Sept–Dec daily 9.30–5pm, Jul–Aug daily 9.30–6pm, rest of year noon–4pm; $6 adults, $4 children, must be 42" tall; 631-661-4876, www. fireislandlighthouse.com).

The Hamptons★

 Tourist information: 877-386-6654. www.discoverlongisland.com.
Dominating a 35mi stretch of Long Island's South Shore, this chain of famous vacation colonies stretches from Westhampton Beach, which rims Shinnecock Bay, to Amagansett.
Once a summer playground for the rich, the Hamptons continue to attract hordes of tourists to their picture-perfect town centers, packed with exclusive boutiques and first-rate restaurants.

The Lobster Roll

1980 Montauk Hwy., Amagansett. Closed Nov–mid-Apr. 631-267-3740. www.lobsterroll.com.
Sand dunes surround this highway shanty on Long Island, midway between Amagansett and Montauk. Regulars, including Barbra Streisand, Kathleen Turner and Alec Baldwin, have taken to calling it "lunch" thanks to a neon sign above the outdoor patio. The restaurant's famous lobster rolls, deep-fried Atlantic cod, and crab cake platter make it more than just a roadside pit stop.

 Note: it's nearly impossible for day visitors to park at most Hamptons beaches during the summer, as all the permits are prepurchased by local residents and renters. One exception is Coopers Beach in Southampton, where you can buy a daily parking pass ($40).

Westhampton Beach

Once a seafaring village, Westhampton is a lively resort where New Yorkers —especially musicians, writers and artists—like to spend their weekends or take up summer residence. The annual Westhampton Beach Outdoor Art Show takes place in early August.
Take a drive along Dune Road, on the narrow barrier beach, to glimpse a variety of house styles, from brown-shingled, white-trimmed New England homes to bungalows. A 15mi-long beach extends from Moriches Inlet to Shinnecock Inlet. *Note: sections of Dune Rd. are extremely narrow and may be impassable following a storm.*

Southampton★

Village maps are available from the Chamber of Commerce (76 Main St.; open Mon–Fri 10am–4pm, Sat–Sun 11am–4pm; 631-283-0402; www.southamptonchamber.com).
This famous resort town is the largest of the Hampton communities and the home of superb estates. Village streets are lined with posh boutiques and upscale restaurants. The esteemed **Parrish Art Museum** focuses on Ameri-

can art of the 19C and 20C, with major holdings of works by American Impressionist William Merrit Chase and the 20C realist Fairfield Porter, as well as by artists who have lived or worked in the area, including Jackson Pollock, Willem de Kooning, Dan Flavin, Roy Lichtenstein, Elizabeth Peyton and Chuck Close. You'll find a regular program of changing exhibits, many featuring works from the permanent collection (& *25 Jobs Lane;* ⊙*open mid-Jun–mid-Sept Mon–Sat 11am–5pm, Sun 1–5pm; rest of year Mon & Thu–Sat 11am–5pm, Sun 1–5pm;* ⊙*closed holidays;* ⊛*$5;* ☎*631-283-2118; www.parrishart.org).*

East Hampton
This town's quaint charm has long attracted writers and artists, several of whom chose to make the local cemetery their final resting place, including Childe Hassam, Jackson Pollock and Stuart Davis. **Main Street**, lined on both sides by magnificent elm trees, boasts several historic structures, including **Guild Hall**, the Hamptons' preeminent cultural institution since 1931. Its busy schedule includes top-shelf art shows, staged readings, music and drama (*no. 158;* ☎*631-324 0806; www.guildhall. org).* At the north end of the street sits Hook Mill, an 1806 windmill. Nearby, the **LongHouse Reserve** is an extraordinary 16-acre sculpture garden with permanent works by Sol LeWitt and Yoko Ono, as well as changing exhibitions (*133 Hands Creek Rd.;* ⊙*open May–Jun & Sept Wed & Sat 2–5pm, Jul–Aug Wed–Sat 2–5pm;* ⊛*$10;* ☎*631-329-3568; www. longhouse.org).*

Sag Harbor★
ℹ*Tourist information:* ☎*631-725-0011. www.sagharborchamber.com.*
With its docks and deep-water harbor nestled in a sheltered cove, this sea town was named port of entry for the US by George Washington. Sag Harbor's charming colonial homes and saltbox cottages preserve a nostalgic flavor of yesteryear. On Union Street, the **Whalers Presbyterian Church** (1918) is considered an outstanding example of

the Egyptian Revival style of architecture. Stop by the **Custom House**, the first customhouse established in New York State, and now a museum (*Main & Garden Sts.;* ↝*visit by guided tour only, late May–early Oct Sat–Sun 1–5pm;* ⊛*$3;* ☎*631-692-4664).* Built as a whaling captain's home, the Greek Revival **Sag Harbor Whaling and Historical Museum** on Main Street has exhibits about the town's whaling days (*no. 200;* &⊙*open mid-May–Oct Mon–Sat & holidays 10am–5pm, Sun 1–5pm;* ⊛*$5;* ☎*631-725-0770; www.sagharborwhalingmuseum.org).*
A short ferry ride from Sag Harbor (as well as from Greenport on the North Fork) lies peaceful **Shelter Island**, a wonderful spot for biking and hiking— nearly a third of the island's 8,000 acres are owned by the Nature Conservancy.

Montauk
ℹ*Tourist information:* ☎*631-668-2428. www.montaukchamber.com.*
Named after the Montauk Indians who once inhabited the area, this town of 4,000 residents is at the eastern-most tip of Long Island, embracing a 10mi strip of woodlands, dramatic cliffs, dunes and white-sand beaches jutting into the ocean. Far more laid back than the Hamptons, it's home to beachfront hotels and motels, seafood restaurants and bars. Be sure to visit the Montauk Point Lighthouse in Montauk State Park; completed in 1796, it is the oldest lighthouse in the state. There's a small museum at its base, and if you're over 41in tall you can climb the 137 steps to the lookout tower for the views (⊙*open early May–early Oct daily & weekends through Dec, weather permitting, hours vary;* ⊛*$9;* ☎*631-668-2544; montauklighthouse. com).* There are seven public beaches in Montauk; two of the most popular are Ditch Plains Beach, Long Island's most famous surfing beach, 2mi east of town, and Hither Hills State Park, 4mi west of town. Nick's Beach is in the heart of the village at the end of South Edison Street.

ADDRESSES

HUDSON RIVER VALLEY
🏠 STAY

$$$$$ Castle on the Hudson – *400 Benedict Ave., Tarrytown. ☎914-631-1980 or 800-616-4487. www.castleonthe hudson.com. 31 rooms.* Resembling a medieval castle, this mansion sits on a hilltop overlooking the river. Inside, stained-glass windows, Oriental rugs and period tapestries soften beamed ceilings and stone walls. Hand-carved four-poster beds draped in goose-down comforters, and custom-made chandeliers decorate the bedrooms. Dinner at **Equus ($$$$)**, in the historic Oak Room, is sure to be a memorable experience.

$$$$$ Mohonk Mountain House – *1000 Mountain Rest Rd., New Paltz. ☎845-255-1000 or 800-772-6646. www.mohonk.com. 267 rooms (includes 3 daily meals).* Overlooking Lake Mohonk, this 1869 Victorian mountain lodge sprawls atop a rocky ridge within a 2,200-acre nature preserve. Guest quarters include antique-filled rooms trimmed in dark wood, family-size suites, or luxurious tower suites complete with a fireplace. Spa facilities, golf, tennis, carriage rides and horseback riding are just some of the many recreational activities available.

$$$ Beekman Arms/Delamater Inn – *6387 Mill St. (Rte. 9), Rhinebeck. ☎845-876-7077. www.beekmandela materinn.com. 73 rooms.* Wide-planked floors and beamed ceilings recall the days when the Beekman Arms—one of the oldest inns in the US—welcomed travelers on horseback. Today it offers 73 rooms with modern conveniences, as well as a cozy restaurant, **The Tavern at Beekman Arms ($$)**, serving updated comfort food like braised short ribs and roasted Long Island duckling. One block away, its sister property, the 1844 **Delamater Inn** comprises seven American Carpenter-style buildings harboring 50 additional rooms, more than half with fireplaces.

🍴 EAT

$$$ Terrapin – *6426 Montgomery St., Rhinebeck. ☎845-876-3330. www.terrapinrestaurant.com. Open daily for lunch and dinner.* **American**. This popular Hudson Valley's restaurant has a prime location at the center of Rhinebeck, in a shingle-style church building dating from 1825. Choose between the sedate, more formal restaurant or the bustling bistro—either way you'll get creative cuisine: dishes like gnocchi with black truffles, salmon with artichoke sauce and creamy garlic soup.

$$$ Xaviar's at Piermont – *506 Piermont Ave., Piermont. Open Fri & Sun for lunch, Wed–Sun for dinner. Closed Mon–Tue. ☎845-359-7007. www.xaviars.com.* **American**. A modern ambience prevails in chef/owner Peter Xaviar Kelly's dining room, where five-course prix-fixe dinners *($100/person)* feature the likes of Hudson Valley foie gras, slow-braised short ribs with English-pea risotto, and dry-aged New York sirloin with gingered shiitake mushrooms and truffled fries. Impressive.

$$ The Red Dot – *321 Warren St., Hudson. Open Wed–Mon for dinner, Sat–Sun for brunch. Closed Tue. ☎518-828-3657.* **American**. City sophisticates and in-the-know locals flock to this friendly-yet-chic restaurant and bar, where you can get a gourmet burger with a cone of supercrisp fries, chicken pot pie, a salmon BLT (bacon, lettuce and tomato) and, for brunch, a terrific eggs benedict. The back garden is a lovely spot.

Culinary Institute of America – 🔖 *See sidebar p316.*

LONG ISLAND
🏠 STAY

$$$$$ 1770 House – *143 Main St., East Hampton. ☎631-324-1770. www.1770house.com. 6 rooms plus a private carriage house. Strict cancellation policy.* Smack in downtown Easthampton, this bed-and-breakfast inn is surprisingly swanky. Rooms have Frette linens, antiques and flat-screen televisions; some have working fireplaces. All but one room have private baths. Guests share the flower-bordered patio. If you're traveling in a group, snag the two-bedroom, two-bath carriage house with living room and butler's pantry. A full breakfast is served daily in season *(Jul–Aug)* and on weekends off-season (continental breakfast on weekdays). The **1770 House Restaurant ($$$$)** wins raves for its innovative preparations and use of local products: look for pan-seared diver scallops, roasted heirloom beets and the like. For more casual fare, try the tavern downstairs.

$$$ Ocean Resort Inn – *95 South Emerson Ave., Montauk. Closed Nov–Mar. ☏631-668-2300. www.oceanresortinn.com. 17 rooms.* The motel itself is nothing fancy—recently renovated rooms are clean, large, comfortable and bright, and some even have jacuzzis. But the location can't be beat. The Ocean Resort is just steps from a pristine white-sand beach with endless views over the Atlantic and a short walk from all the restaurants and shops of Montauk. There's a courtyard for picnicking and a hammock. What more could you need?

$$$ Ram's Head Inn – *108 Ram Island Dr., Shelter Island Heights. Closed Nov–Apr. ☏631-749-0811. www.shelterislandinns.com. 17 rooms.* This sprawling 1929 shingle-style inn, reached via ferry from Sag Harbor or Greenport, has the feel of a relaxed country estate, with Adirondack chairs scattered across a lawn that slopes down to sparkling Coecles Harbor. Rooms are done up in cheerful country decor; four share baths. All guests have free use of the tennis court, fitness center, sauna and private beach equipped with kayaks and sailboats; or you may just want to curl up with a book on one of the plush sofas in the sun room. The inn's restaurant **($$$$)** draws diners from all over the area with dishes like Cedar River Run prime sirloin with arugula, crispy herb polenta and North Fork cabernet. Reservations here, as with the inn, are essential—plan a week ahead for a table, two months ahead for a room.

☏/ EAT

$$$ The Frisky Oyster – *27 Front St., Greenport. Open Wed–Sun for dinner. Closed Mon–Tue. ☏631-477-4265. www.thefriskyoyster.com.* **New American**. This excellent little restaurant blends style and comfort with wild red-flowered wall fabrics and cozy high-backed banquettes. The changing seasonal menu, which may or may not feature oysters, offers smart renditions of bistro favorites like steak frites, as well as dishes with Asian or Italian touches, such as the grilled fig, prosciutto and wild arugula salad and the grilled grouper with shiitake fried rice and Thai papaya salad. Save room for house-made desserts.

$$$ Nick and Toni's – *136 North Main St., East Hampton. Open Wed–Sun for dinner. Closed Mon–Tue. ☏631-324-3550. www.nickandtonis.com.* **Mediterranean**. This Hamptons classic is still going strong. Walls are adorned with folk art, and the wood-burning oven is decorated with colorful mosaic tiles. The chefs draw their inspiration from local products, from the Montauk tuna that comes with white beans and pickled peppers to the Satur Farm baby beets with pomegranates, caperberries and mint. Nick and Toni also run **Rowdy Hall** *($$ 10 Main St., East Hampton; ☏631-324-8555).* A family-friendly gastropub with plenty of outdoor seating in the Parrish Mews and an appropriately convivial feel: try the classic Rowdy burger, fish-and-chips or the French onion soup.

Nick & Toni's

Union Square Greenmarket
©Abraham Nowitz/Apa Publications

Where to Stay

To accommodate its 45 million visitors a year, New York City boasts more than 95,000 hotel rooms. The high price of real estate coupled with tremendous demand makes for what can be astronomical room rates. Visitors interested in staying in Manhattan have access to a variety of lodgings, from trendy Ian Schrager–Philippe Starck creations to the traditional elegance of The Carlyle. Budget-minded travelers will have success finding quality rooms for considerably lower rates by using the discount brokers listed below.

HOTELS
USEFUL CONTACTS

Hotel Reservations Network – *800-715-7666. www.hoteldiscount.com*
Quikbook – *800-789-9887. www.quikbook.com*
Utell – *www.utell.com*
Hotels.com – *www.hotels.com*
Hotwire – *www.hotwire.com*

RATES

Quoted rates do not include the city's substantial **hotel taxes** of 14.75 per cent plus $3.50 per day (for example, with a quoted room rate of $199, you will actually pay $231.85 for that night's stay).
Rate categories below should be taken as a general guideline only. Rates can be higher or lower depending on season, day of the week and volume of advance reservations.
Prices quoted below reflect average cost for a standard double room (two people) in high season (not including city or state taxes). Room prices may be considerably lower in off-season, and many hotels offer discounted weekend rates.

$$$$$	Over $350
$$$$	$250–$350
$$$	$175–$250
$$	$100–$175

PARKING

Guest parking is usually in a nearby garage, and will cost from $20 to $40 per day. More expensive hotels have valet parking.

CALL CHARGES

In-room **telephone charges** can range from 50¢ to as much as $2 for local calls. Be especially prudent when making calls using the hotel's long-distance provider. Some establishments will charge as much as four to five times the usual rate. Even using a long-distance calling card can sometimes incur connection fees.

B&Bs

Many B&Bs in New York are not inns but apartments whose owners rent out rooms; the best come with private baths and complimentary breakfast ($100–$200/night). Entire apartments are also available and can be a terrific value, especially when let by the week or month. Many properties require a two-night stay on weekends; very few allow smoking, and some may not welcome small children.

B&B RESERVATIONS

Affordable New York City
212-533-4001. www.affordablenewyorkcity.com

B&B Network of New York
800-900-8134. www.bedandbreakfastnetny.com

City Lights Bed & Breakfast
212-737-7049. www.citylightsnewyork.com

City Sonnet
212-614-3034. www.citysonnet.com

Manhattan Getaways
212-956-2010. www.manhattangetaways.com

ACCOMMODATION BY AREA
DOWNTOWN

EAST VILLAGE

If you like the feeling of being in a nontraditional, anything-goes atmosphere, you'll appreciate the East Village's edgy feel. Coffeeshops and offbeat little stores beckon everywhere, but the nearby medical centers and NYU also leave their stamp on the district.

$$ East Village Bed & Coffee – *110 Ave. C, between Seventh & Eighth Sts. ☎917-816-0071. www.bedandcoffee.com. 11 rooms.* Rooms in this funky almost-bed-and-breakfast (as the name says, there's only coffee) are bright, clean and individually decorated according to a theme: the Flight Room has maps on the wall and airplanes on the bedspread; the Zen Room has soothing colors and a Buddha statue in the corner. All the rooms share baths.

$$$$$ The Bowery Hotel – *335 Bowery at E. 3rd St. ☎212-505-9100. www.the boweryhotel.com. 135 rooms.* This glam East Village newcomer towers above its neighbors like an off-kilter ziggurat on a once-downtrodden block of the Bowery. The location is convenient to trendy Lower Manhattan neighborhoods (SoHo, Nolita, Greenwich Village, Lower East Side). Within, the decor has a retro feel, updated with luxurious (and distinctly modern) touches like floor-to-ceiling noise-reduction windows, 400-thread-count sheets, high-def TVs, iPod docking stations and rainfall showerheads. The on-site restaurant **Gemma ($$$)** serves up rustic Italian fare nightly for dinner, plus breakfast and lunch on weekends.

FINANCIAL DISTRICT

Business travelers look to the Financial District for accommodations convenient to Lower Manhattan offices and the New York Stock Exchange, but the area's proximity to Battery Park, the Statue of Liberty and South Street Seaport also makes it a good option for leisure travelers.

$$$$ Wall Street Inn – *♿9 South William St. at Broad St. ☎212-747-1500 or 877-747-1500. www.thewallstreetinn.com. 46 rooms.* Business travelers especially

East Village Bed & Coffee

© dominikphoto.com/East Village Bed & Coffee

will find this boutique hotel, located near the New York Stock Exchange, just the ticket. Its business center and workout facility (complete with steam room and sauna) are added draws. The jacuzzi tubs in the more spacious rooms *(seventh floor)* invite relaxation after a busy day. The hotel provides refrigerators in each room, and offers a complimentary continental breakfast.

$$$$$ Ritz-Carlton Battery Park – *♿2 West St. at Battery Pl. ✕ Spa ☎212-344-0800 or 800-542-8680. www.ritz carlton.com. 298 rooms.* Spring for a harbor-view room at this monolith of a hotel towering over Battery Park, and you'll have your own telescope to view New York Harbor and its star attraction, the Statue of Liberty. Guest rooms sport rich fabrics and fine bed linens; bathrooms are awash in marble. Enjoy dinner at the hotel's restaurant, **2 West ($$$$)**, specializing in prime Angus beef. The next day, tone and atone at the hotel's 2,500sq-ft health club.

GREENWICH VILLAGE

You don't have to be a writer, an artist or even a bohemian to appreciate the charms of a stay in the Village. Epicenter of NYU student life and home to the New School University and the Cooper Union, the district has an academic tinge complemented by shopping and dining spots with a pronounced undergraduate flavor.

$$$$ Washington Square Hotel – *103 Waverly Pl., at MacDougal St. ✕ ☎212-777-9515 or 800-222-0418. www.washingtonsquarehotel.com. 150 rooms.* You're smack in the middle of Greenwich Village when you stay at this trim, well-maintained property, which has been family owned and run since 1973. The newly renovated deluxe rooms have art deco-inspired furnishings and pillow-top mattresses, and while they're not fancy, they're large by New York City standards; some even have views of the park. Friendly staff and a cozy bar off the lobby make it feel like a special place.

$$$$$ Maritime Hotel – *363 W. 16th St. at Ninth Ave.* ✕ *℘212-242-4300. www.themaritimehotel.com. 125 rooms.* Designed for the National Maritime Union in 1966 and meticulously renovated in 2003, the Maritime is one of the city's hippest hotels; thanks to its proximity to the shops and clubs of the Meatpacking District, it's especially popular with those in the fashion and entertainment industries. Most of the rooms face the Hudson River, and while they are quite small they have the full complement of amenities—CD/DVD players, 500-thread-count sheets, flat-screen TVs and wireless internet access—along with sizable desks. A clutch of restaurants and bars are on-site, including chic **Matsuri ($$)**, serving black cod and 200 types of sake.

LOWER EAST SIDE

If New York's after-hours scene tops your agenda, try basing yourself on the Lower East Side. Some of the trendiest bars and nightclubs-of-the-moment dot the neighborhood, and the streets are chockablock with great restaurants.

$$$ Off SoHo Suites Hotel –
♿ *11 Rivington St. between Bowery & Chrystie Sts.* ℘*212-979-9815 or 800-633-7646. www.offsoho.com. 38 rooms.* If you'd rather not go out for meals every day—though it'll be hard to resist in this restaurant-laden neighborhood—consider staying at this all-suite hotel. It's located just two blocks south of Houston Street within easy walking distance of a Whole Foods Market. Kitchens are fully equipped, and spacious, newly renovated rooms all have hardwood floors and flat-screen TVs. Economy suites share a bath, so be sure to ask for accommodations with a private bath, if that's your preference.

SoHo
Situated in the heart of Lower Manhattan, SoHo is trend central, drawing shoppers and browsers galore, especially on weekends when fashion-forward boutiques display their wares on the sidewalk.

$$$$$ Soho Grand Hotel –
♿ *310 West Broadway at Grand St.* ✕ *℘212-965-3000 or 800-965-3000. www.sohogrand.com. 365 rooms.* Opened in 1996, the Soho Grand sits at the southwest edge of the arty SoHo neighborhood, a short walk from trendy TriBeCa. Swathed in neutral tones, rooms all have Bose Wave CD/radios, CD libraries, Frette Egyptian cotton linens, flat-screen TVs, minibars and 24hr room service. The swanky **Grand Bar & Lounge** serves contemporary American cuisine and creative cocktails. The Soho Grand welcomes pets, and will even provide a goldfish for your room upon request (and let you take it home if you form a bond).

SOUTH STREET SEAPORT

The South Street Seaport area is a great choice for travelers with kids. Its tip-of-Manhattan location makes it easy to get in line early for Statue of Liberty ferries, and the family-friendly restaurants, attractions and weekend activities at the seaport are just a hop and a skip away.

$$$$ Best Western Seaport Inn –
♿ *33 Peck Slip at Front St.* ℘*212-766-6600 or 800-468-3569. www.seaportinn.com. 72 rooms.* This hotel sits in the South Street Seaport historic district, a cobbled, pedestrian-friendly area full of bars, restaurants and shops just a short walk from the Financial District. Done up country-style with floral prints, guest quarters are well maintained and comfortable. Sixth- and seventh-floor rooms have terraces with incredible views of the East River and Brooklyn Bridge. You'll be treated to a complimentary continental breakfast in the morning and cookies each afternoon. High-speed internet access is available at no charge.

TriBeCa
Trendy restaurants and nightlife boost the appeal of accommodations in this neighborhood, especially during the annual TriBeCa Film Festival in the spring. The streets here make for a pleasant early morning jog or stroll, particularly if you're a fan

of handsome loft and warehouse buildings with terra-cotta and cast-iron facades.

$$$$ Cosmopolitan Hotel – *95 West Broadway at Chambers St. ℘212-566-1900 or 888-895-9400. www.cosmohotel.com. 150 rooms.* The longest continually operating hotel in New York City, dating back to 1850, the Cosmopolitan is located in the heart of TriBeCa. There are some 40 restaurants within a five-block radius, ranging from top-tier places like Bouley to casual neighborhood spots like Bubby's; the Financial District, the World Trade Center site, the West Village and SoHo are all nearby as well. All the rooms come with a private bath, desk, TV and free wireless internet access.

UNION SQUARE/MADISON SQUARE

The streets around Union Square, Madison Square and Gramercy Park appeal to those who prefer a comfortable neighborhood with easy access to both Lower Manhattan and Midtown. If you're staying around here, it's easy to dash out for breakfast at the incomparable Union Square Greenmarket.

$$$$$ The Carlton – &*88 Madison Ave. at E. 29th St.* ✕ ℘*212-532-4100 or 800-601-8500. www.carltonhotelny.com. 317 rooms.* Built in the early 20C, this Beaux-Arts structure was restored, inside and out, to its former splendor in summer 2005. The lobby now has a dramatic three-story waterfall; guest rooms have been fittingly redone with luxurious Scalamandre fabrics and Frette linens, with restful colors, mahogany furnishings, and marble and granite bathrooms rounding out the decor. Amenities include in-room safes, nightly turn-down service, iPod docking stations, flat-screen TVs and free wireless internet access. Some rooms enjoy views of the Empire State Building, located a short stroll away. Located on the ground floor, the hotel's restaurant, **Millesime ($$$$)** serves a French-influenced "seafood brasserie" menu with a focus on seasonal and local ingredients.

$$$$$ Inn at Irving Place – *56 Irving Pl. between E. 17th & E. 18th Sts., Gramercy Park. ℘212-533-4600 or 800-685-1447. www.innatirving.com. 12 rooms.* You won't find the name of the inn on these two 1834 brownstones; just look for the address. Within you *will* find stylish guest rooms appointed with quality 19C furnishings and named for famous New Yorkers like Washington Irving and Sarah Bernhardt, who lived in the neighborhood back then. CD and DVD players share space with iron four-poster or oak beds and overstuffed chairs. There's also wireless internet connection in each room. Continental breakfast is served in the cozy parlor or in your room. Afternoon tea, a real treat, is served in Lady Mendl's Victorian tea salon *(reservations required).* Martinis and nibbles can be had in the downstairs lounge.

MIDTOWN
CENTRAL MIDTOWN

Right in the thick of it and convenient to everything, Central Midtown draws theatergoers and other fans of New York's cultural offerings. If you're staying here, it's a quick return to base from late-night carriage rides in Central Park or evening shows at Carnegie Hall or Radio City Music Hall. And Rockefeller Center is nearby in case you're planning to be part of the outdoor audience at a morning-show taping.

$$$$$ City Club – &*55 W. 44th St.* ✕ℙ ℘*212-921-5500. www.cityclubhotel.com. 65 rooms.* Originally a gentlemen's club, the City Club now feels like an exclusive apartment building, with a discreet lobby, modern decor and attentive service. Rooms are small but luxuriously appointed with black-marble bathrooms, complimentary high-speed internet access, supple linens and DVD players. The sleek on-site **DB Bistro Moderne ($$$)** is renowned for serving the city's most decadent hamburger, stuffed with black truffles and foie gras.

$$$$$ The Royalton – &*44 W. 44th St.* ✕ℙ ℘*212-869-4400 or 800-697-1791. www.royaltonhotel.com. 168 rooms.* In contrast to its historic exterior, dating to 1898, the inside of The Royalton is daringly modern. The first New York product of avant-garde hotelier Ian Schrager and designer Philippe Starck, the decor was recently updated by Charlotte Macaux. Sleek, well-appointed guest rooms are outfitted with long, plush banquettes and crisp linens in cool neutrals; some

Hostels

Hostels are an economical alternative to high-priced Manhattan hotels; and while some can be bare-bones, others are actually nicer than budget hotels. New York hostels average $40 a night for dormitory-style accommodations and $125 a night for a private room. Amenities usually include a community living room, showers, laundry facilities, a kitchen and a dining room or restaurant. Reservations are essential during high season (summer and fall). *For further information, check out the website: www.hostels.com.*

One Bedroom Suite, Roger Smith

Roger Smith

have fireplaces. Bathrooms offer slate- and glass-walled showers or 5ft-wide soaking tubs. Drink and dine at the popular **Forty Four ($$$)**.

EAST MIDTOWN

Architecture buffs feel particularly at home in East Midtown, where iconic buildings and skyscrapers form an eclectic mix of old and new. Swanky Madison and Fifth Avenue stores beckon shoppers, and corporate types also find it convenient to stay here near the office towers.

$$$$$ Roger Smith – *501 Lexington Ave. at East 47th St.* ✗ ℘*212-755-1400. www.rogersmith.com. 130 rooms.* In contrast to the hushed minimalism that defines most upscale hotels, the Roger Smith basks in eccentricity: it runs its own contemporary art gallery on-site and fills the lobby with original work; rooms are individually decorated, some with iron bed frames, others with antique four-posters. Pets and children are welcome, the staff is warm and friendly, and you can check your email on the lobby iMacs.

TIMES SQUARE/THEATER DISTRICT

If the siren song of Broadway has lured you to New York, hotels around Times Square are a smart choice. Based here, you can pop out for dinner, take in a play or a musical, then enjoy a nightcap amid the lights of Times Square. The district also boasts some

of the glitziest shopping experiences in the city.

$$$ Mayfair New York – *242 W. 49th St. between Broadway & Eighth Ave.* ℘*212-586-0300 or 800-556-2932. www.mayfairnewyork.com. 78 rooms.* One of the few family-run hotels in Manhattan, Mayfair New York is located in the heart of Broadway theaters and Times Square nightlife. The entire building is "no smoking." Guest rooms and common areas showcase a collection of rare, historic photos from the Museum of the City of New York. Double-pane windows filter out the street noise. All accommodations come with modern conveniences including high-speed internet connections, hair dryers and computerized wall safes. Service is extremely friendly.

$$$$ Hotel Grace – *125 W. 45th St., between Sixth & Seventh Aves.* ℘*212-354-2323. www.room-matehotels.com. 139 rooms.* Spare, modern furnishings outfit the tiny guest rooms at this budget find, but the platform beds boast quality linens and all rooms have flat-screen TVs and wireless internet access. A youthful air pervades the place, especially at the lobby-level pool. A small workout room with steam room and sauna is open to guests 24hrs a day. There's a complimentary continental breakfast on the mezzanine.

$$$$$ Casablanca Hotel – *147 W. 43rd St. between Sixth Ave. & Broadway.* ℘*212-869-1212. www.casablancahotel.com. 44 rooms.* Surround yourself in a Moroccan-style setting right in the middle of Manhattan. This Broadway–Times Square property opened in 1997, and was recently renovated; guest rooms feature comfortable furnishings as well as high-tech amenities (there's even a telephone in the bathroom). The hotel provides a complimentary continental breakfast, cookies and coffee in the afternoon, use of a nearby fitness facility and a library of DVDs starring New York City.

$$$$$ Iroquois – *49 W. 44th St. between Fifth & Sixth Aves. ℰ800-332-7220. www.iroquoisny.com. 114 rooms.* Popular with the theater crowd, this well-kept 1923 hotel was recently remodeled with modern European furnishings. Plush amenities include goose-down pillows and Frette linens, tubs and showers in all rooms, flat-screen TVs, complimentary newspapers and access to a 24hr fitness center and a Finnish spa for the ultimate in relaxation. The tiny restaurant, Triomphe, is a popular spot with theatergoers.

$$$$$ Muse Hotel – *130 W. 46th St. between Sixth & Seventh Aves. ℰ212-485-2400 or 877-692-6873. www.themusehotel.com. 200 rooms.* This 19-story hotel recently restored its triple-arched, limestone-and-brick facade and redecorated its interior with meticulous attention to detail. Halls are bright and tastefully decorated in pale-green wallpaper; rooms are contemporary yet warmly inviting, with feather beds, L'Occitane bath products, green marble bathrooms and original artwork. Twice-daily maid service, a 24hr fitness room and a daily wine hour in the lobby. It's pet-friendly too.

Muse Hotel

Kimpton Hotels & Restaurants

UNITED NATIONS AREA

Accomodations here draw those with diplomatic business at the UN, as well as visitors in search of a base that's convenient to both the neighborhoods of Lower Manhattan and the swank reaches of the Upper East Side. Handy MTA lines also make it a good choice if you're planning an expedition to Queens or Long Island.

$$$$$ Millennium UN Plaza Hotel New York – *One United Nations Plaza between First & Second Aves. ℰ212-758-1234 or 866-866-8086. www.millenniumhotels.com. 438 rooms.* Sitting directly across from the United Nations, the Millennium offers convenient access to Grand Central Terminal and the Midtown business district as well as fashionable East Side restaurants and boutiques. The hotel's spacious and elegantly appointed guest rooms start on the 28th floor and provide breathtaking views of the New York skyline and the East River. Rich tapestries adorn the lobbies, corridors and guest accommodations. The Millennium is the only Manhattan hotel to have both an indoor tennis court and a glass-enclosed swimming pool. There's also a currency exchange at the front desk, and a full-service health club and fitness center. The Ambassador Grill restaurant serves as a meeting place for many UN dignitaries.

UPTOWN
UPPER EAST SIDE

Museums, art galleries and posh Park Avenue draw culture lovers to the premium accomodations in this wealthy enclave. The area also boasts an impressive collection of restaurants, many helmed by celebrity chefs (and patronized by celebrity clients).

$$$$$ The Carlyle – *35 E. 76th St. at Madison Ave. ℰ212-744-1600 or 888-767-3966. www.thecarlyle.com. 188 rooms.* This elegant hotel has been a fixture of the Upper East Side since 1930. Its guest list includes US presidents and dignitaries from around the world. Unequaled service, comfort and fine furnishings abound at every turn. The esteemed Café Carlyle hosts cabaret performers like Ute Lemper, as well as Woody Allen's Monday night jazz jam. Bemelmans Bar is named for the

Central Park view room, Mandarin Oriental

Mandarin Oriental

writer of the *Madeline* series, Ludwig Bemelmans, who painted the mural that graces the walls therein. Guest rooms may be small in comparison to newer properties, but they are luxuriously appointed with Louis XVI-style furnishings, plush carpets and marble bathrooms; nearly half of the suites have baby-grand pianos.

$$$$$ Hotel Wales – *1295 Madison Ave. between E. 92nd & E. 93rd Sts.* ✕ *☎212-876-6000 or 866-925-3746. www.hotelwalesnyc.com. 46 rooms, 42 suites.* This nicely restored (2000) property, built in 1902, is situated in a pleasant residential/commercial neighborhood within walking distance of Museum Mile. Amenities include a relaxing rooftop terrace, Belgian linens, down comforters on the beds and fresh flowers in the rooms. There's a 24hr fitness room on-site, or for $15 you can use the YMCA nearby. Indulge in the complimentary continental breakfast or head to **Sarabeth's Restaurant**, famed for its delicious breads and pastries.

$$$$$ The Regency – ♿*540 Park Ave. at E. 61st St.* ✕ *☎212-759-4100 or 800-233-2356. www.loewshotels.com. 353 rooms.* Recently treated to a multimillion-dollar renovation, The Regency stands just two blocks east of Central Park on tony Park Avenue. Guest quarters are spacious and luxurious, done in soft beiges with contemporary accents and complete with the latest amenities, from Frette linens to bathroom TVs. Service is the hotel's hallmark: the guest–staff ratio is one-to-one. There's a fitness center, and spa treatments are available.

Singer Michael Feinstein is often on hand to entertain in the lounge.

UPPER WEST SIDE
Performing arts, museums and the grand green swards of Central Park lie open to those who elect to stay on the Upper West Side. It's especially nice in summer, with the abundance of outdoor performing arts.

$$$ Excelsior Hotel – *45 W. 81st St. between Central Park West & Columbus Ave. ☎212-362-9200. www.excelsior hotelny.com. 199 rooms.* A stone's throw from the American Museum of Natural History and Central Park, this family-friendly hotel is decorated French-country style. Rooms in the front of the hotel are brighter; those in the back are quieter. There's wireless internet throughout (for a fee), as well as an entertainment room with fitness center, surround-sound TV and library.

$$$$$ Mandarin Oriental – ♿*80 Columbus Circle at W. 60th St.* ✕ ☰ Spa *☎212-805-8800 or 866-801-8880. www.mandarinoriental.com. 248 rooms.* From its lofty perch on floors 35 to 54 of the Time Warner Center, the Mandarin Oriental boasts wide-angle views of the city, especially of Central Park. All of the soundproofed guest rooms blend Asian color schemes and 1940s-style furniture; flat-panel TVs can be found in the bedrooms and the bathrooms. There's also a full-service spa and fitness center with indoor pool.

$$$$$ On the Ave – ♿*2178 Broadway at W. 77th St. ☎212-362-1100 or 800-509-7598. www.ontheave-nyc.com. 242 rooms, 27 suites.* A recent renovation brought this early-20C hotel luxuriously up to date. Nightly piano music in the lobby is a soothing segue to sleep. In your room you'll find a flat-screen plasma TV and Frette robes; on your bed Italian sheets, down comforters and, on the pillow, Belgian chocolates. Rooms on the top three floors have views of the Hudson River or Central Park; a 16th-floor balcony is dotted with Adirondack chairs for relaxing. Pets are welcome.

Where to Eat

Rest assured that the quality and variety of New York City's cuisine equal the city's prestige as a financial and cultural center. While top restaurants command jet-set prices, the city abounds in ethnic restaurants, bistros, delis and pizza parlors that won't blow your budget.

INTERNATIONAL CUISINE

Long before the Statue of Liberty rose in New York Harbor to welcome immigrants from foreign lands, New York's population was formed of people from different countries, but the city's 19C role as a gateway to America cemented its enduring international character. Newly arrived immigrants quickly formed ethnic enclaves in various parts of the city, perpetuating the cultural and culinary traditions that helped them feel at home in America. One happy result for residents and visitors alike is New York's astounding array of international cuisines.

EASTERN EUROPE

Traditional foods introduced by **Jewish** settlers fleeing persecution in their homelands have become synonymous with New York, particularly on the Lower East Side, the city's first Jewish stronghold. Chewy bagels, eaten plain or topped with cream cheese and lox (smoked salmon), are typical, as are deli favorites like corned beef, pastrami or brisket sandwiches

Russ & Daughters' bagel and lox

Jen Snow/Russ & Daughters

Midtown Carts at Dawn

Midtown lunch breaks have a hero. His name is Zach Brooks. The writer of **http://midtownlunch.com** made it his personal mission to make sense of the 3,000-odd street vendors and cafes in the district. His blog roots out the unsung heroes of lunch for under $10. They don't have to be comfortable or even welcoming, but do have to offer offer good-value, munchable food, from Indian kata rolls to Taiwanese pork chops.

accompanied by tangy coleslaw and sour, drippy pickles. Soft rolls filled with meat or potatoes (knishes) are easy to find here. Tender crepes known as blintzes are a brunch treat; try them filled with sweetened cheese or fruit, topped with sour cream. From Poland and Russia come the beet-and-cabbage soup known as borscht, and stuffed cabbage rolls laced with tomato or mushrooms.

ASIA

Lower Manhattan's Chinatown bustles with first- and second-generation Asian Americans, from not only China but Thailand, the Philippines, Vietnam, Korea and Malaysia as well. Thriving Asian enclaves have blossomed in Flushing (Queens) and other areas as well. **Chinese** specialties include wok-fried meats, seafood and vegetables sauced in innumerable ways and served over rice; juk or congee, a thick rice porridge served with meat and eaten for breakfast; and dim sum, a tasty variety of dumplings (egg rolls, pot stickers, wontons) and other appetizer-size treats. Other Asian favorites to try: Korean barbecue cooked at the table and topped with crunchy vegetables; or a bowl of fragrant Vietnamese pho.

WESTERN EUROPE

Manhattan's Little Italy is New York's best-known (and fast-disappearing) **Italian** neighborhood, but enclaves

Pizzeria in Brooklyn

Y. Kanazawa/MICHELIN

thrive in Bensonhurst (Brooklyn) and Staten Island as well. Pasta is ubiquitous, served in every shape and size and stuffed or dressed with a huge variety of sauces based on meats, fish and vegetables. You'll also find steaks, squid (calamari), sausages simmered with onions and peppers and, of course, pizza. End your meal with luscious tiramisú, a sweet mascarpone cheese-and-cake confection laced with cocoa and brandy; cream-filled cannoli pastries; icy gelato or a crunchy biscotti with espresso.

Greek restaurants abound in New York, but especially in Astoria (Queens), a great place to sample succulent grilled meats and seafood; green salads redolent with olive oil, feta cheese and olives; and tightly rolled marinated grape leaves stuffed with rice and herbs. Baklava, a nut-filled pastry drenched with honey, makes a perfect dessert.

The Scoop

Since April 2003, restaurants, bars and clubs in New York City have been made smoke-free by law. Although jackets may not be required, gentlemen may feel more comfortable wearing one in the more expensive establishments. Reservations are highly recommended. Gratuities are generally not included on the bill; a tip of 15 to 20 per cent is considered standard.

LATIN AMERICA

The Jackson Heights neighborhood in Queens boasts a tempting concentration of **Mexican**, **Peruvian** and **Colombian** restaurants, but Latin American cuisine can be found all over the city. Going far beyond the usual taco-and-burrito fare, New York restaurants serve up authentic marinated and grilled meats, *arroz con pollo* (chicken and rice), spicy chorizo sausages and savory *empanadas*. This is the place to try the citrus-marinated seafood dish known as *ceviche*. For dessert, order a caramel-topped flan.

MIDDLE EAST/NORTH AFRICA

Syrian and **Lebanese** immigrants first settled in Lower Manhattan, but enclaves can now be found in all five boroughs, especially in Brooklyn. Try falafel (a fried fava bean and chickpea patty) or savory grilled meats and vegetables tucked into pita bread or threaded onto skewers (kabobs), served with fresh greens, rice, and hummus; a garlicky puree of chickpeas flavored with tahini and lemon. **Moroccan** specialties include tagines, lamb-based stews slowly simmered with vegetables, fruits and spices, served over couscous.

USEFUL WEBSITES

If you're a serious foodie and want to do some research on your own, visit www.nymag.com, *New York Magazine*'s website, which boasts a quick search engine and hundreds of opinionated reviews. Another great site is www.menupages.com, which has reviews and full up-to-date menus with prices for more than 6,000 New York eateries.

RATES

Listed rates indicate the average cost of an appetizer, an entrée and dessert for one person (not including tax, gratuity or beverages).

$$$$	**Over $75**
$$$	**$50–$75**
$$	**$25–$50**
$	**Under $25**

RESTAURANTS BY AREA

DOWNTOWN

BATTERY PARK CITY

Harbor views and great food are what it's all about in Battery Park City, with dining options ranging from rustic Italian to Chinese.

$$ Gigino at Wagner Park – *20 Battery Pl. at Little West St.* ✆*212-528-2228. www.gigino-wagnerpark.com*. **Italian**. Don't be fooled by the modest entrance underneath the brick lookout platform, Gigino has a vast back deck with expansive harbor views. And with an extensive list of reasonably priced dishes, ranging from wood-oven-fired pizzas to hearty entrées to the signature pasta, spaghetti de Padrino (made with beets, escarole, garlic and anchovy-flavored olive oil), it's sure to satisfy the appetites of every member of la famiglia. The original **Gigino**, with its warm, rustic dining room, is in nearby TriBeCa (*323 Greenwich St. between Duane & Reade Sts.;* ✆*212-431-1112)*.

CHELSEA

Dining options in Chelsea are nothing if not eclectic, with French bistros cozying up to sushi bars, Mexican restaurants and burger joints. Before or after a meal here, be sure to check out Chelsea's tony art galleries.

$$ Bombay Talkie – *189 Ninth Ave. between W. 21st & W. 22nd Sts.* ✆*212-242-1900. www.bombaytalkie.com*. **Indian**. If you enjoy sampling and sharing generous portions of regional Indian classics amid convivial (and sometimes noisy) groups of diners, give this Bollywood-flavored teahouse a try. Traditional naan bread, grain chips and rice puffs precede savory classics like chicken biryani with yogurt dipping sauce, pork vindaloo and abundant vegetarian dishes. Try a cocktail from the bar, where the adventurous East-meets-West approach wins rave reviews.

$$ Gascogne – *158 Eighth Ave. between W. 17th & W. 18th Sts.* ✆*212-675-6564. www.gascognenyc.com*. **French**. If you're craving rustic fare from the southwest of France, make a beeline for Gascogne. Fine cassoulet (a stew of white beans, duck confit and garlic sausage), foie gras, and veal kidneys flamed with Armagnac are examples of the carefully prepared dishes here. In the summer, the delightful, shady outdoor garden is a popular place to dine.

$$ The Red Cat – *227 Tenth Ave. between W. 23rd & W. 24th Sts.* ✆*212-242-1122. www.theredcat.com*. **Contemporary**. The Red Cat combines New England-style decor—wood-paneled walls, red-and-white color scheme—with New American dishes such as pan-roasted organic chicken, sugarcane roasted pork tenderloin and other innovative takes on classic American dishes. Menus change according to the season.

$$ Rocking Horse Cafe – *182 Eighth Ave. between W. 19th & W. 20th Sts.* ✆*212-463-9511. www.rockinghorsecafe.com*. **Mexican**. Mexican folk art and bright colors make a vibrant background for the Rocking Horse's authentic regional Mexican cuisine. Hangar steak, free-range chicken and grilled vegetables provide the filling for burritos, quesadillas and enchiladas at lunch, while the dinner menu selections range from chiltepe-glazed tuna to *chile ancho relleno* and mustard-crusted lamb chops. Just don't eat too much, or you won't have room for the rich *tres leches* cake, topped with sliced bananas and banana cream. Children are welcome here, and the cafe even features a kids' menu.

CHINATOWN

Chinatown's main restaurant drag, Mott Street, blooms with authentic eateries, most of them casual, family-friendly spots. Don't miss the chance to sample dim sum: it's a New York tradition.

$ Great N.Y. Noodletown – *28 Bowery at Bayard St.* ✆*212-349-0923*. **Chinese**. Oodles of noodles is what you'll find at Great N.Y. Noodletown. Served pan-fried, Cantonese-style, or Hong Kong-style in lo mein, inexpensive Chinese noodle dishes take center stage at this no-frills place; but there's also a choice of salt-baked dishes and barbecued meats. Don't wait on the server to take your check; here you have to take your own check up to the cashier to pay before you leave.

$ Oriental Garden – *14 Elizabeth St. between Bayard & Canal Sts.* ✆*212-*

619-0085. **Chinese**. If you're a seafood lover, your meal will greet you at the door—two aquariums full of fish and lobster flank the entrance. Don't like fish? No worries. There's an extensive selection of classic Chinese dishes as well. The little dining room, its walls lined with framed Chinese ideograms, is almost always packed. Just be sure to bring cash; Oriental Garden doesn't accept credit cards for bills under $60.

$ Peking Duck House – *28 Mott St. between Chatham Sq. & Pell St. ℘212-227-1810. www.pekingduckhousenyc.com.* **Chinese**. Food lovers flock to 28 Mott Street for the specialty of the house—the namesake Peking duck. To get it, they must come en masse, since it's prepared only for four or more diners. Topped with a ginger-accented sweet sauce, the delicacy comes with house-made pancakes, cucumbers and scallions. If you're dining solo, or as a couple, try the sea bass or the Szechuan prawns. Then, next time, gather a group of your friends and come back to sample the duck—or head for the restaurant's second location *(236 E. 53rd St. between Second & Third Aves., East Midtown; ℘212-759-8260).*

$$ Dim Sum Go Go – ♿ *5 East Broadway at Chatham Sq. ℘212-732-0797.* **Chinese**. Don't let the Chinese takeout name throw you. This sleek restaurant is more sophisticated than many of its Chinatown counterparts. New wave dim sum is served to order, not on traditional rolling carts. Mushroom and pickled-vegetable dumplings, duck skin and crabmeat wrapped in spinach dough,

or chive and shrimp dumplings in ginger-vinegar dipping sauce are but a sampling of the many choices. Those with heartier appetites will enjoy entrées such as steamed halibut on a bed of braised Chinese leeks and celery, or roast chicken with fried garlic stems.

EAST VILLAGE

The East Village sports a surprising variety of ethnic restaurants, including Italian, Russian, Korean and Japanese. Most are concentrated in the area around First Avenue and points west, and around Tompkins Square Park.

$ Angelica Kitchen – *300 E. 12th St. between First & Second Aves. ℘212-228-2909. www.angelicakitchen.com.* **Vegan**. Health-conscious New Yorkers love the creative vegan fare (no meat or dairy) at this popular East Village eatery. Most of the dishes are simply prepared, letting the flavors of the vegetables (usually local and organic) speak for themselves. Many diners cobble together dinner from the wide assortment of salads, grilled vegetables, tofu and breads (the rice-dense cornbread is a meal in itself), though the most flavorful dishes are often the daily specials, which range from savory stews to tamales. If you're eating solo, take a seat at the community table, where you can read or chat with Angelica's regulars.

$ Soba-Ya – *229 E. 9th St. between First & Second Aves. ℘212-533-6966. www.sobaya-nyc.com.* **Japanese**. Soba-Ya's inexpensive noodle dishes and Zen-like atmosphere appeal to students from nearby New York University. On a cold day, there's nothing like a steaming bowl of soba (Japanese buckwheat noodles, made in-house) to warm you up. Noodles come in steaming bowls of hot broth complemented by your choice of additions from shrimp tempura to meat and vegetables. In warm weather, you'll probably prefer your noodles served cold, with add-on ingredients heaped on top. No matter the season, there's always a good selection of Japanese beer and sake.

$$ Itzocan – *438 E. 9th St. between Ave. A & First Ave. ℘212-677-5856. www. itzocanrestaurant.com.* **Mexican**. Set near Tompkins Square Park, tiny Itzocan is worth seeking out for fresh,

Momofuku Ssäm Bar

©Noah Kalina/Momofuku

well-prepared Mexican food. Burritos and quesadillas fill the menu at lunch, while at dinner the short list of entrées is more upscale (braised flank steak in *chile pasilla*, *semolina epazote* dumplings with roasted poblano peppers). Don't miss the excellent house-made guacamole, and save room for the chocolate mole cake; its rich, chocolatey flavor is kicked up with a soupçon of chile pepper. If you're visiting Museum Mile, check out Itzocan's other location in Spanish Harlem *(1575 Lexington Ave. at E. 101st St.; ℘212-423-0255)*.

$$ Momofuku Ssäm Bar – *207 Second Ave. at E. 13th St. ℘212-254-3500. www.momofuku.com.* **Korean**. Building on his success at nearby Momofuku Noodle Bar *(171 First Ave. at 11th St.)*, chef David Chang introduces New Yorkers to the wonders of the Korean burrito, or ssäm, at this sleekly cacophonous hotspot. In the Momofuku Ssäm, a flour tortilla is stuffed with tender pork, edamame, onions, shiitake mushrooms and kimchi puree. Indeed, pork fills the menu, from the section of country hams to the juicy short ribs to the pork-bun appetizer. There are also sections devoted to local foods, particularly seasonal produce, and to dishes made with offal. FYI: *momofuku* means "little peach" in Korean.

FINANCIAL DISTRICT
Restaurants here cluster around William Street where its curve matches the tip of Manhattan. Business lunches and expense-account dinners are the norm, and steaks, chops and burgers headline the menus.

$$ Les Halles Downtown – *15 John St. between Broadway & Nassau Sts. ℘212-285-8585. www.leshalles.net.* **French**. Chef/author Anthony Bourdain (who penned the restaurant exposé *Kitchen Confidential*) opened this restaurant after the terrorist attack of September 11, 2001—one of the first new restaurants to open in the Financial District at the time. Here he serves up such palate-pleasing French dishes as *steak au poivre* and *coq au vin*. You'll find basically the same menu at his other brasserie, Les Halles on Park Avenue *(411 Park Ave. between E. 28th & E. 29th Sts.; ℘212-679-4111)*.

$ Full Shilling – *160 Pearl St. between Wall & Pine Sts. ℘212-422-3855. www.thefullshilling.com.* **Irish pub**. The Full Shilling serves up traditional Irish pub food, including bangers and mash, shepherd's pie and fish and chips, in a traditional Irish pub setting. (There are some allowances for American taste, from the Cajun chicken sandwich to the mozzarella sticks.) The wonder is that the place is located just steps from the power corridor of Wall Street. Something about the dim lighting, the clatter of plates, and the friendly service seems to melt away stress. A couple of (imperial) pints don't hurt either.

GREENWICH VILLAGE
The blocks right off Houston Street and just west of Washington Square boast a warren of great restaurants, most with an unpretentious, neighborhood feel. French, Japanese and Italian spots rise to the fore.

$$ Pearl Oyster Bar – *18 Cornelia St. between W. 4th & Bleecker Sts. Closed Sun. ℘212-691-8211. www.pearloysterbar.com.* **Seafood**. You can't get fresher fish for the price in Manhattan than at Pearl Oyster Bar. This minnow-size, friendly eatery caters to those in the know with its two long marble counters with side-by-side seats and a small adjoining room with a smattering of bistro tables. Chef/owner Rebecca Charles' signature dish, a gargantuan lobster roll (chunks of fresh lobster moistened with mayonnaise and tucked into a toasted bun) leaves many a Maine lobster shack to shame. Be sure to check out the blackboard specials and save room for the deliciously tart blueberry crumble pie.

$$ Pó – *31 Cornelia St., between Bleecker & W. 4th Sts. ℘212-645-2189. www.po restaurant.com.* **Italian**. Pó is the kind of neighborhood restaurant locals wish they lived around the corner from. Specializing in Tuscan fare with a well-selected, moderately priced wine list, this snug Italian trattoria makes diners feel like welcome guests at a delightful dinner party. The value for money here is hard to beat. Dinner pastas (think white bean ravioli with brown butter sauce, or linguine with fresh clams and white wine) range from $15 to $18. Chef Lee McGrath's six-course tasting menu is a great deal at only $52.

LITTLE ITALY/NOLITA

Mulberry Street between Canal and Broome is the neighborhood's main dining drag. It's closed to vehicles on weekends spring through fall, when authentic Italian bakeries, gelato shops, pizzerias and red-sauce joints set tables out on the sidewalks.

$ Café Habana – *17 Prince St. at Elizabeth St. 212-625-2001. www.cafehabana.com.* **Cuban.** Small, hip and always crowded, this corner diner serves up some of the best skirt steak and fried plantains this side of Havana; runners-up include the grilled corn and egg burrito. For quicker service (expect a long line on weekends and at prime dinner hours) head to the takeout window next door, which has most of the same food and a mean café con leche.

$ Lombardi's – *32 Spring St. between Mott & Mulberry Sts. Open Sun–Thu 11.30am–11pm, Fri–Sat 11.30am– midnight. 212-941-7994. www.firstpizza.com.* Established in 1905, Lombardi's claims to be the first pizzeria in America. Its thin-crust pies (try the clam!) are baked in coal-fired ovens and served on checkered tablecloths. Expect a wait on weekend nights.

$$ Il Palazzo – *151 Mulberry St. between Grand & Hester Sts. 212-343-7000.* **Italian.** Right on Little Italy's main drag, Il Palazzo dishes up a generous selection of classics: veal saltimbocca, chicken cacciatore, rigatoni alla vodka, linguine with clam sauce, shrimp scampi. End your meal with a glass of grappa or vintage port and then head around the corner to Ferrara *(195 Grand St.)* bakery for espresso and gelato.

$$ Nyonya – *199 Grand St. between Mott & Mulberry Sts. 212-334-3669.* **Malaysian.** As Chinatown increasingly engulfs Little Italy, it's not as odd as it might sound to come to the neighborhood for inexpensive and original Malaysian food. This fusion cuisine pairs traditional Chinese ingredients with Malay herbs and spices, resulting in dishes from seafood rice noodles to curried pork spare ribs. For dessert, try the *pulut hitam*, a sweet treat made from black rice and coconut milk.

$$ Pellegrino's – *138 Mulberry St. between Grand & Hester Sts. 212-226-3177.* **Italian.** Pelligrino's is a place that you can take the whole family. The restaurant caters to families with half-portions for children (and others with smaller appetites). Linguini alla Sinatra, the signature dish, overflows with lobster, shrimp, clams, mushrooms and pine nuts in a light red sauce. On a warm summer day, grab one of the sidewalk tables, where you can take in the Little Italy street scene.

LOWER EAST SIDE

Head for Second Avenue, the neighborhood's culinary spine, where you can take your pick of ethnic restaurants, including Korean, Thai, Russian, Mexican and Jewish. There's even a Little India district here, with plenty to sample from India and Bangladesh.

$$ 'inoteca – *98 Rivington St. at Ludlow St. 212-614-0473. www.inotecanyc.com.* **Italian.** Studiously catering to the chic young Lower East Side set, the restaurant offers a superb selection of well-priced Italian wines, some 250 in all, from every region of Italy (an enoteca is a "wine bar" in Italy). Of these, 25 wines are available by the glass. The menu emphasizes small plates and panini (stuffed with the likes of bresaola, fontina and arugula, or roasted vegetables and fresh ricotta). Laid-back little (really little) sister **'ino**, a cheaper but just as trendy alternative, can be found in Greenwich Village *(21 Bedford St. between Downing St. & Sixth Ave.; 212-989-5769)*.

$$ Schiller's Liquor Bar – *131 Rivington St. at Norfolk St. 212-260-4555. www.schillersny.com.* **American.** Looking for a late-night nosh? This bustling white-tiled Lower East Side mainstay, a Keith McNally property, is open until at least 1am every night, and until 3am on Friday and Saturday. The menu choices range from macaroni and cheese with bacon to *moules frites* to lamb curry, supplemented by set daily specials (come Monday for fried chicken, Friday for boiled lobster). The wine list is divided into three sections: cheap, decent and good; according to the restaurant, "cheap" is best.

MEATPACKING DISTRICT

The heat is on in this trendy district, with its ever-increasing number of restaurants helmed by big-name chefs. A few stay open into the wee hours, catering to the after-club crowd.

$$ Fatty Crab – *643 Hudson St. between Gansevoort & Horatio Sts.* ℘*212-352-3592. www.fattycrab.com.* **Malaysian.** Though it's only a few years old, this diminutive restaurant feels like it's been around forever with its dark, well-worn interior, rock music and fanatical following, which keeps the place noisy and crowded at all hours. But chef Zak Pelaccio takes the food seriously, having spent time in Malaysia perfecting his craft. The chile crab is excellent, with large pieces of Dungeness crab in a spicy-sweet tomato chile sauce; so is the fatty duck.

$$ Macelleria – *48 Gansevoort St. between Greenwich & Washington Sts.* ℘*212-741-2555. www.macelleria restaurant.com.* **Italian.** Housed in a reconstructed butcher shop (*macelleria* in Italian), this engaging trattoria with its brick-walled wine cellar offers an outstanding variety of salami, homemade pastas, meat dishes and Italian wines. Start with the iceberg lettuce wedge with gorgonzola and peppercorn dressing, then move on to a pasta dish such as green and white tagliolini with peas and prosciutto, or garganelli with oxtail ragu. Hint for steak lovers: the prime dry-aged porterhouse for two is the same beef that's served at Peter Luger's famed steakhouse in Brooklyn.

$$ Paradou – *8 Little West 12th St. between Greenwich & Washington Sts.* ℘*212-463-8345. www.paradounyc.com.* **French.** Whitewashed walls, high ceilings, and tables fashioned out of vintage French wine crates create an airy, rustic ambience at Paradou (the name means "paradise"). Entrées such as chicken grand-mère, cassoulet and thick-cut pork chops recall the sunny cuisine of the Mediterranean, as do the bowls of plump mussels swimming in tomato-thyme broth. Weekend brunch brings the option of unlimited champagne cocktails; the bellinis and kir royales arrive by the pitcher.

$$ Pastis – *9 Ninth Ave. at W. 12th St.* ℘*212-929-4844. www.pastisny.com.* **French.** Large decorative mirrors, a long zinc bar, bistro tables and walls lined with old advertisements for Pastis create an aura of France circa 1960 here. Like any good French bistro, Pastis serves three meals a day and stays open late. The menu includes all the classics (tripe grantinée, steak tartare), and the cocktail list features drinks made from the restaurant's namesake anise-flavored aperitif, which originated in Marseille. Stop by weekends for the popular brunch.

SoHo

Prince, Sullivan and Grand Streets are the areas to head for if you're dining out in trendy SoHo. The neighborhood attracts its share of hot new restaurants favored by fashionistas, but if you poke about you'll find modest eateries perhaps short on fashion but long on charm.

$$ Blue Ribbon Sushi – *119 Sullivan St. between Prince & Spring Sts.* ℘*212-343-0404. www.blueribbonrestaurants.com.* **Japanese.** A Downtown sushi mainstay, Blue Ribbon Sushi has a vast menu of fresh and buttery raw fish, as well as a kids' menu of assorted yakimono and maki (there's even fried chicken and catfish fingers). Thanks to its no-reservations policy, the waits at the SoHo flagship can be long. If you happen to be staying in Brooklyn, though, you can sample the same grub at the Park Slope outpost (*278 Fifth Ave. between 1st St. & Garfield Pl.;* ℘*718-840-0408*), which is equally popular but larger and less frenetic.

SOUTH STREET SEAPORT

Water Street and Peck Slip welcome families and financial types alike to their tables for excellent steak and seafood. The Seaport itself boasts kid-friendly ice-cream booths and snack stands, plus a few sit-down restaurants for taking a serious break.

$$ Bridge Cafe – *279 Water St. at Dover St.* ℘*212-227-3344. www.bridge cafenyc.com.* **American.** Billing itself as New York's oldest drinking establishment (it's been in business since 1794), Bridge Cafe occupies a cozy 1920s building at the foot of the Brooklyn Bridge. Dishes are based on what's in season—pan-roasted lobster with heirloom apple and celery root salad, for example—and are surprisingly inexpensive, given the quality of the cuisine. Go Sunday for the Bridge Brunch, served from 11.45am to 4pm.

$$ Nelson Blue – 233–235 Front St. at Peck Slip. ☎212-346-9090. www. nelsonblue.com. **New Zealand**. The Southern Hemisphere takes the stage at this intriguing newcomer to the Peck Slip area. Native Maori design touches keep everything laid back and casual, as do the New Zealand beers and Down Under culinary specialties on the menu. Try green-lipped mussels, lamb, even venison dishes, or a saucy meat pie (lamb, chicken or beef) washed down with a pint of Speight's ale.

TRiBeCa

Catering to a local clientele of creative types, trendy TriBeCa is a cool place to eat. Celebrity chefs attract attention to the neighborhood, which can make for a spendy meal, but there are plenty of modest, yet delicious options. Seek them out.

$$ Bread Tribeca – 301 Church St. at Walker St. ☎212-334-0200. www. breadtribeca.com. **Italian**. With its vast windows and simple decor, Bread TriBeCa works well both for an early lunch and for a late dinner. Sandwiches are the specialty here, filled with the likes of Sicilian sardines, handmade mozzarella, and prosciutto di Parma stuffed between Italian ciabatta bread or crusty baguettes. Desserts like the caramelized banana tart, served with vanilla ice cream, are bound to please the most discriminating sweet tooth.

$$ Odeon – 145 West Broadway between Thomas & Duane Sts. ☎212-233-0507. www.theodeonrestaurant.com. **American**. A TriBeCa hotspot since the early 1980s, Odeon has long been a place where the glitterati come to eat. You may still catch a glimpse of big-name entertainers and artists here, but the real draw is the refined cuisine, especially the weekday fixed-price menu at lunch. If you're interested in dining at odd hours, Odeon serves an early-bird brasserie menu of light fare daily until 5.30pm, and a late-bird version from midnight until closing Wed–Sun.

$$$ Locanda Verde – 377 Greenwich St. at North Moore St. ☎212-925-3797. www. locandaverdenyc.com. **Italian**. TriBeCa mainstay Robert De Niro is part-owner of this much-heralded newcomer to the Downtown food scene. Chef Andrew Carmellini's Italian-tavern-themed menu features inventive crostini, crispy pig salad, fire-roasted entrées and his own grandmother's ravioli recipe that led *The New York Times* critic Frank Bruni to quip that he wanted to "swap ancestors" with the chef.

$$$ Nobu Next Door – 105 Hudson St. at Franklin St. ☎212-334-4445. www. myriadrestaurantgroup.com. **Japanese**. Hankering to try the mouth-watering sushi made by Japanese-born chef Nobu Matsuhisa, but you can't get in at his flagship, Nobu? Just go next door, where you'll find essentially the same food at a slightly lower price (be sure to go early to avoid a wait; Nobu Next Door doesn't accept reservations). It's all about texture here: a decor enhanced by black river stones, scorched pine tables and Indonesian market-basket light fixtures harmonizes with the sensual pleasures of clawless lobsters, sea urchins, seafood udon, and mochi ice-cream balls.

UNION SQUARE/MADISON SQUARE

Diners in the know make a beeline for this area, long a nexus of fine dining. Big-name restaurants pepper the blocks, and menu prices play the part so plan accordingly. Locals will tell you it's worth the splurge.

$$ Blue Water Grill – 31 Union Sq. West at 16th St. ☎212-675-9500. www.bluewatergrillnyc.com. **Seafood**. Seafood lovers will revel in the fresh fare at this lively restaurant, which overlooks Union Square. Maine lobster, Maryland crab cakes, and a selection of oysters from the raw bar keep drawing 'em in. There's also sushi and maki rolls. Jazz music enlivens the scene even more, nightly beginning at 6pm in the downstairs lounge, and on Sunday for the restaurant's popular jazz brunch.

$$ Tamarind – 41–43 E. 22nd St. between Broadway & Park Ave., Gramercy Park. ☎212-674-7400. www.tamarinde22.com. **Indian**. There's no mistaking the setting at Tamarind, there are reminders of India everywhere. Cowbells hang in the alcoves of the gleaming-white dining room; a large, wrought-iron wall-hanging from a maharaja's palace greets guests at the entrance. Bustling cooks prepare piquant regional Indian dishes in the glassed-in kitchen. And a good, balanced wine list and a staff of smiling, attentive servers add to Tamarind's appeal. For lighter, less expensive fare, go to the teahouse next door.

$$$ Gotham Bar and Grill – *12 E. 12th St. between Fifth Ave. & University Pl. ☎212-620-4020. www.gothambarand grill.com.* **American**. Gotham Bar and Grill is consistently rated one of New York's finest restaurants, and with good reason. Executive chef Alfred Portale, who studied in France under Michel Guérard, fits the Big Apple to a "T." The pioneer of vertical food, Portale's innovative "skyscraper" presentations are a treat for the eye as well as the palate. The menu changes monthly depending on the market. If you're watching your budget, inquire about the $24 three-course lunch.

$$$ Union Square Cafe – *21 E. 16th St. between Fifth Ave. & Union Sq. West ☎212-243-4020. www.unionsquarecafe.com.* **Italian**. In 1985 veteran New York restaurateur Danny Meyer opened this popular bistro and thus launched a culinary empire that continues to define the Big Apple restaurant scene. USC still packs in crowds every night and it's not hard to see why: the service is friendly and impeccable, the surroundings cool and comfortable, the food imaginative. The high-concept Italian comfort food highlights the best of the nearby Union Square Greenmarket. Don't have a reservation? Belly up to the bar for the same food in a more casual setting.

WEST VILLAGE
The gentrified area north and west of Washington Square Park boasts a fair number of happening restaurants run by happening chefs; if you plan to eat here, be sure to reserve well in advance or prepare to wait.

$$$ Perry Street – *176 Perry St. at West St. ☎212-352-1900. www.jean-georges.com.* **Contemporary**. Marked by impeccable service, sleek surroundings and flawlessly prepared food, Perry Street may well be Jean-Georges Vongerichten's most appealing restaurant. As cool

as it appears at first sight, the decor feels warm and inviting once you're deep into one of the snug chairs or banquettes. The French-inflected New American menu is focused yet inventive, particularly with seafood, and the desserts are divine. Come for the $26 three-course prix-fixe lunch; it's one of the best deals in town. And don't be surprised if you find yourself dining with celebrities: the building, a glass tower by Richard Meier, is full of multimillion-dollar condominiums owned by celebs like Calvin Klein (and sublet by celebrity renters Jim Carrey and Hugh Jackman).

$$ The Spotted Pig – *314 W. 11th St. at Greenwich St. ☎212-620-0393. www. thespottedpig.com.* **Gastropub**. One of the city's most popular restaurants, the Spotted Pig sports a country-cute decor that still manages to be hip, with rustic tables covered in butcher-block paper, pig paraphernalia and other bric-a-brac. Celebrities abound—Bill Clinton allegedly waited a half-hour for a table— but the food's the real star here, with young British expat chef April Bloomfield turning out robust fare like fried calf's livers and rabbit stew. Come early (before 6pm) to avoid the horrendous line; reservations are not accepted. Also be aware that vegetarian options are limited.

MIDTOWN
BROADWAY/TIMES SQUARE/ THEATER DISTRICT
Restaurants here for the most part match the district's theatricality and flair, with over-the-top decor and cuisine. It's a good choice for a splashy night on the town.

$ Azuri Café – *465 W. 51st St. between Ninth & Tenth Aves. Closed Fri night, Sat. ☎212-262-2920. www.azuricafe.com.* **Falafel**. Don't expect to be wined and dined at this Hell's Kitchen hole-in-the-wall. For one thing, it doesn't have a liquor license, and for another, atmosphere is pretty much nonexistent. But for fresh, savory Middle Eastern food, including some of the best falafel, tabbouleh and baba ghanoush you'll find in New York, Azuri can't be beat. Grab a root beer from the cooler and order one of the plates, which will give you an entrée (try the falafel or the vegetable patties) with an assortment of salads and fresh pita bread. Trust the chef; he can be surly with nit-pickers.

$ Carnegie Delicatessen – *854 Seventh Ave. between W. 54th & W. 55th Sts. ☏212-757-2245. www.carnegiedeli.com.* **Jewish kosher**. It's hard to tell what this kosher deli is more famous for: salty service or mile-high pastrami sandwiches. At this New York institution, it's best to endure the former for the latter; split a sandwich if you want to save room for the delicious cheesecake. Be prepared to share your table here; it's all part of the fun. Film buffs will be interested to know that much of Woody Allen's 1983 flick *Broadway Danny Rose* was shot on the premises.

$$ Marseille – *♿630 Ninth Ave. at W. 44th St. ☏212-333-2323. www.marseillenyc.com.* **French**. This bustling bistro within walking distance of Times Square is a terrific spot for pre- and post-theater dining. Offering French cuisine with Moroccan, Turkish and Tunisian overtones, Marseille's menu runs the gamut from bouillabaisse to lamb tagine. The restaurant's art deco setting, embellished with pastel arches, handmade floor tiles and a vintage zinc bar, has a Casablanca feel. Marseille's proximity to theaters means it's busy almost constantly, but the waitstaff manages to handle the crowds with ease. Broadway headliners often drop by after performances.

$$$ Firebird – *♿365 W. 46th St. between Eighth & Ninth Aves. Closed Mon. ☏212-586-0244. www.firebirdrestaurant.com.* **Russian**. Tsar Nicholas would no doubt feel as comfortable in these three elegantly restored town houses as he did in the Winter Palace, and would probably enjoy the cuisine as much too; with dishes like Ukrainian borscht, poached sturgeon and chicken Kiev, not to mention seven kinds of caviar. It's a fun place to watch the pre-theater crowd before walking over to a Broadway show. Or stay to catch the complimentary jazz at the adjacent Firebird Lounge.

$$$ Gallagher's – *228 W. 52nd St. between Broadway & Eighth Ave. ☏212-245-5336. www.gallaghersnysteakhouse. com.* **Steakhouse**. Billing itself as "New York City to the bone," Gallagher's steakhouse opened in 1927 next door to what is now the Neil Simon Theater. Rows of meat carcasses hanging in the meat locker are visible from the street. Inside, a wood-paneled dining room boasts checkered tablecloths, and walls lined with photographs of Broadway stars, politicians and athletes; both human and equine. What's on the menu? Beef, beef and more beef, of the finest quality and cuts.

CENTRAL MIDTOWN
The blocks just below Central Park are rife with hugely popular restaurants. If you crave fine French or Italian cuisine turned out by classically trained experts, set your sights on this primo dining area.

$$$ The Modern – *♿9 W. 53rd St. between Fifth & Sixth Aves. Closed Sun. ☏212-333-1220. www.themodernnyc.com.* **Contemporary**. Operated by Danny Meyer (Gramercy Tavern, Union Square Cafe), this upscale eatery is as well known for its excellent cooking as for its unbeatable location edging the Museum of Modern Art's sculpture garden. A vast glass wall and sprays of colorful flowers add light to the cool space. You can order à la carte at lunch, but dinner is strictly prix-fixe ($98–$140), featuring such creative fare as licorice-poached East Coast halibut. The wine list offers more than 900 selections.

$$$ The Sea Grill – *See Fifth Ave. map. 19 W. 49th St. between Fifth & Sixth Aves. Closed Sun. ☏212-332-7610. www. theseagrillnyc.com.* **Seafood**. Located in Rockefeller Center, the Sea Grill overlooks the famous ice rink, so you can watch the skaters as you dine. There's an international flair to the seafood here; the menu includes Latin-inflected "a la plancha" preparations (on a traditional cast-iron griddle) as well as Asian-, South Asian- and Italian-influenced dishes. A seafood bar and roasted whole Greek daurade round out the offerings.

$$$$ Le Bernardin – *♿See Fifth Ave. map. 155 W. 51st St. between Sixth & Seventh Aves. Closed Sun. ☏212-554-1515. www.le-bernardin.com.* **Seafood**. Expect to spend serious money at this spacious, elegant restaurant, widely acclaimed as one of the city's best; it will be worth the splurge (the chef's tasting menu is $185 per person, without wine). With its coffered ceiling and white-glove service, Le Bernardin also offers a prix-fixe menu that comes almost entirely from the sea. Prepare yourself for chef Eric Ripert's delicately orchestrated dishes, which are divided into sections of "almost raw," "barely touched" and "lightly cooked" on the à la carte menu. *Jackets required.*

EAST MIDTOWN
Dining options are relatively sparse throughout the midtown streets east of Fifth Avenue, but you'll find good steak and seafood restaurants nonetheless. The blocks just south of Grand Central Terminal sport a nice array of world cuisines.

$$$ Maloney & Porcelli – *37 East 50th St. between Madison & Park Aves.* ✆*212-750-2233. www.maloneyandporcelli.com.* **American.** Come here with a big appetite and a good-size wallet. If you're feeling adventurous or just really hungry, try the much-ordered crackling pork shank. This hearty hunk of meat is first deep-fried, then slow-roasted to hold in the juices. It's served with jalapeño-pepper-spiked "firecracker" apple sauce. There's plenty of expertly cooked seafood on the menu as well. Side dishes (fresh-cut French fries, creamed spinach, whipped potatoes) come in portions big enough for two.

$$ El Parador – *325 E. 34th St. between First & Second Aves.* ✆*212-679-6812. www.elparadorcafe.com.* **Mexican.** Don't let the windowless facade turn you away—the upbeat ambience within far outshines your other choices in this restaurant-challenged neighborhood. Order a stiff margarita at the bar, then settle in at a table for some terrific food, from *mole poblano*, the traditional dish of Mexico, to *bouillabaisse veracruzana*, with lobster, shrimp, scallops, clams and mussels in a succulent charred tomato, jalapeño and garlic broth. If nothing strikes your fancy, follow the congenial advice on the menu and "ask for any old favorite dish you like."

UNITED NATIONS AREA
Denizens of Tudor City and the residential towers along the East River head for international cuisine in the streets near the UN and in the neighboring Murray Hill area just to the south.

$$$$ Sushi Yasuda – *204 E. 43rd St. between Second & Third Aves. Closed Sun & holidays.* ✆*212-972-1001. www.sushiyasuda.com.* **Japanese.** Located in a quiet corridor between Grand Central Terminal and the United Nations, Sushi Yasuda owes its popularity to namesake chef Naomichi Yasuda. His insistence on simple dishes based on the freshest products available makes it necessary to change his menu daily. Japanese eel and several selections of *toro* (fatty tuna) number among the specialties, and sushi servings are presented in fresh Hawaiian ti leaves. As for the dining room, it's wrapped in solid bamboo planks, from the walls to the sushi bar.

UPTOWN
CENTRAL PARK
Central Park South features several excellent spots for memorable evenings out, and the park itself boasts what may be New York's most romantic restaurant.

$$ The Boathouse – *On the lake in Central Park (E. 72nd St. & Park Dr. North).* ✆*212-517-2233. Year round for lunch; Apr–Nov for dinner. www.thecentralparkboathouse.com.* **Contemporary.** One of the city's best-kept secrets is hidden inside Central Park. Built in the 1950s, the Loeb Boathouse makes a romantic setting for any special occasion. On a sunny day, there's no better place to dine than on the lakeside veranda. During the colder months, a ski-lodge-style interior room is a cozy getaway. Dishes reflect the city's melting pot culture with everything from jumbo lump crab cakes served with cornichon and caper remoulade to pan-roasted pork tenderloin.

UPPER EAST SIDE
Upscale's the word along Museum Mile and the residential blocks to the east. Look for fine, contemporary French or Asian cuisine in this district.

$$ Candle Cafe – *1307 Third Ave. between 74th & 75th Sts.* ✆*212-472-0970. www.candlecafe.com.* **Vegetarian.** This no-frills eatery specializes in vegetarian cuisine. Freshness and seasonality are prized here, and the cafe uses earth-friendly and healthy organic products in its dishes. Farmers' market entrées include Southwestern chile made with beans and brown rice, chipotle-grilled tofu, and a grilled soy burger. There's also an extensive list of smoothies, elixirs and juices to go with your meal. In 2003, sister restaurant **Candle 79** opened nearby *(154 E. 79th St.).*

$$$ Park Avenue – *100 E. 63rd St. at Park Ave. ✆212-644-1900. www.park avenyc.com.* **Contemporary.** Everything about this posh Park Avenue outpost morphs with the seasons—even the name (Park Avenue Winter, Park Avenue Spring, Park Avenue Summer, Park Avenue Fall). Quarterly menu revamps by executive chef Kevin Lasko bring such delights as soft-shell crabs in spring, vine-fresh tomatoes in summer, and rave-worthy apple pie in fall. A list of more than 250 wines complements the cuisine, and the restaurant offers a generous selection of wines by the glass. The cunning interior design employs moveable panels to bring seasonal transformations to the decor as well.

UPPER WEST SIDE
Long challenged for dining options, the Upper West Side culinary scene is coming along nicely with the arrival of several popular outposts. Set your sights along Columbus or Amsterdam avenues near the Natural History Museum.

$$ Good Enough to Eat – *483 Amsterdam Ave. between W. 83rd & W. 84th Sts. ✆212-496-0163. www.good enoughtoeat.com.* **American.** A white picket fence marks the entrance to this homey little place. Taking a clue from that, you won't be surprised to find that comfort food, just like mom used to make, stars on the menu. This cute eatery, with its exposed-brick walls and folk art accents, serves up bountiful breakfasts, in addition to lunch and dinner.

$$ Ocean Grill – *384 Columbus Ave. between W. 78th & W. 79th Sts. ✆212-579-2300. www.oceangrill.com.* **Seafood.** You'll feel as if you've just boarded an elegant ocean liner when you set foot inside the Ocean Grill's dining room, decked out with photographs of the seashore and porthole windows offering a view of the kitchen. Order

a plate of oysters from the raw bar, simply grilled fish, Maine lobster or the house maki rolls. The "sunset menu" of light fare is served weekdays from 4pm to 5pm; perfect after a day at the American Museum of Natural History, which is right across the street.

$$$ 'Cesca – *164 W. 75th St. at Amsterdam Ave. Closed Mon. ✆212-787-6300. www.cescanyc.com.* **Italian.** 'Cesca is short for Francesca, the name of founder Godfrey Polistina's daughter. The menu emphasizes southern Italian fare such as tuna with white beans, Cerignola olives and preserved lemon; swordfish with caponata; and tripe with red wine and pancetta. These selections are complemented by a list of daily specials. Check out 'Cesca's popular sister restaurant, **Ouest** *(2315 Broadway between W. 83rd & W. 84th Sts.; ✆212-580-8700)*, also on the Upper West Side.

BROOKLYN
International enclaves thrive in Brooklyn, with restaurants and cafes galore. Look for Greek, Russian and Italian especially; New Yorkers regularly travel over the river for the pizza here. And don't forget the up-and-coming DUMBO district, rife with popular restaurants.

$$$$ River Café – *1 Water St. between Furman & Old Fulton Sts. ✆718-522-5200. www.rivercafe.com.* **Contemporary.** Set on a barge on the East River, the cafe has long (since 1977) been renowned for its spectacular views. Be sure to ask for a table by the window, to best enjoy the vistas stretching across the glittering river to Lower Manhattan. Entrées (Colorado rack of lamb, Chilean turbot fillet, grilled dorade fillet) are similar for lunch and dinner; the only difference is that at dinner your only choices are the three- or six-course prix-fixe menus.

Entertainment

New York is famed for its entertainment, especially its nightlife. On any given evening you can attend a star-studded play or a concert, have a drink with a stupendous view, and go dancing into the early hours of the morning. Doing those three things needn't consume your whole travel budget, either. There are plenty of small concert stages and theaters, as well as out-of-the-way lounges and dance clubs with no cover charges. Below is a range of well-regarded venues to consider when making your plans. Most of the most famous performance spaces—**Carnegie Hall**, **Lincoln Center**, **The Carlyle** and **Radio City Music Hall**, for instance—set their schedules well in advance, and allow you to buy tickets online. As Myrna Loy once said, "If you're bored in New York, it's your own fault."

PERFORMING ARTS
BROADWAY THEATER

No trip to New York is complete without taking in a play. Broadway, in fact, is the city's number-one tourist attraction, drawing more visitors than

the Statue of Liberty. Broadway musicals, in particular, are surefire crowd pleasers with audiences of all ages. Aside from a handful of long-running shows —*The Lion King*, *Chicago*, *The Phantom of the Opera* and *Mamma Mia!* among them—shows change regularly. **The Broadway League** website *(www.ilovenytheater.com)* is an excellent source of advance information about shows, providing an easily navigable list of Broadway plays and musicals, along with times, ticket prices and plot synopses; it also allows you to buy tickets. Another source for online theater listings (of all New York City shows) is **TheaterMania** *(www. theatermania.com)*. TKTS, run by the Theater Development Fund, is the preeminent source for day-of-show tickets (🕭 *see sidebar below*).

OFF-BROADWAY THEATER

Many major plays are presented "Off Broadway." Though some of these theaters may be technically in the Theater District, all have fewer than 500 seats. Many have 499. Why? Because union rules are more flexible for Off-Broadway productions than for Broadway shows. So while the houses may be smaller, the overhead costs are

---

Discount Theater Tickets

TKTS is by far the most popular method of obtaining last-minute (usually same-day) discount theater tickets to Broadway and Off-Broadway shows. Tickets generally cost 25 to 50 per cent less than what you'd pay in advance. Choices can be limited, so if you have your heart set on seeing a specific show, it's best to order full-price tickets in advance or to check out the show's **rush ticket** policy. The best advice is to identify several possible shows you'd like to see; chances are TKTS will have discounts to at least one of them. The Theater Development Fund website *(www.tdf.org)* has a helpful list of recently discounted shows. There are two TKTS booths in Manhattan and one in Brooklyn. The **Times Square** booth is under the lighted red steps at Duffy Square *(Broadway & 47th St.; tickets for evening performances year-round Mon & Wed–Sat 3–8pm, Tue 2–8pm, Sun 3pm–30min before performance, tickets for matinees sold Wed & Sat 10am–2pm, Sun 11am–3pm)*. The **South Street Seaport** booth *(corner of Front & John Sts., at the rear of 199 Water St.; Mon–Sat 11am–4pm)* tends to have shorter lines, and you can buy matinee tickets a day in advance. The **Downtown Brooklyn Booth** *(1 MetroTech Center at the corner of Jay St. & Myrtle Ave.; Tue–Sat 11am–6pm)* also features reduced-price tickets to Brooklyn events. TKTS now accepts credit cards in addition to cash, traveler's checks and TKTS gift certificates.

🙂 A Bit of Advice 🙂

To ensure quality entertainment, it pays to do a little scouting out in advance. If you can't, then buy a copy of the latest *Time Out New York* or *New Yorker* (both are available at newsstands citywide) or pick up a free *L Magazine* or *Village Voice*, which can be found in corner newspaper boxes, bookstore vestibules and at visitor information centers. All these publications have extensive listings.

lower (ticket prices are only marginally cheaper, unfortunately). Generally speaking, Off-Broadway shows take more risks than their Broadway counterparts and are less family-oriented; still, many Off-Broadway producers want to launch a hit so big that it must move to Broadway to accommodate audiences. Here are a few highly regarded Off-Broadway theater companies.

Atlantic Theater Company
336 W. 20th St. between Eighth & Ninth Aves., Chelsea. 📞*212-691-5919. www.atlantictheater.org.* The theater founded in 1985 by playwright **David Mamet** presents work by—who else?—David Mamet (among others) in its two spaces, at the address above and at **Stage 2** *(330 W. 16th St.).*

Manhattan Theatre Club
261 W. 47th St. between Broadway & Eighth Ave., Theater District, & at City Center. 📞*212-581-1212 or 212-239-6200. www.mtc-nyc.org.* The crème de la crème of Off-Broadway theater companies, MTC stages new plays at City Center and at the recently restored 650-seat Samuel J. Friedman Theatre on Broadway. Playwrights August Wilson and Athol Fugard have both had their work produced here.

New York Theater Workshop
79 E. 4th St. between Second Ave. & Bowery, East Village. 📞*212-460-5475.*

www.nytw.org. Jonathan Larson's hit musical *Rent* got its start here in 1996 before transferring to Broadway for a 12-year run. Often, though, more serious, often political fare is produced, such as plays by Tony Kushner.

Public Theater
425 Lafayette St. between Astor Pl. and E. 4th St., East Village. 📞*212-967-7555. www.publictheater.org.* The people behind the free summer Shakespeare in the Park festival have also launched such popular Broadway musicals as *Bring in da Noise, Bring in da Funk* and nurtured emerging talent including Pulitzer-winner Suzan-Lori Parks.

OFF-OFF BROADWAY THEATER

This designation goes to venues with fewer than 100 seats. For the most part, these are productions done on a shoestring by playwrights whose work lies far outside the mainstream, or by actors and directors who want to "make theater" from scratch. These shows have short runs, and you can get tickets, usually for under $20 apiece, directly from the theaters. Consult the *Village Voice* for complete listings. A few venues to look for:

The Flea
41 White St. between Broadway & Church St., TriBeCa. 📞*212-226-2407. www.theflea.org.* Avant-garde work, such as that of wordsmith Mac Wellman, is presented in a space run by Jim Simpson, husband of actress Sigourney Weaver.

HERE
145 Sixth Ave. at Broome St., SoHo. 📞*212-647-0202. www.here.org.* This pleasant multi-use venue has three small stages, as well as an art gallery and a cafe. The theaters are often rented out by long-standing Off-Off Broadway companies, as well as actors trying out solo material.

PS 122
150 First Ave. at E. 9th St., East Village. 📞*212-477-5829. www.ps122.org.* A

former public school, this East Village mainstay puts on a range of offbeat performances, many mixing theater with music, dance or film.

CLASSICAL MUSIC

Bargemusic
Fulton Ferry Landing, just south of the Brooklyn Bridge, Brooklyn. ☎718-624-2083 or 718-624-2083. www.bargemusic.org. Though few might have guessed that a coffee barge could be a proper setting for chamber music, native New Yorker Olga Bloom thought it would, and made it so. Since 1977 Bargemusic has been going strong, holding about 220 world-class recitals a year. It's a unique musical evening. To make it an all-Brooklyn night, have dinner at the nearby River Café (👓 *see Where to Eat).*

Carnegie Hall
57th St. & Seventh Ave., Central Midtown. ☎212-247-7800. www.carnegiehall.org. One of the world's most prestigious concert venues, the 1891 hall has three stages for classical music.

Lincoln Center
Columbus Ave. between W. 62nd & W. 65th Sts., Upper West Side. ☎212-875-5456. www.lincolncenter.org. New York's premier cultural center has 12 constituent companies, including the Metropolitan Opera, the New York Philharmonic and the New York City Ballet.

DANCE AND PERFORMANCE

Brooklyn Academy of Music
30 Lafayette Ave. between Ashland Pl. & St. Felix St., Brooklyn. ☎718-636-4100. www.bam.org. Boasting two major performance spaces and a cinema, BAM has become Brooklyn's version of Lincoln Center. But while opera and classical music both have their place here, it's the annual **Next Wave Festival** *(fall & winter)* that garners the headlines, presenting a roster of established and emerging avant-garde dancers and performers.

City Center Theater
131 W. 55th St. between Sixth & Seventh Aves., Central Midtown. ☎212-581-1212. www.nycitycenter.org. This ornate auditorium has been hosting first-rate dance for decades. **The American Ballet Theatre** performs here in the fall, the **Alvin Ailey American Dance Theater** in the winter, The **Paul Taylor Dance Company** in the spring. Twyla Tharp and Merce Cunningham frequently drop in for shorter runs. The Off-Broadway Manhattan Theatre Club puts on plays at two smaller stages here.

Joyce Theater
175 Eighth Ave. at W. 19th St., Chelsea. ☎212-242-0800. www.joyce.org. Modern dancers from such heavy-hitters as the **Martha Graham Dance Company** and the **Ballet Hispanico** take the stage year-round at this 472-seat art deco theater, a former

Brooklyn Academy of Music

Peter Mauss/ESTO/Brooklyn Academy of Music

cinema. A second, smaller space, Joyce SoHo (155 Mercer St. between Houston & Prince Sts.; ☎212-431-9233), nurtures emerging talent.

NIGHTLIFE
CABARET

Cafe Carlyle
The Carlyle Hotel, 35 E. 76th St. at Madison Ave., Upper East Side. ☎212-744-1600. www.thecarlyle.com. Legendary crooner Bobby Short may be gone, but The Carlyle still has a full line-up of name performers like Ute Lemper. The Woody Allen-fronted Eddy Davis New Orleans Jazz Band plays Monday nights (check website for schedule). The cover can top $100—more if you want to be seated close to the stage—with a two-drink minimum. Jackets required for men.

Don't Tell Mama
363 W. 46th St. between Eighth & Ninth Aves., Theater District. ☎212-757-0788. www.donttellmamanyc.com. This Restaurant Row institution offers a rowdy good time as Broadway hopefuls (including the waiters) and intrepid audience members take their turns belting out show tunes in the piano bar; two cabaret theaters have more traditional shows (covers from $10).

Joe's Pub
425 Lafayette St. between Astor Pl. & E. 4th St., East Village. ☎212-967-7555. www.joespub.com. Ensconced in the massive Public Theater building (the former Astor Library), this plush little club makes the most of its limited space, with tight rows of cocktail tables packed near the stage, a middle area of banquettes and a spacious bar area. The emerging and diverse acts range from pop and rock to jazz and cabaret.

Oak Room Supper Club
The Algonquin Hotel, 59 W. 44th St. at Sixth Ave., Central Midtown. ☎212-419-9331. www.algonquinhotel.com. Like the Cafe Carlyle, the Oak Room offers top-notch cabaret in a legendary and elegant setting. The Algonquin, of course, lent its name (and its bar) to the acid-witted writers, including Dorothy Parker and Robert Benchley, who became known as the Algonquin Round Table. More recent performers have included Andrea Marcovicci and John Pizzarelli.

COCKTAIL LOUNGES

Bemelmans Bar
35 E. 76th St. at Madison Ave., Upper East Side. ☎212-744-1600. www.the carlyle.com. A New York classic, mural-bedecked Bemelmans in The Carlyle Hotel has live piano-bar music Tuesday through Saturday nights. Or come early and indulge in an after-museum cocktail; the bartender has concocted a slew of originals.

Campbell Apartment
15 Vanderbilt Ave. between E. 41st & E. 42nd Sts., East Midtown. ☎212-953-0409. You can't help but be amazed when you enter this ornate vaulted space, which executive John W. Campbell turned into a sumptuous office in the 1930s. Today it's a one-of-a-kind bar that feels like a speakeasy, though it's inside Grand Central Terminal. You have to enter the bar from an inconspicuous door on Vanderbilt Avenue, the tiny side street that flanks the east side of the train station.

Lobby Lounge
8 W. 60th St. at Broadway, Upper West Side. ☎212-805-8876. Not your ordinary hotel bar, the Lobby Lounge (on the 35th floor of the Mandarin Oriental Hotel in the Time Warner Center) has one wall made entirely of glass, offering vertiginous views of Central Park and beyond.

Pravda
281 Lafayette St., between Houston & Prince Sts., SoHo. ☎212-226-4944. www.pravdany.com. This subterranean hotspot is the perfect place to retreat for a pre- or post-dinner cocktail downtown. Red banquettes and

flickering candles set a cozy mood. The only things Russian about the place are the Cyrillic posters on the walls and the vodka.

Terroir
413 E. 12th St., East Village. www.wineisterroir.com. A huge selection of Rieslings tops the list at this tiny, unpretentious wine bar. Expect great service, a fun-for-all attitude, and a free taste of sherry if you get there before 6pm. See also their TriBeCa outpost *(24 Harrison St. at Greenwich St.; 212-625-9463).*

World Bar
845 United Nations Plaza (First Ave.) between E. 47th & E. 48th Sts. 212-935-9361. This retro-chic cocktail lounge in Trump World Tower is popular with neighborhood diplomats.

COMEDY

Comix
353 W. 14th St. between Eighth & Ninth Aves., Meatpacking District. 212-524-2500. www.comixny.com. Opened in fall 2006, this is one of the bigger comedy ventures in town, with tiered seating around a stage large enough for sketch troupes but not too big for a single comic. *Daily Show* writers John Oliver and Rob Riggle appear regularly.

Gotham Comedy Club
208 W. 23rd St. between Seventh & Eighth Aves., Union Square–Gramercy Park. 212-367-9000. http://gotham comedyclub.com. One of New York's leading stand-up clubs, Gotham hosts everyone from unknowns to celebrities; as long as they're funny. You be the judge. Jerry Seinfeld has been known to drop in here to test-drive his new material.

Upright Citizens Brigade Theatre
307 W. 26th St. between Eighth & Ninth Aves., Chelsea. 212-366-9176. www.ucbtheatre.com. Saturday Night Live-style sketch comedy and improv, sometimes even with SNL stars, are trotted out nightly here at bargain prices.

DANCE CLUBS

Be sure to check local listings for information about these clubs. Most are open, or popular, only certain nights, and New York clubs have a tendency to disappear without warning.

Cielo
18 Little W. 12th St. between Ninth Ave. & Washington St., Meatpacking District. 212-645-5700. www.cieloclub.com. The sunken dance floor, world-famous DJs and throbbing sound system have drawn legions of clubgoers to this relatively small space in the Meatpacking District.

Love
179 MacDougal St. at W. 8th St., Greenwich Village. 212-477-5683. DJs spin rock, techno and house music depending on the night at this small, underground club. The floor is surprisingly large for such a cozy cave; prepare for some hardcore dancing.

Sapphire
249 Eldridge St. between Houston & Stanton Sts., Lower East Side. 212-777-5153. www.sapphirenyc.com. Sapphire has been spinning funk, hip-hop and house seven nights a week for more than a decade, an eternity in the club world. Happy "hour" lasts from 7pm to 10pm, and the cover is waived on Fridays and Saturdays before 11pm because, you guessed it, things don't really get going until after midnight.

SOB's
200 Varick St. at W. Houston St., Greenwich Village. 212-243-4940. www.sobs.com. Reservations suggested. New York's premier world-music venue, Sounds of Brazil has a tropical decor, a cabana-like bar and a menu featuring Brazilian specialties. Reggae, Latin and hip-hop beats heat up the dance floor nightly. If you show up early on Friday night, you can take a free salsa lesson.

Swing 46

349 W. 46th St. between Eighth & Ninth Aves. ✆212-262-9554. www.swing46. com. Live bands and swing DJs transport clubbers back to the days of the Rat Pack at this 40s-style supper club. The nightly dance lessons will get you up and swinging in no time.

JAZZ AND BLUES

Though you don't have to buy advance tickets to most jazz shows, it's best to make a reservation to ensure you'll get a table.

B.B. King Blues Club & Grill

237 W. 42nd St. between Seventh & Eighth Aves., Times Square. ✆212-997-4144. www.bbkingblues.com. The massive Times Square club has hosted blues greats like Ray Charles, George Clinton and Peter Frampton. The Harlem Gospel Choir accompanies a buffet brunch every Sunday.

Iridium Jazz Club

1650 Broadway at W. 51st St., Theater District. ✆212-582-2121. www.iridium jazzclub.com. Opened in 1994, this sleek spot has won fans with its impressive roster of artists, 600-bottle wine list and state-of-the-art sound system. Legendary guitarist Les Paul played here every Monday night; his memory lives on with Les Paul Tribute Mondays featuring the Les Paul Trio.

Jazz Gallery

290 Hudson St. between Dominick & Spring Sts., SoHo. ✆212-242-1063. www. jazzgallery.org. This terrific little second-floor club is one of the city's great jazz secrets, with none of the commercialism of the larger venues and lots of hardcore regulars. Seats are folding chairs and benches. There's no bar, but you can get a glass of wine in a plastic cup.

Jazz Standard

116 E. 27th St. between Lexington & Park Aves., Union Square–Gramercy Park. ✆212-576-2232. www.jazzstandard.net. There's no minimum food or drink order here, because the owners are

certain you'll want baby back ribs and pan-fried catfish from Blue Smoke restaurant upstairs. Superlative bookings and crystalline sound make this a great choice.

Lenox Lounge

288 Lenox Ave. between 124th & 125th Sts., Harlem. ✆212-427-0253. www.lenoxlounge.com. When film producers search for an authentic Harlem club of the 1930s, they look no farther than the Lounge, as it is commonly known to musicians and locals. Live jazz and blues are played regularly in the Zebra Room.

Smoke

2751 Broadway between W. 105th & W. 106th Sts., Upper West Side. ✆212-864-6662. www.smokejazz.com. One of New York's most popular small clubs offers Monday-night jam sessions, Hammond B3 organ grooves and some of the city's hottest jazz stars (often with no cover charge) in a neighborhood with otherwise slim entertainment pickings.

Village Vanguard

178 Seventh Ave. South, Greenwich Village. ✆212-255-4037. www.village vanguard.com. Photographs of Bill Evans and other jazz greats line the walls, and top-billing jazz musicians take the stage at New York's oldest jazz club, in Greenwich Village. Musicians often drop in after their gigs at other clubs for late-night jam sessions.

ROCK AND POP

Beacon Theatre

2124 Broadway at W. 74th St., Upper West Side. ✆212-465-6500. www.beacontheatre.com. Come see big names like Paul Simon, Van Morrison and the Allman Brothers Band at this wondrous 1929 venue, a stunning, vast and intimate assemblage of rococo curlicues and red velvet.

Bowery Ballroom

6 Delancey St. between Bowery & Chrystie Sts., Lower East Side. ✆212-260-4700.

www.boweryballroom.com. This onetime vaudeville club and shoe store has become a top venue for touring indie-rock bands since opening in 1998. Its main space has a wraparound balcony. In recent years Bowery Presents has expanded to other venues including a larger space, Terminal 5 on Manhattan's West Side (*610 W. 56th St. between Eleventh & Twelfth Aves.; www.terminal5nyc.com*) and the Music Hall of Williamsburg in Brooklyn (*66 North 6th St. between Wythe & Kent Aves., Williamsburg, Brooklyn; www. musichallofwilliamsburg.com*).

Irving Plaza
17 Irving Pl. at E. 15th St., Union Square. ℘212-777-6800. www.irvingplaza.com. Big indie bands like Built to Spill and the New York Dolls, as well as rock legends Tom Jones and Deborah Harry, have played at this newly renovated club, now run by Live Nation.

Madison Square Garden
Seventh Ave. between W. 31st & W. 33rd Sts., Garment District. ℘212-465-6741. www.thegarden.com. The vast space that hosts the New York Knicks and the Westminster Dog Show also welcomes Elton John and Dave Matthews Band when they come to town. Also on-site is a new, smaller space, The Theater at Madison Square Garden, where the last row is less than 200ft from the stage.

Radio City Music Hall
1260 Sixth Ave. at 50th St., Central Midtown. www.radiocity.com. The Rockettes aren't the only ones to grace the stage of this 6,000-seat art deco landmark, part of the Rockefeller Center complex. So do big-name crooners, including Björk, Carly Simon, Alanis Morissette and Tony Bennett. It's worth getting tickets just to see the magical interior.

INDIE ROCK AND AVANT-GARDE
Arlene's Grocery
95 Stanton St. between Ludlow & Orchard Sts., Lower East Side. ℘212-358-1633. www.arlenesgrocery.net.

Named for the Lower East Side bodega it once replaced, the tiny club hosts up to seven bands a night. Go Monday night for punk and heavy-metal karaoke. Bar opens at 1pm, music starts around 7pm, doors close at 4am.

Highline Ballroom
431 W. 16th St. between Ninth & Tenth Aves., Chelsea. ℘212-414-5994. www.highlineballroom.com. Eclectic programming and ear-tingling acoustics define this new industrial-chic venue, opened in 2007 by the owner of the B.B. King Blues Club. Opening night featured Lou Reed; since then the stage has been graced by Diamanda Galas, indie rockers the Arctic Monkeys (at a show attended by P. Diddy), singer-songwriter Suzanne Vega and others.

Knitting Factory
361 Metropolitan Ave., Brooklyn. ℘347-529-6696. www.knittingfactory.com. Legendary home of the musical avant-garde, the club recently moved to new digs in Brooklyn, the better to host great live jazz and rock shows.

Mercury Lounge
217 E. Houston St. between Ludlow & Essex Sts., Lower East Side. ℘212-260-4700. www.mercuryloungenyc.com. A long, dimly lit bar greets visitors to this indie- and roots-rock club. Behind the velvet curtain is an intimate (250-capacity) space with exposed brick walls and a raised stage.

Pianos
158 Ludlow St. between Rivington & Stanton Sts., Lower East Side. www.pianosnyc.com. You'd think that a former piano factory would give patrons plenty of room to spread out. Not so at this bi-level supper club, a magnet for urban hipsters. There are often three bands a night and a DJ. Happy hour 5pm to 7pm, dinner served till 1am.

Shopping

The Big Apple is a shopper's paradise; everything from the functional to the bizarre lies within easy reach. Elite department stores and design studios line Fifth Avenue between 47th and 57th Streets and Madison Avenue between 59th and 79th Streets, where window-shopping is a favored pastime. Trendy boutiques can also be found in SoHo, Nolita, East Village and the West Village. New York City is also home to the nation's wholesale fashion industry, centered in the Garment District on Seventh Avenue, and its diamond wholesale trade, concentrated on Diamond and Jewelry Way (47th St. between Fifth & Sixth Aves.; www.diamonddistrict. org). The Shops at Columbus Circle cover three floors in the Time Warner Center (10 Columbus Circle).

The Official NYC Guide, published by NYC & Company, offers detailed information on the types of shops, their locations and hours of operation.

FIFTH AVENUE

Fifth Avenue south of Central Park routinely ranks among the world's most expensive shopping areas. The blocks are studded with big-name designers, elegant department stores, luxury specialty stores and fine jewelers.

DEPARTMENT STORES

Bergdorf Goodman – 754 Fifth Ave. at 58th St. ℘800-558-1855. www.bergdorfgoodman.com. Department store royalty, BG features exclusive designers for men's and women's clothing, plus a vast selection of shoes and housewares.

Fifth Avenue Shopping

Tiffany & Co.

©JTB/Photoshot

Henri Bendel – *712 Fifth Ave.* ✆*800-423-6335. www.henribendel.com.* Famed luxury department store specializing in high-end clothing and accessories for women.

Lord & Taylor – *424 Fifth Ave.* ✆*212-391-3344. www.lordandtaylor.com.* Upscale and elegant, the grande dame of Fifth Avenue department stores boasts a nice array of brands and complementary personal shopping service.

Saks Fifth Avenue – *611 Fifth Ave.* ✆*212-753-4000. www.saks.com.* A city block square and 10 floors high (one floor is entirely devoted to shoes), the flagship features classy designer fashions in a lovely, historic building.

SPECIALTY STORES

Apple Store – *767 Fifth Ave.* ✆*212-336-1440. www.apple.com.* Up-to-the-nano-second products invite techies on the edge to browse and surf belowdecks after entering through the street-level glass cube.

Cartier – *653 Fifth Ave.* ✆*212-753-0111. www.cartier.com.* The US flagship store of the famed French jeweler is known for its stunning window displays and elegant timepieces.

FAO Schwarz – *767 Fifth Ave.* ✆*212-644-9400. www.fao.com.* A giant wonderland of a toy store welcomes kids of all ages to dream and play.

Gucci – *725 Fifth Ave.* ✆*212-826-2600. www.gucci.com.* Step into the Manhattan outpost of the luxury Italian brand for clothing, accessories and leather goods.

Harry Winston – *718 Fifth Ave.* ✆*212-245-2000. www.harrywinston.com.* Jeweler to the stars, Winston designs over-the-top adornments for the very, very wealthy.

Tiffany & Co. – *727 Fifth Ave.* ✆*212-755-8000. www.tiffany.com.* This iconic jeweler represents the crème de la crème for diamonds, silver and pearls.

TIMES SQUARE

Shopping is synonymous with entertainment around Times Square, where neon signs blaze day and night hawking theme stores, brand outlets and media logos (CBS and MTV have stores here). Don't miss seeing the giant Ferris wheel inside children's mecca **Toys R Us**.

MADISON AVENUE

The stratosphere of New York fashion, the haute blocks of Madison Avenue north of 57th Street are lined with the flagships of world-renowned European and American designers. Boutiques filled with clothing and accessories, crystal and jewels, fine housewares and gifts make for a *ne plus ultra* shopping (or window-shopping) experience.

Baccarat – *625 Madison Ave.* ☎*212-826-4100. www.baccarat.com.* The elegant US headquarters is specially designed to showcase the glittering wares of this legendary French cristallerie.

Barneys – *660 Madison Ave.* ☎*212-826-8900. www.barneys.com.* Edgy looks by several big-name designers reign supreme at this New York fashion mecca.

Betsey Johnson – *1060 Madison Ave.* ☎*212-734-1257. www.betsey johnson.com.* Ultra-feminine designs by the wild child of womenswear stock the racks at this fun and frolicsome boutique.

Calvin Klein – *654 Madison Ave.* ☎*212-292-9000. www.calvinklein.com.* The renowned designer sells high-class (and high-priced) clothing and lingerie for women in a zen-like space.

Daum – *694 Madison Ave.* ☎*212-355-2060. www.daum.fr.* Unique and artistic designs are the hallmark of the fine crystal objects at Daum's Madison Avenue flagship; art collectors shop here.

DKNY – *655 Madison Ave.* ☎*212-223-3569. www.dkny.com.* Casual but classy togs for women take center stage; you'll also find jewelry and fine linens.

Emanuel Ungaro – *1 W. 58th St.* ☎*212-249-4090.* European style informs Ungaro's sophisticated collections for men and women; there's also a line of fine perfumes.

Giorgio Armani – *760 Madison Ave.* ☎*212-988-9191. www.giorgio armani.com.* The famed Italian designer favors clean, sleek lines. Shop here for menswear especially, but also cosmetics.

Polo Ralph Lauren – *867 Madison Ave.* ☎*212-606-2100. www.polo.com.* Here you'll find Lauren's signature American preppy styles for men and women; also housewares and gifts.

Prada – *841 Madison Ave.* ☎*212-327-4200. www.prada.com.* Fashions, leather goods and shoes bear the sleek stamp of this luxury Italian label.

Steuben – *667 Madison Ave.* ☎*800-783-8236. www.steuben.com.* A veritable museum of fine art glassware and one-of-a-kind gifts.

Swarovski – *625 Madison Ave.* ☎*212-308-1710. www.swarovski.com.* Elegant crystal baubles include tabletop items, jewelry and crystal-encrusted sunglasses.

Valentino – *747 Madison Ave.* ☎*212-772-6969. www.valentino.com.* The famed Italian design house creates casual, sporty and formal fashions for women and men.

NEIGHBORHOODS
CRYSTAL DISTRICT

The five-block stretch of Madison Avenue *(from 58th to 63rd Sts.)* is home to the world's richest concentration of crystal decorative objects and jewelry. The big names in this fragile world include Baccarat, Daum, Lalique, Steuben and Swarovski.

TRADEMARK STORES

STORE	ADDRESS	☎	WEBSITE
American Girl Place	609 Fifth Ave.	877-247-5223	www.americangirl.com
Hard Rock Cafe	221 W. 57th St.	212-489-6565	www.hardrock.com
M&M's World	1600 Broadway	212-295-3850	www.mymms.com
NBC Experience Store	30 Rockefeller Plaza	212-664-3700	www.nbcstore.com
NikeTown	6 E. 57th St.	212-891-6453	www.niketown.com
Original Levi Store	1501 Broadway	212-944-8555	www.levi.com
Yankees Clubhouse Shop	393 Fifth Ave.	212-685-4693	www.yankees.com

BOOKSTORES

STORE	ADDRESS	☏	WEBSITE
Bonnie Slotnick	163 W. 10th St.	212-989-8962	www.bonnieslotnickcookbooks.com
bookbook	266 Bleecker St.	212-807-0180	www.bookbooknyc.com
Book Culture	536 W. 112th St.	212-865-1588	www.bookculture.com
Complete Traveler	199 Madison Ave.	212-685-9007	www.ctrarebooks.com
Kitchen Arts & Letters	1435 Lexington Ave.	212-876-5550	www.kitchenartsandletters.com
McNally Jackson	52 Prince St.	212-274-1160	www.mcnallyjackson.com
Rizzoli	31 W. 57th St.	212-759-2424	www.rizzoliusa.com
St. Marks Bookshop	31 Third Ave.	212-260-7853	www.stmarksbookshop.com
Strand Books	828 Broadway	212-473-1452	www.strandbooks.com
Three Lives & Co.	154 W. 10th St.	212-741-2069	www.threelives.com

NOLITA

Mulberry, Mott & Elizabeth Sts. between Broome & Houston Sts. For shopaholics, the acronym for "North of Little Italy" has become synonymous with fashion daring and originality. Young designers fleeing the high rents of SoHo have turned local pizzerias and shoe-repair businesses into trendy boutiques.

57TH STREET

Considered one of the most exclusive shopping streets in the world, 57th between Park and Fifth Avenues is home to art galleries and chic designer boutiques, including **Chanel** *(15 E.*

57th St.; ☏212 355-5050; www.chanel.com) and **Louis Vuitton** *(1 E. 57th St.; ☏212-758-8877; www.louisvuitton.com).*

LOWER MANHATTAN

Known primarily as the financial center of the city, this area offers a varied shopping experience, including famed discount department stores **Syms** *(42 Trinity Pl.; ☏212-791-1199; www.syms.com)* and **Century 21** *(22 Cortlandt St.; ☏212-227-9092; www.c21stores.com).* Festive South Street Seaport incorporates more than 50 boutiques and restaurants, as well as the Pier 17 shopping center.

Bio

LOWER EAST SIDE, EAST VILLAGE, NOLITA

These neighborhoods are chock-full of shops specializing in vintage apparel and clothes by up-and-coming designers. Orchard Street in Lower East Side is the heart of the discount area. Note that many shops may close early on Friday and all day Saturday for the Jewish Sabbath. The greatest concentration of shops in the East Village is along 7th, 8th and 9th Streets between First and Second Avenues; try **Tokio 7** for designer hand-me-downs *(83 E. 7th St.; ☏212-353-8443; www.tokio7. net)*. Nolita's main shopping streets are Mulberry, Mott and Elizabeth Streets. Cool, streamlined **Bio** features directional women's clothing, shoes, and handbags by 30 emerging talents *(29 Prince St.; ☏212-334-3006; www. bio-nyc.com)*.

SOHO AND TRIBECA

Broadway between Houston and Canal is lined with trendy chain stores like H&M, Uniqlo, Forever 21 and Banana Republic. Move west into the heart of SoHo, though, and you'll find more upscale offerings, like **A.P.C.**, an airy, minimalist loft space filled with a well-edited selection of top-quality basics for men and women *(131 Mercer St.; ☏212-966-9685; www.apc.fr)*. More tranquil, TriBeCa is home to upscale interior design stores like **Urban Archaeology** *(143 Franklin St.; ☏212-431-4646; www.urban archaeology.com)*.

GREENWICH VILLAGE

The city's bohemian enclave is known for its quaint boutiques, specialty shops, jazz clubs and coffeehouses. Bleecker Street is lined with Old-World bakeries and Italian grocery stores. NYU students with eclectic tastes flock to the Village's music stores, including **Other Music** *(15 E. 4th St.; ☏212-477-8150; www.othermusic.com)*.

CHELSEA AND GARMENT DISTRICT

Chelsea boasts exclusive art galleries along its west edge between Ninth and Tenth Avenues. On its east edge, between Fifth and Sixth Avenues, you'll find a number of large chain clothing stores, including J. Crew, Anthropologie, Zara and H&M. In between are a number of interior design outfits. Just north of Chelsea sit **Macy's** *(151 W. 34th St.; ☏212-695-*

MUSEUM SHOPS

SHOP	ADDRESS	☏
American Folk Art Museum	45 W. 53rd St.	212-265-1040
American Museum of Natural History	Central Park West at W. 79th St.	212-769-5100
Asia Society & Museum	725 Park Ave. at E. 70th St.	212-288-6400
Cooper-Hewitt, National Design Museum	2 E. 91st St.	212-849-8400
The Frick Collection	1 E. 70th St.	212-288-0700
Guggenheim Museum	1071 Fifth Ave.	212-423-3615
International Center of Photography	1133 Sixth Ave.	212-857-9725
Metropolitan Museum of Art	Fifth Ave. at E. 82nd St.	212-570-3894
Morgan Library & Museum	225 Madison Ave.	212-590-0390
Museum of Modern Art	11 W. 53rd St.	212-708-9700
New York Transit Museum	Grand Central Terminal	212-878-0106
Rubin Museum of Art	150 W. 17th St.	212-620-5000
Studio Museum in Harlem	144 W. 125th St.	212-864-4500
Whitney Museum of American Art	945 Madison Ave.	212-570-3600

FOOD MARKETS

MARKET	ADDRESS	☎	WEBSITE
Agata & Valentina	1505 First Ave.	212-452-0690	www.agatavalentina.com
Chelsea Market	75 Ninth Ave.	212-243-6005	www.chelseamarket.com
Citarella	1313 Third Ave.	212-874-0383	www.citarella.com
Dean & Deluca	560 Broadway	212-226-6800	www.deandeluca.comv
Eli's Manhattan	1411 Third Ave.	212-717-8100	www.elizabar.com
Fairway Market	2127 Broadway	212-595-1888	www.fairwaymarket.com
Gourmet Garage	453 Broome St.	212-941-5850	www.gourmetgarage.com
Grace's Marketplace	1237 Third Ave.	212-737-0600	www.gracesmarketplace.com
Murray's Cheese Shop	254 Bleecker St.	212-243-3289	www.murrayscheese.com
Russ & Daughters	179 E. Houston St.	212-475-4880	www.russanddaughters.com
Zabar's	2245 Broadway	212-787-2000	www.zabars.com

4400; www.macys.com), the world's largest department store, and **B&H**, the city's best camera store, with a vast selection of gadgets and gear *(420 Ninth Ave. at W. 34th St.; ⊘closed Fri night, Sat & major Jewish holidays; ☎212-444-6615; www.bhphoto video.com)*.

UPPER EAST SIDE

A bastion of high-end shopping, the area encompasses upscale fashion boutiques, and is home to world-famous **Bloomingdale's** department store *(E. 59th St. & Lexington Ave.; ☎212-705-2098; www.bloomingdales.com)*.

FLEA MARKETS

For one-of-a-kind collectibles at bargain prices, head to one (or more) of the city's flea markets. One group runs three of the most popular markets: the **Hell's Kitchen Flea Market**, with 170 vendors selling all manner of vintage and retro goods *(W. 39th St. between Ninth & Tenth Aves.; year-round Sat–Sun 9am–5pm)*; the indoor **Antiques Garage** *(112 W. 25th St.; year-round Sat–Sun 9am–5pm)*, with two floors of art, books, photographs, furniture and decorative arts; and the **25th Street Market** *(between Sixth Ave. & Broadway; year-round Sat–Sun 9am–5pm)*, which has

125 vendors of various and sundry items. *For more information: ☎212-243-5343; www.hellskitchen fleamarket.com.*

FOOD AND WINE

New York is a paradise for foodies of both the cooking and the dining persuasions. **Union Square Greenmarket**★ *(⊙ see Union Square)* is the most popular of New York's farmers' markets but there are dozens more sprinkled throughout Manhattan and the five boroughs; check www.grownyc.org for other farm market options. And the city's fine food purveyors are legion, many featuring only-in-New-York specialties to take (or ship) home to your own kitchen.

Acker, Merrall & Condit – *160 W. 72nd St. ☎212-787-1700. www.ackerwines.com.* The venerable wine merchant boasts a huge selection, including many fine and rare vintages, plus a fine assortment of spirits.

Agata & Valentina – *1505 First Ave. at E. 79th St. ☎212-452-0690. www. agatavalentina.com.* This Upper East Side gourmet grocery is foodie heaven, winning raves for its excellent fish, meat and cheese departments; you'll find delicious breads and prepared foods as well.

Appellation – *156 Tenth Ave. between W. 19th & W. 20th Sts. ☎212-741-9474. www.appellationnyc.com.* The enthusiastic owner is committed to showcasing organic and biodynamic wines from all around the world, basing selections on taste first, green second.

Bacchus – *2056 Broadway. ☎212-875-1200. www.bacchuswinestore.com.* You'll find a fun and friendly approach to wine-buying here, plus a broad selection with lots of affordable options.

Chelsea Market – *75 Ninth Ave. between 15th & 16th Sts. ☎212-243-6005. www.chelseamarket.com.* Housed in an 1898 Nabisco factory, the market slots cafes and bakeries in among shops selling flowers, meat, cheeses, wines and other gourmet essentials.

Citarella – *1313 Third Ave. at E. 75th St. ☎212-874-0383. www.citarella.com.* With four locations in Manhattan, Citarella tops everyone's list for fresh, hard-to-find varieties of seafood and meats. The bakery, cheese and produce departments also attract attention for freshness and quality.

Dean & Deluca – *560 Broadway at Prince St. ☎212-226-6800. www.deandeluca.com.* The huge

SoHo flagship store stocks a huge selection of cheeses, breads, pastries and unique pantry ingredients.

Moore Brothers Wine Co. – *33 E. 20th St. ☎866-986-6673. www.moorebrothers.com.* The extremely knowledgeable staff are happy to enlighten you about their small but well-chosen selection of labels from France, Italy and Germany.

Sherry-Lehmann – *505 Park Ave. ☎212-838-7500. www.sherry-lehmann.com.* The friendly staff guide buyers through a vast but expertly selected inventory of wines and spirits.

Zabar's – *2245 Broadway at W. 80th St. ☎212-787-2000. www.zabars.com.* Zabar's stretches a city block and sells unusual foods from around the globe, including more than 600 varieties of imported cheeses.

HOME AND KITCHEN FURNISHINGS

ABC Carpet & Home – *888 Broadway. ☎212-473-3000. www.abchome.com* The Union Square flagship has everything you need to create a plush, elegant home, with six vast and surprisingly serene floors of furniture, accessories and other merchandise.

Conran Shop – *888 Broadway. ☎866-755-9079. www.conran.com.* Well-designed housewares at attractive prices lure shoppers to this branch on the lower level of ABC Carpet & Home.

Moss – *150 Greene St. ☎212-204-7100. www.mossonline.com.* Moss feels more like a gallery than a shop, with scores of eye-catching (and wallet-busting) designs set against the store's crisp white interior.

Property – *14 Wooster St. ☎917-237-0123. www.propertyfurniture.com.* Headquartered in SoHo, Property carries contemporary furniture and accessories by European designers.

Zabar's

Brigitta L. House/Michelin

Sports and Recreation

SPECTATOR SPORTS

It pays to plan ahead if you want to see one of New York's professional sports teams play a home game.

Tickets can generally be acquired through Ticketmaster (☎800-745-3000; www.ticketmaster.com) or the team's website; same-day tickets purchased at the venue may cost slightly more. Late-season games regularly sell out if a team is playing well; early-season games are better for last-minute tickets. If your plans change and you need to swap or sell your tickets, check StubHub (www.stubhub.com).

NY YANKEES

Yankee Stadium (⌖see The Bronx), 1 E. 161st St., The Bronx. MTA *4, B, D train to 161st St./Yankee Stadium. www.yankees.com.* Ticket prices range from $325 for field-level seating to $23 for a spot high in the grandstand's upper deck. There's ample on-site parking at the stadium, but the subway is easy, safe and fast *(25min from Midtown).* Sit-down restaurants include Hard Rock Cafe and NYY Steak.

NY METS

Citi Field, Flushing Meadows-Corona Park, Queens. MTA *7 train to Mets/Willets Pt. www.mets.com.* Field-level center seats cost around $300–$400 depending on the opponent; the cheapest seats (☎$12–$38) are on the upper Promenade level in the outfield.

The subway trip to the stadium takes about 25min from Midtown; LIRR service from Penn Station *(18min)* is also available (check schedules beforehand). If you're driving, arrive at least an hour before game time or you'll have to park in a satellite lot.

NY GIANTS/NY JETS

New Meadowlands Stadium, East Rutherford, NJ. www.giants.com or www.newyorkjets.com. New York City's two football teams play home games at the same new state-of-the-art facility that opened in 2010. New Jersey Transit operates a convenient train directly to the stadium on game days *(25min;* ☎*$10.50 round-trip);* from Penn Station take an NJ Transit train to Secaucus Junction (SEC) and pick up the train to Meadowlands Sports Complex from there. If you're driving, take the New Jersey Turnpike western spur from Lincoln Tunnel or the George Washington Bridge; prepare to park in a satellite lot. Home games sell out to season ticket holders, but you can purchase unused tickets by joining the season-ticket waitlist (☎*no charge)* through the teams' websites, or through ticket brokers. Face-value ticket prices range from $85–$95 (upper level end zone) to $700 (lower level on the 50-yard line). Plan to arrive at least an hour before game time to navigate security checkpoints.

NY KNICKS

Madison Square Garden (⌖see Chelsea). MTA *34th St./Penn Station. www.nba.com/knicks.* Courtside seats can cost as much as $3,000, but most other tickets

HORSE RACING CALENDAR

RACETRACK	SEASON	EVENT	☎/INFORMATION
Aqueduct	Nov–Apr	Thoroughbred racing	718-641-4700 www.nyra.com
Belmont Park	May–mid-Jul & mid-Sept–Oct	Thoroughbred racing and the Belmont Stakes	516-488-6000 www.nyra.com
Meadowlands	Jan–Aug	Harness racing	201-843-2446 www.thebigm.com
Yonkers Raceway	year-round	Harness racing	914-968-4200 www.yonkersraceway.com

Madison Square Garden

Y. Saito/MICHELIN

throughout the venue range from $40 to $240 depending on distance from the court.

MADISON SQUARE GARDEN

Many sporting events ranging from boxing to figure-skating take place at **Madison Square Garden**; contact the box office for information (✆212-465-6741; www.thegarden.com). When events are sold out, you can sometimes get tickets for a fee through a ticket agency *(see Manhattan Yellow Pages)*.

RECREATION

After Central Park, Manhattan's largest recreational facility might be **Chelsea Piers** (♿W. 23rd St & Hudson River; ✗ ✆212-336-6666; www.chelseapiers.com). This impressive complex resides on four former ocean liner piers. In addition to its spa and bowling alley, Chelsea Piers includes:
Golf Club, a heated outdoor driving range with 52 stalls on four tiers *(Pier 59;* 🕐*open Mon–Fri 6.30am–midnight, Sat–Sun 6.30am–11pm;* 💳*starting at $25 for 90 balls;* ✆*212-336-6400).*
Sports Center, which houses a .25mi indoor running track, a weight deck, a rock-climbing wall, basketball courts, a swimming pool, aerobics studios and spa services *(Pier 60;* 🕐*open Mon–Thu 5.30am–11pm, Fri 5.30am–*

10pm, Sat–Sun 8am–9pm; 💳*$50 day pass;* ✆*212-336-6000).*
Sky Rink, an indoor ice-skating arena *(Pier 61;* 🕐*open year-round, call for hours;* 💳*$13.50, $11 children under 13, $8 skate rental;* ✆*212-336-6100).*
Field House, with facilities for gymnastics, soccer, lacrosse and field hockey.

BIKING AND JOGGING

In addition to Central Park, many runners and cyclists make use of the Hudson River Greenway, stretching from Battery Park to Washington Heights. Contact the New York Road Runners Club (✆212-860-4455; ww.nyrr.org) and the New York Cycling Club (www.nycc.org) for information on races and facilities. Bike rentals are available near Central Park and at Gotham Bikes in TriBeCa.

ICE-SKATING

Enjoy skating among the skyscrapers at the following venues in Midtown and in Central Park. There's also a rink at Chelsea Piers (♿*see above).*
The Pond at Bryant Park – *Fifth Ave. between W. 40th & W. 42nd Sts.* 🕐*Open late Oct–Feb Sun–Thu 8am–10pm, Fri–Sat 8am–midnight.* 💳*Free; $13 skate rental.* ✆*212-661-6640. http://thepondatbryantpark.com.*

SPORTS CALENDAR

SPORT/TEAM	SEASON	VENUE	✆/INFORMATION
ⓘ **Baseball**	Apr–Oct		www.mlb.com
NY Mets (NL)		Citi Field	718-507-8499
NY Yankees (AL)		Yankee Stadium	718-293-6000
⬤ **Football**	Sept–Dec		www.nfl.com
NY Giants (NFC)		New Meadowlands Stadium	201-935-8222
NY Jets (AFC)			800-469-5387
✓ **Hockey**	Oct–Apr		www.nhl.com
NY Islanders (NHL)		Nassau Coliseum	800-882-4753
NY Rangers (NHL)		Madison Square Garden	212-465-6073
NJ Devils (NHL)		Prudential Center	800-653-3845
⬤ **Men's Basketball**	Oct–Apr		www.nba.com
NY Knicks (NBA)		Madison Square Garden	212-465-6073
NJ Nets (NBA)		Prudential Center	800-765-6387
⚽ **Soccer**	Mar–Oct		www.mlssoccer.com
NY Red Bulls (MLS)		Red Bull Arena	877-727-6223
🎾 **Tennis**	late Aug–mid-Sept		www.usopen.org
US Open Tennis Championships		USTA National Tennis Center	718-760-6200
⬤ **Women's Basketball**	Jun–Sept		www.wnba.com
NY Liberty (WNBA)		Madison Square Garden	212-465-6766
🎾 **Tennis**	late Aug–mid-Sept		www.usopen.org
US Open Tennis Championships		USTA National Tennis Center	718-760-6200

The Rink at Rockefeller Plaza – ⊙*Open Oct–Apr Sun–Thu 8.30am–10pm, Fri–Sat 8.30am–midnight.* ⊜*$10–$19; $7.50–$12.50 children under 11; $9 skate rental.* ✆*212-332-7654. www.therinkatrockcenter.com.*

Wollman Skating Rink – *Central Park.* ⊙*Open Oct–Apr Mon–Tue 10am–2.30pm, Wed–Thu 10am–10pm, Fri–Sat 10am–11pm, Sun 10am–9pm.* ⊜*$10.50–$15; $5.50–$5.75 children; $6.25 skate rental.* ✆*212-439-6900. www.wollmanskatingrink.com.*

Ice Skating in Central Park

Brigitta L. House/MICHELIN

369

INDEX

INDEX

INDEX

INDEX

INDEX

MAP LEGEND

★★★ **Highly recommended**
★★ **Recommended**
★ **Interesting**

Sight symbols

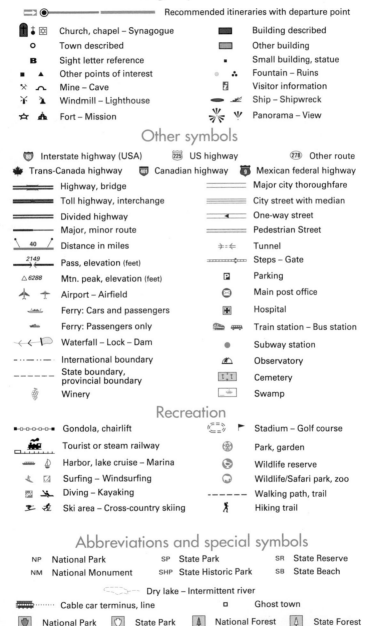

Church, chapel – Synagogue		Building described
Town described		Other building
Sight letter reference		Small building, statue
Other points of interest		Fountain – Ruins
Mine – Cave		Visitor information
Windmill – Lighthouse		Ship – Shipwreck
Fort – Mission		Panorama – View

Recommended itineraries with departure point

Other symbols

Interstate highway (USA)   US highway   Other route
Trans-Canada highway   Canadian highway   Mexican federal highway

Highway, bridge — Major city thoroughfare
Toll highway, interchange — City street with median
Divided highway — One-way street
Major, minor route — Pedestrian Street
Distance in miles — Tunnel
Pass, elevation (feet) — Steps – Gate
Mtn. peak, elevation (feet) — Parking
Airport – Airfield — Main post office
Ferry: Cars and passengers — Hospital
Ferry: Passengers only — Train station – Bus station
Waterfall – Lock – Dam — Subway station
International boundary — Observatory
State boundary, provincial boundary — Cemetery
Winery — Swamp

Recreation

Gondola, chairlift — Stadium – Golf course
Tourist or steam railway — Park, garden
Harbor, lake cruise – Marina — Wildlife reserve
Surfing – Windsurfing — Wildlife/Safari park, zoo
Diving – Kayaking — Walking path, trail
Ski area – Cross-country skiing — Hiking trail

Abbreviations and special symbols

NP National Park   SP State Park   SR State Reserve
NM National Monument   SHP State Historic Park   SB State Beach

Dry lake – Intermittent river

Cable car terminus, line   Ghost town

National Park   State Park   National Forest   State Forest

All maps are oriented north, unless otherwise indicated by a directional arrow.

COMPANION PUBLICATIONS

NORTH AMERICA ROAD ATLAS

A geographically organized atlas with extensive detailed coverage of the US, Canada and Mexico. Includes 246 city maps, distance chart, state and provincial driving requirements and a climate chart.

* Comprehensive city and town index
* Easy to follow "Go-to" pointers

Map 761 USA Road Map

Covers the principal US road network and presents shaded relief detail of the overall physiography of the land.

* Features state flags with statistical data and state tourism office telephone numbers
* Scale 1:3,450,000 (1 inch = approx. 55 miles)

MAP 583 NORTHEASTERN USA EASTERN CANADA ROAD MAP

Large-format map providing detailed road systems; includes driving distances, interstate rest stops, border crossings and interchanges.

* Comprehensive city and town index
* Scale 1:2,400,000 (1 inch = approx. 38 miles)

INTERNET

Michelin is also pleased to offer an online route-planning service:
www.viamichelin.com and www.travel.viamichelin.com

YOU ALREADY KNOW THE GREEN GUIDE,
NOW FIND OUT ABOUT THE MICHELIN GROUP

MICHELIN
A better way forward

The Michelin Adventure

It all started with rubber balls! This was the product made by a small company based in Clermont-Ferrand that André and Edouard Michelin inherited, back in 1880. The brothers quickly saw the potential for a new means of transport and their first success was the invention of detachable pneumatic tires for bicycles. However, the automobile was to provide the greatest scope for their creative talents.

Throughout the 20th century, Michelin never ceased developing and creating ever more reliable and high-performance tires, not only for vehicles ranging from trucks to F1 but also for underground transit systems and airplanes.

From early on, Michelin provided its customers with tools and services to facilitate mobility and make traveling a more pleasurable and more frequent experience. As early as 1900, the Michelin Guide supplied motorists with a host of useful information related to vehicle maintenance, accommodation and restaurants, and was to become a benchmark for good food. At the same time, the Travel Information Bureau offered travelers personalised tips and itineraries.

The publication of the first collection of roadmaps, in 1910, was an instant hit! In 1926, the first regional guide to France was published, devoted to the principal sites of Brittany, and before long each region of France had its own Green Guide. The collection was later extended to more far-flung destinations, including New York in 1968 and Taiwan in 2011.

In the 21st century, with the growth of digital technology, the challenge for Michelin maps and guides is to continue to develop alongside the company's tire activities. Now, as before, Michelin is committed to improving the mobility of travelers.

MICHELIN TODAY

WORLD NUMBER ONE TIRE MANUFACTURER
- 70 production sites in 18 countries
- 111,000 employees from all cultures and on every continent
- 6,000 people employed in research and development

Moving
for a world

Moving forward means developing tires with better road grip and shorter braking distances, whatever the state of the road.

CORRECT TIRE PRESSURE

RIGHT PRESSURE

- Safety
- Longevity
- Optimum fuel consumption

-0,5 bar

- Durability reduced by 20% (- 8,000 km)

-1 bar

- Risk of blowouts
- Increased fuel consumption
- Longer braking distances on wet surfaces

forward together
where mobility is safer

It also involves helping motorists take care of their safety and their tires. To do so, Michelin organises "Fill Up With Air" campaigns all over the world to remind us that correct tire pressure is vital.

WEAR

DETECTING TIRE WEAR

The legal minimum depth of tire tread is 1.6mm.
Tire manufacturers equip their tires with tread wear indicators, which are small blocks of rubber moulded into the base of the main grooves at a depth of 1.6mm.

Tires are the only point of contact between the vehicle and road.

The photo below shows the actual contact zone.

NEW TIRE

WORN TIRE
(1,6 mm tread)

If the tread depth is less than 1.6mm, tires are considered to be worn and dangerous on wet surfaces.

Moving forward
means sustainable mobility

By 2050, Michelin aims to cut the quantity of raw materials used in its tire manufacturing process by half and to have developed renewable energy in its facilities. The design of MICHELIN tires has already saved billions of litres of fuel and, by extension, billions of tons of CO2.

Similarly, Michelin prints its maps and guides on paper produced from sustainably managed forests and is diversifying its publishing media by offering digital solutions to make traveling easier, more fuel efficient and more enjoyable!

The group's whole-hearted commitment to eco-design on a daily basis is demonstrated by ISO 14001 certification.

Like you, Michelin is committed to preserving our planet.

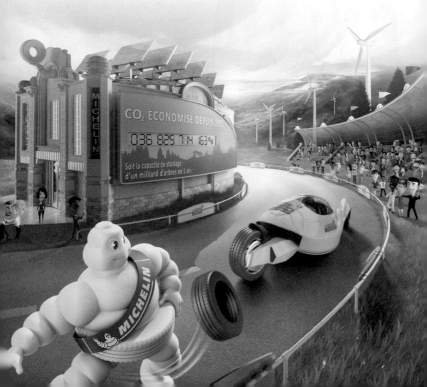

Chat with Bibendum

Go to
www.michelin.com/corporate/en
Find out more about
Michelin's history and the
latest news.

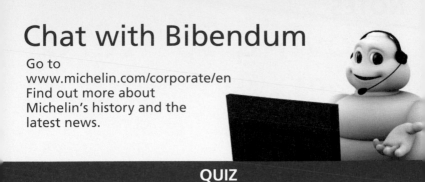

QUIZ

Michelin develops tires for all types of vehicles.
See if you can match the right tire with the right vehicle...

Michelin Travel Partner

Société par actions simplifiées au capital de 11 629 590 EUR
27 cours de l'Ile Seguin - 92100 Boulogne Billancourt (France)
R.C.S. Nanterre 433 677 721

No part of this publication may be reproduced in any form
without the prior permission of the publisher.

© 2013 Michelin Travel Partner
ISBN 978-1-907099-61-8
Printed: July 2012
Printed and bound in France : Imprimerie CHIRAT, 42540 Saint-Just-la-Pendue - N° 201207.0366

Although the information in this guide was believed by the authors and publisher to be accurate
and current at the time of publication, they cannot accept responsibility for any inconvenience,
loss, or injury sustained by any person relying on information or advice contained in this guide.
Things change over time and travellers should take steps to verify and confirm information,
especially time-sensitive information related to prices, hours of operation, and availability.

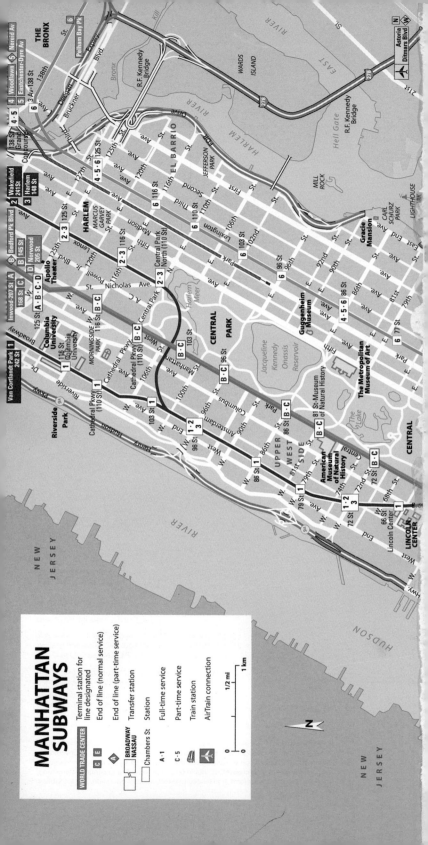